MARK MILLER

The domestication and exploitation of plants and animals

The domestication and exploitation of plants and animals

edited by

PETER J. UCKO

and

G. W. DIMBLEBY

Proceedings of a meeting of the
Research Seminar in Archaeology and Related Subjects
held at the Institute of Archaeology, London University

Aldine · Atherton, Inc.
Chicago/New York

*First published in 1969 by
Gerald Duckworth & Co. Ltd.
and
Aldine Publishing Company
529 South Wabash Avenue
Chicago, Illinois 60605*
ISBN 0–202–33030–3

Library of Congress Catalog Card No.: 70–87945

*Made and printed in Great Britain by
The Garden City Press Limited, Hertfordshire, England*

Contents

The plates are between pp. 550 and 551

Preface

The domestication of plants and animals was one of the greatest steps forward taken by mankind, and although it was first achieved so long ago we still need to know what led to it and how, and even when, it took place. Only when we have this understanding will we be able to appreciate fully the important social and economic consequences of this step. Even more important, an understanding of this achievement is basic to any insight into modern man's relationship to his habitat. In the last decade or two a change in methods of investigating these events has taken place, due to the mutual realization by archaeologists and natural scientists that each held part of the key and neither alone had the whole. Inevitably, perhaps, the floodgate which was opened has resulted in a spate of new knowledge which is scattered in the form of specialist reports in diverse journals.

A meeting of the *Research Seminar in Archaeology and Related Subjects* was held on 18th and 19th May 1968 at the Institute of Archaeology, London University, to discuss the Domestication and Exploitation of Plants and Animals. This meeting was called so that workers in the archaeological, anthropological, and biological fields could bridge the gap between their respective disciplines by personal contact and discussion. The enthusiastic response in itself underlined this need, and the range of papers contributed together forms the most complete coverage available of the subject as a whole. Modern techniques and the result of their application to the classical problems of domestication, selection, and spread of cereals and of cattle are discussed, but so are comparable problems in plants and animals which have not previously been considered in this context.

As is the practice with these seminars, the papers were all circulated beforehand and this book consists of these papers revised by their authors in the light of the discussions which took place. In addition we include several papers which were submitted by participants after the meeting and arose directly from it; these are the contributions by Professor N. A. Barnicot, Mr. S. Payne, Dr. M. L. Ryder, Dr. C. Vita-Finzi, and Dr. W. van Zeist. Professor C. D. Darlington and Dr. P. Ducos were prevented from attending the seminar and so their papers were not discussed in detail at the meeting. Furthermore, as a result of the seminar, our attention was drawn to the important paper by Dr. A. Krapovickas on the groundnut, which we have pleasure in including in this volume in an English translation by Dr. J. Smartt of the Department of Botany of the University of Southampton. We feel that there is a need for a collective work to indicate just where research does stand on the wide front covered by the title of this work and we hope that this book will meet this need.

At the actual seminar meeting we asked Professor S. Piggott to perform the superhuman task of providing a concluding paper to the two-day proceedings. Although Professor Piggott was not asked to summarize the whole content of the symposium, and indeed this would have been an impossible request, we make no apologies for placing his revised contribution as the general conclusion to this book. We have left this particular paper in the style and format of its original presentation at the seminar.

Although we realize that there are differing opinions on taxonomic nomenclature we have found it necessary to standardize and simplify the usage throughout this book. In particular we have omitted references to authorities and we have adopted the binomial nomenclature for both botanical and zoological names. We have followed this procedure in all cases except where sub-specific differences are discussed (e.g. Dr. Clutton-Brock's review of *Canis* remains from Jericho). This simplification was acceptable to the majority of the contributors but we must record that Dr. Ducos would strongly have preferred to have retained the trinomial system (see note 5 on pp. 274-5). We have also had to standardize orthography of sites (e.g. Munhata, Mureybat, etc.).

It will be obvious to the reader that the re-circulation of individual papers and ultimate compilation of this volume has involved an enormous amount of secretarial work. This has been carried out singlehanded by Miss Susan Elizabeth Johnson to whom any expression of thanks must be inadequate. We should also like to thank Mr. Peter Pratt, one of the Seminar's regular members, for generously offering his services for producing Figs. 1-7 on pp. 252-9 and Figs. 1-2 on pp. 474-6 in this book.

Perhaps we may be excused for concluding this Preface on a note of informality. In the happy atmosphere in which this meeting took place we were delighted to find that two of our participants were born poets. We conclude this Preface with their masterpieces, without any editorial comment.

We understand nothing but know much
We plant the seed and know of the harvest
We know our women, to have sons after the reaping,
Children growing after a cycle of harvests,
To watch the flocks and know of flocks unborn.
Born from yesterday we give birth to tomorrow
From the earth, life; from the earth
We take earth, that is life, and make it live
With our fingers, loving the earth, making life
From the mother goddess of earth
From the mother goddess of life.

(Charles A. Reed)

South American Idyll

The courtship of the llama
Embarrasses the farmer.
But it copulates far sooner
Than the kinkier vicuña.

(Stuart Piggott)

PETER J. UCKO
G. W. DIMBLEBY
London 1968

List of participants

J. P. Alcock (Department of Roman Archaeology, Institute of Archaeology, London)

J. Alexander (Department of Extra-Mural Studies, University of London)

B. Allchin (Department of Archaeology and Anthropology, Cambridge)

F. R. Allchin (Institute of Oriental Studies, Cambridge)

A. Ammerman (Department of Prehistoric Archaeology, Institute of Archaeology, London)

E. Anati (Centro di Studi Prehistorici, Valcamonica, Italy)

P. Ashbee (Consultant to the Inspectorate of Ancient Monuments, Ministry of Public Building and Works, London)

M. Avery (Department of Archaeology, Belfast)

G. H. A. Bankes (Department of Prehistoric Archaeology, Institute of Archaeology, London)

N. A. Barnicot (Department of Anthropology, University College London)

R. J. Berry (Department of Biology, Royal Free Hospital Medical School, London)

L. Biek (Inspectorate of Ancient Monuments, Ministry of Public Building and Works, London)

I. M. Blake (Balliol College, Oxford)

H. Bohlken (Institut für Haustierkunde der Universität, Kiel)

S. Bökönyi (Magyar Nemzeti Múzeum, Budapest)

D. M. Boston (Horniman Museum, London)

H. C. Bowen (Royal Commission for Historical Monuments—England)

W. Bray (Department of Prehistoric Archaeology, Institute of Archaeology, London)

D. R. Brothwell (Sub-department of Anthropology, British Museum—Natural History—London)

J. Burton-Page (Department of India, Pakistan and Ceylon, School of Oriental and African Studies, London)

E. Carmichael (Department of Ethnography, British Museum, London)

H. J. Case (Department of Antiquities, Ashmolean Museum, Oxford)

F. Celoria (Department of Archaeology, University of Keele)

R. E. Chaplin (Passmore Edwards Museum, London)

A. T. Clason (Biologisch-Archaeologisch Instituut, Rijksuniversiteit, Groningen)

J. Close-Brooks (Institute of Archaeology, Oxford)

J. Clutton-Brock (Department of Human Environment, Institute of Archaeology, London)

A. M. Copping (Department of Nutrition, Queen Elizabeth College, London)

I. W. Cornwall (Department of Human Environment, Institute of Archaeology, London)

D. G. Coursey (Tropical Products Institute, London)

B. A. L. Cranstone (Department of Ethnography, British Museum, London)

G. Danisman (Department of West Asiatic Archaeology, Institute of Archaeology, London)

C. Delano Smith (Department of Geography, University of Nottingham)

G. W. Dimbleby (Department of Human Environment, Institute of Archaeology, London)

D. M. Dixon (Department of Egyptology, University College London)

R. A. Donkin (Department of Geography, University of Birmingham)

M. S. Drower (Department of Ancient History, University College London)

A. Evans (School of Agriculture, Cambridge)

J. G. Evans (Department of Human Environment, Institute of Archaeology, London)

N. P. Evans (Department of Prehistoric Archaeology, Institute of Archaeology, London)

B. Field (Department of Archaeology and Anthropology, Cambridge)

C. A. Fisher (Department of Geography, School of Oriental and African Studies, London)

K. V. Flannery (Museum of Anthropology, University of Michigan, Ann Arbor)

C. D. Forde (Department of Anthropology, University College London)

P. J. Fowler (Department of Extra-Mural Studies, University of Bristol)

J. P. Garlick (Department of Anthropology, University College London)

C. Grigson (Department of Human Environment, Institute of Archaeology, London)

W. F. Grimes (Institute of Archaeology, London)

J. W. Haldane (Department of Prehistoric Archaeology, Institute of Archaeology, London)

R. Harcourt (Consultant Osteologist, Ministry of Public Building and Works, London)

D. R. Harris (Department of Geography, University College London)

J. G. Hawkes (Botany Department, University of Birmingham)

C. B. Haycraft (Gerald Duckworth & Co. Ltd., London)

F. N. Hepper (Royal Botanical Gardens, Kew, Surrey)

V. P. Hewetson (Department of Botany, University of Durham)

E. S. Higgs (Department of Archaeology and Anthropology, Cambridge)

H. W. M. Hodges (Department of Conservation, Institute of Archaeology, London)

G. W. I. Hodgson (Northern Counties College, Newcastle-upon-Tyne)

M. Hopf (Römisch-Germanisches Zentralmuseum, Mainz)

S. C. Humphries (Warburg Institute, London)

J. B. Hutchinson (School of Agriculture, Cambridge)

G. Jenkins (Plant Breeding Institute, Cambridge)

A. C. Jermy (Department of Botany, British Museum—Natural History—London)

E. R. Jewell (Department of Western Asiatic Archaeology, Institute of Archaeology, London)

P. A. Jewell (Department of Zoology, University College London)

S. E. Johnson (Institute of Archaeology, London)

R. Layton (Department of Anthropology, University College London)

Arlette Leroi-Gourhan (Centre de Recherches Préhistoriques et Proto-historiques, Paris)

H. G. Lloyd (Field Research Station, Ministry of Agriculture, Fisheries and Food, Worplesdon, Surrey)

T. Molleson (Sub-department of Anthropology, British Museum—Natural History—London)

P. Morton-Williams (Department of Anthropology, University College London)

J. P. Moss (Department of Agricultural Botany, University of Reading)

M.-J. Mountain (Department of Archaeology, University of Edinburgh)

D. S. Noble (Department of Western Asiatic Archaeology, Institute of Archaeology, London)

B. A. Noddle (Department of Pharmacology, University of Strathclyde)

T. P. O'Brien (Department of Prehistoric Archaeology, Institute of Archaeology, London)

C. E. Owen (City of Leicester Museums and Art Gallery)

J. P. Owen (J. P. Coy)

A. C. Pal (Department of Indian Archaeology, Institute of Archaeology, London)

S. Payne (Department of Archaeology and Anthropology, Cambridge)

P. Phillips (Department of Prehistoric Archaeology, Institute of Archaeology London)

B. Pickersgill (Department of Agricultural Botany, University of Reading)

S. Piggott (Department of Archaeology, University of Edinburgh)

J. R. Pilcher (Palaeoecology Laboratory, Queen's University, Belfast)

P. Pratt (Department of Architecture and Civic Design, Greater London Council)

E. Pyddoke (Institute of Archaeology, London)

C. A. Reed (Department of Anthropology, University of Illinois at Chicago Circle)

H. Reichstein (Institut für Haustierkunde der Universität, Kiel)

C. Renfrew (Department of Ancient History, University of Sheffield)

J. M. Renfrew (Department of Ancient History, University of Sheffield)

R. Riley (Plant Breeding Institute, Cambridge)

B. K. Roberts (Department of Geography, University of Durham)

A. Rosenfeld (Department of British and Medieval Antiquities, British Museum, London)

M. J. Rowlands (Department of Prehistoric Archaeology, Institute of Archaeology, London)

M. L. Ryder (Animal Breeding Research Organisation, Edinburgh)

G. de G. Sieveking (Department of British and Medieval Antiquities, British Museum, London)

I. G. Simmons (Department of Geography, University of Durham)

J. Smartt (Department of Botany, The University, Southampton)

H. S. Smith (Department of Egyptology, University College London)

M. S. Smith (Department of Nutrition, Queen Elizabeth College, London)

W. G. Solheim (Department of Anthropology, University of Hawaii, Honolulu)

M. Speight (Department of Human Environment, Institute of Archaeology, London)

M. G. Spratling (Department of Prehistoric Archaeology, Institute of Archaeology, London)

W. R. Stanton (Tropical Products Institute, London)

W. T. Stearn (Department of Botany, British Museum—Natural History—London)

W. C. Sturtevant (Office of Anthropology, Smithsonian Institution, Washington)

R. E. Tringham (Department of Archaeology, University of Edinburgh)

J. Turner (Department of Botany, University of Durham)

P. J. Ucko (Department of Anthropology, University College London)

M. Villaret-von Rochow (Musée de Botanique, Lausanne)

C. Vita-Finzi (Department of Geography, University College London)

T. Watkins (Department of Archaeology, University of Edinburgh)

W. Watson (Percival David Foundation of Chinese Art, School of Oriental and African Studies, London)

A. C. Western (Department of Forestry, Oxford)

J. Williams (Department of Anthropology, University College London)

J. Yudkin (Department of Nutrition, Queen Elizabeth College, London)

W. van Zeist (Biologisch-Archaeologisch Instituut, Rijksuniversiteit, Groningen)

D. Zohary (Department of Botany, Hebrew University of Jerusalem)

Additional Papers from

C. D. Darlington (Botany School, Oxford)

P. Ducos (Centre de Recherches d'Ecologie et de Préhistoire, St. André de Cruzières, France)

A. Krapovickas (Facultad de Agronomia y Veterinaria, Universidad Nacional del Nordeste, Corrientas, Argentina)

PETER J. UCKO and G. W. DIMBLEBY

Introduction: Context and development of studies of domestication

Mankind took an immensely long time to learn how to gain food by any other means than hunting, fishing and gathering. Our record of manufactured tools goes back over one million years but evidence of domesticated animals and plants only starts at a date somewhere near the end of the European Ice Age, i.e. after *c.* 10,000 B.C.

So much is fact revealed by archaeological investigation, and this general picture has been long accepted. Two beliefs which do not often receive explicit formulation today but are generally held serve to explain the background to these data; both beliefs are probably overstated and in need of considerable revision and yet both probably still have something of importance to say about human cultural evolution. The first states[1] that only after a considerable time and after considerable cultural experience would man have "learnt" to demand the satisfaction of many culturally derived "needs". In other words, during the first millennia of his existence man would have been content with the satisfaction of his basic (and in most cases, biological) needs —such as hunger/food and cold/warmth—and would have only gradually developed those demands, sometimes called secondary needs, which call for more sophisticated cultural responses—such as handles for equipment, comfortable as well as serviceable dwellings, clothing as well as the camp fire. This belief has been neatly summarized in the adage "needs breed needs". The second belief states[2] that while man lives by hunting, fishing and gathering alone he has little additional time to devote to "luxury" cultural activities, for the greatest part of his day is devoted to searching for food to prevent starvation. In other words, it is held by many prehistorians that only with settled life can develop the characteristics of "civilized" life—such as specialization of labour, accumulation of surplus, sophistication of religious and ritual belief and practice. Both these beliefs can be criticized; in the first place it is only the material equipment found in excavations which can support the claim that it would take several millennia for cultural "development" to emerge and this actual evidence is sadly deficient because of (1) the paucity of material known; (2) conditions of preservation, which make it likely that any material of organic nature has long since perished and that this material is scarcely ever found during excavations; and (3) the fact that material culture and cultural sophistication may not reflect each other. In the second case it is now established that not all hunters and gatherers live at a subsistence level near to starvation conditions; as Hole and Flannery[3] have summarized it: "No group on earth has more leisure time than hunters and gatherers, who spend it primarily on games, conversation and relaxing." The hunters and gatherers of the Upper Palaeolithic certainly had the time, skill and sophistication to decorate weapons, tools and caves with paintings, engravings and low-reliefs[4]; the Hadza women of Tanzania require, on a yearly average, only about two hours in the day for necessary subsistence activities; the Bushmen only make use of a (culturally) selected number of edible berries within the terrain which they occupy; the North-west coast Indians of America are able to rely on their fish supplies to the extent of being able to build large and complex wooden houses in which they live for a considerable part of the year; some groups of Australian aborigines, despite their extremely limited natural resources and their basically "Stone Age" technology, have devised one of the most complex of metaphysical systems of belief held by any human group and have the "time" and interest to decorate rock shelters and material equipment and to celebrate elaborate ritual occasions.

It is in the context of these widely held beliefs and the archaeological fact of a long-lived hunting and gathering tradition that we can best understand and evaluate the claim that the cultural stage when man first became settled in one place and was able to depend on animals and plants which he had domesticated represented a major "revolution" in human cultural development. Commonly this was held to be the stage in development when mankind began to develop those "luxury" activities such as pottery and weaving which characterize the subsequent history of man, and equally the stage in development when religious, social and economic activities really began to flourish. It was Professor V. Gordon Childe who first termed the phrase "Neolithic Revolution" in an attempt to highlight this vital stage in human development; previously the definitions of stages in cultural development had rested almost exclusively on the nature of the material objects found in excavations (and collected together in museum collections) with little regard to the economic and social activities which might be taken to reflect and epitomize.

It is important to recognize that, whatever the various beliefs and theories associated, we are confronted with facts revealed by archaeological research that show that man did manage to change his economic way of life, did manage to settle in one spot and did manage to live in a radically different way from his predecessors and that all this did happen for the first time many thousands of years before Christ. As archaeological discoveries have become more frequent, and as absolute dating methods have been developed, so have our ideas changed as to when exactly this event may first have occurred. It now seems clear that these events must be dated somewhere between 9000 and 7000 years B.C., dates which are much older than anything previously envisaged.

For a long time prehistorians have grappled with the problem of why and how this vital change from nomadic to settled life took place. To Childe the clue lay in the "climatic crisis that ended the pleistocene epoch; the melting of the northern ice sheets . . ."[5], and the subsequent change of environmental conditions. Thus, already some time ago, it became clear that studies of domestication could no longer rely exclusively on archaeological data but would have to combine the findings of botanists, zoologists and environmentalists. Botanists and plant geographers have tried to draw conclusions from the present-day distribution and genetical constitutions of domesticated and wild species of plants but for a long time corroborative facts from the past were rarely found. Several theories have arisen regarding the extent and degree of desiccation which was thought to have followed the Pleistocene period in the Near East and these theories assumed great importance in the light of the locations of several very early sites found only quite recently. It has, for example, been argued that the location of the early "neolithic" site of Jarmo indicates that the wild animals and plants necessary for the first attempts at domestication moved into the hilly flanks of the Fertile Crescent as a response to more desiccated conditions. Others hold that the early "pre-pottery neolithic" site of Jericho shows that plants and animals, as well as humans, responded to the increased desiccation by moving to oases. This repeated emphasis on desiccation as the last full-glacial gave way to the Post-glacial has until recently had little direct evidence to support it. It was probably a rationalization of the observed distribution of these early agricultural sites with the assumption that a full-glacial period in the north and west of Europe would be matched by a pluvial climate in the south-east, so that the subsequent Post-glacial would consequently be drier in that region. It is so easy to think of climatic changes mainly in terms of precipitation, whereas the only overall primary factor is radiant energy, which will be reflected in temperature changes. Precipitation may increase or decrease as temperature rises, according to the geographical situation.

As more direct evidence is obtained, this belief in the pluvial nature of the climate during the Würm glaciation is being seriously questioned. There is accumulating evidence that in the Mediterranean basin and in the Zagros Mountains the climate was arid and cold during Würm II; pollen analyses indicate *Artemisia* steppe[6]. The transition to the Post-glacial is marked by increasing humidity, and relatively humid conditions persisted throughout the first half of the Post-glacial period. It is perhaps significant that the most recently discovered of the very early large agricultural sites, Çatal Hüyük, has moved attention away from direct effects of desiccation and has focused interest on an area, Anatolia, which had not previously been included within the classic Fertile Crescent. We are coming to realize that an apparent increase of aridity, as suggested by archaeological and agricultural criteria, should not necessarily be interpreted as indicating an increase of the aridity of the overall climate. Raikes[7] makes the point that in semi-arid areas the activities of man can lead, and certainly have led, to the extension of near desert conditions without any corresponding change in overall climate. Archaeologists have uncovered more and more prehistoric sites in different areas of the world and new techniques have been devised which have shown that archaeological sites and archaeological materials can be made to yield direct evidence of contemporary crops and herds. Since Childe's first formulation of the concept of the "Neolithic Revolution" all these discoveries have necessitated considerable and continuing revision of our ideas of this event. We have already seen that the evidence now exists to date this occurrence much earlier than Childe had originally envisaged and, as our discoveries have increased in number, so has the geographical area grown wider in which we believe the first steps in domestication may have taken place. It is now clear that pottery manufacture, for example, did not necessarily go hand in hand with domestication and that our remote ancestors originally learnt to cultivate plants and to tame animals long before they made use of baked clay pottery.

For a long time people took Childe's term "Neolithic Revolution" to imply a sudden and drastic change in man's condition and behaviour. Childe himself, however, had written[8] "The term does not imply a single catastrophic change. The Industrial Revolution itself was only the culmination of a gradual process, begun centuries earlier. The prelude to the Neolithic Revolution must have been much longer, and it is less easy to decide what precisely should be termed its culmination." We now have the archaeological evidence to support the view that earliest agricultural activities at least were often halting and varied greatly in extent, specialization and sophistication. A few years ago Professor Braidwood had already suggested[9] such terms as "primary village farming", "settled village farming", "incipient cultivation", and "intensified village farming" to describe the various different forms of early agricultural activity uncovered in prehistoric excavations. It is clear beyond any doubt that domestication was a process extending over several thousand years and that it had its own special characteristics in different areas of the ancient world. Domestication did not, of course, happen only once but has recurred time and time again in different parts of the world and at different times. Domestication as a process still continues.

Notes

1 Harrison, H. S. (1954). Discovery, invention and diffusion, *in* Singer, C. et al. (eds.) *A History of Technology*, I. London. pp. 60–2, and cp. Malinowski, B. (1944). *A Scientific Theory of Culture*. Carolina. pp. 77–93.
2 e.g. Lartet, H. and Christy, H. (1864). Figures d'animaux gravées ou sculptées, *Rev. Archéolog.*, 9; Mortillet, G. (1883). *Le Préhistorique*

Antiquité de l'Homme. Paris. p. 415; see also Childe, V. G. (1952). *New Light on the Most Ancient East.* London. pp. 23, 77, 115.

3 Hole, F. and Flannery, K. (1963). The prehistory of South-western Iran: a preliminary report, *Proc. Prehist. Soc.,* 33, p. 201.

4 See Ucko, P. J. and Rosenfeld, A. (1967). *Palaeolithic Cave Art.* London. pp. 116–23, for the way in which these beliefs affected the acceptance of the real antiquity of palaeolithic art.

5 Childe, V. G. (1942). *What Happened in History.* London. p. 43.

6 e.g. Bonatti, E. (1966). North Mediterranean climate during the last Würm Glaciation, *Nature, Lond.* 209, pp. 984–5; van Zeist, W. (1967). Late Quaternary vegetation history of Western Iran, *Rev. Palaeobot. Palyrol.,* 2, pp. 301–11.

7 Raikes, R. (1967). *Water, Weather and Prehistory.* London.

8 Childe, V. G. (1958). *The Prehistory of European Society.* London. p. 35.

9 e.g. Braidwood, R. and Braidwood, L. (1953). Earliest village communities of South West Asia, *J. World Hist.,* 1 (2); Braidwood, R. J. (1958). Near Eastern prehistory, *Science,* 127 (3312).

W. F. GRIMES

On co-operation

Basic to the whole question of the understanding of the processes by which domestication was achieved are the mutual inter-relationships of the disciplines which from the side of man on the one hand and of "nature" on the other must collaborate closely if progress is to be made. It is not difficult to define the part that each should play. It is the task of the man-aligned disciplines to recover the material and to define its setting in terms both of date and of culture. It is for the natural scientists to apply to that material the methods of analysis which will enable its status to be determined.

It will be self-evident that any discipline concerned with the study of human development in its material and economic aspects may have a contribution to make to the understanding of domestication; but it is probably true to say (again for obvious reasons) that archaeology is best placed at this time to provide information of the kind required. It is perhaps worth noting here the movement that is taking place in archaeological thought in recognising the essential unity of the ecological approach. It is one of the most promising features of the present scene that without in any way detracting from the value and importance of the art-historical, typological and technological aspects man is being viewed more and more as part of an ecosystem in which for some millennia he has played a significant if not a dominant role. The expression, "man another animal in the world of nature" is now coming more widely into use, with the consequence for Britain at least that the ecological approach is achieving for archaeology full status as a science, with the incidental benefit that sources of research grants previously closed are now beginning to be opened.

But this is by the way. The point that the function of the archaeologist must lie in the recovery of evidence and the definition of its setting is emphasized in the present context by the biologists' concern about the relationship of sedentary settlement and domestication. Here it is clear that we have much to learn, with ethnographical analogies to warn us of the danger of too facile conclusions. The Natufians in their progression from a hunting towards a farming economy represent a phase of relatively fixed settlement. In their mode of life can be seen the first steps towards domestication, with the systematic exploitation of the natural resources in plants and perhaps also in animals that were available to them. The sedentary life in itself may in any case be a variable factor, bearing in mind that the Upper Palaeolithic cave-hunters seem to have dwelt for some time on one spot. The problem in their case is to know to what extent depth of deposit represents continuous occupation and how far any one site was a station on a hunting expedition, with the accumulations reflecting successive relatively short visits rather than one long period of fixed habitation.

The overall results of domestication become apparent in the expansion of populations and in the growth of external trade (both phenomena characterizing the advanced Natufians). The recognition of the detail in the progression must depend in the first place on an awareness on the part of archaeologists of the problem. It requires from them the greatest refinement of their own techniques of investigation and observation. It calls for the realization in co-operation with their biologist colleagues of the full potentiality of their natural science material—and this not only in arriving at an understanding of the nature of the changes that took place in the various species as man increased his control over them, but also in assessing their value to man himself, and perhaps above all, their value as food. It is probably a fair guess that the outcome of attempts to define the relationship of domestication and the sedentary life will be to reveal an inter-locking of processes, with some variation from one region to the next within an overall pattern.

The foregoing comments, prompted by consideration of the Natufians, apply far more widely and are by no means confined to matters to do with domestication. As in so many other areas of human activity, the basic problem is one of communication: the creation of a recognition on the part of one group of the needs of another. Recognition is the first crucial link in the chain of action that may bring a solution. It is probably not too much to suggest that in the Near and Middle East an element of inconsistency continues to operate: awareness in some places is countered in others by a situation in which the attention given to human artifacts does not appear to be accompanied by a corresponding regard for the biological evidence. Change here cannot come too soon.

To ask of the excavator that he should broaden his view to take account of non-archaeological evidence is not, however, to suggest (as some archaeologists seem to fear) that the excavator should be expert in the fields covered by the biologists. The excavator should be in contact with the biologist (as well as other scientists) so that the latter may at least be brought in when required; better still—and this is happening with increasing frequency—resident biologists may figure as members of excavating teams. A more distant ideal must be the creation of a class of archaeological scientists prepared to devote their expertise to archaeological ends, capable of keeping pace with progress in the scientific discipline whose language they understand, and alive therefore to the mutually interacting potentialities of developments in the different fields.

It is surely in this direction that the answer must be sought. Archaeologists have in the past frequently had cause to be grateful to scientific colleagues who have been willing to turn aside from their normal work to pursue objectives which must have seemed to lead them up scientific *culs de sac*. In such circumstances the possibilities of development are limited. It is commonly said amongst archaeologists when this subject is discussed that in submitting "scientific" material to the expert they should be able to ask specific questions. But granted that no one wants to devote time to the pursuit of will-o-the-wisps, it may be doubted whether in the end this is a fully profitable way of proceeding. The archaeologist may not ask all the questions; the scientist, in pursuing the questions asked, may be blinded to the other potentialities of the material. The co-operation of archaeologists with natural scientists prepared to steep themselves in the archaeology and to recognize the validity of archaeological evidence as having equal weight with that of their own discipline should act powerfully in seeking answers to questions which are relevant both to the world of man and to the world of nature. Advocacy of such co-operation is of course no new thing and it exists already in a growing number of places; but while mindful of past favours the archaeologist does not come as a supplicant here. The body of knowledge which has been built up by ever-improving methods during this century must be taken into account by researchers in fields bordering or impinging on it. It is unnecessary to labour this point with scientists concerned with problems of domestication, whether of plants or of animals; yet in other contexts there have certainly been cases, some of them very recent, of distinguished scholars operating in such areas of overlap, who have not applied to the archaeological evidence the close attention that they would regard as essential when dealing with the evidence of their own disciplines.

By way of postscript the point is worth making that the problems that attend domestication do not end with early phases. The need remains to follow up the ways in which man used and developed these assets, if only for their bearing upon the difficult question of past populations. The area of co-operation for biologists, ethnographers and archaeologists must for this purpose be extended to take in experiment, which in replicating as far as possible the conditions of the past might produce (amongst other things) more reliable statistical data to exercise some control over the intelligent guesswork which has to serve at the present time; but it would be idle to pretend that the difficulties are not considerable. Matters that immediately present themselves are ploughing techniques, field and soil formation and development, the use of equipment and appliances of all kinds, crop yields, techniques of harvesting and storage; and so on. In Britain growing attention is being paid to site-investigation, which has been moving for some time beyond the field survey stage; and much of what has been done indicates clearly the need for experiment in controlled conditions as a way, perhaps the only way, of accounting for features relating to fields and ploughing practices which are otherwise unexplained[1].

Experimentally, Britain lags behind some European countries, Denmark in particular. The Ancient Agriculture Committee, sponsored by the British Association for the Advancement of Science and the Council for British Archaeology, has, however, made a beginning with some experimentation in ploughing techniques[2] and corn storage[3]. The Committee is now formulating a project for the creation of an experimental farm in which such activities would be co-ordinated as part of a coherent whole. This experimental approach must surely become more widely developed with time. It is the other half, as it were, of the attack on the inter-related problems of man and his environment, bringing benefits to the understanding of more than one aspect of human activity. Inevitably such benefits will go more to the humanists than to the natural scientists. It will nevertheless broaden the basis for co-operation which the investigation of the early stages of domestication shows already to exist.

Notes

1 The inspiration in all recent work may fairly be said to have come from Bowen, H. C. (1961). *Ancient Fields*. London. For a valuable summary of the present position in Britain see Fowler, P. J. and Evans, J. G. (1967). Plough-marks, Lynchets and Early Fields, *Antiquity*, pp. 289–301.
2 Aberg, F. A. and Bowen, H. C. (1960). Ploughing experiments with a reconstructed Donnerupland Ard, *Antiquity*, pp. 144–7.
3 Bowen, H. C. and Wood, P. D. (1968). Experimental storage of corn underground and its implications for Iron Age settlements, *Inst. of Archaeology Bulletin*, 7, pp. 1–14.

Part 1: Origins of domestication

Section 1: Environmental background

DAVID R. HARRIS

Agricultural systems, ecosystems and the origins of agriculture

Progress in the understanding of plant and animal domestication and the evolution of agriculture depends ultimately upon the accumulation of factual evidence from detailed taxonomic, cytological, palynological and archaeological studies. But it is necessary first to consider the problem of domestication in ecological terms. At best this approach provides a unifying conceptual framework within which to investigate the origins of agriculture and the evolution of all agricultural systems. At the least it provides a means of selecting those topics and areas that call most urgently for detailed study and thereby prevents the dissipation of limited time and resources on arbitrarily-chosen investigations.

The ecological approach requires that we conceive of agriculture as an integral part of the environment in which it is practised. This applies equally to techniques of cultivation and harvesting as to crops and livestock: all may be regarded as components of given ecosystems. Thus we recognize agricultural *systems*, whether they are forms of primitive, palaeotechnic cultivation or of modern, neotechnic farming, simply as distinctive types of man-modified ecosystems.

The methodological merit of this approach is that it provides a framework for the analysis of agricultural systems by focusing attention on the properties they share with all other systems, i.e. structure, function, equilibrium and change. We are thus led to ask four fundamental questions about each agricultural system: how is it organized? how does it function? what degree of stability does it have? and how did it evolve through time? There have been few attempts to answer these questions adequately for major agricultural systems of the modern world, such as plantation agriculture, commercial grain farming and commercial livestock ranching, and at present there is insufficient evidence to do so for any of the agricultural systems of the traditional, "non-Western" world. And yet it is the study of traditional agricultural systems, such as shifting or "swidden" cultivation, fixed-plot horticulture, wet-padi cultivation, nomadic pastoralism and forms of mixed grain–livestock farming, that yields the most valid insights into the origins of agriculture. In what follows the relations between agricultural systems and natural ecosystems are explored as a prelude to deductions about the ecological and cultural conditions most likely to give rise to domestication and the initiation of agriculture. These inferences are put forward as an invitation to enquiry and no attempt is made here to test them against the available "facts"[1].

Agricultural systems and ecosystems

In the study of major natural ecosystems at a regional scale a fundamental distinction can be made between generalized and specialized types[2]. The generalized ecosystems are characterized by a great variety of plant and animal species each of which is represented by a relatively small number of individual organisms. Thus the diversity index of the ecosystem—or the ratio between numbers of species and of individuals—is high. Conversely specialized ecosystems have a low diversity index and are characterized by a small variety of species, each of which is represented by a relatively large number of individuals.

In generalized terrestrial ecosystems net primary productivity, or the increment of plant material per unit of time, tends to be high and many ecological niches are available to species at all trophic levels in the food web, from the primary producers (green plants) to the primary, secondary and tertiary consumers (herbivores, carnivores and top carnivores) to the decomposers (macro-organisms such as worms and woodlice and microscopic protozoa, fungi and bacteria). The structural and functional complexity of generalized ecosystems results in their having greater stability, or homeostasis, than specialized ecosystems. Thus the reduction or removal of a component species, whether by natural or human agency, tends to have less effect because alternative pathways for energy flow are available within the system. When alternative food sources exist for many species at each trophic level, population levels fluctuate less widely and changes in one component are less likely to trigger off a sequence of interactions affecting the whole ecosystem. The tropical rain forest is the most highly generalized, productive and stable of major terrestrial ecosystems. It has the highest diversity index, and, although there are very few precise measurements available, net primary productivity of above-ground plant parts reaches 10–20 grams per square metre per day (*c.* 3600–7200 gm/m^2/yr)[3].

By contrast specialized natural ecosystems are much less productive and tend also to be less stable. Among the most specialized of major terrestrial ecosystems are the tundra, the average annual above-ground primary productivity of which is less than 1 gm/m²/day, although during the brief growing season it may rise to 4 gm/m²/day; the mid-latitude grasslands, whose average annual primary productivity ranges from about 0·5 to 2 gm/m²/day; and the boreal forest, with average annual primary productivity of up to about 2·5 gm/m²/day. There is not always an inverse relationship between the degree of specialization of an ecosystem and its productivity—for example, desert ecosystems are characteristically more generalized than tundra, grassland or boreal forest ecosystems and yet their average annual primary productivity is usually less than 0·5 gm/m²/day—but there is nevertheless a general tendency for primary productivity to be higher in the more generalized ecosystems. Certainly a gradient is apparent in major forest ecosystems from the most highly generalized and productive type, the equatorial evergreen rain forest; through the tropical seasonal semi-evergreen and deciduous forests, where species diversity is less and growth limited by a dry season the length and intensity of which increases with latitude; to the more specialized and less productive mid-latitude temperate deciduous and evergreen forests where growth is checked by winter cold.

It is both valid and illuminating to extend this method of analysing natural ecosystems to the interpretation of agricultural systems. It is at once apparent that most modern, neotechnic agricultural systems are highly specialized; they exist to produce maximum numbers of optimum-sized individuals of one or two preferred plant or animal species. Some traditional, palaeotechnic agricultural systems are similarly, if rather less highly, specialized. Wet-padi cultivation and nomadic pastoralism are both dependent on a very limited range of domestic crops and livestock and have evolved special techniques for raising them and for maintaining the productivity of the system (periodic flooding of the rice on the one hand and seasonal migration of the herds on the other). Many traditional agricultural systems, however, are more generalized. They are polycultural rather than monocultural, raising a diverse assemblage of crops in functional interdependence and sometimes integrating livestock into the system as both consumers and fertilizing agents. Shifting swidden cultivation and fixed-plot horticulture are examples of such generalized systems still widely practised in the tropics, while in mid-latitudes mixed farming—involving the production on the same land of crop combinations of grains, roots and livestock—represents a somewhat less generalized system which has become more specialized by reaching a higher level of technical complexity.

From this comparison between natural ecosystems and agricultural systems three principal ways in which the advent of cultivation changes natural ecosystems can be deduced. The mode of change most apparent today is when more or less generalized natural ecosystems have been transformed into specialized artificial ecosystems. This involves a drastic reduction in the diversity index following replacement of most of the wild species of the ecosystem by a relatively small complement of cultivated plants and domestic animals. The transformation may also lead to the selective increase of certain wild species that thrive in the disturbed habitats associated with cultivation and settlement, i.e. both plant and animal "weeds", but by the build-up of their populations at the expense of more vulnerable members of the natural community, the specialized nature of the ecosystem is enhanced and the diversity index remains low. The transformation of generalized natural ecosystems into specialized agricultural systems usually leads to a loss of net primary productivity, but this is not always so. Under modern methods of intensive farming the trend may be reversed. The productivity of sugar cane under intensive cultivation in Hawaii (6700 gm/m²/yr) falls within the upper range of estimates already quoted for the tropical rain forest; and that of a fertilized maize field in Minnesota was found to be approximately equal to the annual net primary productivity of a nearby deciduous oak wood which had been protected from exploitation[4].

The second mode of change—the transformation of specialized natural ecosystems into more generalized agricultural systems—has happened only rarely. The introduction into areas of mid-latitude grassland of a crop-livestock-weed complex associated with a system of mixed farming, as occurred for example during the nineteenth century on the American prairie and the Argentinian pampas, probably resulted in an increase in diversity index, as has the establishment of polycultural irrigation agriculture in certain desert ecosystems in the twentieth century. But in so far as agriculture has intruded into specialized natural ecosystems, and it is of course effectively absent from the boreal forest and the tundra, then it has tended to do so by replacing the natural ecosystem with monocultural cultivation, such as cereal dry-farming or cotton irrigation, resulting in a lowering of the diversity index.

Thirdly, the agricultural utilization of a natural ecosystem may be accomplished by manipulation rather than transformation; not by drastically changing its diversity index but by altering selected components without fundamentally modifying its overall structure. Instead of an artificial ecosystem being created to replace the natural one, cultivation may proceed by substituting certain preferred domesticated species for wild species that occupy equivalent ecological niches. Thus an assemblage of cultivated trees and shrubs, climbers, herbs and root crops may take over spatial and functional roles essentially similar to those fulfilled by wild species of equivalent life-form in the natural ecosystem. Swidden cultivation and fixed-plot horticulture manipulate the generalized ecosystems of tropical forests in this way and in so doing come closer to simulating the structure, functional dynamics and equilibrium of the natural ecosystem than any other agricultural systems man has devised. The substitution for equivalent wild species of domestic animals rather than crops occurs less frequently in manipulated

..

ecosystems. Certain domesticates—notably dogs and pigs—may fulfil a role as scavengers, but this function is normally confined to the immediate vicinity of settlements and does not lead to replacement of the more widely-ranging wild scavengers. The free-range management of pigs in the forests of medieval Europe, and of cattle too in pre-Roman times, may be thought of as an example of partial substitution of domestic for wild scavengers and browsers, as can the brief phase in the late nineteenth century when open-range cattle replaced bison as the dominant herbivores on the grasslands of the North American Great Plains.

It is this third mode of change that has the greatest relevance to the problems of domestication and the initiation of agriculture. The transform-ation of a generalized natural ecosystem into a specialized artificial one implies a long history of technical and social development prior to the crystallization of the agricultural system. Much time must be allowed for the far-reaching genetic and morphological changes involved in the domestication and continued "improvement" of the relatively few highly productive crops and domestic animals on which each specialized agricultural system depends. Likewise the elaboration of complex stratified societies adapted to maintaining the productivity of each system presupposes social evolution extending over long periods of time. Manipulation of natural ecosystems by substitution of preferred domesticates or semi-domesticates for equivalent wild species in appropriate ecological niches is therefore likely to have occurred long before specialized agricultural systems emerged. If so, then we may next ask which natural ecosystems were most readily manipulated in this way?

There is little reason to suppose that early man manipulated specialized natural ecosystems in the course of his earliest experiments in domestication and cultivation. Virtually no crops and few domestic animals, save perhaps the reindeer and the horse, appear to derive from them. Furthermore the areas occupied by such ecosystems lack archaeological evidence of early agriculture. It is much more probable that cultivation began by the manipulation of generalized ecosystems where the high diversity of wild species would be likely to encourage the use of a wide variety of plants and animals for sub-sistence and perhaps to stimulate experiments in their domestication. This conclusion points to forested and wooded lands within low- and mid-latitudes as the most favoured areas. But, in order to determine in which particular habitats within those areas domestication and cultivation are most likely to have begun, it is first necessary to consider how the subsistence economies of non- or pre-agricultural peoples related to natural ecosystems and what their "potential" for plant and animal domestication may have been.

Pre-agricultural economies and ecosystems

The distinction between generalized and specialized ecosystems can be extended to pre-agricultural subsistence economies just as it can to agricultural systems. Thus it is possible to distinguish between the specialized hunters of prehistoric and historic times, whose subsistence depended on the intensive exploitation of relatively few wild species, and the generalized gatherer-hunter-fisher populations who exploited less intensively a broader spectrum of organic resources.

The specialized hunters characteristically occupied specialized natural ecosystems; among those who survived into historic times were the bison- and guanaco-hunters of the North and South American grasslands and the caribou- and sea mammal-hunting Eskimo of the North American boreal forest and tundra. They did so principally through large-scale co-operative hunting of seasonally migrant herds of game. A high degree of mobility was essential to this way of life and both material culture and social organization became intimately adapted to the exploitation of the principal food source. The use of wild plants for food, fibre, and other purposes represented only a minor element in these highly specialized hunting economies. This fact, together with the limiting effect of frequent migration, suggests that their "potential" for plant domestication was virtually nil: a deduction that is in accordance with the lack of archaeological evidence for early agriculture in the specialized natural ecosystems which they occupied. Judging by the failure of the historically surviving specialized hunters to domesticate any of the animals they hunted—despite the apparent suitability of such herd ungulates as the bison, the guanaco and the caribou—animal domestication, too, seems most unlikely to have begun among such peoples; although it is often suggested that the reindeer, and even the dog, may have been domesticated by specialized hunters.

With few exceptions, the generalized gatherer-hunter-fisher populations occupied the more generalized natural ecosystems. They characteristically formed small localized bands who knew their immediate territory intimately and moved less far and less often than the specialized hunters. Occupying mainly forested and wooded areas, they obtained their subsistence from a wide variety of wild plants, non-migrating "small game" and fish. The combination of a less nomadic mode of existence and an intimate familiarity with the plant life of a circumscribed area suggests that plant domestication is most likely to have been initiated by such peoples. Possibly animal domestication was too, although the evidence suggests that domestication at least of the larger herd animals took place after agriculture had become established.

If gatherer-hunter-fishers are the most likely progenitors of plant domestication we may next ask which habitats offered the best opportunities within the generalized ecosystems that they occupied. The suggested answer is the marginal transition zones or ecotones between major ecosystems, especially forest- and woodland-edge situations. Biological productivity tends to be high at both primary and secondary levels in these situations[5] and they offer maximum variation in the availability of species. They are therefore precisely the areas likely to be chosen by generalized gatherer-hunter-fisher populations because they provide optimum access to the most assured and variable supply of wild plants and animals. Upland-lowland margins, varying in scale from small intermontane valleys to the boundaries of major physiographic provinces, may have been particularly favoured as contact zones between contrasted ecosystems: their significance is borne out for example by recent work in Iran and Mexico[6]. Likewise habitats at forest and woodland margins, where tree cover gives way to more open country, are likely to have been preferentially selected. Here, at the boundaries of forest and steppe, forest and savanna, forest and river, and forest and coast, it would have been easier than elsewhere to combine the cropping of animal protein by hunting herbivores or catching fish with the gathering of wild plants. The more assured and better balanced diet thus afforded would also have reinforced tendencies towards sedentary settlement. This in turn would have increased opportunities for the selection of advantageous mutations through many generations of wild and semi-domesticated plants and would thus have favoured the transition from plant gathering to harvesting to full domestication. Furthermore, it would be around permanently or semi-permanently occupied living sites that disturbance of the local ecosystem by man would most readily result in the creation of the open habitats that provided optimum sites for colonization by the weedy ancestors of later cultigens[7].

So we may hypothesize that the most favourable conditions for plant domestication existed among those generalized gatherer-hunter-fisher populations of forest and woodland margins who established relatively permanent settlements based on an assured supply of animal protein (a less diffuse food source than plant protein) and thus created disturbed, open habitats in the vicinity of the occupied area. From what is known of non-agricultural peoples who survived into historic times it appears that the exploitation of fish, both fresh-water and marine, and of aquatic mammals, is likely to support a more sedentary mode of existence than the hunting of terrestrial "small game"; and so it may be that, in some areas at least, riparian and coastal sites have special significance for the earliest phases of plant domestication and cultivation.

Vegeculture and seed-culture

There is one aspect of the generalized agricultural systems of the traditional world that has particular relevance to the origins of both plant domestication and agriculture: the contrast between those systems that are primarily dependent upon seed-reproduced crop plants ("seed-culture") and those that depend mainly on vegetative reproduction ("vegeculture"). The former appears to represent the indigenous mode of agriculture in the drier tropics and sub-tropics of both the Old and New Worlds. Its antecedents are being successfully probed by archaeological and biological investigations in South-west Asia and Middle America, although not yet in other promising areas, such as climatically and ecologically marginal zones between upland and lowland in West Africa, Ethiopia, South-west Arabia, the Indian sub-continent and China. Vegeculture on the other hand has received little attention and this omission represents a major imbalance in our present approach to the problems of plant domestication and agricultural origins.

Vegeculture is most highly developed as an indigenous agricultural system in the humid tropical lowlands of America and South-east Asia. It is also characteristic of the African tropics, but there it is based largely—although not exclusively—on crops introduced from Asia and America. Starch-rich cultigens with enlarged tubers, roots or rhizomes, such as yuca or manioc (*Manihot esculenta*), sweet potato (*Ipomoea batatas*), arrowroot (*Maranta arundinacea*), lleren or allouia (*Calathea allouia*), yautia, ocumo or tania (*Xanthosoma sagittifolium*), arracacha (*Arracacia xanthorrhiza*), "Kaffir potato" (*Coleus* spp.), taro or eddo (*Colocasia esculenta*), "Fiji arrowroot" (*Tacca pinnatifida*) and the yams (*Dioscorea* spp.), comprise the basic crops of humid tropical vegeculture; while in the Andean highland and southward to the extreme limit of cultivation in Chiloé Island there is a unique extension into cool and cold temperate climates of vegeculture based on the potato (principally *Solanum tuberosum*), associated at higher altitudes with three minor root crops: oca (*Oxalis tuberosa*), ulluco (*Ullucus tuberosus*) and añu (*Tropaeolum tuberosum*).

Ecologically the common denominator of the root crops is that, through their ability to store starch, they are well adapted to survive long dry or cold seasons and to mature quickly once the rains begin or the ground warms up. Likewise their wild ancestors—of which at present we have considerable knowledge only for the potato and the yams[8]—must derive from areas of markedly seasonal climate. We may assume therefore that man's first attempts to select forms with larger tubers, roots and rhizomes took place in such areas. Fig. 1 shows the distribution of tropical seasonal climates and it is likely that the climatic province of the tropical lowland root crops is best represented by the two zones with respectively from $2\frac{1}{2}$ to 5 and from 5 to $7\frac{1}{2}$ dry months in the year. The zone of the tropical rain forest itself, where there are fewer than $2\frac{1}{2}$ dry months, can almost certainly be excluded as a homeland of these cultigens and at the other extreme they become ecologically more and more out of place as the dry season lengthens beyond $7\frac{1}{2}$ months in the year.

If these climatic deductions, and the ecological arguments previously advanced, are correct—and they are of course subject to revision in the light of what may be learned about past climatic change in these areas—then we should look for the origins of tropical lowland vegeculture along semi-

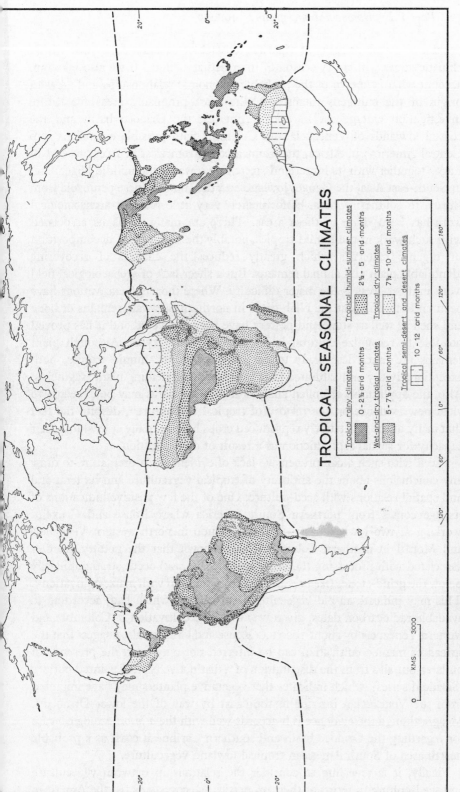

Fig 1 World distribution of tropical seasonal climates
(re-drawn from Map 5, Seasonal Climates of the Earth, by Troll, C. and Paffen, KH., *in* Landsberg, H. E, Lippmann, H, Paffen, KH. and Troll, C. (1963). *Weltkarten zur Klimakunde.* Heidelberg.)

TROPICAL SEASONAL CLIMATES

Tropical rainy climates

0 - 2½ arid months

Wet-and-dry tropical climates

5 - 7½ arid months

Tropical humid-summer climates

2½ - 5 arid months

Tropical dry climates

7½ - 10 arid months

Tropical semi-desert and desert climates

10 - 12 arid months

KMS.   0   3000

deciduous forest margins at riparian, coastal or savanna-edge sites within climatic zones with a dry season of intermediate length. If we also take into account what is known of the probable taxonomic relationships and areas of origin of the cultigens themselves, the most promising areas for future investigation emerge as: in South America, the Orinoco basin and the coastal lowlands of Venezuela and Colombia with possible extensions into Central America; in Africa, the Guinea coast from west of Accra to east of Lagos together with its hinterland stretching towards the middle Niger; and in South-east Asia, the Ganges lowland and the Indo-Chinese peninsula from Burma to southern China. Unfortunately very little relevant archaeological work has been done in these areas. There are many problems associated with such work in the humid tropics, notably the high rate of decomposition of organic materials which greatly reduces the chances of recovering identifiable plant and animal remains. But a sheer lack of archaeological field work in most areas is the major difficulty. Where thorough excavations have been undertaken, as at the Niah caves in northern Sarawak, remains of bone and shell as well as stone and pottery have been recovered and it has proved possible to recognize cultural levels of "Neolithic" type[9]. Although plant remains are much less likely to be recovered in the humid tropics, both exceptionally dry and saturated sites are capable of yielding plant fragments. Also, the application of pollen analysis to tropical floras may be expected to yield new evidence on the history of tropical agriculture[10], despite the fact that many of the vegetatively reproduced crops have partially at least lost their capacity for sexual reproduction as a result of domestication.

Faced with such a comprehensive lack of evidence it is premature to draw any conclusions about the antiquity of tropical vegeculture and its temporal and spatial relations with seed-culture. One of the few positive indications of its age comes from northern South America where Rouse and Cruxent, working at two lowland sites—Rancho Peludo in north-western Venezuela and Momil in northern Colombia—have shown that the pottery griddles associated with processing the bitter manioc (*budares*) occur stratigraphically below the grind-stones (*metates* and *manos*) associated with maize cultivation[11]. This may indicate an old vegecultural substratum which had, according to available radiocarbon dates, given way to maize cultivation in Colombia and western Venezuela by about 1000 B.C. Rouse and Cruxent also suggest that the spread of manioc cultivation can be inferred not only from the presence of budares but also from the distribution of a distinctive type of painted pottery (Saladoid series), which indicates that vegetative planters may have migrated from the Venezuelan interior to the coast by way of the lower Orinoco[12]. Meagre though the evidence is it accords well with the *a priori* ecological case for regarding the Orinoco basin and southern Caribbean coast as a probable hearth area of South American tropical lowland vegeculture.

Finally, it is revealing to consider the relationship between vegeculture and seed-culture in terms of their properties as ecosystems. In the American tropics the distinction between them is broadly reflected in the usage of the terms *conuco* and *milpa*. Milpa is based on seed crops, particularly the uniquely productive combination of maize, beans and squash, and in the past its techniques were normally those of swidden cultivation. Conuco on the other hand is essentially a system of root crop cultivation, often involving the preparation of earth mounds (*montones*) in which stem cuttings and other vegetative parts are planted. It may be practised as a form of swidden, but sometimes fixed-plots are maintained for many years.

Both systems of cultivation are polycultural. A variety of upright, climbing and sprawling crops are grown in close association; in conucos they may be planted together in the same mound. But there are significant differences in the structure and equilibrium of the two systems. The diversity of plants present tends to be greater, their stratification more complex and the canopy of vegetation more completely closed in conuco cultivation: it represents in other words a more highly generalized ecosystem than milpa cultivation. Furthermore, because conuco productivity is focused upon starchy root crops it makes smaller demands on plant nutrients than the relatively protein-rich crops of milpa, notably maize and beans. Less fertility is therefore removed from the soil at harvest and the system has greater inherent stability than milpa. This is further enhanced by the fact that the opportunity for soil erosion is minimal because the ground is seldom if ever bare of plant cover. Provided the soil is deep enough, conucos can be cultivated successfully even on steep slopes without inducing erosion. The milpa ecosystem on the other hand much more easily gets out of equilibrium. The pre-eminence of maize and other nutrient-demanding crops, the less complex stratification and the more open canopy which increases opportunities for weed invasion, all combine to make milpa cultivation less conservative of soil resources and more prone to shift from one temporary clearing to another.

The instability and expansive nature of maize-dominated milpa swidden has been well demonstrated for the Maya lowland of Yucatan[13]; and historically we should expect milpa to exhibit a much greater tendency than conuco to expand into new areas. This may indeed be one of the principal reasons for the predominance of seed-culture over vegeculture in the agricultural systems of aboriginal America at the time of European discovery, related as it would have been to the gradual ascendancy of the seed planters' balanced vegetable diet, based on maize and its associated crops, over the root planters' starch-rich vegetable diet, dependent upon a local supply of animal protein. Thus not only was seed-culture less stable and had a greater inherent tendency to expand, but, by providing a balanced vegetable diet, it allowed expansion to take place into areas where little animal protein was available. Conversely vegeculture created a more stable ecosystem and remained tied to river-bank, seashore, savanna-edge and other ecotone habitats with assured supplies of animal protein. A similar historical pattern of seed-culture expanding into areas of vegeculture is apparent in South-east Asia, where an intrusive rice culture has progressively replaced an indigenous vegecultural system based on yam and taro cultivation[14].

Viewed in this ecological perspective vegeculture appears to be of fundamental importance to our understanding of plant domestication and the beginnings of agriculture. Its antiquity may well equal or even exceed that of seed-culture and until it comes under intensive biological and archaeological study we shall be unable to answer with any confidence the questions of how, where and when agriculture originated.

Notes

1 A general survey of some of the factual evidence relating to agricultural origins in Eurasia, Africa and the Americas will be found in Harris, D. R. (1967). New light on plant domestication and the origins of agriculture: a review, *Geog. Rev.*, **57**, pp. 90–107.

2 The theoretical concepts of ecosystem analysis are fully discussed by Odum, E. P. and H. T. (1959) in *Fundamentals of Ecology*, 2nd ed. Philadelphia, as well as more briefly in (1963). *Ecology*. New York, and by Phillipson, J. (1966). *Ecological Energetics*. London. There have been few attempts to apply ecological principles to the analysis of traditional agricultural systems. The most notable example is the pioneer work of Geertz, C. (1963). *Agricultural Involution: the process of ecological change in Indonesia*. Berkely and Los Angeles.

3 For estimates of net primary production in a variety of ecosystems see Westlake, D. F. (1963). Comparisons of plant productivity, *Biol. Revs. Camb. Phil. Soc.*, **38**, pp. 385–425; and Billings, W. D. (1964). *Plants and the Ecosystem*. London. ch. 7.

4 Ovington, J. D., Heitkamp, D. and Lawrence, D. B. (1963). Plant biomass and productivity of prairie, savanna, oakwood, and maize field ecosystems in central Minnesota, *Ecology*, **44**, pp. 52–63.

5 Ovington, J. D. (1964). Prairie, savanna and oakwood ecosystems at Cedar Creek, *in* Crisp, D. J. (ed.) *Grazing in Terrestrial and Marine Environments*. Oxford. pp. 43–53. Ovington points out that, in the ecosystems he studied, although primary production was highest in the oakwood the savanna was the most efficient ecosystem for creating the greatest mass of potential food for grazing animals.

6 Hole, F. and Flannery, K. V. (1967). The prehistory of South-western Iran: a preliminary report, *Proc. Prehist. Soc.*, **33**, pp. 147–206; Flannery, K. V. (1965). The ecology of early food production in Mesopotamia, *Science*, **147**, pp. 1247–56; Flannery, K. V., this volume, p. 73–100; Flannery, K. V., Kirkby, A. V. T., Kirkby, M. J. and Williams, A. W., Jr. (1967). Farming systems and political growth in ancient Oaxaca, *Science*, **158**, pp. 445–54.

7 For an elaboration of the steps leading to plant domestication and a discussion of the role of "weedy" species in crop ancestry, see Hawkes, J. G., this volume, p. 17–29.

8 See, for example, Hawkes, J. G. (1967). The history of the potato, *J. Roy. Hort. Soc.*, **92**, pp. 207–24, 249–62, 288–302, and 364–5; Coursey, D. G. (1967). *Yams*. London. ch. 2.

9 Harrison, T. (1963–4). 100,000 years of Stone Age culture in Borneo, *J. Roy.Soc.Arts*, **112**, pp. 174–91.

10 See, for example, Laeyendecker-Roosenburg, D. M. (1966). A palyno-

logical investigation of some archaeologically interesting sections in north-western Surinam, *Leidse Geologische Mededelingen*, 38, pp. 31–6.

11 Rouse, I. and Cruxent, J. M. (1963). *Venezuelan Archaeology*. New Haven and London. pp. 5–6 and 53–4.

12 Rouse, I. and Cruxent, J. M. (1963). op. cit. pp. 111–25.

13 Cowgill, U. M. (1962). An agricultural study of the southern Maya lowlands, *Amer. Anthrop.*, 64, pp. 273–86.

14 Spencer, J. E. (1966). Shifting cultivation in Southeastern Asia, *Univ. California Publications in Geog.*, 19, pp. 110–22.

J. G. HAWKES

The ecological background of plant domestication

Introduction

It is a truism of science to say that one cannot solve a problem unless one asks the right sort of questions; and to ask the right questions it is necessary to look at the problem from a particular viewpoint. That viewpoint, so far as the origin of domesticated plants is concerned, is, I am convinced, the ecological one. I shall hope to show that we must look at wild and cultivated plants associated with man as an ecological complex and view this in relation to the ecology of man himself. If we do this we can make considerable progress in understanding the mechanism of domestication, verifying and, when necessary, modifying our hypotheses by reference to exact archaeobotanical data.

It seems fairly certain to us now that domestication of plants and animals started independently in several places at different times, as Helbaek[1] has pointed out. Evidently only certain groups of wild plants were involved in domestication, and Harlan and de Wet[2] show that certain families of plants, especially the Gramineae (grasses) and Leguminosae (beans, peas, etc.) have contributed many major crops; others, such as Cyperaceae, Ranunculaceae, Cactaceae, Caryophyllaceae, Portulacaceae, Berberidaceae, Papaveraceae, Saxifragaceae, Geraniaceae, Onagraceae, Apocynaceae, Asclepiadaceae, Plantaginaceae and many others, have produced no important crops at all.

Then again crops have originated in certain parts of the world only, as was first pointed out by de Candolle[3] who stated: "Agriculture came originally, at least so far as the principal species are concerned, from three great regions, in which certain plants grew, regions which had no communication with each other. These are—China, the south-west of Asia (with Egypt), and inter-tropical America." At a later date Vavilov[4] considerably enlarged on this point by showing that all the major crops originated in the tropical to sub-tropical regions of the world, and in some eleven or twelve centres of origin, based on his concept that centres of diversity could be equated with centres of origin. Although he added further that the origins of plant domestication were to be found in mountain zones in these centres modern research gives some indication that this was probably an over-simplification. We shall return to this point later, but for the moment we can establish quite clearly that cultivated plants arose from a rather restricted number of plant families and in a rather restricted area of the globe. This does not imply, however, that man did not *utilize* all kinds of plants in every area in which he lived. Quite the contrary. All archaeological and ethnobotanical evidence shows clearly that both primitive and relatively advanced peoples have gathered and eaten or otherwise utilized all manner of wild plant products from time immemorial. Even today, we still gather plants, though much less so in our highly industrial urbanized life than was so a hundred years ago[5]. However, the majority of wild plants gathered by mankind have remained firmly wild and have never been domesticated.

Yet some plants, with apparently no more edible or nutritious seeds, fruits or other storage organs than these permanently wild ones were domesticated, and in certain regions of the world only. There must have been, then, in the ancestors of these domesticated plants some special attribute which induced their cultivation. Alternatively, one might postulate that there was some attribute of the peoples of those regions which promoted the invention of agriculture there and nowhere else, but I shall try to develop the thesis that we can look for the basic causes in the plants themselves. Alternative "deterministic" hypotheses which seek to explain the origins of agriculture by postulating a certain stage of mental or sociological development in the peoples concerned or by progressive desiccation of the regions where they lived have not received much support latterly. They will be left to one side for the present though in the end we shall need to return to them, even if in a modified form.

The ancestors of cultivated plants

To arrive at some idea of the attributes of the ancestors of cultivated plants we must look at their closest wild relatives. We clearly cannot study the direct ancestors but only the so-called "ancestral species" which have continued to exist and develop in parallel with the cultivated plants, assuming that these ancestral species have retained many features from the period when domestication took place.

The common factor in cultivated and in closely related wild species is their "weedy tendency", their ecological adaptation to "open", disturbed, or unstable habitats with bare soil and less competition from other plants. This makes use of an ecological, rather than a horticultural definition of weeds, as Bunting[6] and Harlan and de Wet[7] have pointed out, and defines a weed, not in terms of whether it is an unwanted plant competing with those we are trying to cultivate, but one which is adapted to disturbed or open habitats, often requiring high soil nitrogen and able to grow only in those areas where climax forest and grassland have been destroyed.

In a sense, there is very little basic difference between cultivated plant and weed, except that weeds are "unwanted" and cultivated plants are "wanted"; both weeds and crops have the same weedy tendencies, the same ecological adaptation. Weeds, also, may seem to be more agressive than cultivated plants but this is not true in every case, and in primitive agricultural systems it is difficult often to distinguish between weed and crop.

If then the growth and habitat requirements of the cultivated plants and their present-day closely related wild relatives are similar, we can safely assume that the original ancestor of the cultivated plant will have possessed similar ecological characteristics. Vavilov[8] was convinced that "the wild species and varieties most akin to the cultivated plants, form one ecological group with the latter" and cites as examples barley, wheat, oats, lentils, melon, carrot and hemp, all of which possess wild relatives of similar ecological requirements.

How then did the ancestors of our cultivated plants survive in pre-human or pre-agricultural times, given that they were unable to grow in dense plant communities of perennial trees, shrubs or herbs? Evidently they were restricted to disturbed soil along river banks, on gravel, rocks, screes, landslide areas and places where the poor and intermittent rainfall was insufficient to support a vegetation of a perennial nature (scrub deserts, dry intermont basins, for instance). Plants with weedy tendencies may well have evolved in or near the great glaciers which covered vast areas of the northern hemisphere after and during the great Pleistocene glaciations. Other disturbed habitats are provided by the results of overgrazing of herbivores, traffic on game trails, animal trampling and bedding areas, the work of burrowing animals, etc.[9] Clearly there were plenty of disturbed or open areas before the advent of man and he himself only enlarged and multiplied such areas, thus providing many more opportunities for plants with weedy tendencies to spread and increase in numbers. Even before the invention of agriculture, as Sauer[10] and others have suggested, man may have acted as an agent for ecological change by burning vegetation and clearing or trampling it near his camps and trails.

To go back to a point that was made earlier, man has always apparently been a food gatherer (apart from a hunter) and no doubt he gathered weed seeds along with the rest. Yet, curiously enough, some groups of weeds have never become domesticated whilst other plants most obviously were domesticated because of their ecological weediness. Thus, Englebrecht[11] put forward the view that certain primary crops offered themselves to the earliest collecting peoples by growing near their temporary settlements as "habitation weeds", favoured by the high nutritive status of the soil. Such plants sought man out as much as he sought them out, because of their specific manurial requirements.

For example, Sinskaja[12] from a study of hemp (*Cannabis sativa*) showed that weed hemp, just as cultivated hemp, required a very richly fertilized soil and that it was always to be found around the camps of the nomads in the Altai where the soil had been enriched by cattle during the winter, as well as

in kitchen gardens and in rubbish heaps. She drew attention to the wide variation of wild hemp, which followed man's wanderings through the Old World,
postulating that in times of famine man selected for use the forms with less
shattering fruits and higher oil content. Sinskaja pointed out that in the Altai,
one could see all the details of hemp cultivation and she postulated that the
following four stages, which can now be seen simultaneously, followed each
other chronologically when hemp was first cultivated. (1) The plant occurred
only in the wild. (2) It spread from its original wild centres to populated
places. (3) Hemp then began to be utilized by the population. (4) It was finally
cultivated.

Vavilov[13] sums up by stressing that the primitive ancestral forms of cultivated plants already possessed tendencies which induced man to cultivate
them, that man took what was offered to him and that for many plants the
process of their introduction into cultivation took place almost independently
of his will.

This has sometimes been called the "rubbish heap" hypothesis of the
origin of agriculture since it assumes that plants with weedy tendencies
colonized kitchen middens and rubbish heaps and were thus gathered by
primitive man and, imperceptibly perhaps, brought into cultivation[14]. It
does not, however, explain the exact processes of cultivation or throw light on
the following points: (a) Why were plants domesticated only comparatively
recently, some 9000 years ago, and thus for only 0·5% of the total 2 million
years of man's developmental history? (b) Why were only certain plants
cultivated originally from the very wide range of gathered plants and the
fairly wide range of plants with weedy tendencies? (c) Why were the origins
of agriculture restricted to certain areas of the world, even though weeds
seem to be fairly widespread and especially abundant in the northern temperate
belts where agriculture did *not*, in fact, originate?

These questions are not easy to answer, but I think it would be helpful to
consider the following points:

(i) Recent thinking has rightly placed emphasis on the role of weeds in the
evolution of cultivated plants subsequent to their domestication as well as in
the origin of agriculture by the colonization of rubbish heaps. Perhaps, however, we have been a little too enthusiastic about weeds from the ecological
point of view and should look again at the whole situation rather more
critically.

(ii) The ancient primary crops such as wheat, barley, maize, etc., originated
in mountains and for the first two species the direct descendants of their
ancestors are still alive and available for study. We can therefore look more
closely at these species rather than at all weeds, with a view to solving the
problem of agricultural origins.

(iii) The closely related wild relatives of these cereal species grow as weeds
of fields and cultivated land, whilst other species in the same genus are not
found in such habitats but in compact soils on dry slopes.

Origins of seed agriculture

How did the ancestors of the cultivated cereals survive in pre-agricultural times ? To avoid competition with other plants it is evident that they could only grow and survive in poor thin soil on rocks, amongst stones or in sands and gravels, as we have already stated. Furthermore, it seems necessary for them to have been confined to regions with a well-marked wet and dry season, since if the rainfall was continuous such areas would quickly become covered by lush rain forest or dense grasses.

These plants, ancestors of our cultivated plants, were opportunists; they needed to germinate and grow quickly when the rains came in the spring and when the ground warmed up, but equally, they needed to complete a full life cycle and mature their seeds before the ground dried out in the summer. Thereafter the seeds lay dormant in the soil, germinating perhaps a little in the autumn rains, and growing again in the spring to set a new crop of seeds in the early summer. At the same time they were extremely sensitive to competition from other vegetation and for this reason were restricted to areas such as I have just described.

It is interesting to note that most of the ancient Old World seed crops were domesticated in the mountains of the subtropics from about 25° to 45°N where these climatic conditions, with a cold winter, wet spring and autumn and a hot dry summer are to be found. The seeds needed to survive the long hot dry season in a well-baked thin soil, and there must consequently have been a strong selection pressure for large seeds with large food reserves to resist the drying out and grow quickly when the rains came again. In these soils and under these conditions nothing with small seeds would survive well, but nor would large perennial plants either, so these ecological weeds, the ancestors of our cultivated plants, were able to grow and survive under these special conditions without competition from trees or herbaceous perennials.

Such plants, as we have already stated, were pre-adapted for cultivation, and with their weedy tendencies, their need for "open" rich soil conditions, naturally colonized the bare ground and rubbish heaps provided by man. Since they had already evolved large food reserves they were of particular interest to man, who no doubt ate them in preference to the smaller-seeded weeds and wild plants when he could find them. We thus have the two attributes here: (1) "weediness", and (2) large food reserves which enabled them to survive in very dry summer conditions in poor thin soil free from competition with perennial plants. These two factors together seem to me to be the key to the domestication of Old World mountain seed crops.

To primitive man it must have seemed little short of miraculous to find that plants needed for food sprang up by his very huts and paths. Perhaps it is not too far-fetched to suggest that this situation might have been the basis for so many folk-legends which attributed the beginnings of agriculture and the introduction of useful plants to gods or supernatural beings[15].

I suggest, therefore, that seed agriculture was developed in three distinct stages:

1 *Gathering and colonization*

In this first stage the pre-adapted wild plant species with weedy tendencies which were ecologically adjusted to growth in areas with well-marked wet and dry seasons and which possessed rather larger food reserves than normal began to colonize areas around dwelling places and were gathered from here and elsewhere by man, still at the food gathering stage.

All evidence points to the fact that primitive peoples were extremely untidy, so that no doubt seeds were dropped by mistake round their dwellings after they had gathered them from afar. As the plants established themselves the collecting range was diminished and man's collecting and foraging began to be confined more and more to the vicinity of his dwellings where, in the richer nitrogenous soil, the weedy plants established themselves readily. Thus gathering changed imperceptibly into harvesting but as yet there was no planting. In this way a kind of symbiosis resulted from the ecological requirements of the plants on the one hand and the food needs of man on the other.

2 *Harvesting*

This is the second stage, where a build-up of mutations conduced towards more efficient harvesting by the selection of cereals with non-brittle rhachis and in the selection of poor or defective capsule dehiscence in flax, peas, beans and other plants. Thus, unconscious selection by man of the plants with less efficient dispersal methods took place since it was the seeds of these that were automatically more efficiently gathered. Such plants would have been at a disadvantage in the wild, and indeed cereals such as maize lack all methods of natural dispersal and depend entirely on man.

3 *Sowing (planting)*

As a third and final stage sowing as well as harvesting must have taken place. This is an active process which involves the careful retention of seeds and the concept of placing them in the more or less prepared soil of fields or gardens round the dwellings. Probably this came very late when already a high level of social and cultural organization in the primitive "agriculturalists" had been attained. Prior to this stage one could visualize that although seeds from non-brittle cereals and non-dehiscent capsules might have been gathered for consumption only the wild type forms with brittle spikes or dehiscent capsules actually formed the basis of next year's crop, since the others were wholly eaten. At that stage, then, there must have been strong selection pressure *against* the non-brittle rhachis. Not until some of the harvested seeds were kept for active sowing did the selection pressure change *in favour* of non-brittle spikes and *only at that point could the crop be considered to be truly domesticated.*

Origin of root and tuber agriculture

We have been speaking consistently about plants that reproduce from seeds and have neglected all mention of those that reproduce vegetatively. It has been postulated at various times that agriculture based on roots and tubers preceded that based on seeds and fruits, since in the former case the operations of planting and harvesting are almost identical, whilst in the latter these processes are very dissimilar. This sounds on the face of it to be a reasonable and logical hypothesis, but there is no concrete evidence to support it so far as I am aware. It would seem more likely that seed agriculture developed in those areas where suitable seed plants were available and where the ecological conditions for it were suitable, mainly, as we have seen, in the northern subtropical mountain belt of the Old World and in the northern tropical belt of the New World, as Sauer[16] has pointed out. Root and tuber agriculture seems to have developed chiefly in the tropics, though one cannot make too rigid a distinction between the two, and there are many regions where seed and tuber agriculture go on side by side.

Tropical root crops must have originated also in areas with a well-marked wet and dry season, since the plant stores up in its underground organs sufficient food reserves to tide it over the dry period. Large food reserves are a distinct advantage to a plant in a tropical environment which needs to grow extremely quickly when the rains begin in order to compete with trees and shrubs; small seeded cereals, on the other hand, would grow more slowly, and it is therefore quite likely, as Sauer and others have pointed out, that agriculture in the tropics was based primitively on root and tuber cultures, developing in or on the edges of the dry forest zones, probably at low altitudes. Harris[17] considers that the marginal contact zones between major ecosystems (ecotones) may have great significance for the beginning of vegeculture. It seems that the detailed processes may well have been similar to those I have already described for seed cultures, with the three phases of (1) Gathering and colonization, (2) Harvesting, and (3) Planting following in chronological succession.

Sauer has correctly pointed out the enormous emphasis placed on root and tuber agriculture in the New World, as compared with the Old. Not only is there an abundance of tropical tubers (yams, canna, manihot, sweet potatoes, etc.) but we find also a wide range of high mountain cool temperate tuber crops (potatoes, oca, ulluco, arracacha, añu, etc.). This is all the more surprising when we consider that they may have arisen in competition with maize. However, recent discoveries on maize domestication have shown that it may have been first domesticated in Meso-America, and only later spread southwards to the area of the Andean root and tuber crops. Secondly, these latter are cultivated in general at altitudes higher and cooler than are suitable for really efficient maize cultivation and they do not therefore compete with it as much as might be supposed at first glance.

We can postulate the same three stages for the high altitude root and tuber crop domestication as before; my own researches on the potato have shown that in one or two places relics of stage two still exist (in Venezuela and Colombia) where plants are *harvested* from year to year but are never *planted* or are only re-planted when the soil becomes so depleted that the yields drop too low to make it worth continuing to grow the plants in the same place. It is of interest to note further that the one example of continuous harvesting with no planting that I was able to discover was in a kitchen garden near a house, where the soil was continually enriched by household rubbish and the excreta of household animals. This situation seems to me to be a relic (or at least a model) of the early stage two (Harvesting) of agriculture, described above.

Stage one (Colonization and gathering) can be seen very frequently, since wild as well as weed potato species are constantly colonizing areas around fields and settlements. Many of these are eaten if there is a crop failure, and would no doubt be cultivated if their yield and flavour were better; in fact one can go further and state that the really good plants have already been domesticated whilst the poor or mediocre ones still seem to be presenting themselves for domestication, in the same way as the ancestors of the better sorts which were successfully domesticated many thousands of years ago.

An interesting point that might be worth examining here and which Dr. Harris has kindly brought to my attention is whether there are likely to be significant differences in the rate of evolution of root and tuber crops as compared with seed crops. The former reproduce vegetatively and do not therefore benefit from the effects of sexual reproduction which brings with it genetic segregation and a potentially greater rate of change. We must remember that most primitive tuber crops are capable of sexual reproduction and seedlings arise spontaneously, whose tubers will be incorporated in the crop. On the other hand, the advanced Old World cereals are self-fertilizing and an exchange of genes is not then possible between individuals. This would slow down the rate of change. Maize, however, is a cross-fertilizing seed crop and most certainly exhibits an enormous amount of variation. On the whole, I doubt whether any conclusions can be drawn on the length of domestication of vegetatively versus sexually reproducing crops from this line of enquiry.

Primary and secondary crops

Vavilov[18] has shown that a number of domesticated plants were not cultivated directly from the wild but arose in a rather different manner at a later stage as weeds of cultivation. He thus divides cultivated plants into two distinct groups of crops.

1 *Primary crops*, comprising all those ancient crops that, so far as we know, were domesticated directly from wild plants (even though the wild plants possessed strong weedy tendencies). Examples of this group are wheat, barley, rice, soyabean, flax and cotton. To those we could also add maize and potatoes.

2 *Secondary crops*, which originated as weeds in admixture with the primary crops, and generally at a much later stage. Examples of these are rye, oats, *Eruca sativa* and a number of other minor crops. These became adjusted to growth in various primary crops (e.g. rye in soft and club wheats and oats in emmer—*Triticum dicoccum*) and mimicked them in a number of physiological and morphological characters through the effect of unconscious artificial selection.

As the principal crops were taken into areas further north or at higher altitudes they were less well-adapted to the harsher climatic conditions and poorer soils; the weeds on the other hand, were better adapted to such conditions and hence the percentage of weeds increased until finally the weed became the crop and the crop the weed. This hypothesis had also been advanced by Englebrecht[19] though it was not documented as fully by him as by Vavilov.

In a rather different way the tomato can also be thought of as a secondary crop since it apparently spread northwards from Peru through the New World tropics to Mexico as a weed of maize and bean fields. It was actually brought into cultivation in Mexico, though it may have persisted as a garden weed for a very long time.

Important crops such as oats and rye thus originated as weeds, just as, in a sense, the primary crops such as wheat and barley originated because of their weedy tendencies. In addition, most of our crops in their centres of diversity, and even outside, are associated with very closely associated weed species, some so close that they are often thought of merely as weed forms of the same species. These weeds, as Harlan[20] rightly points out, represent rapidly evolving races which are able to exchange genes with the crop through occasional bursts of hybridization[21]. They act as reservoirs of variability and are of the greatest importance in the evolution of the crop itself. They are thus of great importance to the plant breeder in his search for valuable genetic variation, and Vavilov in his use of weed forms for breeding set a pattern which many other breeders have followed.

Mountains as the home of agriculture

Vavilov[22] counters the views of Metchnikov that cultivated plants originated first in the great river basins of the Nile, Ganges, Euphrates, etc., by stating that the entire racial diversity of the field and vegetable crops studied by him is concentrated in mountainous districts. It is well known now that agriculture in these large river valleys had already reached a high level of sophistication, depending for success on meteorological prognostication and a knowledge of geometry and surveying so as to predict the time of water flow and to conduct the water through a proper system of irrigation channels. Vavilov further points out that mountains supply optimum conditions for differentiation of races and varieties, for the preservation of diverse ecotypes and for manifesting varietal diversity. He points also to the fact that mountains are excellent isolators, providing a wide range of different conditions, isolated valleys and all the essential prerequisites for rapid evolution, both in wild and in cultivated plants. He also emphasizes the importance of the varied ethnic composition of the mountain inhabitants of S.W. Asia, the Caucasus and N.W. India, contrasting that with the poor ethnic diversity of the peoples of the Alps and Pyrenees, which he thinks might explain the absence of variation in the cultivated plants of those latter areas. Helbaek[23] concurs with Vavilov in considering that the natural habitats of the primary crops of S.W. Asia, wheat, barley, flax, etc., are the mountains, where adequate rainfall for non-irrigation agriculture exists. On the other hand, the basins of the Nile and Euphrates-Tigris do not answer to these requirements; furthermore, it cannot be demonstrated that the wild progenitors of the plants mentioned ever existed in these valleys.

The tropical lowlands as the home of agriculture

Because of this well substantiated thesis that the mountains of south-western Asia, the Caucasus and parts of the Himalayas were the cradles of agriculture for many crops we have hitherto assumed that all agriculture began in mountains, believing as we do that it arose more than once and was based on a wide variety of different plants. It is certainly thought that the cool-temperate root and tuber crops of the Andes were first domesticated in the mountains and that maize also was cultivated primarily in rather dry medium altitude valleys of Meso-America. However, it seems doubtful whether we can extrapolate the hypothesis to include tropical root and tuber crops or tropical grain crops[24]. We should do better to consider that their origins lay in the lowland tropical belt, in areas of intermittent rainfall with a well-marked dry season and probably on the forest-savanna margins or in low stony hills where the soil cover was poor. Here again, competition with climax forest or grassland would be considerably reduced, as we saw for the subtropical mountain seed crops. By examining a map of the wet/dry belts in tropical latitudes we could, I think, limit our search for the regions of origin of many wide-spread tropical crops. Added to this we should consider the distribution areas of the nearest wild relatives as de Candolle[25] did, so as to clarify and define more exactly the areas in which the cultivated plants were first domesticated.

Prerequisites for agriculture in human societies

In embarking on this subject as a botanist, I realize that I am treading on extremely thin ice. Yet one or two points might be worth making, if for no other reason than to promote discussion.

Many social anthropologists have made the point that agriculture cannot originate until man takes up a sedentary life, presumably engaged in fishing or restricted by the terrain of mountains from roaming for great distances. Since few cultivated plants and certainly none of the primary crops are derived from maritime plants it can therefore be assumed that the fishing was carried out in fresh-water rivers or lakes. This must surely apply to lowland tropical crop origins since one would hardly assume that there were sufficient fish in small mountain streams for the upland pre-agriculturalists to make use of them.

A second point often made is that the incentive to cultivate the land was from surplus and not from hunger. I have attempted to show that there was no incentive involved in the three stages of agriculture as I have set them out, but that the process, once started, was practically automatic. Good plants appeared, as if by magic or as a gift from the gods, and gathering changed imperceptibly into harvesting and thence into planting.

Nevertheless a large unsolved problem still exists, which I mentioned before but which I have not attempted to solve. Why in fact did it take man so long to become an agriculturalist, some 99·5% of his total period on earth as a distinct species? Fossil evidence, such as the wild maize pollen from peat below the City of Mexico with a radiocarbon dating of 80,000 years, shows that the plants were available long before their domestication took place. The problem is thus taken out of the botanist's sphere and handed firmly back to the ethnologist and social anthropologist. It seems that one may need to bring in concepts of the correct stage of sociological or tool-making development in order to explain this, and since we have already stated that agriculture needed a settled mode of existence before it could begin we must assume that man did not develop such a settled mode of existence until some 9000 years ago, and then only in certain places. When this stage in human development was reached agriculture could then begin, if the right plants were also available.

Conclusions

In this paper I have tried to show the importance of an ecological approach in solving problems of domestication, building on the work of Vavilov and others, and putting forward a number of points of my own for discussion.

Cultivated plants and their ancestors are, from one point of view, nature's misfits. They cannot form a part of climax vegetation but must needs take advantage of disturbed open soils or rocky areas of such poor soil quality that nothing without the tenacious powers of quick growth and ability to store large quantities of food could survive. Not all plants with weedy tendencies could have been cultivated but it seems certain now that without weedy tendencies no plant could have been cultivated primitively, nor could it have come in at a later stage as a secondary crop. Once the main food crops had been domesticated many other lesser crops, garden plants, flowers and trees were brought into cultivation. With these, no doubt the basic pre-requisites were quite different, and I should go beyond my brief to discuss them here. We have been interested in trying to solve the problem of how agriculture first arose, for the agricultural revolution has undoubtedly been, together with the use of tools and the discovery of fire, one of the most important phenomena in the history of mankind.

Notes

1 Helbaek, H. (1959). How farming began in the Old World, *Archaeology*, 22, pp. 183–9.
2 Harlan, J. R. and de Wet, J. M. J. (1965). Some thoughts about weeds, *Econ. Bot.*, 19, pp. 16–24.
3 de Candolle, A. (1855). *Géographie Botanique Raisonée*. Paris; de Candolle, A. (1882). *Origin of Cultivated Plants*. English trans. London, published 1884.
4 Vavilov, N. I. (1926). Studies on the origins of cultivated plants, *Bull. Appl. Bot. Pl.-Breed.*, 16, pp. 1–245.
5 See Schwanitz, F. (1966). *The Origin of Cultivated Plants*. (Trans. from German edition of 1957.) Cambridge, Mass.
6 Bunting, A. H. (1960). Some reflections on the ecology of weeds, *in* Harper, J. L. (ed.) *The Biology of Weeds*. Oxford.
7 Harlan, J. R. and de Wet, J. M. J. (1965). ibid.
8 Vavilov, N. I. (1926). ibid.
9 Harlan, J. R. and de Wet, J. M. J. (1965). ibid.
10 Sauer, C. O. (1952). *Agricultural Origins and Dispersals*. New York.
11 Engelbrecht, T. (1916). Über die Entstehung einiger feldmässig angebauter Kulturpflanzen, *Geogr. Z*, 22, pp. 328–34; quoted by Darlington, C. D. (1963). *Chromosome Botany and the Origins of Cultivated Plants*. (2nd ed.) London.
12 Sinskaja, E. N. (1925). Field crops of Altai, *Bull. Appl. Bot. Pl.-Breed.*, 14, pp. 367–70; quoted by Vavilov, N. I. (1926). ibid.
13 Vavilov, N. I. (1926). ibid.

14 See Sauer, C. O. (1952). ibid.; See Anderson, E. (1954). *Plants, Man and Life*. London.

15 Thus, de Candolle, A. (1882). op. cit. p. 1, states: "The traditions of ancient peoples, embellished by poets, have commonly attributed the first steps in agriculture and the introduction of useful plants, to some divinity, or at least to some great emperor or Inca." See also Darlington, C. D. (1963). op. cit. p. 133.

16 Sauer, C. O. (1952). ibid.

17 Harris, D. R., this volume, pp. 3-15.

18 Vavilov, N. I. (1926). ibid.

19 Engelbrecht, T. (1916). ibid.

20 Harlan, J. R. (1965). The possible role of weed races in the evolution of cultivated plants, *Euphytica*, 14, pp. 173–6.

21 See also Hutchinson, Sir J. (ed.) (1965). *Essays on Crop Plant Evolution*. Sect. 7, Crop plant evolution: a general discussion. Cambridge.

22 Vavilov, N. I. (1926). ibid.

23 Helbaek, H. (1960). Ecological effects of irrigation in ancient Mesopotamia *Iraq*, 22, pp. 186–96.

24 See, for example, Harris, D. R. (1967). New light on plant domestication and the origins of agriculture: a review, *Geog. Rev.*, 57, pp. 90–107.

25 de Candolle, A. (1855). ibid.

C. VITA-FINZI

Geological opportunism

We do not know how, or to what extent, primitive man responded to climate; we shy away from thinking that any such response was decisive. Yet geologists, palynologists and their colleagues continue to devote their energies to expressing their findings in climatic terms for the benefit of the archaeologist. And this even when their client is becoming increasingly convinced that climatic change does not appear to account for "significant subsistence shifts . . . in the archaeological record"[1] and that human populations at the hunting gathering stage, in that they do not *a priori* live at starvation level[2], are not vulnerable to climatic blackmail.

An unfortunate corollary of this climate-oriented approach (which, incidentally, pervades most studies concerned with the Pleistocene) is that workers in diverse fields try to employ climatic terms as their *lingua franca* even when the climatic implications of their findings are not necessarily comparable or related. Consider, for example, a situation where the pollen spectrum within a sediment has been grossly distorted (the use of this term is not meant to imply that an ideal, undistorted spectrum necessarily exists) by anomalous winds blowing from a highland during a particular season, whereas the sediment that harbours the pollen has been laid down by an isolated downpour falling in a lowland area. The reduction of both sets of data to climatic terminology is unlikely to reveal how they are associated. The theme of the present paper is that, at least as regards the study of plant and animal domestication and the history of agriculture, some of the indicators that are defective in the reconstruction of ancient climates may directly furnish us with information on past conditions which is as relevant as climate to the issues at stake and sometimes more so.

To pursue a little further the hypothetical illustration given above, the fact that deposition was accomplished by flood-flow may in itself be of primary significance. Two cases where this proves to have been the case at a time which might be deemed "sensitive" in terms of early agriculture will be mentioned in the hope that other workers may be encouraged to consider the primary implications of geological (and analogous) evidence while shelving its secondary, climatic connotations.

The first example is that of the Tesuque Valley in New Mexico, which displays two alluvial terraces. The older of the two, which stands 18–20 feet above the stream, has yielded a radiocarbon date of 2230 ± 250 years from a sample found at a depth of 13 feet; pottery found on its surface suggests that deposition had ended by A.D. 1200–1250. Miller and Wendorf state: "While deposition of the high-terrace alluvium was occurring, the floodplain of Rio Tesuque would have been an excellent area for the practice of flood-water farming (Bryan 1929)[3]. The numerous villages located by the archaeologic survey indicate that the valley supported a large population during this period. Later, when the high terrace was trenched by erosion, the area suitable for floodwater farming was greatly reduced[4]."

The second example is that of the upper Wadi Hasa in Jordan[5]. Near Qal'at el Hasa the floor of this valley is underlain by an alluvial deposit (the Hasa Formation) which has a maximum thickness of 5 m. and which has yielded Kebaran artifacts and, one metre below its surface, charcoal dated to 3960 B.P. As pre-Kebaran upper palaeolithic remains, though present in an older fill nearby, appear to be absent from the Hasa Formation, its deposition may be placed somewhere between 10,000 and 2000 years ago, with the bulk of it laid down by 4000 B.P. The character of the fill—a well-bedded silty fine sand—suggests deposition by periodic flooding. This leads to a conclusion similar to that reached by Miller and Wendorf with regard to the Tesuque high terrace, namely that "for a period of several millennia Wadi Hasa was endowed with broad, undissected valley floors, subject to periodic silt deposition by floods, conditions reminiscent of those exploited by the Navahos in New Mexico (Bryan, 1954:16)"[6]. The repeated reference to Bryan deserves some comment.

To judge from Bryan's illustrations, the chief prerequisite for floodwater farming is an undissected alluvial floor, since diversion is the means by which the floodwaters are exploited. In the instances he gives, drinking water could be obtained from surface depressions and from an easily tapped high water-table; the valley vegetation furnished fuel and timber. Continuing aggradation was significant only in so far as the cultivable area was thereby progressively increased, but the renewal of fertility by silt deposition, which we have come to associate with Nilotic flood cultivation, apparently played no significant part in the exploitation of Chaco Canyon.

Now it is true that aggradation would here seem to have been occasioned by a moister climatic interlude; yet the hazards of drought remained although, as today, their role was simply to "limit the number of people and fix their standards of living"[7]. In other words the climatic factor is relevant in this context only in that it inhibited erosion; it was the non-degrading situation which, in Bryan's words, "afforded a locality for the initiation and development of a civilization based on agriculture"[8], or as one might say in today's more moderate parlance, provided "lands of high water-retention, where soil moisture helped the planted cereals to survive annual fluctuations in rainfall"[9]. This kind of situation can be detected in the stratigraphic record without the need to opt for any of the theories advanced to explain the alternation between erosion and deposition in semi-arid environments; yet it tends to be eclipsed by the search for causes.

The *geological opportunism* exhibited by the inhabitants of Chaco Canyon, and possibly by those of the Tesuque Valley and Wadi Hasa, evidently changes in scope as technology progresses. If Cleopatra's nose had been shorter, there would have been no Actium, and Nicopolis would not have been built to commemorate Augustus' victory; but the city could only survive with the help of a long aqueduct. Even then its economic survival cannot have been easy; the rich plain of Arta which lies at its door did not come into being until the Middle Ages[10], and could not be fully exploited until modern drainage had cured its swamps and their malaria[11]. The plain is thus irrelevant to the problem of Nicopolis, but this became clear only when it had been dated.

So far we have considered soils which in some way favour or require some particular agricultural mode of operation. More generally, one can contribute to the problems central to this volume by considering the *total available cultivable land* during the period in question. In many parts of the Old World, for example, extensive areas of soil are localized on a small number of datable alluvial deposits[12]. While it is impossible to state categorically that the valleys were composed of bare bedrock prior to the deposition of these alluvial bodies, one can at least specify when they came into being by means of archaeological, radiocarbon or other dating techniques. In Iran, for example, there have been two major periods of alluvial accumulation, of which the earlier took place roughly between 40,000 and 10,000 years ago[13]. Even without postulating depositional conditions propitious to floodwater farming it is difficult to evade the conclusion that this period was more favourable to experiments in agriculture than, say, the current phase of downcutting. What is more, aggradation ultimately both called for, and made possible, the excavation of *qanats*[14]. In this respect geological change can be said to have prompted something more than opportunism.

The formation of China's loess deposits is analogous in that on its date hinge a number of theories regarding early exploitation of the land[15]. But it has to be remembered that soil may be lost as well as gained, and in ways more decisive than merely by a decline in its fertility or an increase in its salinity. Raikes has suggested that Beidha may have been abandoned principally because its soil was eroded[16]. There may be other early farming sites where erosion has removed all traces of advantageous geological conditions; but there are many (some of them already excavated) where the evidence has survived.

Notes

1 Flannery, K. V., this volume, pp. 73–100.
2 Flannery, K. V., this volume, ibid.
3 Bryan, K. (1929). Floodwater farming, *Geog. Rev.*, **19**, pp. 444–56.
4 Miller, J. P. and Wendorf, F. (1958). Alluvial chronology of the Tesuque Valley, New Mexico, J. *Geol.*, 66, pp. 177–94.
5 Vita-Finzi, C. (1966). The Hasa Formation, *Man*, **1**, pp. 386–90.
6 Bryan, K. (1954). The geology of Chaco Canyon, New Mexico, *Smithsonian Misc. Coll.*, **122** (7).
7 Bryan, K. (1954). op. cit. p. 46.
8 Bryan, K. (1954). op. cit. p. 45.
9 Flannery, K. V., this volume, ibid.
10 Higgs, E. S. and Vita-Finzi, C. (1966). The climate, environment and industries of Stone Age Greece; Part II, *Proc. Prehist. Soc.*, **32**, pp. 1–29.
11 *Admiralty Handbook of Greece*. (1945). **3**, p. 36.
12 Vita-Finzi, C. (1969). *The Mediterranean Valleys*. Cambridge.
13 Vita-Finzi, C. (In press). Quaternary alluvial chronology of Iran, *Geol. Rdsch.*
14 Wulff, H. E. (1968). The Qanats of Iran, *Scientific American*, **218**, pp. 94–105.
15 Smalley, I. J. (1968). The loess deposits and Neolithic culture of northern China, *Man*, **3**(2), pp. 224–41.
16 Raikes, R. L. (1966). Beidha. Prehistoric climate and water supply, *Palestine Exploration Quarterly*, **98**, pp. 68–72.

W. van ZEIST

Reflections on prehistoric environments in the Near East

Introduction

In all discussion of the domestication of plants and animals in the Near East, prehistoric environments and especially changes in the environment play an important part. The stimulating theory that a general desiccation of North Africa and South-west Asia after the last glacial period was a direct factor in the origin of domestication has, of course, been abandoned. This by no means implies, however, that the question as to how far changes in climate may have affected the evolution of food production is no longer important. Further, the distribution of the wild ancestors of the domesticates in earlier times would have depended upon the environmental conditions. Harlan and Zohary are quite correct in warning that the domestication of cereals may not have taken place where the wild species were most abundant[1]. On the other hand, it is not likely that farming started outside the distribution area of wild cereals.

At present, there is a serious discrepancy between demand and supply of information on the Late Quaternary[2] climatic and vegetational history of the Near East. One tries in such a case to make the utmost of the little information on palaeo-environment so far available; but this easily results in generalizations and far-reaching conclusions which are not justified at the present state of knowledge. Besides, the same palynological information is not infrequently brought forward as evidence for more or less contradictory opinions.

In this paper I shall try to suggest along what lines palaeobotanical information may be utilized in reconstructing prehistoric environments. This discussion will inevitably lead to an attempt to reconstruct the distribution of the major vegetational units in the past. I wish to stress that one should not rely too heavily on these reconstructions, since they are based on too scanty evidence. They are mainly intended to serve as illustrations of the reasoning pursued. It is to be hoped that in the not too remote future speculations on palaeo-environments in the Near East can be replaced by more firmly established conclusions.

The locations of prehistoric settlements and of pollen-diagram sites referred to in this paper are shown in Fig. 3.

The present natural vegetation zones

A satisfactory reconstruction of the vegetation in earlier times requires a sufficiently dense network of pollen diagrams covering the region concerned. Although the prospects for more palaeobotanical data from the Near East are not discouraging, the scarcity of pollen-bearing sediments will always force us to reconstruct the Late Quaternary vegetational history of this part of the world on less ample information than is the case, for example, for western Europe.

When only fairly scattered palaeobotanical information is available, the present distribution of the natural vegetation types can be very useful in reconstructing vegetational patterns of the past. By natural vegetation we understand the plant cover which would be present if man had not exercised his influence. As a consequence of human activity for many thousands of years, which often resulted in the complete destruction of the original plant cover over large areas, the determination of the natural vegetation type can be difficult and may lead to differences of opinion.

The distribution of the major vegetational units in the Near East is shown in Fig. 1. It should be stressed that this vegetation map provides a very generalized picture. Moreover, the delimitation of the vegetational units is often more or less arbitrary.

The vegetation zones are determined by precipitation and temperature. Forests constitute the natural vegetation in regions with sufficient precipitation and, at the same time, where temperatures are not too low. In steppe and desert-steppe areas, the climate is too dry for trees. At high elevations, where alpine vegetations are found, low temperatures and especially the short growing season prevent tree growth. Frequently between the forest and the steppe a transitional zone with a steppe-forest vegetation is to be distinguished or at least postulated.

In reference to the vegetational units distinguished in Fig. 1 the following remarks can be made. The forest vegetations can be divided into two major ecological groups. Mesic forests occur in areas receiving sufficient precipitation spread over the whole year, while xeric forests must endure a more or less severe dry period in the summer. Mesic forest types, which are characterized by a large number of deciduous tree species, are found in the regions adjoining the Black Sea and the Caspian.

Within the summer-dry forests, a distinction is made between those which do not tolerate cold (Mediterranean vegetations) and the temperate to hardy forest vegetations. The thermophilous Mediterranean vegetations consist largely of evergreen trees and shrubs and of pines.

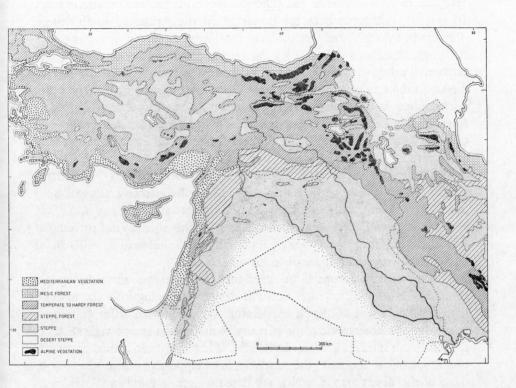

MEDITERRANEAN VEGETATION
MESIC FOREST
TEMPERATE TO HARDY FOREST
STEPPE FOREST
STEPPE
DESERT STEPPE
ALPINE VEGETATION

0   300 km

Fig 1 Vegetation map of the eastern Mediterranean region
(adapted from vegetation maps for Iran (Bobek, H. (1951). Die natürlichen
Wälder und Gehölzfluren Irans, *Bonner Geographische Abhandlungen*, **8**;
Zohary, M. (1963). On the Geobotanical Structure of Iran, *Bull. of the Research Council of Israel*, **11d**, Suppl.), Turkey (Louis, H. (1939). Das natürliche Pflanzenkleid Anatoliens, *Geogr. Abhandh.*, **3**, Reihe, Heft **12**), Syria
(Pabot, H. (1957). Rapport au gouvernement de Syrie sur l'écologie végétale
et ses applications, FAO Rapport No. **663** (Rome)), Lebanon (Pabot, H. (1959).
Rapport au gouvernement du Liban sur la végétation sylvo-pastorale et son
écologie, FAO Rapport No. **1126** (Rome)), and Palestine (Zohary, M. (1962).
Plant Life of Palestine, New York).)

The temperate to hardy summer-dry forest belt includes a few regionally different types. In the Zagros Mountains of western Iran and north-eastern Iraq, the deciduous Persian oak (*Quercus persica*) is the most common tree[3]. In general, deciduous oaks are dominant in the forests of south-eastern Turkey, but in this area tree junipers can likewise play an important part. Although deciduous oaks are by no means absent in south-western and western Turkey, tree junipers and pine are the main constituents of the forest. In the south-west, cedar (*Cedrus libani*) and Cilician fir (*Abies cilicica*) are common at higher elevations, between 1000 and 2000 m.[4] The cedar-forest zone in Lebanon and western Syria is likewise included in the temperate to hardy forest belt[5]. In northern Turkey, deciduous oaks as well as pine play an important part in the summer-dry forests.

The extent of the original steppe-forest vegetation is most difficult to establish. This is because these areas have been under intensive cultivation for many years. Louis[6] does not distinguish a separate steppe forest in Turkey and it looks as if Pabot's[7] criteria for delimiting this zone do not correspond with those of Bobek[8] and Zohary[9]. Among the trees and shrubs which are at home in the steppe forest are pistachio and almond.

The last ecological zone to be mentioned is the steppe where aridity is a common feature. Since steppes occur at elevations ranging from 200 to more than 1500 m. above sea level, temperature conditions can differ quite considerably. A characteristic plant of many Near Eastern steppe vegetations is the sagebrush species *Artemisia herba-alba*. Where the mean annual precipitation drops below 100 mm., the relatively rich steppe vegetations give way to those of the desert steppe, which are much poorer in number of species as well as in overall plant cover.

The palynological information

To date, the most complete published palaeobotanical record for the Late Quaternary in the Near East, is that from Lake Zeribar, situated in the Zagros Mountains of western Iran, at an elevation of *c.* 1300 m.[10] The natural vegetation in the Lake Zeribar area is the Zagrosian oak forest. Since the palaeobotanical results obtained from the Lake Zeribar sediment cores fill a key-position in the discussions on the Late Quaternary climatic and

Fig 2 Generalized pollen diagram for sediments from Lake Zeribar, western Iran
(van Zeist, W. and Wright, H. E. (1963). Preliminary pollen studies at Lake Zeribar, Zagros mountains, south-western Iran, *Science*, **140**, pp. 65–7; van Zeist, W. (1967). Late Quaternary vegetation history of western Iran, *Rev. Palaeobot. Palynol.*, **2**, pp. 301–11. The diagram shows the ratio between arboreal and non-arboreal pollen and some selected pollen types. The radiocarbon dates (Yale Radiocarbon Laboratory) between brackets are from the lower part of the I-13 core.)

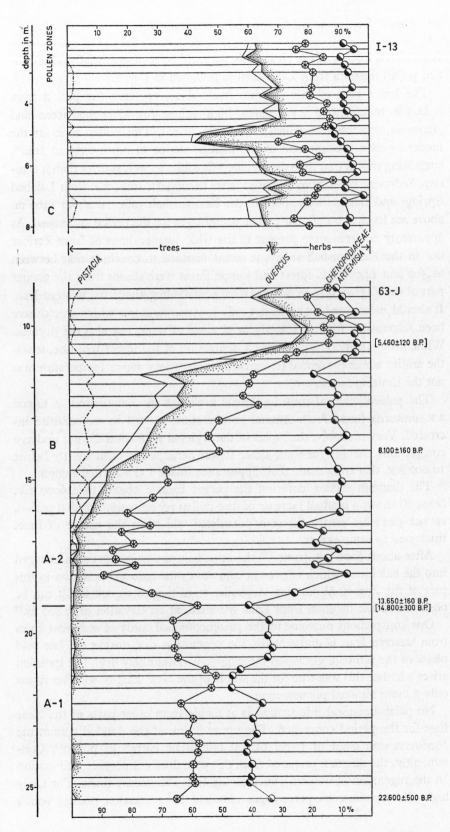

vegetational history of the Near East, they will be reviewed briefly. A simplified pollen diagram from Lake Zeribar is shown in Fig. 2.

The lower part of this diagram (zone A-1), covering the period from *c.* 22,500 to *c.* 14,000 B.P., shows high values for Chenopodiaceae and *Artemisia*, whereas tree pollen is virtually absent. This pollen zone fits the modern pollen precipitation of the plateau steppe of north-western Iran[11], suggesting that at that time the climate was cooler as well as drier than it is today. Sediment cores from two other sites in western Iran, *viz.* from Lalabad Springs and Lake Nilofar, both in the Kermanshah valley at about 1300 m. above sea level, show similar pollen assemblages for the period concerned. As apparently no trees were present in the wide surroundings of Lake Zeribar nor in the Kermanshah valley, it seems justified to conclude that between 22,500 and 14,000 B.P. forest and steppe forest were absent from the greater part of the Zagros, if trees had not disappeared altogether from western Iran. It should be stressed that it is not only low temperatures which would have been responsible for this scarcity or absence of trees, but also the dryness. While lower temperatures caused a depression of the upper tree line, it was the aridity which prevented tree growth at elevations where temperature was not the limiting factor.

The palaeobotanical record suggests a change in climate from *c.* 14,000 B.P. onwards (zone A-2). Annual precipitation as well as temperature increased. Very probably, the aspect of the regional vegetation did not undergo conspicuous changes for some time. It was perhaps not until shortly before 10,000 B.P. that trees made their appearance in the Lake Zeribar region.

The diagram section covering the period from *c.* 10,000 to *c.* 6000 B.P. (zone B) shows a gradual increase of tree-pollen percentages. For that period, an oak-pistachio steppe forest is postulated which, in the course of time, thickened to some extent.

After about 6000 B.P. (zone C) the open oak-pistachio vegetation changed into the oak forest which at present constitutes the natural vegetation in this part of the Zagros Mountains. A similar transition to an oak forest can be observed in the diagram from Lake Mirabad, at an elevation of *c.* 800 m.[12]

One conspicuous outcome of the palaeobotanical study of sediment cores from western Iran is undoubtedly the conclusion that during the last cold phase of the ultimate glaciation the climate was definitely dry. The question arises whether this was true for the whole of the Near East or whether it was only a more regional phenomenon.

No palaeobotanical information is available from other parts of the Near East for the period concerned. The upper 80 m. of the Ashdod core at the Mediterranean coast of Israel turned out to be barren of pollen[13]. Consequently, the diagram prepared from this core does not provide information on the vegetation of western Israel during Late Pleistocene times. The fairly high Chenopodiaceous percentages obtained for regression phases, which would correspond with glacial periods, could indicate that also during earlier glaciations periods with a dry climate occurred.

On the other hand, pollen diagrams from Ioannina, in north-western Greece, and from Tenagi Philippon, in north-eastern Greece, demonstrate that the dry climate of the last part of the ultimate glaciation was not confined to western Iran[14]. The Ioannina diagram points to a steppe forest or to a mosaic of forest and steppe for the period between *c.* 30,000 and 14,000 B.P., while the Tenagi Philippon diagram reflects a steppe-like vegetation during the last glacial period.

The pollen evidence from both western Iran and northern Greece suggests that between *c.* 30,000 and 14,000 years ago, the climate in the Near East was not only colder than it is at present, but that it was also considerably drier. This conclusion is supported by Bobek's geomorphological studies, which suggest that on the interior plateau of Iran, the influence of continentality has been strengthened rather than weakened during the cold spells of the Pleistocene[15].

From his geological studies in Libya Hey concluded that between 32,000 and 12,000 B.P., temperatures were lower and the winters wetter than they are today[16]. This would indicate that the climatic conditions in North Africa during the Late Pleistocene were not wholly comparable with those in the Near East.

The reconstruction of the past vegetation

What would have been the vegetation in the Near East for the period between *c.* 35,000 and 14,000 B.P., assuming that over the whole region the climate was cooler as well as drier than it is today? It has already been stated that the palynological study of sediment cores in western Iran leads to the conclusion that during the period concerned, at least the greater part of the Zagros must have been treeless. Since it was dryness which would have prevented tree growth at lower elevations, it is apparent that the Mesopotamian and Syrian lowland, where temperatures were higher and precipitation lower than in the mountains, would not have been at all suitable for trees.

Climatic conditions in the interior of Turkey would not have differed much from those in western Iran during the last cold spell of the ultimate glaciation. Consequently, at that time the larger part of Turkey would also have been covered by treeless vegetations.

It is likely that forests and steppe forests were confined to a few areas, which at present receive appreciable amounts of rain at lower elevations. The precipitation map (Fig. 3) indicates that such areas could have been found in the mountains along the Mediterranean in Lebanon, western Syria and south-western Turkey. Furthermore, the mountainous regions adjoining the Black Sea and the Caspian would have supported forest vegetations.

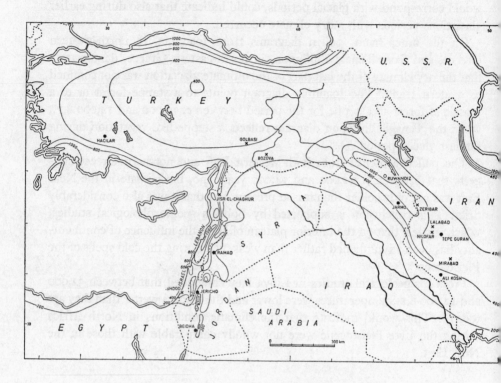

Fig 3 Precipitation map of the eastern Mediterranean region
(The isohyets for Iran and Iraq are redrawn from Wright, H. E. (1961).
Pleistocene Glaciation in Kurdistan, *Eiszeitalter und Gegenwart,* 12, Fig. 1.
The isohyets for Palestine are redrawn from Zohary, H. (1963). *Plant Life of
Palestine,* New York, Map 3. The isohyets for Syria are drawn from an un-
published precipitation map kindly made available by Dr. Y. I. Barkoudah
(Damascus). Data for Turkey is taken from Walter, H. (1955). *Die Klima-
Diagramme der Türkei,* Stuttgart; and data for Lebanon is taken from Pabot,
H. (1959). Rapport au gouvernement du Liban sur la végétation sylvo-
pastorale et son écologie, FAO Rapport No. 1126, (Rome). The location of early
neolithic sites (10,000–8000 B.P.) which yielded botanical evidence for farming
(●) and of pollen-diagram sites (×) is likewise shown. The diagrams from
Bozova and Gölbasi, in south-eastern Turkey, cover only the last 3000 years
(van Zeist, W., Timmers, M. W. and Bottema, S. (In press). Studies of
Modern and Holocene Pollen Precipitation in South-eastern Turkey,
Palaeohistoria, 14), and for that reason they are not discussed in this paper.
The study of the sediment core from Jisr-el-Chaghur, in north-western Syria,
is in its initial stage.)

In the Ruwandiz area, at the foot of a very high and massive section of the Zagros-Taurus mountain arc, mean annual precipitations of *c.* 1000 mm. are reported for stations at about 1000 m. above sea level[17], suggesting that there also tree growth could have continued in the dry and cold period prior to 14,000 B.P. In this connection it must be mentioned that in the same area, Wright observed Pleistocene cirques at 1500 m., which are attributed to the last glacial phase[18]. It is clear that a snowline at about 1500 m. cannot be reconciled very well with a possible occurrence of trees between let us say 800 and 1200 m. If the snowline depression was caused by a decrease in temperature alone, the mean annual temperature must have dropped at least 12°C. Since at lower elevations there is no geologic or palaeontologic evidence for a temperature depression of 12°C, Wright remarks "that it is probable that the glaciation was the result of increased snowfall as well as moderately lower temperature". However, the palynological results indicate that the last cold phase of the Pleistocene was dry, implying that a temperature depression of 12° would hardly have been large enough to effect this extensive glaciation. For that reason it seems justified to assume that the last major snowline depression must not be correlated with the cold phase from between *c.* 30,000 and 14,000 B.P., but with an earlier and moister glacial phase. It should be emphasized that this Pleistocene tree refuge area in north-eastern Iraq is a very hypothetical one. I only wish to point to the possibility that here climatic conditions may have enabled tree growth.

It is obvious that not only the steppes and desert steppes, but also the alpine vegetations covered considerably larger areas than they do today.

After about 14,000 B.P. trees started to spread from their refuge areas. It is not impossible that the Late-Pleistocene forests along the Black Sea and the Caspian did not contribute essentially to the reforestation of the Near East as the summer-dry climate of the interior was too unfavourable for the trees from these mesic forests. Most probably it was the forests along the Mediterranean in Lebanon, western Syria, and south-western Turkey—and the refuge area in north-eastern Iraq, if this existed at all—which provided the trees which were going to re-occupy large parts of the Near East.

As for the vegetation between *c.* 10,000 and 8000 B.P., the period in which the beginning and early spread of agriculture in the Near East took place, the following can be said. The pollen record for western Iran indicates that during the period concerned, steppe forests were found in areas where nowadays the Zagrosian oak forest constitutes the natural vegetation. This would imply that 10,000 to 8000 years ago the vegetation in the Zagros Mountains had a "drier" character than it has today. Assuming that the same was true for the whole of the Near East, the present summer-dry forest region in the interior of Turkey would wholly or for the greater part have been covered with steppe-forest vegetations. Since steppes would have occupied the present steppe-forest areas, the belts in which tree growth took place were narrower than they would be today if there had been no human interference.

In short, between *c.* 10,000 and 8000 B.P., the vegetation would generally have been more open than later in the Postglacial (from about 6000 B.P. onwards).

Although it is admitted that the above outline of the vegetational pattern in early post-glacial times is very speculative, the fact remains that the palaeobotanical evidence suggests that at least in western Iran the climate during this period was drier than it is today. What does this "dryness" mean? It is obvious to think first of less precipitation. However, the geographical position of the neolithic sites of Ali Kosh in Iranian Khuzistan, Ramad near Damascus, and Beidha in western Jordan, which yielded botanical evidence for the cultivation of crop plants and which date from well before the introduction of irrigation farming, cannot be reconciled with the assumption of less rainfall.

At Ali Kosh, the growing of emmer wheat and barley must have constituted a major component of the economy in the period between *c.* 8700 and 8000 B.P.[19] At present, the annual precipitation at Ali Kosh amounts to about 300 mm. With a decrease of the precipitation dry farming in this area would soon become marginal and it would no longer provide a dependable food supply. It is difficult to imagine how the inhabitants of Ramad (*c.* 8000 B.P.) could have depended to a large extent upon dry farming if the precipitation was less than the present amount of *c.* 250 mm. per year[20]. It is not likely that at Beidha (*c.* 8950–8550 B.P.) agriculture played an important part, but the mere fact that plants were cultivated indicates that the mean annual rainfall cannot possibly have been less than the estimated 200 mm. of today[21].

The site of Jericho, with a mean annual precipitation of 140 mm.[22], will not be considered. It is unlikely that dry farming was ever possible there. Consequently, one must assume that the barley, wheat and pulses, recovered from pre-pottery neolithic layers at Jericho (*c.* 10,000–8500 B.P.)[23], had been traded with farmers from the more moisture receiving uplands.

The greater dryness suggested by the pollen assemblages in zone B of the Zeribar diagram could be explained by assuming that during that period the annual precipitation was not less than it is today, but that as a result of higher temperatures, or of a longer rainless period, the summers were drier. The indications for intermittently low water levels in Lake Zeribar during pollen zone B support this hypothesis[24]. The great summer dryness could have prevented the establishment of forests in the larger part of the Zagros and in other areas.

On the other hand, in the warm and summer-dry regions of the Near East, cereals and legumes complete their vegetation cycle before it becomes really hot, just as do the other annuals. For that reason a greater dryness during the summer will not affect these crop plants. It is the precipitation in the autumn, winter and spring which determines whether dry farming is possible.

Finally, a few speculations can be made concerning the distribution of wild einkorn (*Triticum boeoticum*), wild emmer (*Triticum dicoccoides*), and wild barley (*Hordeum spontaneum*) in the past. In south-eastern Turkey, northern

Iraq, and western Iran, primary habitats of wild wheats and barley are found in the forest belt. Wild barley may also be common in the steppe-forest zone below the deciduous oak forest, and, moreover, this species penetrates the steppe and desert steppe in wadi bottoms[25].

It has already been set forth that in the last cold phase of the Pleistocene, forest and steppe forest were probably obliterated from the greater part of the Zagros-Taurus mountain arc, if trees had not disappeared altogether. This would imply that in this region a zone where climatic conditions are favourable for wild cereals did not exist or that at least it was greatly diminished. If forest or steppe forest could survive in the Ruwandiz area, one may assume that wild cereals also found a refuge there. Furthermore, wild barley occurred probably in the wadis of the low and relatively warm steppes and desert steppes. Western Syria, Lebanon and adjacent areas would certainly have provided suitable habitats for wild emmer and barley. It is not unlikely that in western Turkey, where at present primary habitats of wild einkorn are met with, this species survived in the coastal area.

Like the trees, wild cereals would have spread from their refuge areas after 14,000 B.P. The distribution of wild wheats and barley at about 10,000 B.P. or soon afterwards would not have differed much from that of today. It has been suggested that palaeobotanical and archaeological evidence together lead to the conclusion that between 10,000 and 6000 B.P. the precipitation in the autumn, winter and spring can hardly have been less than it is at present, but that the summers were drier. Since summer dryness does not affect annuals such as wild cereals, one may assume that the areas which in early post-glacial times provided suitable habitats for these species were to a large extent the same as the present-day ones[26].

Notes

1 Harlan, J. R. and Zohary, D. (1966). Distribution of wild wheats and barley, *Science*, **153**, pp. 1074–80.

2 The Quaternary, the youngest main period of the geological time scale, is subdivided into the Pleistocene and the Holocene or Postglacial. The Pleistocene/Holocene border is dated to 10,300 B.P.

3 Bobek, H. (1951). Die natürlichen Wälder und Gehölzfluren Irans, *Bonner Geographische Abhandlungen*, **8**; Zohary, M. (1963). On the Geobotanical Structure of Iran, *Bull. of the Research Council of Israel*, **11d**, Supplement.

4 Louis, H. (1939). Das natürliche Pflanzenkleid Anatoliens, *Geographische Abhandlungen*, 3. Reihe, Heft 12.

5 Pabot, H. (1957). Rapport au gouvernement de Syrie sur l'écologie végétale et ses applications FAO Rapport No. **663**, Rome; Pabot, H. (1959). Rapport au gouvernement du Liban sur la végétation sylvo-pastorale et son écologie, FAO Rapport No. **1126**, Rome.

6 Louis, H. (1939). ibid.

7 Pabot, H. (1957). ibid.

8 Bobek, H. (1951). ibid.

9 Zohary, M. (1963). ibid.
10 van Zeist, W. and Wright, H. E. (1963). Preliminary Pollen Studies at Lake Zeribar, Zagros Mountains, South-western Iran, *Science*, 140, pp. 65–7; van Zeist, W. (1967). Late Quaternary Vegetation History of Western Iran, *Rev. Palaeobot. Palynol.*, 2, pp. 301–11; Wasylikowa, K. (1967. Late quaternary plant macrofossils from Lake Zeribar, Western Iran, *Rev. Palaeobot. Palynol.*, 2, pp. 313–18.
11 Wright, H. E., McAndrews, J. H. and van Zeist, W. (1967). Modern pollen rain in western Iran, and its relation to plant geography and quaternary vegetational history, *J. Ecol.*, 55, pp. 415–43.
12 van Zeist, W. (1967). ibid.
13 Rossignol, M. (1962). Analyse pollinique de sédiments marins Quaternaires en Israël. II.—Sédiments Pleistocènes, *Pollen et Spores*, 4, pp. 121–48.
14 Bottema, S. (1967). A late quaternary pollen diagram from Ioannina, North-western Greece, *Proc. Prehist. Soc.*, 33, pp. 26–9; van der Hammen, T., Wijmstra, T. A., and van der Molen, H. (1965). Palynological study of a very thick peat section in Greece, and the Würm-glacial vegetation in the Mediterranean Region, *Geologie en Mijnbouw*, 44, pp. 37–9.
15 Bobek, H. (1963). Nature and Implications of Quaternary Climatic Changes in Iran, *UNESCO-WMO-Symposium on Changes of Climate, Rome* Oct. 1961, pp. 403–13.
16 Hey, R. W. (1963). Pleistocene Screes in Cyrenaica (Libya), *Eiszeitalter und Gegenwart*, 14, pp. 77–84.
17 Wright, H. E. (1961). Pleistocene Glaciation in Kurdistan, *Eiszeitalter und Gegenwart*, 12, pp. 131–64 (Table 2).
18 Wright, H. E. (1961). ibid.
19 Hole, F. and Flannery, K. V. (1967). The Prehistory of South-western Iran: a preliminary report, *Proc. Prehist. Soc.*, 33, pp. 147–206.
20 de Contenson, H. and van Liere, W. (1964). Sondages à Tell Ramad en 1963. Rapport Préliminaire, *Annales Archéologiques de Syrie*, 14, pp. 109–24; de Contenson, H. and van Liere, W. (1966). Seconde campagne à Tell Ramad. Rapport Préliminaire, *Annales Archéologiques Arabes Syriennes*, 16, pp. 167–74; van Zeist, W. and Bottema, S. (1966). Palaeobotanical investigations at Ramad, *Annales Archéologiques Arabes Syriennes*, 16, pp. 179–80; Vogel, J. C. and Waterbolk, H. T. (1967). Groningen radiocarbon dates VII, *Radiocarbon*, 9, pp. 107–55.
21 Kirkbride, D. (1966). Five Seasons at the Pre-Pottery Neolithic village of Beidha in Jordan, *Palestine Exploration Quarterly*, 98, pp. 8–61; Helbaek, H. (1966). Pre-Pottery Neolithic farming at Beidha, *Palestine Exploration Quarterly*, 98, pp. 61–6.
22 Zohary, M. (1962). *Plant Life of Palestine*. New York. (Table 1.)
23 Kenyon, K. M. (1960). Excavations at Jericho, 1957–58, *Palestine Exploration Quarterly*, 92, pp. 88–108; see Hopf, M. this volume, pp. 355–9; Stuckenrath, R. (1963). University of Pennsylvania Radiocarbon Dates VI, *Radiocarbon*, 5, pp. 82–103; Barker, H. and Mackey, J. (1963). British Museum natural radiocarbon measurements IV, *Radiocarbon*, 5, pp. 104–8.
24 Wasylikowa, K. (1967). ibid.
25 Harlan, J. R. and Zohary, D. (1966). ibid.
26 After the manuscript had been submitted, I became acquainted with the publication of two pollen diagrams from the Bolu area, in north-western Turkey (Beug, H.-J. (1967). Contributions to the postglacial vegetational history of northern Turkey, *in* Cushing, E. J. and Wright, H. E. (eds.) *Quaternary Paleoecology*, pp. 349–56). Beug's results do not require the reconsideration of any of the viewpoints set forth in this paper.

DANIEL ZOHARY

The progenitors of wheat and barley in relation to domestication and agricultural dispersal in the Old World

Introduction

Students of the origin of old world cultivated plants will probably remember the present decade as the "archaeological decade". The recent archaeological activity in Western Asia clearly shows that by 7000 B.C. farming villages had been established over the wide arc spanning the western flanks of the Zagros Mountains in Iran and Iraq, Southern Anatolia, spreading southward into Palestine[1]. More important, in several excavations, such as Jarmo in Iraq, Ali Kosh and Tepe Sabz in Iran, Çatal Hüyük and Hacilar in Anatolia, and Beidha in Jordan, a considerable amount of plant remains has been un-earthed. These have been critically examined and brilliantly identified by several workers and particularly by Hans Helbaek of the Danish National Museum[2]. It is now well established that the neolithic agricultural development in Western Asia depended primarily on domestication and subsequent cultivation of three species of cereals: (1) Einkorn wheat (*Triticum monococcum*), (2) Emmer wheat (*Triticum dicoccum*), and (3) Two-row barley (*Hordeum vulgare* ssp. *distichum*). Thus we have a definite answer to the cardinal question: what were the primitive crops at the initiation of agriculture. In terms of the origin of Old World cultivated plants, these archaeological finds are no doubt the critical "missing links" which enable us to reconstruct the events of domestication more definitely.

Now that the identity of the West Asiatic principal early crops is well established, the genetical and botanical information concerning relationships between tame and wild cereal species can be reassessed, and the evolution of cultivated types more soundly understood.

First, we have ample botanic and genetic evidence to determine definitely what are the wild ancestors of the neolithic primitive cultivated cereals. Following this, the distribution, ecology and various biological characteristics of the wild species can be surveyed, in order to find out whether they might have some bearing on the questions of where, when and how crop domestication began and developed in the Old World.

The present paper starts with a survey of the wild ancestors, reviewing the main genetic reasons why these wild plants should be considered as progenitors of the barley and wheats cultivated by the neolithic farmers. It continues with a review of their distinct ecology and several other biological traits, stressing features relevant to domestication and to the spread of agriculture.

Einkorn wheat

It is now clear that wild *Triticum boeoticum* (Pl. VIII) is the only candidate for the ancestry of cultivated einkorn, *T. monococcum*. The reasons for this can be summarized as follows: both wild and cultivated einkorns are morphologically similar. Both have diploid chromosome numbers ($2n = 14$), and domesticated and wild einkorns show close genetic affinities: hybrids between wild *T. boeoticum* and cultivated *T. monococcum* are completely fertile, and chromosome pairing in meiosis is normal. Genetically, the two types should be regarded as mere races and not as fully separated species.

The main distinguishing trait between wild einkorn and cultivated einkorn lies in the biology of seed dispersal. This difference is conspicuously reflected in the morphology of the rachis of the ear. In wild einkorn we have brittle ears; and the individual spikelets disarticulate at maturity to disperse the seed. In cultivated einkorn, this essential adaptation to wild conditions no longer exists. The mature ear stays intact and breaks only upon threshing. Survival depends on reaping and sowing.

Wild *T. boeoticum* shows a relatively wide distribution area. It is spread over Western Asia and penetrates also into the Southern Balkans (Greece, Turkey, Syria, North Iraq, Transcaucasia). Its distributional centre lies, however, in the Fertile Crescent Belt of Southern Turkey, Northern Iraq and adjacent territories in Northern Syria, a second, smaller centre being found in West Anatolia. In these centres, wild einkorn is massively spread as a component of open herbaceous oak park-forests and steppe-like formations. In addition to such primary habitats, wild einkorn also occurs as a weed, occupying secondary habitats such as edges of cultivation and roadsides. Sometimes it even invades fields of cultivated cereals. Edaphically, wild einkorn shows definite affinity to basaltic soils, marls and limestones. Further away from the centres, this wild wheat is less common and much more sporadic in its distribution. Significantly, in these peripheral areas, it is mainly restricted to segetal or secondary habitats, i.e. sites which were not available before the opening up of these areas by agricultural activity.

The wide geographic range of wild einkorn is also paralleled by wide morphological variation and ecotypic adaptation to a relatively wide climatic amplitude. *T. boeoticum* is distributed from the low, warm, summer-dry foothills of the Euphrates basin, to the elevated cool and continental plateaux and mountain ridges of Anatolia. In Turkey, its altitudinal amplitude is 0–1600 m.; in Iran and Iraq, 600–2000 m.

Two main eco-geographic races have been recognized by botanists in wild einkorn. A relatively small and usually one-seeded race is characteristic of the cooler Balkans and Western Anatolia, while a larger race with two-seeded spikelets is found in the warmer, summer-dry areas of Southern Turkey, Iraq and Iran. However in Anatolia, all inter-gradations and intermediates between these two extremes occur, often forming mixed, variable populations. The small one-seeded race is usually referred to as *T. boeoticum* ssp. *aegilopoides* (or *T. aegilopoides* in older floras), while the larger two-seeded race is commonly called *T. boeoticum* ssp. *thaoudar* (or *T. thaoudar* in older floras). Fig. 1 shows the known distribution of wild einkorn as assessed from field surveys and botanic collections[3]. The shaded areas in this map indicate the regions in which wild einkorn massively occupies *primary habitats*, i.e. areas in which it should be considered genuinely wild. Dots outside the shaded areas represent sites in which *T. boeoticum* occurs today exclusively as a segetal plant, i.e. places to which this grass apparently spread after the initiation of agriculture.

Emmer wheat

Genetic and morphological evidence clearly indicate that cultivated emmer (*Triticum dicoccum*) is derived from wild emmer (*T. dicoccoides*) (Pl. VIII). As in the previous case of einkorns, here too, we are confronted with a pair of closely related wild and domesticated types. *T. dicoccum* and *T. dicoccoides* both have tetraploid chromosome numbers ($2n = 28$), and hybrids between them are fully interfertile. Wild emmer also shows striking morphological similarity to cultivated emmer. Thus genetically, these two wheats (as well as the more evolved, naked *T. durum* wheats) are again not fully separated species, but rather races or sub-species of a single species complex. Also here, domesticated and wild emmers are mainly separated from one another by their distinct seed dispersal biology. Wild emmer has the typical brittle spike characteristic of all wild cereals and the individual spikelets serve as the seed dissemination units. In cultivated emmer the mature ears stay intact; they are separated only by threshing, and are thus fully dependent on man for their survival.

T. dicoccoides is more restricted in its distribution and ecology than wild einkorn. Its range covers Israel, South Syria and Transjordan (see Fig. 2), and its centre is found in the catchment area of the Upper Jordan Valley, i.e. the slopes of Eastern Galilee and Gilead facing the Sea of Galilee, the adjacent basaltic plateaux of Golan and Hauran, and further north to the eastern slopes of Mt. Hermon. In this area, *T. dicoccoides* is indeed common, particularly in places which have not been severely overgrazed.

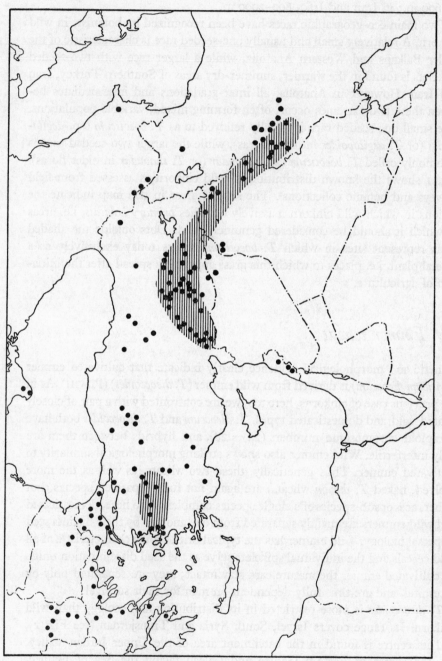

Fig 1 Distribution of wild einkorn *Triticum boeoticum*.
Dots represent known sites, and the areas in which primary habitats occur are shaded. (Adapted from Harlan, J. R. and Zohary, D. (1966). Distribution of wild wheats and barley, *Science*, 153, pp. 1074–80.)

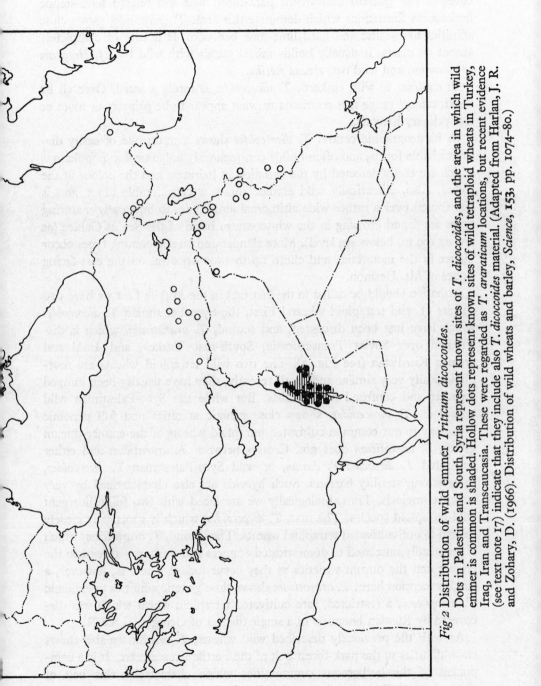

Fig 2 Distribution of wild emmer *Triticum dicoccoides.*
Dots in Palestine and South Syria represent known sites of *T. dicoccoides,* and the area in which wild emmer is common is shaded. Hollow dots represent known sites of wild tetraploid wheats in Turkey, Iraq, Iran and Transcaucasia. These were regarded as *T. araraticum* locations, but recent evidence (see text note 17) indicate that they include also *T. dicoccoides* material. (Adapted from Harlan, J. R. and Zohary, D. (1966). Distribution of wild wheats and barley, *Science,* 153, pp. 1074–80.)

Wild emmer occurs here as a common annual component in the herbaceous cover of the *Quercus ithaburensis* park-forest belt and related semi-steppe herbaceous formations which dominate this area. *T. dicoccoides* shows close affinities to basaltic and hard limestone bedrocks. It is rare or completely absent on marls. It usually builds mixed stands with wild barley, *Hordeum spontaneum*, and wild oat, *Avena sterilis*.

In contrast to wild einkorn, *T. dicoccoides* is rarely a weed. Over all its distributional range it is restricted to what appear to be primary or more or less primary habitats.

In its geographic centre, *T. dicoccoides* shows a multitude of easily distinguishable forms, and often builds conspicuously polymorphic populations which are easily detected by the variation in hairiness and the colour of the spikes. Also, climatically wild emmer shows a considerable range and is distributed over a rather wide altitudinal amplitude. Robust early maturing types are found growing in the winter-warm basin of the Sea of Galilee (as low as 100 m. below sea level). More slender and later blooming types occur higher in the mountains and climb up to 1500–1600 m. on the east-facing slopes of Mt. Hermon.

Attention should be called to the fact that in the Middle East we have two species of wild tetraploid wheats! First, the Syro-Palestinian *T. dicoccoides* which have just been discussed, and second, *T. araraticum*, which is distributed over Soviet Transcaucasia, South-east Turkey, and Iraqi and Iranian Kurdistan (see Fig. 2). The two wild tetraploid wheats are morphologically very similar and, until recently, they have usually been lumped together and confused by botanists. But while the Syro-Palestinian wild tetraploid, *T. dicoccoides*, shows close genetic affinities and full genomic homology to our common cultivated tetraploid wheats of the emmer-durum group, *T. araraticum* does not. Crosses between *T. araraticum* and either cultivated *T. dicoccum-T. durum*, or wild Syro-Palestinian *T. dicoccoides*, show strong sterility barriers. Such hybrids are also characterized by very irregular meiosis. Thus, biologically we are faced with two fully divergent wild tetraploid species. The first, *T. dicoccoides*, which is genetically closely related to our cultivated tetraploid wheats. The second, *T. araraticum*, which is genetically unrelated to domesticated emmers and durums—at least to the emmer and the durum varieties as they occur today! There is, however, a single exception here: *T. araraticum* shows close genetic affinities to endemic *T. timopheevi*, a restricted, rare cultivated tetraploid wheat which was discovered by Russian botanists in a single district of Georgia, U.S.S.R.

As with the previously described wild wheats, *T. araraticum* also shows close affinities to the park-forest belt of the Fertile Crescent arc. It is a component of the herbaceous communities which characterize this belt of vegetation. As far as we know, the distribution of *T. araraticum* is rather sporadic. It has never yet been found to form the same extensive masses and "wild fields" that so characterize the other two wild wheat species, *T.*

boeoticum and *T. dicoccoides*. It is almost always found mixed with *T. boeoticum*, where the latter usually prevails. In South Turkey, North Iraq, and West Iran, it grows in what seem to be genuine primary habitats (*Quercus brantii* forest belt) as well as at the edges of cultivation. In Transcaucasia, its distribution is much more restricted, and is apparently found only in places highly disturbed by man's activity.

Barley

It is now clear that only a single genuinely wild species of barley is closely related to the various cultivated barley forms, and should be regarded as their sole ancestor[4]. This is two-row brittle *Hordeum spontaneum*. *H. spontaneum* has the same chromosome number as cultivated barley *H. vulgare*. Both are diploids ($2n = 14$); hybrids between them are fully fertile and show regular pairing in meiosis. Again, from a genetic point of view, wild *H. spontaneum* and the various forms of cultivated *H. vulgare* did not diverge to the extent of representing fully independent, separated species.

Wild barley, *H. spontaneum*, shows wider distribution than the wild wheats. It is spread over a wide area in the East Mediterranean basin and the West Asiatic countries, penetrating east as far as Turkmenia and Afghanistan[5]. Like wild einkorn, wild barley occupies, at present, both primary habitats and segetal, man-made habitats. Its distribution centre lies in the Fertile Crescent Belt, i.e. in a wide arc, starting from Israel and Transjordan in the south-west, stretching north towards South Turkey, and bending south-east towards Iraqi Kurdistan and South-west Iran (see Fig. 3). In this general area, and only here, *H. spontaneum* is massively and continuously spread over primary habitats. It constitutes an important annual component of open formations, and is particularly common in the summer-dry belt of the deciduous oak park-forest, east, north and west of the Syrian desert and the Euphrates basin, and the slopes facing the Jordan rift valley. From here, *H. spontaneum* spills over to the drier and warmer deserts. In the Fertile Crescent countries, *H. spontaneum* also occupies a whole array of secondary man-made habitats, i.e. opened-up Mediterranean maquis, abandoned cultivation, edges of fields and roadsides. Further west (Aegean region and Cyrenaica) and further east (North-east Iran, Soviet Central Asia and Afghanistan), *H. spontaneum* is rare and much more sporadic in its distribution; it rarely builds even local masses and seems to be completely restricted to segetal habitats or to sites which have been drastically churned by man's activity. Thus, in these peripheral areas, wild barley does not seem to be genuinely wild! As in the case of wild einkorn, it apparently spread to these locations as a weed, as a consequence of agricultural activity.

In general, wild barley does not tolerate extreme cold and it is only occasionally found above 1500 m. It is thus almost completely absent from the

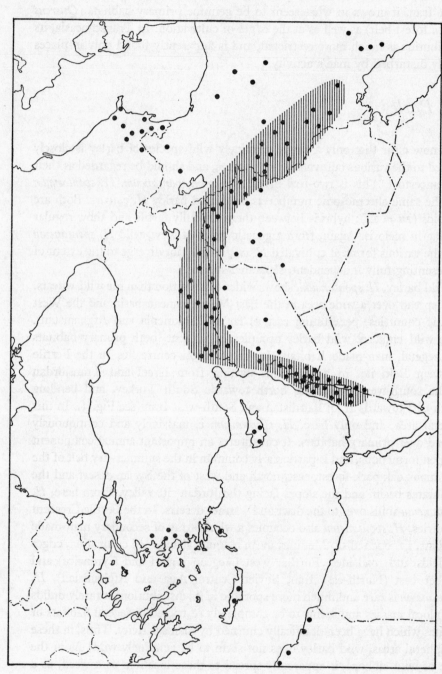

Fig 3 Distribution of wild barley *Hordeum spontaneum*.
Dots represent known sites, and the areas in which primary habitats occur are shaded. (Adapted from Harlan, J. R. and Zohary, D. (1966). Distribution of wild wheats and barley, *Science*, 153, pp. 1074–80.)

elevated continental plateaus of Turkey and Iran. On the other hand, it is somewhat more xeric as compared with the wild wheats and penetrates relatively deep into warm steppes and deserts. Morphologically too, *H. spontaneum* is quite variable and several distinct races can be distinguished. Robust types with extremely large seeds and extraordinarily long awns occur in the catchment area of the Upper Jordan Valley, often in close association with similarly robust *T. dicoccoides* forms.

A much more slender desert type is found in the drier steppes and in desert dry water courses. This race is sporadically spread from the Negev to the steppic plateaux of Transjordan, northward to the Turkish border, and eastward to Iran and Afghanistan. It is a small, grassy type with kernels only half the size of the robust races of the Eastern Galilee. All intermediate types between these extremes are widely spread in Palestine, Syria, Turkey and Iran.

Until recently, cultivated six-row barley, *H. vulgare* ssp. *hexastichum*, was considered to have arisen not from *H. spontaneum*, but from what was regarded as a second wild progenitor, brittle six-row *H. agriocrithon*. Brittle six-row barley plants have been collected in several localities in the Middle East, either as weeds in cultivation or as scattered individuals in *H. spontaneum* stands, growing at edges of barley cultivation. Recent analysis[6], however, has demonstrated that such six-row *agriocrithon* plants could not be considered as an independent, genuinely wild species. Indeed, it was found that they are not adapted to survive under true wild conditions. They were demonstrated to be secondary hybrid derivatives, resulting from occasional spontaneous hybridization between six-row cultivated *H. vulgare* and two-row wild *H. spontaneum*. These finds seem to have settled the controversy of the monophyletic vs. diphyletic origin of cultivated barleys. The botanical and genetic evidence is well corroborated by the archaeological finds. As amply stressed by Helbaek[7], the earlier archaeological deposits contain only two-row barleys. Six-row barley appears later. It seems clear now that cultivated six-row barley is derived from two-row cultivars, and that the sole wild ancestor of all cultivated barley is *H. spontaneum*.

Ecology and population structure of wild cereals

The first fact that should be emphasized is that *Hordeum spontaneum*, *Triticum boeoticum* and *T. dicoccoides* are common plants in their distribution centres. Frequently they build extensive, massive stands. In fact, all these three wild cereals are important herbaceous constituents of the "sub-Mediterranean" oak park-forest vegetation belt that arches over the Syrian desert and the Euphrates basin. This belt receives a considerable amount of rain (400–1000 mm.)—but only in winter. The summer here is very warm and dry. The vegetation is characterized by a lush growth of annuals in winter and spring.

In the few places where the oak park-forest is still preserved, thick herbaceous cover occupies the openings between the well-spaced trees (*Quercus ithaburensis* in the west, and *Q. brantii* in the east). Where the trees have been destroyed or heavily coppiced, the herbaceous cover is even more uniform, and a steppe-like landscape prevails in places unoccupied by agriculture. Particularly rich in annuals are the hard limestone and basaltic bedrocks with their relatively heavy soils. These rock formations occur over considerable parts of the "sub-Mediterranean" oak park-forest belt. *H. spontaneum, T. boeoticum, T. dicoccoides,* as well as several species of oats (*Avena*) and goat-face grasses (*Aegilops*), are frequently dominant annuals here. They are particularly conspicuous in places which have not been heavily overgrazed (such places are uncommon today in the Near East!). Under heavy grazing pressure, the wild cereals are greatly repressed, and their place is often taken by less palatable herbs. Significantly, when the grazing pressure is relaxed, the wild grasses usually re-establish their dominance within a few years.

Thus in the *Q. ithaburensis* and *Q. brantii* formations and related park-forests or "moist steppes", that stretch from Palestine to South Turkey and Iraqi and Iranian Kurdistan, one finds extensive "natural fields" of wild cereals. Conspicuous examples of such massive stands occur on the basaltic plateaus and the hard limestone slopes of Eastern Galilee and adjacent Gilead and Golan. When the State of Israel was established two decades ago, grazing had been regulated in the Upper Jordan Basin. Consequently, winter growth of the wild cereals here is now largely unimpaired. All over the slopes facing the Jordan Valley, from sea level near the Sea of Galilee to the elevated hills near the town of Safad, *H. spontaneum, T. dicoccoides* and *Avena sterilis* are spread in masses. On uncultivated slopes, natural fields of these wild cereals extend over many kilometres. In their growth and total mass, these wild fields of wheat, barley and oats are not inferior to their cultivated counterparts. These robust wild forms can be favourably compared with their cultivated relatives in grain production also. In rainy years, well developed wild Eastern Galilee stands (of *T. dicoccoides* mixed with *H. spontaneum*) are estimated to produce some 50–80 kg. of grain per dunam (1000 sq. metres). This does not fall far behind the yields which local cultivated durum and barley varieties produce in this region—under wooden plough agriculture (i.e. 50–150 kg. per dunam).

Similar extensive "fields" of wild cereals are spread over the wide arc north and east of Palestine—i.e. Syria, Southern Turkey and east into Northern Iraq and Western Iran. But in the centre and eastern flank of the arc, species composition is somewhat different. Wild barley, *H. spontaneum,* is present everywhere. But Palestinian tetraploid wild emmer, *T. dicoccoides,* is replaced in Turkey, Iraq and Iran by diploid wild einkorn *T. boeoticum*—with an occasional admixture of tetraploid *T. araraticum.* Conspicuous "fields" of wild cereals with such composition are common in Gaziantep, Malatya, Diyarbakir, Siirt provinces of Southern Turkey, and Jebel Sinjar, and the

700–1400 m. altitude zone of the Zagros ranges in Irbil-Sulaymaniya provinces of Iraqi Kurdistan. They also occur in the Shahabad-Ilam area in adjacent Western Iran. All over these hilly areas, the large robust types of two-grained wild einkorn. *T. boeoticum* ssp. *thaoudar* prevail. Turkey, in particular, is very rich in wild einkorn. The basaltic formations which characterize Diyarbakir province harbour extensive, almost pure stands of this wild diploid wheat[8].

There is, however, a very conspicuous phenological difference between fields of wild cereals and their cultivated counterparts. As already stressed, ears of the wild cereals disarticulate immediately upon maturation. Under the dry hot weather that characterizes the end of the growing season in the Near East, this process is very abrupt. In a given site and for a given wild cereal, plants mature quickly and simultaneously. Thus, wild cereal fields showing masses of maturing ears shed their fruits and turn into barren dry stalks within one or two weeks! There is only a very limited time interval in which the grain of wild cereals can be effectively collected. If an extremely dry warm spell ("hamsin") happens to occur at maturation time (and these spells are quite frequent in this season) shedding of fruit can be completed in a matter of two or three days, and the potential harvesting time shortened even more.

But differences in maturation time do exist between different cereals and in different localities or ecological niches. In Israel, in mixed stands, *H. spontaneum* matures some one to three weeks earlier than *T. dicoccoides*. Plants growing in sites with deep heavy soil mature somewhat later than those occupying shallow soils. Considerable differences in the ripening time occur, however, in different altitudes. Maturation of wild emmer at the sea level belt near the Sea of Galilee, occurs around the end of April, while higher up in the Safad area (alt. 700–800 m.) stands mature around 15th–20th May. In the adjacent east-facing slopes of Mt. Hermon (alt. 1400–1600 m.), ripening occurs still later—in early June. Similar altitudinal clines occur in Turkey, Iraq and Iran. Therefore, in regions with varied topography, altitudinal amplitude compensates for the abrupt shedding. Collectors can start their harvest in lower elevations and proceed gradually to climb the higher slope, and effective harvesting time is extended to last four to six weeks.

Seed dispersal and germination of the wild cereals

As has already been pointed out in the previous sections wild wheats and barley have fragile spikes, and their ears disarticulate immediately upon maturity. The fragility of the spike is, in fact, the main diagnostic character that serves for distinction of wild cereals from their cultivated counterparts. But what is less emphasized is that the brittleness is only the most conspicuous reflection of one of the major adaptations of these wild cereals to their wild environment: their specialization in seed dispersal. As annuals under Mediterranean summer-dry conditions, these wild cereals are heavily dependent on efficient mechanisms to disperse and plant their seed, protect them in the long dry summer, and facilitate effective germination when rains start in the subsequent season. The spikelet in wild wheats and the triplet in the wild barley are, in fact, specialized arrowshaped seed dissemination units which very effectively insert the mature fruiting units into the soil. The elongated shape of the spikelet or the triplet, the sharpness of its base (the rachis segment), the hairiness and the scabrosity of the unit, the strong awns it bears, and the sterile lateral spikelets in the barley's triplet, are all essential elements of the dissemination and planting device. Immediately after ripening, the individual spikelets (in wild wheats) and the individual triplets (in wild barley) fall to the ground and operate as effective arrow-like devices for one way "migration" of the seed into the soil. Fruit burial is a quick process; it is completed a few weeks after shedding. The summer aspect of the wild cereal "fields" is characterized by dry, barren stalks and effectively inserted fruits. Only the big awns remain protruding from the ground.

Another major adaptation of the wild cereals to their environment is regulation of germination and facilitation of rapid development of seedlings. In *T. dicoccoides* and *T. boeoticum* ssp. *thaoudar*, the dispersal unit (i.e. the spikelet) contains two kernels. The first germinates in the ensuing winter; in the second, germination is usually inhibited and only occurs a year later, safeguarding these annuals against the hazards of droughts. In barley, where only one seed occurs in each dispersal unit, differential inhibition of germination occurs between triplets of the same ear.

Wild wheats and barley are also characterized by a relatively larger seed, which are as big, or almost as big, as their cultivated counterparts. This is, apparently, also a necessary adaptation to the conditions under which these cereals germinate and start to develop in nature. In the lush, herbaceous communities of the oak park-forest belt, rapid growth commences immediately after the first effective autumn rain. A big seed, with a mass of storage material, is an obvious asset in the fierce competition for space and light which occurs here at the beginning of the growing season.

The size of the kernel in the wild wheats and barley is, so to speak, a pre-adaptation for domestication. The wild cereals produce attractive large quantities of big, easy-to-collect-and-store kernels. The main developments under domestication were not selection for bigger seed, but the breakdown of the seed dispersal mechanism and the "wild type" regulation of germination. Both are essential for survival under wild conditions; but they are useless, and even damaging, under domestication.

Places of origin of the early cultivated cereals

If we assume that the main climatic and vegetation belts which are distinguishable today in the Near East had more or less the same distribution some 10,000 years ago, the data presented in this paper on the wild cereals may provide clues to possible centres of early domestication.

One of the main aims of this paper was to emphasize that at present, we already possess ample information on the distribution, ecology and biology of the wild cereals. More important, on the basis of the field information and general geobotanical knowledge of the Near East, it is possible to assess fairly accurately where these wild progenitors occupy primary habitats in contrast to places where they occur exclusively as weeds. Of course, only in primary habitats are these grasses genuinely wild. Only here (i.e. in the "centres") could they have existed prior to the advent of agriculture.

The conclusion was reached[9] that einkorn wheat was probably domesticated in South-east Turkey, and emmer wheat in the Upper Jordan watershed. Barley could have been domesticated almost anywhere within the arc that spans the Fertile Crescent. Furthermore, since wild barley occurs also in relatively dry places, barley domestication could have started in less humid sites in this belt.

It is also clear that in the centres of their distribution, wild einkorn, wild emmer and wild barley are widely spread and their big kernels and massive stands could have been an obvious attraction to collectors. Harlan[10] amply records the remarkable yields of wild wheat he harvested in Turkey. Wild fields of all the three cereals may have been harvested long before the start of agricultural practices.

Collection stage versus cultivation

If wild wheats and barley were indeed collected in their respective centres long before they were domesticated, the question naturally arises as to whether we can distinguish between the collection stage and the advent of domestication. In other words, can we recognize domestication soon after it began? Biologically speaking, perhaps the best way to define domestication and to contrast it with the stage of collection is as follows:

When a cereal is harvested and *all* the grain yield obtained is used as food we are dealing with a *collection stage*; when a cereal is harvested and later one *part* of the yield is used as food, while a second *part* of the grain is *intentionally planted* by man, we are dealing with *domestication*.

From the point of view of population genetics and considerations of selection pressures, these two situations are diametrically opposed. Under the system of collection the wild stands maintain themselves spontaneously, i.e.

their existence depends entirely upon the wild mode of seed dispersal. When wild stands are being harvested grains from the less brittle plants which constitute these populations have of course a better chance to be gathered by man while the more brittle plants donate relatively more seed for the start of the successive generation. Mere collection of wild stands would therefore actively select for quick-shattering forms. By contrast, artificial planting would mean selection in exactly the opposite direction. Non-brittle mutants which were lethal in the first situation become advantageous under the second system. Compared to the brittle forms, they have a better chance of contributing their seed for subsequent generations. Genes for non-brittleness are thus strongly selected for by the system of harvesting-and-planting! Thus under domestication, one should expect establishment of non-brittle cereals whether or not the cultivator is conscious of this trait. Furthermore, theoretically, such a shift from brittle to non-brittle spikes should be fast, and if the planted populations of wheats and barley were large enough, it could have been accomplished in a matter of only a few generations.

In summary, the notion that man first discovered brittle mutants in wild cereal fields, realized their potentialities and subsequently introduced cultivation, is apparently a gross over-simplification. Non-brittle mutants were not the cause of domestication but rather an immediate result, the consequence of a change in the biological system when planting was introduced.

The fact that several times (as Helbaek found in Beidha) both brittle and non-brittle cereals have been found mixed together, is not necessarily an indication that we are dealing with the real beginnings of domestication. Early farmers were no doubt both collectors and cultivators, and the collection of wild cereals could have added to the harvest obtained from the cultivated plots for a long time after the advent of domestication. The critical indication that cultivation was practised is of course the presence of some non-brittle material.

Aegilops squarrosa *and the origin of bread wheats*

Hexaploid wheats or bread wheats (*Triticum aestivum*) are exclusively cultivated forms. They do not have wild counterparts in nature. Helbaek's[11] finds in Anatolia, Iran and Mesopotamia indicate that these wheats started to appear one to two millennia after the early start of domesticated einkorn and emmer. Cytogeneticists have fully analysed the mode of formation of *T. aestivum*[12]. Bread wheat has been demonstrated to be a hybridization-and-fusion product. It contains two sets of chromosomes (genomes A and B) present in the emmer-durum wheats and a third set (genome D) found in a wild goat-face grass *Aegilops squarrosa*. In other words, hexaploid $(2n = 42)$ *T. aestivum* was formed by hybridization and subsequent chromosome doubling—which fused tetraploid $(2n = 28)$ emmer-durum wheats with diploid $(2n = 14)$ *Ae. squarrosa*.

Since no wild hexaploid wheat occurs in nature, it seems plausible to assume that the formation of the bread wheats occurred only *after* the advent of wheat agriculture, and that wild *Ae. squarrosa* combined with a cultivated tetraploid wheat to form a new cultivated wheat species.

The first conspicuous fact about *Ae. squarrosa* is that this goat-face grass is the easternmost diploid species in the *Triticum-Aegilops* group. Although its centre lies in the South Caspian area, it is widespread and very common in Northern Iran and adjacent Transcaucasia and Transcaspia (see Fig. 4). Further away from this centre, *Ae. squarrosa* spreads westward as far as Eastern Turkey and the Syrian Desert steppes, and eastward to Pakistan and Kashmir. In Soviet Central Asia it is recorded as far east as Kirghizia and adjacent parts of Khazakstan.

Like wild barley and wild einkorn, *Ae. squarrosa* occupies both primary and segetal habitats. But only in the centre of its distribution, i.e. North Iran, and adjacent Transcaspia and North Afghanistan, is this plant a frequent component in genuine steppes and "forest-steppe" formations. At the same time, it is a noxious follower of agriculture and a common weed in cereal fields. Towards the periphery of its distribution, it is almost exclusively a weed. Here, too, we are faced with a case of a wild progenitor which apparently largely expands its distribution with the opening-up of the land by agriculture.

Both morphologically and ecologically, *Ae. squarrosa* shows an extraordinarily wide amplitude and is represented by a multitude of forms. Its exact ecological range still requires detailed study. But it is clear that in its distribution centre, this diploid occurs over a strikingly wide range of rather continental climatic conditions, from the dry sage-brush steppes of the elevated Iranian and Afghan plateaus, to the margins of deserts, and to the temperate rain-soaked Hyrcanic forest belt at the southern coast of the Caspian Sea.

In summary, the morphological variation and ecological amplitude of *Ae. squarrosa* are exceptionally wide; they exceed those of the other diploid species in the *Triticum-Aegilops* group. Furthermore, in contrast to the more "Mediterranean" wild emmer, this diploid extends its range into the cold continental steppes of Central Asia. It is also a successful and agressive weed in cereal fields. As a weed, it greatly expanded its distribution—beyond the area of its primary habitats.

As already pointed out by Zohary *et al.*[13], these features provide clues to the place of origin of bread wheat *T. aestivum* and explain some of its ecological characteristics.

At the start of neolithic agriculture, the two contributors that fused to form the hexaploid wheats were evidently geographically isolated. Wild emmer *T. dicoccoides* was restricted to Palestine and Syria. *Ae. squarrosa* apparently did not spread westward from North Iran. Contacts between the tetraploid

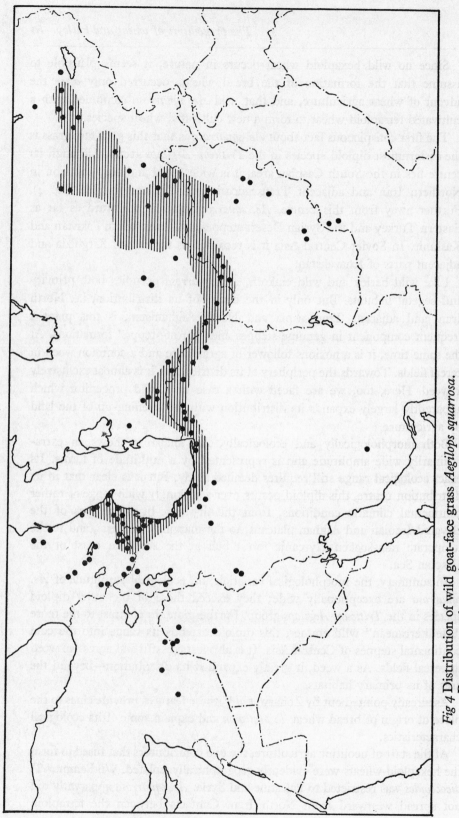

Fig 4 Distribution of wild goat-face grass *Aegilops squarrosa*.
Dots represent known sites, and the areas in which primary habitats occur are shaded. (Adapted from Zohary, D., Harlan, J. R. and Vardi, A. (1968). The wild diploid progenitors of wheat, *Euphytica*.

wheats and *Ae. squarrosa* could have been established only after the domestication of emmer and the spread of wheat agriculture to North Iran and Armenia. If this be true, the most likely place of origin of hexaploid wheat should have been somewhere near the south-west corner of the Caspian Sea. Several additional lines of evidence point to the same conclusion. As already mentioned, there is no wild hexaploid wheat in nature. Furthermore, Kihara and his group[14] have demonstrated that synthetic hexaploids between *T. dicoccoides* and *Ae. squarrosa* are weak dwarf plants, resulting from a dwarf gene which occurs in most strains of wild emmer. In contrast, this dwarf gene has not been found in cultivated emmer-durum varieties, and the synthetic hexaploids between the cultivated tetraploid and *Ae. squarrosa* develop normally.

Ecologically, the addition of the D genome greatly changed wheat adaptation. The tetraploid wheats (emmer-durum group) were derived from a "Mediterranean" progenitor, i.e. were adapted to the mild winters and warm, rainless summers which characterize the Mediterranean basin. The incorporation of the D genome rendered hexaploid wheat far more adaptive to extreme continental conditions and sub-humid temperate climates. This is most likely the main factor that facilitated the wide distribution and the apparent success of hexaploid cultivated wheats over the more continental plateaux of Asia and the colder and mesophytic areas of Europe.

The conspicuous weedy tendencies of *Ae. squarrosa* should have been another asset. When *Ae. squarrosa* was added to the cultivated wheat, it did not greatly change the already acquired adaptation of the latter to thrive under agricultural conditions. Adjustment of the new hexaploid wheats to cultivation was therefore relatively easy.

Self-pollination and its significance

Both wild and cultivated wheats and barleys are predominantly self-pollinated. Self-fertilization in these plants is ensured by the precocious dehiscence of the anthers—prior to the opening of the florets. Cross-pollination occurs occasionally, but it is a rare event amounting to only a few promils of the total pollinations. Thus in their mating system wheats and barleys differ from the majority of the plant species—which are cross-pollinated.

Was it a mere chance that the first plants which were successfully domesticated in West Asia were selfers? There is good reason to assume that this was not the case, and that at the initiation of the Middle Eastern agriculture self-pollinated plants were better suited or "preadapted" to domestication in comparison to cross-pollinated plants.

The first obvious advantage of self-pollination is the isolation established by this mating system. Self-pollination splits the population into independent pure lines. Under such a system two forms (e.g. brittle wild barley and a cultivated non-brittle barley) can co-exist in the same area. They do not face the danger that the less common type will be swamped by the more common one. If indeed domestication of cereals in the Middle East started in the same regions where the wild progenitors were common, effective isolation of the initial cultivated crop was a necessity. Self-pollinators had this advantage. Cross-pollinators did not. Under a system of cross-pollination the initial small patches of the crop would have been exposed to massive pollination by wild type pollen. Swamping would result and maintenance of the identity of the cultivated variety would be difficult. It is therefore not surprising that the first plants which were successfully domesticated in the Middle East were all selfers. Cross-pollinated crops (e.g. rye) appeared only later.

It is also important to note that wheats and barleys are not obligatory selfers but just predominantly self-pollinated. Rare cross-pollination occurs in these plants. Such a mating system is admirably suited for rapid evolution and the establishment of new forms. Inbreeding would lead to the fixation of numerous lines, and the more attractive of them could have been easily selected and maintained by man. The occasional cross-pollination would have provided the crop with genetic flexibility—the possibility of combining and reshuffling genes originating from different lines and different sources.

Introgression and its effects

In the Mediterranean basin and in the Near East, the cultivated cereals and their wild relatives are genetically not completely isolated from one another. Over wide areas they grow side by side, and occasionally hybridize. In fact, such spontaneous hybridization is followed by introgression, i.e. by gene-flow from the wild entities to the cultivated entities. For wheat and barley, the picture can be summarized as follows.

Most conspicuous are the genetic relationships between the pairs of domesticated crop and wild ancestor. In Israel, for example, wild *Hordeum spontaneum* frequently comes into contact with cultivated barley (*H. vulgare*). At edges of cultivation, roadsides and similar habitats, sporadic hybrid swarms between cultivated and wild barleys occur rather frequently, and gene-flow from wild to cultivated, and vice versa, has been demonstrated[15]. Similar relationships are found in Israel between wild *T. dicoccoides* and its genetically close related *T. durum*; while in Thrace and Western Anatolia, this type of spontaneous hybridization still occurs between wild *T. boeoticum* and cultivated *T. monococcum*.

In the wheats, introgression occurs, not only between the interfertile domesticated and wild pairs, but also with more alien wild species. In fact, polyploid *T. durum* and *T. aestivum* have been found to hybridize in nature with some dozen different species of *Aegilops* and *Triticum*, such as *Ae. cylindrica*, *Ae. triuncialis*, *Ae. variabilis* and *Ae. longissima*. Furthermore, cultivated wheats also hybridize with their diploid progenitors, i.e. *T. boeoticum*, *Ae. speltoides* and *Ae. squarrosa*. Such spontaneous interspecific hybrids are largely sterile, but significantly not completely so. They do set some seed! Subsequent backcrossing to the cultivated species results in effective introgression. Gene-flow from the wild species to the cultivated polyploid wheat is quite common and apparently contributes considerably to the genetic variation of the cultivated forms. As already stressed by Zohary[16], polyploid wheats should be considered as "genetic sponges". Polyploidy buffers the hybridization process and makes it possible for these plants to incorporate genetic material from numerous different wild species.

In the last decade, natural hybridization and introgression between cultivated cereals and their wild relatives have been intensively studied and the details of the mechanisms clarified, at least in wheats and barleys. It now seems apparent that this process played a decisive role in the rapid evolution and successful dispersal of the cultivated cereals. It effectively enriched the initial cultivated crop with a wide range of genetic variation. The build-up of variation in the cultivated crops was thus not an independent process. Initial cultivated crops were able to utilize successfully the extensive gene pools of their wild relatives.

Each initial crop should therefore be envisaged as a sponge. After the initial domestication (i.e. its becoming dependent on man) it most probably absorbed genetic variation from adjacent wild relatives. This enlarged its adaptive range and subsequently made it possible for it to spread and to adapt itself to new areas. Then a new cycle of hybridization was possible with additional locally adapted wild species—until the full range was achieved[17].

Notes

1 Braidwood, R. J. and Howe, B. (1960). Prehistoric investigations in Iraqi Kurdistan, *in Studies in Ancient Oriental Civilization*, 31, Oriental Institute, Chicago, pp. 38–50; Hole, F., Flannery, K. V. and Neely, J. (1965). Early agriculture and animal husbandry in Deh Luran, Iran, *Current Anthropology*, 6, pp. 105–6; Mellaart, J. (1961). Excavations at Hacilar, *Anatolian Studies*, 11; Mellaart, J. (1962–5). Preliminary reports on Çatal Hüyük, *Anatolian Studies*, 12–15; Kirkbride, D. (1966). Five seasons at the pre-pottery neolithic village of Beidha in Jordan, *Palestine Exploration Quarterly*, 98, pp. 8–72.
2 Helbaek, H. (1966). Commentary on the phylogenesis of *Triticum* and *Hordeum*, *Econ. Bot.*, 20, pp. 350–60.
3 Harlan, J. R. and Zohary, D. (1966). Distribution of wild wheats and barley, *Science*, 153, pp. 1074–80.
4 Zohary, D. (1960). Studies on the origin of cultivated barley, *Bull. Res. Counc. Israel*, Sect. D, 9, pp. 21–42.
5 Harlan, J. R. and Zohary, D. (1966). ibid.
6 Zohary, D. (1960). ibid.; Zohary, D. (1963). Spontaneous brittle six-row barleys, their nature and origin, *Proc. First Internat. Barley Genetics Symp.*, Wageningen, pp. 27–31.
7 Helbaek, H. (1959). Domestication of food plants in the Old World,

Science, **130**, pp. 365–72; Helbaek, H. (1960). Ecological effects of irrigation in ancient Mesopotamia, *Iraq,* **22**, pp. 186–296.

8 Harlan, J. (1967). A wild wheat harvest in Turkey, *Archaeology,* **20**, pp. 197–201.

9 Harlan, J. R. and Zohary, D. (1966). ibid.

10 Harlan, J. R. (1967). ibid.

11 Helbaek, H. (1966). ibid.

12 Riley, R. (1965). Cytogenetics and the evolution of wheat, *in* Hutchinson, Sir J. (ed.) *Essays on Crop Plant Evolution.* Cambridge. pp. 103–25.

13 Zohary, D., Harlan, J. R. and Vardi, A. (1968). The wild diploid progenitors of wheat, Ms. sent to *Euphytica.*

14 Kihara, H. (1965). The origin of wheat in the light of comparative genetics, *Jap. J. Genetic.,* **40**, pp. 45–54.

15 Zohary, D. (1960). ibid; Zohary, D. (1963). ibid.

16 Zohary, D. (1965). Colonizer species in the wheat group, *in* Baker, H. G. and Stebbins, G. L. (eds.) *The Genetics of Colonizing Species.* New York. pp. 404–21.

17 New finds, pertaining to the distribution of *Triticum dicoccoides* have been recently reported on by Rao, P. S. and Smith, E. L. (1968). Studies with Israeli and Turkish accessions of *Triticum turgidum* L. emend. Var. *dicoccoides* (Koern). Bowden, *Wheat Inform. Service,* **26**, pp. 6–7. These workers performed a cytogenetic analysis in several Turkish wild wheats, recently collected by J. R. Harlan. Their results indicate clearly that the wild tetraploid wheats in Southern Anatolia are not cytogenetically uniform, and they do not belong exclusively to the *araraticum* type as was previously assumed by Harlan and Zohary. Instead these Turkish collections contained both *araraticum* and *dicoccoides* types! Thus wild tetraploid wheats which have close cytogenetic affinities to cultivated *T. dicoccum* and *T. durum* are not exclusively confined to Palestine and South Syria. They also occur in Southern Turkey and possibly also in adjacent Iraq. We need, of course, further clarification of the spatial, ecological and genetic relationships between *araraticum* and *dicoccoides* types in Turkey, Iraq and Iran before a final decision can be made on whether *dicoccoides* wheats in these areas are genuinely wild, or secondarily derived. But all in all Rao and Smith's data raise grave doubts whether Palestine and South Syria are the sole location in which domestication of emmer wheats could have taken place. The north and north-east parts of the arc again become candidates.

C. D. DARLINGTON

The silent millennia in the origin of agriculture

Recent advances in the widely separated fields of archaeology and genetics lead us to question some of the ideas about the origin of agriculture which may have earlier seemed most acceptable. One of these is the idea that the domestication of animals in general preceded the cultivation of plants. Another is the idea that agriculture arose independently in many different regions both of the Old World and the New, regions which only later coalesced. A third is the idea that agriculture began in the easiest way with the easiest crops, that is with the root crops of tropical regions.

These ideas have been ably expounded by Sauer, Coon, von Wissmann[1] and others. They may now be most critically reconsidered in relation to the second theory, that of the independent regional origins of crops. The view that agriculture arose in several places independently follows almost directly from Vavilov's theory of crop origins. On a basis of his own expeditions to Afghanistan, Abyssinia and Mexico, Vavilov[2] suggested, in 1926, that every species of crop plant had been taken into cultivation at a particular centre which was marked by a recognizable region, usually very mountainous, where it displayed a maximum of variation today.

There were some nine of these centres which might seem to have contributed by fusion to give in the bronze age six main world divisions in the character of agriculture like those shown for crop plants by Kuptsov[3]. And these we might have supposed were independent in origin. The studies of the last forty years, historical and geographical, have however led us to believe that Vavilov's centres of diversity were not so much primary as secondary, not so much sites of origin as places of development. For example, emmer wheat and barley had not arisen from wild plants in Abyssinia but in Syria. Sesame and cotton had not arisen in Afghanistan but in Africa[4].

One source of new understanding was in Vavilov's own later work in the course of which agricultural and genetical evidence took the place of his earlier and simpler botanical notions. Another source was in evolutionary views due partly to Darwin[5] and partly to a German geographer Engelbrecht[6]. On these views the main evolution of crop plants, unlike that of domesticated animals, was due to the *unconscious selection* of the cultivator. The activities of cultivation, tilling and sowing, reaping and threshing, inherently and selectively altered the conditions of survival of the crop plant without any such intention on the part of the cultivator. The crops themselves were in this way thoroughly transformed in the course of a few thousand seed generations during which nothing very striking might seem to be happening. These transformations were silent and unconscious. They took place in parallel in wheat, rice, maize, hemp and many other crops at different times and in different parts of the earth.

One of the most striking unconscious changes arising in this way was the breakdown in most seed crops of the inbreeding inhibition. This mechanism of breeding control by genetic incompatibility corresponds in effect to the incest taboo in man, and is characteristic of the wild ancestors of crop plants[7]. Another unconscious change on quite a different scale was the supplanting of crops by their own weeds. It now appears that crops have been supplanted in this way whenever they have been carried, as has happened most obviously in Europe, into new climatic or ecological regions for which they were constitutionally unsuited[8].

Vavilov's imprisonment and premature death in 1943 prevented him from developing this work and above all from seeing its implications in terms of the dated archaeology and the new genetics which give us the foundation for our present ideas. What we see today is the decisive evidence (of Braidwood, Mellaart, Helbaek, and others[9]) that agriculture in the Old World arose in a single connected region, a Nuclear Zone, of Anatolia, Iran and Syria before 7000 B.C. And that it arose here at a time when no other region of the Old World shows evidence of any similar settled life. The question for us is therefore how agriculture could come into existence about four thousand years later in India and in Abyssinia with partly different crops, and in China at first with entirely different crops. Could the origin have been independent? Or had cultivators moved from the old area to the new areas adopting new crops as they moved?

From the point of view of the crops the answer to this question now presents little difficulty. The crops could have been carried over by advancing cultivators in Africa and Asia just as they were over shorter distances in Europe. Wheat often passed over to new regions unchanged. Hexaploid wheats seem to have reached India in the third millennium B.C. and China in the second millennium. Tetraploid wheats came to Abyssinia probably before the first millennium. But in all the new countries wheat was partly replaced by its own weeds, rye, oats, and buckwheat in the northern regions, and in each southern region by its own millets. Gradually in India the division of the country into three regions, depending on wheat, rice and sorghum has been stabilized[10].

From the point of view of the land, and the means of migration, it may be thought that such an expansion of agriculture presents a greater difficulty. In the Oxus and Tarim basins desert sand has now largely smothered the routes that would have been followed. We have however the evidence of former oases on these routes[11] and we know that they were used as regular and important means of communication until the time of the Han Dynasty in China. The deterioration of vegetation that must be assumed is of course what we should expect to have followed grazing by the animals of the passing farmers as well as of the intruding pastoral nomads[12]. Both the peasant and the herdsman evidently spoilt their habitats and hence spoilt the prospects for later generations.

The passage of crops and stock across central Asia damaged the vegetation and effectively closed the road which the first passage had opened. Similarly, the passage of cattle and men across central Africa to the Cape promoted those diseases of cattle and men which again effectively closed the road that their passage had opened. In a word, the unexampled movements of the neolithic expansion seem to have led to reactions which interrupted the movements themselves and broke the world up into the isolated fragments of later ages, those same geographical regions described by Kuptsov[13].

These views of crop evolution in quite a different sense bear on the problem of the evolution of man himself. We know how closely primitive peoples identify themselves with their crops and stock. We also know how closely they are adapted to meeting the needs and exploiting the gifts of those plants and animals. We may see examples in Galton's[14] (1853) or Raglan's[15] accounts of the pastoralist in Africa and in Freeman's account[16] of the rice grower in Borneo. The processes by which these different types of human being have evolved may now be seen as connected with the unconscious selection by which their crops and stock have also evolved. Men, crops and stock had become overwhelmingly and continuously dependent on one another for their survival. Their fitness was therefore an integrated property and their relationship reciprocal. In the silent millennia during the expansion of agriculture the men themselves were transformed by the new relations with the plant and animal world which they themselves were in process of establishing[17].

The evolution of man, crops and stock in these millennia was thus, I suggest, a matter of mutual selection, a kind of process in animal and plant adaptation where all parties to the transaction effectively modify one another. The characters it produces are all stable when fixed in position, but unstable when new factors are introduced into the situation. The hybridization of cultivators and hunters would be the most universal of these new factors during the expansion of agriculture. It would also be indispensable for adaptation to new climates. And it evidently gave rise to new genetic combinations, new races with new habits of living, such as those long recognized in neolithic and bronze age Britain.

The appearance of many new types of men making use of many new crops and stock made possible expansions of the new combinations from the Nuclear Zone. Each combination, like all races of men and animals, naturally had its own ecologically favoured habitat and different combinations certainly moved at different speeds. Pastoralists always covered the ground faster than settled cultivators and even, in Africa, went in different directions[18]. Different types of people thus sorted themselves out.

One of the new differences of type that were sorted out was that between grain and root farmers. How profoundly contrasted were the selective and evolutionary effects of these two ways of working and living may be seen from considering what happens today. The grain farmer, especially if he works in a temperate climate and with a temperate calendar, depends for his success on tilling and manuring the soil, sowing the seed, weeding and protecting the crop, reaping the harvest, thrashing, winnowing and eventually storing the grain. This success depends in turn on his own skill and forethought and on what he has learnt from the inventions of his ancestors. If he neglects or mistimes or otherwise falls short in any of these operations, failure and famine are the penalty that he and his progeny pay. On the other hand he may make improvements in managing or choosing his crop or his soil, in fashioning or using his tools, his hoes, sickles or riddles, and in fixing the calendar for the days and seasons of his work. In all these things his success brings a higher yield, and hence a greater prosperity for a larger population; and if his children are intelligent enough to learn from him they will propagate a more diligent and more skilled population.

By contrast the root farmer can and need do very little to improve his lot. He cannot select his seed for he grows his crop direct from the roots. He can find improved roots in the wild. With great yams, sweet potatoes and bananas (which are in the same case, for they must be seedless) this is just what he has done. With manioc too he can devise means of extraction of the toxic principle. But having done these few things he can go no further. Nor is he much encouraged to do so for with these crops Nature takes care of everything for him.

Of course Nature can fail. So the potato farmers in Ireland discovered in 1846 when they could be partly saved from starvation only by imported foreign grain, grain which they did not themselves know how to cultivate[19]. But the vast extension of root and banana farming in the tropics shows us that the simplest and easiest methods have been able to propagate and preserve great populations in India, Africa, South America and Polynesia. These populations fed and prospered on the root crops distributed from Southeast Asia. But that great distribution and expansion came only during the last 2000 years after grain growing had been brought to South-east Asia from the Indus valley. It was later and it was derivative.

Summing up: it was the industrious and prudent grain farmer whose expansion created the peasant communities of Europe, Egypt, India and China (as well as of Mexico and Peru) on which the great civilizations seem to have been based. Root cultivation, on the other hand, as Burkill puts it[20], in relation to manioc, "advances that part of the population which contributes least to the common good". Easy cultivation does not select for either foresight or industry. That seems to be why South-east Asia was not a centre of origin of agriculture.

While the great expansions of crops and stocks were being prepared certain industrial experiments were being promoted and chains of reaction were being set in motion by the new grain crops. They present a problem first enquired into by Braidwood, Oppenheim and others[21]. For example, fruit growing could lead to the fermentation of wine which could be contained and kept in gourds. But it did not lead to any wider development. Barley, on the other hand, used as the basis of malting and hence of the brewing of beer, would lead to the production of yeast which in turn could be applied to the baking of bread made from the flour of bread wheat which had been ground in stone querns and kneaded into dough. And the use, first of flat stones, and then of ovens, for baking this bread could be connected with the invention of pottery and the smelting of ores. All the more so because both of these, together with bread wheat, seem to have had a single district of origin on the northern side of the Nuclear Zone, in Anatolia, and to have arrived much later on the southern side, in Palestine.

If we assume a single origin for pottery as well as for agriculture, the later distribution of pottery also sets us an important problem. Pottery is useful or indispensable in the preparation and preservation of most human foodstuffs. It is particularly useful in the preparation of grain by boiling as opposed to baking. The materials for its manufacture are also almost universal. This is perhaps why the making of pottery has repeatedly spread from its centre of origin in the Nuclear Zone deep into Asia and Africa far outside the area of grain growing. It has been carried, like pastoralism far in advance of agriculture itself and by hybridization it has often passed into the hands of otherwise largely palaeolithic people.

Owing to their joint or integrated adaptation, the genetic possibilities that we can expect from particular kinds of crops, stock and men are, I suggest, somewhat precise. For this reason their behaviour, their movements and their evolution are precisely limited. They have their rules, and if we bear in mind that these rules are all connected many conjectures which seem beyond examination may become useful working hypotheses.

Notes

1 Coon, C. S. (1954). *The History of Man*. New York and London; Sauer, C. O. (1952). *Agricultural Origins and Dispersals*. New York; Wissmann, H. von. (1957). Ursprungsherde und Ausbreitungswege von Pflanzen und

Tierzucht und Ihre Abhängigkeit von der Klimageschichte, *Erde Kunde* 11, pp. 81–94 and 176–93.

2 Vavilov, N. I. (1926). Studies on the origin of cultivated plants, *Bull. App. Bot.*, **16** (2), pp. 139–248.

3 Kuptsov, A. (1955). Geographical distribution of cultivated flora and its historical development, *Bull. All Union Geog. Soc.*, **87**, pp. 220–31.

4 Burkill, I. H. (1953). Habits of man and the origins of the cultivated plants of the Old World, *Proc. Linn. Soc.*, **164**, pp. 12–42; Harlan, J. R. and Zohary, D. (1966). Distribution of wild wheats and barley, *Science*, **153**, pp. 1074–80; Harris, D. R. (1967). New light on plant domestication and origins, *Geog. Rev. (N.Y.)*, **57**, pp. 90–107; Hutchinson, J. B. (1962). History and relationship of the world's cottons, *Endeavour*, **21**, pp. 5–15; Vavilov, N. I. (1950). The origin, variation, immunity and breeding of cultivated plants, *Chron. Bot.*, **13**, pp. 1–366.

5 Darwin, C. (1868). *Animals and Plants under Domestication*. London.

6 Engelbrecht, Th. (1916). Uber die Entstehung einiger feldmässig angebauter Kulturpflanzen, *Geog. Z.*, **22**, pp. 328–34.

7 Darlington, C. D. (1943). Genetics and the evolution of the mating system in man, *Ann. Eug.*, **12**, pp. 44–5.

8 Darlington, C. D. (1943). *Chromosome Botany and the Origins of Cultivated plants* (2nd ed.). London.

9 Braidwood, R. J. and Howe, B. (1960). Prehistoric investigations in Iraqi Kurdistan, *Studies in Ancient Oriental Civilisation*, Oriental Institute, Chicago, **31**; Helbaek, H. (1959). Domestication of food plants in the Old World, *Science*, **130**, pp. 365–72; Helbaek, H. (1966). Commentary on the phylogenesis of *Triticum* and *Hordeum*, *Econ. Bot.*, **20**, pp. 350–60; Mellaart, J. (1967). *Çatal Hüyük*. London.

10 Burkill, I. H. (1953). ibid.

11 Wissmann, H. von. (1957). ibid.

12 Darling, F. Fraser (1956). Man's ecological dominance through domesticated animals on wild lands, *in* Thomas, W. L. (ed.) *Man's Role in changing the face of the earth*. Chicago.

13 Kuptsov, A. (1955). ibid.

14 Galton, Sir F. (1853). *Narrative of an Explorer in Tropical South Africa*. London.

15 Raglan, Lord (1939). *How Came Civilisation?* London; Raglan, Lord (1962). Prehistoric Men—what can we know of them, *Rat. Annual*, pp. 31–41.

16 Freeman, J. D. (1955). *Iban Agriculture*. London.

17 Darlington, C. D. (1963). Psychology, genetics and the process of history, *Br. J. Psych.*, **54**, pp. 293–8; Darlington, C. D. (1967). The genetics of society as "human society and genetics", *in* Kuttner, R. E. (ed.) *Race and Modern Science*, New York; Darlington, C. D. (1969). *The Evolution of Man and Society*. London.

18 Payne, W. J. A. (1964). The origin of domestic cattle in Africa, *Emp. J. Exp. Agric.*, **32**, pp. 97–113.

19 Woodham-Smith, C. (1962). *The Great Hunger*. London.

20 Burkill, I. H. (1951). The Greater Yam in the service of man, *Adv. Sci.*, **7**, pp. 443–8.

21 Braidwood, R. J. *et al.* (1953). Did man once live by beer alone?, *Amer. Anthrop.*, **55**, pp. 515–26; Hartman, L. F. and Oppenheim, A. L. (1950). On beer and brewing techniques in ancient Mesopotamia, *J. Amer. Or Soc.* Suppl. **10**.

KENT V. FLANNERY

Origins and ecological effects of early domestication in Iran and the Near East

Introduction

Late in the Pliocene period there began a series of movements of the earth's crust, which caused the central plateau of Iran to be drawn closer to the stable massif of Arabia. The land between, caught in the grip of these two far-heavier formations, was compressed and folded into a series of parallel mountain ridges or anticlines. Gradually the centre of this compressed zone collapsed and subsided, so that the parallel ridges, trending from north-west to south-east, appear to rise out of it like the successive tiers of a grandstand, eventually reaching the Arabian and Iranian plateaus to either side. The sunkland in between, still settling and filling with the erosion products of the mountains, became the rolling and irregular plain known as Mesopotamia; the parallel ridges to the east of it are the Zagros Mountains[1].

The result was an area in which altitudinal differences produce a great number of contrasting environments in a relatively limited geographic area—a mosaic of valleys at different elevations, with different rainfall, temperature, and vegetational patterns. Like some of the other areas where early civilizations arose—Mesoamerica and the Central Andes, for example—the Near East is a region of "vertical economy", where exchanges of products between altitude zones are made feasible and desirable by the close juxtaposition of four main environmental types: high plateau (*c.* 5000 ft.), intermontane valleys (1500–4000 ft.), piedmont-steppe (600–1000 ft.), and alluvial desert (100–500 ft.). A similar pattern arose in the Levant, where the same late Pliocene tectonic movements produced the great Jordan Rift Valley, flanked by the wooded Lebanon-Judean mountains and the arid Syrian Plateau. It was in this kind of setting that the first steps toward plant and animal domestication were made.

Stages in Near Eastern prehistory

In a recent article, Frank Hole and I have divided the prehistory of Western Iran into three main adaptive eras[2]. The first was a period of semi-nomadic hunting and gathering, which lasted until roughly 10,000–8000 B.C. The second era we have called the period of early dry-farming and Caprine domestication, and it seems to have involved predominantly emmer wheat (*Triticum dicoccum*), two-row hulled barley (*Hordeum distichum*), goats (*Capra hircus*), and sheep (*Ovis aries*). This period lasted until about 5500 B.C., and its hallmarks are already familiar to members of this symposium: permanent villages, early hornless sheep, goats with medially-flattened and/or helically-twisted horn cores, and cereal grain samples which show a mixture of wild (tough-glumed, brittle rachis) and domestic (brittle-glumed, tough-rachis) characteristics. The third adaptive era was one which involved the previously-mentioned cultivars plus bread wheat (*Triticum aestivum*); six-row barley which might be either hulled or naked (*Hordeum vulgare*); lentils; grass peas; linseed; domestic cattle (*Bos taurus*); pigs (*Sus scrofa*); and domestic dogs (*Canis familiaris*), and featured irrigation in those zones where its use was feasible without elaborate technology. This era culminated, in the lowlands at least, in the rise of walled towns, about 3000 B.C.[3]

There is no reason to believe that the entire Near East went through these eras synchronously; in addition, evidence suggests that each of the cultivars may have appeared earlier in some areas than in others. Nevertheless, with these caveats in mind, I find this framework useful enough so that I will follow it in this paper, and apologize in advance for viewing the rest of South-western Asia through Iranian eyes. The stages are, it should be emphasized, ones of farming adaptation: they imply nothing about level of social and political development. They allow, in other words, for the simultaneous existence of tiny four-acre villages in Kurdistan and immense, 32-acre sites like Çatal Hüyük in Anatolia.

The basic argument of the paper is as follows. An important change in subsistence pattern, midway through the Upper Palaeolithic in the Near East, set the stage for domestication of plants. This shift, which represented a trend toward "broad spectrum" wild resource utilization, continued long after cultivation had begun. In this sense, our Western view of early cultivation as a drastic change or "improvement" in man's diet is erroneous, as is the frequently-cited notion that early agriculture gave man a "more stable" food supply. Given the erratic nature of rainfall in south-west Asia, the era of early dry-farming was still one of unpredictable surpluses and lean years, with considerable reliance on local wild products. I suggest that early caprine domestication, apart from its food aspects, represented a way of "banking" these unpredictable surpluses in live storage, analogous to the use of pigs by Melanesian peoples[4] or the exchange of imperishable, exotic raw materials which characterized early village farmers in Mesoamerica[5]. Early irrigation modified this pattern, and also aggravated environmental destruction to the point where the return to a wild resource economy would have been nearly impossible. It also set the stage for both dramatic population increases in the lowlands and "ranked" or stratified societies in which a hereditary elite controlled the small percentage of the landscape on which the bulk of the food was produced. A bit of indulgence on the reader's part will be required by the fact that in a paper of this length only the meagrest documentation can be offered for these points of view.

Prime movers and subsistence change

A basic problem in human ecology is why cultures change their modes of subsistence at all. This paper, while not relying on the facile explanation of prehistoric environmental change, is hardly destined to settle that problem. The fact is, however, that for much of South-west Asia we have no evidence to suggest that late Pleistocene or post-Pleistocene environmental changes forced any of the significant subsistence shifts seen in the archaeological record. I will therefore use, as one possible mechanism, a model of population pressure and disequilibrium relative to environmental carrying capacity, drawn from recent enthnographic data on hunting and gathering groups.

A growing body of data supports the conclusion, stated with increasing frequency in recent years, that starvation is not the principal factor regulating mammal populations[6]. Instead, evidence suggests that other mechanisms, including their own social behaviour, homeostatically maintain mammal populations at a level *below* the point at which they would begin to deplete their own food supply. The recent conference on "Man the Hunter", held at Chicago in 1966, made it clear that this is probably also true of human populations on the hunting-gathering level[7]. In addition, a number of current ethnographic studies indicate that, far from being on a starvation level, hunting-gathering groups may get all the calories they need without even working very hard[8]. Even the Bushmen of the relatively desolate Kalahari region, when subjected to an input-output analysis[9], appeared to get 2100 calories a day with less than three days' worth of foraging per week. Presumably, hunter-gatherers in lusher environments in prehistoric times did even better. This is not to say that palaeolithic populations were not limited by their food supply; obviously, they were. But *in addition*, they engaged in behaviour patterns designed to maintain their density below the starvation level.

What, then, would persuade a hunter-gatherer to modify his subsistence pattern significantly—for example, to adopt agriculture? In the course of this paper I would like to apply the equilibrium model recently proposed by Binford[10] as a means of explaining post-Pleistocene changes in the archaeological record. This model will be used to offer tentative explanations for subsistence changes which took place in the Near East at the three critical points mentioned in the start of this paper: the Upper Palaeolithic, the beginning of domestication, and the beginnings of irrigation.

Binford, drawing on both Birdsell and Wynne-Edwards, postulates that prehistoric hunting populations, once reasonably well-adapted to a particular environment, tended to remain stable at a density below the point of resource exhaustion. He argues that their adaptation would change only in the face of some disturbance of the equilibrium between population and environment. Two kinds of disturbances might take place: either (1) a change in the physical environment which would bring about a reduction in the density of chosen plant and animal foods, or (2) a change in demography which would raise local human populations too close to the carrying capacity of the immediate area. The first kind of disturbance might be reflected in the palynological record; the second might be reflected in a shift in site density and settlement pattern in the archaeological record. Disturbances of both kinds occurred in the prehistoric Near East, but it is perhaps the second kind which is most useful theoretically, because it does not rely on the *deus ex machina* of climatic change, an event which does not seem to have taken place with sufficient frequency to explain all (or even most) prehistoric cultural changes[11].

Binford points out that, even in the hunting-gathering era, certain areas supported higher populations than others because of their high level of edible resources. Butzer[12] makes the same point, singling out the "grassy, tropical deciduous woodlands and savannas; the mid-latitude grasslands; (and) the lower latitude Pleistocene tundras" as having the optimal carrying capacity for hunting-gathering populations. In the case of the Near East, for example, it would appear that the mixed oak woodland of the Levant Coast supported higher upper palaeolithic populations than some of the treeless inland steppe areas, at least where survey has been comparably extensive. One sees, therefore, a mosaic of "optimal" habitats, with a somewhat higher carrying capacity and population density, separated by "less favourable" habitats with a somewhat lower carrying capacity and population density. Binford argues that one source of stimulus for culture change is the cyclical demographic pressure exerted on these marginal habitats by their optimal neighbours. It is the optimal habitats which are regional growth centres; it is in them that populations rise, followed by buddings-off and emigrations of daughter groups before the carrying capacity has been strained[13]. They are the "donor systems"; the marginal habitats are the "recipient systems". And it is in the marginal habitats that the density equilibrium would most likely be periodically disturbed by immigrations of daughter groups, raising populations too near the limited carrying capacity. Thus Binford argues that pressures for the exploitation of new food sources would be felt most strongly *around the margins* of population growth centres, not in the centres themselves.

The "broad spectrum" revolution

The first change I would like to deal with took place in the upper palaeolithic period, before 20,000 B.C., and amounted to a considerable broadening of the subsistence base to include progressively greater amounts of fish, crabs, water turtles, molluscs, land snails, partridges, migratory water fowl (and possibly wild cereal grains in some areas ?).

The Upper Palaeolithic of the Near East has a number of chronological phases and regional variants, from the "Antelian" and "Kebaran" of the Mediterranean Coast[14] to the "Baradostian" and "Zarzian" of the Zagros Mountains[15]. Its environmental context in the coastal Levant may have been an open Mediterranean woodland not unlike today's[16], while the Zagros Mountains seem at that time to have been treeless *Artemisia* steppe[17]. In both areas, hunting of hoofed mammals accounted for 90% of the archaeological animal bones, and when weights of meat represented are calculated, it appears that ungulates contributed 99%[18]. In the Zagros, archaeological settlement patterns suggest that the basic residential unit was a "base camp" composed of several families, which shifted seasonally; from this base, hunting parties made periodic forays to "transitory stations", vantage points from which they stalked and eventually killed game, which was then cut up into portable sections at temporary "butchering stations"[19]. There are indications that a similar pattern may have characterized the Levant. On the basis of multi-variant factor analysis of flint tools, Binford and Binford[20] have described the various living floors of Rockshelter I at Yabrud as brief "work camps" made at varying distances from a base camp, sometimes for hunting, sometimes for processing plant material. Near the Wadi Antelias, where Ksar Akil was presumably the "base camp", Ewing[21] describes "hunting sites on the surface higher up in the mountains", some of which may be analogous to the transitory stations or butchering stations of the southern Zagros.

Midway through the "Antelian" or "Baradostian" phases, one can see the aforementioned trend toward increasing use of small game, fish, turtles, seasonal water fowl, partridges, and invertebrates—the latter including terrestrial and marine snails, freshwater mussels, and river crabs. It would be oversimplified to view this as a "shift from large to small game", for even at late palaeolithic sites, ungulates contributed 90% of the meat supply. The trend is rather from exploiting a more "narrow spectrum" of environmental resources to a more "broad spectrum" of edible wild products. This "broad spectrum" collecting pattern characterized all subsequent cultures up to about 6000 B.C., and I would argue that it is only in such a context that the first domestication could take place. It is a pattern in which everything from land snails (*Helix* sp.) to very small crabs (*Potamon* sp.), and perhaps even cereal grasses, was viewed as potential food. It was also accompanied by a number of "pre-adaptations" for early cultivation.

One of these was the development of ground stone technology. At sites like Ksar Akil in Lebanon[22] and Yafteh Cave in Iran[23], small coarse grinding stones occasionally appear; abraders are increasingly common in later Zarzian sites in the Zagros, where they come to include grooved rubbing stones.[24] Evidence suggests that these implements were at first used mainly (but not necessarily solely) for milling ochre. However, the ground stone technology was there, and when man eventually turned to the cereal grasses, he had only to adapt and expand a pre-existing technology in order to deal with grain processing.

Still another "pre-adaptation" for what was to follow can be detected in the later stages of the Palaeolithic in the Near East: the development of storage facilities, which are not at all well-represented in earlier phases. In the Zarzian level at Shanidar Cave, for example, "several pits . . . which may have been storage pits" are reported by Solecki[25]. These features increase with time; many sites of the period 9000–7000 B.C. are reported to have subterranean pits, e.g. Zawi Chemi Shanidar[26], Karim Shahir[27], and Mureybat[28]. Some were plastered, evidently for storage, e.g. at Aïn Mallaha[29], while others may have been used for roasting grain over heated pebbles, e.g. at Mureybat[30]. In any event, these subterranean pits seem to be a feature of the broad-spectrum collecting era, and would presumably have been more effective for storing or processing invertebrate or vegetal foods (snails, acorns, pistachios, etc.) than for any activity connected with ungulate hunting.

It seems unlikely that the shift to a broad spectrum pattern was a direct result of environmental change. It is true that the earlier Pleistocene "big game" of the Near East—elephant, rhinoceros, hippopotamus, and so on— had vanished, but as pointed out by Howell[31], these species disappeared midway in the Mousterian period, that is, many thousands of years before we can see any substantial increase in the use of fish, invertebrates, and (possibly) vegetal foods. Moreover, use of these latter foods is more striking in some areas than others. For example, in the Levant area none of the Mount Carmel caves shows much in the way of invertebrate foods[32], while "thousands" of *Helix* snails are reported from Ksar Akil in the Wadi Antelias[33]. In the Zagros, certain caves like Palegawra[34] have more abundant remains of snails, mussels, and crabs than do those in other areas; we recovered virtually no land snails from our Khorramabad Valley caves[35].

Regional variations like those mentioned above suggest that Binford's model of disturbed density equilibrium may not be far wrong: pressure for the use of invertebrates, fish, water fowl, and previously-ignored plant resources would have been felt most strongly in the more marginal areas which would have received overflow from the expanding populations of the prime hunting zones, raising their densities to the limit of the land's carrying capacity. At this point they would tend to turn, I suggest, not to small *mammals*—which do not appear to be a very secure resource anywhere in the Near East—but to those smaller resources which are readily and predictably available in some quantity at certain seasons of the year. These are water fowl, fish, mussels, snails, and plants. Many of these resources are storable, and though small, are not to be scoffed at. Land snails, for example, although less rich in protein than ungulate meat, are actually much richer in calcium[36], especially in limestone mountain regions, since they use lime to synthesize their protective mucous[37]. Mussels supply vitamin A and acorns and pistachios are very high calorie foods, much more so than wild game[38]. Present data tentatively suggest that the "broad spectrum revolution" was real, that it was nutritionally sound, and that it originally constituted a move which counteracted disequilibria in population in the less favourable hunting areas of the Near East. Once established, however, it spread to and was eventually taken up even by the favourable areas. And one other aspect of it might be noted: the invertebrate (and vegetal?) foods involved are ones which could easily have been collected by women and children, while the men continued ungulate hunting. The broad spectrum collecting pattern may therefore have contributed to the development of division of labour in the late Pleistocene and early post-Pleistocene era.

Early dry farming

The environmental context of early domestication

The "broad spectrum" revolution set the cultural stage for domestication, and with the close of the Pleistocene the oak woodland belt expanded over the upland Near East, even into areas of the Zagros which had formerly been tree-less steppe[39]. This "optimum" wild resource zone, which includes the densest stands of edible nuts, fruits, and wild cereal grasses had apparently been present in the Levant throughout the last glaciation[40], but was now available over a much wider area.

A number of environmental characteristics of this zone today (which presumably have characterized it since the Pleistocene drew to a close) should be mentioned here, for they are variables which affected man's use of the region and set the environmental stage for domestication. Low average precipitation inhibits dense forest growth, but cool, moist air from the Mediterranean in winter results in enough rain (or snow) to guarantee some spring growth of edible grasses and legumes. Hot, dry air circulating out of Eurasia in the summer (plus even hotter local winds off Arabia) produces a prolonged rainless period which inhibits the growth of perennials; most of the vegetation thus consists of annuals which have a peak growing season in March or April, after which they must be harvested in a three-week period. This set the seasonal collecting pattern. Further, like most arid or semi-arid regions, the zone has a low vegetation diversity index[41], which means that certain species (like wild cereal grasses) may form nearly pure stands. This is true of the fauna as well; while the number of mammalian species is low (relative to wetter areas), many of these are species which tend to form herds, e.g. sheep, goat, gazelle, and onager. Harlan and Zohary[42] have discussed the implications of the nearly-pure cereal stands, and Reed[43] has considered the pre-adaptive role of "herd behaviour" in the ungulates which were first domesticated.

The origins of cultivation

The beginning of cultivation is a second shift which may have taken place in the less favourable valleys and wadis around the periphery of the zone of maximum carrying capacity.

For many years it was assumed, quite logically, that domestication must have begun in the zone where the wild ancestors of the domesticates are most at home. Then, in an eye-opening paper, Harlan and Zohary[44] revealed that "over many thousands of hectares" within this zone "it would be possible to harvest wild wheat today from natural stands almost as dense as a cultivated wheat field". Harlan[45] then proceeded to do just that: armed with a flint-bladed sickle, he harvested enough wild wheat in an hour to produce one kilo of clean grain—and the wild grain, after chemical analysis, proved to be almost twice as rich in protein as domestic wheat. Harlan and Zohary[46] therefore closed with a warning: "Domestication may not have taken place where the wild cereals were most abundant. Why should anyone cultivate a cereal where natural stands are as dense as a cultivated field? . . . farming itself may have originated in areas adjacent to, rather than in, the regions of greatest abundance of wild cereals."

Harlan's wild wheat harvest also suggested that a family of experienced plant-collectors, working over the three-week period when wild wheat comes ripe, "without even working very hard, could gather more grain than the family could possibly consume in a year"[47]. Such a harvest would almost necessitate some degree of sedentism—after all, where could they go with an estimated metric ton of clean wheat?

This was, of course, what archaeologist Jean Perrot[48] had been saying for years about the Natufian culture in Palestine—that they had been semi-sedentary, based on intensive wild cereal collection. A further suggestion of this nature has since come from Tell Mureybat, a site on the terrace of the Euphrates River in inland Syria, dating to *c.* 8000 B.C. Preliminary analyses of carbonized barley and einkorn wheat from pre-pottery levels at the site—which have clay-walled houses, grinding stones, and roasting pits presumably used to render the cereal glumes brittle for threshing—suggest that the grain may be all wild[49]. Such data indicate that sedentary life based on wild cereal collecting and hunting may be possible, and that consequently pressures for domestication may not be as strong in the heart of the wild cereal habitat as elsewhere.

This impression is reinforced by the fact that some of our most ancient samples of morphologically domesticated grain (e.g. emmer wheat) come from "marginal" habitats well outside the present wild range of that plant; for example, in the Wadi Araba region[50] and the Khuzistan steppe[51], in areas where dense stands could only be produced by deliberate cultivation. It is possible, therefore, that cultivation began as an attempt to produce artificially, around the *margins* of the "optimum" zone, stands of cereals as dense as those in the *heart* of the "optimum" zone. Binford had already suggested that this might have taken place in response to population pressure exerted on the marginal habitats by expansion of sedentary food-collectors from the heart of the wild cereal zone. It appears that efforts at early cultivation were probably soon reinforced by favourable mutations in the cereals themselves, such as toughening of the rachis, polyploidy, and loss of tough glumes.

The spread of the early dry-farming complex across the Near East is striking; where surveys are adequate, it appears that very few environmental zones were without farming communities at this time, although population densities were higher in some areas than others. In the Zagros Mountains, densities of sites are highest in intermontane plains with a high sub-surface water table and frequent marshy areas[52], suggesting that a critical resource sought by early farmers were lands of high water-retention, where soil moisture helped the planted cereals to survive annual fluctuations in rainfall. At Ali Kosh on the lowland steppe of south-west Iran, early farmers planted their cereals so near swamp margins that seeds of club-rush (*Scirpus*) were mixed in with the carbonized grain samples[53]. This is analogous to the practices of early farmers in parts of arid highland Mesoamerica, who also utilized permanently-humid bottomlands and high-water table zones[54]. Such types of farming may also have facilitated the spread of agriculture out of the Near East and into Europe, which took place sometime during this time period.

More complicated techniques accompanied the extension of early dry-farming to its limits in very marginal habitats to the north-east (e.g. the Turkoman steppe), and the south-west (e.g. the Wadi Araba region). At Beidha, in the south Jordan desert, it is possible that farming sites were located in such a way as to take advantage of rainfall run-off concentrated by steep nearby cliffs[55]. On the Turkoman steppe, early cultivators used small "oasis" situations where streams from the Kopet Dagh formed humid deltas along the base of the mountain range[56]. In all such cases, where rainfall agriculture must have been pushed to its absolute limit, barley seems to have been the main crop[57]; otherwise, wheat was preferred.

A detailed look at the early dry-farming diet

In archaeology, one concrete example is often worth more than a whole chapter of generalization. At this point, I would therefore like to present in some detail our dietary data from the site of Ali Kosh, a small early dry-farming village on the Khuzistan steppe of south-western Iran[58]. Excavations at Ali Kosh produced *c.* 45,000 carbonized seeds, which on analysis by Helbaek (n.d.) could be grouped into 40-odd species of plants; it also produced more than 10,000 identifiable bones from approximately 35 species of animals. I have listed only the most common categories in Table 1. In

TEPE ALI KOSH (7500–5600 B.C.)

(a)Emmer wheat	Caper
(a)Two-row barley, hulled	Pistachio
(a)(Rare traces of other cultivars)	Gazelle
	Onager
(a)Goats	Pig
(a)Sheep	Aurochs
Small wild legumes (*Astragalus, Trigonella, Medicago*)	Fox (and other small mammals)
	Miscellaneous birds
Wild two-row barley	Ducks and geese
Goat-face grass (*Aegilops*)	
Ryegrass (*Lolium*)	Water turtles
Wild oat grass (*Avena*)	
Canary grass (*Phalaris*)	Fish (carp, catfish)
Vetchling (*Lathyrus*)	
Shauk (*Prosopis*)	Freshwater mussels

Table 1 Most common foods recovered in debris at Ali Kosh, an early village in the plain of Deh Luran, south-western Iran.(b)

(a) Domesticated items.
(b) See Helbaek, H. (In press). Plant-collecting, dry-farming, and irrigation agriculture in prehistoric Deh Luran, in Hole, F., Flannery, K. V. and Neely, J. A. Prehistory and human ecology of the Deh Luran plain, *Memoirs*, Univ. of Michigan, Museum of Anthropology; See Hole, F. and Flannery, K. V. (1967). The prehistory of south-western Iran: a preliminary report, *Proc. Prehist. Soc.*, 33 (9), pp. 147–206.

addition, I have estimated the pounds of usable meat represented by minimum individuals of each type of animal, using the system proposed by White[59] and adult weights taken from Walker[60] and my own field notes (Table 2). A further chart (Table 3) gives average representative nutritional values for some of the important plant and animal foods at the site, taken from Platt[61], plus some estimates of the amount of each food source needed to make a kilogram.

Three periods of the early dry-farming era were represented at the site of Ali Kosh. These have been called the Bus Mordeh (7500–6750 B.C.), Ali Kosh (6750–6000 B.C.), and Mohammad Jaffar (6000–5600 B.C.) phases[62]. Counts of the animal bones and carbonized seeds by species will be given in the final reports on the site[63]. I can present here only an abbreviated summary of the results.

The subsistence pattern in the earliest, or Bus Mordeh phase, had five main aspects: (1) the cultivation of cereals, whose grains amounted to only

Animal	Estimated adult weight (kg.)	TEPE ALI KOSH						TEPE SABZ (all phases)	
		Bus Mordeh Phase		Ali Kosh Phase		Moh. Jaffar Phase			
	Kg. of usable meat	Minimum no. of individuals	Kg. of usable meat	Minimum no. of individuals	Kg. of usable meat	Minimum no. of individuals	Kg. of usable meat	Minimum no. of individuals	Kg. of usable meat
Sheep/Goat	50 / 25	(49)	1225	(102)	2550	(40)	1009	(44)	1100
Gazelle	50 / 25	(16)	400	(59)	1475	(18)	450	(18)	450
Onager	350 / 175	(3)	525	(12)	2100	(4)	700	(8)	1400
Aurochs	800 / 400	(3)	1200	(6)	2400	(2)	800	—	—
Domestic cattle	500 / 250	—	—	—	—	—	—	(9)	2250
Pig	100 / 70	(2)	140	(3)	210	(3)	210	(5)	350
Wolf (?)	26 / 13	—	—	(2)	26	(2)	26	—	—
Red fox	9 / 4·5	(2)	9	(3)	13·5	(7)	31·5	(6)	27
Hyaena	40 / 20	—	—	—	—	(1)	20	—	—
Wild cat	1 / 0·5	—	—	(2)	1	(2)	1	(1)	0·5
Marten	1 / 0·5	—	—	—	—	—	—	(1)	0·5
Weasel	0·2 / 0·1	—	—	—	—	(1)	0·1	—	—
Hedgehog	0·8 / 0·4	—	—	(2)	0·8	(1)	0·4	(1)	0·4
Duck-size birds	1·5 / 1	—	—	—	—	(2)	2	—	—
Goose-size birds	2 / 1·4	(2)	2·8	(2)	2·8	(1)	1·4	(1)	1·4
Partridge-size birds	0·2 / 0·14	(1)	0·14	(6)	0·84	(7)	0·98	(6)	0·84
Hawk-size birds	1 / 0·7	—	—	—	—	—	—	(2)	1·4
Turtle	0·5 / 0·25	(8)	2	(4)	1	(4)	1	(4)	1
Fish	0·5 / 0·25	(29)	7·25	(47)	12·25	(44)	11	(4)	1
Crab	0·01 / 0·005	—	—	(3)	0·015	(3)	0·015	—	—
Mussel	0·01 / 0·005	(123)	0·62	(166)	0·83	(111)	0·56	(8)	0·04

(a) For method of calculation, see White, T. (1953). A method of calculating the dietary percentage of various food animals utilized by aboriginal peoples, *American Antiquity*, 18 (4). pp. 396–8.

Table 2 Estimated kilograms of usable meat represented in middens at Ali Kosh and Tepe Sabz, in the plain of Deh Luran, Iran. Broken down by category of animal, and cultural phase (except in the case of Tepe Sabz).[a]

| Food | Estimated value per kilogram of edible portion | | | | | | | | Approximate amount needed for 1 kilo |
	Calories	Protein (gm.)	Fat (gm.)	Carbohydrate (gm.)	Calcium (mg.)	Iron (mg.)	Vitamin A (IU)	Vitamin C (mg.)	
Wheat	3440	115	20	700	300	35	—	—	±33,000 grains
Barley	3390	120	20	680	350	40	—	—	±45,000 grains
Lentils	3390	240	10	590	700	70	1000	—	±25,000 lentils
Lathyrus	2930	250	10	460	1100	56	700	—	Tens of thousands
Small wild legumes	3350	290	52	500	1800	220	—	—	>1,000,000 seeds
Miscellaneous wild grasses	3880	120	75	680	600	50	—	—	>30,000 grains
Pistachio	6260	200	540	150	1400	140	1000	—	±2750 nuts
Almond	6570	200	590	120	1500	35	—	—	±1000 nuts
Goat	1450	160	90	—	110	25	—	—	1/25 of one animal
Sheep	1490	170	90	—	110	25	—	—	1/25 of one animal
Gazelle	1450	160	90	—	110	25	—	—	1/25 of one animal
Onager	2020	190	140	—	100	30	—	—	1/175 of one animal
Aurochs	2020	190	140	—	100	30	—	—	1/400 of one animal
Domestic cattle	2020	190	140	—	100	30	—	—	1/250 of one animal
Pig	3710	140	350	—	100	20	—	—	1/70 of one animal
Ducks/Geese	1390	190	70	—	150	15	—	—	1 bird (or less)
Turtle	790	160	10	20	1000	10	—	—	4 turtles
Fish	950	180	25	—	500	10	—	—	4 fish
Mussels	700	100	20	30	1500	100	200	—	200 mussels

(a) Based on tables given by Platt, B. S. (1962). Tables of representative values of foods commonly used in tropical countries, *Medical Research Council, Special Report Series*, 302, H.M.S.O.

Table 3 Estimated values of some of the foods commonly eaten at Ali Kosh and Tepe Sabz, in the plain of Deh Luran, Iran.(a)

about 3% of the carbonized seeds, but because of their greater size constituted perhaps a third of the total weight of plant food; (2) collecting of small wild legume seeds of clover-alfalfa type, which constituted about 94% of the carbonized seeds, but amounted probably to no more than a third of the total weight of plant food; (3) collecting of the seeds of wild grasses, constituting only about 1% of the carbonized seeds and about 15% of the weight of plant food; (4) herding of domestic goats and sheep, whose bones constituted about 67% of the faunal material, but which contributed only about a third of the total weight of meat represented (see Table 2); (5) hunting of wild ungulates, which accounted for only 25% of the animal bones, but contributed more than 60% of the total weight of meat.

The remainder of the food supply was made up by elements such as nut meats, fruits, small mammals, fish, water fowl, and mussels, which although nutritionally important constituted a small percentage of the total weight of meat and plant food. Unfortunately, in the absence of coprolites, we have no way of calculating what percentage of the diet was made up by plant foods and what percentage was meat. It appears, however, that the Bus Mordeh villagers ate a good deal more meat than the average modern Iranian peasant; Watson[64] reports that animal bones are "rather rare" on village dump heaps today.

Nowadays, as May[65] points out, "most Iranian meals are of the one-pot type", with many ingredients thrown in, such as grain, lentils, meat, onions, etc. This may also have been true prehistorically—at least during the later part of the dry-farming era, when cooking pots are known. The early cereals (emmer wheat and two-row hulled barley) are largely unsuitable for bread-making, and their grains seem to have been pounded up and eaten right along with fragments of the woody spikelet base[66]. A lack of scorched or carbonized bone suggests that most meat was cooked after it had been cut off the carcass, or else boiled; there is little evidence to indicate direct roasting of the meat while still on the bone. Thus, it is possible that a typical meal of the early dry-farming era consisted of a gruel of cereal grains, spikelet bases, wild legumes, and chunks of ungulate meat cooked up together.

During the three periods represented at Ali Kosh, the only significant change in meat resources seems to have been an increase of sheep relative to goats; hunting was just as important when the site was abandoned as when it was founded. On the other hand, the changes in plant species percentages through time are more striking. They reflect (1) increases in cultivated cereal grains, (2) decreases in the use of local wild legumes, (3) increases in crop weeds, and (4) increases in plants typical of fallowed agricultural land (see below). In Tables 2 and 3 I have added comparative data from a nearby site, Tepe Sabz, which was occupied during the later era of simple irrigation farming (5500–3700 B.C.).

In terms of total food supply, hunting and wild plant collecting were not "supplements" to the Bus Mordeh diet; they were major subsistence strategies. Most of the total weight of meat and plant foods of this period came from wild resources. These resources had been available throughout the preceding Upper Palaeolithic period, and some of them (e.g. aurochs meat, pistachios, small wild legumes) are intrinsically richer in calories, protein (or both) than most of the domestic foods eaten in the Bus Mordeh phase. In this sense, there is no reason to believe that the early "food-producers" were significantly better nourished than their "food-collecting" ancestors. Nor was their subsistence base necessarily more "reliable"; attempts at dry-farming in the Deh Luran plain today meet with failure two or three years out of every five[67].

The one real advantage of cereal cultivation is that it increases carrying capacity of the land in terms of kilograms per hectare. Dry farming of wheat in northern Khuzistan, for example, yields an average of 410 kilos per hectare[68]. This is equal to the weight of usable meat from sixteen sheep, or the weight of more than 400 million small legume seeds. There is probably no other food in the Bus Mordeh phase debris which will produce as many kilos from so small an area as the cereals. Cultivation thus represented a decision to replace the native, high-protein wild legume ground cover with a lower-protein grass which would grow more densely and probably was less work to harvest, in spite of the risk of crop failure.

Nutritional aspects of early dry-farming in Iran

Still another fact which emerges from an examination of Tables 1–3 is that the early farmers of south-western Iran were still in the "broad spectrum" era: they made a living by *diversifying* their subsistence strategies, rather than concentrating on one food source. In fact, the synergistic effect of their various food combinations—ungulate meat, grasses, legumes, nut meats, mussels and so on—probably resulted in better nutrition than would specialization on a narrower range of products.

Highest on the list of calorie-producing foods used at Ali Kosh and Tepe Sabz were the almonds and pistachios, followed by cereal grasses and wild legumes. The wild legumes, judging by analyses of *Trigonella*[69], seem to have been higher in protein than most other food sources. Most calories probably came from these plant foods, since none of the meat sources (with the possible exception of pig) has a very high caloric value.

Minerals like calcium came from a variety of foods: mussels, water turtles, fresh water crabs, almonds, and pistachios. The mussels, pistachios, and various of the wild legumes are also good vitamin A sources. (It is interesting to note, however, that all these calcium-vitamin A sources probably became insignificant once the milking of domestic animals was established—an event for which we still have no archaeological evidence.)

None of the foods listed in Table 3 is a decent vitamin C source; the fruit of the wild caper (*Capparis*) probably filled this role. Other sources existed in the environment, and probably were used, although it cannot be proved archaeologically. These include fresh ungulate liver, the fruit of the jujube tree (*Zizyphus*), and the growing shoots of *Medicago* and other wild legumes[70]. In short, combinations of the twenty or so major foods used by the early dry farmers probably left them far better nourished than today's Iranian villager.[71]

Cropping, herding and erratic rainfall in the dry-farming era

One aspect of dry-farming in western Iran—or elsewhere in the Near East, for that matter—is that its outcome is unpredictable. Our figure of 410 kilos per hectare for northern Khuzistan is an average; in a good year the yield might be 1000 kilos, in a bad year almost nothing.

We have already mentioned the hazards of dry-farming in the Deh Luran plain. Watson[72] gives roughly similar figures for Iranian Kurdistan, where annual rainfall is higher (but still erratic). There a farmer may plant 300 kilos of wheat, and if the rain comes on time and in sufficient amounts, he might even get a ten-fold yield (3000 kilos). On the other hand, Watson's informants lost their entire wheat crop in 1958, 1959, and 1960 because of insects. What early farmers needed, therefore, was a way of levelling out the years of unpredictable bumper crops.

Primitive peoples, in the prehistoric record and in the ethnographic present, seem to use three main methods for dealing with unpredictable surpluses. They can store them; they can convert them into craft items of imperishable, exotic raw materials, which can be used as media of exchange during lean years[73]; or they can convert them into live storage, i.e. domestic animals, which can be used either directly (as food) or for inter-group exchanges which set up reciprocal obligations and maximize sharing during lean years[74]. These second two alternatives amount to a kind of "banking" of surpluses[75].

While early farmers in Mesoamerica relied fairly heavily on exchanges of exotic raw materials[76], the early Near Eastern farmers seem to have used mainly storage and domestic animals. Sheep and goats, for example, may be purchased with agricultural surpluses in good years, then exchanged for grain in lean years. They may be allowed to graze on growing cereal grain fields in good years[77], and at some time periods were fed stored or surplus barley[78]. Archaeological and ethnographic evidence suggest that plant cultivation and animal herding, far from being two separate subsistence activities, are interrelated in ways which help "bank" surpluses and even out the erratic fluctuations of the Near Eastern environment.

Effects of early cultivation on the wild plant cover

One effect of cultivation was an extensive alteration of the native plant cover of areas like the south-west Iranian steppe, which may actually have prevented a return to previous food-gathering patterns.

We have mentioned already the heavy dependence of Bus Mordeh phase farmers on local wild plants between 7500 and 6750 B.C. Nine-tenths of the seeds identified by Helbaek from these levels were from small annual legumes and wild grasses native to northern Khuzistan. Most abundant were the clover-like legumes *Medicago* (wild alfalfa), *Astragalus* (spiny milk vetch), and *Trigonella* (a small plant of the pea family, related to fenugreek); but they also collected oat grass (*Avena*), Bermuda grass (*Cynodon*) and Canary grass (*Phalaris*). However, these wild plants have the same general growing season as wheat and barley, which the Bus Mordeh people cultivated, and they also compete for the same alluvial soil with low salinity which the cereals require. As cultivation of wheat and barley increased, therefore, these wild legumes and grasses assumed the status of weeds, and were removed to make way for cultivated grains.

Their place did not remain unfilled for long, however—what happened was that new crop weeds from the mountains were introduced, probably in imperfectly cleaned batches of grain brought down to the steppe. These included various strains of *Aegilops* (goat-face grass), *Lolium* (ryegrass), and other grasses. Once established, the newcomers proved stubborn; Adams[79] reports that today ryegrass is one of the major crop weeds requiring eradication in the Mesopotamian lowlands.

One of the native plants which did not compete with the cereal crops was *Prosopis*, a woody perennial legume with an edible pod, related to the mesquite plant of the American West. Adams points out that *Prosopis* matures in a different season of the year from the cereals, and its deep root system survives even after ploughing. This woody wild legume may therefore even *increase* along with cultivation and fallow land, and Helbaek has in fact detected an increase in *Prosopis* seeds through time through three periods at Ali Kosh. Evidently the early cultivators responded in a reasonable way: as *Prosopis* increased, they ate more of it.

Fallowing practices also modified the landscape in other ways. Today in Khuzistan, three-fourths of all arable land is fallow during any given year. Helbaek's study of carbonized seeds from the Mohammad Jaffar Phase at Ali Kosh indicate that by *c.* 6000 B.C. such fallowing systems were already taking their toll of the previously dominant grasses and legumes, which were increasingly being replaced by pasture plants like mallow (*Malva*), plantain (*Plantago*), fumitory (*Fumaria*) and bedstraw (*Galium*).

The tiny annual legumes retreated to the margins of the cultivated land and the talus slope of the mountains. Their role as a major human food was played out by 6000 B.C. But they were not forgotten or ignored; they became food for sheep and goats. Today, from Iran west across the Near East, and even as far as the Tuareg Country of North Africa[80], *Astragalus* and *Trigonella* have become two of the most common plants collected as fodder for domestic caprines. Man continues to derive energy from them, but through an animal converter.

Early irrigation farming

Origins of irrigation

Irrigation may be yet a third example of an innovation which took place in a less-favourable habitat adjacent to an area of population growth. Our earliest evidence for this new technology comes not from the well-watered uplands of Kurdistan and Luristan, where early dry-farming was so successful, but from the lowland steppe of Khuzistan, a treeless plain receiving only 300 mm. of annual rainfall.

There is some reason to believe that the Khuzistan steppe was, indeed, receiving overflow populations from the mountain woodland. One line of evidence is the aforementioned field weeds in early levels at Ali Kosh—including *Aegilops* and *Lolium*, which are more at home in the mountains than on the steppe. The implication is that the whole complex, both cereals and field weeds, came into the steppe from the uplands. Another line of evidence is the strong resemblance of steppe artifact assemblages to those in the mountains[81].

Although survey has been far from exhaustive, what we know of the Zagros region at that time does suggest that population densities were higher in the large intermontane valleys than on the steppe[82]. Under conditions of rainfall agriculture, the carrying capacity of the steppe is limited, soil salinity is an ever-present danger, and considerable fallowing is required. Parts of the steppe, however, had great potential for irrigation: areas like the upper Khuzistan plains, where "increased surface gradients and widespread under-lying gravel deposits provide sufficient natural drainage . . . to minimize the problems of salinization and waterlogging that usually attend irrigation agriculture"[83]. Once irrigation appeared, the steppe greatly increased its carrying capacity and became, in fact, the dominant growth centre of the Zagros region between 5500 and 4000 B.C. Yet, interestingly enough, this new mode of production did not spread rapidly out of south-west Asia as earlier systems of dry-farming had: it seems to have been a peculiarly Near Eastern development.

Early irrigation on the lowland steppe was accompanied by a shift in settlement pattern[84]. Instead of locating sites near the margins of swampy areas, where the high water table could be used to ameliorate fluctuations in rainfall, some villages now occurred in linear arrangements along fossil stream courses from which water could be drawn by small, shallow canals. Table 4 lists the major plant and animal food sources from Tepe Sabz, an early irrigation site in south-western Iran.

Archaeological evidence for early irrigation comes from a variety of approaches. It was Adams[85] who first pointed out that there were alignments of later prehistoric sites in Khuzistan (5500–3500 B.C.) which seemed to

TEPE SABZ (5500–3700 B.C.)

(a)Emmer wheat	Shauk (*Prosopis*)
(a)Two-row barley, hulled	Caper
(a)Bread wheat	Pistachio
(a)Einkorn wheat	Almond
(a)Six-row barley, hulled	
(a)Six-row barley, naked	Gazelle
(a)Linseed	Onager
(a)Lentils	Pig
(a)Grass peas	
(a)Goats	Fox (and other small mammals)
(a)Sheep	Miscellaneous birds
(a)Cattle	
Goat-face grass (*Aegilops*)	Water turtles
Ryegrass (*Lolium*)	
Vetchling (*Lathyrus*)	Fish

Table 4. Common foods recovered from Tepe Sabz, in the plain of Deh Luran, south-west Iran.[b]

(a) [Domesticated items.
(b) See Helbaek, H. (In press). Plant-collecting, dry-farming, and irrigation agriculture in prehistoric Deh Luran, in Hole, F., Flannery, K. V. and Neely, J. A. Prehistory and human ecology of the Deh Luran plain, *Memoirs* Univ. of Michigan, Museum of Anthropology.

follow such water courses south into the zone where rainfall alone is inadequate for cultivation. Implications of the settlement pattern were that irrigation, consisting of the simple breaching of the natural levees of small streams flowing at the surface of the plain, enabled prehistoric farmers to partially counteract the erratic and frequently inadequate rainfall of the steppe. A similar survey by Wright[86], recently undertaken in the vicinity of Ur, shows that Ubaid baked-clay sickles and sickle fragments found on the land surface tend to be restricted to a band five kilometres wide to either side of fossil stream channels, giving us an estimate of the area watered by the small canals serving the fields.

Ecological effects of irrigation

Irrigation in Khuzistan, according to Adams[87] tends to increase crop yields from 410 kilos per hectare to 615 kilos per hectare. In addition, the actual physical size of the crop plants themselves seems to have been increased. For example, Helbaek's studies suggest that seeds of flax or linseed (*Linum bienne*) grown by rainfall alone have a maximum length range between 3·29–4·03 mm., while irrigated flax has a maximum length range of 4·39–6·20 mm. Flax seeds of this large size do not appear in the Deh Luran deposits until 5500–5000 B.C., after which they are present in large numbers[88]. However, as many authors have already pointed out, irrigation if unaccompanied by proper drainage may bring salt to the surface through capillary action in areas which were not previously saline. Agriculture then necessitates a strategy in which the advantages of irrigation water are weighed against soil salinity. One strategy employed in the lowlands of Iran and Mesopotamia was to concentrate on barley, which has a shorter growing season and higher salt tolerance than wheat. It is no accident that barley and sheep (see below), with their relatively greater ability to withstand the rigours of the hot, dry, saline lowland steppe and alluvium, were among the most important food resources of Elamite civilization[89].

One by-product of irrigation was that the canal became a new semihumid niche on which specialized plants could be grown, apart from those which the water was originally intended to irrigate. It is known, for example, that onions and date palms were grown on canal banks in early historic times in Mesopotamia[90]. Unfortunately, the canal vegetation is also served as a haven for crop pests such as the bandicoot-rat (*Nesokia indica*) which otherwise would have been less abundant in the region.

Sheep versus Stipa: *a by-product of the origins of wool*

An interesting chain of events followed the domestication of *Ovis orientalis*, an animal which still roams the foothills and intermontane plains of the Zagros and Taurus ranges in herds of up to fifteen individuals. These sheep have a coat which is reddish-buff above, white below, and is little different from that of a deer or gazelle. The coat is composed of hair from two kinds of follicles: "primaries", which produce the visible coat, and "secondaries", which produce the hidden, woolly underfur[91].

In the wild, these sheep use a number of wild grasses as forage. One of the best of these is a plant known as *Stipa*, or "feathergrass", which grows over much of the area from the Khuzistan and Assyrian steppes to the high mountains of the Iran-Iraq border. Many species of *Stipa* are classed by Pabot[92] and others as among the better forage species in terms of nutrition. *Stipa* has a rather interesting seed implantation mechanism: the seed has a sharp callus, which easily penetrates the soil, and a number of short stiff hairs which oppose its withdrawal. The bent and twisted awn of the seed, which is hygroscopic, serves as a driving organ, twisting and untwisting with changes in humidity. Thus, over a period of alternating wet and dry days, the feathergrass seed literally "screws itself into the ground".

Now, to set the stage, let us domesticate *Ovis orientalis* in the Zagros area sometime between 9000 and 8000 B.C. It appears (at the present state of our knowledge) that the first genetic change following domestication was the loss of horns in some sheep, probably females. One hornless sheep specimen is known from the Bus Mordeh phase in the Deh Luran plain of Iran, dating to about 7500 B.C.[93], and others are known from early villages near Kermanshah, Iran and in Anatolia[94]. A later change, and one still not radiocarbon dated[95], was the appearance of wool in domestic sheep, which we know took place prior to 3000 B.C.[96] Ryder[97] has shown that this was brought about when the "secondary" follicles increased in number and changed their spacing, causing the "underfur" to become the principal component of the sheep's coat.

It has long been known that sheep survive high temperatures and desertic conditions better than most other domestic animals. Recent studies by Schmidt-Nielsen[98] and his associates suggest that this is due to a number of factors: a "panting" mechanism which "permits an efficient ventilation of the upper respiratory tract, where most of the evaporation takes place"[99] and also —believe it or not—their wool. Thermometers were used to measure the internal, skin-surface, and outer-wool temperatures of sheep exposed to extreme conditions of heat and sun. It was observed that while the wool temperature reached 87°C, skin temperature remained at 42°C; in other words, "4 cm. of wool sustained a gradient of 45°C between tip and skin"[100]. It appears that while wool acts not only as a reflection to divert light and heat rays, but also as a layer of insulation which allows air circulation to cool the skin without exposing it to the sun. There may thus be some adaptive advantage for woolliness in domestic sheep maintained in captivity in hot climates, especially if they are deprived of a chance to spend the mid-day hours in the shade of a thicket, as they do in the wild. (Obviously, however, the *extreme* degree of woolliness in modern breeds is an artificial condition maintained by man, since feral sheep rapidly lose it.)

One of the side-effects of this process becomes apparent when woolly sheep are allowed to graze in meadows of *Stipa*: the feathergrass seed catches in the wool and often, through the same process of wetting and drying with which it plants itself, may burrow right into the animal's skin, causing considerable discomfort and even infection[101]. In some parts of Iran today, for example, shepherds even avoid taking their flocks into areas dominated by this plant[102], which must have been one of the most useful foods of the hairy wild sheep. Such little ecological chains of events give us some idea of how complex the whole process of domestication must have been.

Effects of changing land-use on sociopolitical structure

An interesting relationship appears when one plots the increasing population of prehistoric Iran against today's figures for different kinds of land use, as I have done in Table 5. It would appear that while early dry-farming and irrigation were pushing population densities up at a rapid rate, the relative amount of land which could be considered "prime", or "highly productive" was decreasing with equal rapidity. Let me explain.

Hole and I[103] have already presented estimates of population densities for parts of south-western Iran during the prehistoric era. These estimates are based on numbers of sites recovered by our surveys and those of Adams[104], using figures of approximately 100 persons per 1-hectare village site, and so on; it is presumed that whatever inaccuracies are present apply equally to all

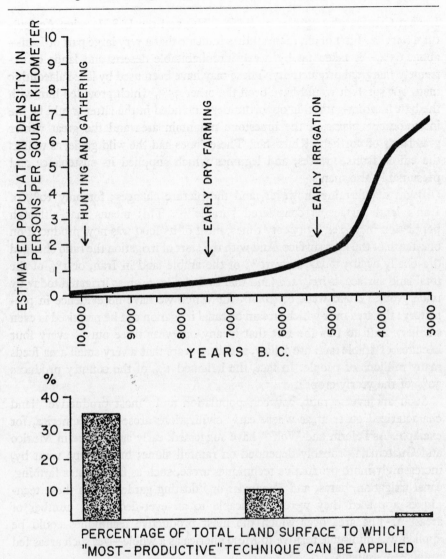

Table 5 Inverse ratio between population growth and percentage of total land surface to which "most productive" technique (hunting-gathering, dry-farming, early irrigation) could be applied at various stages of Iranian prehistory.

periods, so the general shape of the population growth curve should be reasonably reliable. Briefly, our estimates go from 0·1 persons per square kilometre in the late Palaeolithic, to 1–2 persons per square kilometre under conditions of early dry-farming, and up to 6 or more persons per square kilometre after irrigation appears in the archaeological record. In other words, population increased at least sixty-fold in the space of about six thousand years.

Now consider the figures given by May[105], which are based on the 1956

Iranian Census, plus studies by FAO-WHO and the U.S. Foreign Agricultural Service. First of all, these studies indicate that a very large part of Iran—about 65%—is taken up by nearly uninhabitable deserts and lands of extremely marginal productivity. These may have been used by late Palaeolithic man, but surely it would have been the other 35% which provided him with the best hunting-gathering opportunities; included in the latter would be the intermontane plains of the limestone mountain area and the great winter grasslands of northern Khuzistan. These zones had the wild game, as well as the edible fruits, grasses, and legumes which supplied its sustenance and presumably also man's.

Begin dry-farming, however, and the picture changes; for only 10% of Iran's land surface is considered "arable"[106]. This means that although population increased by twenty times, most of its food was now produced on one-tenth of the land surface. And with the start of irrigation the ratio changed drastically again; today, only 10% of the arable land in Iran, or 1% of the total land surface, is irrigated (and that includes large areas irrigated today by underground chain wells or *qanats*, for which we have no evidence in prehistory; the area over which stream or canal irrigation can be practised is even smaller). Add to this the fact that in any one year three out of every four hectares of arable land are fallow, and it appears that a very small area feeds many millions of people. In fact, the irrigated 1% of the country produces 30% of the yearly crop[107].

Such an inverse ratio between population and "most productive" land characterized other areas where early civilizations arose—Mesoamerica, for example. As Palerm and Wolf[108] have suggested, early agriculture in Mexico and Guatemala probably depended on rainfall alone; but as time went by, increasingly more productive techniques arose, such as flood-water farming, canal irrigation, dams, and *chinampas* or "floating gardens". As these techniques appeared they were "applicable to an ever-decreasing number of areas"[109]. The area over which the most productive techniques could be applied was miniscule relative to Mesoamerica as a whole—yet such areas fed millions of Indians.

Perhaps the most important consequence of the inverse ratio is that it set the stage for social stratification. As May[110] has pointed out, one of the salient characteristics of Near Eastern agriculture is what he politely calls "inequitable systems of land ownership and tenure". It is not just that 100% of the food is produced on 10% of the land; it is the fact that in some cases 1% of the population owns the 1% of the land which produces 30% of the food. This kind of differential access to strategic resources, including the means of production, is at the heart of "ranked" or "stratified" society. It is not a result of agricultural success, or "surplus", but a product of the widening gap between the size of the population and the size of the critical land surface on which it was most dependent. It is probably no accident that highly stratified societies followed this adaptive era in the alluvial lowlands of the Near East.

Conclusions

Like many semi-arid mountain regions, the Near East is a mosaic of woodland or parkland areas, relatively rich in wild products, surrounded by steppes or grasslands which are less rich in wild products. The changes leading to intensive food production are here viewed as a series of responses to disturbances of density equilibrium in human populations around the margins of the favoured areas, caused by the fact that those areas were the zones of population growth and emigration. Obviously, a definition of "favourable" depends on the technological level at the time: i.e. hunting, wild plant collecting, early dry-farming, or early irrigation.

Recent ethnographic studies do not indicate that hunters and gatherers are "starving", or that starvation is the major factor limiting their populations. Nor does the archaeological record in the Near East suggest that the average Neolithic farmer was any better nourished than the average Palaeolithic hunter. Moreover, over much of the Near East, farming does not necessarily constitute a "more stable" subsistence base or a "more reliable" food supply. The real consequence of domesticatį on was to (1) change the means of production in society, (2) make possible divisions of labour not usually characteristic of hunter-gatherers, and (3) lay the foundations for social stratification by continually reducing the zone of "optimum" productivity while allowing the population to expand at a geometric rate. It also (4) increased man's potential for environmental destruction, so that eventually it would have been impossible for him to return to his former means of subsistence, had he wanted to.

In this respect, early Eastern agriculture represents yet another example of the "second cybernetics"[111]. Starting with a relatively stable configuration of plant and animal species at 10,000 B.C., early cultivation took two genera of cereal grasses and two genera of small ungulates out of their habitat and artificially increased their numbers while they underwent a series of genetic changes, many of which were favourable from man's standpoint. These favourable changes made feasible a still greater investment of human labour in the cereals and caprines, and a greater artificial expansion of their range at the expense of other species. At this point, the ecosystem was no longer cybernating, or "stable"; all former rules which had kept species in check were off. What had been a minor deviation from equilibrium at 8000 B.C. had been amplified into a major subsystem at 5000 B.C., by which time irrigation had been employed to produce single-species stands of cereals where none had even existed in the wild. When equilibrium was momentarily reached again, perhaps around the time of the Sumerian state, a great many species—like the aurochs, the onager, and the red deer—had been driven completely on to marginal land. Today they are locally or universally extinct in the Near East. The new niches opened up by agriculture and irrigation were not for them, but for the crop pests and weeds which accompanied the cereals into foreign habitats and became, in some cases, part of the dominant biota. So great was the change in the Near East that today we see its original configuration only in the pollen record and the Palaeolithic bone debris.

Notes

1 Lees, G. M. and Falcon, N. L. (1952). The geographical history of the Mesopotamian plains, *Geog. J.*, **118**, pp. 24–39.
2 Hole, F. and Flannery, K. V. (1967). The prehistory of south-western Iran: a preliminary report, *Proc. Prehist. Soc.*, **33** (9), pp. 147–206.
3 Adams, R. M. (1962). Agriculture and urban life in early south-western Iran, *Science*, **136**, p. 114.
4 Lees, S. H. (1967). Regional integration of pig husbandry in the New Guinea highlands, *Paper presented at the Michigan Academy of Sciences, Annual Meeting 1967*.
5 Flannery, K. V. (1968). The Olmex and the Valley of Oaxaca: a model for inter-regional interaction in Formative times, *Conference on the Olmec, Dumbarton Oaks*, Washington, D.C., 27th October 1967.
6 Wynne-Edwards, C. V. (1962). *Animal Dispersion in relation to Social Behaviour*. Edinburgh.
7 Birdsell, J. B. (1966). Some predictions for the Pleistocene based upon equilibrium systems among recent hunters, Statement for conference, "*Man the Hunter*", University of Chicago, 6–9th April 1966.
8 McCarthy, F. D. (1957). Habitat, economy, and equipment of the Australian Aborigines, *Aus. J. of Sci.*, **19**, pp. 88–97; Bose, S. (1964). Economy of the Onge of Little Andaman, *Man in India*, **44** (4), pp. 298–310, Calcutta; Lee, R. B. (1965). Subsistence ecology of !Kung Bushman. *Ph.D. Dissertation, University of California, Berkeley*.
9 Lee, R. B. (In press). !Kung Bushmen subsistence: an input-output analysis. To appear in Vayda, A. P. (ed.) *Human Ecology: an anthropological reader*, American Museum of Natural History.
10 Binford, L. R. (1968). Post-Pleistocene adaptations *in* Binford L. R. and Binford, S. R. (eds.) *New Perspectives in Archaeology*, Chicago.
11 Binford, L. R. (1968). ibid.
12 Butzer, K. W. (1964). *Environment and Archeology: an introduction to Pleistocene geography*. Chicago.
13 Birdsell, J. B. (1957). Some population problems involving Pleistocene man, *Cold Spring Harbor Symposia on Quantitative Biology*, **22**. The Biological Laboratory, Cold Spring Harbor. pp. 47–69.
14 Howell, F. C. (1959). Upper Pleistocene stratigraphy and early man in the Levant, *Proc. of the American Phil. Soc.*, **103**, (1), pp. 1–65.
15 Solecki, R. S. (1964). Shanidar Cave, a late Pleistocene site in northern Iraq, *Rep. of the VIth Inter. Congress on the Quaternary*, **4**, pp. 413–23.
16 Rossignol, M. (1962). Analyse pollinique de sédiments marins Quaternaires en Israël, II—Sédiments Pleistocènes, *Pollen et Spores*, **4** (1), pp. 121–48; Rossignol, M. (1963). Analyse pollinique de sédiments Quaternaires dans la plaine de Haifa, Israel, *Israel J. of Earth Sciences*, **12**, pp. 207–14.
17 van Zeist, W. and Wright, H. E., Jr. (1963). Preliminary pollen studies at Lake Zeribar, Zagros Mountains, south-western Iran, *Science*, **140**, pp. 65–9; van Zeist, W. (1967). Late Quaternary vegetation history of western Iran, *Rev. of Palaeobot. and Palynol.*, **2**, pp. 301–11.

18 Flannery, K. V. (1965). The ecology of early food production in Mesopotamia, *Science*, **147**, pp. 1247–56.
19 Hole, F. and Flannery, K. V. (1967). ibid.
20 Binford, L. R. and Binford, S. R. (1966). A preliminary analysis of functional variability in the Mousterian of Levallois facies, *Amer. Anthrop.*, **68** (2, part 2), pp. 238–95.
21 Ewing, J. F. (1949). The treasures of Ksar 'Akil, *Thought*, **24**, Fordham University, p. 276.
22 Ewing, J. F. (1951). Comments on the report of Dr. H. E. Wright, Jr., on his study of Lebanese marine terraces, *J. of Near Eastern Studies*, **10**, p. 120.
23 Hole, F. and Flannery, K. V. (1967). ibid.
24 Hole, F. and Flannery, K. V. (1967). ibid.; Garrod, D. A. E. (1930). The Palaeolithic of southern Kurdistan: excavations in the caves of Zarzi and Hazar Merd., *Bull. of the American School of Prehistoric Research*, **6**, pp. 9–43.
25 Solecki, R. S. (1964). op. cit. p. 417; Solecki, R. L. (1964). Zawi Chemi Shanidar, a post-Pleistocene village site in northern Iraq, *Rep. of the VIth Inter. Congress on the Quaternary*, **4**, pp. 405–12.
26 Solecki, R. S. (1964). ibid.; Solecki, R. L. (1964). ibid.
27 Braidwood, R. J. and Howe, B. (1960). Prehistoric investigations in Iraqi Kurdistan, *Studies in Ancient Oriental Civilization*, Oriental Institute, Chicago, **31**.
28 van Loon, M. (1966). Mureybat: an early village in inland Syria, *Archaeology*, **19**, pp. 215–16.
29 Perrot, J. (1966). Le gisement Natufien de Mallaha (Eynan), Israël, *L'Anthropologie*, **70** (5–6), pp. 437–84.
30 Braidwood, R. J. and Howe, B. (1960). ibid.
31 Howell, F. C. (1959). op. cit. table 10.
32 Garrod, D. A. E. and Bate, D. M. A. (1937). *The Stone Age of Mt. Carmel: excavations at the Wadi el-Mughara*, **I**. Oxford.
33 Ewing, J. F. (1949). op. cit. p. 262.
34 Reed, C. A. and Braidwood, R. J. (1960). Towards the reconstruction of the environmental sequence in north-eastern Iraq, *in* Braidwood, R. J. and Howe, B. op. cit. p. 169.
35 Hole, F. and Flannery, K. V. (1967). ibid.
36 Platt, B. S. (1962). Tables of representative values of foods commonly used in tropical countries, *Medical Research Council, Special Report Series*, **302**, Her Majesty's Stationery Office.
37 Hesse, R., Allee, W. C. and Schmidt, K. P. (1951). *Ecological Animal Geography*. New York.
38 Platt, B. S. (1962). ibid.
39 van Zeist, W. and Wright, H. E. (1963). ibid.
40 Rossignol, M. (1962). ibid.; Rossignol, M. (1963). ibid.
41 Odum, E. P. and Odum, H. T. (1959). *Fundamentals of Ecology*, 2nd ed. Philadelphia. p. 281.
42 Harlan, J. R. and Zohary, D. (1966). Distribution of wild wheats and barley, *Science*, **153**, pp. 1075–80.
43 Reed, C. A. (1959). Animal domestication in the prehistoric Near East, *Science*, **130**, pp. 1629–39; Reed, C. A. (1960). A review of the archaeological evidence on animal domestication in the prehistoric Near East, *in* Braidwood, R. J. and Howe, B. op. cit. pp. 119–46.
44 Harlan, J. R. and Zohary, D. (1966). op. cit. p. 1078.
45 Harlan, J. R. (1967). A wild wheat harvest in Turkey, *Archaeology*, **20** (3), pp. 197–201.
46 Harlan, J. R. and Zohary, D. (1966). ibid.
47 Harlan, J. R. (1967). op. cit. p. 198.
48 Perrot, J. (1966). op. cit. pp. 480–3.

49 van Loon, M. (1966). ibid.
50 Kirkbride, D. (1966). Five seasons at the pre-pottery Neolithic village of Beidha in Jordan, *Palestine Exploration Quarterly*, 98 (1), pp. 8–72.
51 Helbaek, H. (In press). Plant-collecting, dry-farming, and irrigation agriculture in prehistoric Deh Luran, *in* Hole, F., Flannery, K. V. and Neely, J. A. Prehistory and human ecology of the Deh Luran plain, *Memoirs*, Univ. of Michigan, Museum of Anthropology.
52 Hole, F. and Flannery, K. V. (1967). ibid.
53 Helbaek, H. (In press). ibid.
54 Flannery, K. V., Kirkby, A. V., Kirkby, M. J. and Williams, A. W., Jr. (1967). Farming systems and political growth in ancient Oaxaca, *Science*, 158, pp. 445–54.
55 Kirkbride, D. (1966). ibid.
56 Masson, V. M. (1965). The Neolithic farmers of Central Asia, *Acts, VI Inter. Congress of Pre- and Proto-historic Sciences*, 2, pp. 205–15.
57 Helbaek, H. (1966). Commentary on the phylogenesis of *Triticum* and *Hordeum*, *Econ. Bot.*, 20, pp. 350–60; Helbaek, H. (1966). Pre-pottery Neolithic farming at Beidha, *in* Kirkbride, D. Five seasons at the pre-pottery Neolithic village of Beidha in Jordan, *Palestine Exploration Quarterly*, 98 (1), pp. 61–6; Masson, V. M. (1965). ibid.
58 Hole, F. and Flannery, K. V. (1967). ibid.
59 White, T. (1953). A method of calculating the dietary percentage of various food animals utilised by aboriginal peoples, *American Antiquity*, 18 (4), pp. 396–8.
60 Walker, E. P. (1964). *Mammals of the World*. Baltimore.
61 Platt, B. S. (1962). ibid.; Obvious difficulties were encountered in finding values for some of the wild foods at Ali Kosh. For gazelle meat, I have used the values for lean goat meat; for onager, those for lean beef. Small legume values are those given for fenugreek (*Trigonella* sp.), etc.
62 Hole, F. and Flannery, K. V. (1967). ibid.
63 Helbaek, H. (In press). ibid.; Hole, F., Flannery, K. V. and Neely, J. A. (In press). ibid.
64 Watson, P. J. (1966). Clues to Iranian prehistory in modern village life, *Expedition*, 8 (3), p. 13.
65 May, J. M. (1961). *The Ecology of Malnutrition in the Far and Near East*. New York. p. 370.
66 Helbaek, H. (In press). ibid.
67 Hole, F. and Flannery, K. V. (1967). op. cit. footnote 6.
68 Adams, R. M. (1962). op. cit. p. 110.
69 Platt, B. S. (1962). ibid.
70 Platt, B. S. (1962). ibid.
71 May, J. M. (1961). op. cit. p. 373; the synergistic value of food combinations was brought home to me in 1963 while I worked closely in the field with my friend and colleague, Frank Hole, excavating the paleolithic caves of Iran's Khorramabad Valley. As we sat in our camp in the evening —partaking of barley in its most appealing form—we used to share a large paper sack of Kurdistan pistachios (*Pistacia atlantica*). Wild products being what they are, the 1963 pistachio crop was riddled with small live caterpillars which had bored into the nuts and lay waiting for the unwary eater. I examined each pistachio carefully as I opened it, and as a consequence had to discard about half; but I noticed that Hole was able to eat 100% of the ones he selected, and I commented on his luck. To which he replied: "I'm just not looking." I later learned that a kilo of dried caterpillars may contain 3720 calories, 550 grams of protein, 2700 milligrams of calcium, and a generous supply of thiamine, riboflavin, and iron (see Platt, B. S. (1962). ibid.). In fact, the protein content is double that of the pistachios themselves, and a combination of the two foods

probably has a synergistic effect exceeding the value of the nuts alone. Hole's wise decision to diversify his subsistence base brought him out of the field season a good thirty pounds heavier than me.

72 Watson, P. J. (1966). ibid.
73 Harding, T. G. (1967). *Voyagers of the Vitiaz Strait: a study of a New Guinea trade system.* Seattle; Flannery, K. V. (1967). ibid.
74 Lees, G. M. (1967). ibid.; Rappaport, R. A. (1967). Ritual regulation of environmental relations among a New Guinea people, *Ethnology,* **6** (1), pp. 17–30.
75 Lees, S. H. (1967). ibid.
76 Flannery, K. V. (In press). ibid.
77 Adams, R. M. (1965). *Land behind Baghdad: a history of settlement on the Diyala plains.* Chicago. p. 14.
78 Adams, R. M. (1962). op. cit. p. 115.
79 Adams, R. M. (1965). op. cit. p. 5.
80 Nicolaisen, J. (1963). Ecology and culture of the pastoral Tuareg, *National-museets Skrifter,* **9,** Copenhagen.
81 Hole, F., Flannery, K. V. and Neely, J. A. (In press). ibid.
82 Hole, F. and Flannery, K. V. (1967). ibid.
83 Adams, R. M. (1962). op. cit. p. 110.
84 Hole, F., Flannery, K. V. and Neely, J. A. (In press). ibid.
85 Adams, R. M. (1962). op. cit.
86 Wright, H. T. (1967). The administration of rural production in an early Mesopotamian town. *Ph.D. Dissertation. University of Chicago.* pp. 38–9.
87 Adams, R. M. (1962). ibid.
88 Helbaek, H. (1960). The paleoethnobotany of the Near East and Europe, *in* Braidwood, R. J. and Howe, B. (1960). op. cit. pp. 99–118; Helbaek, H. (1960). Ecological effects of irrigation in ancient Mesopotamia, *Iraq,* **22,** pp. 186–96; Helbaek, H. (In press). ibid.
89 Adams, R. M. (1962). ibid.; Hole, F. and Flannery, K. V. (1967). ibid.
90 Adams, R. M. (1960). Early civilizations: subsistence and environment, *in* Kraeling, C. H. and Adams, R. M. (eds.) *City Invincible: a symposium on urbanization and cultural development in the ancient Near East.* Chicago. pp. 269–95.
91 Ryder, M. L. (1958). Follicle arrangement in skin from wild sheep, primitive domestic sheep and in parchment, *Nature, Lond.* **182,** pp. 781–3.
92 Pabot, H. (1960). *The Native Vegetation and its Ecology in the Khuzistan River Basins.* Khuzistan Development Service, Ahwaz, Iran.
93 Hole, F. and Flannery, K. V. (1967). op. cit. fig. 8.
94 Personal communication from S. Bökönyi and D. Perkins, Jr.
95 Textiles from Çatal Hüyük, once thought to be perhaps the earliest wool know, have been examined now by Ryder, M. L. (1965). Report of textiles from Çatal Hüyük, *Anatolian Studies,* **15,** pp. 175–6, and it appears that they are mostly flax fibre.
96 Hilzheimer, M. (1941). Animal remains from Tell Asmar, *Studies in Ancient Oriental Civilization,* **20,** Univ. of Chicago, Oriental Institute.
97 Ryder, M. L. (1958), ibid.
98 Schmidt-Nielsen, K. (1964). *Desert Animals: physiological problems of heat and water.* Oxford.
99 Schmidt-Nielsen, K. (1964). op. cit. p. 99.
100 Schmidt-Nielsen, K. (1964). op. cit. p. 97.
101 Reeder, J. R. (1967). Grasses, *Encyclopedia Britannica,* 1967 edition, **10,** p. 700.
102 Pabot, H. (1960). ibid.
103 Hole, F. and Flannery, K. V. (1967). ibid.
104 Adams, R. M. (1962). op. cit.
105 May, J. M. (1961). op. cit.

106 May, J. M. (1961). op. cit. p. 357; Cressey, G. B. (1960). *Crossroads: land and life in South-west Asia*. Chicago.

107 May, J. M. (1961). ibid.

108 Palerm, A. and Wolf, E. (1957). Ecological potential and cultural development in Mesoamerica, *in Studies in Human Ecology*, *Social Science Monographs*, 3, Pan American Union, Washington, D.C. pp. 1–37.

109 Palerm, A. and Wolf, E. (1957). op. cit. p. 36.

110 May, J. M. (1961). op. cit. p. 343.

111 Maruyama, M. (1963). The second cybernetics: deviation-amplifying mutual causal processes, *American Scientist* 51 (2), pp. 164–79; Flannery, K. V. (1968). Archaeological systems theory and early Mesoamerica, *in Anthropological archaeology in the Americas*, Anthropological Society of Washington.

P. A. JEWELL

Wild mammals and their potential for new domestication

It is a remarkable fact, to which allusion is made by many authors, that so few species of the world's rich mammalian fauna have been domesticated by man. Most of these species, moreover, were domesticated anciently and when, in the Neolithic, the four major meat producers, sheep, goats, cattle and pigs, were under control, domestication for this purpose was practically at an end. Innumerable alternative species of large herbivore were available for domestication but an insignificant number were taken in hand: in Asia several species of bovini were domesticated and many of them fulfil a role similar to that of cattle; reindeer are outstanding in having been domesticated to meet the exigencies of a particular environment; and horses, camels and llamas have come to serve functions other than food supply. In many areas the inferiority of the domestic stock in fitness and in productivity must have been obvious, yet in his migrations man has always attempted to take his exotic beasts with him. He has preferred to endure their low productivity rather than attempt the revolution of mastering new species.

Now, however, man has been brought to the point where he is obliged to take a new look at his stock. The need arises from his own prodigious increase in numbers and his increasing demands for meat[1]. All the species that could once be hunted are becoming less and less available: natural habitats have been relentlessly destroyed and the majority of the world's mammalian species, certainly the large herbivores, are faced with extinction. Rather than lose species by default man must review his total animal resources and amongst other actions initiate a new phase of domestication in order to exploit those resources to the full[2]. Success in this process would be a key factor in meeting the impending catastrophe of a world shortage of food.

Present meat-producing domestic animals are all members of the order Artiodactyla and it is within this same order that the greatest potential for new domestication lies. A broad examination of all mammals suggests five orders within which species should be domesticated for various purposes: primates for medical research; rodents for research, for certain types of small-scale intensive meat production, and as furbearers; carnivores as furbearers;

and the two ungulate orders, Perissodactyla and Artiodactyla for meat production.

Of the families in the Perissodactyla only the Equidae appear suitable for domestication, and of these only zebra remain undomesticated. It is known from past successes that zebra can be tamed and trained to pull waggons[3]. The animals are not now needed for draught but as will be discussed below they should be considered as possible meat producers.

The order Artiodactyla comprises 194 species[4]; ninety-two of these species are indigenous to Africa and special attention will be given to domestication in that continent. It would be remiss, however, not to mention the potential for domestication in the very large family that is excluded from Africa, namely the deer. There are forty-one species of deer but only one species, the reindeer, *Rangifer tarandus*, has been domesticated. The unique value of this species lies in its exploitation of the tundra. But another deer, the elk, *Alces alces*, could well be the best meat producer to exploit the taiga and other northern, but not extreme arctic zones. Great progress has in fact already been made in its domestication and in the Pechero-Ilych Park of northern Russia a large herd of elk are under careful management and selection. and show most of the attributes required of domestic animals[5]. Probably other species of deer merit domestication and their special role would be that of controlled browsers in the temperate forest zone.

Potential in Africa

The greatest concentrations of wild large herbivores, and greatest assemblages of species, are in Africa. But many of Africa's human populations, typifying developing countries, suffer from lack of animal protein in their diets[6]. The African situation is also a challenging one because it is peculiar that no indigenous species (apart from the ass in North Africa) have been domesticated there. The major factors contributing to this situation would seem to be as follows: (*a*) the relatively recent incursion of agricultural peoples into southern Africa; (*b*) the abundant prey species available for hunting and until recently providing an alternative meat supply; (*c*) the presence of several powerful carnivores, the lion, leopard, hyaena and hunting dog which have presented a severe obstacle to attempting new domestications; (*d*) tradition and folk lore which distinguish between wild beasts and those that "chose to follow man", and social customs associated with established domestic species that strongly encourage conservatism. The prejudices engendered by these factors are not confined to black Africans. White settlers and the instigators of veterinary policies have proved to be just as inflexible and instead of treating meat production in Africa as a biological problem, they have pursued programmes of prodigious game slaughter in an effort to make the ranges safe for familiar, but unsuitable, domestic animals

Limitations to the productivity of domestic stock

Cattle, sheep, goats and pigs have an evolutionary adaptation to the environments in which they originated and a limited ability to adapt to new ones. The protection afforded by careful husbandry and by veterinary medicine has permitted an enormous extension of their range, but in some environments their efficiency is reduced to marginal levels and diseases may offer absolute barriers. The most outstanding example of limitation by disease is tsetse-borne trypanosomiasis infection in Africa. The disease renders 4·15 million square miles of land unavailable to cattle (representing about 37% of the total land area of Africa)[7], but indigenous wild mammals are well adapted to the parasites. Tremendous effort is expended to try and increase the area in which cattle can be safely moved and one of the major means of implementing this policy has been "game elimination", on the supposition that certain species of wild mammals act as a reservoir for the disease. Millions of head of antelopes, buffalo and other species have been slaughtered with variable and only partial success. The cost in squandered protein resources is not usually taken into account in assessing these schemes.

A second limitation to livestock efficiency lies in the physiology and feeding behaviour of the animals concerned. Much of Africa is arid and hot and animals must cope with these exigencies[8]. Many breeds of domestic animals, particularly cattle of zebu stock, respond reasonably well, but indigenous large mammals are better equipped having evolved finely adjusted behavioural and physiological adaptations to these environmental extremes. Several species cope with heat stress by tolerating considerable fluctuations in body temperature and thus lessening the need to lose water: buffalo and oryx provide examples[9]. The eland voids faeces of low moisture content and this enables it to gain more preformed water. If eland and ox were eating the same succulent acacia leaves, and were deprived of drinking water the eland would achieve the better water balance. An estimated 4 litres of water per 100 kg. body weight per day is available to the eland from food and metabolic sources so that the animal can be almost independent of surface water[10]. The ruminants have evolved an effective means of nitrogen conservation by urea-recycling through the salivary glands[11], and the species adapted to arid environments can be expected to be particularly efficient in this regard. Amongst domestic stock in the tropics, fertility is often low but wild mammals exhibit a remarkably high reproductive capacity as has been shown in studies on wildebeest, eland and hartebeest[12].

Finally, in their selectivity towards the plants that they graze or browse, indigenous mammals probably exhibit superiority over exotic species, and the antelopes can select a high proportion of the most nutritious parts of plants. The more important aspect of food-plant use, however, is that exhibited by a community of indigenous herbivores which can exploit the

5—DOPAA • •

habitat far more efficiently than husbanded groups of cattle, sheep and goats. Lamprey[13] has documented the manner in which a community of herbivores are separated ecologically and use different parts of a complex environment. The major species in his study of E. African savannah woodland were harte-beest, waterbuck, wildebeest, buffalo, zebra, impala, Grant's gazelle, warthog, eland, lesser kudu, rhino, dikdik, elephant and giraffe. Of these the first three are grass feeders; buffalo, eland and kudu take a fair proportion of herbs and shrubs; warthog tackle sedges; and elephant and giraffe concentrate on shrubs and trees. This spatial separation is augmented by a separation in the time and season at which species use different areas, giving rise to a grazing succession[14]. These communities can reach a very high biomass and the carrying capacity of most savannah areas is considerably greater for a complex of indigenous herbivores than for ranched domestic species[15].

Game cropping

In Africa, biologists have been greatly concerned with the kinds of facts presented above. If communities of indigenous wild mammals have a much higher potential productivity than domestic stock then means of harvesting their yield must be devised. Game cropping[16] is the method employed and many successful schemes are in progress in Uganda, Kenya, Rhodesia and Zambia. The technical problems of cropping are, however, very great: hunt-ing and killing without excessive disturbance is difficult; it is difficult to maintain quality in handling and processing meat in the field; transport and haulage are very costly. Nevertheless, from a biological point of view, the system has one great advantage which is that the several herbivores involved are free to move and select food plants, water and shelter, in accord with the way these are best provided by the habitat. The system can make a very big contribution to meat production and as an "extensive" system of game ranching is likely to find a permanent place in the economy. Its role however is different from what would be achieved by newly domesticated species, and these methods of exploitation must be seen as complementary.

Domesticating new species in Africa

One species of African large herbivore is now domesticated. This is the eland *Taurotragus oryx*. It has long been bred and studied in the Ukraine[17] and many small herds are kept in southern Africa[18]. It shows high fertility, good live weight gains, and excellent carcass qualities[19], and even in those attributes usually thought of as resulting from domestication such as docility, ease of handling, and restraint by fences, the eland is superior to range cattle. Eland thrive under conditions of food, water and tsetse fly infestation in which cattle cannot survive; they can be milked, moreover, and their milk has peculiar and superior keeping properties of great value in a tropical environment[20].

An even greater prize for domestication may exist in the giant eland, *T. derbianus*, a form indigenous to W. Africa, and formerly extending in range as far as the Sudan[21]. The survival of this species is endangered, however, and in a visit from Nigeria to the Cameroons in 1966 I was not able to assure myself that any still survive.

The blesbok, *Damaliscus dorcas*, has not reached the same stage of subjugation as the eland, but, on the other hand, the species exists entirely as dispersed herds on S. African range-land, where they belong to the land-owners, and none survive in the wild state. They are small hartebeests, that can exploit sour veld more effectively than cattle[22], that breed and thrive well in dry conditions and are easily restrained by fences. They can be managed by being rounded up and impounded in corrals.

The hartebeests in general form an extremely promising group of species that should be domesticated. Their radiation in Africa has produced divergent types that are likely to show particularly valuable adaptations to local environments. Hybrids occur where geographical races overlap and the two genera, *Damaliscus* and *Alcelaphus*, can be regarded as forming clines through the continent. Hybrids have been reported between the genera[23].

The domestication of the African buffalo, *Synceros caffer*, is long overdue. It fills a niche that is very similar to the domestic ox, but has all the advantages of being indigenous. Having a very wide distribution throughout Africa the species must, in its many local forms, have immunity to a wide range of trypansomiases and other infections. Tame buffalo have often been reared[24] and the fierceness of the wild animals should not be a deterrent to mastering them. The progenitors of cattle, *Bos primigenius*, were quite as ferocious, and other species of bovini, such as the gaur, *B. gaurus*, have been domesticated despite their formidable disposition. Buffalo are larger than range cattle, make good live weight gains, give high carcass yields[25] and naturally herd closely.

The warthog, *Phacochoerus aethiopicus*, should be mentioned because it is unaffected by African swine fever which makes pig-farming difficult. Warthogs are easy to tame and in grubbing for roots and tubers they exploit a food-source not touched by other species. Experimental rearing and handling will be required in order to decide which species of African swine, whether warthog, bush-pig, *Potamochoerus porcus*, or giant forest hog, *Hylochoerus meinertzhagen*, is best suited to domestication.

The wildebeest, *Connochaetes gnou*, zebra, *Equus burchelli*, and small gazelles are the dominant grazers of the great open savannah areas of E. Africa, and whilst the small animals complement the large, the wildebeest and zebra would appear to compete for available grazing. In such a situation it would be essential to study both wildebeest and zebra, and examine the efficiency of their ecological adaptations in order to decide which might be the best domestic producer. Other factors, such as the acceptability of the meat for human consumption, of course enter such decisions. It might be found that domestic eland could replace these species in many situations, but to achieve overall maximum productivity the principle of ecological separation must be respected. For this same reason, although it might appear extravagant of effort, it will probably prove economically rewarding to domesticate the small gazelles.

Examples will not be multiplied, but it is obvious that many other species must be considered as candidates for domestication. Selection will depend on the geographical area, and ecosystem, of intended use, and on the success achieved with pioneer species.

General considerations

It may be supposed that the process (in prehistoric times) by which our present stock were domesticated was a protracted one in which much ingenuity, and a great expenditure of human effort was involved. If new domestication is to be effective it must be done quickly, on a large enough scale to demonstrate its economic feasibility and every device of animal control and breeding will need to be used. The foundation stock of tamed animals should be large so that individuals can be rigorously screened for suitable breeding stock. Desirable behavioural traits must first be sought (docility, acceptance of restraint, low aggressiveness, etc.) and intensive behavioural studies of the species concerned should be initiated early. Techniques of artificial insemination should be worked out immediately for each species, just as they are currently being worked out for the asiatic buffalo, *Bubalus bubalus*. Males with desirable characters can then sire increased progeny. Immobilizing and tranquillizing drugs could be used in many ways to aid handling.

Certain types of social behaviour in wild ungulates may be incompatible with ordinary methods of husbandry. It is notable that existing domestic herbivores are gregarious species that exhibit dominance hierarchies within their social groups, and this organization is well seen in feral cattle[26], feral sheep[27] and wild gaur[28]. Many species of African buck, however, exhibit territorial behaviour[29] in which the males take possession of certain areas of land and exclude other males. It has been suggested[30] that this behaviour would be unfavourable in domestic stock, but whilst superficially this might appear likely it seems to me that a better understanding of the whole social organization of territorial species would indicate ways of overcoming the difficulties, and even of turning them to advantage. The dominant males in a herd of some newly domesticated species, if firmly attached to small territories, could offer focal points of attraction keeping the herd together. The effect that territoriality has in dispersing animals through both favourable and less favourable terrain can promote more intensive use of the habitat[31]. Secondary males, not required for breeding, could be castrated and this would presumably reduce conflict.

Hybridization could prove a valuable means of manipulating domestic forms. The hartebeests form clines of two genera, and hybrids between local geographical races occur naturally[32]. There appear to be no certain records of African buffalo crossing with cattle, but they might interbreed with other bovines. These hybrids, even if sterile, could be expected to exhibit many useful characters, and their production might provide a means of circumventing some of the problems of domesticating buffalo.

Present-day domesticated forms of cattle, sheep and goats, differ markedly from their wild progenitors and one of the most significant changes that has been exhibited is a diminution in size[33]. Such a change may have accompanied selection for docility as well as have been induced by poor feeding conditions in captivity. Any newly domesticated species can be expected to change or be deliberately changed, in the directions of, for example, improved bodily proportions for meat production and reduced horn size.

If the developments discussed above do take place they will yield information of a very valuable kind for archaeologists. The opportunity will exist to study directly the effects of domestication and selection on a variety of large mammals, particularly incidental changes in the skeleton. It should also be noted that current ecological studies of large mammals, and investigations that would be stimulated by new economic uses, could have much relevance to an understanding of the ecology of prehistoric man. The work of Laws and Parker[34] on the elephant, for example, has led them to suggest that this species has been a major agent, together with climate, man and fire, in modifying the environment of prehistoric Africa.

The likelihood of physical and behavioural changes serves to emphasize that domestication cannot be regarded as a form of conservation for species threatened with extinction. Morris[35] comments, referring to domesticated animals: "Their numbers are dramatically increased. In terms of world populations they are tremendously successful. But it is a qualified success. The price they have paid is their evolutionary freedom. They have lost their genetic independence and . . . are now subject to our breeding whims and fancies." Domestication is a way of greatly increasing the exploitation of species that have long been our prey. At the same time it could accelerate the extermination of the wild form over the range where the domesticated form is used, and for the same reasons of competition and interference with domestic stock as happened in the past[36]. It will then become of even greater importance to keep truly wild populations in existence in National Parks, and protected by appropriate hunting laws, so that they can remain available for study in relatively natural environments, and can provide invaluable reserves of genetic material.

Notes

1 FAO reports, and information summarized by Crawford, M. A. (1968). The possible use of wild animals as future sources of food in Africa, *Vet. Rec.*, 82, p. 305.

2 Jewell, P. A. (1968). Climate versus man and his animals, *Nature, Lond.* 218, pp. 993–4.

3 Bigalke, R. C. (1965). Can Africa produce new domestic animals ?, *New Scientist*, 374.

4 Morris, D. (1965). *The Mammals*. London.

5 Yazan, Y. and Knorre, Y. (1964). Domesticating elk in a Russian National Park, *Oryx*, 7, pp. 301–4.

6 Latham, M. (1965). *Human Nutrition in Tropical Africa*. FAO, Rome; and see references in Crawford, M. A. (1968). op. cit.

7 Phillips, J. (1959). *Agriculture and Ecology in Africa*. London. pp. 63–72; Deshler, W. (1963). Cattle in Africa: distribution, types, and problems, *Geog. Rev.*, 53, pp. 52–8.

8 McDowell, R. E. (1968). Climate versus man and his animals, *Nature, Lond.* 218, p. 641.

9 Bligh, J. and Harthoorn, A. M. (1965). Continuous radiotelemetric records of the deep body temperature of some unrestrained African mammals under near natural conditions, *J. Physiol.*, 176, pp. 145–62.

10 Taylor, C. R. and Lyman, C. P. (1967). A comparative study of the environmental physiology of an East African antelope, the eland, and the Hereford steer, *Physiol. Zool.*, 40, pp. 280–95.

11 Livingstone, H. G., Payne, W. J. A. and Friend, M. T. (1962). Urea excretion in ruminants, *Nature, Lond.* 194, pp. 1057–8.

12 *Symposium on Biology of Reproduction in Mammals*, Nairobi, 1968. *Symp. Soc. Reprod. Fert.* (In press).

13 Lamprey, H. E. (1963). Ecological separation of the large mammal species in the Tarangire Game Reserve, Tanganyika, *East Afr. Wildlf. J.*, 1, pp. 63–92.

14 Vesey-Fitzgerald, D. F. (1960). Grazing succession among East African game animals, *J. Mammal.*, 41, pp. 161–72.

15 Talbot, L. M., Payne, W. J. A., Ledger, H. P., Verdcourt, L. D. and Talbot, M. H. (1965). The meat production potential of wild animals in Africa, *Commonwealth Bureau An. Breed. Gen. Tech. Comm.*, 16, p. 42.

16 Talbot, L. M., Payne, W. J. A., Ledger, H. P., Verdcourt, L. D. and Talbot, M. H. (1965). ibid.

17 Uspenskii, G. A. and Saglanskii, A. D. (1952). *Domestication of the eland in the U.S.S.R.* Summary in *Rhod. J. Agric. Res.*, 1, p. 87.

18 See Bigalke, R. C. (1964). ibid.

19 Zyl, J. H. M. van. (1962). The meat production of South African game animals. 1. The eland, *Fauna and Flora*, 13, pp. 35–40; Skinner, J. D. (1967). An appraisal of the eland as a farm animal in Africa, *Anim. Breed. Abst.*, 35, pp. 177–86.

20 Treus, V. and Kravchenko, D. (1968). Methods of rearing and economic utilization of eland in the Askaniya—Nova Zoological Park, *Symp. Zool. Soc. London*, 21, pp. 395–411.

21 Sidney, J. (1965). The past and present distribution of some African ungulates, *Trans. Zool. Soc., London*, 30, pp. 1–396.

22 Kettlitz, W. K. (1967). The Blesbok, *Fauna and Flora*, 18, pp. 36–46.

23 *D. dorcas* × *A. buselaphus*; Kettlitz, W. K. (1967). ibid.

24 Bigalke, R. C. and Neitz, W. O. (1954). Indigenous ungulates as a possible source of new domesticated animals, *J. S. Afr. Vet. Med. Ass.*, 25, pp. 45–54.

25 Zyl, J. H. M. van and Skead, D. M. (1964). Meat production of South African game animals. 2. The African buffalo, *Fauna and Flora*, **15**, pp. 34–40.
26 Schloeth, R. (1958). Cycle annuel et comportement Social du taureau de Camargue, *Mammalia*, **22**, pp. 121–39.
27 Grubb, P. and Jewell, P. A. (1966). Social grouping and home range in feral Soay sheep, *Symp. Zool. Soc., Lond.* **18**, pp. 179–210.
28 Schaller, G. (1967). *The Deer and the Tiger*. Chicago.
29 Uganda Kob, see Buechner, H. K. (1963). Territoriality as a behavioural adaptation to environment in Uganda Kob, *Proc. XVI Int. Congr. Zool.*, **3**, pp. 59–63; Waterbuck, see Kiley-Worthington, M. (1965). The waterbuck in East Africa, *Mammalia*, **29**, pp. 177–204.
30 Hale, E. B. (1962). Domestication and the evolution of behaviour, *in* Hafez, E. S. E. (ed.) *The Behaviour of Domestic Animals*. London.
31 Jewell, P. A. (1966). The concept of home range in mammals, *Symp Zool. Soc., Lond.* **18**, pp. 85–109.
32 Sidney, J. (1965). ibid.
33 Jewell, P. A. (1962). Changes in size and type of cattle from prehistoric to medieval times in Britain, *Z. Tierzücht Zücht Biol.*, **77**, pp. 159–67; Jewell, P. A. (1963). Cattle from British archaeological sites, Man and Cattle, *Occ. paper Roy. Anthrop. Inst.*, **18**, pp. 80–91.
34 Laws, R. M. and Parker, I. S. C. (1968). Recent studies on elephant population in East Africa, *Symp. Zool. Soc., Lond.* **21**, pp. 219–359.
35 Morris, D. (1967). *The Naked Ape*. London.
36 Zeuner, F. E. (1963). *A History of Domesticated Animals*. London.

I. G. SIMMONS

Evidence for vegetation changes associated with mesolithic man in Britain

Introduction

In Britain the case for neolithic and later forest clearance is unequivocably established but is has been customary to regard mesolithic man as a hunter, fisher, and collector, who did not affect his environment beyond his immediate surroundings. Godwin[1] says, "He was one component of the ecosystem, dependent upon the forest, rivers and lakes for food, surrounded and dominated by the forest". The example of Star Carr[2] is quoted: here the pollen record was affected very little by the felling of birch trees to make a platform and only a few ruderal pollen were present. But Star Carr is but one type of habitat used by mesolithic man, representing a lowland "wet" site, i.e. in close contact with a lake and in a generally damp area. Other environments include lowland "dry" sites, such as Addington, Kent[3], Selbourne[4], and Iping Common[5], many of them being heathland today. In addition there are numerous instances of mesolithic finds, often in large quantities, on the moorlands. Bodmin Moor, Dartmoor, the Pennines, and the North York Moors are examples[6]. The discovery of a lack of environmental modification as typified by Star Carr, does not mean that a similar culture may not have had a definite effect in a different habitat and it is proposed here to concentrate on some investigations in the uplands. Here, the general pattern of finds is the discovery of large numbers of microliths on the soil surface or stratified at a peat-soil interface.

Pollen-analytical evidence

1 *Dartmoor.* Investigations by the author[7] of a streamside exposure at 1500 ft. (457 m.) not far from the source of the Blacklane Brook revealed a phase during late zone VI which was interpreted as representing forest recession. The deposit was amorphous blanket peat above a wood layer and the evidence for an opening in the forest consisted of a sudden peak in

Pteridium which was coincident with an occurrence of *Artemisia* and a large peak in Gramineae, followed by curves for several helophytes and for *Prunus-Sorbus* type (probably *S. aucuparia*); though generally declining, the *Corylus* curve also shows a peak at the point. After the initial explosion, the values recede slightly but do not revert to their former absence. In this particular context of time and locality the hypothesis of a clearance due to fire (*Calluna* disappears) during the mesolithic cultural period was suggested. Its stratigraphic position suggests that it occurred in conjunction with the changeover from forest to blanket mire; and the general unlikeliness of lightning fire being a causative agent here allows the possibility that mesolithic man was in some way concerned, but it is not implied that the use of fire was deliberate. A parallel occurrence, characterized especially by a high (10% of AP) peak of *Rumex*, along with *Artemisia* and Compositae pollen, is seen at site PA.2. This is near Postbridge (1200 ft.), where mesolithic implements have been found.

2 *Stump Cross, near Grassington, Yorks.*   This site[8] is important because mesolithic flint flakes are stratified into muds. At the level of a flake charcoal is found, and an *Artemisia* grain (cf. Blacklane on Dartmoor, *supra*, but there is no *Pteridium* response); the *Corylus* curve rises sharply and there is a kink in *Ulmus*. The time context is early zone VIIa. Walker is inclined to see these changes in pollen frequency as resulting from blanket mire inception due to climatic change but they would equally well bear the interpretation of the opening of a forest.

3 *The North York Moors.*   Recent and hitherto unpublished work has been carried out by the author on Egton High Moor, part of the central watershed of this upland (Figs. 1, 2, 3). The most important site is at North Gill, 1215 ft. (370 m.) where the base of the blanket peat shows a *Polytrichum* peat (2–5 cm. thick) which is in some places overlain by a peat deposit consisting largely of charcoal (this is also up to 5 cm. thick). An amorphous blanket peat then covers all. Detailed pollen analyses through the sequences

mineral soil→*Polytrichum* peat→amorphous peat, and
mineral soil→charcoal peat→amorphous peat,

reveal similar patterns. In the amorphous peat at the horizon of the charcoal, there are peaks in *Pinus* (30% of AP, hitherto at 5%) with a fall-off in *Quercus* and *Alnus*; *Betula*, *Fraxinus* and *Corylus* are high, as is *Salix*, and grains of *Artemisia*, and *Rumex*, and spores of *Pteridium* are found. Afterwards, the *Pinus* declines and *Quercus* regains its values, along with very high *Alnus* frequencies. The *Artemisia* and *Pteridium* values remain low but do not disappear. Analyses through the charcoal peat itself are equally revealing: the same peaks of *Pinus* are found, along with high *Betula*, *Corylus*, but low *Quercus*. The more detailed (2 cm. interval) analysis shows that *Sphagnum* more or less disappears at the horizon of the ruderal pollen types (*Plantago lanceolata*, *Senecio* type, *Rumex* and Chenopodiaceae). Forest regeneration is shown by higher values of *Quercus*, *Corylus*, and *Alnus*, diminution of the ruderals and the come-back of *Sphagnum*.

All this is consistent with an opening of the forest, which was probably temporary, although there are hints, as on Dartmoor, that some land may have remained open. The time context is early to mid VIIa and so the association of this phase with mesolithic man is hard to resist, especially since this is an area of so many artefacts. Dimbleby[9] came to similar conclusions in the same region when as a consequence of soil pollen analyses he suggested that fire resulted in an increase of *Betula* and *Corylus* (this is confirmed by the present analyses, although they suggest these were not permanent effects), increase of grass and *Calluna* beneath a lighter canopy (borne out for Gramineae, but not on the whole for *Calluna*), and decrease of alder (again, a temporary flourishing is suggested rather than a permanently increased presence). Dimbleby's suggestion of a lighter canopy is possibly corroborated by the presence of *Melampyrum*, which Iversen[10] has interpreted as indicating the formation of partial clearings in formerly virgin forests.

Evidence from analogous situations

This method of reasoning has many pitfalls, not least the use of present-day cultural practices as analogies for the past, but in the case of the accounts of early European travellers in the deciduous and mixed forests of the Eastern seaboard of North America we may perhaps be more certain of its usefulness, where although agriculture was practised, hunting and fishing was still an important part of the economy. The effects of the Indians on their environment as a result of these pursuits was often clearly recorded.

Even the palaeolithic populations of the late-glacial period, Lawrence *et al.*[11] suggested, may have prolonged the successional stages. But the evidence for vegetation change in the eastern woodlands is much stronger[12].

The nomadism of some of the tribes did not, it appears, prevent them from affecting the ecology: "temporary dwellings of a nomadic family band might be occupied by a small partially cleared area, while semi-permanent villages occupied clearings of considerable magnitude . . . as much as 100 or 150 acres"[13].

It seems likely that populations here were larger than was likely in mesolithic England although the reports of an annual cycle of migration (seashore in summer, deep woods hunting camps in autumn and winter and rivers in spring) do not conflict with our conception of the life a pre-agricultural hunting, fishing, and gathering group.

The use of fire by the Indians was apparently deliberate: in the Hudson River and Lake Champlain regions the woods were burned in the autumn and again in the spring in order to make hunting easier, to improve the growth of grass and to surround game. Inland from Narragansett Bay, a

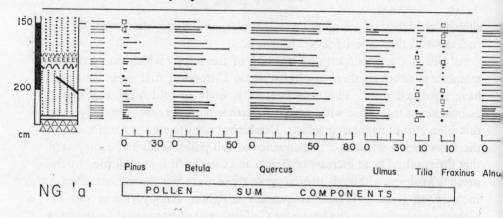

NG 'a'

POLLEN SUM COMPONENTS

Fig 1 The basal part of the North Gill "a" profile, through the *Polytrichum* peat (horizontal lines) into the amorphous peat (dots). Note the two peaks of *Pinus* which are found again in North Gill "b". This is the tree

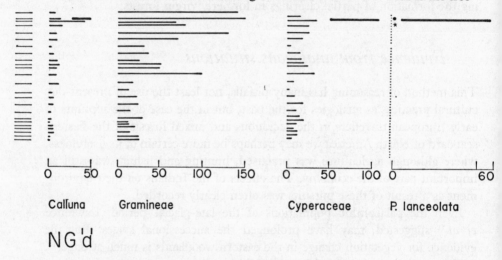

Calluna   Gramineae   Cyperaceae   P. lanceolata

NG 'd'

Fig 2 North Gill "a" profile, non-tree pollen; symbols as in Fig 1. Note the

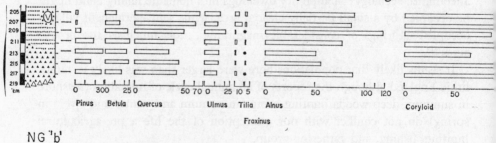

NG 'b'

POLLEN SUM COMPONENTS

Fig 3 North Gill "b" profile, through the charcoal peat (black triangles) into the amorphous peat (black dots; with charred twig marked "V"). Note the two 30% *Pinus* peaks, and the correspondence of the *Quercus* fall-

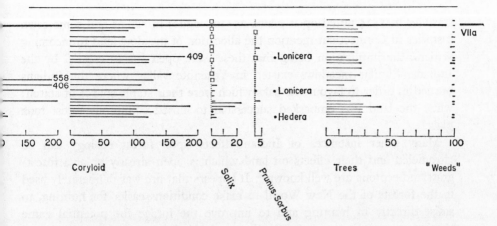

pollen diagram; an open square = 1% frequency, a large dot = present but less than 1%. The *Ulmus* decline can be clearly seen.

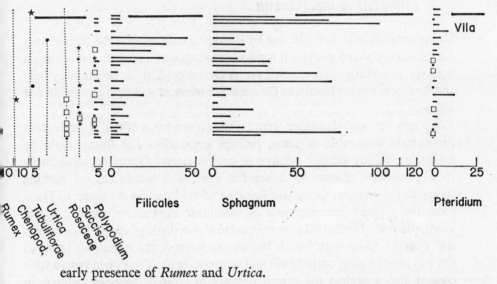

early presence of *Rumex* and *Urtica*.

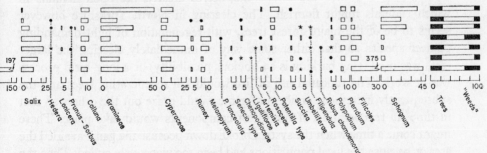

off with the rise in the "weeds", especially *Rumex, Melampyrum*. Black dots indicate frequencies of less than 1%, stars pollen found in scanning but not included in the count.

traveller in 1524 noted open plains 25–30 leagues in extent and some town histories in Connecticut mention the allocation of meadow land to incoming settlers, the implication being that these were open spaces created by the Indians. Similar meadows existed in Yosemite valley where the Indians burned in order to favour the oaks which were their staple source of starch; when the land was emparked succession to closed coniferous forest took place[14].

Many other instances of Indian effects upon forest ecology can be chronicled and their effects on land which is open already or at a forest-grassland ecotone are well known[15]. It appears that fire was deliberately used in the forests of the New World to make conditions easier for hunting, to assist directly in hunting and to improve the forage for potential game species.

Towards a mechanism

Using both the evidence afforded by analogous cultures and the fragmentary hints from the pollen analyses it is possible to suggest an ecological mechanism whereby mesolithic man effected forest clearance. This is preliminary only and doubtless improvements to the sequence outlined will be suggested in due course.

We may suppose that there were on the higher parts of our uplands areas particularly favourable to game, perhaps seasonally. The forest might be broken or slightly thinner because of environmental factors or, more likely these sites were known to mesolithic man, who would set up hunting camps in the vicinity. Grieg and Rankine[16] found that on the flanks of Dartmoor the greatest concentrations of mesolithic implements were at spring heads and at the North Gill sites referred to above single grains of *Potamogeton* and *Typha latifolia* were found. In order to improve the terrain for hunting, fire was used to clear underbrush and to corral game. Thus open spaces were created and doubtless the camps themselves created the open habitats in which ruderals might flourish. The clearing in North Yorkshire however seems to be of the major forest trees, with regeneration of light-demanding pioneer species so that either some way of immediately clearing the larger trees was used (ring barking is an obvious possibility) or a long-term process was at work. The repeated use of fire would kill regenerating trees and the subsequently increased numbers of game would graze out the others so that in time no regeneration of the forest components would take place. There might come a time when the system broke down because the game avoided the area or because the local populations had been too vigorously culled. Then the clearing created would colonize back to forest, via *Corylus*, *Betula* and *Fraxinus* stages. In some circumstances it is not inconceivable that soil deterioration had set in, preventing the regrowth of the high forest to its

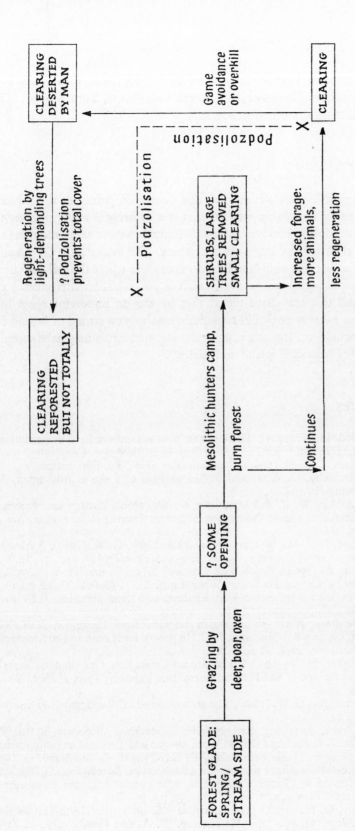

FIG 4 A possible mechanism for the sequence of clearing by Mesolithic man in upland areas

former condition. This would account for the continued open space indicators at Blacklane (Dartmoor) and North Gill (North York Moors). This is shown schematically above as Fig. 4.

Conclusion

Although more evidence is needed, this discussion points to the possibility of clearance by mesolithic man in what was to become a marginal environment. Irreversible effects were probably limited to these areas and that is why Star Carr does not fall into such a category. The evidence so far assembled points to the fact that only in upland areas or areas where the soil was changed easily by rapid pedogenic processes such as podzolization after clearance (on high ground this may have meant that he was an important agent in the inception of blanket bog), did mesolithic man exert a strong or lasting effect on his environment. But at a rough estimate, such areas may have comprised about five-eighths of England and Wales[17].

Notes

1 Godwin, H. (1965). The beginnings of agriculture in Western Europe *in* Hutchinson, J. (ed.) *Essays on Crop Plant Evolution.* Cambridge.

2 Clark, J. G. D. (1954). *Excavations at Star Carr.* Cambridge.

3 Dimbleby, G. W. (1963). Pollen analysis of a site at Addington, Kent. *Grana Palynol.,* 4, 140–8.

4 Rankine, W. F. and Dimbleby, G. W. (1960). Further excavations at a Mesolithic site at Oakhanger, Selborne, Hants., *Proc. Prehist. Soc.,* 26, pp. 246–62.

5 Keef, P. A. M., Wymer, J. J. and Dimbleby, G. W. (1965). A Mesolithic site on Iping Common, Sussex, England, *Proc. Prehist. Soc.,* 31, pp. 85–92.

6 Fox, A. (1964). *South-West England*; Elgee, F. and H. W. (1933). *The Archaeology of Yorkshire*; Wainwright, G. J. (1960). Three microlithic industries from South-west England and their affinities, *Proc. Prehist. Soc.,* 26, pp. 193–201.

7 Simmons, I. G. (1964). Pollen diagrams from Dartmoor, *New Phytol.,* 63, pp. 165–80; Simmons, I. G. (In press). Early man and environment on Dartmoor, *Proc. Prehist. Soc.*

8 Walker, D. (1956). A site at Stump Cross, near Grassington, Yorkshire, and the age of the Pennine microlithic industry, *Proc. Prehist. Soc.,* 22, pp. 23–8.

9 Dimbleby, G. W. (1961). The ancient forest of Blackamore, *Antiquity,* 35, pp. 123–8.

10 Iversen, J. (1964). Retrogressive vegetational succession in the Post-glacial, *J. Ecol.,* 52 (Suppl.), pp. 59–70; and Personal communication.

11 Lawrence, D. B., Schoeniker, R. E., Quispel, A. and Bond, G. (1967). The role of *Dryas drummondii* in vegetation development following ice recession at Glacier Bay, Alaska, with special reference to its nitrogen fixation by root nodules, *J. Ecol.,* 55, pp. 793–813.

12 Day, G. M. (1953). The Indian as a factor in the North-eastern forest, *Ecology,* 34, pp. 329–346; Niering, W. A. and Goodwin, R. H. (1962).

Ecological studies in the Connecticut Aboretum Natural Area. I. Introduction and Survey of vegetation types, *Ecology*, 43, pp. 41–54.

13 Day, G. M. (1953). op. cit. p. 330.

14. Gibbens, R. P. and Heady, H. F. (1964). The Influence of Modern Man on the vegetation of the Yosemite valley, *Calif. Agri. Bull.*, 36.

15 Stewart, O. C. (1956). Fire as the first great force employed by man, *in* Thomas, W. L. (ed.) *Man's Role in Changing the Face of the Earth.* London. pp. 115–33.

16 Grieg, O. and Rankine, W. F. (1956). A stone age settlement system near East Week, Dartmoor, *Proc. Devon Arch. and Expl. Soc.*, 5, pp. 8–25.

17 The full profiles, of which figs. 1–3 are extracts, are published in Simmons, I. G. (In press). Pollen diagrams from the North York Moors, *New Phytol*, 68.

Part II: Methods of investigation

Section 1: Domestication and exploitation of plants

J. ALEXANDER

The indirect evidence for domestication

Botanists, zoologists and archaeologists interested in the problems of domestication have naturally been concerned with the "*direct*" evidence, which may be "cultural" or "non-cultural". Direct cultural evidence is precise literary references, drawings, paintings and carvings, specialized tools, and cultivation systems. Indirect cultural evidence includes the actual remains of plant cultigens preserved by carbonization, matrix impressions, silica skeletons, and the bones, teeth, horns or antlers of animals. Unfortunately, some archaeologists have accepted a number of other cultural traits associated with early farming communities in Europe, Western Asia and Northern Africa as diagnostic of the beginnings of domestication, when these are, at best, only "*indirect*" evidence and of very limited value; "*indirect*" non-cultural evidence from botany and zoology has been little considered. It may be of use to examine here the restrictions which should be placed on some kinds of cultural interpretation and the increasing importance which should be attached to the non-cultural. Before doing this the central role of the field archaeologist in solving these problems may be stressed. Evidence of any kind can only come from carefully excavated and well-dated sites, and whilst the techniques of excavation may be learnt by botanists and zoologists who are prepared to serve a full archaeological apprenticeship, the evidence will not be obtained without it. For the foreseeable future, progress must be by teams of workers led by archaeologists.

The *indirect cultural* evidence comprises most of the material found in excavations, for it takes its final proof of being connected with farmers or pastoralists, from non-cultural evidence. How unreliable is indirect cultural evidence has been made clear by ethnology, which has been too little regarded by prehistorians. Cultural evidence has been overemphasized in the past because of the historical accident that much of the early work has been done in Western Europe—where the cultural evidence has special validity. This region received its knowledge of farming from outside and its first farmers possessed skills, in particular those of making pottery and ground-stone tools, which were the product of millennia of development elsewhere. It was these skills which enabled them to be identified and they were in fact isolated culturally before it was certain that they were farmers. When criteria established in Western Europe are applied to other parts of the world the results can be unfortunate.

With the exception of Australia, some husbandry of indigenous plants and animals existed in all continents in the historic present (sixteenth century A.D.). The range and variation in methods of cultivation and equipment was very wide and by analogy, any attempt by prehistorians to take a particular cultural trait out of its local setting and to infer a relationship between it and any particular plant or animal domestication is unsound.

Examples of some of the more striking points still often disregarded by archaeologists may be listed.

Societies without domesticated plants or animals who use:

1 Digging sticks; America[1], Australia[2], Asia[3], Africa[4].
2 Grinding stones; America[5], Australia[6], Asia[7].
3 Ground stone tools; Australia[8].
4 Irrigation including dams and channels, and fences for wild plants; America[9].
5 Pottery; Asia[10], America[11], Africa[12].
6 Storage pits[13], metal[14], long-settled villages, elaborate social organizations and substantial houses, all in North America[15].

Societies with domestic plants and animals who lack the following:

1 Ground stone tools or any other farming equipment leaving durable evidence; America[16].
2 Pottery; in the Pacific[17].
3 Grinding stones; Africa[18].

This suggests that the most cultural traits should be considered only as part of larger complexes of facts. In detail these may be discussed under the following headings:

1 *Clearing the land.* This will be necessary in most parts of the world and may need tools different from those used by hunter/gatherers. These may not be specialized enough to be direct evidence of clearance (indeed no tools at all may be used) but the heavy component of late glacial and early post-glacial lithic industries should be studied with this use in mind. The apparent

abandonment in West Africa of many of the clearing tools when the work was finished[19] is interesting, for it might lead to identifying clearing systems here and elsewhere. The signs of wear on stone tools should also be considered with this use in mind[20].

2 *Preparation of the land, planting or sowing.* This will usually be done with such tools as digging sticks, hoes, rakes and ploughs. Only in the case of the plough are these specialized enough to be precisely linked with full agriculture, and digging sticks will always be particularly difficult to assess[21]. Stone, bone, antler or wooden hoes, are on ethnographic evidence, rarely used for planting[22] although widely used for mounding-up. It seems possible that a limited role should be accepted for many of those found in excavation.

Sowing as opposed to planting and the relationship of this to cultivation techniques might be suggested by a study of these tools.

3 *Harvesting.* The variety of reaping methods known from ethnography includes many which leave no durable evidence[23]. Some of these methods are also used by gatherers and this makes durable harvesting tools difficult to assess.

Reaping knives and sickles, unless a study of the wear on them gives precise evidence[24], are relatively valueless, unless supported by non-cultural evidence.

4 *Processing and storing.* Many crops need treatment if they are to be kept, and if grown in quantity, need special stores. It is possible in the excavation of settlements that features connected with these processes will be identified, and since quite elaborate ones are, as has been mentioned[25] used by gatherers, they may belong to incipient as well as long established agricultural societies. Seed-crops may need threshing and winnowing floors, drying racks or ovens; roots, tubers and rhizomes may need graters, squeezers or heating bowls. None of these will be conclusive without non-cultural evidence. Storage may leave good archaeological evidence as clamps and pits or above ground stacks or stores. The special designs of these may be recognizable in plan and construction in well-established agricultural/vegecultural societies but in initial ones will need the support of non-cultural evidence.

In this context Forde's observation that storage in the tropics is largely unnecessary except where large accumulations are needed for social purposes[26] is interesting.

5 *Cooking and preparation for eating.* Grinding, pounding or grating is necessary for many food crops but since all these techniques are used by gatherers, they cannot, of themselves, be indicative of domestic crops, or even of food preparation. They are also used for preparing paints and poisons. In cooking, much specialized equipment may be highly suggestive of particular crops; for example interior-heated ovens in wheat and barley growing areas or baking plates in manioc growing ones. Only in association with non-cultural evidence are they conclusive.

6 *Evidence of animal keeping.* Durable equipment seems less common,

from ethnographic parallels, for animal-keeping than for agriculture and a wider range of motives seems to lead to their being kept. Evidence from the form of containers (milk or cheese holders) is of course unreliable without non-cultural evidence[27]. In some societies byres and corrals may be recognized with the help of other kinds of non-cultural evidence.

The *indirect non-cultural* evidence has been much less considered than the direct. This is unfortunate for it is probably from it, and not from the cultural evidence that the beginnings of domestication in most areas will be recognized. Hope of future advance lies in the increasing interest being shown by natural scientists. With their help, an increasingly wide range of research techniques may be tried on each new final-glacial or early post-glacial site as it is discovered. The field archaeologist must have discussed the theoretical possibilities of applying specialized knowledge and techniques from many disciplines before excavation begins. This will mean a kind of collaboration very different from the rather formal post-excavation one which has usually taken place in the past. Only when the relationships are intimate and discussion is wide ranging will the possible uses of highly specialized techniques be realized[28]. Some of the more oblique evidence so far recovered may be considered as examples.

In the *botanical* sciences two kinds of indirect evidence may be instanced. Any disturbance of a natural vegetation cover will provide growth opportunities for plants not normally dominant. In agricultural clearings, selective weeding may further favour particular small or low-growing plants. This phenomenon has been much studied and complexes of weeds in fields of different crops in all parts of the world[29] are well known. Their occurrence in excavated pollen spectra or, particularly, in macroscopic collections, might sometimes indicate not only cultivation but even the kind of crops being grown. The possibility of recognizing regularly cropped pasture by its selective weeds must be considered[30].

Refinements in sampling techniques for pollen study have meant that thin successive, even annual strata of deposition, can be recognized and sampled. These may reveal very local and temporary disturbances in a vegetation cover, and in conjunction with domestic plant and weed pollens can identify human interference with it for agriculture[31]. Alternatively, variations in the proportional representation of plants in the natural spectrum may be attributable to man.

Much of what has just been said for plants is true for molluscs. *Molluscan* evidence can be used either as complementary to the botanical or, in its absence, as an alternative to it[32]. Disturbances in a vegetation cover will profoundly alter the molluscan spectrum and make the change recognizable in stratified deposits. Species favouring cultivated fields or even particular crops[33] may also be distinguishable. The presence of other species may also indicate the presence of animals. The possibilities of the study of specialized molluscan pests needs much further attention by archaeologists.

Entomological evidence must become of increasing importance in the future[34]. Many insects are even more limited in their tolerance of vegetation change than molluscs, and also more selective in their feeding habits[35]. Identifiable fragments of insects, mainly cuticles and legs, occur in sites of all ages[36] and in a variety of wet, dry, acid and non-acid conditions. From the evidence of insect pests, the kind of crops being grown or the kind of animals being kept, may be identifiable, as may be buildings used as stores (for example, as cereal granaries) or byres (for sheep, goats or cattle).

Parasitology may also play a much greater part in identifying farming in the future. The survival of parasites either as eggs[37], or spores[38], is now well attested and since parasites such as Nematodes are usually highly selective in their hosts, they might well help to give some indication of the crops or animals present.

Zoology can provide an indirect evidence of plant agriculture by showing the presence of vertebrate pests; concentrations of rodent bones for example may indicate cereal granaries. Indirect zoological evidence of animal husbandry has been much considered in recent years and it may be that too much attention has been paid to it in considering the beginnings of domestication[39]. The ageing and sexing of excavated animal populations has been much developed but much less is known of the difference between tame and wild herds, or of the exploitation of the latter by hunting societies[40]. The effects of castration upon bone and other tissues may well be of more use in the future distinguishing early or intermediate stages of domestication[41].

One kind of indirect *geological* evidence may be cited here. The human clearance of hillsides in regions of torrential rain can quickly lead to sheet erosion, and this in association with other kinds of evidence, could indicate farming[42].

In conclusion it may be suggested that attention has perhaps been too much concentrated upon a looking-backwards from established farming communities in attempts to see traits present in them in their ancestral societies[43]. An analogy might be made with some of the earlier approaches of physical anthropology to the problems of human evolution. If more attention was paid to late glacial and immediately post-glacial societies, using the methods of study suggested by ethnography, and implementing them by the techniques of a number of natural science disciplines, the balance might be restored.

Notes

1 Paiute (Great Basin): Forde, C. D. (1964). *Habitat, Economy and Society.* London.
2 Bindibu (Central West Australia): Thomson, D. F. (1964). Some wood and stone implements of the Bindibu tribe of Central West Australia, *Proc. Prehist. Soc.*, **30**, pp. 404–8.

3 Veddas (Ceylon): Allchin, B. (1966). *The Stone Tipped Arrow*. London. p. 128.
4 Bushmen and others.
5 Forde, C. D. (1964). ibid.
6 Thomson, D. F. (1964). op. cit.
7 Allchin, B. (1966). op. cit.
8 Warramunga (Central Australia): Spencer, B. and Gillen, F. (1913). *Across Australia*. London, p. 368.
9 Paiute: Forde, C. D. (1964). ibid; Kwakiutl (British Columbia): Forde, C.D. (1964). ibid.
10 Andaman Islanders: Radcliffe-Browne, A. R. (1964). *The Andaman Islanders*. London; Veddas: Allchin, B. (1966). op. cit.
11 Yokut (Great Basin): Forde, C. D. (1964). ibid.
12 Bushmen and others.
13 Paiute: Forde, C. D. (1964). ibid.
14 North-west Coast tribes generally: Forde, C. D. (1964). ibid.
15 Olson, R. (1927). *Adze, Canoe and House Types of the North West Coast*. Washington.
16 Hopi (Arizona): Forde, C. D. (1964). ibid.
17 South Solomon Islanders: Forde, C. D. (1964). ibid.
18 Ambo (Zambia): Stefaniszin, B. (1964). *The Ambo*. Livingstone; and Sub-Saharan Africa generally.
19 Davies, O. (1958). West Africa, *COWA Area Report*, **2**, p. 1.
20 As suggested by Dr. Ruth Tringham.
21 For example, hoes among the Chenchu (South India): Allchin, B. (1966). op. cit. p. 111. Weights, unless found on digging sticks, are unreliable evidence since similar objects have other uses, e.g. loomweights, mace heads, net sinkers.
22 Forde, C. D. (1964). op. cit., p. 379.
23 For example, beaters and baskets.
24 As suggested by Dr. Ruth Tringham.
25 Paiute: Forde, C. D. (1964). op. cit.
26 Forde, C. D. (1964). op. cit., p. 380.
27 The recent identification of polypeptic acids in pot sherds may be of significance here.
28 For example, the recent identification of polypeptic acids in pot sherds.
29 Salisbury, Sir E. (1961). *Weeds and Aliens*. London. Thirty-nine families of weeds in wheatfields and fourteen in temperate grassland are listed.
30 The same kind of identification is possible in the tropics, see Adams, L. and Baker, J. (1962). Weeds of the cultivated and grazing lands of Ghana, *in* Wills, W. (ed.) *Agriculture and Land Use in Ghana*.
31 Dimbleby, G. W. (1967). *Plants and Archaeology*. London. p. 148.
32 Evans, J. Molluscs in chalk soils, Unpublished paper presented to the *Research Seminar in Archaeology and Related Subjects*, 1967.
33 For example, the East African "Banana" snail.
34 Sparks, B. (1963). Non-marine mollusca and archaeology, *in* Brothwell, D. R. and Higgs, E. (eds.) *Science and Archaeology*. London.
35 For example, "Yam" beetles (*Heteroligus* sp. and *Prionoryctes* sp.) or *Aspidoproctus*. Jerath, M. (1965). Yam pests and their known parasites and predators in Nigeria, *Nig. Dept. of Agric. Research*, Memo. **83**.
36 From Inter-glacial deposits onwards.
37 Pike, A. and Biddle, M. (1966). Parasite eggs in mediaeval Winchester, *Antiquity*, **40**, p. 293.
38 Levy, J. (1958). Vegetable complex of Coffin, *Proc. Prehist. Soc.*, **23**, p. 162.
39 Herre, W. (1963). The science and history of domestic animals, *in* Brothwell, D. R. and Higgs, E. ibid.

40 Detailed surveys of large collections of wild animal bones, as for example at Solutré or Mount Carmel, need to be undertaken.
41 For example, the recent identification of castrated reindeer from antler tissue.
42 As perhaps at Nok; Fagg, B. A. B. (1959). The Nok culture in prehistory, *J. Niger. Hist. Soc.*, **1.**
43 See the use of the term "neolithic" in Central Asia; Mongait, L. (1958). *Archaeology in the U.S.S.R.* London.

D. M. DIXON

A note on cereals in ancient Egypt

This paper is confined to noting briefly some of the evidence on cereals in ancient Egypt down to the Ptolemaic period. This is considered, somewhat arbitrarily perhaps, under two headings, Direct and Indirect evidence. Under the former is included the archaeological-botanical and artistic evidence and under the latter the textual evidence. Limitations of space have precluded discussion of such matters as ancient Egyptian agricultural implements, granaries, etc., and no attempt is made to discuss the origins of the various species, or the route(s) by which they may have entered Egypt[1].

Direct evidence

The staple wheat species of Egypt was emmer, *Triticum dicoccum*. Indeed, until fairly recently it was the only species of wheat reported from Egypt from neolithic times down to the Ptolemaic period. All finds of emmer wheat known up to 1940 have been listed, with references by V. and G. Täckholm[2]. According to Percival[3], fragments of wood and ivory carvings (natural size) of cereal spikes found in the tomb of Djer at Abydos probably represent emmer rather than barley, as stated by Petrie[4].

Spelt, *T. spelta*, which is frequently mentioned in discussions of Egyptian wheat, and often appears in translations of Egyptian texts, has never been found in Egyptian grain deposits.

In 1948 the top of an uncarbonized spike of wheat was found in a grave at the neolithic site of El-Omari. In Debono's preliminary report on the excavations[5], Mrs. Täckholm refers to this specimen as *Triticum monococcum*, einkorn, and elsewhere[6] she states "When I saw this ear, I got the impression that what we had here was quite another type of wheat, not met with earlier at the excavations, viz. *T. monococcum* L." The spike was subsequently submitted to E. Schiemann, E. Tschermak, and H. Kihara, all of whom agreed that it was *T. monococcum*[7]. In 1951 Täckholm published[8] the results of her examination of the plant material discovered by Firth in 1927 in rooms opening off an underground gallery near the north enclosure wall of the Step

Pyramid complex at Saqqara. The bulk of this material consisted of "extremely well preserved" wheat and barley, including complete spikes of both cereals. Among these, Täckholm encountered "once more the type of *T. monococcum*. As a matter of fact, a detailed investigation of the material proved to me that a fair portion of the material consisted of *T. monococcum*. Again, another cereal find from Icheti's tomb, Saqqara, from the VIth Dynasty, excavated by J.-P. Lauer also seems to be *T. monococcum*[9]."

Samples from the Step Pyramid galleries were submitted to Åberg, who stated in his report[10] that a detailed study of the "two markedly different types" of wheat specimens sent to him "clearly showed that two species were represented, namely *Triticum monococcum* L. and *Triticum dicoccum* Schübl.". After describing the characters of the wheat identified as *T. monococcum*, Åberg remarks that it "seems to be rather closely related to the variety which Percival (1921) described as var. *vulgare* Kcke.". He concludes with the words "At the present time there is therefore no doubt but what the ancient Egyptians knew about *Triticum monococcum* and even used it for cultivation[11]".

The grain discovered during the excavation of Icheti's tomb at Saqqara was examined by Helbaek[12]. The material submitted to him consisted of two whole spikes and twenty-six major portions of such. Helbaek remarks that "On the whole it must be admitted that these spikes, to a superficial observation, are extremely deceptive and, so far as size is concerned, suggestive of Einkorn. This impression does not, however, stand up to a close morphological scutiny[13]." After close examination and comparison, he concluded that the alleged einkorn among the Icheti wheat was emmer, *T. dicoccum*. "In spite of a certain dimensional conformity with recent einkorn, the morphological discrepancies are too great for referring any part of the find to this species[14]."

In the light of his examination of the Icheti wheat, Helbaek went on to suggest that the einkorn from the Zoser galleries was also emmer, and cast doubt on the identification of the Omari specimen as einkorn[15]. These doubts were later confirmed when he examined (1955) the Zoser material and the Omari spike. His view, therefore, is that "no valid evidence for the presence of einkorn in Egypt has so far been offered[16]".

Authenticated finds of any species of naked wheat prior to the Graeco-Roman period are extremely rare, and most authorities are now inclined to regard only finds from that period as certainly identified naked wheats. A number of finds of naked wheat have from time to time been reported[17], but most of them have proved on further examination to be threshed emmer.

Among the material obtained from two of the Fayûm neolithic granary pits excavated by Caton-Thompson were some charred grains which Percival (alone of the three cereal specialists who examined them) identified as *Triticum vulgare* (i.e. *T. aestivum*), bread wheat[18]. These determinations were greeted with some scepticism, and subsequently Percival modified his opinion. He stated[19] that the straw from which the lining of the pits was derived came from a wheat, and that although it was not possible to be quite certain of the kind, "it is unlike any form of Emmer and *resembles* the straw of Bread wheat". Kew, however, reported that the particular wheat from which the straw lining was derived could not be identified. Of the carbonized grains Percival says they were "naked grains of a kind of wheat" and that "in general form and size" they "resemble grains of some forms of Bread wheat, but in some points they differ slightly from modern Bread wheats". Among the material he examined were "one or two spikelets with chaff resembling that of emmer, and containing carbonized, blunt-ended grains somewhat like those of *T. vulgare*; the significance of these finds I cannot appraise". Percival did "not feel justified in naming these carbonized grains as grains of *T. vulgare* with certainty". "I . . . hesitate to commit myself to the naming of these (i.e. the straw and carbonized grain) as undoubtedly specimens of *T. vulgare*."

It certainly seems very unlikely that the Fayûm Neolithic people were growing bread wheat, which was apparently unknown to the neolithic people at Merimde, the vast bulk of the grain found at that site being emmer. Bread wheat was likewise unknown in the predynastic period and in dynastic times—notwithstanding Unger's claim to have identified grains of a naked wheat, which he termed *T. vulgare* var. *antiquorum*, in mud bricks from one of the Dahshur pyramids and from the town ruins at Tell el-Maskhuta (Nineteenth Dynasty).

However, a few years ago evidence did come to light for the existence of naked wheat in neolithic Egypt. At the middle and late neolithic sites of Merimde-Beni Salâme and El-Omari were found a number of carbonized grains which were identified by Helbaek[20] as club wheat, *T. compactum*, a hexaploid naked wheat. "With their greater thickness, blunt and rounded shape, and the steeply placed embryo", they differed sharply from emmer grains found at these sites; and Helbaek thinks that "for all the distortion caused by the process of carbonization Emmer grains would not arrive at this shape, and it seems justifiable to list Club wheat among the cultivated plants of Neolithic Egypt[21]."

At both Merimde and El-Omari, however, the grains of club wheat formed but a small proportion of the grain found, the bulk of it being emmer and hulled barley. It seems, therefore, that "Club wheat was not intentionally cultivated, but occurred as a stray occupant of the field. . . . It was probably brought to Egypt together with the other crop plants at the beginning of agriculture, but since it is never encountered in deposits of later periods previous to the Graeco-Roman epoch, it was obviously a race that did not thrive in the local conditions obtaining there[22]."

Turning now to the dynastic period, it may be noted that Schulz[23] considered as certain the identification as naked wheat of grains of Twelfth Dynasty date found by Schweinfurth at Drâ Abu el-Naga, Thebes, and of others from the tomb of Rahotep at Meir, also Twelfth Dynasty.

Schiemann[24] thought she recognized *T. durum*, macaroni wheat, a tetraploid naked species, in material of Eighteenth Dynasty date from Deir el-Medineh, but owing to the smallness of the sample, the determination was only provisional.

From Graeco-Roman times a number of certainly identified examples of *T. durum* are known[25] and it is not until this period that the species can be considered as established in Egypt.

Barley has been used as a foodstuff in Egypt since very early times. Examination of the abdominal contents of a large number of bodies of predynastic date from Naga ed-Dêr in Upper Egypt showed that almost every one contained husks of barley. Barley frequently occurs in tombs and settlements of all periods, usually alongside emmer. The barley grown in Egypt anciently seems to have been much the same as that grown at the present time.

According to Jackson[26], the material from the neolithic granary pits excavated by Caton-Thompson in the Fayûm consisted of a mixture of two-rowed and six-rowed types of barley. Most finds of ancient Egyptian barley fall within the group of four-rowed and six-rowed types. According to Mrs. Täckholm, who lists all the finds of four- and six-rowed barley known up to 1940[27], the red, white, and black barleys mentioned in the Egyptian texts were probably four-rowed forms.

Reference has already been made to the wooden and ivory carvings of cereal spikes found in the tomb of Djer at Abydos by Petrie, who described them as representing "bearded barley". As already noted, however, they probably represent emmer wheat. An entire barley plant was found in the coffin of Amenophis I at Drá Abu el-Naga.

According to Täckholm, naked barley was known in ancient Egypt, the oldest example being grains from the neolithic settlements in the Fayûm excavated by Caton-Thompson[28]. Neither chaff nor spikelets have been discovered, and consequently it has not been possible to determine to which of the three known types of naked barley the grains belong, viz. *Hordeum distichum* var. *nudum*, *H. tetrastichum* var. *coeleste*, or *H. hexastichum* var. *revelatum*. Helbaek, however, says that naked barley does not occur in ancient Egypt: "Many reports on Egyptian grain postulate the occurrence of Naked barley in prehistoric and dynastic deposits. No documentation has ever been published, and according to my experience, which includes examination of many grain finds, the postulate is unfounded[29]."

Among the barley finds listed by Täckholm are a number of instances of germinated barley. According to some, this was used for beer-making, but as we shall see later, Nims thinks that malt may also have served as a primary food in addition to being used in making beer. Others, however, think that the barley was germinated exclusively for funerary rites. Loret[30], for example, describes a hollow pyramid model, now in the museum at Florence, containing germinated barley along with a picture of Osiris, and he points out that the germination of the barley figured in the funeral rites of the month of Khoiak in memory of Osiris's death.

During the Eighteenth Dynasty the objects known as "Osiris-beds" occur in tombs. For example, in the so-called "Treasury" in the tomb of Tut'ankhamūn was a "huge black oblong box containing a figure of Osiris swathed in linen". This "Osiris-bed" or "germinated figure of Osiris" consists of a wooden frame moulded in the form of this deity, hollowed out, lined with linen, filled with Nile silt, and planted with barley[31]. This was moistened, the grain germinated, and the inanimate form became green and living—thus symbolizing the resurrection of Osiris, and of course of the deceased. The life-size effigy found in Tut'ankhamūn's tomb was completely bandaged in the same way as a mummy.

Other examples of "Osiris-beds" with germinated barley are known: two were found in the tomb of Yuya and Thuyu, measuring 1·63 m. and 1·73 m. respectively in length[32]. Another specimen, 1·78 m. long and 68 cm. wide, was found in the tomb of Mahirper at Thebes[33]. In the Cairo Museum is an empty specimen from the tomb of Horemheb[34], and in the Egyptian Museum at Stockholm is a small "Osiris-bed", of unknown date, dug in a brick about 25 cm. long and filled with germinated barley[35].

Possibly a necklace of germinated barley found by Maspero on the mummy of Kent at Sheikh 'Abd el Qurnah (Dyn. 20) also symbolized resurrection[36].

Despite Unger's claim[37] to have recognized some ancient Egyptian representations as dura, *Sorghum vulgare*, this cereal has not been identified on the monuments, not has its grain been found in a Pharaonic context. In the Agricultural Museum in Cairo is a panicle of dura said to have been found at Gebelein, but Mrs. Täckholm remarks on its rather fresh appearance[38]. In the Botanical Museum at Berlin-Dahlem was a piece of culm labelled *Sorghum vulgare* Pers. said to have come from the tomb of Nib-ari(?), Valley of the Kings, Thebes, Eighteenth Dynasty; no collector is indicated[39]. Unger[40] states that dura stems were found together with papyrus at Saqqara and that Rosellini found dura grains at Thebes, the latter of which were said to have been determined by a Dr. Hannerd. Both records, however, are very dubious, and the position at present therefore is that there is no evidence that dura was cultivated in Pharaonic Egypt.

Schweinfurth was probably correct in suggesting that it was not cultivated in Egypt before the Roman-Byzantine period; and the only authentic ancient instances of dura grain seem to be those found by de Garis Davies in the Coptic Monastery of Cyriacus at Thebes, dating from the sixth to seventh centuries A.D. These were determined by Schweinfurth[41].

Although *Pennisetum typhoideum* (pearl or bulrush millet), *Setaria italica*, *Panicum miliaceum* (proso-millet, or broom corn millet), and *Echinochloa frumentacea* all occur in Egypt at the present day, not one of them has been identified among the ancient plant remains. A caryopis without seed found by Unger in a mud-brick from the town-wall of El Kab[42] probably belongs to a *Panicum* species (the brick is said, though on what grounds is not clear, to be probably of Second Intermediate date), but apart from this, no species of *Panicum* is known from ancient Egypt.

The only species of *Setaria* so far reported from ancient times is *S. verticillata* which occurs at the present day as a weed in gardens, cultivated ground, and waste places. In the Museum at Kew is a well-preserved specimen of this species with a complete panicle, which was found in a flower garland excavated by Petrie at El Lahun. According to Mrs. Täckholm it is probably Twelfth Dynasty, though there is no date on the accompanying label[43].

The only species of *Echinochloa* known from ancient Egypt is *E. colonum*, grains of which were identified by Netolitzky among the intestinal contents of some predynastic bodies excavated by Reisner at Naga ed-Dêr[44]. Judging by the quantity and purity of the grains, it is perhaps possible that at that time the plant was cultivated locally as a cereal.

It would appear reasonable to suppose that the rice-plant may have been known to the inhabitants of the Lower Nile Valley, where suitable conditions for its growth existed in the swamps of Upper Egypt and especially the Delta.

In 1752 Count de Caylus[45], a member of the Académie des Belles-Lettres, gave an account of a large bronze figure of Osiris in his possession. The figure, he says, was coated with a thin layer of gilded plaster; intermixed with the plaster as a binder, were rice stalks. De Caylus was not alone in his belief that the straws came from the rice plant; some years earlier, in 1739, the figure had also been examined by a M. de Bose, another Academician, who arrived at the same conclusion.

The present location of the statuette is unknown, nor is it possible to date it very closely on the basis of de Caylus's illustration. The base, and therefore any inscription it may have borne, was missing. The piece could as well be Saite or Ptolemaic.

Daressy[46] was inclined to accept the findings of the two eighteenth-century savants; Täckholm, on the other hand, thinks the identification as rice very unlikely[47]. Whatever the truth of the matter, apart from this one alleged case, rice has not been found in connection with ancient Egypt. It does not occur in the tombs and no representations have been recognized on the monuments. It is not mentioned in the texts and its Coptic name is identical with and clearly derived from the Arabic *el arouz*. It seems clear that rice was not cultivated in Egypt until some time after the Arab conquest of the country.

However, this is not to say the Egyptians of Pharaonic times could not have known of the rice plant or its grains; they may well have known about rice, though from what source they might have derived their knowledge and whether the rice was wild or cultivated would be a matter of conjecture. What is clear, on present evidence, is that the plant was not cultivated in Pharaonic Egypt. The explanation could be that by the time the Egyptians became acquainted with rice, whenever that may have been, they had already been growing wheat and barley for a long time and were perfectly satisfied with these crops, which are in fact much more nutritious than rice, which has the additional disadvantage that it cannot be made into flour.

Indirect evidence

Linguistic evidence may often furnish information not supplied by the archaeological material. A good example (though not a cereal) is the case of the chick pea or Bengal gram (*Cicer arietinum*), which has been cultivated for centuries in India, the Near East, and southern Europe. The archaeological evidence for the cultivation of this species in ancient Egypt seems to be extremely meagre[48]. Examination of the linguistic evidence, however, shows that *C. arietinum* was cultivated in the Nile Valley at least as far back as the New Kingdom. Among a number of plants listed in a school text[49] of this time is one called in Egyptian *ḥrw-bik*, lit. "falcon-faces", and a comparison of the chick pea, with its "hook" or "beak", with Egyptian representations of hawks' heads puts the identification beyond all doubt (Pl. v). Indeed, it would be difficult to think of a more apt name[50].

Turning now to cereals, the word for "barley" was *ıt*, which occurs from the First Dynasty onwards[51]. Frequently found are the expressions "Upper Egyptian barley" and "Lower Egyptian barley[52]", which probably refer to the geographical provenance of the grain rather than to any botanical differences. One may compare the market descriptions *baladi beheiri* "Lower Egyptian" and *baladi saıdi* "Upper Egyptian" applied at the present time to the grain of Egyptian cone wheat, *Triticum pyramidale*, according to its origin[53]. At a later date (Dynasty XX onwards) a compound expression occurs quite commonly, viz. *ıt-m-ıt*, literally "barley as barley". Two slightly differing explanations of this term have been proposed: according to Černý[54], "prices, especially small sums, were often expressed by means of equivalent quantity of barley. In order to avoid this conception of the word 'barley' one mostly said 'barley as barley' (i.e. 'barley in the form of actual barley') when speaking of barley *in natura*." Gardiner[55] suggests that by Ramesside times *ıt* had in addition to its meaning "barley" acquired the more general meaning of "corn" (one may compare the use of *ḥḏ* = "silver" and "money in general"). When it was desired to specify "barley", as opposed to corn in general, the term *ıt-m-ıt* was employed.

Another common cereal name is *bdt*, later *bty*, which also occurs in the First Dynasty[56]. It obviously cannot denote "barley", the name for which, as we have just seen, was *ıt*. In any case the two names occur alongside one another on a First Dynasty seal-impression[57]. Nor can it denote "spelt" since this is not attested archaeologically in Egyptian grain finds. Now it has been noted that apart from a few stray instances of club wheat in neolithic sites, all the grain deposits found in Egypt, from the neolithic period down to

Roman times, consisted of emmer. There can be no doubt, therefore, that *bdt* is the Egyptian name for this cereal.

In a list of cereal names included in the Onomasticon of Amenope (Dynasty XX) are seven different kinds of *bty*. Gardiner[58] regarded the enumeration of these seven kinds as showing that "*bdt* cannot be tied down to one single botanical species, so that there may be some justification for the alternative rendering 'spelt' that is often adopted". Spelt, we repeat, is not attested from Egypt. Of the seven kinds of *bdt* (*bty*) named, four are distinguished by their colour, viz. "white", "black", "red", and "orange-red"(?)[59]. It seems clear that Gardiner bases his view mainly on these varied colours, which doubtless refer to some prominent or obvious feature of the *bdt* in question, most likely the grain. These different colours, however, in no way tell against their all being emmer. Emmer grains do vary in colour; according to Percival[60], the colour is chiefly white, red, or yellowish, or gradations thereof—pale red, reddish-yellow, amber, and even (in some Abyssinian varieties) a deep purple.

In a discussion of Ramesside texts relating to the transport and taxation of corn, Gardiner[61] drew attention to "a remarkable habit of Egyptian scribes applicable, not only to Ramesside times, but also to the Eighteenth Dynasty: whenever black and red ink are both being used, red ink is employed for *bdt*-wheat and black for *it-m-it* 'barley'; though subsequently when both kinds of grain are being added together as *šs* 'corn' red ink may be used[62]". So firmly rooted was this habit that it actually occurs in a mere story. Hence wherever this contrast of colours occurs in connection with corn, it is reasonable to conclude that the black amount refers to barley, and the red amount to emmer. Furthermore, since in these Ramesside texts discussed by Gardiner the amounts written in black are both smaller and fewer than those in red, most payments in corn, and especially tax-payments, were made in emmer, not barley.

During the Old and Middle Kingdoms the leading cereal was barley, emmer being second, judging from the common expression *it bdt* "barley and emmer". This expression occurs still in the New Kingdom but the relative importance of the two cereals was already reversed.

From the Twenty-fifth Dynasty and through the Persian Period emmer was the main cereal. For example, in the Adoption Stela of Nitokris, dating from the reign of Psammetichus I, "3 khar of first-class emmer" are given to Nitokris "from the temple of Rēʿ-Atum in the Hekʿadje nome, . . . after it has been offered in the (divine) presence, every day, and the god has been satisfied therewith[63]". The pre-eminence of emmer is likewise attested in the Demotic papyrus from El-Hibeh, known as the "Petition of Peteêsi" (Dem. P. John Rylands IX), which dates from the reign of Darius I; as well as in other Demotic papyri from this site[64].

Another word denoting some cereal is *swt*. While it appears to denote a wheat of some kind, its precise meaning is not clear. If it be not a general term for wheat, it is difficult to suggest what it could be. It was distinct from *it* and *bdt*, for on a stela dated to year eight of Ramesses II, the king bragging of his concern for the welfare of his workmen, says: "Upper Egypt continually conveys for you to Lower Egypt and Lower Egypt conveys for you to Upper Egypt, barley, emmer, *swt*-wheat, salt(?), and beans in immense quantity[65]". Täckholm[66] says *swt* denoted naked wheat, but admits that such wheats were of "but little importance in Egypt until the Ptolemaic period". As we have just seen, however, and as Mrs. Täckholm herself notes, *swt* occurs very commonly from at least the Old Kingdom onwards. It cannot denote macaroni wheat, *T. durum*, since as we have seen this is not attested in Egypt until the Graeco-Roman period. Nor, it seems, can it denote einkorn, as Mrs. Täckholm suggested in a later publication[67]. Spelt, too, is ruled out. Helbaek[68] suggests that *swt* denotes "a variety of Emmer which perhaps while alive was distinguished by some character that does not readily appear from the material in the mummified state". If so, we must wait for the morphologists to point out the finer distinctions in the emmer material already recovered. There is, of course, the possibility that over the centuries *swt* (earlier *zwt*) may have changed its meaning.

A not uncommon term for some form of cereal is *bš3*, which occurs, along with wheat and dates, on Second Dynasty stelae[69]. From the Third Dynasty through to the Twelfth it appears as a label on granaries depicted on funerary monuments. From the Fourth Dynasty dates usually occur in the same scenes, often, though not always, in adjacent bins. The pairing of *bš3* and dates occurs also in four accounts in the Kahun papyri[70], in an account in P. Boulaq 18, and in the Moscow Mathematical Papyrus[71]. Despite this association with dates, however, and the existence of the Coptic ˢBHHⲱ ᴮBEⲱ meaning "unripe figs", there seems little doubt that *bš3* was a cereal, not a fruit[72]. Thus in two Old Kingdom tombs are scenes depicting men reaping a cereal which looks somewhat like barley. Above the scenes is the legend "beer for he who cuts the *bš3*". *Bš3* is mentioned in Old Kingdom tombs in bread- and beer-making scenes, but it is not quite certain with which activity the *bš3* is to be connected. In two tombs, however, is the legend "grinding *bš3*". The verb used, *tiš*, is known only from these examples, and according to the *Wörterbuch*, its cognate or derivative *tš(3)* "to crush" is used in connection with grain only in the process of beer-making. Proof that *bš3* was used in beer-making is afforded by the references in P. Math. Rhind 71 and in the above-mentioned Moscow Mathematical Papyrus, where, as already noted, it is associated with dates. There is apparently no technical objection to dates having been used as an ingredient in beer.

For reasons already given, *bš3* cannot have been spelt. That it was an old generic name for "barley" seems ruled out by the circumstance that in various Old Kingdom representations of granaries it is shown together with Upper Egyptian barley and Lower Egyptian barley. In a review of Gardiner's discussion of the question[73] Nims[74] suggested that *bš3* was a "word for any grain set aside for or specially prepared for beer-making" and that it might mean "malt". In a later article on the bread and beer problems of the Moscow Mathematical Papyrus, he cites[75] as additional support for his view Oppenheim's study of brewing in Mesopotamia[76] in which the latter shows that malt was used there from the Sumerian period onwards, and served as a primary food as well as for brewing. In view of the fact that malt (sprouted barley) has been found in Egyptian tombs, Nims suggests that a similar development probably took place also in Egypt[77]. The occurrence on Second Dynasty stelae of wheat, dates, and malt (*bš3*) is an indication, according to Nims, of the use of malt as a primary food. He cites too an inscription in the tomb of Neferhotep at Thebes, Eighteenth Dynasty, which refers to the making of an "Osiris-bed", i.e. a seed-bed in the form of that deity. The inscription runs: "4th month of the Inundation, day 19. The day of moistening the *bš3* and spreading out the bed of Osiris NN[78]." In the Moscow Papyrus the *bš3* mentioned in connection with the beer problems would not be a new element, but "only Upper Egyptian barley which has been 'sprouted' or 'malted' in preparation for brewing[79]".[80]

Notes

1 A much fuller treatment will appear in the author's *The Food Plants of Pharaonic Egypt* (in preparation) and references here have therefore been kept to a minimum.
2 Täckholm, V. and G. (1941). *Flora of Egypt*, **1**. Cairo. pp. 242–6.
3 Percival, J. (1921). *The Wheat Plant*. London. pp. 186–7.
4 Petrie, W. M. F. (1901). *The Royal Tombs of the Earliest Dynasties*, Part II. London. p. 23; pls. 5, 16; 6, 17 = pl. 34, 82–3.
5 Debono, F. (1948). El Omari (près d'Hélouan). Exposé sommaire sur les campagnes des fouilles 1943–1944 et 1948, *Annales du Service des Antiquités de l'Egypte*, **48**, p. 568 and pls. 7, 2.
6 Lauer, J.-Ph., Täckholm, V. Laurent, Åberg, E. (1951). Les Plantes découvertes dans les souterrains de l'enceinte du roi Zoser à Saqqara (IIIe Dynastie), *Bull. de l'Institut d'Egypte*, **32**, p. 127.
7 Lauer, J.-Ph. *et al.* (1951). ibid.
8 Lauer, J.-Ph. *et al.* (1951). ibid.
9 Lauer, J.-Ph. *et al.* (1951). op. cit. pp. 127–8.
10 Lauer, J.-Ph. *et al.* (1951). op. cit. pp. 156–7.
11 Lauer, J.-Ph. *et al.* (1951). op. cit. p. 157.
12 Helbaek, H. (1953). *Queen Icheti's Wheat. A Contribution to the Study of Early Dynastic Emmer of Egypt* [Det Kongelige Danske Videnskabernes Selskab, Biologiske Meddelelser, bind 21, 8]. Copenhagen.
13 Helbaek, H. (1953). op. cit. p. 6.
14 Helbaek, H. (1953). op. cit. p. 10.
15 Helbaek, H. (1953). op. cit. p. 11.
16 Helbaek, H. (1955). Ancient Egyptian Wheats, *Proc. Prehist. Soc.*, **21**, pp. 94–95.
17 References in Täckholm, V. and G. (1941). op. cit. p. 254.
18 Caton-Thompson, G. and Gardner, E. W. (1934). *The Desert Fayum*. London. pp. 46–7.
19 Caton-Thompson, G. and Gardner, E. W. (1934). ibid.

20 Helbaek, H. (1955). op. cit. pp. 93–4.
21 Helbaek, H. (1955). op. cit. p. 94.
22 Helbaek, H. (1955). ibid.
23 Reference in Täckholm, V. and G. (1941). op. cit. p. 254.
24 Reference in Täckholm, V. and G. (1941). ibid.
25 Täckholm, V. and G. (1941). op. cit. pp. 254–5.
26 In Caton-Thompson, G. and Gardner, E. W. (1934). op. cit. p. 48.
27 Täckholm, V. and G. (1941). op. cit. pp. 287–92.
28 Percival, J. (1936). Cereals of Ancient Egypt and Mesopotamia, *Nature*, *Lond.*, **138**, pp. 271–272.
29 Helbaek, H. (1959). Domestication of food plants in the Old World, *Science*, **130**, No. 3372,pp. 6 and 8, n. 29.
30 Loret, V. (1892). *La Flore Pharaonique*. 2nd Edit. Paris. p. 24.
31 Carter, H. (1933). *The Tomb of Tut. Ankh. Amen*, III. London. p. 61 and pl. 64.
32 Quibell, J. E. (1908). *Tomb of Yuaa and Thuiu*. Cairo. pp. 35–6 Nos. 51022–3.
33 Daressy, G. (1902). *Fouilles de la Vallée des Rois*. Cairo. pp. 25–6, pl. 7, No. 24061; cf. p. 170, Nos. 24664–5, 24667 (from the tomb of Amenophis II).
34 Anon. (1934). *The Egyptian Museum, Cairo. A Brief Description of the Principal Monuments*. Cairo. p. 76 (No. 3840. B).
35 Determined by V. Täckholm.
36 Schweinfurth, G. (1887). Die letzten botanischen Entdeckungen in den Gräbern Ägyptens, *Botanische Jahrbücher für Systematik, Pflanzengeschichte und Pflanzengeographie*, herausg. von A. Engler, 8, p. 12.
37 Unger, F. (1860). Botanische Streifzüge auf dem Gebiet der Culturgeschichte, *Sitzungsberichte der Kaiserlichen Akademie der Wissenschaften in Wien, Math.-Naturwissenschf. Classe*, **38**.
38 Täckholm, V. and G. (1941). op. cit., p. 537.
39 Täckholm, V. and G. (1941). ibid.
40 Unger, F. (1860). ibid.
41 Winlock, H. E. and W. E. Crum. (1926). *The Monastery of Epiphanius at Thebes*. I. New York. p. 61.
42 Unger, F. (1862). Botanische Streifzüge auf dem Gebiete der Culturgeschichte. V. Inhalt eines alten ägyptisches Ziegels an organischen Körpern, *Sitzungsberichte der Kaiserlichen Akademie der Wissenschaften in Wien, Math.-Naturwissenschf. Classe*, **45**. p. 81.
43 Täckholm, V. and G. (1941). op. cit. p. 460. (Several other specimens with panicles were found in graves of the Christian period at Antinoe, *c.* fifth century A.D.)
44 Netolitzky, F. (1914). Die Hirse aus antiken Funden, *Sitzungsberichte der Kaiserlichen Akademie der Wissenschaften in Wien, Math.-Naturwissenschf., Klasse*, **33**, pp. 741, 755 (referred to here under the old name *Panicum colonum* L.).
45 Caylus, de (1752). *Recueil d'antiquités Egyptiennes*. Paris.
46 Daressy, G. (1922). Le Riz dans l'Egypte Antique *Bull. de l'Institut d'Égypte*, **4**, p. 37.
47 Täckholm, V. and G. (1941). op. cit. p. 412.
48 Apart from one find of post-Pharaonic date (second to third century A.D.) and another of uncertain date mentioned by Gardener Wilkinson, I know of no published references to finds of *C. arietinum* in Egypt.
49 Papyrus Anastasi IV, 8, 10 = P. Lansing, 11, 5. English transl. *in* Caminos, R. (1954). *Late Egyptian Miscellanies*. London. pp. 164 and 410.
50 Keimer, L. (1929). "Falcon-face", *Ancient Egypt*, 1929, pp. 47–8.
51 e.g. Emery, W. B. (1958). *Great Tombs of the First Dynasty*, III. London. p. 60, pls. 37, 18; 83, 3.

52 cf. Sethe, K. (1907). Die Namen von Ober- und Unterägypten und die Bezeichnungen für Nord und Sud, *Z. für ägyptische Sprache und Altertumskunde*, 44, p. 19.
53 Täckholm, V. and G. (1941). op. cit. p. 232.
54 Černý, J. (1934). Fluctuations in Grain Prices during the Twentieth Egyptian Dynasty, *Archiv Orientálni*, 6, p. 175, n. 1.
55 Gardiner, A. H. (1941). Ramesside Texts relating to the Taxation and Transport of Corn, *J. Egyptian Archaeology*, 27, p. 24, n. 3.
56 e.g. Emery, W. B. (1958). op. cit. p. 36.
57 Emery, W. B. (1958). op. cit. p. 36, pls. 37, 18.
58 Gardiner, A. H. (1947). *Ancient Egyptian Onomastica* II. Oxford. p. 222*.
59 On the rendering "orange-red" for *kt*, see the discussion in Gardiner, A. H. (1947). op. cit. pp. 222*–3* and the references there cited.
60 Percival, J. (1921). op. cit. p. 191.
61 Gardiner, A. H. (1941). op. cit. pp. 19–73.
62 Gardiner, A. H. (1941). op. cit. pp. 26–7.
63 Caminos, R. A. (1964). The Nitocris Adoption Stela, *J. Egyptian Archaeology*, 50, pp. 75–6.
64 Griffith, F. Ll. (1909). *Catalogue of the Demotic Papyri in the John Rylands Library, Manchester*, III. Manchester. p. 78, n. 11.
65 Hamada, A. (1938). A stela from Manshîyet eṣ-Ṣadr, *Annales du Service*, 38, pp. 217–30.
66 Täckholm, V. and G. (1941). op. cit. p. 253.
67 Lauer, J.-Ph., Täckholm, V. Laurent, Åberg, E. (1951). op. cit. p. 128.
68 Helbaek, H. (1953). op. cit. p. 13.
69 Saad, Z. Y. (1957). *Ceiling Stelae in Second Dynasty Tombs*. Cairo. Nos. 15, 17, 18, 19; pls. 26, 21, 22, 23.
70 Griffith, F. Ll. (1898). *Hieratic Papyri from Kahun and Gurob*. London. Pls. 15, 66, 67; 18, 3, 4; 19, 3, 4.
71 Nims, C. F. (1958). The bread and beer problems of the Moscow Mathematical Papyrus, *J. Egyptian Archaeology*, 44, pp. 56–65.
72 Gardiner, A. H. (1947). op. cit. II. pp. 223*–4*.
73 Gardiner, A. H. (1947). ibid.
74 Nims, C. F. (1950). Egyptian catalogues of things, *J. of Near Eastern Studies*, 9, pp. 261 ff.
75 Nims, C. F. (1958). op. cit. p. 63.
76 Hartman, L. F. and Oppenheim, A. L. (1950). On beer and brewing techniques in Ancient Mesopotamia, *J. Amer. Or. Soc.*, Suppl. 10.
77 Nims, C. F. (1958). op. cit. p. 63.
78 Nims, C. F. (1958). ibid. (quoted).
79 Nims, C. F. (1958). ibid.
80 *Bš3*, *swt*, and other cereals used in bread-making and brewing, are discussed in some detail by H. Wild in an article (1966, Brasserie et panification au tombeau de Ti, *Bull. de l'Inst. fr. d'Arch. orientale*, 64, pp. 95 ff.), which came to hand too late to be utilised in the foregoing paper. Mrs. Täckholm has since accepted Helbaek's identification of the alleged einkorn from El-Omari and Saqqara as emmer (Personal communication and cf. Täckholm, V. (1964), *Favaas Blomster*, Stockholm).

ARLETTE LEROI-GOURHAN

Pollen grains of Gramineae and Cerealia from Shanidar and Zawi Chemi

Much work has been done which shows us the geographical distribution of the wild grasses which are ancestral to cultivated cereals; these grasses are found over vast areas in the Middle East, but we need more localized evidence and especially their relation to prehistoric sites. The variation of their geographical distribution during the Würm climatic oscillations is still not known; most of our information concerns the present although something is known about their distribution during the last ten thousand years.

Although both pollens and grains are found in prehistoric excavations, it is only the latter which have been studied. Of course, in so far as they are available at all, it is the grains and seeds which yield the more precise information about species and evolution of cultivated types. However, despite the difficulties of studying pollen, they can reveal vital information. For a site which is clearly pre-agricultural, by its industry (Mousterian for example) or by radiocarbon dating, it is only pollen analysis which can, except in the most exceptional circumstances, suggest the existence of an ancient "cereal type" in the pollen grains of wild grasses.

Two different measurements allow us to divide grass pollens into different types; the first being the diameter of the grain and the second, the external diameter of the annulus (or ring) encircling the pore.

1. Small grains, less than 40μ, on average from 20μ to 35μ, annulus smaller than 8μ, generally 5μ to 6μ; such grass pollens belong to wild species.

2. Middle size grains from 40μ to 45μ (and even 50μ), annulus reaching 10μ: "Cerealia type"; such grains comprise wild species, wild ancestors of cultivated species and cultivated species.

3. Grains larger than 50μ and annulus from 10μ to 13μ; most of these belong to cultivated species which have been domesticated for some time. The problem comes with the second group, for "Cerealia type" grain can be either cultivated or wild. Inspection of their morphology can help to distinguish between them, and can even differentiate species, but it can hardly be used for old and fossil pollens[1].

If the "Cerealia type" pollens are found throughout a long pre- and early agricultural sequence, it is difficult to establish the beginning of agriculture. The inception of agriculture may be marked by an increase in the percentages of "Cerealia types" or by the presence of very large types, but great difficulties are involved in their study. In the Zeribar lake deposits, van Zeist has shown that, in this region of Iran, "Cerealia type" pollens existed more than 20,000 years ago[2].

If, on the other hand, as at Shanidar in northern Iraq (see the excavations by R. Solecki[3]), such "Cerealia type" pollens are absent or very rare during pre-agricultural periods, there are two possible explanations. First, this may be due simply to climatic fluctuations in the Zagros mountains during the Würm glaciation in which the lowering in altitude of vegetational zones excluded their growth. Similarly their later appearance may also be due to natural causes (changes in temperature or dryness) during which the vegetational zones were submitted to new variations. Second, the later appearance of such pollens may be due to human agency associated with the diffusion of agriculture. It seems that it is the latter explanation which appears to have operated at Shanidar.

Shanidar Cave

Palynological results were obtained from twenty-two samples from the different occupation levels of Shanidar Cave. Despite the presence of a thinly wooded environment (whose fluctuations have been used for assessing some climatic variations), herbaceous plants are abundant throughout suggesting steppe, savannah or steppe-park so that it has been possible to analyse them throughout the stratigraphic sequence (even the earliest level). All the Gramineae pollen grains have been measured (see Table 1).

In all the samples from the Mousterian, the Baradostian (Upper Palaeolithic) and the mesolithic levels, the grain sizes are small, rarely reaching 38μ and 8μ for the annulus. There are only three exceptions where a pollen grain exceeds 40μ and the annulus 9μ. It therefore appears that grasses with large pollen grains were not characteristic of the nearest local flora but they may have occurred only rarely, or they may have existed at some distance from the cave. Studies concerning the dispersal of grass pollen, which is anemophilous, yielded some information. J. Heim has shown that, beyond a few kilometres from the fields, the percentage of Cerealia pollens is very low[4].

There is only one sample from the lower part of the Proto-Neolithic level and its exact stratigraphic context is not known. The pollen diagram from 1 m. to the surface shows striking differences from those of lower levels, for there are numerous "Cerealia type" pollens, a few of them exceeding 50μ. Although there is a decrease in the tree pollen values, there is not sufficient evidence to suggest a significant climatic change. But, as van Zeist has commented, the introduction of new wild species (such as *Aegilops*) from a nearby area may

SHANIDAR

Level	Gramineae grain diam. <40μ ann. diam. <8μ	"Cerealia type" grain diam. <40μ ann. diam. >8μ	>40μ >8μ	Total nos. of pollens
Recent (A)				
0·60 m.	203	73	36	364
Proto-Neolithic (B1)				
0·50 m.	212	25	20	377
0·70 m.	128	15	25	726
1·00 m.	215	11	19	525
Bottom	36	2	1	151
Mesolithic (B2)				
2·85 m.	22			70
Baradostian				
3·00 m.	20			61
3·40 m.	7			24
3·75 m.	4			25
4·00 m.	54	1		361
Mousterian				
4·25 m.	7			36
4·35 m.	3			13
6·30 m.	3			10
6·40 m.	4			28
7·30 m.	10			66
7·50 m.	20			71
7·57 m.	15		1	61
Neanderth. IV	22			min. 1816
8·60 m.	12			188
9·65 m.	18		1	107

Table 1 Wild Gramineae and "Cerealia type"; number of pollen grains.

possibly be due to minor climatic fluctuations; the possibility of a change in the flora due to animal domestication must also be kept in mind. Yet the sudden appearance of numerous large "Cerealia type" pollens seems to be due to human action which, at Shanidar, could be the first evidence of agriculture.

Zawi Chemi

In her paper on the village site of Zawi Chemi (c. 4 kilometres from Shanidar Cave), R. L. Solecki[5] noted that throughout the whole of the main layer (B) the same material culture (Proto-Neolithic) was found; a long occupation of the site is suggested. Domesticated sheep appear late in the sequence and, as polished and chipped celts occur only towards the top of the deposit, we may suppose the evolution of the industry to have lasted perhaps for even a few thousand years. Unfortunately the one carbon-14 date available

(10,870 B.P.) was estimated from charcoal which came from a different area from our samples.

The Proto-Neolithic level is more than two metres thick in some parts of the excavation and is covered by *c.* 0·50 m. of recent deposits. Here it is much easier than at Shanidar to follow the botanical progression since we have more than fifteen samples from the various sub-levels (see Table 2).

ZAWI-CHEMI

Level	Gramineae grain diam. <40μ ann. diam. <8μ	"Cerealia type" grain diam. <40μ ann. diam. >8μ	>40μ >8μ	Total nos. of pollens
Recent				
(F1) 0·25 m.	7			101
0·25 m.	55		2	1226
0·30 m.	61		2	2022
(C4)^(a) 0·50 m.	2			40
Proto-Neolithic				
0·90 m.	110	1 +	5	697
0·95 m.	12	3 +	2	419
1·00 m.	61	3 +	4	556
polished celts 1·20 m.	116	2 +	2	422
(C4) 1·60 m.	6			86
domestic sheep? 1·70 m.	38			377
1·90 m.	84	4 +	5	501
1·95 m.	29	3		705
2·05 m.	34	4 +	1	632
(C4) 2·15 m.	28	2 +	4	241
2·20 m.	51	1 +	1	602
(C4) 2·21 m.	13			376
2·35 m.	83			365
2·45 m.	22			112

(*a*) The samples without numbers are all from area B4.

Table 2 Wild Gramineae and "Cerealia type"; number of pollen grains.

Throughout layer B, no change can be seen in the tree pollen group which remains very low. There is a slight fluctuation in the composition of the herbaceous pollens; Chenopodiaceae increase from the bottom to 1·95 m. at which point they constitute 41% of the total pollen. Above this level they decrease rapidly. Gramineae increase in percentage after the Chenopodiaceae maximum. This change may be due either to human agency or to a variation from a drier to a wetter climate.

From the bottom until *c.* 2·20 m., the grass pollen grains are still small (still no agriculture?); above this, larger pollen grains appear, rarely exceeding 45μ, but with annulus as large as 8·5μ or even 10μ. At 1·90 m., the percentage of grass increases; there was only one pollen grain larger than 50μ and this remains a unique specimen from the Zawi Chemi Proto-Neolithic. In the higher sublevels of this main culture there is a series of large grains as well as the small grains which characterized the beginning of the deposit; this fact, and more especially the larger size of the annulus, suggest the introduction of agriculture.

The Proto-Neolithic level from Shanidar Cave, where similar artifacts are found, appears to be somewhat more evolved—with respect to the pollens—in its uppermost part. The percentage of grass pollen is higher and seems undoubtedly due to the proximity of a cultivated field. The sizes of the pollen grains are, on average, similar to those from the Proto-Neolithic of Zawi Chemi, yet, with a low, although constant, proportion of grains exceeding 50μ.

Recent levels

The "recent" level at Shanidar gives us the surest example of agriculture; c. 55% of the grass pollens are larger than 40μ or have a large annulus which may reach as much as 12μ in diameter. Furthermore, some of them have a thick exine or a strongly marked pitting. It is possible that this larger grain size may have been due to improvement of locally cultivated varieties but it seems also that it may be the result of the introduction of new species[6].

Not all recent levels yield many "Cerealia type" grains; at Zawi Chemi, between 0·25 m. and 0·30 m., only four pollen grains of this type were found among more than 3000 grains, while the Composites predominated. It is worth noting that the site is actually located in a wheat field, so that no, or very little mixing could have taken place.

A large number of pollen analyses are needed to shed light on several outstanding problems concerning the Near East: e.g. the vegetational history and its connection with fluctuations of temperature and precipitation during the Würm glaciation and the Holocene; the extent to which the distribution of the wild ancestors of cereal species at the beginning of plant domestication differed from their known present distribution; the evolution of pollens of cultivated forms which should be investigated by a joint study of the pollens and grains from Pre-ceramic and Early Neolithic sites.

Notes

1 Beug, H. J. (1961). *Leitfaden der Pollenbestimmung.* 1. Stuttgart.
2 van Zeist, W. (1967). Late Quaternary vegetation history of western Iran, *Rev. Palaeobot. Palynol.*, 2, pp. 301–11.
3 Solecki, R. S. (1963). Prehistory in Shanidar valley, northern Iraq, *Science*, Jan. 18, 139, No. 1551, pp. 179–93.
4 Heim, J. (1962). Recherches sur les relations entre la végétation actuelle et le spectre pollinique récent dans les Ardennes belges, *Bull. Soc. R. Bot. Belgique*, 96, pp. 5–92.
5 Solecki, R. L. (1964). Zawi Chemi Shanidar, a post-pleistocene village site

in northern Iraq, *Rep. VIth Intern. Congr. Quatern. Warsaw*, 1961, pp. 405–512.

6 W. R. Stanton has pointed out that the change in pollen size could be due to agronomic changes; the distance travelled by the pollen decreases with the larger size of grain, so larger pollens are only possible with a high density of planting. G. W. Dimbleby has pointed out that the maize pollens of *c.* 80,000 years ago are of the same order of size as today, as maize is self-pollinating; see Hawkes, J. G., this volume p. 27.

J. M. RENFREW

The archaeological evidence for the domestication of plants: methods and problems

Introduction

During the past ten years a substantial quantity of cereal grains and seeds have been recovered in excavations of the earliest neolithic village sites in the Near East and South-east Europe. These plant remains, dating to before 5000 B.C., shed new light on the origins and development of plant domestication in the Old World and are of the greatest interest to agricultural botanists and plant geneticists as well as to prehistorians. Most of the palaeoethnobotanical material from the Near East has been examined and identified by Dr. Hans Helbaek (Copenhagen), and a glance at the references for this paper will reveal the extent to which all students of these problems are indebted to his work. Other early deposits chiefly in Southern Europe have been studied by Dr. Maria Hopf, Dr. Willem van Zeist and by the present author.

This paper sets out to make a complete and comprehensive survey of all the finds of palaeoethnobotanical material so far published which comes from sites dating to before 5000 B.C. in the Old World, and also includes several hitherto unpublished finds examined by the author, belonging to this period. It is proposed first to describe the nature of the material—preserved by carbonization, as grain impressions or silica skeletons—and this will be followed by an outline of the methods used for identification of the material. Special reference will be made to the differences between wild and domesticated forms, and the extent to which these can be recognized in the palaeoethnobotanical material. It was thought useful to follow this with a catalogue of the finds so far available, giving details of the material from each site, which form the basis for this discussion. The finds thus set out will then be analysed for each species found—giving the archaeological evidence for domestication. Comparison of these results with modern theories of plant genetics reveals various discrepancies and the problems raised will be considered.

Methods

The survival of the evidence

The palaeoethnobotanical material survives from the period of the beginnings of agriculture in three different forms: as carbonized material, impressions in mud-daub and coarse pot sherds, and as small fragments of silica skeletons in ash and carbon detritus. (For a general discussion of these forms of preservation see Helbaek[1].)

The bulk of the material we are considering was preserved by carbonization. The grain and seeds were converted to carbon while more or less retaining their characteristic shape as a result of overheating near a hearth, or in a parching oven (the primitive glumed wheats in particular needed to be parched before they could be threshed and winnowed satisfactorily[2]); or by a house fire in the area in which they were stored. They did not become carbonized by spontaneous combustion[3]. The carbonized material from these early sites consists of whole spikelets of wheat (e.g. Hacilar) and barley (e.g. Jarmo), spikelet forks of wheat (e.g. Ali Kosh), rachis fragments of naked wheat (e.g. Çatal Hüyük), and of barley (Ali Kosh), and carbonized grains and seeds (e.g. Çatal Hüyük and most of the early finds in Greece and Bulgaria).

Two important finds, however, were preserved as impressions in mud-daub in the construction of walls and roofs of houses, where the mud had first been mixed with straw and chaff (perhaps sweepings from the threshing floor). At Jarmo impressions of wild and domesticated emmer wheat spikelets were recovered from baked clay and mud-daub. Impressions form the chief source of evidence for the Pre-Pottery Neolithic husbandry at Beidha, where a primitive and transitional form of hulled two-row barley was the chief species found. At Argissa-Maghula in Thessaly Dr. Maria Hopf found impressions of einkorn and emmer wheats and hulled six-row barley. Impressions in pottery have also been found from this early period. In this case the spikelets and grains became incorporated in the wet clay as the pot was being built and were then burnt out when the vessel was fired, thus leaving a perfect mould of the grain from which a latex cast can be obtained. Such impressions of emmer wheat spikelets and internodes, and florets of hulled barley were found in coarse ware sherds of phase A in the 'Amuq.

Occasionally associated with impressions of grain in mud-daub and coarse sherds there occur silica skeletons of small fragments of the epidermis and glumes which can be identified on microscopic examination. The cell walls of the epidermis of grass seeds and those of some other plants contain silica which is deposited during the growth of the cell. This silica remains when the organic material disappears due to burning or to natural decay. When embedded in mud-daub or mud bricks or objects of baked clay these silica skeletons may survive indefinitely, forming an exact replica of the plant cell and retaining all the characteristics of the walls and pits of the epidermis[4]. In the 'Amuq finds silica skeletons of the dorsal pale, the glume and an internode of emmer wheat were found together with those of a wild oat pale and the epidermis of rye grass[5]. Fragments of silica skeletons are also occasionally found in deposits of ash and carbon detritus for example fragments of wheat and barley epidermal cells were found at Jarmo[6].

Methods and problems of identification

The early plant remains are identified by a careful study of the minute details of morphology preserved in the grains and seeds and comparison with the corresponding parts of fresh plants of the same species. The examiner must also be aware of the different forms of distortion which may occur due to the form of preservation of the material. In all forms of preservation the techniques of identification are based solely on the correlation between the morphology of the ancient grains and seeds with that of their modern counterparts. Direct evidence for the structure of the chromosomes are not obtainable[7].

The first plants to be domesticated by man in the Old World appear to have been the cereals wheat and barley. In the period with which we are concerned three species of wheat, *Triticum monococcum*, *Triticum dicoccum*, and *Triticum aestivum* became established as fully domesticated crops, and both hulled and naked varieties of two- and six-row barley were also grown. In Thessaly oats and millet may also have come into cultivation at this period. Also present on many of the early sites are various representatives of the pulses especially peas, lentils and vetch, and although these have not been studied so intensively it seems likely that peas and lentils at least had been domesticated by 5000 B.C. Another crop which falls outside the categories mentioned so far is flax which appears to have come into cultivation in the Near East certainly before the end of our period.

Wheat. The earliest finds consist of the glumed diploid einkorn and tetraploid emmer wheats and their wild ancestors; these can be shown to be genetically more primitive than the naked hexaploid bread wheat and club wheat which also occur before 5000 B.C.[8] The chief difference between wild and domesticated glume wheats lies in the fragility of the rachis; the wild species have a brittle rachis enabling individual spikelets to disarticulate on ripening and thus disperse the seeds. The domestic forms of the glume wheats also have a brittle rachis, but it tends not to break up into spikelets until threshed. Thus it seems that the earliest farmers selected their seed grain from those spikes which remained intact until the whole ear was ready for harvesting. Besides the brittleness of the rachis other features of the wild einkorn *T. boeoticum* and wild emmer *T. dicoccoides* are the great size, coarseness and extreme hairiness of their spikelets and their long ripening period, so that the uppermost grains may have dispersed before the lower ones on the same spike have ripened. In the case of wild einkorn two varieties are known: there is a small single-grained race which is found chiefly in the Balkans and western Anatolia, *T. boeoticum* ssp. *aegilopoides*, and a larger twin-grained variety occurring in S. Turkey, Iraq, and Iran *T. boeoticum* ssp. *thaoudar*[9]. The spike of the cultivated einkorn, *T. monococcum*, tends to be shorter and more compact than that of the wild species. The grains, though still pointed at both ends, are shorter and broader than those of *T. boeoticum*[10]. Both single and twin grained forms of *T. monococcum* occur on the early sites.

Wild emmer differs from wild einkorn in being on the whole much larger, and in having invariably two grains ripening per spikelet. The spike is thus less compressed laterally. The glume has a single prominent keel contrasting with the wild and cultivated forms of einkorn which have two keels to their glumes[11]. Most forms have a very hairy rachis. Cultivated emmer tends to have a more or less glabrous spike in contrast to *T. dicoccoides*, and the head is shorter, denser, and less hairy and the grains much plumper than in the wild species[12]. Thus the wild wheat species may be distinguished from each other and from their cultivated progeny. The chief differences between cultivated einkorn and emmer grains may be briefly summarized as follows: grains of einkorn tend to be very narrow indeed averaging about 1·5–2 mm., and in the single-grained varieties they have a rounded profile in both dorsal and ventral aspects. The grains of two-grained einkorn are closer to those of emmer, being flattened ventrally, but are distinguished by their shortness and narrowness. Caryopses of emmer are plumper than those of einkorn and have a characteristic hollow in the ventral aspect.

The hexaploid wheats have no wild progenitor to correspond with *T. boeoticum* or *T. dicoccoides*. They are derived from emmer probably through crossing with a species of *Aegilops*[13]. The hexaploid wheats which concern us here are the naked *T. aestivum* (bread wheat) and *T. compactum* (club wheat). They are distinguished from the foregoing cultivated species by having much shorter, fatter, more rounded grains, with the greatest width near the embryo. There is a marked difference in the spikelet fragments too—instead of forming a "fork" as in einkorn and emmer where the keels of the glumes and the rachis internode adhere firmly together as a single unit, bread and club wheat spikelets break quite differently with the rachis segments adhering together whilst the glumes and keels have invariably disintegrated[14]. The grains of club wheat are shorter and plumper than those of bread wheat and the rachis segments also tend to be shorter due to the denser ear form.

Barley.   The earliest cultivated barley found seems to belong to the two-row variety and undoubtedly has derived from the wild *Hordeum spontaneum*. Both wild and domesticated forms are found in the earliest deposits. The differences between these forms are not very great. The domestic variety has a tough rachis that does not break during threshing, whereas the wild form has a brittle rachis breaking up into discreet spikelets on maturity each consisting of one median fertile grain with a lateral sterile floret on either side. The fragility of the rachis—the major distinctive feature of the wild two-row barley—is only controlled by two genes[15]. In discussing the transitional forms of two-row barley occurring at Beidha Helbaek states that the cultivated form has larger grains[16]. The lateral florets of *H. spontaneum* are pedicellate and not sessile as in cultivated varieties, and the pales are not wrinkled: these features are found in the barley at Jarmo[17].

The Beidha finds, besides the transitional form of *H. spontaneum* which showed signs of having been cultivated if it had not reached the point where it could be described as fully domesticated, also revealed a mutant of two-row barley which must have arisen due to domestication—the naked form—but there is no clear evidence as to the spikelet type[18]. The first indisputable evidence of naked six-row barley comes from Aceramic Hacilar, but Helbaek would like to consider all the early finds as belonging to this type[19]. The status of the wild six-row barley, *H. agriocrithon*, in the origin of the six-row domesticated form has been the subject of much controversy since its discovery in Tibet (1938) and Palestine (1954). The question is which is the more primitive condition, six- or two-row, or could they have evolved side by side[20]? If as Zohary and others maintain the two-row variety is the most primitive then the first demonstrable mutation in barley found in the palaeoethnobotanical material is remarkably complex. The sterile lateral florets became fertile at the same time as the pales lost their cohesion to the caryopsis. This mutation made the grain completely dependent on man for its reproduction since the primitive means of dispersal within the hulled spikelet was now lost. The fact that rachis internodes do not occur in the early deposits, with the exception of Jarmo where several internodes were found adhering together, suggests that the axis was no longer brittle.

Naked barley is distinguished from the hulled form by having much wider grains, which lack the longitudinal striations of the palea veins and have minute transverse rippling of the surface. The six-row form is distinguished by having distinctly twisted lateral grains, the twist being most noticeable in the ventral aspect.

Two other cereals may have come into cultivation at this early period although both are represented by very few finds. They both occur on Aceramic Neolithic sites in the fertile plain of Thessaly in Central Greece.

Broom corn millet. The wild ancestor of *Panicum miliaceum* is not certainly known; Helbaek has postulated *Panicum callosum* Hochst., the Abyssinian wild species, as a possibility[21]. The find from the Aceramic levels at Argissa-Maghula[22] is of carbonized grain measuring $1 \cdot 9 \times 1 \cdot 9 \times 1 \cdot 0$ mm. which corresponds with those for the cultivated form[23].

Oats.   An exceptionally large oat grain was found in the Aceramic Neolithic
levels at Achilleion in Thessaly. Unfortunately the diagnostic lemma base,
and the point of insertion of the awn were broken away so that the species
cannot be ascertained. However the size of the grain 9·2 × 3·3 × 2·5 mm.
suggests a cultivated form cf. *Avena sativa/Avena byzantina*[24]. It is interesting
to note in passing that the wild oat *Avena ludoviciana* has been identified at
Pre-Pottery Neolithic B Beidha[25], and that wild oats (species not given) occur
in the Ali Kosh and Mohammad Jaffar phases at Alik Kosh[26] and also in
'Amuq A[27].

Besides the domestication of cereals it seems likely that some of the pulse
crops were beginning to come under cultivation before 5000 B.C.

Lentil.   The lentil is the most frequently found of the pulses on these early
sites. The domestic form *Lens esculenta* is probably derived from *Lens
nigricans,* and this latter form was found at Argissa[28]. It is not possible without
measurements to say whether the finds from Pre-Pottery B Jericho, Jarmo,
Aceramic Hacilar, Ceramic Hacilar and Tepe Sabz are wild or cultivated. The
Ghediki lentils were probably cultivated as they measured 4·1–3·2 × 3·5–3·3
mm.[29] compared with 2·66 × 2·48 mm. at Argissa[30]. The two deposits of
lentils from Azmaska in Bulgaria contained small seeds averaging 2·7 × 2·4
mm. and must probably be considered wild[31].

Peas.   The wild purple pea, *Pisum elatius,* is known from Aceramic Hacilar
and Çatal Hüyük[32] while on the other sites it is the field pea, *Pisum sativum*
var. *arvensis,* which is represented. It occurs at Pre-Pottery B Jericho, Jarmo,
Çatal Hüyük, Can Hasan, Ghediki and Sesklo. Measurements of the peas
from the last three sites are available:

Can Hasan   max. diam. 4·4 mm.   length of hilum 1·9 mm.
Ghediki   4·1–3·5 × 3·8–3·4 × 3·5–3·0 mm.
Sesklo   4·2–3·7 × 3·5–2·9 × 3·8–2·9 mm.

Vetch.   Although all the finds of vetch from these early sites probably
represent wild plants it is interesting to note that *Vicia ervilia* which was later
cultivated, already occurs at Çatal Hüyük[33]. *Vicia narbonensis,* the ancestor of
the horse-bean, occurs, at Beidha[34]. The earliest record of cultivated horse-
bean, *Vicia faba,* is from Pre-Pottery B Jericho. Other sites where vetches
have been found are Ali Kosh (Mohammad Jaffar Phase), Tepe Sabz, and
Jarmo.

Flax.   Finds of seeds of *Linum usitatissimum* occur on two sites within our
period: Tepe Sabz and Tell es-Sawwan. The one measurable seed from the
latter site was 4 mm. long and 2·4 mm. broad[35].

Catalogue of finds before 5000 B.C. of domesticated plants in the Near East and South-east Europe

The finds can be divided into the following regional groups: Iran and Iraq, Zagros, Palestine, Syria, Anatolia, Greece and Bulgaria.

I IRAN AND IRAQ

1 *Ali Kosh* (Deh Luran plain, Iranian Khuzistan)

(a) *Bus Mordeh Phase* 7500–6750 B.C.

The plant remains obtained by Hole and Flannery using flotation techniques to recover the carbonized grain from the earliest level at the site, were identified by Helbaek, and a preliminary discussion appears in Helbaek[36] and Hole and Flannery[37]. The following species have been identified: *Triticum boeoticum*[38], *T. monococcum*[39] represented by a few battered grains, *T. dicoccum*[40] small grains and spikelet forks, *Hordeum spontaneum*[41], naked barley ?two-row[42]. Besides these cultivated species a number of wild pulses were collected: *Medicago*, *Astragalus*, and *Trigonella*[43].

(b) *Ali Kosh Phase* 6750–6000 B.C.

T. dicoccum and *H. distichum* are the chief crops in this phase; two grains of six-row barley were also found[44]. The same wild pulses were collected as in the previous phase and in addition the following wild grasses were represented: *Aegilops*, *Lolium*, wild oats and canary grass[45].

(c) *Mohammad Jaffar Phase* 6000–5500 B.C.

Emmer wheat and hulled two-row barley remain the chief cultivated plants, and they are joined in the plant record by plantain, mallow, vetch, wild oat, and canary grass[46]. The detailed report on these finds is awaited with great interest.

2 *Tepe Sabz* (Deh Luran, Iranian Khuzistan)

Sabz Phase 5500–5000 B.C.

T. aestivum[47], hulled six-row barley[48] and hulled two-row barley[49] are the cereals represented at this site, and "irrigated" flax is also represented[50]. The following pulses were found—lentil, vetch and vetchling[51].

3 *Tepe Guran* (Luristan)

The deposit of grain was found in a domed oven in a mud-walled house dating between 6200–5500 B.C. The grain was identified by Helbaek as chiefly *H. distichum* with a few grains of *H. spontaneum*[52].

4 *Tell es-Sawwan* (on the Middle Tigris in Iraq)

The grain was found in a defensive moat 2 m. below its upper level, dating from 5800–5600 B.C. Finds from this site are described in Helbaek[53]. *T. monococcum*—a single grain, *T. dicoccum*—grains 6·3 mm. long and roughly as wide as thick. *T. aestivum*: the grains were 4–5 mm. long and plumper than the emmer grains. Naked six-row barley grains were 4–5 mm. long, rounded and plump with a finely corrugated skin, and there were a few hulled six-row grains also present. The grains of hulled two-row barley were 4·5–6·5 mm. long. Three seeds of flax were also present: the only measurable grain was 4 mm. long and 2·4 mm. wide.

II THE ZAGROS

1 *Jarmo* (Iraqi Kurdistan)

The grain comes from the early farming village dated to *c.* 6750 B.C. Various wheats were found: *T. aegilopoides* (i.e. *T. boeoticum* ssp. *aegilopoides*), "smaller type with convexly curved ventral and dorsal sides"[54]; *T. monococcum*, carbonized grains[55], *T. dicoccoides*, impressions in clay[56], "straight, flat-bottomed" grains and spikelets[57]; *T. dicoccum*, spikelets (impressions) illustrated by Helbaek[58] and grains.

Hordeum spontaneum made up the bulk of the find. The kernels were hulled, straight and unwrinkled, some specimens consisting of the median fertile floret with one of the lateral male florets attached[59]. The lateral florets are not sessile as in modern two-row barley, but have a short pedicel. Interestingly, it appears from some axis portions, consisting of three internodes, that the spike was not brittle as in the wild form, but had attained at least a certain degree of toughness.

The following pulses were also represented: field pea[60]; lentil[61]; and blue vetchling[62].

Grains and fragments of the "sturdy" glumes of *Aegilops* sp. were also identified.

2 *Matarrah* (Kurdish uplands)

The finds are dated to the Hassunah period, *c.* 5750 B.C. Two species are recorded: *H. distichum*, long straight barley grains, and impressions of two-row spikes[63]; *T. dicoccum*[64].

PALESTINE

1 *Beidha* (Southern Jordan)

The finds are from the Pre-Pottery Neolithic "B" village. *T. dicoccum*, impressions of spikelets with glumes and curving keels (not straight as in the wild species). Some spikelets were larger and coarse as in the wild form, others small. The variation was considered typical of genetical transition[65]. The carbonized grains varied in length from 5 to 10 mm.[66]

H. spontaneum was found with grains of considerable size, exceeding that of the wild species, but retaining the brittle rachis[67]. Whole spikelets were found with sterile laterals as well as fertile median grains[68].

Naked grains, with width/length index exceeding 0·50 were found[69]. The softly rounded surface is devoid of longitudinal striations of palea veins, and in one, the shell is minutely rippled, establishing that these are naked grains. Since no two-row naked barley is known in antiquity, these are probably from six-row barley[70].

The wild pulses collected include *Vicia narbonensis*, *Medicago* and *Onobrychis crista-galli*[71].

Amongst the weeds, the following grass species were noted: *Aegilops* sp., *Lolium* sp., and *Avena ludoviciana*[72].

2 *Jericho* (Jordan valley)

(a) Pre-Pottery Neolithic A

In the earliest Pre-Pottery levels excavated by Dr. Kathleen Kenyon, Dr. Maria Hopf has identified the cultivated hulled two-row barley *H. distichum* and emmer wheat *T. dicoccum*.

(b) Pre-Pottery Neolithic B

In this level Dr. Maria Hopf has identified *H. distichum*, *T. monococcum* and *T. dicoccum* among the cereals, and the pulse crops *Pisum* cf. *sativum*, *Lens culinaris* and *Vicia faba*[73].

(c) Pottery Neolithic

H. distichum, *T. monococcum* and *T. dicoccum* continue to be cultivated.

SYRIA

1 *'Amuq A* (Plain of Antioch)

Cereal remains were found as impressions and fragments of silica skeletons in heavily chaff-tempered "coarse simple ware", dated to *c.* 5750 B.C.

Species found were *T. dicoccum* spikelet and internode, the internode measured 2·93 mm. from the lower tip to the articulation scar, and was 1·60 mm. wide just under the scar. The glume was 8·00 mm. long[74]. Hulled barley was represented by a poorly preserved small floret, possibly a sterile floret[75]. Oat, *Avena* sp., occurred as a silica skeleton of epidermal cells of pales. Microscopic examination showed the cells to be sinuate walled, the crests and waves being thickened with the connecting parts thin and fairly straight. The isodiametric cells are lobed all round, which indicated that the species here is not *A. sativa*, *A. barbata*, or *A. fatua*, since the cells are too slender[76]. Also found were grains of *Lolium* sp. cf. *gaudium*.

2 Tell Mureybat (on bank of Euphrates, N. Syria)[77]

During the excavations of the site by Dr. M. N. van Loon in 1964 and 1965 finds of carbonized seeds were made, which have been studied by Dr. van Zeist and W. A. Casparie. The levels containing the seeds have carbon-14 dates ranging from 8050 to 7542 B.C. Among the eighteen types of seeds identified cultivated plants are not represented, but of interest to us are seeds of wild einkorn and wild barley which were discovered. The wild einkorn is the two-grained variety *T. boeoticum* ssp. *thaoudar* and there are no examples of *T. boeoticum* ssp. *aegilopoides*.

The grains measured:

Length	4·83 mm.	(3·8–6·0 mm.)
Breadth	1·30 mm.	(0·9–1·6 mm.)
Thickness	1·33 mm.	(1·0–1·7 mm.)

They are slender, spindle-shaped seeds showing the greatest width in the middle of the grain, while the ends are more or less pointed.

The wild barley *H. spontaneum* is represented by a small number of grains which are rather flat on the dorsal side, with a comparatively small thickness and more or less angular cross-section. The maximum width of the grain is in the middle; it tapers to a narrow base and the width decreases only slightly towards the apex. The following measurements were obtained for these grains:

Length	5·44 mm.	(3·8–6·7 mm.)
Breadth	1·89 mm.	(1·5–2·1 mm.)
Thickness	1·26 mm.	(1·0–1·6 mm.)

3 Tell Ramad (Syria)[78]

The Pre-Pottery Neolithic B levels of this site, excavated in 1963, have yielded remains of cultivated plants. Hulled two-row barley *H. distichum*, emmer wheat *T. dicoccum*, einkorn *T. monococcum*, and club wheat *T. compactum* and lentil *Lens culinaris* have been identified by van Zeist and S. Botteina.

ANATOLIA

1 Çatal Hüyük (Konya Plain)

Vast quantities of carbonized grain were found in levels VI to II, *c.* 5850–5600 B.C. Helbaek has identified the following domesticated plants: *T. monococcum*. The grains are small[79] and it is the two-grained variety which is represented[80]. *T. dicoccum.* This species is represented by grains and inter-nodes. The grains are of exceptionally large size[81], measuring up to 9 mm. in length and with extraordinary short, broad internodes and coarse heavy glumes[82]. *T. aestivum.* The grains were identified thus as shorter, broader and fatter than normal emmer spikelets. The rachis segments remain united and the glumes and keels disintegrate, revealing a naked wheat rather than hulled or glumed wheat[83]. *H. spontaneum.* Present as "introduced weed"[84]. *H. vulgare* var. *nudum.* Present in "great volumes"[85]. The grains seem to belong to compact spikes, of the small-grained variety[86]. Of the pulses, peas—*Pisum elatius* and *P. sativum* var. *arvensis,* vetch—*Vicia noeana* (a common variety in this locality) and *V. ervilia,* were also present[87].

2 Mersin (Cilicia)

The material was brought back to England from Mersin by Prof. V. G. Childe, and is now at Reading University. Its stratigraphical position is not well documented, but it is considered to belong to a level not later than the Hassunah period[88]. The material has been identified by Helbaek as dense-eared hulled six-row barley, the first known occurrence of this form.

3 Aceramic Hacilar (Plain of Burdur, west-central Anatolia)

The finds have been set at about 7000 B.C. *T. boeoticum.* Typical grains were found sporadically in the deposits[89]; a small form of *T. dicoccum*[90]; naked six-row barley. Also present were several pulses, *P. elatius*[91], vetchling and lentil[92].

4 Late Neolithic or Chalcolithic Hacilar

The precise context for this material has not been reported, but the date is quoted as *c.* 5800–5000 B.C.

T. monococcum. Large quantities, chiefly twin-grained[93]; *T. dicoccum.* Whole carbonized spikelets practically intact[94]; *T. aestivum.* Rachis fragments[95]; naked six-row barley was much cultivated. Both two- and six-row hulled forms of barley were also found. The only pulse crop so far recorded from this phase is lentils[96].

5 Can Hasan (Konya Plain)

Two deposits of grain were found in neolithic level 5, dated *c.* 5250 B.C. The first consisted of hulled six-row barley, with grains measuring 5·7 × 3·2 × 2·5 mm. (average), and *Triticum* sp., the grains being too fragmentary for more specific identification. The other deposit consisted of *Pisum sativum* var. *arvensis,* the field pea which measured average 4·4 mm. diameter measured along the hilum, and the length of the hilum averaged 1·9 mm.[97]

GREECE

1 Knossos (Crete)

Finds of grain come from Stratum X which dates to *c.* 6100 B.C. Naked hexaploid wheat, emmer and barley are present but no further details are given[98].

2 Ghediki (E. Thessaly)

Finds from the Aceramic Neolithic levels which probably date between 6000–5000 B.C. yielded *T. monococcum*, the single-grained form, measuring 5·5 × 2·0 × 3·0 mm.[99]; *T. dicoccum*, the chief cereal cultivated, average L. 5·2, B. 2·9, T. 2·5 mm.[100]; *H. distichum* average L. 5·8, B. 2·9, T. 2·3 mm.[101]; *H. distichum* var. *nudum* L. 6·0, B. 2·7, T. 2·0 mm.[102] The pulses represented are *Pisum* sp. measuring average 3·9 × 3·5 × 3·3 mm., *Vicia* sp. 4·5 × 4·4 × 4·4 mm. and *L. esculenta* L. 3·8 × B. 3·4 mm.[103]

3 Achilleion (S. Thessaly)

Finds in the Aceramic Neolithic levels, 6000–5000 B.C., comprise *T. dicoccum* average L. 6·0, B. 2·6, T. 2·7 mm.[104], and *Avena* sp. L. 9·2, B. 3·3, T. 2·5 mm.[105] It was identified on the basis of the hairy covering of the caryopsis revealed where the lemma and palea were broken away. Unfortunately the pales were broken at diagnostic places so that the species could not be ascertained.

4 Sesklo (S. E. Thessaly)

Two deposits of carbonized grains were found in the Aceramic levels (6000–5000 B.C.). One deposit consists of *T. dicoccum* (av. L. 5·7, B. 3·0, T. 2·3 mm.), *H. distichum* L. 5·5, B. 3·1, T. 2·0 mm. and some peas *Pisum* sp. 3·8 × 3·4 × 3·2 mm. The second deposit also contained *Pisum* sp. averaging 3·9 × 3·2 × 3·2 mm.[106]

5 Argissa Maghula (Central Thessaly)

Finds from the Aceramic layers consist of both grain impressions and carbonized grains dating 6000–5000 B.C. The species represented are *T. monococcum* (carbonized grain measured 6·0 × 2·3 × 2·7 mm.[107]); grain impression of two-grained einkorn 6·4 × 3·0 × (2·5) mm.[108] and impressions of spikelet forks measuring (10·2) × 4·8; (11·0) × (3·8); (9·0) × (3·0); (8·3) × (4·0); (8·0) × (4·0); (7·0) × (5·0) mm.[109] *T. dicoccum* represented by impressions of spikelet forks: (11·0) × (6·2); (5·0) × (5·0); (7·2) × (4·5) mm. *H. vulgare* carbonized grain measured (4·8) × 2·6 × 2·0 mm.[110] and grain impression (6·8) × (3·8) mm.[111] "*H. vulgare* L. *polystichum* var. *tetrastichum*" is represented by the impression of a rachis (18·0 × (2·5) mm. of which a single rachis segment measures L. 3·5 mm.[112] cf. *Panicum miliaceum* was represented by a small rounded seed 1·9 × 1·9 × 1·0 mm. with the embryo broken away[113]. Lentils, *L. nigricans*, represent the only pulse found. The carbonized seeds measured av. 2·66 × 2·48 × 1·7 mm., and they are thought to belong to the wild species on the basis of their size[114].

6 *Nea Nikomedeia* (W. Macedonia)

Carbonized grain and grain impressions found at this Early Neolithic village dated *c.* 6200 B.C. These finds are not yet published in detail but a preliminary report in Rodden and Rodden[115] indicates that wheat, barley and lentils were cultivated. *T. monococcum*, *T. dicoccum*, *H. vulgare* var. *nudum*, *Lens culinaris*, *Pisum sativum* and *Vicia ervilia* have been identified by van Zeist among the carbonized material.

BULGARIA

1 *Azmaska Moghila* (Maritza valley)

Finds from the Early Neolithic levels (Karanovo I culture) at this site yielded grains dating to *c.* 5000 B.C. The following species were identified by Dr. Maria Hopf in material sent to the Berlin Radiocarbon Laboratory[116], *T. monococcum*, *T. dicoccum*, and *T. aestivum*, and the pulses, *Lathyrus* cf. *cicera*, and *V.* cf. *angustifolia*.

Samples were also examined by the author in the Stara Zagora Museum in the summer of 1966[117]. The following species were identified: *T. monococcum* L. 5·2, B. 2·0, T. 2·5 mm., *T. dicoccum*, spikelet forks and grains, the latter measuring 6·6 × 3·1 × 2·7 mm., and *L. nigricans*, which formed the bulk of two deposits, averaging 2·7 × 2·4 mm.

2 *Karanovo* (Maritza valley)

The earliest levels of this site (Karanovo I culture dating *c.* 5000 B.C.) yielded large quantities or carbonized grain. These included *T. monococcum* (both single and twin-grained varieties): the single-grained type measures av. L. 5·9, B. 2·1, T. 3·1 mm., and the twin-grained form L. 6·2, B. 2·0, T. 2·8 mm. *T. dicoccum* is represented by spikelet forks, glume fragments and grains. The caryopses measured L. 6·6, B. 3·1, T. 2·8 mm.

Tentative conclusions and problems arising from the results outlined above

1 *Wheat*

(a) *Triticum monococcum.* Its wild ancestor *T. boeoticum* is recognized at Tell Mureybat, Ali Kosh (Bus Mordeh phase), Jarmo, and Aceramic Hacilar. The domesticated form *T. monococcum* is not found very widely nor in great numbers on these early sites. However, it is found at Ali Kosh (Bus Mordeh phase), Tell es-Sawwan, Jarmo, Çatal Hüyük—where it is very abundant[118]— and also at Late Neolithic Hacilar[119]. In Europe it is present at Ghediki and Argissa in Thessaly and Tell Azmak and Karanovo in Bulgaria. It is interesting to note that the two-grained variety derived from *T. boeoticum* sp. *thaoudar* occurs at Çatal Hüyük, Hacilar[120], Argissa[121], and Karanovo I[122]. Helbaek has postulated on this basis that "west-central Anatolia was the primary centre of conscious development and selection of the cultivar and that this selection took place about 6000 B.C."[123] This certainly seems likely for the two-grained variety, but the single-grained species occurs nearly a millennium earlier in Iran, at Ali Kosh where it is associated with its wild ancestor.

One problem arises from the modern distribution of wild einkorn: the small usually single-grained "race" is characteristic of the southern Balkans and west Anatolia, whilst the larger usually twin-grained race *T. boeoticum* sp. *thaoudar* is found in south Turkey, Iraq and Iran[124]. Harlan and Zohary stress however that wild einkorn seems to be most at home in south-east Turkey on the basaltic cobble, e.g. on Karacadag. Granted that the twin-grained race may have been domesticated in south Anatolia and spread into Europe from there as a cultivable crop, it seems that we must postulate a single-grained *T. boeoticum* sp. *aegilopoides* growing further east than its modern distribution to account for the finds at Ali Kosh and Jarmo, considerably older than the other deposits considered. This brings us up against a problem that at present seems difficult to solve: what were the distributions of the wild cereal grasses at the time of the earliest plant domestications? This problem is not wholly or satisfactorily answered by plotting modern distributions, although these may be taken to indicate the general area for consideration.

(*b*) *Triticum dicoccum.*   Whereas einkorn is domesticated by cultivation and selection from wild einkorn, emmer is slightly more complex in its make-up. The wild species *T. dicoccoides* has two genome components AA and BB—the A genome being derived from einkorn, and B possibly from a species of *Aegilops*, possibly *Ae. speltoides*[125]. The chromosomes of hybrid AB would be doubled—since the fourteen chromosome hybrid would be sterile as the chromosomes of the "A" and "B" genomes would not pair normally[126]— giving rise to a new tetraploid wild species *T. dicoccoides* with genomes AABB. *T. dicoccoides* probably arose long before man began to domesticate plants in the Old World. The area in which it arose probably lies somewhere close to the overlap in the distribution of *Ae. speltoides* and *T. boeoticum*, i.e. in a broad arc from the south-east shores of the Black Sea, through Eastern Turkey and down the shores of the East Mediterranean as far as Mt. Carmel. The most easterly point of this arc lies at the headwaters of the river Tigris.

Two races of wild emmer have been distinguished: that found in Turkey, Iraq, Iran and the U.S.S.R. is never found in great abundance, but often occurs associated with wild einkorn and wild barley as a minor component of the grassland flora in the lower oak-woodland belt[127]. This race is rather small, and not much larger than wild einkorn. The other race distinguished has a distribution centred on the Upper Jordan valley, and is remarkable for its large size and robustness. It occurs in massive stands on basaltic and hard limestone slopes. Harlan and Zohary postulate that this race, now found in the Upper Jordan valley, was the ancestor of the modern tetraploid wheats, and that the Turkish-Iraqi race was of little importance for the early domestication of cereals. It has been shown that this Turkish-Iraqi race is closest to *T. timopheevi*, a half weed, half cultivated wheat of Soviet Georgia and Armenia[128]. It is of interest to note that the only palaeoethnobotanical find of *T. dicoccoides* so far is from Jarmo in the Zagros region of Iraqi Kurdistan, while at Beidha in Southern Jordan no wild emmer is present. The chief crop there seems to have been hulled two-row barley transitional between the wild and domestic forms. The emmer at this site however shows great variation in size suggesting that it represents a period of "genetical transition"[129].

Emmer is the most widely found of all the early domesticated cereals. Among the sites at present under consideration it is present at all except Tepe Sabz, Tepe Guran and Mersin. In the early deposits at Ali Kosh and Aceramic Hacilar the grains are small but characteristic[130], at Beidha the grains range in length from 5–10 mm. At Çatal Hüyük the grains are large, up to 9 mm., with short, broad internodes to the spikelets and heavy glumes[131]. In Thessaly the average length of carbonized emmer grains of the Aceramic Neolithic ranges from 5·2 mm. (Ghediki) to 6·0 mm. (Achilleion)[132]. In the Maritza valley of Bulgaria the average length is larger than in Greece[133] at Azmaska Moghila, 6·7 mm. and at Karanovo I, 6·8 mm.

(c) *Triticum aestivum.* Unlike *T. monococcum* and *T. dicoccum*, Bread wheat has no wild ancestor. Its genome complement AABBDD is derived from *T. dicoccoides/T. dicoccum* (AABB) with another *Aegilops* species. This was probably *Ae. squarrosa* as Riley has indicated[134]. He suggests, on the basis of high frequency of *Ae. squarrosa* in sample of wheat at Chalus on the Caspian, that the initial hybridization may well have occurred under conditions of cultivation. "If this were so", he continues, "the first hexaploid wheat may have been a free-threshing type resembling *T. aestivum.*" On the other hand, McFadden and Sears have synthesized the hulled hexaploid *T. spelta* from *T. dicoccoides* and *Ae. squarrosa*[135] and *T. aestivum* is thought to have arisen either by gene mutation in *T. spelta* or through natural crossing of different forms of *T. spelta*[136]. The archaeological evidence here strongly suggests that *T. aestivum* arose in the Near East, Anatolia and South Europe without any connection with *T. spelta*, an association not recorded even in later prehistory from this area. The earliest find of the species is at Çatal Hüyük, 5800–5600

B.C., closely followed by Late Neolithic Hacilar. Further east it occurs in the find from Tell es-Sawwan, 5800–5600 B.C., and at Tepe Sabz from about 5200 B.C.[137] The earliest occurrence in Europe at Knossos at about 6000 B.C., followed by Tell Azmak[138]. Even in Central Europe, where both bread and spelt wheat occur in archaeological contexts, the spelt follows bread wheat by about a thousand years.

T. compactum, closely related to *T. aestivum*, is known from Tell Ramad in Pre-Pottery Neolithic B levels.

2 Barley

(a) *Two-row barley* (Hordeum distichum). All varieties of two-row barley derive from *H. spontaneum*, the wild, hulled two-row form, which is chiefly distributed at present in an arc stretching from the northern tip of the Red Sea via Israel, Syria, South Turkey, North Iraq, and South-west Iran on the Persian Gulf[139]. It is this wild form, showing some evidence of cultivation, which occurs at Ali Kosh (Bus Mordeh phase), Tepe Guran, Jarmo, Beidha, and Çatal Hüyük. The Beidha find is perhaps the most interesting: tens of thousands of impressions of this species were found. They are ascribed to this wild species partly by virtue of the brittle rachis, but the grains are very much larger than the normal wild form, so that Helbaek[140] has spoken of "cultivated wild barley".

H. spontaneum has been identified among the grains found at Tell Mureybat. At Jarmo, *H. spontaneum* has been identified both from impressions and carbonized remains. Here finds of rachis fragments with three internodes joined together suggest that the axis was no longer brittle—as a result of cultivation of selection. This feature allows us to describe the Jarmo barley as the earliest "domesticated" two-row barley yet found. It still corresponds to the wild *H. spontaneum* in that the lateral florets are pedicellate and not sessile, and the pales are not wrinkled[141].

Fully domesticated hulled two-row barley occurs at many sites of slightly later date: Ali Kosh (Ali Kosh and Mohammad Jaffar phases), Tepe Sabz, Tepe Guran, Tell es-Sawwan, Matarrah, Late Neolithic Hacilar, Ghediki, and Sesklo.

It is interesting to note that another form, the naked variety of barley, occurs in extremely early contexts (Ali Kosh in the Bus Mordeh phase and Beidha as well as Ghediki in Thessaly). Naked barley does not occur wild and thus these forms must be considered as domesticates. Helbaek states[142] that "there is no evidence for two-row naked barley in antiquity", and so identifies the Beidha and Ali Kosh specimens as six-row. This seems unlikely, however, when the rest of the material with which they were found is hulled two-row barley, albeit the wild form. The Ghediki grain was considered two-row on the basis of a similar association. Only finds of the rachis segments with adhering pales would solve this matter satisfactorily.

(*b*) *Six-row barley* (Hordeum vulgare).   The whole question of the origins of six-row barley has been the subject of controversy since de Candolle and Koernicke in the nineteenth century suggested that *H. spontaneum* might be the ancestor of both the two- and six-row forms, although de Candolle also suggested the possibility of a hypothetical wild six-row form which would be the antecedent of the cultivated six-row form. Since then, allegedly wild six-row barley has been found in Tibet, and in Palestine *H. agriocrithon* was found in 1954. It has been accepted by many authorities as the long-sought primitive, wild progenitor of cultivated barley[143]. No finds of *H. agriocrithon* are yet reported from archaeological deposits.

The earliest form of six-row barley yet found appears to be naked. A curved (lateral) grain of naked six-row barley was found at Aceramic Hacilar, and naked six-row barley occurs in great quantities at Çatal Hüyük, *c.* 5600 B.C.[144] It appears also at Tell es-Sawwan, *c.* 5800–5600 B.C.[145] Thus it appears (if we disregard the Ali Kosh and Beidha finds noted above) that naked six-row barley comes into its own as a cultivated crop chiefly in Anatolia, and that if it is derived from *H. spontaneum* the three mutations giving a firm rachis, fertile lateral grains and naked caryopses had occurred as a consequence of domestication at least before 7000 B.C. (Aceramic Hacilar). Finds of hulled six-row barley occur slightly later: at Ali Kosh (Ali Kosh phase), Tell es-Sawwan, and Tepe Sabz in the Near East, Mersin, Late Neolithic Hacilar and Can Hasan in Turkey, and Argissa-Maghula in Thessaly. This again is curious, for if six-row barley was derived from the wild hulled *H. agriocrithon* one might expect to find the hulled form domesticated even earlier. This does not appear to be the case from the palaeoethnobotanical material so far examined.

So far the archaeological evidence supports the case for *H. spontaneum* as the ancestor of both two- and six-row barleys. The domesticated two-row barleys seem to have emerged first at Jarmo (hulled) and possibly at Beidha (hulled) and in the Ali Kosh phase at Ali Kosh (naked). The hulled form was widely cultivated from about 6000 B.C. in the Near East and Southern Europe. The earliest six-row barley (naked form) appears in Anatolia around 7000 B.C. and was established in Thessaly after 6000 B.C. Hulled six-row barley occurs by 6000 B.C. at Ali Kosh (Ali Kosh phase) and Argissa in Thessaly. It is subsequently found at Tepe Sabz, Tell es-Sawwan, Mersin, Late Neolithic Hacilar, and Can Hasan. It thus appears that there was no significant time lag between the emergence of domesticated two- and six-row forms, and that both occur, in their naked and hulled varieties, very shortly after domestication.

3 *Broom corn or proso-millet* (Panicum miliaceum)

Only one possible find of this species is known for the period in question. It was from Argissa-Maghula[146], with seeds measuring 1·9 × 1·9 × 1·0 mm.

The wild ancestor of the species is not known[147] although Helbaek has suggested that the Abyssinian wild species *Panicum callosum* Hochst., which closely resembles it morphologically, may be involved[148]. The earliest find previously recorded was from the Jemdet Nasr period in Mesopotamia, dated around 3000 B.C.[149] This form of millet was widely grown in Central Europe from around 2000 B.C.[150]

4 Oat (Avena *sp.*)

Finds of wild oat grains are not unusual at these early sites—at Ali Kosh (Ali Kosh and Mohammad Jaffar phases), Beidha, 'Amuq A. Only at Beidha has the species been identified, as *Avena ludoviciana*. The find at Achilleion would normally have been considered wild, but for the exceptionally large size of the caryopsis, measuring 9·2 × 3·3 × 2·5 mm. As the diagnostic parts of the lemma were broken away, more precise identification was not possible. But on size alone it looks as though this might have been a domesticated form. If so it is very much earlier than any other find. *A. strigosa* and *A. sativa* were cultivated in central and northern Europe at the beginning of the first millennium B.C.[151]

5 The pulses

(a) *Pea.* Finds of the field pea, *Pisum sativum* var. *arvensis* and the rough-seeded purple pea, *P. elatius*, are quite common on these early sites. The former is known from Jarmo, Çatal Hüyük, and Can Hasan, and is probably the species represented in the Aceramic levels at Ghediki and Sesklo in Thessaly. *P. elatius* is known chiefly from Hacilar, and in smaller quantity at Çatal Hüyük. Bertsch and Bertsch consider *P. elatius* as the wild species from which the cultivated field and garden peas derive[152]. Whether any of these finds can be considered fully domestic is an open question, but field peas were certainly cultivated in the Late Neolithic of Europe[153].

(b) *Lentil.* The lentil is the most widely found form of pulse seed on these early sites. It occurs at Jarmo and Tepe Sabz in the Near East, at Aceramic and later Hacilar in Anatolia, at Ghediki, Argissa and Nea Nikomedeia in Greece, and at Karanovo I and Tell Azmak in Bulgaria. The domestic form, *Lens esculenta*, is probably derived from the wild *L. nigricans*, and is distinguished from it by the larger size of its seeds. Hopf[154] describes the Argissa finds as *L. nigricans* on the basis of the size of the carbonized seeds, 2·66 × 2·48 × 1·7 mm. The finds from Ghediki are larger (3·8 × 3·4 mm.) and may be domesticated. At Tell Azmak, lentils formed the bulk of two sizeable deposits, but the seeds measured only 2·7 × 2·4 mm. which suggests that they may not have been domesticated.

(c) *Vetch.* The early finds of vetch belong chiefly to wild species, but it is interesting to note that *Vicia ervilia* was already known at Çatal Hüyük. It became an important crop later in Anatolia and neighbouring regions[155]. Unspecified vetch and vetchling are known from the Mohammad Jaffar phase at Ali Kosh and the Sabz phase at Tepe Sabz. Blue vetchling was found at Jarmo, and *V. narbonensis* at Beidha. *V. noeana*, a common weed in the vicinity of Çatal Hüyük was also found in the neolithic deposits besides *V. ervilia*, and a large-seeded vetch was present in Aceramic levels at Ghediki in Thessaly. It is interesting to note that the horse-bean, *V. faba*, was not culti-vated until later[156] although its wild ancestor was present in the Beidha finds.

6 Flax

Two finds of flax seeds are known from this early period, from Tell es-Sawwan and Tepe Sabz. The former find contained a seed measuring 4·0 × 2·4 mm. corresponding to *Linum usitatissimum*, and comparing well with the previous earliest finds from Arpachiyah and Tell Brak (seed length, 3·84 and 4·03 mm. respectively) reported by Helbaek[157]. Fibres from textiles at Çatal Hüyük have been identified variously as flax and wool, and in the absence of any finds of seeds, the presence of flax at that site cannot yet be regarded as established. The wild ancestor of flax, *L. bienne*, occurs naturally in the Kurdish foothills, and it seems likely that it was domesticated in this region, and subsequently spread into temperate Europe[158]. It is not possible to say whether flax was first cultivated for its oily linseeds or for the fibres of its stem.

Conclusion

The finds discussed above comprise the evidence as it now stands which bears on the domestication of the earliest crop plants of the Old World (see Table 1). They provide a somewhat complex picture of early husbandry, which cannot conveniently be summarized in a few words. The wide variety of crops at many early sites over a large area is, however, an obvious feature.

Many of the finds here listed have been reported only in a preliminary way, and few of them illustrated in detail. We do not have full details and measure-ments of the earliest forms represented, and their publication will be of great importance. More finds will be needed as well, before we can understand the full range of variation between the wild species, on the one hand, and the cultivated varieties on the other. As yet no systematic study of "intermediate" forms has been possible, and the rather close similarity in some cases between the domesticates and their prototypes offers little hope of documenting in detail the process of domestication as fully as Mangelsdorf has been able to do for maize.

The complex picture of early plant husbandry documented by these finds suggests that the "Early Neolithic" period which they represent was preceded by a lengthy period of experimentation before these crops—which still form the basis of our agriculture today—were finally selected and domesticated. The great lack in our knowledge here arises from the absence, up to now, of finds of crop plants from the period immediately preceding what we now know as the "Early Neolithic". Although there are indications that both the Natufians and the Karim Shahir people were exploiting food plants, we do not know what these were. Future finds, therefore, may not only fill in the details of the outline picture already available for the "Early Neolithic" period: they may set the beginnings of agriculture back a millennium, or several millennia, earlier than present evidence allows. Undoubtedly the most valuable step towards increasing our understanding of early agriculture

Sites	Dates—B.C.	Wild Einkorn	Einkorn	Wild Emmer	Emmer	Bread wheat	Wild 2-row barley	Hulled 2-row barley	Naked 2-row barley	Hulled 6-row barley	Naked 6-row barley	Oat	Millet	Pea	Lentil	Vetch	Flax
Ali Kosh (B.M.)	7500–6750	x	x	–	x	–	x	–	x?	–	–	–	–	–	–	–	–
Ali Kosh (A.K.)	6750–6000	–	–	–	x	–	–	x	–	x	–	Wd	–	–	–	–	–
Ali Kosh (M.J.)	6000–5600	–	–	–	x	–	–	x	–	–	–	Wd	–	–	–	x	–
Tepe Sabz (Sabz)	5500–5000	–	–	–	–	x	–	x	–	x	–	–	–	–	x	x	x
Tepe Guran	6200–5500	–	–	–	–	–	x	x	x	–	–	–	–	–	–	–	–
Tell es-Sawwan	5800–5600	–	x	–	x	x	–	x	–	x	x	–	–	–	–	–	x
Tell Mureybat	8050–7542	x	–	–	–	–	x	–	–	–	–	–	–	–	–	x	x
Tell Ramad	c. 7000	–	x	–	x	C	–	x	–	–	–	–	–	–	x	–	–
Jericho, P.P. Neo.	c. 7000	–	x	–	x	–	–	x	–	–	–	–	–	x	x	x	–
Beidha, P.P. Neo. B.	c. 7000	–	–	–	x	–	x	–	x?	–	–	Wd	–	–	–	x	–
Jarmo	c. 6750	x	x	x	x	–	x	–	–	–	–	–	–	x	x	x	–
Matarrah	c. 5500	–	–	–	x	–	–	x	–	–	–	–	–	–	–	–	–
'Amuq A	c. 5750	–	–	–	x	–	–	B	–	–	–	Wd	–	–	–	–	–
Mersin, E. Neo.	c. 5750	–	–	–	–	–	–	–	x	–	–	–	–	–	–	–	–
Çatal Hüyük, VI–II	5850–5600	–	x	–	x	x	x	–	–	–	x	–	–	x	–	x	–
Aceramic Hacilar	c. 7000	x	–	–	x	–	–	–	–	–	x	–	–	x	x	x	–
Ceramic Hacilar	5800–5000	–	x	–	x	x	–	x	–	x	x	–	–	–	x	–	–
Can Hasan, L. Neo.	c. 5250	–	–	–	W	–	–	–	–	x	–	–	–	x	–	–	–
Knossos, Stratum X	c. 6100	–	–	–	x	x	–	B	–	–	–	–	–	x	–	–	–
Aceramic Ghediki	c. 6–5000	–	x	–	x	–	–	x	x	–	–	–	–	x	x	x	–
Aceramic Sesklo	c. 6–5000	–	–	–	x	–	–	x	–	–	–	–	–	–	x	–	–
Aceramic Argissa	c. 6–5000	–	x	–	x	–	–	–	–	x	–	x	–	–	x	–	–
Aceramic Achilleion	c. 6–5000	–	–	–	x	–	–	–	–	–	–	–	x	–	x	–	–
Nea Nikomedeia	c. 6200	–	–	–	W	–	–	B	–	–	–	–	–	–	x	–	–
Karanovo I	c. 5000	–	x	–	x	–	–	–	–	–	–	–	–	–	x	–	–
Azmaska Moghila, E. Neo.	c. 5000	–	x	–	x	–	–	–	–	–	–	–	–	–	x	–	–

W = Wheat unspecified   B = Barley unspecified   Wd = Wild form   C = Club wheat

Table 1   Finds of domesticated plants and related species from the Near East and Europe before 5000 B.C.

would be the excavation of more sites from this shadowy period from the tenth to the eighth millennium B.C., and the application of flotation and other techniques to recover such plant evidence as they may contain.

None the less, we should not undervalue the great advance which has taken place in our knowledge in the period, less than two decades, since Professor R. J. Braidwood's pioneering excavations at Jarmo. At first solely through the work of Hans Helbaek, and more recently with that of other scientists also, our knowledge of Early Neolithic plant husbandry has reached the stage that the developments documented through the archaeological finds can be compared (and sometimes contrasted) with the developments put forward on less pragmatic grounds, by plant geneticists. These comparisons have already proved very fruitful, to both disciplines, and it seems very likely that they will lead, over the next few decades, to an agreed and perhaps fairly complete understanding of the domestication of food plants in the Old World[159].

Notes

1 Helbaek, H. (1963). Palaeo-Ethnobotany, *in* Higgs, E. S. and Brothwell, D. R. (eds.) *Science in Archaeology*. London. pp. 180–5.
2 Harlan, J. R. (1967). A wild wheat harvest in Turkey, *Archaeology*, 20 (3).
3 Helbaek, H. (1952). Early crops in Southern England, *Proc. Prehist. Soc.*, 18, pp. 194 ff.
4 Helbaek, H. (1960). Cereals and Weed Grasses in phase A, *in* Braidwood, R. J. and Braidwood, L. J. *Excavations in the Plain of Antioch, I.*, Appendix II, Chicago, p. 540.
5 Helbaek, H. (1960). ibid.
6 Helbaek, H. (1959). How farming began in the Old World, *Archaeology*, 12, p. 188.
7 Helbaek, H. (1966). Commentary on the phylogenesis of *Triticum* and *Hordeum, Econ. Bot.*, 20, p. 350.
8 Helbaek, H. (1960b). The Palaeoethnobotany of the Near East and Europe, *in* Braidwood, R. J. and Howe, B. *Prehistoric Investigations in Iraqi Kurdistan*, Chicago, p. 104.
9 Harlan, J. R. and Zohary, D. (1966). The distribution of wild wheats and barleys, *Science*, 153, p. 1078.
10 Peterson, R. F. (1965). *Wheat*. New York. pp. 10–12.
11 Peterson, R. F. (1965). ibid.
12 Peterson, R. F. (1965). ibid.
13 Peterson, R. F. (1965). op. cit. p. 85.
14 Helbaek, H. (1966). op. cit. fig. 8, p. 356.
15 Harlan, J. R. and Zohary, D. (1966). ibid.
16 Helbaek, H. (1966b). Pre-Pottery Neolithic farming at Beidha, *Palestine Exploration Quarterly*, 98 (i), p. 62.
17 Helbaek, H. (1960b). op. cit. p. 108.
18 Helbaek, H. (1966). ibid.
19 Helbaek, H. (1966). ibid.
20 Bell, G. D. H. (1965). The comparative phylogeny of the temperate cereals, *in* Hutchinson, Sir J. (ed.) *Essays on Crop Plant Evolution*, Cambridge.
21 Helbaek, H. (1960b). op. cit. p. 113.

22 Hopf, M. (1962). Bericht uber die Untersuchung von Samen und Holz-kohlenesten von der Argissa-Magula aus den präkeramischen bis mittel-bronzezeitlichen Schichten, *in* Milojčic, V., Boessneck, J., and Hopf, M. *Die deutschen Ausgrabungen auf der Argissa-Magula in Thessalien.* Bonn. p. 102.

23 Bertsch, K. and Bertsch, F. (1949). *Geschichte unseres Kulturpflanzen.* Stuttgart. p. 85.

24 Renfrew, J. M. (1966). A report on recent finds of carbonized cereal grains and seeds from Prehistoric Thessaly, *Thessalika*, 5, p. 23.

25 Helbaek, H. (1966b). ibid.

26 Hole, F. and Flannery, K. V. (1967). The prehistory of southwestern Iran: a preliminary report, *Proc. Prehist. Soc.*, 33, pp. 147 ff.

27 Helbaek, H. (1960). ibid.

28 Hopf, M. (1962). op. cit. pp. 101 ff.

29 Renfrew, J. M. (1966). ibid.

30 Hopf, M. (1962). op. cit. pp. 104–6.

31 Renfrew, J. M. Unpublished investigation.

32 Helbaek, H. (1964). First impressions of the Çatal Hüyük plant husbandry, *Anatolian Studies*, 14, p. 122.

33 Helbaek, H. (1964). ibid.

34 Helbaek, H. (1966b). ibid.

35 Helbaek, H. (1965). Early Hassunan Vegetable at es-Sawwan near Samarra, *Sumer*, 20, pp. 45 f.

36 Helbaek, H. (1966). ibid.

37 Hole, F. and Flannery, K. V. (1967). ibid.

38 Helbaek, H. (1966). ibid.

39 Helbaek, H. (1966). ibid.

40 Helbaek, H. (1966). op. cit. p. 352 and fig. 4.

41 Helbaek, H. (1966). op. cit. p. 357.

42 Helbaek, H. (1966). ibid.

43 Hole, F. and Flannery, K. V. (1967). ibid.

44 Hole, F. and Flannery, K. V. (1967). ibid. Helbaek (1966) op. cit. p. 357.

45 Hole, F. and Flannery, K. V. (1967). ibid.

46 Hole, F. and Flannery, K. V. (1967). ibid.

47 Helbaek, H. (1966). op. cit. p. 354.

48 Helbaek, H. (1966). op. cit. p. 358 and fig. 12.

49 Hole, F. and Flannery, K. V. (1967). ibid.

50 Hole, F. and Flannery, K. V. (1967). ibid.

51 Hole, F. and Flannery, K. V. (1967). ibid.

52 Meldgaard, J., Mortensen, P. and Thrane, H. (1963). Excavations at Tepe Guran, Luristan, *Acta Arch.*, 34, p. 112, n. 17.

53 Helbaek, H. (1965). ibid.

54 Helbaek, H. (1959b). Domestication of food plants in the Old World, *Science*, 130, pp. 365 ff.

55 Helbaek, H. (1960b). ibid.; Helbaek, H. (1960c). Ecological effects of irrigation in Ancient Mesopotamia, *Iraq*, 22, pp. 186 ff.

56 Helbaek, H. (1966). ibid.

57 Helbaek, H. (1959). op. cit. p. 184.

58 Helbaek, H. (1959b). ibid.

59 Helbaek, H. (1959). op. cit. p. 187.

60 Helbaek, H. (1959b). op. cit. fig. 8; Helbaek, H. (1959). op. cit. p. 189.

61 Helbaek, H. (1959). ibid.

62 Helbaek, H. (1959b). ibid.

63 Helbaek, H. (1960b). op. cit. p. 109.

64 Helbaek, H. (1959b). ibid.

65 Helbaek, H. (1966b). ibid.

66 Helbaek, H. (1966). ibid.

67 Helbaek, H. (1966b). ibid.
68 Helbaek, H. (1966). ibid.
69 Helbaek, H. (1966b). ibid.
70 Helbaek, H. (1966). ibid.
71 Helbaek, H. (1966b). ibid.
72 Helbaek, H. (1966b). ibid.
73 For details of these finds, see Hopf, M., this volume, pp. 355–9.
74 Helbaek, H. (1960). ibid.
75 Helbaek, H. (1960). ibid.
76 Helbaek, H. (1960). ibid.
77 van Zeist, W. and Casparie, W. A. (1968). Wild Einkorn, wheat and barley from Tell Mureybit in Northern Syria, *Acta Bot. Neerl.*, 17 (1), pp. 44–53.
78 van Zeist, W. and Botteina, S. (1966). Palaeobotanical investigations at Ramad, *Annales Arch. Arabes Syriennes*, 16, pp. 179–80.
79 Helbaek, H. (1964). op. cit. p. 121.
80 Helbaek, H. (1966). op. cit. p. 351 and fig. 3.
81 Helbaek, H. (1964). op. cit. p. 121.
82 Helbaek, H. (1966). op. cit. p. 352 and fig. 4.
83 Helbaek, H. (1966). op. cit. p. 354 and fig. 6.
84 Helbaek, H. (1964). ibid.
85 Helbaek, H. (1966). op. cit. p. 357.
86 Helbaek, H. (1964). op. cit. p. 121.
87 Helbaek, H. (1964). ibid.
88 Helbaek, H. (1959b). ibid.
89 Helbaek, H. (1966). ibid.
90 Helbaek, H. (1966). op. cit. p. 352 and fig. 4.
91 Helbaek, H. (1964). ibid.
92 Helbaek, H. (1966b). op. cit. p. 63.
93 Helbaek, H. (1966). ibid.
94 Helbaek, H. (1966). op. cit. p. 353.
95 Helbaek, H. (1966). op. cit. fig. 7.
96 Helbaek, H. (1961). Late Bronze Age and Byzantine crops at Beycesultan in Anatolia, *Anatolian Studies*, 11, p. 82.
97 Renfrew, J. M. (1968). A note on the neolithic grain from Can Hasan, *Anatolian Studies*.
98 Evans, J. D. (1964). Excavations in the Neolithic settlement of Knossos 1957–60, Part I, *Annual Brit. Sch. Arch. Athens*, 59, pp. 132 ff. See identifications by Helbaek.
99 Renfrew, J. M. (1966). op. cit. p. 22.
100 Renfrew, J. M. (1966). ibid.
101 Renfrew, J. M. (1966). ibid.
102 Renfrew, J. M. (1966). ibid.
103 Renfrew, J. M. (1966). op. cit. p. 23.
104 Renfrew, J. M. (1966). ibid.
105 Renfrew, J. M. (1966). ibid.
106 Renfrew, J. M. (1966). ibid.
107 Hopf, M. (1962). op. cit. pp. 104–6.
108 Hopf, M. (1962). ibid.
109 Hopf, M. (1962). ibid.
110 Hopf, M. (1962). ibid.
111 Rodden, R. J. and Rodden, J. M. (1964). A European link with Çatal Hüyük: uncovering a seventh millennium settlement in Macedonia. Part I, *Illustrated London News*, 11th April, pp. 565 ff.
112 Hopf, M. (1962). ibid.
113 Hopf, M. (1962). ibid.
114 Hopf, M. (1962). ibid.
115 Rodden, R. J. and Rodden, J. M. (1964). ibid.

116 Kohl, G. and Quitta, H. (1966). Berlin Radiocarbon Measurements II, *Radiocarbon*, 8, pp. 27 ff.
117 Renfrew, J. M. Unpublished investigation.
118 Helbaek, H. (1964). op. cit. p. 121.
119 Helbaek, H. (1966). ibid.
120 Helbaek, H. (1966). ibid.
121 Hopf, M. (1962). op. cit. pp. 104–6.
122 Renfrew, J. M. Unpublished investigations.
123 Helbaek, H. (1966). op. cit. p. 352 and fig. 4.
124 Harlan, J. R. and Zohary, D. (1966). ibid.
125 Peterson, R. F. (1964). op. cit. p. 83.
126 Peterson, R. F. (1965). ibid.
127 Harlan, J. R. and Zohary, D. (1966). op. cit. p. 1079.
128 Harlan, J. R. and Zohary, D. (1966). ibid.
129 Helbaek, H. (1966b). ibid.
130 Helbaek, H. (1966). op. cit. p. 352 and fig. 4.
131 Helbaek, H. (1966). ibid.
132 Renfrew, J. M. (1966). ibid.
133 Renfrew, J. M. Unpublished investigations.
134 Riley, R. (1965). Cytogenetics and the evolution of wheat, *in* Hutchinson, Sir J. op. cit. p. 106.
135 Peterson, R. F. (1965). op. cit. p. 85.
136 Peterson, R. F. (1965). op. cit. p. 100.
137 Helbaek, H. (1966). op. cit. p. 354.
138 Kohl, G. and Quitta, H. (1966). ibid.
139 Harlan, J. R. and Zohary, D. (1966). op. cit. p. 1075.
140 Helbaek, H. (1966b). op. cit. p. 61.
141 Helbaek, H. (1960b). op. cit. p. 108.
142 Helbaek, H. (1966). op. cit. p. 356 and fig. 8.
143 Bell, G. D. H. (1965). op. cit. p. 84.
144 Helbaek, H. (1966). op. cit. p. 356 and fig. 8.
145 Helbaek, H. (1964). ibid.
146 Hopf, M. (1962). op. cit. pp. 104–6.
147 Bertsch, K. and Bertsch, F. (1949). ibid.
148 Helbaek, H. (1960b). op. cit. p. 113.
149 Helbaek, H. (1959b). op. cit. p. 371.
150 Bertsch, K. and Bertsch, F. (1949). op. cit. p. 90.
151 Helbaek, H. (1960b). op. cit. p. 114.
152 Bertsch, K. and Bertsch, F. (1949). op. cit. p. 165.
153 Bertsch, K. and Bertsch, F. (1949). op. cit. p. 168.
154 Hopf. M. (1962). pp. 104–6.
155 Helbaek, H. (1961). ibid.
156 Helbaek, H. (1959b). op. cit. p. 371.
157 Helbaek, H. (1960b). op. cit. p. 193.
158 Helbaek, H. (1960b). op. cit. p. 114.
159 The author gratefully acknowledges the help she received from Dr. D. Theochares (prehistoric grain from Thessaly), Professor D. Dimitrov, Dr. G. Georgiev, Dr. Mikov, and the Director of the Stara Zagora Museum for the earliest Bulgarian material; and Mr. David French for the neolithic material from Can Hasan.

RALPH RILEY

Evidence from phylogenetic relationships of the types of bread wheat first cultivated

The interpretation of phylogeny from interchanges

The comparison of chromosome structure in different plant genotypes provides a means of assessing relative phylogenetic positions, and in the wheat group interchange differences are most useful for this purpose. In the origin of an interchange, segments are exchanged reciprocally between chromosomes that are usually completely unrelated in their genetic functions. Thus two chromosomes, with the linearly arranged order of segments ABCDEF and UVWXYZ, might undergo an exchange to give rise to chromosomes with the new structures ABCXYZ and UVWDEF. Chromosomes with structures altered in this way may become fixed in populations derived from the individuals in which they first occurred. In some instances it is possible to recognize experimentally which is primitive and which derived.

Differences between individual plants or plant populations, due to interchanges, can be recognized from the behaviour of chromosomes at meiosis in hybrids between them. Where the parents differ by the presence of an interchange, instead of all the chromosomes associating in pairs, or bivalents, four chromosomes associate together in a quadrivalent. These four chromosomes will be the two from one parent with the original structure and the two from the alternate parent with the interchanged structure. In this way interchange differences can be readily recognized and used to trace phylogenies and work of this kind has been carried out in wheat[1].

The method can be explained by discussing the relationships of the four wheat varieties, Chinese Spring, V220, Holdfast, and Cappelle-Desprez. From meiosis in hybrids the following relationships were established:

Chinese Spring × V220—no quadrivalent = no interchange difference,
Chinese Spring × Holdfast—one quadrivalent = one interchange difference,
Chinese Spring × Cappelle-Desprez—two quadrivalents = two interchange differences,

Holdfast × Cappelle-Desprez—one   quadrivalent = one   interchange difference.

The relationships established from meiosis in the hybrids can be illustrated diagramatically, using one or two lines to represent one or two interchange differences respectively, as follows:

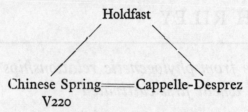

Clearly the chromosome structures of Chinese Spring and V220 are more like that of Holdfast than like that of Cappelle-Desprez. Although there is no internal evidence as to which is primitive and which derived, it is apparent that a chromosome structure like that of Holdfast must have been intermediate to whichever of the other two states is derived.

The archetypic chromosome structure of wheat

Triticum aestivum, the most widely cultivated wheat, has 42 chromosomes that were derived in evolution from the 28-chromosome emmer wheat, *T. turgidum*, and from the 14-chromosome, weed grass *Aegilops squarrosa*. The complete sets of chromosomes of both these species are present in *T. aestivum*, but, because many forms of wheat differ from each other due to the presence of interchanges, their original ancestral structure may have been modified.

Obviously interest attaches to the recognition of forms of *T. aestivum* with the primitive chromosome structure. This requires the establishment of 42-chromosome forms in which there are no interchanges relative to emmer in the chromosomes derived from emmer, and in which among the remaining chromosomes there are similarly no interchanges relative to the chromosomes of *Ae. squarrosa*. From the study of meiosis in hybrids, *T. aestivum* ssp. *vulgare* variety Chinese Spring was shown to have no interchange differentiation relative to either *T. turgidum* ssp. *dicoccoides* or *Ae. squarrosa*. Consequently the ancestral chromosome structure of the 42-chromosome wheats is present in Chinese Spring.

Forms of T. aestivum

There are a number of subspecies of *T. aestivum*, the 42-chromosome wheat, that are separated on the basis of major morphological distinctions, although the differences between them are generally simply inherited[2]. These sub-species are:

T. aestivum ssp. *vulgare*	bread wheat
T. aestivum ssp. *compactum*	club wheat
T. aestivum ssp. *spelta*	large spelt or dinkel wheat
T. aestivum ssp. *sphaerococcum*	Indian dwarf wheat
T. aestivum ssp. *macha*	
T. aestivum ssp. *vavilovi*	

Faced with this range of variation an interesting question concerns the form that was first available for agricultural use, since presumably all diverged from a single prototype at the 42-chromosome level. Any subspecies which does not possess the primitive chromosome structure can presumably be dismissed from this role, so that it is important to ascertain how widely the primitive structure is distributed.

The distribution of the primitive chromosome structure

The primitive chromosome structure of *T. aestivum* ssp. *vulgare* Chinese Spring was used as a standard against which the structures of other forms were compared in hybrids. The results were as follows:

Number of interchange differences from the primitive structure	Subspecies	Comments
None	*vulgare*	one form from Kashmir (in 1930)
	spelta	two forms from Baktiari region of Iran (in the 1950's)
One	*vulgare*	seven forms, European, Chinese, Indian, and American
	spelta	two European, and three Baktiari forms
	compactum	
	vavilovi	
Two	*vulgare*	one French form
	macha	
	sphaerococcum	

So far as this limited exploration goes, only subspecies *vulgare* and *spelta* have the primitive chromosome structure and there is thus no evidence that any of the other subspecies could have been available to the first cultivators. Of course a wider survey might reveal that some of the other subspecies have similar ranges of structural variation to those that have been observed in *vulgare* and *spelta*. Arguments supporting some other subspecies as the most primitive would, however, certainly be aided by the demonstration in it of forms with the primitive structure, since the present evidence favours *vulgare* or *spelta*.

The only forms of *spelta* with the primitive structure were collected in the Baktiarian area of Iran by Professor H. Kuckuck[3]. Other forms of *spelta* from the same area differed from the primitive structure by a single interchange, as did the two central European forms studied. If the same interchange proves to be present in the European and Baktiarian forms, then it must have existed formerly in a continuous population, or in a common pool, that is now relict in these widely disjunct areas. If the interchanges were all the same it would demonstrate the antiquity of *spelta*, showing that the European and Iranian forms did not arise independently from *vulgare*.

The two forms of *vulgare* with the primitive structure both came from the more easterly range of the subspecies. Chinese Spring probably came from the Chungking region of China, while the other variety, V220, was obtained from Kashmir. Kashmir is within the area in which 42-chromosome wheat could have been first formed—this area being delimited by the distribution of *Ae. squarrosa*. However the present results can be taken as no more than a hint that the primitive chromosome structure in *vulgare* may have been better preserved in the eastern part of its present area of distribution.

Work on chromosome structures has so far shown that either *vulgare* or *spelta* may have been the first 42-chromosome form. This approach is not capable of discriminating between them, but a study of the geographical distribution of the primitive structure, in both forms, might well provide information that would assist the choice.

Notes

1 Riley, R., Coucoli, H. and Chapman, V. (1967). Chromosomal inter-changes and the phylogeny of wheat, *Heredity*, 22, pp. 233–48.
2 Mackey, J. (1954). The taxonomy of hexaploid wheat, *Svensk. bot. Tidskr.*, 48, pp. 579–90.
3 Kuckuck, H. (1959). On the findings of *Triticum spelta* L. in Iran and on the arising of *Triticum aestivum*-types through crossing of different *spelta*-types, *Wheat Inf. Serv.*, 9–10, pp. 1–2.

WILLIAM C. STURTEVANT

History and ethnography of some
West Indian starches

The traditional classificatory rubrics of western science and everyday discourse are becoming less suitable as we learn more about the range of alternative possibilities in the relations between man and the living world around him. Concepts such as "domestication", "cultigen", "ornamental", "agriculture", "horticulture", or "irrigation" refer to bundles of cultural, biological, and historical variables which can now be seen to occur in various combinations in different places and different periods, combinations which are inadequately classified by these and many similar terms. It is probably time to abandon the broader rubrics in order to concentrate on defining and analysing more specific variables, examining their changing associations in different instances and their functional and historical interrelations with features from other spheres such as sociological, economic, ecological, and biological ones.

Classificatory criteria such as whether a species can survive without human care, whether a species has been genetically modified through man's activities, or the extent to which his biotic environment has been intentionally or unintentionally changed by man, are cultural as well as biological. The cultural variables are of several major sorts, including for plants, (1) ethnoscientific features, i.e. those related to folk botanical concepts, including folk taxonomies; (2) techniques of protection, selection, planting, cultivation, collection, and harvesting; (3) techniques of processing, after collection or harvesting; (4) storage and preservation methods; (5) utilization or consumption techniques. In addition there are of course relevant or correlative features of general technology, economics, settlement patterns, social organization, religion and mythology, and so forth.

While I think the time has come for ethnographers, archaeologists, geographers, and historians to make an intensive effort to sort out and specify the cultural variables involved in the care, modification, and use of plants and plant products by human societies everywhere, I am not prepared myself to search the vast quantity of pertinent literature. Rather, I want to examine here one narrow example: the shifting associations of processing and utilization techniques with three species in one relatively restricted culture-area over a period of about 450 years[1].

The region involved is the West Indies, especially the Greater Antilles— the islands of Puerto Rico, Jamaica, Hispaniola (present-day Haiti and the Dominican Republic), and Cuba—with some attention to some of the Lesser Antilles (Dominica, Barbados, St. Vincent, the Virgin Islands, and the Grenadines). When the Spanish arrived here in the 1490s, the Greater Antilles, except for a few corners, were densely populated by groups of Arawakan-speaking Indians largely sharing the same culture; for convenience I refer to these as "Taino", without distinguishing the closely similar "Sub-Taino". This label is unambiguous, even though it may be etymologically inappropriate as Sauer has recently objected[2]—his suggested replacement, "(Island) Arawak", is inappropriate because of possible confusion with the culturally quite distinct Arawak of the South American mainland. The Lesser Antilles were occupied by a different cultural group for whom the label "Island-Carib" has become standardized (the men's form of speech here contained many Carib loan words, yet the language, like Taino, belonged to the Arawak rather than the Carib family).

Although many islands in the Lesser Antilles were depopulated early in the colonial period, social and cultural continuity with the aborigines has been maintained through two surviving Island-Carib groups, one on Dominica and the other, displaced, in British Honduras. The Taino population of the Greater Antilles was almost entirely destroyed within thirty years of Columbus's first discovery, and the few remnants were rapidly assimilated, genetically, socially, and culturally, into the newly-forming creole societies of European and African origin which replaced the Indians. Despite what was a biological and cultural disaster, there is a surprising continuity of Indian cultural traits. This is most evident in the names and uses for domesticated and wild plants, where even modern ethnographic data often help us to interpret and fill out the description of aboriginal culture which can be reconstructed from documentary and archaeological sources. Of course, many new plants and new techniques were introduced in the subsequent centuries; but this has been a long period of documented history through which many of the changes can be traced in detail.

The dense and highly developed neolithic-level aboriginal Taino population was primarily supported by intensive agriculture, probably of the swidden type[3]. The crops belonged to that tropical South American complex which emphasized vegetative reproduction and the use of roots (in the ordinary rather than the technical botanical sense of this last word)[4]. The most important were *Manihot esculenta* (manioc) and *Ipomoea batatas* (sweet-potato). Other "root" crops were *Xanthosoma sagittifolium* (yautía, an aroid), *Calathea allouia* (lirén, of the arrowroot family), and probably a species of *Canna*. Maize was present but of secondary importance, as were the other seed crops normally found with it in the aboriginal New World: one or more beans (probably *Phaseolus lunatus* and *P. vulgaris*) and a squash or pumpkin (perhaps *Cucurbita moschata*). Other domesticated food plants included *Capsicum* sp(p). (red pepper), *Arachis hypogaea* (peanut), and, in Jamaica but not Hispaniola, *Ananas comosus* (pineapple). Many other plants were used for food or other purposes, and several of these were domesticated. However, there is often doubt as to species identification and degree of domestication. In recent centuries many important domesticates originating in tropical Africa and South-east Asia have been introduced, among them bananas, yams, taro, sugar cane, millet, ackee, mango, and breadfruit. Many utilization techniques have also changed, partly through influences from European, West African, and non-Antillean American Indian cultures.

Manioc

Manioc is today an important food crop in most parts of the tropical world. All other species of its genus are wild plants of the American tropics. *Manihot esculenta* Crantz is usually supposed to have first been domesticated in north-eastern South America; the principal botanical specialist on the plant now thinks that Mexico-Guatemala is at least as likely to have been the centre of origin. The starch-rich tubers of this plant contain varying amounts of a toxic cyanogenetic glycoside. Those varieties which have little, or where it is concentrated in the rind which is removed in peeling, are called "sweet"; varieties with higher amounts more evenly distributed are called "bitter" and require special processing techniques to remove or render the poison harmless. Formerly, the sweet varieties were distinguished as *M. aipi*, *M. dulcis*, or *M. palmata*, and the bitter ones as *M. utilissima*. It is now known that the toxicity is not associated with morphological features of the plant, and that it often varies with soil and climatic conditions and the age of the plant. All varieties are now considered to belong to one species, *M. esculenta*[5].

The methods which the Taino were using to prepare food from bitter manioc when Europeans first arrived in the sixteenth century can be specified with some certainty, using descriptions by contemporary Spanish observers[6], comparative data on modern South American Indian ethnography, a little archaeological evidence, and survivals into modern times of artifacts and terminology among the non-Indian successor populations of the West Indies.

The Taino raised manioc in large hills constructed in swidden fields. An important characteristic of the plant is that, like many wild crops but unlike most cultigens, storage techniques are relatively unimportant because it can be harvested over a very long period. Thus the tubers were taken out of the ground with a digging stick as they were needed, anywhere from ten months to three years after the cuttings had first been planted[7]. These tubers were then peeled with mussel or scallop shells, and pulped by grating. A grater made from a stone covered with shark skin yielded a finer flour for a better quality bread, called "jaujau"; in nineteenth-century Cuba a board sheathed in shark skin was still used as a grater, and the finest bread was known there into the present century as "casabe de levisa", "shark cassava"[8]. Pulp for the ordinary bread, "casábi", was more coarsely grated. Here there are some difficulties in determining the nature of the graters. Judging from comparative evidence[9] one would expect a grater made from a board with inset stone chips (or, less likely, with inset or carved wooden points, or inset fish bones, thorns, or teeth), and there are indeed archaeological examples of two-handled hardwood graters with inset stone chips from Hispaniola and Cuba, and the type survived into modern times in Cuba, Puerto Rico, and Dominica[10]. In addition, monolithic basalt graters with one face roughened by pecking are relatively common in Hispaniola archaeology (although they do not occur in Cuba); this type seems unnecessarily difficult to construct, but it is partially paralleled by graters of rough granite slabs documented for South America[11]. But neither of these types is unequivocally described in sixteenth-century written sources on the Taino. The only detailed early description (of a type other than the one covered with shark skin) is difficult to understand: Las Casas tells us that the Indians grate manioc roots "on some rough stones on a kind of frame, which they call guariqueten, the penultima short, which they make of poles and canes placed as a base for some palm leaves or coverings, which are like deer skins; finally, in this way they grate it in a trough so that the mass does not fall"[12]. Does "rough stones" refer to a monolithic or stone-chip grater (as the archaeological and comparative ethnographic evidence would imply), used in a trough made of, or set on, a basketry and palm leaf mat? Or is this a grater made of stone chips set in a basketry framework, perhaps tied or stuffed with palm fibre (a more logical interpretation, but a type otherwise entirely unknown), and used in a (presumably wooden) trough? With Las Casas' "guariquetén" should be compared with the modern Puerto Rican Spanish term "guariquitín", meaning "a plaited cane bed used by the poor"; the same word occurs in the Dominican Republic, as "guarequetén" or "guariquitén", but here defined as a large wooden vessel for grated manioc pulp—by an author who also cites the pertinent passage in Las Casas, making one wonder whether his definition applies to modern usage or is an interpretation of Las Casas' ambiguous description[13].

In any case, the grated pulp was next left overnight in a trough covered with palm leaves. The next day it was stuffed into cylindrical basketry presses, loosely plaited of palm leaves or tree bark, seven to nine feet long and the diameter of a man's arm or thigh, with a "handle" on each end. This artifact, here called "sibucán", is clearly the same as the diagonally-twilled basketry manioc press with a loop on each end, usually called "tipití" in the literature on South America where it is still widespread[14]. One end of this press was suspended from a tree branch, and weight applied to the other end

—either several stones hung from it, or two or three women seated on the outer end of a pole some twelve feet long run through the lower loop of the press with the inner end inserted in a hole low in the trunk of the tree from which the press was hung. As the press stretched, the juice, called "hyen", was expressed through the interstices of the basketry. Untreated, this juice was poisonous, and there are records of its use by Cuban and Hispaniola Indians in committing suicide. Boiled to eliminate the poison, the juice was used as a sauce for flavouring other dishes. The modern Dominica Island-Carib settle out starch from the milky fresh expressed juice, and either return this to the meal or use it to make fine cassava cakes; the Taino may also have done this, for there is a sixteenth-century mention of "anaiboa" as manioc "flour" from which a fine porridge, "like blanc-mange", was made with milk, while in modern Cuban Spanish "naiboa" is the term for the white, starch-bearing expressed manioc juices, and a related term, "anaiboa", "naiboa", or "neiboa" today means "sticky" in the Dominican Republic[15].

The damp pulp from which the poison had been removed by pressing, was sifted through the "hibís", a basketry sieve made from thin strips of cane, in order to break up the larger lumps and remove fibres and ungrated bits. The sifted pulp or flour was placed on a hot "burén", a large circular flat pottery griddle an inch or so thick, attached with clay or mud to three or four stones supporting it over a fire. The damp meal coagulated with the heat and the cakes thus formed were turned over with thin wooden paddles after cooking for about fifteen minutes on one side, to cook on the other. For ordinary casábi, the meal was spread over the burén to a depth of an inch and a half, leaving an inch or two space around the rim; the finished cake was about a third of an inch thick. The jaujau type was spread much thinner. When removed from the griddle the cakes were flexible, but they became very hard after drying in the sun for several hours to a day or two, and would then last two or three years if kept dry. Before eating the cake was broken up with the fingers and the bits softened by dipping in a pot of liquid.

The Spanish in the Antilles rapidly adopted cassava as a staple food and substitute for wheat bread, and before 1550 they had introduced screw presses to Hispaniola as more efficient substitutes for the basketry sibucán[16]. From very early in the colonial period Jamaica was especially important as a centre of production and export of cassava[17]. In the seventeenth century many of the French colonists in the Lesser Antilles also preferred cassava to European wheat bread. Here the roots were pulped on graters of pierced copper a foot and a half long and eight or ten inches broad, attached to a board, with the lower end resting in a vessel. An improved tool was also in use: a large wheel with the grater on the circumference, crank-turned by two Negro slaves while a third applied the roots (an almost identical rotary grater was also replacing the manual grater in Brazil by 1648, among those who could afford it)[18]. The pulp was pressed in two ways: placed in cloth sacks squeezed beneath a pole with one end inserted in a hole in a tree (a stump is illustrated) and stone weights placed on the opposite forked end, which took seven or eight hours, or else, more commonly, the juice was expressed in an hour by placing the pulp in a wooden "canot" some four feet long, one and a half feet wide, and three feet deep, with holes in the sides and a fitted board lid on which were placed stones pressed down by a similar forked branch. The pressed flour was passed through an Indian-made basketry sieve called "hebechet" (the term, "hébichet", and the artifact survive among the Dominica Island-Carib)[19]. A round cast-iron plate about a half inch thick (among the Indians, a pottery griddle) was heated over a fire. On this the sifted meal was spread about an inch thick, which was turned to cook on the other side after it had formed a cake, then removed and sun dried (Pl. IV A)[20]. A similar process was used in the 1730s and 1740s to produce "le pain des Negres & des Sauvages" in Haiti: the roots were pulped on a copper grater, pressed for twenty-four hours to remove the poisonous juice, and cooked as flat thin cakes on an iron plate[21].

There are also good eighteenth-century descriptions of Jamaican techniques. Here the roots were washed, scraped, pulped on an iron grater in a tub or trough, then pressed in hair, linen, or palmetto bags placed on flat stones and squeezed with a plank inserted in a notch in a tree trunk with weights on the other end. The "farine" or "farina" was then dried in the sun, pounded in a large wooden mortar, and baked over a fire on "a flat, broad round iron, commonly called a baking-stone", "bestrewed with the sifted meal to whatever size or thickness people pleased to have the cakes made: this agglutinates as it heats, grows gradually harder, and when thoroughly baked, is a wholesome well-tasted bread" which was eaten buttered while hot or used in puddings. A similar process was evidently used in Barbados. The expressed juice was boiled, the viscous scum skimmed off, and the remainder diluted with water and drunk or used as a sauce. The scrapings from the fresh roots of bitter manioc were applied for the treatment of ulcers. The poisonous juice as it fermented became infested with "worms" called "topuea"; these the Indians and Negroes dried and powdered and stealthily transferred, as a supposedly deadly poison, from beneath the poisoner's thumb-nail to a victim's food bowl[22].

In the modern West Indies, manioc roots are processed in two ways. One of these is a direct descendant of the Indian and Colonial method; essentially the same techniques are described for Cuba, Jamaica, Puerto Rico, and the French islands[23]. The roots are washed and peeled, then pulped by rubbing them against a rapidly revolving circular grater. The pulp is placed in bags or baskets and pressed to remove the juice—in Jamaica, at least, with the simple lever press of a plank with one end inserted in a notched tree trunk and the other end weighted with rocks, resting on the basket of pulp on a pile of stones. The meal is sifted to remove fibres and ungrated bits, then cooked on flat metal plates over a fire, constantly stirred to yield cassava meal or formed in flat cakes which bake into cassava bread. One type of tapioca is obtained by settling the starch out of the expressed juice, decanting the fluid and heating the starch on flat pans until the individual grains burst and then coagulate into tapioca pellets. Boiling the juice into a syrupy consistency destroys its poison, and it is then used as a peppery sauce known as "cassareep".

The second process yields starch for industrial purposes or for two forms of tapioca; the same technique is used also in Brazil, Malaya, and elsewhere. It involves machinery of varying complexity, but the process is basically the same everywhere: "it is a wet milling process, water being used to convey the starch throughout the system and to wash away impurities. Briefly, it involves washing the roots to remove foreign matter, destroying their cellular structure so as to liberate the starch, screening off the fibrous material, separating the starch from the water-soluble impurities and protein by gravitational means [decanting the fluid], and drying"[24]. The result is known as cassava starch or tapioca flour. Flake tapioca is produced by heating the damp starch on metal plates until the starch grains swell and coagulate into irregular flakes; to make pearl tapioca, the damp starch is shaken on a cloth frame to form it into pellets, then toasted on metal plates[25].

A very simple variant process is used in the Jamaican countryside, where the pulp from scraped and grated roots is mixed with water, "strained through a towel held by two persons", the milky liquid collected beneath and settled for an hour or two, and the water poured off leaving the starch which is either dried briefly, salted, and baked into "pot bammie", or dried several days, broken up in a mortar, sifted, mixed with flour, and cooked into "dumplings"[26].

Manioc is an extremely important food crop in Africa, where it was evidently introduced from Brazil in the latter sixteenth century. But the American utilization techniques did not travel with the plant: the grater is rare and the tipití absent; manioc starch and tapioca are usually unknown and cassareep is nowhere prepared[27].

On the other hand, the method for removing starch from grated manioc pulp by washing it and settling out the starch grains is not recorded from the Greater Antilles during the contact period or immediately after, and was undoubtedly introduced there by the Spanish. It is an ancient European method for getting starch from wheat[28], and this may well be the source. It might also be a European introduction of an Amazonian Indian process, for Brazilian Indians in the seventeenth century got "vipeba" or "farinha fresca" by settling from water in which manioc roots had soaked for four or five days[29]. Historical investigations of early South American Indian techniques are required, and the Antillean data warn us not to project modern ethnographic information back into the past without using the historical sources which are available.

Arrowroot

True arrowroot, *Maranta arundinacea*, is an herbaceous perennial with rhizomes rich in starch. These are however covered with scales containing an acrid or bitter substance which must be carefully peeled off before use, and the cellular structure of the rhizomes is so tough that more thorough grinding or maceration to release the starch grains is required than is the case with manioc[30].

All species in the genus are American, and *M. arundinacea* itself occurs wild in Brazil, northern South America, and perhaps Central America. It is now widespread in cultivation throughout the tropics of both hemispheres[31]. However, although many tribes of the South American tropical forest have cultivated it in recent times as a food plant[32], the history of its domestication has not yet been investigated and we cannot be sure that it was cultivated anywhere by pre-Columbian Indians.

The species is frequently listed in modern sources as one of the plants cultivated by the aboriginal Taino. This is an error; correcting the record by an examination of how the mistake became established, and stating the evidence against the supposition, provides a simple example of the necessity for returning to original sources for the history of domestication.

The best way to identify the plants which the sixteenth-century Spanish sources mentioned as used by the Taino, is to compare the morphological characterizations of the early writers with modern botanists' descriptions, and to compare the early Taino names with modern Antillean Spanish popular plant terminology and its referents. The latter is nearly always the crucial point, for the early authors' plant descriptions are usually inadequate, while the Taino names they give for useful plants, wild or cultivated, were mostly adopted by the Spanish invaders.

The early accounts describe two West Indian plants which modern authors have erroneously identified as arrowroot. One of these is the "lirén" or "llerén", said to be a cultivated plant with a starchy root which was eaten raw or cooked[33]. This was definitely *Calathea allouia*, for the description of the plant fits this species well enough and the same uses and the same or similar names are attested for it in the modern Antilles: "llerén, lerén, lirén, lairén", or "leirén", in Puerto Rico, Cuba, and the Dominican Republic[34]. Botanists agree with this equation, but the anthropologists Lovén and Friederici were misled by the older synonym *Maranta allouya* into thinking that the plant was *M. arundinacea*, and this misidentification was followed by Roumain and Rouse. The same error was made by Sapper, who even added "hier heimisch". Sauer pointed out that the early descriptions of lirén "clearly" do not refer to *M. arundinacea* "but may refer to *Calathea allouia*", yet he left the question open and has recently included arrowroot in a list of aboriginal Antillean domesticates under the name "ararú" (see below on this term)[35].

The other plant sometimes identified as arrowroot is one which Peter Martyr called "cabaióes" and merely described as "like onions"; Oviedo wrote the same Taino name as "cauallos", which he says resemble the lirén but are somewhat larger, "grow in poor and thin soils. . . . [and are] wholesome food and enjoyed by the Indians. It is a wild fruit and it comes up and grows through the care of nature alone"[36]. The last point would seem to eliminate *M. arundinacea*, which does not occur wild in the Greater Antilles except as an escape from cultivation[37]. Probably this was a species of *Canna*; *Xanthosoma violaceum* has also been suggested, but this seems less probable if Oviedo's "like lirén" means the whole plant, rather than just its edible underground portion[38].

These are evidently the only contact-period descriptions which might refer to arrowroot. Furthermore, it is surely significant that nowhere today does a Taino name for it survive. The common names in use are all (with one barely possible exception) of clearly post-Columbian application. In Spanish-speaking areas the plant is usually known as "yuquilla" ("little manioc") or "sagú" ("sago", a term of Malayo-Polynesian origin); other names are "raíz americana" ("American root"), "maranta", "salop" or "salep" or "sulup", and "touola" or "tulola"[39]—only the last is of unknown origin, and it does not occur in the sixteenth-century literature. The French name "herbe aux flèches" is apparently a loan-translation from a now-lost Island-Carib name. The most common term is the English "arrowroot" and its derivatives, Spanish "arrurruz", Portuguese "araruta", Dutch "arraroot" or "arrowroot" or "pijlwortel", German "Pfeilwurz", and a great variety of terms used in South-east Asian languages whose shapes are so close to the English word that this must be their ultimate source[40]. Martius suggested that the English term is derived by folk etymology from mainland Arawak "aru-aru", "starch of starch" ("aru" or "haru" being the name for both manioc and moriche palm starch)[41]; but as we shall see, the signification of the English name is clear enough so that its resemblance to Arawak must be coincidental. Bartlett, on the other hand, tentatively suggested that the English name derives from "araru" or a similar form in an Indonesian language[42], although the American origin of the plant plus the etymology of the English name means that the direction of borrowing was just the reverse of what Bartlett suggests.

The earliest recognizable description of the plant in the West Indies was published by du Tertre in 1654. According to him, soon after a French governor had made peace with them in 1641 the Island-Caribs, evidently largely from Dominica, brought to him in Guadeloupe "une plante qu'ils appelloient en leur langue, l'herbe aux flèches (ie n'ay pû retenir le mot Sauvage)". The leaves and flowers of this plant as described by du Tertre agree well with modern botanists' characterizations of *Maranta arundinacea*. Unfortunately he does not say whether the Indians cultivated the plant. But he does specify that "the savages value this plant highly, and not without considerable reason; because we discovered by everyday experience the rare and admirable qualities which it possesses: its root pounded and applied to wounds of arrows poisoned with manchineel [*Hippomane manchinella*], entirely allays the venom and even stops incipient gangrene, relieves all kinds of inflammation, as also the swelling caused by stings of the wasps of Guadeloupe, which is rather dangerous"[43]. A similar source is indicated by Sir Hans Sloane, who in 1696 described "Indian arrow root" under the Latin phrase Canna Indica radice alba alexipharmaca, adding that he had seen the plant in 1687–8 in gardens in Jamaica and other Caribbean islands and had heard that it grew wild in Dominica; he also cited a description by Gómara, first published in 1552–3, which merely says that the Caribs of Santa Marta in Colombia used "the juice of the root" of an undescribed plant as an antidote for poisoned arrow wounds, for blindness, and for curing the evil-eye. In 1707 Sloane described the plant at greater length—a description recognized by modern botanists as referring to *Maranta arundinacea*—summarized du Tertre's account of its properties, and added:

> This plant was first brought from the Island *Dominica*, by Colonel *James Walker*, to *Barbados*, and there planted. From hence it was sent to *Jamaica*, being very much esteem'd for its Alexipharmack qualities. That Gentleman observed the Native *Indians* used the Root of this Plant with success, against the Poison of their Arrows, by only mashing and applying it to the poison'd wounds.[44]

According to Barham, a Jamaica physician writing before 1711, the plant Sloane labelled Canna Indica was called "arrow root" because it was first known as an Indian antidote for poisoned arrow wounds, for which the juice was taken internally and the bruised root was used as a poultice on the wound. "This was discovered by an Indian, taken after he had wounded an European with one of these poisoned arrows, whom they tortured until he promised to cure him, which he did effectually with the root of this plant." Barham cited two cures by applications of the bruised root, of bites by a poisonous black spider, one on the finger and another a woman bitten "at the necessary-house, upon the buttock", and a case of accidental poisoning in which two or three men died but one was saved by drinking two glasses of juice from bruised arrowroot root. He also considered arrowroot an efficacious remedy for several other ills:

> I have seen this root frequently given in malignant fevers with great success, when all other things have failed. When I make up *lapis contrayerva* for my own practice, I always put in a good quantity of it. I have given it decocted, but it is best in powder, which causes sweat; the dose is from a drachm to two. . . . It hath no manner of ill taste or smell; it works by sweat and urine, and yet it is a great cordial; it provokes the terms, and clears lying-in women; it drives out the small-pox or measles; and if it was

candied as eringo-root, it would make a pleasant preserve, for it possesses the like prolific virtues.[45]

Before 1750 arrowroot was also used medicinally in Barbados—"the juice of this [root] is exceeding cold, and, being mixed with Water, and drunk, is looked upon to be a Preservative against any Poison of an hot Nature"—but also "out of this Root is made likewise the finest starch, far excelling any made with Wheat" and this latter is the earliest mention of a non-medicinal use. By 1774 in Jamaica, although still used chiefly as a medicine, the roots were also "washed, dried, and reduced to an impalpable powder" which "makes an excellent starch; and has been used as a *succedaneum* for the common sort", and the plant is one of a list of "wholesome and palatable viands". The first description of the method of converting the roots into starch was published in 1787. Relying on his own observations in Jamaica, William Wright described *Maranta arundinacea* as a plant of the "gardens and provision grounds", the year-old roots of which were dug, washed, "and then beaten in large deep wooden mortars to a pulp" which was thoroughly stirred in water in a large tub. The fibrous parts were removed and discarded, and the milky water strained through "a hair sieve, or coarse cloth". The starch was settled out, the supernatant water drained off, and the starch remaining rewashed and settled again, then "finally dried on sheets in the sun". Wright does not mention the uses of this starch, although "a decoction of the fresh roots makes an excellent ptisan in acute diseases". Somewhat later, arrowroot starch was described as used in Jamaica as "a warm alexipharmic", to "resist the force of poisons", and "administered in infusions to the sick", but also "it has been sometimes known to be used for food when other provisions were scarce"[46].

Although specimens of arrowroot seeds were first sent to England (from Mexico) before 1732, the first large shipment of starch, presumably from Barbados or Jamaica, is dated 1799. Shortly thereafter, the starch in milk was recommended as an infant food, having "lately been introduced into England". Its use here is illustrated by the fact that a writer in 1846 cited Barham and Wright in order to suggest that a plant known in England as a source of edible starch might also be useful as an antidote for poisons. In the same year a French pharmacologist noted that what the English called "Indian arrow-root" had been imported from Jamaica for a dozen years or so, that he had determined this starch to be exactly the same as that of "*Maranta arundinacea* cultivated in the other Antilles", and the plant had also been transported to India where it was grown for commercial starch. In fact, it may have been grown for starch in Bengal as early as 1813 (although there are Old World plants, such as *Tacca pinnatifida*, which have also been called "arrow root")[47].

In 1823 a Danish pharmacist in St. Croix, Virgin Islands, reported that arrowroot was there grown for its starch which had long been generally used as a household and hospital remedy "against catarrhal illness, diarrhoea, dysentery, and in every other illness where mucilaginous remedies are employed" (use as an antidote not being mentioned), and that it was considered a household necessity as a sick food (mixed with Madeira or Port, sugar, and cinnamon or nutmeg), for starching clothes, and as a substitute, presumably in puddings, for sago, tapioca, and "Persian salep". In St. Croix the starch was prepared by washing the roots after the scaly rind was removed, pulping them in a grating mill or by pounding in a stone mortar, mixing the pulp with water and pouring this through a sieve into a second vessel, repeatedly washing and sieving the mass remaining in the sieve, and settling the starch out of the mixture which passed through the sieve. After the supernatant water was poured off the settled starch, the latter was mixed with fresh water and again settled out, and this process of washing and settling was repeated until the supernatant water remained clean. The starch was finally spread out to dry in the sun. The resulting product, if properly washed and unadulterated, was preferred to manioc starch. "The [arrowroot] salop which is prepared on the Danish and English islands is generally unadulterated; that which comes from Puerto Rico, on the other hand, is uncleanly prepared and mixed with cassava and other kinds of starch, reportedly from bananas and plantains, potatoes, and other starch-bearing plants." During the 1830s there is another, briefer, report of arrowroot starch used in sick diets and for starching clothes in the Virgin Islands, a statement that the plant was grown in large quantities in a few localities in Cuba, and a report that small amounts were raised by Negroes in Antigua[48]. Thus before 1840 the plant was grown in English, Danish, French, and Spanish areas of the Antilles, and the starch was exported to Europe at least from English and French islands.

In the middle of the last century the chief exporters of arrowroot starch were Bermuda and St. Vincent. In Bermuda the roots were grated against a hand-operated wheel, the circumference of which was sheathed with a grating surface of punctured "tinned iron". The pulp was washed in a mechanically turned cylindrical sieve, the starch settled out, rewashed and sifted several times, and the caked starch broken up and dried in the sun. Although a few years before 1845 all mills in Bermuda were hand-operated, in that year a large establishment used horse-driven machinery, and about 400,000 lb. of starch per year were produced on the island. In the same year the methods used in St. Vincent were well described. Here the roots were peeled by hand, ground to a pulp in a mill consisting of two pairs of brass rollers, and the starch washed from the pulp in large copper cylinders with sieve bottoms containing rotating paddles driven by a water wheel. The starchy water was strained, settled, washed and resettled several times, and the starch sediment finally sun dried and packed. This latter method was in use in Bermuda by the 1880s. In St. Vincent the initial peeling was abandoned, and a rotating cylinder set with saw blades replaced the brass rollers[49].

Arrowroot has been cultivated for its starch, sometimes for export, in many places in recent years: especially in various West Indian islands and in Bermuda, but also in Brazil, the Guianas, Mexico, West Africa, Natal, Madagascar, Mauritius, Réunion, India, Ceylon, mainland South-east Asia, Indonesia, the Philippines, and Guam[50]. Apparently only in South-east Asia are the whole rhizomes used as food, prepared by boiling or roasting[51] (probably harvested young so as not to be too woody, although the starch content is also lower then).

However, large scale cultivation of the plant survives only in St. Vincent in the Lesser Antilles, which has exported some five to ten million pounds of starch yearly over at least the last thirty years, over two-thirds of each year's export going to the United States, under one-third to the United Kingdom, and the remainder mostly to other West Indian islands. In the most modern starch factory in St. Vincent, the roots are first washed, then cut into bits which are rasped and crushed to a pulp which is mixed with water and passed in a continuous flow on to vibrating sieves; the residue on the sieves is re-crushed and re-sieved twice; the "starch milk" which passes through the sieves is pumped into a centrifuge separator, the starch from this is washed, sieved through fine wire cloth, and re-centrifuged, and the resulting starch is mixed in water with sulphurous acid (which retards fermentation) and then settled in tanks from which the supernatant water is later drained, the top layer of the sediment hosed away to remove the remaining fibres, and the starch finally dried in a mechanical steam drier. The starch is exported as an ingredient (sometimes a minor one) for arrowroot biscuits, and for use in puddings and dietetic foods; some arrowroot starch is used as a face powder base and in glues[52].

Earlier uses have survived in West Indian folk medicine: the roots are pounded for poultices for wounds and ulcers in Dominica, and washed, grated, and boiled to make a gruel for treating diarrhoea in Jamaica; in the Grenadines arrowroot is even still used as an antidote for manchineel poison-ing, not of course from poisoned arrows, but a suspension of the starch taken internally when the fruit has been eaten and starch poultices applied to external burns from manchineel juice[53].

The historical development in the West Indies seems clear: an Indian antidote for poisoned arrow wounds, adopted by non-Indians as an antidote for other poisons then extended to other medicinal uses, then used as a food for the sick at about the same time as it became a source of starch for other purposes with starch gaining techniques very likely transferred from those used with manioc.

Zamia

Zamia, the most widespread and variable of the New World cycad genera, consists of twenty to thirty poorly understood species ranging from peninsular

Florida through the Greater Antilles, southern Mexico, Central America, and northern South America as far as the Mato Grosso of Brazil. The plants have a crown of pinnate evergreen leaves ranging up to a metre or more in length which spring from a short cylindrical or tuberous stem. This starch-rich stem sometimes weighs several pounds, and is subterranean in all the eight or so closely similar Antillean species. Evidently the stems, leaves, and seeds of all species are poisonous—probably a toxic glycoside is involved; the variety of production techniques shows that either fermentation or washing of the pulped stems eliminates or reduces the toxicity sufficiently to allow human consumption[54].

The fundamental source for the identification of *Zamia* as a plant used by the Taino is Las Casas' sixteenth-century account of Hispaniola. His description of "guáyaga" is a good characterization of the *Zamia* plant: "the roots are like fat squills; the shoots and leaves which come from them out of the ground, about two or three spans [long], somewhat resemble the dwarf fan-palms of Andalusia, although they are narrower and smoother and more delicate than those of the dwarf fan-palm". The identification is clinched by the name (reported also by an earlier source, as "guaiega" described as "round roots . . . like truffles, and larger"), which survives as a name for *Zamia* in the modern Dominican Republic in the form "guayiga" or "guáyiga". Another name, "guáyaro" and variants, is given by Las Casas and others for a wild "root" eaten by the Indians of Hispaniola; this may also have been *Zamia*, since one early source describes its preparation as strikingly like that used for guáyaga, and since variants of "guáyaro" survive today in Cuba as names for *Zamia*. However, in modern Puerto Rico the latter name is applied to a wild yam, *Rajania cordata*, and both Las Casas and Peter Martyr seem to distinguish the two names as referring to different plants in early Hispaniola[55].

According to Las Casas, the guáyaga was an important food resource of the Taino of the Higuey region of Hispaniola. They collected the stems from wild plants, grated them "on some rocks rough like rasps" (presumably monolithic or stone-chip graters), and shaped the pulp into balls which were put in the sun for one to three days until they began to rot and became blackish and wormy. The balls were then flattened into small cakes which were baked on a clay griddle supported with stones over a fire (evidently the burén used for cooking cassava)—"and if it is eaten before it becomes black and is not full of or with some or many worms, the eaters will die".

The historical connections between the Indian preparation of *Zamia* in Hispaniola and the modern methods there and elsewhere in the Antilles are most readily traced through eighteenth-century descriptions of Puerto Rican methods. Two processes were used along the south coast of that island, where *Zamia* was a food of the poor and in times of famine: the stems were grated, the pulp allowed to rot in water, then dried and sifted, and formed into small leaf-wrapped loaves roasted on hot coals, which were black when eaten or;

else the grated pulp was piled to rot, breed worms, and dry out into a dark red mass which was then ground to a powder and shaped into small loaves[56]. A similar process is reported for the mid-nineteenth century: the pulp from grating was heaped up and covered with banana leaves for three or four days while it fermented and worms grew in the interior; the mass was then broken open and the worms gradually "disappeared" as it dried into a coarse, dark flour, which was ground up and used to make small loaves. But by this time *Zamia* was also used here for starch production with techniques probably transferred from those used to gain manioc starch: the stems were washed and grated, the pulp stirred in water and the liquid strained through a cloth or sieve, the starch settled out and rewashed two or three times before being sun dried. The starch was used only for starching clothes. The pulp and juice from grating and the wash-water from starch production were all used to treat sores, ulcers, and buboes[57]. Today wild *Zamia* still yields a scarcity food in parts of Puerto Rico, where the peeled stems are grated on a tin grater, the pulp being caught in a bowl of salted water and then squeezed dry in a rag, salt added, and formed into small leaf-wrapped loaves which are baked in ashes[58]. The rotting stage which provided the main link with Indian methods has been dropped, although the use of the pulp for small leaf-wrapped loaves eaten in times of food scarcity has persisted at least since the eighteenth century.

For the Dominican Republic we have only nineteenth- and twentieth-century reports of the use of *Zamia*. Soldiers of the French army besieged in the city of Santo Domingo in 1808 presumably heard that bread could be made from the plant, for they attempted to transfer the techniques they knew for making cassava, but with fatal results because squeezing the juice out of *Zamia* pulp will not remove the poison. We have two good accounts of the preparation of starch from wild *Zamia* here, a brief one dated 1872 and a very full one from 1952–4. The stems are washed, peeled (now, but not in the nineteenth century), and grated on a piece of sheet metal roughened with nail holes and loosely attached to a wooden paddle. The pulp is then washed three times in a burlap sieve suspended from four posts, the starch-bearing water settled for twenty-four hours and decanted leaving the starch which is rewashed and strained through broadcloth, and finally settled again. The starch is dried for several days suspended in cloth wrappings which are occasionally twisted and squeezed. The remaining hard ball is broken apart and spread out during a final sun drying. The starch is mainly sold in the cities for starching clothes (in the nineteenth century it was also exported to Curaçao and St. Thomas for the same purpose). But some of it is eaten, combined with various ingredients in several recipes, although leaf-wrapped loaves are not reported from this island. Here there is no survival of the aboriginal Hispaniola processing techniques, but simply continuity in the food use of the same wild plant[59].

Zamia starch was sold in Jamaica markets in the early nineteenth century, some of it evidently imported from the nearby Cayman Islands[60]. It is still used for food in the Caymans, a clear porridge being made from starch extracted by grating on perforated tin graters, washing the pulp, and settling the starch from the wash water[61]. In western Jamaica *Zamia* grows wild, but it is also cultivated to some extent in household gardens—the only report from the Antilles of cultivation of the genus for food or starch. Two other starch-yielding plants, tous-les-mois (*Canna* sp.) and arrowroot, are also grown here, and the starch gaining process is the same for all three: the stems are peeled, washed, and grated on a metal grater perforated with nail holes; water is added to the pulp which is then squeezed in a cloth, and the starch-bearing water collected in a bowl where the starch settles out. The water is then poured off, and salt and lime juice added to the starch to bleach it before it is dried in the sun. It is eaten as a gruel, cooked with water, milk, and sugar[62].

For Cuba we have only brief statements in the nineteenth and twentieth centuries that starch was extracted from *Zamia* stems by grating, washing, settling, and drying, and was used for starching clothes, for industrial purposes, and to make a sweetmeat. In eastern Cuba, the starch (?) of *Zamia* is also used in medicinal baths[63]. There are only brief references, beginning in 1838, for the use of *Zamia* starch as food and for starching clothes in the Bahamas[64].

Conclusion

We have examined first a true cultigen of aboriginal times, taken over by the European and African settlers of the West Indies; second, a plant only doubtfully aboriginally domesticated and that not in the Greater Antilles but introduced there from the Lesser Antilles by Europeans; and third, a wild plant of the region used by both Indians and their successors. All three have starch-rich "roots" which are not used for food after simple cooking, but rather require special preparation techniques either because they are toxic or because they are tough and woody, or both.

The aboriginal preparation techniques for bitter manioc and *Zamia* were quite different, although they shared two artifacts, the grater and the burén. Both are toxic; with manioc, the poison was removed by squeezing out the juice, whereas with *Zamia* it was removed by fermentation. The Europeans introduced a new technique for gaining starch, by washing the pulp and settling the starch out of the wash-water. This technique was apparently first applied to manioc, from which it was transferred to *Zamia*. In the latter case the new method also was an effective substitute for fermentation as the means for eliminating the toxicity of the root. Thus the preparation techniques for both plants changed, yet remained at least as similar to each other; in recent folk usage they still share a similar grater, and now also the washing and settling technique, but the burén has been dropped from *Zamia* preparation methods. The Europeans also introduced a new plant, arrowroot, at first not for its starch but for medicinal purposes adopted with the plant from the Indians of the Lesser Antilles. Once adopted the use changed, starch for food and other purposes being gained from the roots by techniques transferred from those used with manioc. One result was that the new plant was incorporated into the peasant agricultural repertoire to such an extent that modern anthropologists have erroneously assumed that it, like the manioc its uses now resemble, is a survival of a Taino domesticated food plant.

This case-history demonstrates—what is not in doubt, but is often overlooked—that there need not be a constant association between plants, the artifacts used in their preparation, and the uses made of the products. The use of the burén or griddle in the preparation of a product from a wild plant is perhaps relevant to the interpretation of archaeological pottery griddles as evidence on the history of manioc domestication. The change from a medicinal to a food use of one of these plants reminds us that any ethnobotanical field study shows a remarkable number of non-food uses of plants, for medicine, for the manufacture of artifacts, and for a wide variety of other purposes (e.g. personal adornment and perfume; weights and measures; punk and tinder; fish poisoning; various symbolic, magical, and religious associations). Any of these uses may be the basis for domestication or selection, even though ultimately a plant may be used mainly or entirely as a source of food.

The West Indies, as the first site of modern European colonial expansion, may be unusual in the extent of historical documentation available. But in much of Africa, Asia, and Oceania, as well as the New World, there are also historical records covering several centuries. Too often, modern ethnographic data are used to interpret the archaeological evidence in regions where historical documents would help to peel off the major recent changes due directly or indirectly to this European expansion.

Notes

1 This paper is part of a long-term study of the historical economic botany of the Antilles and Florida; in particular, the section on *Zamia* is a summary of the Antillean chapter of a monograph to deal with the utilization history of this genus throughout its range. The author is especially indebted to S. W. Mintz, the late J. M. Goggin, and J. W. Thieret, for bibliographic and other suggestions.

2 Saucer, C. O. (1966). *The Early Spanish Main.* Berkeley and Los Angeles. pp. 37, 185–6.

3 Sturtevant, W. C. (1961). Taino agriculture *in* J. Wilbert (ed.) The evolution of horticultural systems in native South America, *Antropológica Supplement Public*, **2**, Caracas: Soc. de Ciencias Naturales La Salle, pp. 69–82; Sauer, C. O. (1966), op. cit., pp. 51–2, doubts it, but I still think that the scanty evidence points towards shifting rather than permanent fields.

4 For a valuable discussion of the contrast between the vegetative and seed complexes of New World agriculture, including hypotheses on the origins,

spread, and correlates of the vegetative type, see Sauer, C. O. (1959). Age and area of American cultivated plants, *Actas del XXXIII Congreso Internacional de Americanistas*, 1, pp. 215–29, San José.

5 Rogers, D. J. (1965). Some botanical and ethnological considerations of *Manihot esculenta*, *Econ. Bot.*, 19 (4), pp. 369–77; Johnson, R. M. and Raymond, W. D. (1965). The chemical composition of some tropical food plants IV. Manioc, *Tropical Science*, 7 (3), pp. 109–15; Chadha, Y. R. (1961). Sources of starch in Commonwealth territories III: Cassava, *Tropical Science*, 3 (3), pp. 101–13.

6 Especially Las Casas, B. de. (1909). Apologética historia de las Indias. *Historiadores de Indias*, 1. *Nueva Biblioteca de Autores Españoles* 13, pp. 29–31 (chapter 11); Oviedo y Valdés, G. F. de (1851). (1520–57) *Historia General y Natural de las Indias*, 1, Madrid: Real Academia de la Historia, pp. 269–71 (book 7, chapter 2); Cobo, B. (1890). (1653) *Historia del Nuevo Mundo*, 1. Sevilla. pp. 351–4 (book 4, chapter 7).

7 Sturtevant, W. C. (1961). ibid.

8 Pichardo, E. (1862). *Diccionario Provincial Casi-Razonado de Vozes Cubanas*. 3rd ed., Habana. p. 130; Suárez, C. (1921). *Vocabulario Cubano . . .* Habana. p. 121.

9 e.g., Nordenskiöld, E. (1919). An ethno-geographical analysis of the material culture of two Indian tribes in the Gran Chaco, *Comparative Ethnographical Studies*, 19, Göteborg, p. 79 and map 11; Roth, W. E. (1924). An introductory study of the arts, crafts, and customs of the Guiana Indians, *Bur. of Amer. Ethnol. Annual Rep.*, 38, pp. 277–80; Bennett, W. C. (1949). Household furniture, *in* Steward, J. H. (ed.) *Handbook of South American Indians*, 5, p. 26.

10 The archaeological examples: Fewkes, J. W. (1907). The aborigines of Porto Rico and neighboring islands, *Bur. of Amer. Ethnol. Annual Rep.*, 25, p. 194; Harrington, M. R. (1921). Cuba before Colombus, *Indian Notes and Monographs* [*Miscellaneous* 17], New York. p. 98 and pl. 6; Herrera Fritot, R. (1947). Tres tipos de objetos indoarqueológicos de Santo Domingo, *Revista de Arqueología y Etnología*, época 2, año 2, nums. 4–5, pp. 125–42, Habana, pp. 127, 137. The modern survivals: Pichardo, E. (1862). ibid.; Bachiller y Morales, A. ‖(1883). *Cuba Primitiva; origen, lenguas, tradiciones e historia de los indios de las Antilles Mayores y las Lucayas*. 2nd ed., Habana. p. 372; La Torre y Huerta, C. de. (1890). Conferencia científica. *Anales de la Real Academia de Ciencias Médicas, Físicas y Naturales de la Habana, Revista Científica*, 27, p. 328; Coll y Toste, C. (1907). *Prehistoria de Puerto-Rico*. San Juan. p. 250; Taylor, D. (1938). The Caribs of Dominica, *Anthropological Papers*, 3, *Bur. Amer. Ethnol. Bull.*, 119, p. 137.

11 Nordenskiöld, E. (1919). op. cit. pp. 82–4.

12 Las Casas, B. de. (1909). ibid.

13 Malaret, A. (1917). *Diccionario de provincialismos de Puerto Rico*. San Juan. p. 82; Malaret. (1946). *Diccionario de Americanismos*, 3rd ed., Buenos Aires. p. 454; Tejera, E. (1951). *Palabras Indíjenas de la Isla de Santo Domingo* (con adiciones por Emilio Tejera, prólogo de Pedro Henríquez Ureña). Ciudad Trujillo. p. 242.

14 See, for example, the description and a distribution map in Métraux, A. (1928). *La Civilisation Matérielle des Tribus Tupi-Guarani*. Paris. pp. 103–4, 114–15. A recent study of the modern South American distribution of this and other methods for squeezing manioc pulp is Dole, G. E. (1960). Techniques of preparing manioc flour as a key to culture history in tropical America, *in* Wallace, A. F. C. (ed.) *Men and Cultures*. Philadelphia. pp. 241–8.

15 Taylor, D. (1938). op. cit. p. 138; Echagoian. (1864). Relación de la Isla Española enviada al rey D. Felipe II, por el licenciado Echagoian, oidor de

la Audiencia de Santo Domingo, *Col. de Documentos Inéditos Relativos al Descubrimiento, Conquista y Colonización de las Posesiones Españolas en América y Oceanía*, 1, Madrid, p. 17; Suárez, C. (1921). op. cit. p. 375; Pichardo, E. (1862). op. cit. p. 188; Tejera, E. (1951). op. cit. p. 391.

16 Las Casas, Oviedo y Valdés and Cobo (see note 6) all comment on the substitution; Las Casas mentions the screw press.

17 Cundall, F., and Pietersz, J. L. (1919). *Jamaica under the Spaniards: abstracted from the archives of Seville.* Kingston. pp. 2, 4, 5, 10, 15, 19, 35, etc.

18 Piso, W. (1648). De medicina brasiliensi, *in* Ioannes de Laet (ed.) *Historia Naturalis Brasiliae* . . . Leiden. p. 53.

19 Taylor, D. (1938). op. cit. pp. 128–9. The term has spread from the Lesser Antilles to Haiti, for Mintz, S. W., tells me (*in lit.*, June, 1968) that "bičet" is the Haitian Creole term for "tray", including a winnowing tray.

20 Tertre, J. B. du (1654). *Histoire Generale, des Isles des Christophe, de la Guadeloupe, de la Martinique, et Autres dans l'Amerique.* . . . Paris. pp. 178–184; Tertre. (1667). *Histoire Generale des Antilles Habités par les François* . . . , II, Paris. pp. 112–18 and plate facing p. 419.

21 Desportes, J. B. R. P. (1770). *Traité ou Abrégé des Plantes Usuelles de S. Domingue.* Vol. 3 of his *Histoire des maladies de S. Domingue.* Paris. p. 223.

22 Long, E. (1774). *The History of Jamaica* . . . , III, London. pp. 772–8; Browne, P. (1789). *The Civil and Natural History of Jamaica,* London. pp. 349–50; Wright, W. (1787). An account of the medicinal plants growing in Jamaica, *London Medical Journal*, 8 (3), pp. 262–3; Barham, H. (1794). *Hortus Americanus: containing an account of the* . . . *vegetable productions of South-America and the West-India Islands, and particularly of the island of Jamaica* . . . Kingston. pp. 34–5; Hughes, G. (1750). *The Natural History of Barbados.* London. p. 150.

23 Cunliffe, R. S. (1916). Yuca; su cultivo, variedades, contenido en almidón y fabricación, *Rep. de Cuba, Secretaría de Agricultura, Comercio y Trabajo, Estación Experimental Agronómica, Santiago de las Vegas, Boletín* No. 34, Habana, pp. 19–20; Cook, O. F. and Collins, G. N. (1903). Economic plants of Porto Rico, *Contributions from the U.S. National Herbarium,* 8 (2), p. 184; Nicholls, H. A. (1929). *A Text-Book of Tropical Agriculture.* 2nd ed., rev. by Holland, J. H., London. pp. 430–3; Beckwith, M. W. (1927). Notes on Jamaican ethnobotany. *Publics. of the Folk-lore Foundation,* 8, Poughkeepsie: Vassar College, pp. 42–3; Pairault, A. (1900). Plantes comestibles féculentes cultivées aux Antilles, *Bull. de l'Assoc. des Chimistes de Sucrerie et de Distillerie de France et des Colonies,* 17 (1–2), p. 80.

24 Wurzburg, O. B. (1952). Root starches other than those of white and sweet potato, *Econ. Bot.,* 6 (3), pp. 211–15.

25 Cunliffe, R. S. (1916). op. cit. pp. 20–8; Nicholls (1929). op. cit. p. 433; Burkill, I. H. (1904). The tapioca plant: its history, cultivation and uses; a review of existing information, *Agricultural Ledger,* 11 (10), pp. 135–8; Everington, E. (1912). Cassava starch and its uses, *West Indian Bulletin, The Journal of the Imperial Dept. of Agric. for the West Indies,* 12 (4), pp. 527–9; Schery, R. W. (1947). Manioc—a tropical staff of life. *Econ. Bot.,* 1 (1), pp. 20–5.

26 Beckwith, M. W. (1927). op. cit. p. 42.

27 Jones, W. O. (1959). *Manioc in Africa.* Stanford. pp. 32, 102.

28 Brautlecht, C. A. (1953). *Starch: its sources, production and uses.* New York. p. 2.

29 Piso, W. (1648). op. cit. pp. 53–4.

30 Bailey, L. H. (ed.) (1912). *Cyclopedia of American agriculture. II Crops.* New York. p. 199; Wurzburg, O. B. (1952). op. cit. p. 152.

31 Schumann, K. (1902). Marantaceae. 11. Heft (IV. 48), *in* A. Engler (ed.)

Das Pflanzenreich...Leipzig. pp. 125–6; de Candolle, A. (1883). *Origine des Plantes Cultivées*. Paris. pp. 64–5; Bernegg, A. S. von (1929). *Tropische und Subtropische Weltwirtschaftspflanzen; ihre Geschichte, Kultur und volkswirtschaftliche Bedeutung. I. Teil: Stärke- und Zuckerpflanzen*, Stuttgart. p. 273; Bois, D. (1927). *Les Plantes Alimentaires chez tous les Peuples et à travers les Ages; histoire utilisation, culture*. 1. Paris. p. 459.

32 Lowrie, R. H. (1948). The tropical forests: an introduction, *in* Steward, J. H. (ed.) *Handbook of South American Indians*, 3, p. 1; Nimuendajú, C. (1948). The Cawahíb, Parintintin, and their neighbors, *in* Steward, J. H. (ed.) op. cit. p. 295.

33 Oviedo y Valdés, G. F. de (1851). op. cit. pp. 279–80 (book 7, chapter 6); Las Casas, B. de (1909). op. cit. p. 29 (chapter 10); Cobo, B. (1890). op. cit. p. 357 (book 4, chapter 9); Santa Cruz, Alonso de (1918). *Islario General de Todas las Islas del Mundo*. Madrid. p. 458.

34 Britton, N. L. and Wilson, P. (1923). Botany of Porto Rico and the Virgin Islands, *Scientific Survey of Porto Rico and the Virgin Islands*, 5, New York. p. 178; Pichardo, E. (1862). op. cit. pp. 161–2; Maza, M. G. de la (1889). *Diccionario Botánico de los Nombres Vulgares Cubanos y puerto-riqueños*. Habana. p. 110; Malaret, A. (1931). *Diccionario de Americanismos*. 2nd ed., San Juan. pp. 317, 325, 514; Abad, J. R. (1888). *La República Dominicana; reseña general geográfico-estadística*. Santo-Domingo. pp. 69, 333.

35 Colmeiro, M. (1892). Primeras noticias acerca de la vegetación americana . . . , *Ateneo de Madrid, Conferencias*, Madrid. p. 29; Barrett, O. W. (1928). *The Tropical Crops* . . . New York. p. 381; Lovén, S. (1935). *Origins of the Tainan Culture, West Indies*. Göteborg. p. 369; Friederici, G. (1947). *Amerikanistisches Wörterbuch, Univ. Hamburg, Abhandlungen aus dem Gebiet der Auslandskunde*, 53. Reihe B., *Völkerkunde, Kulturgeschichte und Sprachen*, 29, pp. 346–7; Roumain, J. (1942). Contribution à l'étude de l'ethnobotanique précolombienne des Grandes Antilles, *Bull. du Bureau d'ethnologie de la Rép. d'Haiti*, 1, p. 40; Rouse, I. (1948). The Arawak, *in* Steward, J. H. (ed.), *Handbook of South American Indians*, 4, p. 523; Sapper, K. (1934). Geographie der altindianischen Landwirtschaft. *Petermanns Mitteilungen*, 80, pp. 41–4, 80–2, 118–21; Sauer, C. O. (1950). Cultivated plants of South and Central America, *in* Steward, J. H. (ed.), *Handbook of South American Indians*, 6, p. 511; Sauer, C. O. (1966). op. cit. p. 54.

36 Anghiera, P. M. d' [Peter Martyr] (1574). *De Rebus Oceanicis et Novo Orbe, decades tres* . . . Cologne. p. 301 (decade 3, book 9); Oviedo y Valdés, G. F. de (1851). op. cit. pp. 284–5 (book 7, chapter 15).

37 Britton, N. L. and Wilson, P. (1923). op. cit. p. 177; Schumann, K. (1902). op. cit. p. 126.

38 The suggested identification as arrowroot is in Colmeiro, M. (1892). op. cit. p. 37, and in Barrett, O. W. (1928). op. cit. p. 380—both for "cauallos"; on p. 30 of the same work, Barrett suggests *Canna* for "cabaióes"; *Xanthosoma* is suggested by Gordon, B. Le Roy (1957). Human geography and ecology in the Sinú country of Colombia, *Ibero-Americana*, 39, pp. 101–2.

39 "Yuquilla" in Cuba: Pichardo, E. (1862). op. cit. pp. 231–2; Maza y Jimenez, M. G. de la, and Roig y Mesa, J. T. (1914). Flora de Cuba (datos para su estudio), *Rep. de Cuba, Sec. de Agric., Comercio y Trabajo, Estación Experimental Agronómica, Santiago de las Vegas, Boletín* No. 22, Habana, p. 27; Suárez, C. (1921). op. cit. p. 466; "yuquilla" in Puerto Rico: Cook, O. F. and Collins, G. N. (1903). op. cit. p. 266; Malaret, A. (1917). op. cit. p. 150; Otero, J. I., and Toro, R. A. (1931). Catálogo de los nombres vulgares y científicos de algunas plantas puertorriqueñas, *Gob. de P.R., Depto. de Agric. y Trab., Estación Experimental Insular, Río Piedras P.R., Boletín* No. 37, San Juan, p. 29; "sagú" in Cuba:

Pichardo, E. (1862). ibid.; Maza, M. G. de la and Roig, J. T. (1914). ibid.; Suárez, C. (1921). ibid.; La Sagra, R. de (1831). *Historia Económico-Política y Estadística de la Isla de Cuba* . . . Habana. p. 82; Roig y Mesa, J. T. (1928). Diccionario botánica de nombres vulgares cubanos. *Rep. de Cuba, Sec. de Agric., Comercio y Trabajo, Estación Experimental Agronómica, Santiago de las Vegas, Boletín* Num. 54, Habana, pp. 628, 725: "sagú" in the Dominican Republic: Abad, J. R. (1888). op. cit. pp. 69, 334; "raíz americana" in Cuba: Suárez, C. (1921). op. cit. p. 442; "maranta" in Puerto Rico: Grosourdy, R. de (1864). *El médico Botanico Criollo.* 4. Paris. p. 371; Britton, N. L. and Wilson, P. (1923). op. cit. p. 177; Otero, J. and Toro, R. A. (1931). ibid.; "maranta" in Haiti: Barker, H. D. and Dardeau, W. S. (1930). *Flore d'Häiti; clé et description des ordres-familles et genres des Spermatophytes d'Häiti* . . . Porte-au-Prince. p. 60—but these are instances of a "common" name invented rather than collected by botanists, for the Linnaean genus was named in honour of Bartolommeo Maranta, a sixteenth-century Venetian botanist and physician (Miller, P. and Martyn, T. (1807). *The Gardener's and Botanist's Dictionary* . . . new ed. London *s.v.* Maranta; Bailey, L. H. (1949). *Manual of Cultivated Plants* . . . rev. ed. New York. p. 292; "West-Indian salep": Bernegg, A. S. von (1929). ibid.; "salop" in the Virgin Islands: Benzon, P. E. (1823). Om den vestindiske Salop, dens Dyrkning, Tilberedelse og almindelige Egenskaber, *Tidsskrift for Naturvidenskaberne*, 2, pp. 158–72; Schomburgk, R. H. (1833). Berichte über die Kulturpflanzen Westindiens, *Linnaea*, 8, p. 264; "sulup" in Puerto Rico: Grosourdy, R. de (1864). op. cit. 3, p. 141—these are variants of a term, evidently ultimately derived from Arabic, which is applied in India and the Near East to dried orchid tubers and starch made from them (Watt, G. (1908)). *The Commercial Products of India*, London. pp. 962–3; Yule, H. and Burnell, A. C. (1903). *Hobson-Jobson: a glossary of colloquial Anglo-Indian words and phrases* . . . new ed. London. [reprinted 1968, London], p. 784; Brautlecht, C. A. (1953). op. cit. p. 285); "touala" in Jamaica: Cook, O. F. and Collins, G. N. (1903). op. cit. p. 185; "tulola" is cited for Cuba by both Maza, M. G. de la (1889). op. cit. p. 102, and Roig, J. T. (1928). op. cit. p. 669, although the same two authors writing jointly (1914, op. cit. p. 17) give this word with the note, "we doubt the name".

40 Dutch "arraroot" is given by Boldingh, I. (1914). *The Flora of the Dutch West Indian islands*, II, *Curaçao, Aruba and Bonaire*, Leiden. p. 19; many of the South-east Asian and Malaysian terms are listed in Heyne, K. (1927). *De Nuttige Planten van Nederlandsch Indië*. 2nd ed. Batavia. pp. 507–8, and in Brown, W. H. (no date) [between 1935 and 1941]. Useful plants of the Philippines. *Commonwealth of the Philippines, Dept. of Agric. and Commerce, Manila, Technical Bull.*, 10 (1), p. 483; to these may be added Burmese ádálu'.

41 Martius, C. F. P. von (1867). Zur Ethnographie Amerika's zumal Brasiliens, Vol. 1 of his *Beiträge zur Ethnographie und Sprachenkunde Amerika's zumal Brasiliens*. Leipzig. p. 689 note; for "haru" and "aru", see Roth, W. E. (1924). op. cit. p. 216.

42 Bartlett, H. H. (1953). English names of some East-Indian plants and plant products, *Asa Gray Bull.*, 2 (2), pp. 159–62.

43 Tertre, J. P. du (1654). op. cit. pp. 151–2.

44 Sloane, H. (1696). *Catalogus Plantarum quae in Insula Jamaica sponte proveniunt* . . . *adjectis aliis quibusdam quae in insulis Maderae, Barbados, Nieves, & Sancti Christophori nascuntur* . . . . London. p. 122; Gómara, F. L. de (1749). *Historia de las Indias. Historiadores primitivos de las Indias Occidentales* (Andres González de Barcia. ed.), 2, Madrid, pp. 63–5 (chapter 71); Sloane (1707). *A Voyage to the Islands Madera, Barbados*

Nieves, S. Christophers and Jamaica . . . 1, London. pp. 253–4; among modern botanists recognizing this description are Schumann, K. (1902). op. cit. p. 135, and de Candolle, A. (1883). op. cit. p. 65.

45 Barham, H. (1794). op. cit. pp. 6–8.
46 Hughes, G. (1750). op. cit. p. 221; Long, E. (1774). op. cit. pp. 759, 855; Wright, W. (1787). op. cit. pp. 269–70; Browne, P. (1789). op. cit. pp. 112–13.
47 Miller, P. and Martyn, T. (1807). op. cit., *s.v.* Maranta; Anonymous (1893). Arrowroot, *Bull. of Misc. Info., Royal Gardens, Kew*, 82, 83, pp. 331–3; Hamilton, W. (1846). On the Maranta arundinacea, and its applications as an antidote to animal and vegetable poisons, *Pharmaceutical Journal and Transactions*, 6 (1), pp. 25–8; Guibourt, [G.] (1846). Nouvelles considerations sur l'amidon, l'arrow-root et le sagou . . ., *Journal de Pharmacie et de Chimie*, troisième série, 9, pp. 191–8; Milburn, W. (1813). *Oriental Commerce* . . . 2. London. p. 207.
48 St. Croix: Benzon, P. E. (1923). ibid.; later Virgin Islands: Schomburgk, R. H. (1833). op. cit. pp. 264–5; Cuba: La Sagra, R. de (1831). ibid.; Antigua in 1837: Harris, D. R. (1965). Plants, animals, and man in the Outer Leeward Islands, West Indies . ., *Univ. of Calif. Publ. in Geography*, 18, p. 113.
49 Cogswell, C. (1845). On the arrow-root of Bermuda. *London and Edinburgh Monthly Journal of Medical Science*, 5 (10), pp. 789–96; Ure, A. (1845). *Recent Improvements in Arts, Manufactures, and Mines: being the second edition of a supplement to the third edition of his Dictionary.* London. pp. 8–10; Saunders, W. (1882). Report of the Superintendent of Gardens and Grounds, *Report of the [U.S.] Commissioner of Agriculture for the Years 1881 and 1882*, p. 226; Anonymous (1893). St. Vincent arrowroot, *Bull. of Misc. Info., Royal Gardens, Kew*, 80, pp. 191–204.
50 Bernegg, A. S. von (1929). op. cit. p. 275; Bois, D. (1927). ibid.; Burkill, I. H. (1935). *A Dictionary of the Economic Products of the Malay Peninsula.* London. p. 1424; Raymond, W. D. and Squires, J. (1959). Sources of starch in colonial territories II: Arrowroot (*Maranta arundinacea* Linn.), *Tropical Science*, 1 (3), pp. 182–92; Safford, W. E. (1905). The useful plants of Guam . . . *Contributions from the U.S. Natl. Herbarium*, 9, pp. 318–19.
51 Indonesia: Heyne, K. (1927). ibid.; Malaya: Burkill, I. H. (1935). ibid.; Philippines: Brown, W. H. n.d., op. cit. p. 438; Burma: author's field notes, 1955.
52 Raymond, W. D. and Squires, J. (1959). ibid.
53 Nicholls, H. A. (1929). op. cit. p. 434; Beckwith, M. A. (1927). op. cit. p. 11; Howard, R. A. (1952). The vegetation of the Grenadines, Windward Islands, British West Indies, *Contributions from the Gray Herbarium of Harvard Univ.*, 174, p. 98.
54 Schuster, J. (1932). Cycadaceae. Heft 99 (IV. I), *in* Engler, A. (ed.) *Das Pfanzenreich* . . . . Leipzig. pp. 150–60; Whiting, M. G. (1963). Toxicity of cyads, *Econ. Bot.*, 17 (4), pp. 270–302.
55 The sixteenth-century accounts are: Las Casas, B. de (1909). op. cit. pp. 11, 29 (chapters 3, 10); Las Casas, B. de (1951). *Historia de las Indias.* México and Buenos Aires. 1, pp. 419, 462 (book 1, chapters 106, 121), 2, p. 265 (book 2, chapter 17); Oviedo y Valdés, G. F. de (1851). op. cit. p. 284 (book 7, chapter 16); Anghiera, P. M. d' [Peter Martyr] (1574). ibid.; and Ansanus, T. *et al.* (1867), Carta que escribieron varios Padres de la órden de Santo Domingo, residentes en la isla Española . . ., *Colección de Documentos Inéditos* . . . [*del Archivo*] *de Indias.* pp. 419, 430; the modern popular terminology is in: Boyrie Moya, E. De, Krestenson, M. K. and Goggin, J. M. (1957). *Zamid* starch in Santo Domingo . . , *Florida Anthropologist*, 10 (3–4), pp. 17–40; Barker, H. D. and Dardeau, W. S

(1930). op. cit. p. 3; Abad, J. R. (1888). op. cit. p. 73; García, J. G. (1876). *Memorias para la historia de Quisqueya ó sea de la antigua parte española de Santo Domingo* .... Santo Domingo. p. 250; Roig, J. T. (1928). op. cit. p. 348; Britton, N. L. and Wilson, P. (1923). op. cit. pp. 164–5; Grosourdy, R. de (1864). op. cit. **3**. p. 137; and Maza, M. G. de la (1889). op. cit. p. 78.

56 Miyares González, F. (1954). *Noticias particulares de la Isla y Plaza de San Juan Bautista de Puerto Rico*. Río Piedras. pp. 79–80; Abbad y Lasierra, I. (1866). *Historia Geográfica, Civil y Natural de la Isla de San Juan Bautista de Puerto-Rico*. new ed. San Juan. pp. 252, 438.

57 Grosourdy, R. de (1864). op. cit. **3**, pp. 144–5.

58 Mintz, S. W., *in lit.* 9/9/1957, reporting his field inquiries.

59 Prenleloup, L.-A. (1872). Remarques sur quelques *Zamia* et leurs produits, *Bull. de la Soc. Vaudoise des Sciences Naturelles*, **11** (67), pp. 277–82, Lausanne; Boyrie Moya, E. de *et al.* (1957). ibid.

60 Pereira, J. (1854). *The Elements of Materia Medica and Therapeutics*, **2**. 3rd Amer. ed. Philadelphia. pp. 283–4; Smith, J. (1882). *A Dictionary of Popular Names of the Plants which furnish the Natural and Acquired Wants of Man* ... London. p. 362.

61 Lewis, C. B. (Inst. of Jamaica, Kingston), *in lit.* 3/7/1954 to J. M. Goggin.

62 Davenport, W. H., *in lit.* 20/8/1955, reporting his field inquiries.

63 Pichardo, E. (1862). op. cit. p. 272; Maza, M. G. de la, and Roig, J. T. (1914). op. cit. p. 25; Suárez, C. (1921). op. cit. p. 529; Roig y Mesa, T. J. (1945). *Plantas Medicinales, Aromáticas o Venenosas de Cuba*. Habana. p. 511.

64 Lindley, J. (1838). *Flora Medica; a botanical account of all the more important plants used in medicine* ... London. p. 550; Jackson, J. R. (1864). Cyads. *Intellectual Observer*, **5** (4). p. 252; Gifford, J. (1912). *The Everglades and Other Essays relating to Southern Florida*. 2nd ed. Miami. p. 171.

M. VILLARET-von ROCHOW

Fruit size variability of Swiss prehistoric Malus sylvestris

The study of prehistoric apples in Switzerland is at the moment confined to size comparisons of carbonized fruit-halves from different neolithic and bronze age sites with a few present-day specimens. Unfortunately wild crab apple trees, belonging to *Malus sylvestris* ssp. *sylvestris*, have become rare in western Switzerland; they are scattered about the Jura and the Prealps, are even less frequent on the Swiss Central Plain (Schweizerisches Mittelland) and occur sometimes in hedges in the Rhone Valley. In 1967, we gathered from one tree in a Carpinion forest reservation "Bois de Chênes" near Nyon, twenty specimens of fruit. They show a wider range of variability than the statistics published by K. and F. Bertsch[1] which were based on sixty wild apples from Beuron/Württemberg (see Fig. 1). Our specimens were cut and carbonized in the laboratory at 220–240°C. We noticed considerable shrinkage (about 25% in breadth and 28% in length) and, in connection with this, the characteristic somewhat flattened shape of most of our crab apples became even more pronounced. The maximum size of our material found in 1967 corresponds, after carbonization, astonishingly well with the limit values given by Oswald Heer[2]; they lie within 27 mm. breadth and 24 mm. length. Basing results only on dry herbarium materials, I formerly fixed the maximum size of recent crab apples as 31 × 28 mm.[3]; but as it would be better to compare prehistoric collections with carbonized present-day specimens, the values given by Heer would seem to be much more suitable.

Shape and size of apple pips vary greatly in *M. sylvestris* (*sensu stricto*) and hitherto have not yielded any reliable relationship to fruit size. Since the increase in volume of fruit is in most cases due to an increase in the breadth of the fruit (only a small percentage of the fruit are oblong or show a tendency to increase in length), the breadth of the fruit has been chosen as an approximate criterion for fruit-size (Fig. 1). The percentage of oblong forms is mentioned in the descriptions which follow.

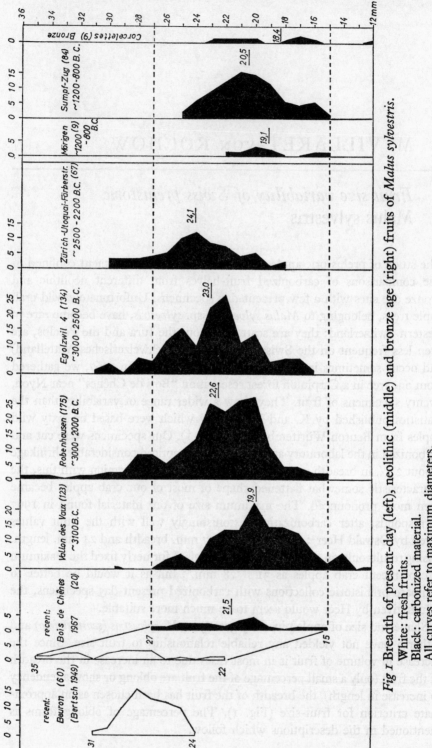

Fig 1 Breadth of present-day (left), neolithic (middle) and bronze age (right) fruits of *Malus sylvestris*.
White: fresh fruits.
Black: carbonized material.
All curves refer to maximum diameters.
Underlined numbers : arithmetic means.

The prehistoric samples in Fig. 1 refer to the following sites:

(A) Neolithic

1 *Vallon des Vaux* (Chavannes le Chêne, Vaud): rock-shelter in calcareous Molasse sandstone from which about 400 apples were collected during the excavation by Dr. M. Sitterding in 1966. The site is considered to be among the oldest neolithic localities in western Switzerland (Chasséen pottery). Age: *c.* 3200 B.C. The fruit material shows an exceptionally high number of oblong specimens (28·5%) as well as very small crab apples. With reference to the latter, we cannot follow K. and F. Bertsch's[4] suggestion that one small specimen found in a Bandkeramik site at Böckingen represented "*Malus paradisiaca*" or "*Malus praecox* Borkh[5]".

2 *Robenhausen:* older museum collections of Heer's and Messikommers' classic "lake-dwelling" at Kanton Zürich which are now in the Musée d'Archéologie Lausanne (109 specimens), the Landesmuseum Zürich (eighteen specimens), and the Historisches Museum Bern (thirty-one specimens). Seventeen specimens which were measured by Neuweiler[6] have been added to the graph in Fig. 1. Approximate age: between 3000 and 2000 B.C., Cortaillod to Schnurkeramik.

3 *Egolzwil 4:* excavation by the Landesmuseum Zürich in 1960 (134 specimens examined). Frequency of oblong specimen 15%, some pear-shaped. Approximate age: between 3000 and 2500 B.C.

4 *Zürich-Utoquai-Färberstrasse:* excavated by Kantonale Denkmalspflege Zürich in 1962. All the fruit specimens were found in the lowest Horgen level and they are especially well preserved, with large fleshy parts. Only one specimen is longer than it is broad (see Fig. 2). Approximate age: between 2500–2200 B.C.

(B) Bronze age

5 *Mörigen/Kanton Bern:* collection of the Historisches Museum Bern (nine specimens). Even the small specimens contained normally developed seeds. Approximate age: between 1200–800 B.C.

6 *Sumpf-Zug:* excavated by Dr. J. Speck[7] and collections now in the Kantonales Museum für Urgeschichte Zug (eighty-four specimens examined). The fruit are typically-shaped crab apples, only three of which are longer than they are broad. Even the smallest ones have been cut carefully in halves. Age: about 1200–800 B.C. This settlement was occupied for at least 200 years and was gradually enlarged[8].

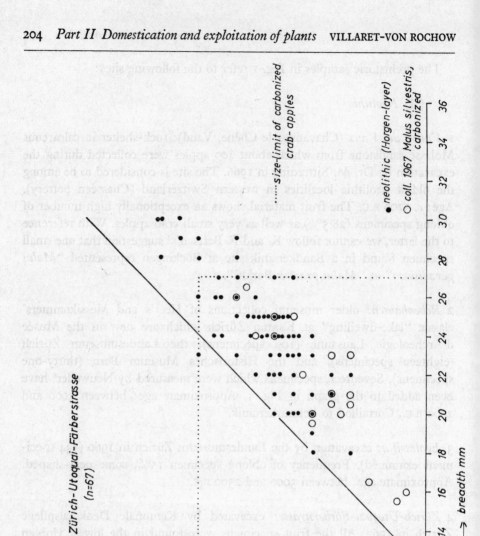

Fig 2 Shape and size diagram from Zürich-Utoquai-Färberstrasse.
Fruit of flattened broad shape lie under the diagonal.
The Horgen material is similar to the present-day specimens (circles); the high arithmetical mean of the former (24·1 mm.) is partly due to the absence of very small fruit.

7 *Corcelettes* near Grandson/Vaud: museum collection of Musée d'Archéologie, Lausanne (nine specimens, all of them cut).

As far as can be seen from the material examined, only a low percentage of the total number of fruit found in any of the settlements lie beyond the range of present-day crab apples. None of the curves in Fig. 1 indicate a significant frequency maximum outside the crab apple class. Moreover, very large specimens appear to be restricted to only a few neolithic localities, and only one or two specimens reach a maximum of 36 mm. breadth (Robenhausen: one specimen at Landesmuseum Zürich; Wangen: one specimen according to Bertsch[9]; and one further specimen (III, 1) from Bodman seems to be of considerable size[10]). Among the oblong fruits, the "longer lake dwelling apple" described by Heer and figured in one specimen from Robenhausen has only been observed in one specimen from Burgäschisee-Süd[11].

Swiss settlements of the late bronze age until now have only yielded a small *Malus sylvestris*-type (total numbers examined: 102). Instead of an increase in size which could have been caused by selection and cultivation, we observe, on the contrary, a decrease in size (see Fig. 1: arithmetic means of breadth: 19·1; 20·5; 18·4 mm.). Whatever the interpretation of large size neolithic apples should be, there is as yet no evidence at all of a progressive evolution up to the late bronze age.

Heer and Neuweiler both suggested that there was cultivation of apples in the Swiss neolithic period, but their arguments were based on quite different views. Heer[12] laid particular stress on the high numbers, and great importance of, wild, acid crab apples for the Swiss lake-dwelling people before suggesting that a "considerable number" of larger apples, found only at Robenhausen by the author, probably represented a "cultivated variety". Basing his conclusion on his general experience and some few measurements, Neuweiler[13] noticed a gradual transition between the small and the large-size fruit so that he could not accept them as a separate variety. But further on in the same article Neuweiler—surprisingly enough—returned to de Candolle's old idea[14] that the large quantity of stocked prehistoric apples suggested apple cultivation.

Meanwhile the general picture of Swiss neolithic husbandry has repeatedly shown its mixed character: besides cereals, flax, opium poppy and other crops, considerable numbers of wild fruit have been collected (such as hazel nuts (*Corylus avellana*), raspberries (*Rubus idaeus*), acorns (*Quercus* spp.) and sloes (*Prunus spinosa*)), for instance at Auvernier near the end of the neolithic period, where they are associated with large numbers of apple pips. Thus, several kinds of wild fruit still played an important role during the Swiss neolithic period and therefore the presence of large quantities of apples cannot be taken as evidence that they also were not wild.

Notes

1 Bertsch, K. and F. (1949). *Geschichte unserer Kulturpflanzen*. Stuttgart. pp. 1–275.
2 Heer, O. (1865). Die Pflanzen der Pfahlbauten, *Neujahrsbl. Naturf. Ges. Zürich a.d.J. 1866*, 68, pp. 1–54.
3 Villaret-von Rochow, M. (1967). Frucht- und Samenreste aus der neolithischen Station Seeberg, Burgäschisee-Süd, *Acta Bernensia*, 2 (4), Fig. 13.
4 Bertsch, K. and F. (1949). ibid.
5 Bertsch, K. (1961). Einheimische Wildäpfel, *Jb. vaterl. Naturkde Württemberg*, 116, pp. 185–94.
6 Neuweiler, E. (1924). Pflanzenreste aus den Pfahlbauten des ehemaligen Wauwilersees, *Mitt. Naturf. Ges. Luzern*, 9, pp. 301–23.
7 Speck, J. (1955). Die Ausgrabungen in der spätbronzezeitlichen Ufersiedlung Zug-"Sumpf", *in Das Pfahlbauproblem. Monographien zur Ur- und Frühgeschichte der Schweiz*, 11, Basel, pp. 275–334.
8 Huber, B. and Merz, W. (1962). Jahrringchronologische Untersuchungen zur Baugeschichte der urnenfelderzeitlichen Siedlung Zug-Sumpf, *Germania*, 40, pp. 44–56.
9 Bertsch, K. and F. (1949). op. cit. p. 97.
10 See Bertsch, K. and F. (1949). op. cit. Fig. 49, which is classed among "cultivated neolithic apples".
11 Villaret-von Rochow, M. (1967). op. cit. pl. IV, Figs. 10 and 11.
12 Heer, O. (1865). ibid.
13 Neuweiler, E. (1924). ibid.
14 de Candolle, A. (1883). *L'origine des Plantes Cultivées*. Paris. pp. 1–377.

Section 2: Domestication and exploitation of animals

R. J. BERRY

The genetical implications of domestication in animals

When early man discovered that there were certain advantages in conserving certain animals near to his dwelling place, he was entering into the first phase of domesticating them[1]. At this juncture, the only sign of domestication available to the archaeologist would be ecological[2]. However there is frequently too small an amount of material available for determining if animal remains found in association with man represent a random sample of a wild-living population or one drawn from a "domesticated" population. In practice it is necessary to ask the question: what criteria can be used to characterize a domesticated form?

This question pre-supposes that domestication involves change; some of this change will be inherited and some will be environmentally determined. Whatever the cause, there are two questions that must be faced in any attempt to specify characters by which domesticated forms can be recognized. These are:

1 Are there any known morphological changes which inevitably accompany domestication?
2 Can the same changes arise by any other mechanism besides domestication?

This paper is an attempt to suggest answers to these questions. I have used animal examples, but the same arguments can almost certainly be applied to plants[3].

Changes which follow domestication (see Fig. 1)

A number of traits have been claimed to be characteristic of domesticated forms. Zeuner[4] has summarized the more important of these:

1 *Size:* early types of domesticated animal tend to be smaller than their wild relations and "small size is used as a diagnostic character in prehistoric deposits where wild and domesticated forms are liable to occur together".

2 *Colour:* wild colouration is exceptional in most domesticated animals. In particular "piebaldness in the animals depicted by early man is definite evidence of domestication".

3 *Changes in the skull:* "the most important effects of domestication are exhibited by the skull, mainly because they are easily recognizable in fossil material from ancient dwelling sites. . . . The rule is that the facial part of the skull tends to be shortened relative to the cranial, which is but little affected." This may cause correlated changes in the dentition, and "at a very early stage of domestication the teeth became smaller than they are in wild forms. . . . With progressive shortening of the face, teeth which are already in the state of reduction may disappear entirely, such as the first pre-molars and third molars". Horn size tends to decrease.

4 *Post-cranial skeleton:* no changes which reliably indicate domestication are accepted, but "in domesticated cattle, weak muscle-ridges and poorly defined facets of the joints make it comparatively easy to recognize specimens of domesticated origin, and also in the domesticated pig, where the epiphyses of the limb bones do not fuse with the diaphyses until long after maturity is reached". The number of caudal vertebrae is almost invariably reduced in domesticated forms, except in sheep where an "increase in the number of tail vertebrae beyond twelve is a virtually certain character of domestication".

5 *Hair:* the greatest changes are associated with the underlying shorter hairs, especially in species which have a large amount of wool in the wild forms.

6 *Soft parts:* the development of local fat accumulations (as in the hump of camels) has usually been favoured under conditions of domestication; the size of the brain relative to the rest of the body may be reduced, some parts being affected more than others; musculature may be increased (as in draught or racing horses) or reduced (as with the chewing muscles of carnivores).

7 *In general*

   (*a*) New characters are rarely produced, but existing ones selected.
   (*b*) Pathological conditions are often favoured.
   (*c*) Under domestication, growth rates are frequently affected, producing allometric and often neotenous changes.

Zeuner discusses each of these points, mentioning exceptions. The crucial question is to what extent some or all of these changes, which are undoubtedly associated with domestication in certain forms, may be regarded as generally diagnostic of the state.

Observed changes upon domestication: the Norway rat

The most intensive studies of domestication have been carried out on the grey or Norway rat (*Rattus norvegicus*)[5]. This work helps to put into perspective the suggestions summarized above, and is important because it involved domestication alone without associated selection for economic or aesthetic characters.

The Norway rat seems to have been introduced to Britain about 1730 and to North America about 1775. It was probably taken into captivity about 1800[6]. At that time rat-baiting was popular in England and France. Recently trapped rats were placed in a pit and a terrier let loose amongst them. The spectators bet on the time required by different terriers to kill the last rat. Large numbers of rats had to be caught and held in readiness for such spectacles. Richter[7] has written of records which indicate that albinos were removed from such collections and retained for breeding and exhibition.

This was the beginning of the domestication of most modern strains of laboratory rats, and no more is known of the process than for any other animal. However, in 1919 H. D. King[8] began a "repeat" of the domestication of the species. He took into his laboratory 16 male and 20 female wild-caught rats, and the study of their descendants is still continuing, more than fifty generations later.

The first results of laboratory breeding of King's "captive-greys" were associated with reproductive performances. The early generations were marked by a high degree of female sterility (only 6 of the original 20 females bred) and infant mortality, and it was necessary to foster the first generation young on to "well-domesticated" mothers. It was suggested that the infertility of the wild females and the relatively high proportion of sterile animals was due to disturbance of the nervous system brought about by fear and confinement in cages. However the incidence of female sterility declined from 37 to 6% in the first eight generations, and all the females chosen for breeding from the thirteenth generation onward were fertile.

As the proportion of fertile females increased, so did the length of the reproductive period: the time between the birth of the first and last litter in the twenty-fifth generation was more than double that in the first (440 days as compared with 204 days). This was achieved by females becoming pregnant at an increasingly early age, and also breeding later in life. Since litter size remained approximately constant (*c*. 6·0 young per litter)[9], this had the effect that fecundity increased from an average of 23·1 young per female in the first generation to an average of 63·3 young in the twenty-fifth generation.

Mean adult weight increased fairly steadily to a gain of about 20% over the first twenty-five generations, so that the rats became slightly heavier on average than those of the long-established Wistar albino strain. Individual rats attaining an adult weight considerably above the generation average appeared in increasing numbers as the generations progressed. These exceptionally large individuals were tentatively attributed to the segregation of genes acting mainly during adult life. However the variability of body weight at all ages decreased over the generations, presumably due to an increase in genetical homogeneity. Body weight increased proportionally more than body length over the first ten generations, and during this time the pituitary gland increased in weight and the thyroid decreased.

The docility of the rats increased over the generations, but even at the forty-third generation they were not so tame as Wistar albinos. Farris and Yeakel[10] showed that King's strain were highly susceptible to audiogenic seizures, and were more emotional or fearful than Wistar albinos in a standard open-field psychological test. The "captive-grey" rats often exhibited nervous or savage behaviour (jumping, squealing and biting) towards humans. Farris and Yeakel suggested that the different responses of the two strains might be due to the genetical constitutions of the founding members of each. Keeler and King[11] have attempted to analyse the consequence of genetical substitutions in King's "captive-grey" strain by studying differences between mutants and non-mutants for eight mutations which appeared in the strain (six affecting coat colour or hair structure, one producing waltzing behaviour, and one shortening the tail). Each of the sub-strains derived from different mutants exhibited a characteristic behaviour, and each produced a range of anatomical modifications in mean gland weights or skeletal measurements. The conclusions were that the characteristics of the "fully-laboratorized" Wistar albino strain could have been achieved by substitution of the hooded, black (non-agouti) and albino allelomorphs into the "captive-grey" genotype, the most important one being that of the black allelomorph. (For example, 73% of blacks tickled on the nose with a fine brush exhibited no rage-reaction, as compared with only 15% of their agouti sibs[12].)

Now these findings cannot distinguish between the pleiotropic effects of a gene and close linkage of a gene with loci affecting temperament and behaviour. Keeler was inclined to accept the first explanation, largely because eighteen of the more well-known strains of laboratory rats were homozygous for black, seemingly too great a number to have acquired the allelomorph by chance incorporation. However, neither Stone[13] nor Bendig and Braun[14] could find any difference in response between coloured and albino segregants in various behavioural tests, and Broadhurst[15] found that black animals of an F_2 generation were more timid than their agouti sibs. It would appear, therefore, that the agouti locus is more likely to be linked with genes affecting behaviour than to affect it directly.

Another approach to the domestication of animals is to compare domesticated with wild forms. Richter[16] has done this for the Norway rat, comparing rats trapped around Baltimore city with Wistar albinos. He found no obvious differences between the two forms as regards external appearance, structure of skeleton or growth rate to about 300 days. After this, the wild rats grew faster and attained a heavier final weight. The greatest differences were in the weights of the internal organs, endocrine glands especially, which were generally lighter in the laboratory rats. In particular, the adrenals of the laboratory animals weighed on average only one quarter to one half of their weight in the wild animals, the biggest difference being in the extent of the cortex. This anatomical difference had physiological consequences in that wild rats could not survive for long after adrenalectomy, even when given additional salt, whereas most laboratory rats did survive. The deaths were quite sudden and appeared to result from an inability to cope even with normal laboratory stresses. On the other hand, the glomerular zone of the adrenal cortex has a mineral salt regulating and conserving function, and wild rats were able to tolerate a diet with a low salt content which was deleterious to laboratory rats.

The adrenal lipids of laboratory rats were easily depleted by fighting or X-irradiation, but these stresses had no apparent effect on the adrenal lipid content of wild rats. The greater secretory capability of the latter probably explains the fact that wild rats are little affected by gonadectomy, whereas laboratory rats treated thus show an almost complete cessation of spontaneous activity, although this is restorable by treatment with cortisone. It is interesting that these hormonal differences are exactly those which might be expected as a correlated consequence of selecting for earlier and more efficient breeding in domesticated rats (see below).

Changes "mimicking" domestication

The Norway rat increased its body weight by a fifth in the first twenty-five generations of domestication. Since different parts of the body have different growth rates, this means that there is plenty of possibility for change in proportions producing many of the changes discussed by Zeuner[17]. A factor enhancing such allometric changes is that one of the most potent effects of domestication in any species is selection for earlier sexual maturity by breeding from the first maturing young[18]. However, extremely rapid change in body size may occur under natural conditions completely independently of domestication. This is most apparent when the stabilizing influence of gene flow is removed from a species, usually when it colonizes an island[19]. Foster[20] has shown that in general larger animals (carnivores, artiodactyls and lagomorphs) decrease in size when isolated, while smaller animals (rodents) increase. This tendency is well illustrated by the races of rabbits (*Oryctolagus cuniculus*) and field-mice (*Apodemus sylvaticus*) on islands round the British coast. Island rabbits may be about 20% lighter than their mainland neighbours[21], while island field-mice may be twice the size of their neighbours[22]. Moreover, these size differences may arise quickly: the house mouse (*Mus musculus*) on the Welsh island of Skokholm have been isolated for only

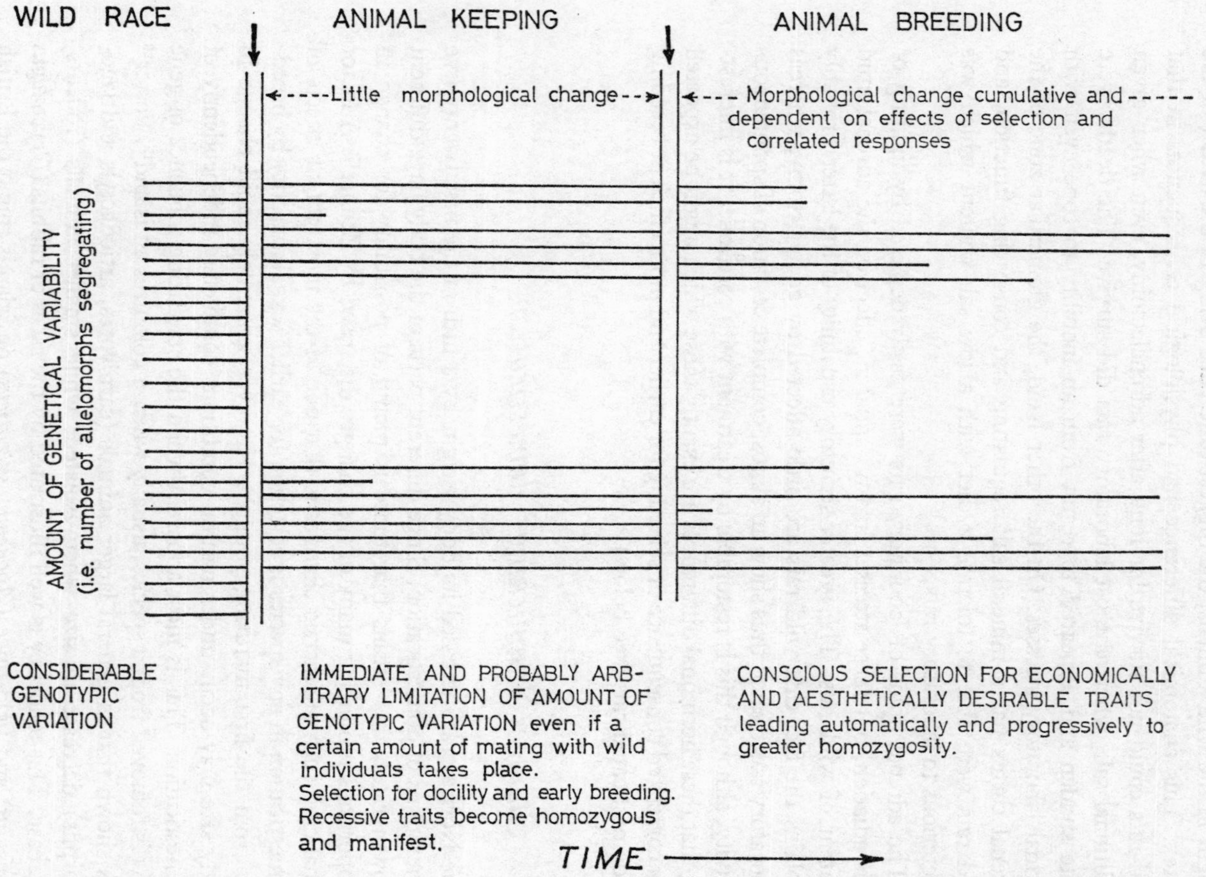

WILD RACE   ANIMAL KEEPING   ANIMAL BREEDING

Little morphological change

Morphological change cumulative and dependent on effects of selection and correlated responses

AMOUNT OF GENETICAL VARIABILITY (i.e. number of allelomorphs segregating)

CONSIDERABLE GENOTYPIC VARIATION

IMMEDIATE AND PROBABLY ARBITRARY LIMITATION OF AMOUNT OF GENOTYPIC VARIATION even if a certain amount of mating with wild individuals takes place. Selection for docility and early breeding. Recessive traits become homozygous and manifest.

CONSCIOUS SELECTION FOR ECONOMICALLY AND AESTHETICALLY DESIRABLE TRAITS leading automatically and progressively to greater homozygosity.

TIME

Fig 1 Diagrammatic representation of the genetical changes taking place in a group of animals as it undergoes domestication.

seventy years, but they are 20% longer and heavier than their closest main-land relatives[23]. There seems little doubt that increased size is an adaptive character for small mammals on islands[24], and that there is sufficient size variation present in natural populations to enable the mean size of individuals to be fairly rapidly adjusted by natural selection[25].

The analogy between the origins and characteristics of island and domesti-cated races can be pushed some way[26]: both experience greatly restricted gene-flow with the bulk of their relatives; both undergo adaptation to a specialized environment; and this adaptation is largely dependent upon the genetical variation available in the founding members of the form in ques-tion[27]. This means that different organisms will differ in their responses to the same conditions (e.g. change of size of rabbits and mice on islands) making it impossible to formulate a general rule of the changes expected when a common selective pressure (such as domestication) is applied. Furthermore, the response to the same pressure will depend on the available allelomorphs in the gene-pool, and may differ from locality to locality. For example, DDT resistance in house-flies has arisen independently in many different parts of the world—and by at least four different biochemical (or genetical) mechanisms[28]; the tail of house mice is a heat regulating organ and becomes shorter relative to body length northwards through the British Isles—but in the Faeroes the tail is 20% longer than in Shetland mice, and is approxi-mately the same length as in southern English mice[29]. The consequences of these considerations is that even within a single species, it may be extremely difficult to lay down criteria to distinguish between domesticated and non-domesticated forms. Zeuner regarded wild coat colour as uncommon and piebaldness as distinctive of domesticated forms, but many laboratory strains of the Norway rat have wild-type coat colour; Searle[30] has described a cline in blotched tabby in Western European cats; Hebridean field mouse races all arose from the same stock yet differ considerably in their coat colour and extent of ventral white colouration[31]; and wild house mice are polymorphic for allelomorphs affecting belly colour and spotting[32]. Tooth loss may have nothing to do with a trend towards smaller jaws[33]. Even pathological allelo-morphs can be common in non-domesticated forms: this is well known in man[34], but high frequencies of deleterious allelomorphs are often found in other forms (most American populations of house mice contain many recessive lethal allelomorphs of the *t*-series—Dunn; over 70% of Skokholm house mice have spina bifida occulta—Berry)[35].

Genetical diversity of populations

We are still suffering a hangover in our thought from the old type concept of a species, and its genetical corollary that individuals are homozygous at virtually all loci. This "classical" idea of population genetics implied that natural variation is extremely limited, and in the context of archaeology any specimens which "deviated" (usually on subjective grounds) from the normal, or which bore a resemblance to modern domesticated forms, could be regarded as evidence for domestication. It is becoming increasingly clear that homozygosity is not the normal state of affairs for many loci[36], and that perhaps 10–20% of loci are normally heterozygous[37]. This means that a considerable amount of variation will arise in every generation as a consequence of segregation and recombination[38], although most of the extreme variants will be eliminated before they can contribute to the next generation[39]. As a consequence exact and rapid adaptive response to environmental change is possible and inevitable[40]. Unless this change involves selection of an allelomorph with obvious phenotypic effects, this adaptation might not be easily detectable. On the other hand, correlated phenotypic responses due to linkage are almost certain (cf. the apparent pleiotropic effects of non-agouti in the Norway rat).

Usually domestication involves selection for some desirable quality, such as egg laying ability, coat texture or meat yield. Most artificial selection will produce a distinctive phenotype. However there is no reason to believe that domestication *per se* will alter the phenotype[41] or even a major part of the genotype[42]. The Norway rat illustrates this point well.

Another example is the difficulty of distinguishing between the skulls of coyotes and domestic dogs, even though these forms are normally regarded as belonging to two species (*Canis latrans* and *C. familiaris* respectively). Howard[43] has described a method for separating the two, but it is based on a fairly sophisticated character (the ratio between the palatal width and the length of the upper molar tooth-row), and Howard had available 194 skulls of known identity. Domestication is primarily the establishment of a stock breeding under manageable conditions (this is exemplified by the husbandry of animals in zoos)[44], and hence a domesticated form is really a local ecotype of a species. As such it is adapted to a greater or less extent for human use, and may have become too specialized for life in the wild[45].

I began this paper by asking two questions. The rather destructive answer to these questions must be that it is not possible to recognize any traits which inevitably accompany domestication, and, even worse, most of the criteria by which domestication has been claimed to be recognizable, may occur as a result of processes which have nothing to do with domestication. This does not mean that domestication changes can never be recognized in any particular well-known form (such as pig or sheep), but it does mean that it is impossible to extrapolate from (say) cows to horses or even between extreme forms of the same species (such as Indian and European cattle). The conclusion and moral to which we are forced is that domestication should never be claimed from archaeological material unless there is a clear and continuous lineage with modern forms, or unless cultural remains provide incontrovertible evidence of domestication[46].

Notes

1 See Bökönyi, S., this volume, pp. 219–29.
2 See Bökönyi, S. ibid. and Chaplin, R. E., this volume, pp. 231–45.
3 Salisbury, Sir E. (1961). *Weeds and Aliens*. London; Heiser, C. B. (1965). Sunflowers, weeds and cultivated plants, *in* Baker, H. G. and Stebbins, G. L. (eds.) *The Genetics of Colonizing Species*. New York and London; Jones, D. A. (1967). Polymorphism, plants and natural populations, *Sci. Prog., Oxf.*, 55, pp. 379–400; Stebbins, G. L. (1967). Adaptive radiation and trends of evolution in higher plants, *Evolutionary Biology*, 1, pp. 101–42.
4 Zeuner, F. E. (1963). *A History of Domesticated Animals*. London. Chapter 3; Klatt, B. (1927). Entstehung der Haustiere, *in* Baur, E. and Hartmann, M. (eds.) *Handbuch der Vererbungswissenschaft*, 3. Berlin.
5 Robinson, R. (1965). *Genetics of the Norway Rat*. London.
6 Donaldson, H. H. (1924). *The Rat: Data and Reference Tables*. 2nd ed. Philadelphia.
7 Richter, C. P. (1954). The effects of domestication and selection on the behaviour of the Norway rat, *J. nat. Cancer Inst.*, 15, pp. 727–38.
8 King, H. D. and Donaldson, H. H. (1929). Life processes and size of body and organs of the gray Norway rat during ten generations in captivity, *Amer. anat. Mem.*, No. 14; King, H. D. (1939). Life processes in gray Norway rats during fourteen years in captivity, *Amer. anat. Mem.*, No. 17.
9 Batten, C. A. and Berry, R. J. (1967). Parental mortality in wild-caught house mice, *J. anim. Ecol.*, 36, pp. 453–63.
10 Farris, E. J. and Yeakel, E. H. (1943). The susceptibility of albino and gray Norway rats to audiogenic seizures, *J. comp. Psychol.*, 35, pp. 73–80; Farris, E. J. and Yeakel, E. H. (1945). Emotional behaviour of gray Norway and Wistar albino rats, *J. comp. Psychol.*, 38, pp. 109–18.
11 Keeler, C. E. and King, H. D. (1942). Multiple effects of coat colour genes in the Norway rat, with special reference to temperament and domestication, *J. comp. Psychol.*, 34, pp. 241–50.
12 Keeler, C. E. (1942). The association of the black (non-agouti) gene with behaviour in the Norway rat, *J. Hered.*, 33, pp. 371–84.
13 Stone, C. P. (1932). Wildness and savageness in rats of different strains, *in* Lashley, K. S. (ed.) *Studies in the Dynamics of Behaviour*. Chicago.
14 Bendig, A. W. and Braun, H. W. (1951). The influence of the genotype on the retention of a maze habit in the rat following electroshock convulsions, *J. comp. Physiol. Psychol.*, 44, pp. 112–17.
15 Broadhurst, P. L. (1960). Studies in psychogenetics: applications of biometrical genetics to the inheritance of behaviour, *in* Eysenck, K. J. (ed.) *Experiments in Personality. I. Psychogenetics and Psychopharmacology.* London.
16 Richter, C. P. (1954). ibid.
17 De Beer, G. R. (1958). *Embryos and Ancestors*. 3rd ed. Oxford.
18 Spurway, H. (1952). Can wild animals be kept in captivity?, *New Biology*, 13, pp. 11–30.
19 Mayr, E. (1954). Change of genetic environment and evolution, *in* Huxley, J., Hardy, A. C. and Ford, E. B. (eds.) *Evolution as a Process*. London. Kurten, B. (1959). Rates of evolution in fossil mammals, *Cold Spring Harbour Symp. quant. Biol.*, 24, pp. 205–15.
20 Foster, J. B. (1964). Evolution of mammals on islands, *Nature, Lond.*, 202, pp. 234–5.
21 Lloyd, H. G. Personal communication.
22 Berry, R. J., Evans, I. M. and Sennitt, B. F. C. (1967). The relationships

and ecology of *Apodemus sylvaticus* from the Small Isles of the Inner Hebrides, Scotland, *J. Zool. Lond.*, **152**, pp. 333–46; Berry, unpublished.

23 Berry, R. J. (1964). The evolution of an island population of the house mouse, *Evolution*, **18**, pp. 468–83.

24 Cook, L. M. (1961). The edge effect in population genetics, *Amer. Nat.*, **95**, pp. 295–307; Corbet, G. B. (1961). Origin of the British insular races of small mammals and of the "Lusitanian" fauna, *Nature, Lond.*, **191**, pp. 1037–40.

25 Crowcroft, P. and Rowe, F. P. (1961). The weights of wild house mice (*Mus musculus* L.) living in confined colonies, *Proc. zool. Soc., Lond.*, **136**, pp. 177–85.

26 Baker, H. G. and Stebbins, G. L. (1965). (eds.) *The Genetics of Colonizing Species*. New York and London.

27 Mayr. E. (1954). ibid.; Berry, R. J. (1967). Genetical changes in mice and men, *Eug. Rev.*, **59**, pp. 78–96; Parsons, P. A., Hosgood, S. M. W. and Lee, B. T. O. (1967). Polygenes and polymorphism, *Molec. Gen. Genet.*, **99**, pp. 165–70.

28 W. H. C. (1964). Genetics of vectors and insecticide resistance, *Wld. Hlth. Org. techn., Rep. Ser.*, **268**, 40 pp.

29 Berry, R. J. (1964). ibid.; Berry, R. J. (1967). ibid.

30 Searle, A. G. (1964). The gene-geography of cats. *J. Cat Genet.*, **1** (5), pp. 18–24.

31 Delany, M. I. (1964). Variation in the Long-tailed field-mouse (*Apodemus sylvaticus* L.) in north-west Scotland. I. Comparison of individual characters, *Proc. roy. Soc. B.*, **161**, pp. 191–9; Berry, R. J., Evans, I. M. and Sennitt, B. F. C. (1967). ibid.

32 Dunn, L. C., Beasley, A. B. and Tinker, H. (1960). Polymorphisms in populations of wild house mice, *J. Mammal.*, **41**, pp. 220–9.

33 Brothwell, D. R., Carbonell, V. M. and Goose, D. H. (1963). Congenital absence of teeth in human populations, *in* Brothwell, D. R. (ed.) *Dental Anthropology*. London; Berry, R. J. (1968). The biology of non-metrical variation in mice and men, *in* Brothwell, D. R. (ed.) *The Skeletal Biology of Earlier Human Populations*. London.

34 Polman, A. (1950). Anencephaly, spina bifida and hydrocephaly. A contribution to our knowledge of the causal genesis of congenital malformations, *Genetica*, **25**, pp. 29–78; Blumberg, B. S. (1961). (ed.) *Genetic Polymorphisms and Geographic Variations in Disease*. New York and London; Berry, R. J. (1961). Genetically controlled degeneration of the nucleus pulposus in the mouse, *J. Bone jt. Surg.*, **43B**, pp. 387–93; Berry, R. J. (1967). ibid.

35 Dunn, L. C. (1955). Widespread distribution of mutant alleles (*t*-alleles) in populations of wild house mice, *Nature, Lond.*, **176**, pp. 1275–6; Berry, R. J. (1964). ibid.

36 Lerner, I. M. (1954). *Genetic Homeostasis*. Edinburgh.

37 Harris, H. (1966). Enzyme polymorphisms in man, *Proc. roy. Soc. B.*, **164**, pp. 298–310); Lewontin, R. C. and Hubby, J. L. (1966). A molecular approach to the study of genic heterozygosity in natural populations. II. Amount of variation and degree of heterozygosity in natural populations of *Drosophila pseudoobscura*, *Genetics*, **54**, pp. 595–609; Milkman, R. D. (1967). Heterosis as a major cause of heterozygosity in nature, *Genetics*, **55**, pp. 493–5.

38 Mather, K. (1943). Polygenic inheritance and natural selection, *Biol. Rev.*, **18**, pp. 32–64; Mather, K. (1953). The genetical structure of populations. *Symp. Soc. exp. Biol.*, **7**, pp. 76–95.

39 Haldane, J. B. S. (1959). Natural selection, *in* Bell, P. R. (ed.) *Darwin's Biological Work*. Cambridge; Berry, R. J. and Crothers, J. H. (1968).

Stabilizing selection in the Dog whelk (*Nucella lapillus*), *J. Zool., Lond.*, **155**, pp. 5–17.

40 Kettlewell, H. B. D. (1961). The phenomenon of industrial melanism in Lepidoptera, *Ann. Rev. Entomol.*, 6, pp. 245–62; Dobzhansky, T. (1963). Genetics of natural populations. XXXIII. A progress report on genetic changes in populations of *Drosophila pseudoobscura* and *Drosophila persimilis* in a locality in California, *Evolution*, **17**, pp. 333–9.

41 Bader, R. S. (1956). Variability in wild and inbred mammalian populations, *Quart. J. Fla. Acad. Sci.*, **19**, pp. 14–34.

42 Fisher, R. A. (1935). Dominance in poultry, *Phil. Trans. roy. Soc. B.*, **225**, pp. 195–226.

43 Howard, W. E. (1949). A means to distinguish skulls of coyotes and domestic dogs, *J. Mammal.*, **30**, pp. 169–71.

44 Spurway, H. (1952). ibid.

45 Leopold, A. S. (1944). The nature of heritable wildness in turkeys, *Condor*, **46**, pp. 133–97; Gillett, J. D. (1967). Natural selection and feeding speed in a blood-sucking insect, *Proc. roy. Soc. B.*, **167**, pp. 316–29.

46 My thanks are due to Mr. D. R. Brothwell, Professor H. Grüneberg, Dr. P. A. Jewell and Dr. A. G. Searle for their comments and criticisms, and to Mr. A. J. Lee for drawing the figure.

S. BÖKÖNYI

Archaeological problems and methods of recognizing animal domestication

Domestication is an extremely complicated process. In essence it is nothing other than man's special interference in the life of certain animal species, but this interference has been really varied. Although man has interfered in the life of some animal species by hunting them or driving them out from their living places, (for example, the cave bear in the Pleistocene) from a very early date, domestication is an interference of a quite different kind. There is no doubt that the purpose of earliest domestication was to secure animal protein reserve for the human population, that the domesticated animals served as living food conserves, and finally that man killed these animals just as he did his other quarry, the wild animals. But capturing animals, keeping them in corrals and killing them at the appropriate time does not amount to domestication; domestication implies something more. Its essential criterion is that man intends to breed the captured individuals of a certain wild species. The word "domestication" presumes the propagation of animals that man keeps in captivity, or more exactly man's breeding of animals under artificial conditions. And this is a real difference in comparison to the wild, hunted animals, for in connection with the latter, primitive man had only one purpose: to kill as many of them as possible.

I would define the essence of domestication as: the capture and taming by man of animals of a species with particular behavioural characteristics, their removal from their natural living area and breeding community, and their maintenance under controlled breeding conditions for profit.

In this respect it seems useful to examine the main phases of animal breeding that began with domestication. One can distinguish two main phases (1) animal keeping, and (2) animal breeding.

Animal keeping is the primitive form of animal breeding without purposeful selection or the control of feeding. Its most important characteristics are that: (*a*) in a given population there is only one breed, and (*b*) the domestic animals are of a primitive type and—in the case of mammals—their size is small in comparison to that of the wild form. The origins of selective breeding, however, do go back to prehistoric times, for with the introduction of castration of some males (from the late neolithic on) man was practising a certain selection (i.e. he selected some males for breeding and excluded others). However, this process was not conscious selection for higher productivity (e.g. for size, strength, speed, meat production, milk yield, wool, etc.).

The basis of real *animal breeding* is purposeful selective breeding and the control of both quantity and quality of feeding. It begins when man treats his domestic animals as individuals and not only as a herd. The beginnings of real *animal breeding* varied in time for different species; it started earlier for horse and dog than for cattle. It was first applied to all domestic animals in classical Greece and was widely practised by the Romans. With the fall of the Roman Empire, real animal breeding disappeared but it has become dominant again since the Late Middle Ages. The best criteria for recognizing this advanced phase are: (*a*) that different breeds live together in a population, (*b*) that the size of animals increases but dwarf breeds also appear, and (*c*) that the productivity of animals increases.

Domestication as a process involves three main factors: the man who carries it out, the wild animal that has been domesticated, and the domesticated animal that is the result. At first, one might think that it is only man who is the positive factor: he influences the animal, he transforms it from the wild state into the domesticated one, he multiplies its numbers, he takes it to distant regions, he restricts or kills off its wild forms, etc. This is undoubtedly the main line of development but beside this the whole process includes a range of complex interactions. These influences can be clearly seen not only on the domesticated animal—both on the individuals and on the whole populations—but also on the wild ancestors and even on man, on human populations and on the whole society.

There is no need to enumerate in detail these effects and changes for other papers in this book deal with them. But it is useful to examine the whole picture and in this way to try to determine for example what kind of differences existed between the fauna of prehistoric sites with animal keeping (apart from hunting) and the fauna of early sites with local domestication (apart from hunting and with or without animal keeping). It would be very interesting to examine questions like: what kind of factors determine the animal husbandry of a certain prehistoric culture, or in what ways are the qualitative and quantitative features of animal husbandry characteristic of a certain prehistoric culture or period, or to what extent can the origin, relationship, and movement of animals and peoples be determined from the type and development of animal husbandry and from its relation to hunting, etc. These questions have been rather neglected in recent research, and are therefore very well worth discussing.

With regard to the first question, there is certain evidence for animal keeping on a prehistoric settlement if:

1 the proportion of age groups of a domesticable species is not the same as found normally in the wild population;
2 the proportions of the sexes of a domesticable species is not the same as found normally in the wild population;
3 domesticated species appear which have no wild ancestors in that particular region, at least since the Pleistocene;
4 morphological changes appear in domesticated animals;
5 there are artistic representations of domesticated animals;
6 there are objects associated with animal husbandry.

Among these criteria the last four are the most reliable but the first two are the most interesting. The last four require that a certain time has passed during which either domesticated species spread to distant areas, or morphological changes developed[1]. Although it is well known nowadays that the time required for such a development is not very long (in South-west Asia hornless sheep and goats with twisted horns appeared as early as the eighth millennium B.C., and longifrons-/brachyceros-/cattle were identified in the Carpathian Basin in the sixth millennium B.C., and a good example of how fast domestic animals have spread is that sheep and goat and probably pig arrived in south-eastern Europe from their centre of domestication in South-west Asia as early as the seventh millennium B.C.), it is vital that reliable methods for distinguishing domesticated animals from their wild ancestors in the early period of domestication, when morphological changes had not yet developed, should be found. At the same time it is vital that such methods should be found for those species where morphological changes occurred only thousands of years after their first domestication (e.g. the horse).

Arcikhowski[2] was the first to attempt to distinguish wild and domesticated forms on the basis of differences in the proportions of age and sex groups. According to Arcikhowski the appearance of very old animals, the equal proportion of males and females and the lack of vertebrae and breast-bones indicated a wild population, while on the other hand the lack of old animals, the overwhelming majority of females (a great part of the males were killed as young animals or castrated; castration was introduced in animal keeping quite early) and the occurrence of whole skeletons indicated a domesticated population. This is without doubt a very intelligent principle by which to distinguish populations especially because it associates the differences in age and sex proportions with the occurrence or lack of certain kinds of bones (the hunter leaves the parts of the body which are poor at the place of killing, whereas domesticated animals are killed actually on the sites and their whole skeletons are therefore found *in situ*), and it could probably be extended to the study of the very early domestication of sheep and goats.

Perkins[3] deduced the domesticated state of the sheep of the proto-neolithic (10,870 ± 300 B.P.) Zawi Chemi Shanidar from the sudden increase of the proportion of immature animals. Coon[4] was the first who advanced the thesis that a high proportion of young animal bones was a proof of a domesticated population, and this has increasingly become an axiom particularly in Near Eastern archaeology. But Hopkins[5] has proved by statistical methods that in this respect there were significant differences between the uppermost (B_1 = proto-neolithic) and the next (C = Baradostian) layer of Shanidar Cave, and that the difference between layer C and the layers at Zawi Chemi Shanidar was also significant, but that the difference between the lowermost layer D (Mousterian!) of the cave and the top two layers of Zawi Chemi was not significant. "No one, I think, would argue that the Neanderthals from Shanidar Cave were domesticating sheep, and yet statistically they may have been killing a high percentage of immature animals"[6], but it is possible that the high proportion of young animals was somehow connected with a special type of hunting. Despite this, I am of the opinion that an increase in the number of immature animals in an early neolithic site shows (however incompletely) evidence of domestication, simply because in somewhat later periods of the neolithic this has occurred together with morphological changes in undoubtedly domesticated populations. I am convinced that it would be useful to combine this method—like that of Arcikhowski[7]—with the study of changes in sex groups and of the spectrum of bone kinds.

We have so far looked at the evidence which shows that animals were kept on prehistoric settlements. The next step is to determine what kinds of proof of local domestication can be found in the material found on a prehistoric site. This has a special importance not only for the determination of early domestication but also for secondary domestication in later times. It is well known that the progress of domestication did not end with the taming of the first animals; on the contrary, as the techniques of domestication spread man tried to tame the wild animals of new and different regions. On the other hand, throughout the neolithic man was forced to domesticate, because at that period when animal husbandry was still incipient and hunting was gradually on the decrease it would have been impossible to supply the growing human population with meat and at the same time to increase the domestic stock. Moreover neolithic man recognized quite early that domesticated stock was the basis of "wealth", and he attempted to raise it as efficiently as he could. And this led again to domestication. And at last when at the end of the neolithic he discovered new uses for his domesticated animals (milk, wool, draught, etc.) there broke out a "fever of domestication" in the whole of Europe[8]. When at the end of this "fever" the aurochs, the wild ancestor of the most important domesticated animals of Central and Western Europe at that time, was getting rarer man switched over to the swine which has been domesticated till the most recent times. Despite this switch the aurochs was still domesticated after prehistoric times, albeit very rarely. Virgil mentioned that in North Italy after a cattle epizootic the peasants captured and domesticated aurochs to replace their domestic stock. Likewise, mediaeval chronicles record that an aurochs bull, which was captured and tamed in Hungary, was used to draw in the heavy foundation-stones of the cathedral of Strassbourg[9] and its horn still hung on one of the pillars of the cathedral till the Great French Revolution.

And now the question: what is the evidence for local domestication in the material of a site?

1 Remains of both wild and domesticated forms on the site.
2 The existence of transitional forms between the wild ancestor and the domesticated animal.
3 Changes in the proportions of age and sex groups in the wild form.
4 Representations of scenes of capture.

The first point needs no further explanation. As regards the second point, transitional forms can be of two different kinds: (a) hybrids of the wild and domesticated form, (b) newly domesticated individuals (more common). If there exist skulls, or larger skull fragments, in the case of cattle it is not too difficult to distinguish the two types[10]. While the second type is a small-scale form of the wild cattle, the first type shows none of the well determined and rather standard proportions of the wild form. It has for example large horns on a small skull or, exactly the contrary, long horns with a wavy frontal ridge between the horns, or an uneven forehead, etc. (Such a disproportion was probably characteristic of the whole body but until now we have no whole skeletons to prove this.)

In the case of local domestication, transitional individuals bridge the differences between the wild and domestic forms of a particular animal species. For sheep and goats this question has yet to be studied; however such types should be identifiable at least in the form, cross-section, twisting, etc., of the horns. However, in the case of pig and cattle, transitional individuals can already be very well identified. In the case of pig and cattle, domestication causes a considerable decrease of size which can be recognized in the extremity bones which are found abundantly on prehistoric settlements. In the cattle material of a settlement without local cattle domestication (Seeberg, Burgäschisee-Süd, Switzerland, early neolithic, Cortaillod culture[11]) there is a gap between the series of measurements of wild and domestic cattle. On the other hand, on a site with large-scale cattle domestication (Berettyószentmárton, Hungary, late neolithic, Herpály[12]) there are many transitional forms. On the frequency diagrams for the cattle bones of this site these animals are transitional between the wild and domesticated cattle. The differences between the two sites are shown in Table 1.

Transitional forms like these occur also among the pigs of prehistoric European sites but as the pig was generally far rarer than cattle in prehistoric sites, its domestication was less important, and its numbers were much smaller.

On sites with local domestication there are interesting changes in the proportions of age and sex of wild forms. Modern experiments prove, and

Metacarpus Breadth of proximal end		50–51	52–53	54–55	56–57	58–59	60–61	62–63
Seeberg, Burgäschisee-Süd[a]	domesticated	2	2	1	4	0	0	0
	wild	0	0	0	0	0	0	0
Berettyószentmárton[b]	domesticated	0	0	0	1	3	3	3
	wild	0	0	0	0	0	0	0

Metacarpus Breadth of proximal end		64–65	66–67	68–69	70–71	72–73	74–75
Seeberg, Burgäschisee-Süd	domesticated	0	0	0	0	0	0
	wild	0	1	3	4	2	0
Berettyószentmárton[b]	domesticated	3	4	0	0	0	0
	wild	0	0	1	5	1	1

Metacarpus Breadth of proximal end		76–77	78–79	80–81	82–83	84–85	86–87
Seeberg, Burgäschisee-Süd	domesticated	0	0	0	0	0	0
	wild	1	0	0	0	0	0
Berettyószentmárton[b]	domesticated	0	0	0	0	0	0
	wild	3	6	0	1	0	1

Table 1

(a) Boessneck, J., Jéquier, P. and Stampfli, H. R. (1963). Seeberg, Burgäschisee-Süd. Die Tierreste, *Acta Bernensia*, **2** (3).

(b) Bökönyi, S. (1962). Zur Naturgeschichte des Ures in Ungarn und das Problem der Domestikation des Hausrindes, *Acta Arch. Hung.*, **14**, pp. 175–214; Bökönyi, S. and Kubasiewicz, M. (1961). *Neolithische Tiere Polens und Ungarns in Ausgrabungen*, **I**. Das Hausrind. Budapest-Szczecin.

there is also prehistoric evidence for this, that only young animals can be domesticated. Therefore prehistoric man had to capture young animals to tame them. But, on the other hand, the wild adult individuals tried to protect their young, and man had therefore to kill the adults in order to capture the young. Consequently it is logical that in the material of sites with large-scale domestication there should be only a few (or even no) bones of immature wild individuals and that the overwhelming majority of the domesticable wild species should be adult, mature or even senile animals. And this is exactly what we find. For example at Berettyószentmárton (with large-scale cattle domestication) among 1106 aurochs bones of identifiable age there were only ninety-five (8·6%) immature individuals and 1011 (91·4%) of adult and senile animals. On the other hand, at Seeberg-Burgäschisee-Süd (without cattle domestication) 26% (judging from the mandibles, even 55%) of the aurochs bones were of immature individuals[13]. This latter example shows clearly that this type of selection did not operate and that, on the contrary, the hunters tried to kill the young animals which were the easier prey.

In the wild the proportion of male and female animals is normally 1:1. This ratio should also exist in the bone material of the wild ancestors of the domesticated animals in prehistoric sites. But in one form of hunting[14] which eventually led to domestication, man began to husband the wild herd just like his domesticated stock; he protected the herd against its natural enemies (amongst which were other human hordes), saved the young and female individuals, and if he wanted to kill any he chose the old animals, and first of all the superfluous males. There is a good example of this at the site of Asiab (West Iran, *c*. eighth millennium B.C.) with its very beginning of goat domestication. At this site judging from horn cores, there were almost only male individuals among the wild goats. Or again in Berettyószentmárton the greatest number of the aurochs bones were of bulls, while in Seeberg-Burgäschisse-Süd bones of aurochs cows were probably in the majority.

As for representations of the capture of animals these are comparatively late. For example, the famous golden cups of Vaphio (1550–1450 B.C.) show the capture of bulls at a time when cattle had been domesticated for at least 4500 years (and it is not even sure if the bulls represented were really wild animals).

It is obvious that of the four criteria mentioned above it is the second one which is of decisive importance. In other words it is the occurrence of transitional individuals which is the best evidence for local domestication. Domestic stock, individuals with well-determined criteria of advanced domestication are theoretically not essential. But only theoretically, because in practice there are some sites where such an initial stage of domestication is not observable. The same is true for the changes in the proportions of age and sex groups of the wild forms. These changes are associated only with that type of domestication which developed from hunting. But since the domestication of the most important animals has its origin in hunting, there can be no doubt that these types of changes can be observed in the populations of wild ancestors if there is enough bone material available.

The third group of questions concerns the relations between man, human population, society and domestication and animal husbandry. To study these questions it is necessary to examine the animal husbandry of the whole prehistoric and early historic population in a certain area. The Carpathian Basin, and particularly Hungary, seems to be a good territory for this purpose. The Carpathian Basin is a closed geographical unit, and Hungary has roughly homogeneous environmental and climatic conditions. Furthermore, and particularly important, the bone material of Hungary's *c*. 400 prehistoric and early historic sites was studied with the same method and from the same view points. (This material also served very well as a basis for synthesizing the material of Central and Eastern Europe.) In these investigations only the material from settlements was used, for it was this material that accurately reflected not only the qualitative but also the quantitative composition of the domesticated fauna. The essence of the method was the study qualitatively, and above all quantitatively, of the species in the domesticated fauna. They (together with the hunted fauna) give us valuable information about the development of one of the most important sections of the economy. It can be proved that the great periods of prehistory and early history and many prehistoric cultures or groups of cultures, had their own typical animal husbandry (which is reflected in the proportions of domesticated species). And this husbandry was at least as characteristic of them as the form or decoration of their pottery, etc. The great periods of prehistory and of early history (and in some cases their sub-phases and even certain cultures) can be very well distinguished from each other on the basis of the development of their animal husbandry.

The species composition of animal husbandry also yields information about the relationship and migrations of cultures; e.g. the relations of the neolithic of South-west Asia and that of Greece are well-known. At Argissa-Maghula[15] and Nea Nikomedeia[16], the two early neolithic settlements in Greece, with animal bones which have been identified, the proportions of species in the domesticated fauna are the same: an animal husbandry based on sheep and goat as in the early neolithic of South-west Asia. The domesticated fauna contains at least 70% sheep and goat, while pig and cattle (the latter in all likelihood domesticated first in South-west Europe in the seventh millennium B.C.) are far less common, and dog seems to be extremely rare. The same form of animal husbandry extended as far as the Northern Balkans and even as far as the Carpathian Basin (see Table 2). But while the early neolithic people of the Southern Balkans hardly hunted, in the wet and swampy environment of the Carpathian Basin they acquired a quite considerable part of their meat by hunting and fishing. The original type of animal husbandry was deeply rooted in the traditions of the human population for they clung to it even in an unfavourable environment (sheep and goat were not animals of the swamps). And this is the best evidence to show that in this case we are dealing with the migration northwards of a type of animal husbandry together with a human group and not the simple taking over of a particular domesticated species. Beyond the Carpathian Basin this type of animal husbandry based on sheep and goat is not found.

This alien form of animal husbandry was unable to develop further (for lack

	Wild animals %	Domesticated animals %	Cattle %	Sheep/goat %	Pig %	Dog %
Argissa-Maghula(a) (Greece)	0·92	99·08	4·76	84·15	9·99	0·18
Nea Nikomedeia(b) (Greece)	7·00	93·00	14·55	70·45	14·77	0·23
Ludas-Budzak (Yugoslavia)	20·92	79·08	13·13	86·13	0·37	0·37
Maroslele-Pana (Hungary)	32·96	67·04	26·52	70·16	1·66	1·66
Gyálarét (Hungary)	26·95	73·05	30·37	63·56	4·67	1·40
Röszke-Ludvár (Hungary)	59·18	40·89	17·96	76·41	1·64	3·99
Deszk-Olajkut (Hungary)	19·84	80·16	29·39	70·21	0·20	0·20

Table 2

(a) Boessneck, J. (1961). Haustierfunde präkeramisch-neolithischer Zeit aus Thessalien, *Z. Tierzücht. ZüchtBiol.*, **76**, pp. 39–42.

(b) Higgs, E. S. (1962). The fauna of the early neolithic site at Nea Nikomedeia, Greek Macedonia, *Proc. Prehist. Soc.*, **28**, pp. 271–4.

of domesticable wild forms of its leading elements, the sheep and goat) and was unable to maintain itself later than the end of the first third of the neolithic. From this time on cultures of local origin developed their own forms of animal husbandry. These were based on cattle and pig, animals which had their wild forms in the Carpathian Basin, and could therefore be domesticated locally. In this type of animal husbandry, cattle were the leading element and pig generally occupied the second place. These cultures practised large-scale domestication, with which their hunting was also associated: aurochs was the main hunted animal (see the second group of questions above: the adult animals were killed and the young ones captured).

The late neolithic cultures which had a local origin (Herpály culture, Lengyel culture, etc.) practised a similar form of animal husbandry. Their settlements are, however, easily distinguishable from earlier ones on the basis of the sudden increase of hunting. This was connected with a new "fever of domestication" with a large-scale domestication of cattle.

And so for every period and phase of Hungarian prehistory there is a typical form of animal husbandry reflected in the particular proportions of the animal species.

There is yet another question: what kind of information can the type of animal husbandry found tell us about the migrations of cultures or peoples? There is another good example from the Carpathian Basin: during the Holocene there were three important south-eastern incursions into this region. The first was the Körös culture at the beginning of the neolithic, the second the Badener culture at the end of the Copper Age or at the beginning of the Bronze Age, and lastly the Turks at the end of the Middle Ages. Despite the gaps of three thousand years between these incursions all three brought with them exactly the same form of animal husbandry based on sheep and goats (see Table 3). The bone material of their settlements can only be distinguished by the domestic breeds kept on them, by the occurrence of horse and domestic birds on Turkish sites, and by the decrease in hunting.

	Wild animals %	Domesti- cated animals %	Cattle %	Sheep/ goat %	Pig %	Dog %	Horse/ birds %
Körös cultura (average)	33·60	66·40	21·00	77·31	0·72	0·97	—
Budapest-Andor utca (Badener culture)	6·81	93·19	34·31	41·72	22·58	1·29	—
Buda-Pasha palace (Turkish)	1·03	98·97	10·45	86·16	0·35	0·48	2·56

Table 3

The proportions of species in a domesticated fauna also tell us something about the way of life of certain human populations. It is quite clear that nomadic peoples firstly breed animals which can easily be driven, while, on the other hand, settled peoples keep mainly animals which can be confined.

Adaptation of animal husbandry to changes in ways of living is clearly seen from the Early Middle Ages. From the point of view of animal husbandry the early mediaeval settlements of Central and Eastern Europe can be divided into two groups. The first group consists of the Slavonic and German villages and towns, while the second group includes the Hungarian villages and the settlements of certain newly settled peoples of the Pontic region. The animal husbandry of the first group was characterized by having pig and cattle (alternately) as its leading elements, whereas sheep and goat were much rarer, and horse was either very rare or entirely absent. In the animal husbandry of the second group, cattle or sheep/goat were the most common domesticated animals, and the horse also was common, whereas pig was extremely rare. Certain differences in the uses of the domesticated animals existed in the two groups. For example, the horse was not eaten by people of the first group, whereas it was eaten by people of the second group, and whilst for the people of the first group cattle were almost exclusively draught animals, they were also kept for meat by people of the second group, etc. There was no essential difference between the animal husbandry of the Slavs and Germans in the first group or that of the Hungarians and Pontic peoples in the second group. This shows that the differences between the animal husbandry of the two groups were not of ethnic origin, but existed simply as a result of changes in the way of life, slowly followed by changes in the animal husbandry of the newly settled peoples.

Since Celtic and Roman times settlement types and the class-structure have also caused changes in the animal husbandry. There are fundamental differences between the domesticated fauna of Celtic villages and towns (oppidums) and that of Roman villas, castles, military stations or native villages. (It was in the Celtic towns, Roman villas and castles that the first beginnings of a civilized way of life occurred, while in Celtic villages, Roman military stations and native villages under Roman rule, people continued their prehistoric way of life.) In the Middle Ages there were sharp differences between the animal husbandry of villages, towns, royal or episcopal residences and the nobleman's manor-houses. The animal husbandry of villages always lagged behind that of towns, etc., but in addition to this the animal husbandry of towns demanded emphasis on those species which did not need too much place and did not require too much food (e.g. pig, hen). In general it has been the hen which has been the domestic animal of urbanization since the Celts. A difference caused by the class-structure was that since the Romans, imported animals (peacock, guinea-fowl, etc.) have appeared in the animal husbandry of villas, royal residences, etc.

The problems discussed in this paper are only a small sample of the questions which arise in connection with domestication and early animal breeding. Some of them have been touched upon also in other papers, but I think it has been useful to raise them in this way because I am convinced that approaching these questions from different angles can help to solve them.

Notes

1 Unfortunately animal representations and objects connected with animal husbandry (e.g. bridles) appear quite late in the archaeological record.
2 Arcikhowski, A. W. (1947). *Introduction to Archaeology.* (In Russian.) Moscow.
3 Perkins, D. (1964). Prehistoric fauna from Shanidar, Iraq, *Science*, 144, pp. 1565–6.
4 Coon, C. S. (1951). *Cave Explorations in Iran, 1949.* Philadelphia.
5 Hopkins, J. (1967). Identification of the domestication of animals without morphological changes. Manuscript, Chicago.
6 Hopkins, J. (1957). ibid.
7 Arcikhowski, A. W. (1947). ibid.
8 Bökönyi, S. (1968). *The Historical Development of Animal Breeding in Central and Eastern Europe.* (In Hungarian with English summary.) Agrártört, Szemle.
9 Szalay, B. (n.d.). The Hungarian aurochs. The history of the aurochs (*Bos primigenius* Boj.) in Hungary. (In Hungarian.) Manuscript.
10 Bökönyi, S. (1962). Zur Naturgeschichte des Ures in Ungarn und das Problem der Domestikation des Hausrindes, *Acta Arch. Hung.*, 14, pp. 175–214.
11 Boessneck, J., Jéquier, P. and Stampfli, H. R. (1963). Seeberg, Burgäschisee-Süd. Die Tierreste, *Acta Bernensia*, 2 (3). Bern.
12 Bökönyi, S. (1959). Die frühalluviale Wirbeltierfauna Ungarms. (Vom Neolithikum bis zur La Tène-Zeit), *Acta Arch. Hung.*, 2, pp. 39–102.
13 Boessneck, J., Jéquier, P. and Stampfli, H. R. (1963). ibid.
14 Pohlhausen, H. (1953). Nachweisbare Ansätze zum Wanderhirtentum in der niederdeutschen Mittelsteinzeit, *Z. f. Ethnol.*, 78, pp. 64–82. Begleiten.
15 Boessneck, J. (1962). *Die Tierreste aus der Argissa-Magula vom präkeramischen Neolithikum bis zur mittleren Bronzezeit. Die deutschen Ausgrabungen auf der Argissa-Magula in Thessalien.* Bonn.
16 Higgs, E. S. (1962). The fauna of the early neolithic site at Nea Nikomedeia Greek Macedonia, *Proc. Prehist. Soc.*, 28, pp. 271–4.

RAYMOND E. CHAPLIN

The use of non-morphological criteria in the study of animal domestication from bones found on archaeological sites

The study of the history of man's exploitation of animals is severely hampered by our lack of knowledge concerning the biology of the species involved and the dearth of adequately documented specimens from archaeological excavations.

Many studies concerned with the recognition of animal domestication from bones have relied on morphological criteria. This is not surprising since the problem has generally been approached from an anatomical standpoint. These criteria are however of limited value when studying the sequence leading to, and the consequences of, domestication.

The morphological approach presupposes that changes produced by domestication will be reflected in the skeleton. In practice it would appear that only a few bones of the body may be so affected. Morphological changes which may be observed are not necessarily a result of domestication and it is therefore desirable that contemporary examples of wild species from the same region should be available to ascertain whether other factors may be involved. These points have generally been ignored by archaeologists despite the clear evidence of rapid changes in the size of wild species in the post-glacial period[1]. Until contemporary deposits of true wild animals have been found and studied (as opposed to those bones found on excavations and identified as wild) the interpretation of changes observed in the bones, as being the result of domestication, can be no more than speculation. It is of course also necessary to demonstrate that such changes are not part of the normal variation within the population associated with sex and age or due to the simultaneous exploitation of different populations. Problems like these can only be satisfactorily worked out on a few types of bone which usually form but a small proportion of a large quantity of fragments. As a result of this, the study of domestication on many sites had had to be done with samples that were totally inadequate for the problems involved. These cautions emphasize once again both the need for anatomical and ecological investigations of living populations to provide objective data on relevant species and the need for the excavation of palaeozoological deposits rather than just cultural ones[2].

Even where sample size requirements are met, morphological criteria only permit the recognition of a late stage in the domestication story. The earliest stage recognizable is that where changes have been produced and this is at an unknown distance in time or space from the initial success. The answers to such questions as when and how domestication occurred can only come from a study of earlier material in the stratigraphical sequence using other criteria.

Another aspect of the problem of morphological criteria is concerned with the sequence of domestication. If the changes being studied are the product of say twenty-five generations, the length of time involved will vary between species. The time required to produce a given number of generations is a product of the time from birth to puberty plus the gestation period of the next offspring. In roe deer, for example, the generation time is 14 months (birth to puberty) plus 10 months (gestation), the first offspring being produced 24 months after the birth of the parent. In red deer this is 36 or 48 months, depending on puberty[3]. Another vital factor in this, for example, is the degree of selection pressure that was being exerted; pigs, for example, still strongly resembled their wild ancestors in Europe long after specialized strains of sheep, cattle and horses had been developed. This is of course a gross oversimplification of the problem since it is unwise to make interspecific comparisons of such variable phenomena. It does however serve to underline the fact that our view of the sequence may be distorted by the use of morphological criteria.

If we are to study the events leading to domestication and its significance to the community, a method of recognizing domestication[4] and of quantifying all animal exploitation is necessary. Domestication is only a pattern of animal exploitation and can therefore be recognized by reference to the parameters which define that pattern. In studying domestication it is also necessary to consider certain specialized usage patterns which, whilst they may not constitute domestication, may usefully be termed incipient domestication.

For ungulates in particular, the following parameters may be used to characterize the nature and scale of the exploitation.

1 The species involved
2 The minimum number of each species
3 The age of these animals
4 The sex of these animals
5 The frequency of the different bones of each species
6 The size of the animals.

In the methodology outlined below the species involved, the number of animals and their age and sex are essential parameters. At this point I would like to make some general observations on the use of these parameters and also to comment on the other two as they are relevant to much of what is discussed in this volume, but they do not receive detailed consideration below[5].

The frequency of occurrence of the different bones greatly assists in the identification of the type of site involved (e.g. a field butchering camp) and the recognition of "trade". The value of this technique for the investigation of hunting practices is shown by the work on North American palaeo-Indian sites[6]. This has also been used in the study of a Saxon farm site in London[7] where it showed that the most valuable joints of mutton had disappeared from the site. This is illustrated in Fig. 1 and relevant details are given below[8].

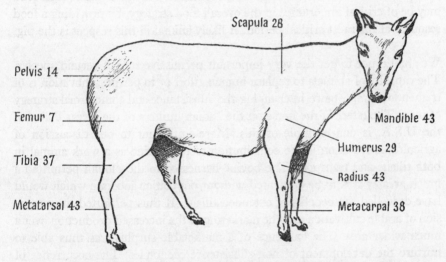

Fig 1 The minimum number of animals identified from the principal bones of the body of the sheep found on a Saxon site, Whitehall, London.
(This sketch, by Mr. John Atkinson, approximates the type of female sheep from the site)

Although this method is useful for understanding hunting practices and for illustrating marketing or the disposal of meat, it does not provide a basis for the recognition of domestication. The size of the animal will normally determine whether it is butchered on the spot instead of the whole carcase being brought back to the dwelling site intact. Even where there is a temporal shift in the bone frequency spectrum from field dressing to site dressing, this may mean no more than a change in hunting area, technique or cultural practices.

The minimum number of animals is now the generally accepted basis for all quantity studies, it having been amply demonstrated on many occasions how misleading are the results of studies using the fragments method.

The minimum number of animals may either be used alone or as a basis for further calculation depending on what aspects of species "importance" are being studied. Archaeologists commonly refer to the importance of a species without specifying what the animals were important for. Some common measures of importance, meaningful in the archaeological context are the number of animals in relation to accommodation, fodder, mobility, etc., the amount of food produced (not only meat, but milk, blood, visceral organs, etc.[9]) and the provision of raw materials. The quantities involved are obtained by extrapolation from the minimum number, taking into account the age, sex and size of the animals involved. We should remember that in the most simple terms at least a hundred sheep may only be the body weight food equivalent of ten bovines. In terms of resources (food + raw material + work) one species may be of overwhelming importance though its numbers are few. In other cases an animal that contributes little in terms of total food may be of critical importance in the overall food strategy, by providing a food resource at the most critical period. A likely animal in this respect is the pig.

We should not forget the very important permissive role of certain species. The capacity of animals to replace human effort or to permit innovation is of tremendous importance in changing the subsistence and commercial strategy of man. The effect of the horse on the Indian hunters of the Great Plains of the U.S.A. is one example of this. More important to our discussion of agricultural evolution is the contribution of the bovine as a work animal in both tillage and transport. The bovine harnessed to the plough permitted a much greater area to be cultivated without population increase which would have cancelled the benefits of extended tillage. It thus permitted the expansion of arable cultivation and the marketing of the increased production over a much wider area. The existence of a marketable surplus was thus able to nurture the development of non-subsistence economies. The occurrence of domesticated bovines has a far greater significance than just a shift from hunting to keeping. We should bear in mind the exceptional importance of this enabling factor even if, through lack of evidence of its action, we cannot prove and quantify it in the same way as we do the basic animal production.

In many human groups when we think of the animals we must consider that food may have been the predominant need supplied by them. In such cases it is clearly useless to talk in terms of importance by reference to the number of head walking around. What is important is the total contribution of this species to the diet. Again, in relation to agriculture, it is misleading to talk in terms of shifts in species importance without reference to the exploitation being practised. If, for example, there is a numerical increase of sheep whilst cattle numbers stay static, this may have arisen as a result of the inception or extension of wool production rather than as a result of the extension of overall meat production. This is more likely to have been achieved by an extension of cattle numbers if this species could supply it efficiently within the strategy of production. Here we must bear in mind the relative difficulties of extending and stabilizing meat production. The small species with their different breeding biology and development patterns may be more efficient in producing short term increases and needs, though this strategy raises other problems in relation to the suitability of the habitat and the need for supervision, etc.

This type of interpretation of the bone evidence is just that—interpretation—it represents one person's view of the evidence. Generally it represents the best fit to our prejudices. It is therefore disturbing to find a trend in some recent literature towards the presentation of little more than the author's interpretation and lacking the fundamental evidence which would enable others to assess the data in the light of their theories.

In a herd of animals, various age and sex structures will optimize the production of such commodities such as meat, milk, fleece, etc. In the case of sheep optimum all-commodity production is likely to be achieved by a herd consisting almost entirely of females and castrates, which are kept until they are worn out and unlikely to survive another winter. Males, because of their greater size, yield more meat and wool than a castrate but they may well be disruptive to the herd. A more efficient use of the herd may however be to keep only the females for the bulk of the wool (plus breeding, milk and residual meat) and to remove castrated animals when they reach an economic carcase weight (having of course also collected the wool clip). Any exploitation for the basic animal product on a rational basis gives rise to specific age and sex structures in the population. Population models according to the basic parameters can be built up for any type of exploitation or survival strategy. Such models are valuable tools in interpreting the economy behind the bone assemblage. The exploitation patterns quoted here are the result of work on Roman and later sites. In quoting them I do not wish to imply that such patterns will be found on the earliest domestication sites but merely to demonstrate the strength of these methods in an archaeological context.

As in the domesticated animals the nature of the parameters for wild species will be characteristic for particular situations. The population age structure of a wild herd of deer, for example, is a property of that species and its habitat, and man's activity[10]. Fig. 2 illustrates the age and sex structure of a wild herd of roe deer in Denmark described by Anderson[11], details of which are given below[12]. If environmental evidence is available a prediction of this can be made within certain limits. This will greatly assist in understanding incipient domestication and the level of exploitation involved. As domestication is a movement away from the wild and a transference of both stock and ideas from one environment to another, the way in which man was exploiting the wild animals will strongly influence his approach to the problems of utilization in captivity.

Man's exploitation of a wild population is governed by his needs, his technical skill, his hunting skill and the biology and behaviour of the animal population.

If we assume, as I think we must, a close knowledge of the territory and species therein, it is probable that hunting skill is largely static. In the absence

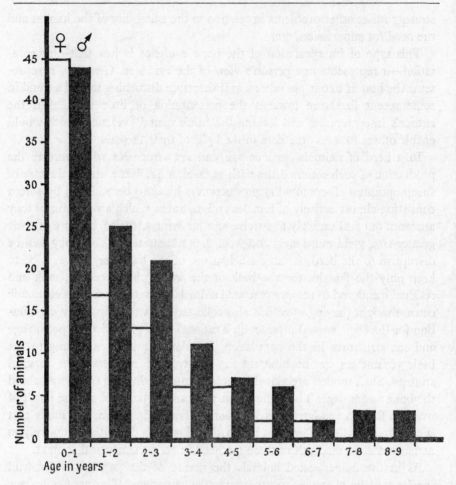

Fig 2 The age and sex structure of a herd of wild roe deer (*Capreolus capreolus* L) at Kalo, Denmark, based on the extermination of the herd.

of evidence for the introduction of superior weapons we may reasonably assume that this factor is also constant. In any case, improved weapons, etc., mostly affect the quantity and more rarely the nature of what is killed.

Thus our two major variables are man's needs (modified by religious needs where necessary) and the biology of the animal population. We are thus able to construct models of animal populations to show which animals are likely to be killed and to formulate certain hypotheses which will assist in assessing the exploitation.

Any sample of bones derived from a human occupation site does of course reflect some degree of human need. Certain needs and their consequences are however of particular relevance to domestication.

The amount of time and effort needed to capture an animal is not proportional to its size; thus in the quest for food man tends to exert a choice for the largest ungulates available that are consistent with his needs, abilities and efforts. Depending on relative abundance however the same quantity of meat may be more easily obtained from several animals of a smaller species. Further, some species can survive much higher cropping rates than others. Animals with long pre-pubertal periods such as the elephants contrast sharply with the medium sized ungulates in this respect. Given hunting aids such as dogs, the emphasis in hunting may be shifted to those species that are amenable to herding by dogs such as reindeer, saiga, sheep and goats, etc., away from cattle, pigs and deer, which are not so amenable to hunting in this way. A desire for a particular raw material such as wool or antler may also influence hunting and it would be of value to know the extent to which this affected the ecology of the region. Preferential culling of male animals in a polygamous species such as red deer or sheep is beneficial to the population since it increases the reproduction rate[13], a fact which would not go unnoticed. Thus, whether deliberate or not (a fact which we can never know) such a beneficial exploitation should perhaps be regarded as incipient domestication. Such patterns are identifiable in bone samples by reference to the parameters given.

If selective hunting is not practised the cull should be random in regard to the numbers of animals in any age and sex group. We may therefore predict for a given species the likely proportions of each age and sex group when no selection is practised. Adjustment must be made for differences in behaviour and biology between the sexes. From the sort of data that is given in Fig. 2 it is possible to estimate the frequency with which a sex or age group is likely to be encountered. This can then be modified in the light of behaviour patterns such as that of the red deer herd which is usually led by an old hind. Being the leader, the old hind is the one most likely to be caught by capture devices set on lines of movement.

In some cervids a selection bias for antlers may be recognized by comparison of the age structure of the males with that of the females. Since the female shows no obvious external indication of her age the female sample should reflect the random picture. The age structure of a sample of male fallow deer killed in road accidents in Epping Forest[14], is shown in Fig. 3 this may be compared with the age structure of a sample of male fallow deer obtained by purposeful culling in a park herd shown in Fig. 4. These patterns require detailed study of the individuals and populations in order to explain them. The park herd is only explicable in terms of the purpose of the cull and the ability of the stalker to identify the relevant criteria in living animals[15].

Careful consideration must be given to the age structure and seasonal distribution of the males and female[16]. In polygamous species this can vary considerably between the sexes. The mortality rate often varies considerably and this is not so much occasioned by the direct effects of fighting males but the aftermath. During the rutting season males lose condition as a result of which many fail to survive the spring. In some species there is a marked

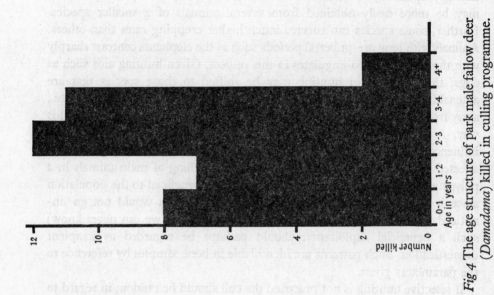

Fig 4 The age structure of park male fallow deer (Damadama) killed in culling programme.

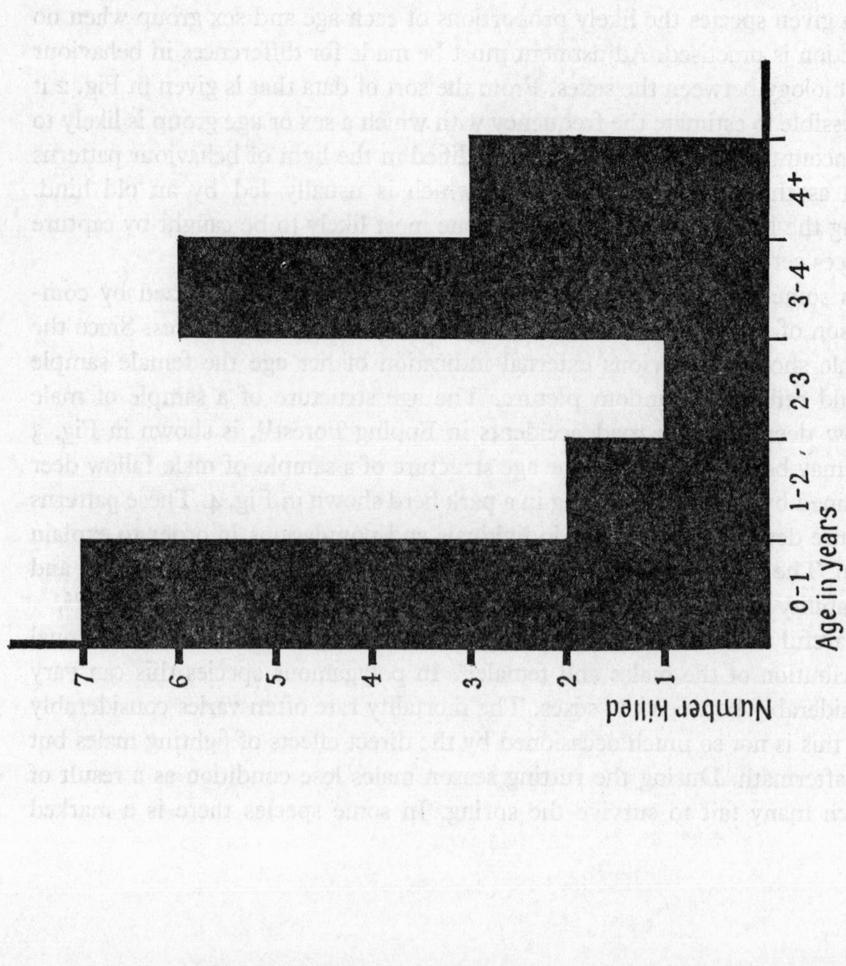

Fig 3 The age of wild male fallow deer (Dama dama) killed in road accidents in Epping Forest.

seasonal separation of the sexes for much of the year. It must be borne in mind however that often the young (pre-pubertal) males form part of the female herd[17].

In conclusion we can say that in assessing the nature of the exploitation of a wild species by man the most important parameters are the age and sex of the animals in the sample, the structure of which must be explained against the biology and behaviour of the species.

Despite exerting a fairly strong influence on the wildlife population prehistoric man is unlikely to have created any strong imbalance or brought many species near extinction. However, where man had concentrated on a particular species, either as a result of environmental or ecological factors or the use of canids for hunting, some form of wildlife management (incipient domestication) was being exerted. In the case of animals like the reindeer it is an almost invisible step to full domestication.

It is not known whether sedentary domestication was generally preceded by a phase of semi-nomadic domestication. We must be careful not to over-generalize about such events for the history of domestication of each species was probably different amongst different groups and in different environments. It is possible that semi-nomadic domestication is the result of the evolution of hunting techniques with specialization as a result of the adoption of the dog. We may on this basis suggest why man was able, in certain areas, to have reached a stage of semi-nomadic/nomadic herding of reindeer, sheep and goats, and possibly gazelles. This is however a blind alley of cultural evolution and there is as yet little evidence that this is a significant general stage of the transition from hunting to domestication.

An alternative view of the domestication of the sheep and goat lies in their relationship to cultivation. The full potential of tillage to the community is only realized when this is sedentary though it does not preclude seasonal hunting (which can be identified from the bones). The effect of tillage is to insert into the environment patches of concentrated luxuriance which few herbivores can resist. Thus, with the adoption of tillage the species valued for hunting become the enemies of the cultivator. The necessity of crop protection, however, must have been a welcome innovation for the animals came into the fields and no longer had to be pursued! To be a successful cultivator however one had to virtually exterminate the game, and meat and raw materials would become scarce locally. It is perhaps at this stage that the most valuable species were brought into captivity. Some support for this view is obtained by a consideration of which species were the most usable and which were actually chosen in this early period.

In South-west Asia there would seem to be three contenders—pigs, goats and sheep. The pig would seem to be the least amenable of the three because of its weak social structure. Sheep and goats are relatively small and can be handled by one man, they breed regularly and have a short generation period. These qualities are also shared by the pig. Sheep and goat are social species, handleable with the aid of canids, this contrasts with the remainder of the fauna—cattle, pigs, deer, etc., where this is more weakly developed.

The herding of reindeer in the north is a logical extension of their hunting in a zone which does not favour tillage and to which domestic species are ill adapted. In other geographical zones away from South-west Asia, other species might have been more attractive. The choice however may not always have had to be made since in Europe, by the time tillage had spread to any extent, it was already accompanied by successfully domesticated ungulates, both large and small. It thus appears that in Europe and South-west Asia it is just those animals that we would expect to be most suitable that are the earliest domesticated ungulates on present evidence. We do, however, need to know much more about animal exploitation and its relationship to settlement and cultivation in pre-domestication times by methods outlined above.

The hypothesis involving tillage implies that full domestication is an immediate step and that from the outset man must exert his control by containment and in ensuring that food is available and that the environment will enable them to breed and flourish. Inherent in this new relationship are two potentially disruptive factors, one, the problem of the sex ratio of the offspring and the disruptive effect of sexually mature males, the second, the need for a take-off from the population for food. There are two ways of dealing with the problem of the male. Either the removal of the majority of males before puberty or their castration. The optimum production from the herd is obtained by the latter method though there is possibly little difference between killing intact males when they reach optimum pre-pubertal condition and the killing of castrates when they reach optimum condition. The overall management of the herd for meat and fleece production in the case of sheep consists of the keeping of the females into old age which are killed when they are unlikely to survive the lean period. This provides annual crops of wool and lambs, and also residual meat. The males, either as castrates or intact animals are killed for meat as described above since they are of less value than females and reach optimum value at a particular weight and time. We must, I think, give credit to these early farmers/herders for the rational use of their flock and I think the pattern outlined above is not beyond their ability. This type of system is clearly recognizable archaeologically since there is a considerable disparity between the components of the relevant parameters between the wild and domesticated systems of exploitation. These utilization patterns are well demonstrated at the Saxon farm in Whitehall, London. Provisional age structure data of unsexed bones is shown in Figs. 5–7 for cattle, pigs and sheep. Despite the slight inconsistencies[18] in the data occasioned by the methods used, clear differences in the strategy are apparent between the species. These differences are readily explained on the lines noted above.

The sex and age structures of this domesticated system are quite distinct. The majority of the animals fall into two groups, one, predominantly of male

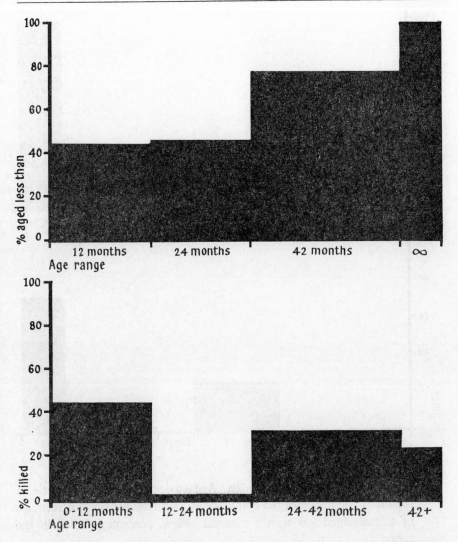

Fig 5 Saxon farm, Whitehall, London. Age at death of domestic pigs as
shown by the fusion of the epiphyses of long bones. Above, percentage
of animals aged less than *x* months. Below, percentage killed in age
range.

and castrates, are killed quite young, and another group, predominantly of
females, are killed in old age. One of the critical points to be noted is that a
trimodal sex structure will be present but it must be remembered that the
intact male is likely to be represented only by about two to four animals per
hundred. Adequate samples are therefore large. Limits to the recognition of
sex are set by bones whose growth is not yet completed. These immature
bones have not as far as I am aware been investigated for sexual differences.
There are enormous difficulties surrounding any attempt to age animals

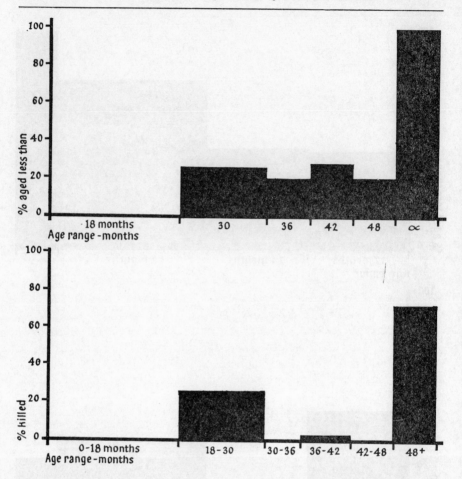

Fig 6 Saxon farm, Whitehall, London. Age at death of domestic cattle as shown by the fusion of the epiphyses of long bones. Above, percentage of animals aged less than *x* months. Below, percentage killed in age range.

absolutely. This however does not invalidate the method since we are only concerned with the relative age and sex structure of the population and this can be obtained from either dental criteria[19] or the use of the sequence of fusion of the epiphyses of long bones[20]. Depicted graphically this latter is shown as the number above or below the age. Much work has now been done on sexual dimorphism in bones and it should not be difficult to interpret the distribution patterns of measurements and ratios obtained from the sample.

It has been seen that the exploitation of domestic and of wild populations is characterized by particular features of the age and sex classes within the population which are sufficiently different to be detectable in groups of sub-fossil bone. Further parameters given above enable both a description and a

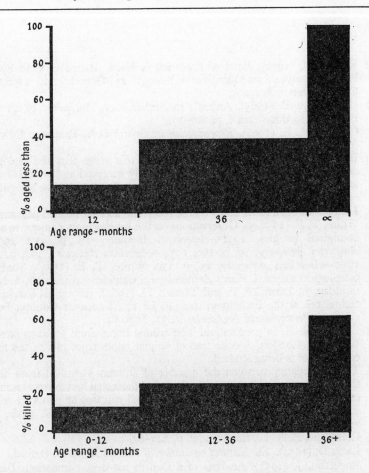

Fig 7 Saxon farm, Whitehall, London. Age at death of domestic sheep as shown by the fusion of the epiphyses of the long bones. Above, percentage of animals aged less than *x* months. Below, percentage killed in age range.

quantification of the exploitation of animals by man to be made. It is suggested that this approach is particularly necessary when seeking to study the man/animal relationship and therefore also to the study of the origins and history of domestication in particular.

Notes

1 Kurtén, B. (1959). *Rates of Evolution in Fossil Mammals*. Cold Spring Harbor Symposia on Quantitative Biology. **24**; Genetics and Twentieth Century Darwinism, 205.

2 Chaplin, R. E. (1965). Animals in Archaeology, *Antiquity*, **39**, p. 204; Berry, R. J., this volume, p. 207–17.

3 Chaplin, R. E. (1966). *Reproduction in British Deer*. Passmore Edwards Museum, London.

4 It is perhaps worth bearing in mind at this stage that the biological definition of domestication that is generally accepted and which is used in this book does not provide a single criteria for its objective recognition on archaeological sites until a very late period.

5 I am preparing a fuller study on the recording and use of such parameters.

6 White, T. E. (1952–5). Observations on the butchering technique of some aboriginal peoples. 1952—*American Antiquity*, **17**, p. 337. 1953—*American Antiquity*, **19**, p. 160. 1954—*American Antiquity*, **194**, p. 254. 1955—*American Antiquity*, **21**, p. 170. White, T. E. (1953). Studying osteological material, *Plains Archaeological Conference Newsletter*, **6**, 1953; Guilday, J., Parmalee, P. and Tanner, D. (1962). Aboriginal butchering techniques at the Eschelman site (36 La 12), Lancaster County, Pennsylvania, *Pennsylvania Archaeologist*, **32**, 2: p. 59.

7 Chaplin, R. E. in preparation. The animal bones from a Saxon farm in Whitehall, London. A collection of animal bones from pits of the ninth century A.D. is being studied.

8 The discrepancy between the number of animals identified from bones that would have had little meat on them and those that had the most is interpreted as indicating the "export" of dressed carcases or joints from this site. This analysis for practical reasons is limited to cranial, girdle and limb bones.

9 Cranstone, B. A. L., this volume, p. 247–63.

10 Lack, D. (1954). *The Natural regulation of Animal Numbers*. Oxford.

11 Anderson, J. (1953). Analysis of a Danish roe-deer population. *Danish Rev. of Game Biology*, **2**, p. 127.

12 The data redrawn from Anderson, J. (1953). ibid, is based on the total extermination of a wild herd of Roe deer. A great deal of very important information is contained in this paper which should be consulted in full. The data given here should not be used without reference to the original work.

13 Anderson, J. (1953). ibid.

14 Chaplin, R. and Chapman, D. (1963). A preliminary report on some fallow deer (*Dama dama*) from Epping Forest, *Essex Naturalist*, **31** (1), p. 148; Chaplin, R. and Chapman, D. (1966). Report on fallow deer (*Dama dama L*) obtained from Epping Forest during May-December 1964, *J. of Zoology*, **148**, p. 561.

15 Chaplin, R., and White, R. (1969). The use of tooth eruption and wear, body weight and antler characteristics in the age estimation of wild and park male fallow deer (*Dama dama*), *J. of Zoology*, **157**, p. 125.

16 Grubb, P. and Jewell, P. A. (1966). Social grouping and home range in feral soay sheep, *in* Jewell, P. A. and Loizos, C. (eds.) *Play, Exploration and Territory in Mammals*, Symposia of the Zoological Society of London, Number **18**, London; Lowe, V. P. W. (1966). Observation on the dispersal of red deer on Rhum, *in* Jewell, P. A. and Loizos, C. ibid.; Darling, F. Fraser (1937). *A Herd of Red Deer*, Oxford.

17 Grubb, P. and Jewell, P. A. (1966). ibid.

18 In detail almost any of this type of graph can be misleading because of the present limits of our knowledge and techniques for age estimation. The present graphs Figs. 5–7 are based on the fusion of the epiphyses of the long bones. The data depicted here is based on the percentage of a particular bone type that is or is not fused. The sequence in which the epiphyses fuse is generally accepted as a constant but the true age at which they fuse is extremely variable. This is discussed more fully in Chaplin, in preparation and Silver, I. (1963). The ageing of domestic animals, *in* Brothwell, D. R. and Higgs, E. S. (eds.) *Science in Archaeology*. London. The ages given on the lower axis of the graph are in general the upper limits of the range of variation in modern stock quoted by Silver, I. (1963). ibid. In Fig. 6 no attempt has been made to remove the minor inconsistencies in the centre. This is due to the fairly small sample of relevant criteria in that range. Notwithstanding these cautions these graphs give a reliable indication of the general structure of the husbandry on this site.

19 Chaplin, R. E., in preparation; Chaplin, R. and White, R. (1969). ibid.

20 Silver, I. (1963). ibid.

B. A. L. CRANSTONE

Animal husbandry: the evidence from ethnography

I must begin by defining my brief. My main concern is with the types of economies in which livestock play a part; with the connection (sometimes the contradiction) between the economic value of an animal and the prestige which it enjoys or confers; with the efficiency (or lack of it) with which the economic possibilities of animals are exploited; with the techniques used by man in handling animals and in obtaining from them what he desires. I am dealing mainly with animals as providers of food or raw materials, not with draught or pack animals, or with animals as sources of power. I shall hardly enter the very wide fields of the effects of stock-keeping on social and political institutions and on the way of life of peoples who depend largely on their livestock, or of the restrictive effect this way of life may have on their material culture.

The place of animals in some representative societies

Most people who practise some form of agriculture keep domestic animals which provide food, raw materials, or power: that is to say, which are not merely pets, or aids in hunting, but are valued for their meat, milk, blood, hides, wool or other products, or for their ability to pull or carry. Among peoples who practise shifting cultivation and who lack the plough the number of animals kept and their economic importance tend to be relatively small, for the level of agricultural technique is not sufficiently high to produce a surplus of food to support them. It is true that the animals often forage for themselves, as in the case of the mithan[2] of Assam or the Melanesian pig, but they usually return at night or at least at intervals to be fed. In these conditions domestic and wild or feral animals often inter-breed, and in appearance may be indistinguishable. Indeed the Nagas of Assam encourage this interbreeding to improve the stock, and supply salt-licks in the forest in order to attract the wild bulls, the domesticated females being driven out to them[3]. Since few animals can be kept there is little or no deliberate use of manure on the fields, though cattle may graze on stubbles after harvest. Many peoples at this agricultural level do not understand the value of manure.

Among plough cultivators the situation is rather different. The use of the plough implies the use of draught animals. Among plough cultivators grain crops are usually the staple, which means that there are stubbles, or straw, or by-products on which cattle can be fed, and improved techniques may provide a surplus to human requirements which can be fed to animals. Animals tend to be kept under closer control, because the land suitable for cultivation is likely to be fully and permanently utilized, and so there is less scope for animals to forage and more need to ensure that they do not damage crops, fences or terraces. Under these conditions of closer confinement opportunities for interbreeding with wild animals will be much less frequent. Moreover the greater density of settlement may result in wild animals of the same species being exterminated in the locality. It then becomes more likely that selective breeding will take place[4].

The animals which provide manure may not be in the same ownership as the stubbles on which they feed. The cattle-keeping Fulani of the savannah zone between the southern borders of the Sahara and the forest provide an example of a symbiotic relationship with the settled agriculturalists. They migrate southwards in the dry season in search of pasture and water, and northwards in the wet season to avoid tsetse fly. Except on the edge of the desert they depend largely on the sedentary peoples, pasturing their cattle on the stubbles or corraling them on the fallows, making gifts to the cultivators before entering their territory, and obtaining vegetable foods in exchange for milk products[5].

Animals are often of great importance to settled agricultural peoples not only for draught purposes but also to provide power for water-raising or milling machinery. But their direct contribution to the food supply may be rather small, though important in a protein-deficient diet.

Many shifting cultivators value their domestic animals as much for ritual as for purely economic reasons. This is true of the Nagas of Assam and their mithan[6], and in many parts of Melanesia pigs are regarded in this light: some tribes of the New Guinea highlands kill hundreds at periodical ceremonies.

The New Hebrides provide some good examples. Layard[7] describes the role of pigs in Vao, a small island off the east coast of Malekula. The upper canines of boars are knocked out so that the tusks of the lower jaw grow round in a circle, pierce the flesh of the cheek and re-enter the jaw. In some cases they re-emerge to form a second complete circle or even more. It is not surprising that the physical condition of these boars is usually poor. "Circle-tuskers" are essential for sacrifice and ceremonial presentation. The only pig-meat eaten is that of sacrifices. So some boars are gelded and sacrificed before the tusks re-enter the jaw; their value is much less, but they provide more meat. For this reason pigs are often killed in pairs, a circle-tusker and a gelding. The circle-tusker is of value only while alive, and only if its tusks are in good condition; if a tusk is broken the pig is worth little. Its physical condition does not affect its value, but after death its tusks are worthless.

It often happens that a man does not possess suitably tusked boars when he requires them, and it is necessary to borrow. The boar must be repaid later with a boar with tusks of the stage of development which those of the borrowed boar would by then have reached. This may entail borrowing again. Tusked boars thus become almost a form of currency, and a complex network of obligation comes into being. It appears too that the importance of pigs is such that land which might be used for cultivation is left to provide foraging ground for them.

Sows are not eaten by either sex. Women may not, because pigs are killed only in the context of ritual in which women have no part. Men may not, because sows being female are ritually dangerous to them. Layard says of the cultivation of tusks: "This practice lies at the base of the natives' whole overt religious life, gives rise to the chief form of currency, and so largely regulates all their economic activities, and . . . permeates every aspect of life"[8].

The Sakau district of north-west Espiritu Santo, as described by J. R. Baker[9], presents a somewhat different picture. Here there is the remarkably high proportion of about ten to twenty hermaphrodite pigs per hundred males. The degree, or form, of their intersexuality varies. Four forms are distinguished and named. All are sterile, but grow tusks. Apparently the natives have to operate on piglets of one form to allow them to pass urine—an interesting example of veterinary technique. A man purchasing promotion in rank (on which political and social power depend) must kill both tusked boars and hermaphrodites, and they are required also for presentation, for example in obtaining a wife. As in Vao pigs are borrowed. Since boars and hermaphrodites only are of value many female piglets are killed instead of being kept for breeding, as would seem logical to us. Here women and children may eat the flesh of hermaphrodites.

Among pastoral peoples the picture is somewhat different. Full pastoral nomadism is an Old World way of life practised in areas in which either insufficient rainfall or a short summer growing season makes agriculture impossible or unattractive. Pastoral nomads are economically dependent on their animals, and they cannot, therefore, totally ignore economic considerations in relation to them. This dependence forces them, or a section of the group, to lead a nomadic life in search of pasture and water, but it is not always necessary for the whole group to move. Among the Lapps the old people, women and children live relatively settled lives while the younger men tend the herds (this is to some extent a recent development), and the camels of the Ahaggar Tuareg may be at pasture in the Sudan five hundred miles from the oases where the flocks of goats and sheep are based and the slaves tend the gardens[10].

The animal which has the greatest economic value for a pastoral people is often not that which has the greatest prestige. The Tuareg keep camels, goats and sheep, a few horses, and in the south a few cattle and donkeys. The camel is the prestige animal, a subject (with war and love) for poetry. Formerly the Tuareg lived partly by raiding and by exactions from caravans, and for these activities camels were essential, as they still are for trading activities. But economically goats are much more valuable. There are ten times as many goats as sheep, the latter being bred mainly for slaughter, and regarded as more appropriate for sacrifice by this rather superficially Moslem people. There seem to be about thirty to forty goats per person (perhaps excluding slaves).

The Rwala bedouin of the Syrian desert[11] keep camels and horses. Here it is the camel which is economically vital, but the horse which has the prestige. Horses are used for repelling raids, in the vicinity of the camp; but camels are ridden for long-distance raiding. Few stallions are kept, mares being preferred for riding. The horse is unsuited to desert conditions; it has to be specially fed, and foals receive all the mare's milk and camel's milk in addition. The bedouin are the suppliers of camels to the settled peoples, and the camel is practically their only saleable product.

On the steppes of Russian Turkestan the Kazak[12] kept horses, sheep, a few goats, and bactrian camels (their traditional way of life is now largely if not entirely obsolete). Sheep, of the fat-rumped and fat-tailed breeds, form the majority of the livestock and provide the main food supply, but the Kazak too value the horse more highly. However, unlike the Arabs, the Kazak prefer to ride geldings. Mares are milked, and their flesh is eaten, but both are luxury foods. Sheep too are milked, and the milk made into butter and cheese. The climate is unsuitable for cattle, but a few are kept for their milk: beef is disliked and rarely eaten. Sheep and horses are herded separately, since horses need better grazing. Sheep provide wool, which is made into felt. Camels are mainly used as pack animals, but the hair which they shed in the spring is used in weaving rugs and hangings for the felt-covered tents called *yurt*. Sheep are herded by boys, who often ride oxen.

Among the East African herding peoples it is cattle which have, and confer, prestige. The Masai[13]—who are exceptional for this area in that they do not also cultivate—have nearly as many sheep as cattle, but sheep are far less highly esteemed. Both sheep and cattle provide milk, blood and meat. However, the Masai have two types of cattle: a smaller sort with horns of lyre form, and a larger type with shorter horns. The latter yield nearly twice as much milk, but the former are more highly valued. Among East African cattle-keeping people generally a man's prestige depends on the size of his herd, not on the quality of his beasts.

The Nuer[14] of the swamp and savannah country on both sides of the upper Nile both cultivate and herd cattle. They are pastoral in outlook, and before the outbreak of rinderpest in the late nineteenth century apparently relied more heavily on their cattle than they do now. In 1930 there were about ten cattle and five sheep and goats to a byre—that is, to a family unit. Millet and maize are cultivated, and fishing is important in the dry season and in bad years. Among the Nuer cattle have undisputed ritual pre-eminence. They play a part in all social processes and relationships. Fathers provide cows to obtain wives for their sons, and another son cannot marry until the herd has been built up again. Men have an intimate knowledge of the peculiarities of their beasts, and take their names from the ox given by their father at their initiation. Songs are sung in praise of oxen and girls. Cattle, sheep and goats are never killed purely for meat; they are sacrificed as a means of making contact with the spirits. But the pretext may be a thin one, and any animal which dies goes into the pot, so meat is eaten more commonly than by many herding peoples.

An indication of the real importance of a domestic animal can be gained from the number of specialized terms relating to it. The Tuareg have twelve or more terms to indicate the age and sex of goats and at least seventeen for their colour[15]. The Nuer have six main terms for the shape of the horns of their cattle; ten main colour terms and at least twelve for combinations of white and grey; and others denoting age and sex[16]. The Lapp reindeer herders —who have no other domestic animal of economic significance—have about fifty names for colours and the distribution of patches of colour, almost as many for varieties of antler form, and dozens for age and sex. This has a very practical application: by using a combination of these terms it is possible to designate any individual animal among thousands[17].

Variation of efficiency in the exploitation of livestock

The degree of efficiency with which peoples exploit the possibilities offered by their livestock varies greatly. The Nuer seem to be markedly successful in this respect. Their staple foods are milk and millet. Cows' milk is drunk fresh or eaten with millet porridge. It is also left to sour in gourds, which are not cleaned so that the acids remain to curdle the milk. It is accumulated, sometimes for several weeks (in which case ox's urine is added as a preservative), and then is boiled to make a yellow cheese which will keep for months if sealed in a gourd with cattle-dung. The whey is drunk by women and boys. The milk of sheep and goats is used only by children.

Blood is obtained from cattle by binding the neck so that a vein becomes congested, and piercing it with a small knife. Women boil the blood to thicken it; men let it coagulate and roast pieces in the embers.

The Nuer depend on their cattle not only for food. Their country lacks timber, stone and iron. Cattle provide skins, from which bedding, drums, shields and thongs are made; bones, made into beaters, pounders, scrapers and other tools; horn from which spoons and spear heads are formed; dung, used as fuel, for plastering walls and floors, for dressing wounds; the ashes of dung are used as a mouth-wash and tooth powder and for dressing the hair and skin; urine has uses in washing, making cheese and dressing skins.

The Masai use milk and blood, and make butter but not cheese. They also use the milk, blood and meat of sheep. Blood is obtained by shooting into the vein of the neck a special arrow with a stop below the point which prevents it penetrating too far (Fig. 1). There are restrictions on eating meat: it

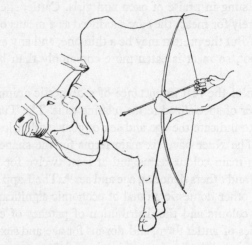

Fig 1 Drawing blood from the neck vein of an ox by shooting into it an arrow with a stop below the point. Masai.
(after Hollis, A. C. (1905). *The Masai: their language and folklore.* Oxford. Pl. XI.)

must not, for instance, be eaten on a day on which milk is consumed. The Bantu-speaking peoples of south-east and south Africa do not draw blood, nor do they make cheese. The Fulani depend heavily on milk, do not use blood, and eat meat only on ceremonial occasions.

The Rwala bedouin depend mainly on camel's milk drunk fresh or sour, or boiled and made into cheese. Many families when in the desert live solely on milk for long periods. Meat is rarely eaten. Wheat or sorghum and dates are obtained from the settled peoples on the desert fringes. Among the Tuareg only the camel herdsmen depend substantially on camel's milk. They make no cheese and little butter. Those living in the oases, however—the majority—consume a good deal of goat's milk, which is drunk fresh or sour and made into butter or hard cheese, the latter being pounded and mixed with food or water. Little meat is eaten: occasionally a camel foal is killed for a festival, and barren she-goats or castrated he-goats are killed. Sheep are bred mainly for slaughter, but are few in number. Millet, dates and figs and other vegetable foods are available in the oases, and herdsmen sometimes collect and grind wild grass seeds.

The Kazak keep mares mainly for their milk, which is made into *kumiss*.

It is poured into a skin bag, a wood paddle is inserted and the neck is closed tightly round it. The paddle is agitated for several hours and then the milk is left to sour for about four days. The result is a slightly intoxicating and very nourishing drink which keeps for a long time. The bags have been known to burst, with devastating results. Sheep's milk, which is much more plentiful, is soured or made into butter or cheese. Soft cheese is mashed in water when milk is scarce; hard cheese largely replaces meat in winter and spring. The older sheep are killed off in the autumn, but at other times meat is a luxury.

Most of the Lapps now regard reindeer as a cash crop, selling the meat in the urban markets. The herds are allowed to wander in spring and summer and become mixed, and little use is made of their milk. Formerly the method was more intensive: the herd was kept separate and under control, and does were milked from spring to autumn. This method, though it exploited the potentialities of the reindeer more fully, was in some ways less efficient; it led to overcropping of the lichens in the more restricted area available to a family's herd, and the spread of disease was more rapid. Moreover it required the co-operation of the whole family, which is no longer possible for social reasons.

It will be clear, then, that pastoral peoples vary greatly in the degree to which they exploit their animals. Few are able to eat meat regularly. Most depend heavily on milk and milk products. All obtain some vegetable food. The peoples mentioned also vary greatly in the bases of their economies. The Rwala and the Lapps depend almost entirely on camels and reindeer respectively. The Kazak and the Tuareg have several species. The Nuer, though they think of themselves as cattle people, also cultivate and fish. Sections of many pastoral peoples—often those who have lost their herds through disease or other misfortune—live settled lives and trade vegetable products with their nomadic relatives.

The reindeer, the last animal of major economic importance to be domesticated, provides examples of varying degrees of domestication[18]. It is used in various ways from Scandinavia to the Bering Strait. In the east of Siberia and in America the Yukaghir and the Eskimo did not domesticate it, though some depended heavily on the wild herds. The half-wild reindeer of the Chukchi roam at will, followed by the herders. They cannot be milked or used for riding or for drawing sledges; they provide only meat and skins, and the Chukchi depend also on fishing and sealing. The sedentary Yakut and the Samoyed use them as pack animals and to draw sledges, but not for milking or riding. The Tungus live by a combination of hunting and pastoralism. They use reindeer for drawing sledges, as pack animals and for riding (a good buck will carry 150 lb. for fifty miles in a day). They milk them, but do not make butter or cheese. They rarely kill them for meat. Families with only a few reindeer use them to extend the range of their hunting and fishing. The Skolt Lapps of Norway and Finland have small herds which they manage by the more intensive method described above, and rely also on fishing and hunting. Finally the extensive methods of the mountain Lapps have enabled them to extend southwards down the previously uninhabited plateaux of central Scandinavia.

So far only Old World peoples have been mentioned, for pastoralism is exclusively an Old World way of life. In America the only domestic animals directly of interest in the present context are the two South American Camelidae, the llama and the alpaca[19]. The llama is of great importance in the Andean zone as a pack animal. It is hardy, tolerant of thirst, and suited to high altitudes. A strong male will average fifteen to twenty miles a day for many days carrying more than 100 lb. (this is only a little more than a good dog will pull, in favourable conditions; but the conditions in which the two animals are employed are quite different). The llama also provides meat, wool and hides, and its dried dung is important as fuel in the largely treeless zone in which it is found. It is not ridden or milked. The armies of the Incas seem to have been accompanied by herds of llamas to serve as a mobile meat-supply. Llamas were apparently castrated to obtain more tasty meat and longer wool, but it seems uncertain whether this was a pre-Columbian practice.

The alpaca, a smaller species, is kept mainly for its wool, but also for its meat, hides and dung.

The vicuna, a wild species, provides superlative wool. The reason for the failure of the Indians to domesticate it seems to be that before mating it goes through an elaborate and protracted courtship ritual, which is inhibited by captivity. The llama and alpaca have similar but apparently less elaborate mating behaviour. One wonders whether similar difficulties have prevented the domestication of other species.

Animal-management techniques

We now come to techniques of animal management. These can be divided conveniently into those concerned with controlling breeding, those concerned with obtaining milk for human use, and a miscellaneous group.

There are several reasons for not allowing animals to breed freely and promiscuously. In harsh environments young born at certain seasons may have a reduced prospect of survival. The Kazak fit leather aprons to their rams in the spring, since autumn-born lambs have little chance. The Masai practise the same method. The Tuareg divide their flocks of goats into two and arrange for the kids to be born at two seasons, depending on the expected availability of pasture, so as to spread the milk yield over a longer period. The prepuces of he-goats and rams which are not to be allowed to breed are bound with a cord (Fig. 2)[20].

It seems to be rather unusual for males to be selected for breeding in order to pass on valuable characteristics. The Nuer, however, choose bull-calves for

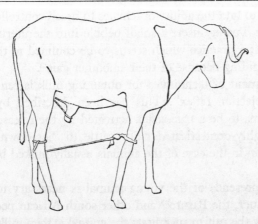

Fig 2 Prevention of mating. A ram, the prepuce of which has been bound
with a cord and tied back to its scrotum; its front and back legs have
been hobbled together with the same object. Tuareg.
(after Nicolaisen, J. (1963). *Ecology and Culture of the Pastoral Tuareg*.
Copenhagen. Fig. 25.)

breeding from the calves of the best milking cows and castrate most of the
remainder, leaving one entire to about thirty or forty cows.

Castration is the most usual method of controlling breeding. It has the
effect, too, of rendering the animals easier to handle and affects their
metabolism. The Lapps castrate most of the reindeer bucks and use them for
draught and pack purposes and as bell-reindeer which lead the herd. The
Tuareg say that castrated camels grow larger humps and fatten more quickly,
and are more enduring and stronger as riding animals. They are also less
dangerous, since bull-camels in rut sometimes attack people.

The method of castration in general use among cattle-keeping peoples, and
applied to other animals such as camels and horses, is by opening the scrotum
and removing the testicles. Some African herdsmen use a knife, others the
blade of a spear. In New Guinea pigs are castrated in this way with a bamboo
knife. All too often authors (including professional anthropologists) have
recorded the practice without describing the method.

A second group of methods involves damaging or destroying the testicles
without removing them. Sometimes the scrotum is bound with a cord
beforehand so that the testicles atrophy. The Lapps wrap the scrotum in
cloth and bite or chew it; the result is often a partial castration which however
renders the animal docile and more easily tamed[21]. The Sonjo of Tanzania
are irrigation agriculturalists who also keep flocks of goats. They castrate all
males at about six months, the only exceptions being those—apparently fairly
numerous—whose testicles do not descend. The method is to strangulate the
scrotum with a bow-string, and then to crush the testicles with an elongated
stone implement especially shaped and smoothed for the purpose[22]. The
Masai castrate rams by pounding the testicles between two stones.

It is unusual to find the ability of females to breed controlled or destroyed. However, some Tuareg insert a small pebble into the uterus of she-camels with this object; a practice which seems to be confined to those who prefer she-camels for riding because of their smoother gait[23].

The development of techniques for obtaining milk is rendered necessary by the "milk-ejection reflex". This has been described by Amoroso and Jewell[24]; it seems to be a true reflex activated by the release of a hormone. Stimulating highly-domesticated dairy cattle to "let down their milk" is less difficult than in the case of the animals usually milked by less advanced peoples.

Usually the presence of the young animal is necessary to start the flow of milk. The Nuer, the Basuto[25] and other south African peoples[26], and the Tuareg all allow the calf to suck first; the animal is then milked, after which the calf is allowed to return to the udder. Difficulty arises if a calf dies, or is killed for eating or to conserve milk for human use. Many peoples then skin the calf, stuff the skin with straw or grass and bring it to the mother. The Nuer rub the dummy with the mother's urine to give it the "right" smell. The Rwala sometimes kill a camel calf at birth, smear another with its blood and bring it to the she-camel; or if a strange calf is to be suckled they tie up the mother's nostrils so that she cannot smell it. I have seen a reference to a method practised in the north of England, where the skin of a dead calf was mounted on a rocker so that it would butt against the udder in a realistic manner.

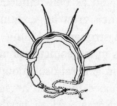

Fig 3 Weaning. A ring armed with thorns which is tied round the calf's muzzle. Nuer.
(after Evans-Pritchard, E. E. (1940). *The Nuer*. Oxford. Fig. 6.)

Sometimes the calf is allowed all the mother's milk for a period after birth. This may be especially necessary if pasture is poor.

Another method of activating the milk-ejection reflex is by stimulation of the genital tract, either manually or by inflating the vagina with air. At the present time these practices are especially typical (or have been most frequently recorded) of the cattle-keeping peoples of north-east and east Africa, but they have been observed in Asia and Europe and are of great antiquity. They have been described by Lagercrantz[27] and by Amoroso and Jewell.

In order to conserve milk for human use it may be necessary to accelerate

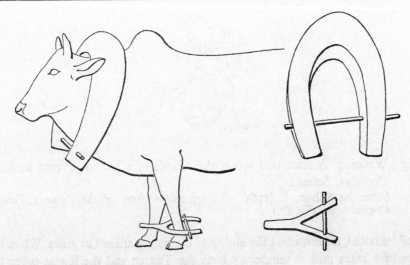

Fig 4 Animal-management techniques of the Gonds of Madhya Pradesh.
Heavy wood neck-ring, to accustom the beast to a yoke; hobble applied
to animals given to straying.
(after MS drawing by Rai Bahadur Hiralal, by permission of the Trustees
of the British Museum.)

the weaning process. The young animal may be totally separated from the
mother or its access may be restricted. The Tuareg keep kids in an enclosure
or tether them and release them only at certain times to be suckled.

There are two main groups of devices associated with weaning: those
which make suckling painful for the mother, and those which make it difficult
or impossible for the young animal. The Nuer tie a ring armed with thorns
round the calf's muzzle so that it pricks the udder (Fig. 3). The Gonds of
Bihar, about sixty years ago when they were adopting a settled peasant life,
used a device made from four pointed sticks, tied behind the calf's head
(Fig. 4). An Indian colleague tells me that he has seen this in use by Hindu
peasants, and points out that it prevents not only sucking but also grazing
near ground level. In fact it enforces selective grazing. The Rwala insert a
sharp peg under the nostrils of a camel-calf to prick the udder. The Tuareg
tie the skin of a hedgehog to the muzzle of a kid. They also place a stick
across the mouth, like a bit, and tie it behind the horns (Fig. 5); or pass a stick
through the kid's cheeks. A stick is passed through the nasal septum of the
calves of cattle (Fig. 6). In the case of camel calves they pierce the upper lip
and pass through it a length of root, which is then knotted at each end. This
makes suckling painful for the mother; but more important (and like the two
latter methods described for kids), it prevents the calf from sucking by
admitting air. The Tuareg also make cuts on the noses of calves, of both
camels and cattle, which make sucking painful for them. These methods, it

Fig 5 Weaning. A stick tied across the mouth of a kid to prevent sucking.
Chawiya, Sahara.
(after Nicolaisen, J. (1963). *Ecology and Culture of the Pastoral Taureg.*
Copenhagen. Fig. 19.)

will be noted, do not affect the ability of the young animal to graze. When the
need for extra milk is temporary both the Tuareg and the Rwala cover the
udder of a she-camel with a pouch or net (Fig. 7). The Lapps smear the
udders of reindeer does with excrement to discourage the fawns.

Insects are a major pest to most domesticated animals, causing, at best,
loss of milk, and often seriously affecting their condition. The annual migrations of the Lapps to the plateaux and of the Kazak from the river valleys
where they spend the winter to the open steppes are governed as much by the
need to escape from insects as by the requirements of pasture. The Nuer
confine their cattle at night in byres, all the chinks of which are plugged with
dung. Smoky dung fires are made inside. The cattle are described as emerging
in the morning dazed and staggering. Mosquitoes sometimes cause the
reindeer of the Tungus to stampede. The herder builds a smudge fire round
which the herd congregates by day, grazing by night. The annual southward migration of the Fulani is in search of pasture and water in the dry
season, but their return northwards in the wet season is enforced by the
tsetse fly. The Bavenda of the north Transvaal keep their cattle in kraals until
the middle of the morning to avoid ticks. Their cattle suffer from flies and

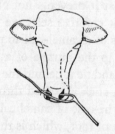

Fig 6 Weaning. A forked stick passed through the nasal septum of a calf,
to make suckling painful for the cow. Tuareg.
(after Nicolaisen, J. (1963). *Ecology and Culture of the Pastoral Tuareg.*
Copenhagen. Fig. 31.)

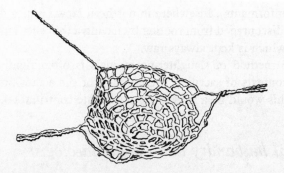

Fig 7 Goat's hair net bag which is tied over the udder of a she-camel to conserve her milk for human use. Tuareg.
(after Nicolaisen, J. (1963). *Ecology and Culture of the Pastoral Tuareg*. Copenhagen. Fig. 41.)

heat in confinement, but the Bavenda say that the ticks, which are a major danger to cattle, go underground as the day gets hotter[28].

There remains a number of miscellaneous techniques and devices which deserve mention.

Animals are sometimes hobbled, usually to prevent their wandering too far while grazing during a halt: a practice, therefore, applied to beasts being used for riding, pack transport or draught rather than to herds under the care of a herdsman. The Gonds (and, no doubt, Indian villagers) applied a form of wooden hobble to cattle which had a habit of wandering from the herd (Fig. 4). The Tuareg hobble camel calves during weaning so that they cannot keep up with their mothers when grazing. Many peoples tie the hind legs of cows during milking with a "spancel". Hobbles are used on rams by the Tuareg to prevent or impede breeding.

The catching of incompletely domesticated or trained animals may present difficulty. When holding their annual round-ups, at which they sort their reindeer by their ear-marks, the Lapps drive them into stockades and lassoo them. The Kazak catch horses from the herds for riding by means of a noose on the end of a pole, used from horse-back.

Some African peoples train the horns of their cattle for aesthetic reasons. The Dinka do this by paring away a portion of the surface so that the horn grows in the desired curve[29]; the Nuer make an oblique cut in the horn, which achieves the same object.

The practice of identifying animals by ear-marking is widely spread, being recorded from, for example, the Lapps[30], the Sonjo[31] and the Tuareg[32].

In New Guinea, where pigs normally forage freely, gardens are often fenced to keep them out; but even so some pigs become adept at gaining entry. The peoples at the headwaters of the Sepik apparently blind such pigs by levering out the eye with a stick, piercing it "to let out the water", and allowing it to return to the socket (I have not seen this, but I heard of it from reliable informants). Elsewhere in northern New Guinea these trouble-some pigs are discouraged from rooting by having a thin slice cut from the tip of the snout, which is kept always raw.

Finally, the method of slaughtering animals is often rigidly prescribed, especially in contexts of sacrifice, presentation or the acquisition of prestige or rank. But this would be a subject for a separate contribution.

Animal husbandry and the archaeologist

The interaction of material and non-material aspects of culture is always complicated, and there is no space here for discussion of the effects of dependence on animal husbandry on other aspects of social and economic life. However, in the present context a few comments of special relevance to archaeology may be justified.

That full pastoral nomadism leads to impoverishment of material culture has often been remarked. Nomads must travel light. They are not likely to use pottery, or numbers of metal vessels, or any but the simplest household goods. Their dwellings must be portable. Non-functional art objects—made for purely ritual or decorative purposes—are likely to be absent. Their clothing and utensils are often made from animal products: skins, wool, horn, bone. In the environments in which many of them live even wood is scarce.

Many of their artefacts, being of perishable materials, would be unlikely to survive in an archaeological context. This is true of all the devices shown in Figs. 2 to 7.

But this point must not be pressed too far. The more complete the direct dependence of a people on their animals, as in the case of the Bedouin or the Kazak, the more essential is contact with other peoples. I have said that all nomads obtain some vegetable food. The Kazak obtained many other goods—luxuries as well as necessities—from the towns or from itinerant traders. The Bedouin trade their camels not only for grain but for rifles and ammunition, cloth for their tents, and all sorts of utensils. Only the very poorest bedouin families lack a set of vessels for preparing and serving coffee. Moreover, although non-functional art may be lacking among such peoples, decora-tion is applied to harness-trappings and weapons and wealth may be con-verted into jewellery.

Paradoxically, those whose dependence on their animals is less total are sometimes more restricted in the range if not in the bulk of their material culture, perhaps because being more self-sufficient they have less need to establish contacts with other peoples. The Nuer provide an example.

Settlement patterns, which are often relatively simple for peoples who live mainly by agriculture, may become more complex when animal husbandry is of greater economic importance. Most pastoral nomads have a base. The Tuareg have the oases with their gardens where women, children and the elderly remain and where craftsmen practise their trades. The Kazaks spent the winter in scattered family groups in river-valley sites which were clan property and to which they returned each year, living in semi-sub-terranean houses with turf or stone walls. There were also groups who practised irrigation agriculture in the valleys and were permanently settled. These included some poor Kazak families who lacked livestock as well as people of different origins. The Lapps, too, have their settlements, occupied mainly by the elderly, women and children, in more recent times in the neighbourhood of "church villages", where they made huts of sods supported by a timber frame.

The Rwala have no similar base. To some extent the villages of the desert fringe, near which they camp during July and August, fulfil the same function. However, some Rwala spend even these hottest months at desert water-holes. They are the most completely nomadic of the peoples considered here.

The Nuer, with a much more widely based economy, present a rather different picture, but among them too the village sites, situated on sandy ridges above flood level, are occupied only for part of the year. During the early part of the dry season, when the floods have receded, the young people lead a nomadic life with the herds while the elderly and the children remain in the village and tend the crops. When the harvest is completed and the pasture withers in the drought all congregate together at riverside camps, returning to the villages as the floods rise again.

Clearly village sites which are occupied permanently or for part of every year could be expected to yield archaeological evidence. The same is true of camping sites which for various reasons are occupied year after year: the Rwala camp at wells, which are themselves artefacts, being made or improved by man. But the route of the Kazak during spring and summer varies each year according to the incidence of showers and, therefore, of pasture, and the same is true of the herding groups of the Tuareg and the Rwala. Many of their camp sites would leave little trace.

If in a certain area evidence should be found for both a settled life and a nomadic herding life, analogy with the peoples discussed here suggests that a number of different explanations have to be considered. It could indicate the presence of two distinct peoples each exploiting the natural environment in different ways, as in the case of the Fulani and the settled peoples among whom they move in the southern part of their range. It could result from groups of the same people leading differently based lives, as in the case of the Fulani and the Kazak, each of whom have settled elements. It could suggest a life similar to that of the Tuareg, many of whom live permanently in the oasis settlements while others tend the herds at great distances. Or it could represent different phases of an annual cycle, as in the cases of the Nuer and the nomadic Kazak.

Animals are the only form of wealth which is self-mobile. People who depend heavily on animals are, therefore, usually warlike, because they

have to be prepared to defend their herds. This is especially true of those
whose animals are able to travel far and fast: horses, camels, cattle. It is less
true of sheep and goat herders; and one rarely hears of raiders driving off
herds of pigs. People who herd the more mobile animals must themselves be
mobile. The Kazak and Tuareg mount their sheep and goat herders on oxen,
but clearly only horse- and camel-riders can herd horses and camels. It is this
mobility, combined with hardihood, which has caused the nomads to be
dreaded by the settled peoples throughout history. However they usually
threaten only their neighbours, for their way of life discourages the development of large political units or centralized control, and their chiefs are
unable to gather large numbers or to hold them together. It is only when
they have been welded into a coherent force by a leader of genius that they
have spread far from their own habitat.

Notes

1 Valuable background material will be found in Forde, C. D. (1964).
   Habitat, Economy and Society. London; Birket-Smith, K. (1960). *Primitive
   Man and his Ways*. London; Mourant, A. E. and Zeuner, F. E. (eds.)
   (1963). *Man and Cattle*. Roy. Anthrop. Inst., London; Zeuner, F. E.
   (1963). *A History of Domesticated Animals*. London.
2 The mithan is usually considered to be the domesticated form of the gaur.
3 Zeuner, F. E. (1963). Op. cit. pp. 253–5.
4 Of course there are exceptions to any such generalizations. The pigs of
   the medieval villager certainly foraged in the woods and must surely have
   interbred with the wild pig.
5 Stenning, D. J. (1959). *Savannah Nomads*. London.
6 See, e.g. Mills, J. P. (1926). *The Ao Nagas*. London; Stonor, C. R. (1950).
   The feasts of merit among the Northern Sangtam tribe of Assam, *Anthro-
   pos*, 45.
7 Layard, J. (1942). *Stone Men of Malekula*. London.
8 Layard, J. (1942). Op. cit. p. 240.
9 Baker, J. R. (1929). *Man and Animals in the New Hebrides*. London.
10 Birket-Smith, K. (1960). ibid.; Nicolaisen, J. (1963). *Ecology and Culture
   of the Pastoral Tuareg*. Nat. Mus. of Copenhagen.
11 Musil, A. (1928). *The Manners and Customs of the Rwala Bedouins*. New
   York.
12 Forde, C. D. (1964). op. cit. ch. XVI.
13 Forde, C. D. (1964). op. cit. ch. XIV.
14 Evans-Pritchard, E. E. (1940). *The Nuer*. Oxford.
15 Birket-Smith, K. (1960). op. cit. p. 158.
16 Evans-Pritchard, E. E. (1940). op. cit. pp. 41–5.
17 Collinder, B. (1949). *The Lapps*. Princeton. pp. 92–5.
18 Forde, C. D. (1964). op. cit. ch. XVII.
19 Gilmore, R. M. (1950). Fauna and ethnozoology of South America, *in*
   Steward, J. H. (ed.) *Handbook of South American Indians*, 6, pp. 429–54.
20 For the animal-management techniques of the Tuareg, see, especially,
   Nicolaisen, J. (1963). ibid.
21 Collinder, B. (1949). op. cit. p. 112.
22 Gray, R. F. (1963). *The Sonjo of Tanganyika*. London. p. 40.
23 Nicolaisen, J. (1963). op. cit. p. 70.

24 Amoroso, E. C. and Jewell, P. A. (1963). The exploitation of the milk-ejection reflex by primitive peoples, *in* Mourant, A. E. and Zeuner, F. E. (1963). ibid.
25 Ashton, H. (1952). *The Basuto.* London. pp. 135-6.
26 Schapera, I. (ed.) (1937). *The Bantu-speaking Tribes of South Africa.* London. pp. 137-41.
27 Lagercrantz, S. (1950). East Hamitic milking customs, *in Contribution to the Ethnography of Africa.* Studia Etnografica Upsaliensia, 1, Lund.
28 Stayt, H. A. (1931). *The Bavenda.* London. p. 39.
29 Grunnet, N. T. (1962). An ethnographic-ecological survey of the relation-ship between the Dinka and their cattle, *Folk,* 4.
30 Collinder, B. (1949). op. cit. p. 91.
31 Gray, R. F. (1963). op. cit. p. 40.
32 Nicolaisen, J. (1963). op. cit. pp. 138-40 and Fig. 100.

P. DUCOS

Methodology and results of the study of the earliest domesticated animals in the Near East (Palestine)

Introduction

The beginning of the domestication of animals established a new relationship between man and animals which, over a certain time, introduced on the one hand changes in domesticated species which took on new morphological characteristics, and on the other hand an evolution of human culture in which new ways of life were adopted as a response to the success in gaining control of a part of the essential meat supply. In order to assess objectively the beginnings of domestication it is necessary to concentrate on this very relationship; it is clear that anatomical features cannot serve to reveal the beginnings of domestication for domesticated species only undergo transformation after a considerable number of generations, while indirect archaeological evidence (equipment, architecture, a sedentary existence) is not sufficient to actually prove primitive domestication.

In order to investigate the beginnings of domestication in Palestine we have applied a method which uses neither archaeological nor anatomical data. Some of the general principles of this method were announced in 1961 and detailed applications have since been fully published[1]. To summarize, the method of acquiring animals (in an ethnological sense) can be ascertained numerically from analysis of bone collections. The data is of different kinds and new criteria can be isolated: the frequency of different parts of the skeleton, the frequency of species, the frequency of different age groups, are the criteria which we used in our analyses, the two last being the most important.

Review of Palestinian prehistory

Following the microlithic industries of the Palestinian Mesolithic (known as the Natufian) come the first neolithic assemblages, which were found by Garstang in his famous excavation at Jericho. Jericho, with its stratigraphy subsequently confirmed and made more precise by Miss K. Kenyon, remains one of the type sites for Palestinian prehistory.

Two Pre-Pottery Neolithic levels (PPN-A and PPN-B), dated by C-14 to the eighth and the seventh millennium respectively, are followed by a Pottery Neolithic which is contemporary with the Middle Neolithic of Byblos, in other words which is dated to the middle of the fifth millennium. On this evidence there was a break of more than a thousand years in the stratigraphy of Jericho.

Perrot's work at Hagoshrim and Beisamun and his excavations at Munhata at first suggested that these sites filled the break in the Jericho sequences, but detailed analysis of the material has shown that the same hiatus does exist at Munhata; levels 3–6 are contemporary with PPN-B at Jericho, while Munhata 2 is already contemporary with the Middle Neolithic of Byblos, and therefore does not pre-date the Pottery Neolithic of Jericho. As the other sites (Hagoshrim and Beisamun) can be dated to the fifth millennium it is necessary to accept this break as common to the whole valley of the Jordan.

In Palestine the fourth millennium is the period of the Ghassoulian which was found by Neuville and Mallon at the site of Teleilat-Ghassoul on the banks of the Dead Sea and which is now better known from Perrot's excavations at Beersheba. The Ghassoulian corresponds to the "Chalcolithic" with metal objects appearing for the first time in a context which otherwise is essentially still Neolithic.

Research into the beginnings of animal domestication

Bone assemblages from Ghassoulian sites show that at this time (the fourth millennium) the different Palestinian cultures knew and practised animal domestication in a form which one cannot call archaic. On the one hand the domesticated species are already very different from wild species: cattle are small and very similar to the *brachyceros* breed; pigs are smaller than any wild forms of *Sus scrofa* with certain new cranial characteristics which class them with turbary pig, although there are certain differences between them; sheep are heavier than turbary sheep; goats have twisted horns and are also smaller than wild bezoar goats. On the other hand analysis of the distribution curves of age groups shows that animals were not only killed for food, but were also kept for their milk and wool; a considerable number of young animals were killed. Finally, a comparison of the different sites indicates a tendency to specialization in animal domestication; on the one hand cattle and pigs, and sheep and goats on the other. This is a complex picture and shows that the beginnings of domestication must have been prior to the fourth millennium and that investigation of the beginnings of animal domestication must concentrate on the populations which lived after the archaeological hiatus of the sixth millennium (Pottery Neolithic) or even on those which preceded the hiatus (Pre-Pottery Neolithic and Natufian). Some of the recent excavations by the French archaeological mission in Israel have offered the opportunity to study this problem under particularly fruitful conditions, for several sites have been excavated which were very rich in animal bones. These sites fall within a well-defined geographical area, the upper valley of the Jordan at the levels of lakes Tiberias and Hulah, and they date from both before and after the archaeological hiatus. This communication is concerned with the preliminary analyses of this series of excavations which have only just been completed.

The period before the archaeological hiatus is represented at Aïn Mallaha and in the lower levels (3–6) at Munhata; the period following the hiatus (the Pottery Neolithic) is represented at Hagoshrim, Beisamun and level 2 at Munhata.

Table 1 summarizes the different proportions of species found at the various sites.

	Aïn Mallaha	Munhata 5–6	Hagoshrim	Beisamun	Munhatta 2
Cervids	33·4	rare	3·8	1·7	0·0
Gazelles	44·6	34·1	11·9	7·2	21·4
Cattle	3·3	(4·9)	63·5	35·9	18·7
Large Caprinae[b]	1·6	45·5	14·2	29·4	26·9
Small Caprinae	0	0	0	0	13·3
Pigs	14·2	11·1	5·6	24·4	15·2

(a) The proportions given for Munhata 5–6 are still provisional and may have to be modified to a certain extent after further analysis.

(b) *Capra hircus* + *Ovis orientalis*.

Table 1 The proportions of different species[a]

The presence of *Ovis orientalis* requires some explanation, for the existence of this species has never been mentioned in scientific publications on Palestine. However, it must be borne in mind that Bate's[2] and Vaufrey's[3] studies of prehistoric fauna are not particularly illuminating in this respect. It is of course very difficult to distinguish morphologically between *Ovis* and *Capra* except on the basis of a few parts of the skeleton. In the series described by Bate there is only one single bone which is distinctive of *Capra*, that is the ankle bone of *hircus* type. In the Judean desert collections described by Vaufrey[4] there is not a single distinctive piece and Vaufrey writes "it seems that the bones are those of ibex".

If one considers, for example, the scatter diagram of Caprinae first phalanges at Munhata 5–6 (Fig. 1) it is clear that two species of large Caprinae are present. The same scatter diagram is obtained for Munhata 2 with, in addition, a clustering which corresponds with the small Caprinae; these latter are virtually the only ones found in the Ghassoulian. Scatter diagrams for Beisamun are similar to those of Munhata 5–6. The large Caprinae include

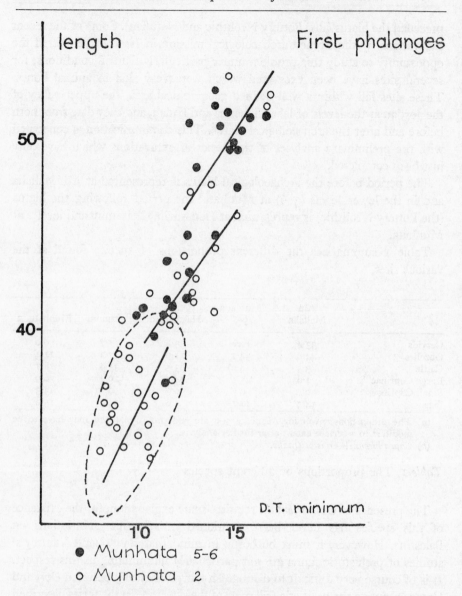

Fig 1 Scatter diagram of Caprinae first phalanges.
  The interrupted line shows the distribution of phalanges of small Caprinae from Bir-es-Safadi (*Capra hircus* and *Ovis aries*). The existence of two species of large Caprinae is clear. Small Caprinae only appear in Munhata 2.

two species: the larger one is *Capra hircus* and the other belongs to the genus *Ovis*, for horn cores have been found at Munhata, admittedly not securely stratified, and also at Beisamun where their stratigraphic position is certain. A study of these horn cores shows that they belong to a sheep of the urial group and of the species *Ovis orientalis*.

  The first point to be noticed is the decrease in frequency of the cervids;

whereas they are very plentiful in the Natufian of Aïn Mallaha, they are not found in Munhata 2. This decrease is so marked that we cannot just infer less emphasis on hunting; what must have occurred was a general decrease of cervids in Palestine (they are found again on later sites, but are always few) probably due to the disappearance of forest. We cannot argue in the same way about the gazelle which maintained its important position, especially at Munhata, the southernmost site and the one which is therefore closest to the semi-arid zone.

Other features to be noted in Table 1 are:

1 the increase of cattle in Pottery Neolithic sites;
2 the increase of Caprinae from the Pre-Pottery Neolithic onwards;
3 the more or less constant proportions of pigs;
4 the exceptional nature of Hagoshrim with its very high proportion of cattle;
5 the presence of small Caprinae at Munhata 2; a demonstration of this can be illustrated by a comparison of the first phalanges of the Caprinae from Munhata 2 with those from Munhata 5–6.

None of the animals at Aïn Mallaha were domesticated. It is only possible to determine age groups for gazelles and boars and these are similar to those for wild populations except for the rarity of young animals up to one year old, a feature which can easily be explained with reference to actual hunting tradition. Cervids, gazelles and pigs make up more than 90% of the species found, and it is unreasonable to suggest that one of the species which is found only rarely at this site (for example, cattle) should have been domesticated.

At Munhata 5–6 pigs are slightly less frequent than at Aïn Mallaha and cattle only just more frequent. The large Caprinae, which are very frequent, reveal an age distribution which is rather different from that of wild populations, with maxima for the classes between 1–2 years and between 2–4 years. However, a X^2 test, which measures the probability that this difference is not due to chance, shows that this is not significant (13·93). The age groups of pigs at Beisamun is very similar to that at Aïn Mallaha ($X^2 = 9·95$); the distribution of cattle there is like a wild distribution except for the rarity of the group of animals between 2–4 years and the abundance of animals between 4–6·5 years; finally, the distribution of Caprinae is similar to a wild distribution with a X^2 of 10·69 which is not significant.

The only age group distribution which can be determined at Hagoshrim is for cattle, and this is very different from a natural distribution ($X^2 = 40·04$). Young animals are rare (less than 10%), old animals practically non-existent, and the bulk of the animals found are adults of between 4–9 years old. This exceptional distribution goes hand in hand with a particularly high proportion of cattle.

The distribution of pigs at Munhata 2 is very different from that of both Aïn Mallaha and Beisamun and is characterized by a very high proportion of individuals less than one year old. The distribution is similar to that of the chalcolithic site of Metzer. The X^2 is significant (44·46). The distribution of cattle is identical to that at Beisamun ($X^2 = 8·35$); that of Caprinae accentuates the characteristics of the distribution of this group at Munhata 5–6, but this time with a highly significant X^2 (94·05).

The interpretation of these results will include comparative material from other sites but from the outset will be based on one observation. For each of the three groups there are two fundamental distribution types:

1 for the pigs (Fig. 2), a distribution which is close to a wild distribution (Mallaha, Beisamun) and a distribution with a markedly high proportion (more than 40%) of individuals under one year of age (Munhata 2, chalcolithic Metzer).

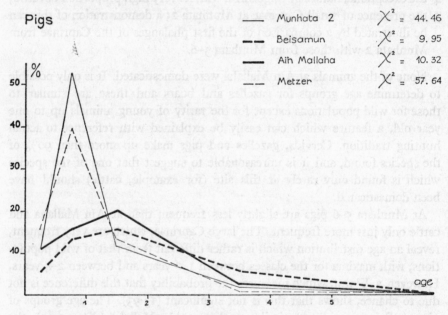

Fig 2 The age group distribution of pigs.

2 for cattle (Fig. 3), a distribution which is similar to a wild distribution with, nevertheless, a paucity of the age group 2–4 years which appears to be compensated by an abundance of the age group 4–6·5 years. This distribution type is found also at Beisamun, Munhata 2 and elsewhere at Tell Mureybat (Syria, Pre-Pottery), in Ghassoulian sites and in Bronze Age Palestine. There is also a distribution with a clear peak where practically all the animals are adults, and this is the distribution type at Hagoshrim, at Çatal Hüyük (Anatolia), and at Roucadour (France, Neolithic) for the *brachyceros* breed (whereas at this latter site the *primigenius* breed has a distribution of the first sort).

3 for the Caprinae (Fig. 4), there are two different distributions as for cattle. The distribution which is similar to the wild one is found at Beisamun and also at Bir-es-Safadi (Ghassoulian); the distribution with a maximum of age groups 1–3 years is found at Munhata 2 and perhaps also at Munhata 5–6.

The pig distribution which shows a clear peak of young animals under one year of age clearly indicates domestication based on the consumption of very young animals and the preservation of some adult animals for purposes of reproduction.

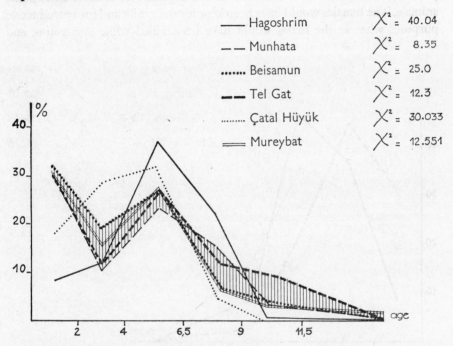

―――― Hagoshrim X^2 = 40.04
― ― Munhata X^2 = 8.35
••••••• Beisamun X^2 = 25.0
▬▬ Tel Gat X^2 = 12.3
•••••••• Çatal Hüyük X^2 = 30.033
═══ Mureybat X^2 = 12.551

Fig 3 The age group distribution of *Bos taurus*.
The hatched zone represents either hunting activities or evolved husbandry.

It is the distribution of cattle at Hagoshrim, and at Çatal Hüyük, which proves domestication, for the difference from a wild distribution cannot be explained in any other way. On the other hand the other distribution type is less conclusive. To see in this distribution type the results of hunting activities is not satisfactory for the same distribution type is found in Bronze Age sites such as Tel Gat and Tel Nagila where it is impossible that hunting occurred, not only because these were urbanized civilizations but also because in this southern area at this time (Tel Nagila is in the semi-arid zone) no wild cattle existed. It is also difficult to infer the effects of domestication from this distribution, for after all, is this not the same distribution type as found at Tell Mureybat (Pre-Pottery, North Syria) where cattle are considerably less frequent than an animal of genus *Equus* which must at this time have been wild and where we are without doubt dealing with the activities of hunters ?

It is therefore necessary to admit that the significance of this second distribution type is still unclear and that two sorts of activity could have resulted in such a distribution. Such a convergence is not difficult to understand; that hunting should reveal a distribution close to the wild distribution is consistent with the principles of the method. However, when we are dealing with an evolved type of animal domestication, such as at Tel Gat, it is probable that there was a difference in the exploitation of male and female animals. The females would have been kept for their milk and for reproductive purposes whereas the males would have been killed while still young and

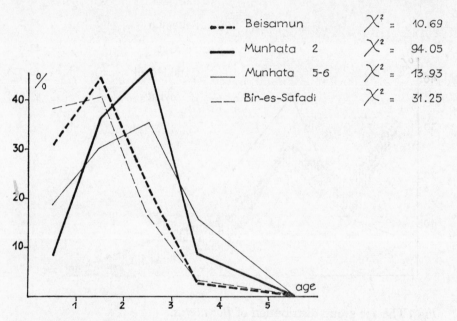

Fig 4 The age group distribution of Caprinae.

only a few adults would have been kept to ensure reproduction. In this way the distribution curve is made up of these two independent and inverse distributions (that of the males and that of the females) so that the deficiencies of one are compensated for by the abundances of the other with the result that overall it becomes similar to a wild distribution.

The same arguments can be applied to the Caprinae distributions to which the same domestication practices apply. To explain the significance of cattle at Munhata, at Beisamun, and the significance of Caprinae at Beisamun, we must consider some other factors.

The domestication of cattle at Hagoshrim (and also at Çatal Hüyük) is of an archaic kind; its only aim was to provide meat and the absence of young

animals shows a great reluctance to kill animals which had not yet contributed to the increase of the herd. It follows that it is difficult to conceive
that cattle should have been domesticated in a more sophisticated and
efficient way at Beisamun and Munhata 2 for these two sites are not much
later in date, the proportion of cattle at Munhata 2 is fairly low, and the
proportion of gazelles shows that hunting was still important. In the same way
we must admit that the Caprinae at Beisamun were hunted for their
domestication at Munhata 2 is still of an archaic type.

Conclusion

We can now summarize the evidence for the beginnings of animal domestication in Palestine.

In the Pottery Neolithic period, after the archaeological hiatus, we find
on the one hand hunters, as at Beisamun, and on the other hunter-pastoralists,
as at Munhata 2 where the domestication was of Caprinae and pigs and at
Hagoshrim where a kind of cattle specialization may have occurred. In the
Pre-Pottery Neolithic period and in the Natufian animal domestication does
not appear to have existed, except perhaps in the case of the Caprinae
at Munhata 5–6 (about which it is not possible to be definite at the
moment).

These conclusions refer to a clearly defined geographical area, the Upper
Jordan valley, from Lake Tiberias to Lake Houlah. How can they be reconciled
with what is known about the semi-arid zone where an earlier domestication
has been identified by myself at El Khiam and by Perkins at Beidha? It is
absurd to suggest that domestication was known in southern Palestine in the
seventh millennium, then disappeared and only reappeared again in the fifth
millennium. This situation takes us to an hypothesis about the archaeological
hiatus of the sixth millennium. This hiatus may perhaps correspond to a
decrease in population density in the area, but it seems excessive to suggest
the total disappearance of people from Palestine during this period. The
hiatus could equally well correspond to a period of proto-husbandry which
would be the activity of nomadic populations. Such people would leave so
few remains that archaeologists would only recognize them under exceptional
circumstances. During the fifth millennium the Upper Jordan valley would
have seen the transition to settled agriculture, possibly as a result of contacts
between newcomers and existing nomadic populations. This is of course
only an hypothesis whose truth can only be confirmed in two ways: by the
discovery of some sixth millennium habitation sites in Palestine, and by the
study of domestication in the Neolithic settlements of the Syria–Lebanon
zone.

It is important, finally, to note the separate existence of houses and villages
on the one hand, and animal domestication on the other. It is not possible to

see domestication as the result of a sedentary way of life, for villages existed for several thousands of years before domestication occurred. In the same way it is necessary to note that the domestication of animals does not appear to have been the result of an increase in aridity which reduced the availability of wild fauna. If the decrease in the number of cervids argues for a decrease in forestation, then the increase in the number of cattle and wild Caprinae argues for a climate which was perhaps more humid than in the Natufian. The fact that the cultures which settled in Palestine were diversified, with differing food-producing bases, proves that we should find elsewhere older groups of people practising domestication, perhaps even in the sixth millennium. It remains true, nevertheless, that the domesticated species at Munhata 2 and at Hagoshrim are very similar to wild forms (it is only at Munhata 2 that we find some Caprinae which are smaller than wild forms and these cannot have been the only ones to have been domesticated) which shows that, although it is probable that there were older centres of domestication, the upper regions of the Jordan valley were a focus of domestication in the fifth millennium B.C.[5]

Notes

1 Ducos, P. (1965). Contribution à l'étude des origines de la domestication, *Thesis, Faculté des Sciences de Bordeaux;* Ducos, P. (1968). L'origine des animaux domestiques en Palestine, *Pub. de L'Inst. de Préhist. de l'Univ. de Bordeaux,* 4.

2 Bate, D. M. A. (1937). The fossil fauna of the Wadi-al-Mughara caves, *in* Garrod, D. A. E. *The Stone Age of Mount Carmel,* I. Oxford. pp. 134–240.

3 Vaufrey, R. (1951). Etude paléontologique, I. Mammifères, *in* Neuville, R. Le Paléolithique et le Mésolithique du Désert de Judée, *Arch. de l'Inst. de Paléontologie Humaine,* 24, pp. 198–217.

4 Vaufrey, R. (1951). ibid.

5 I must specify my position on the use of trinomials in referring to domesticated animals. The argument against using sub-specific names for domesticated animals depends on the fact that their differentiation is of a different kind from the different geographical forms of wild species. But such an argument leads to paradoxical postulates. If one calls wild cattle *Bos primigenius* and domesticated cattle *Bos taurus,* it follows that one accepts that domestication of the species *primigenius* has led to morphological changes which resulted in a new species, *taurus,* and one cannot deny the possibility that domestication has in addition led to the creation of sub-species. The opposite approach which would call the domestic pig *Sus scrofa* is also paradoxical, for 22 sub-species of wild *Sus scrofa* are recognized. Domesticated pigs differ morphologically from all the wild sub-species even more than do the wild forms between themselves and surely these domesticated pigs can be considered as one or more sub-species.

    Bohlken, H. (1961). Haustiere und Zoologische Systematik, *Z. Tierzücht. ZüchtBiol.,* 76 (I), pp. 107–13, has shown the necessity of using a trinomial classification for domesticated animals and has proposed a scheme which, although subject to discussion, has the merit of showing the phylogeny of these forms. Until general agreement is reached, I would prefer to use a trinomial classification in deference to the rules agreed in the International Code of Zoological Nomenclature.

In view of the editorial policy adopted throughout this book, I have agreed not to use the trinomial nomenclature. The terms *primigenius* and *brachyceros* are used here as subspecific names, and the large Caprinae *Capra hircus* is, in fact, *Capra hircus aegagrus*.

CAROLINE GRIGSON

The uses and limitations of differences in absolute size in the distinction between the bones of aurochs (Bos primigenius) *and domestic cattle* (Bos taurus)

Introduction

One of the most obvious differences between domestic and wild cattle is that the domestic cattle (*Bos taurus*, in this case) are almost all smaller than their wild ancestor, the aurochs (*Bos primigenius*). Bohlken[1] showed how very close wild and domestic taurine cattle are in their skull characters; indeed he saw no reason for their classification as separate species. Fig. 1, in which measurements of some aurochs cows have been added to Bohlken's graph of basal length plotted against palatal length for aurochs bulls and modern domestic cattle of both sexes, shows that in spite of some overlap a reduction in size is one of the most obvious effects of domestication. The question therefore arises whether it is justifiable to use small size as diagnostic for domestication when cattle bones are excavated from archaeological sites.

It must first be stressed that this paper is not concerned with the formulation of a general principle on the effect of domestication, but merely with the distinction between the bones of *B. taurus* and *B. primigenius*.

Comparisons between the dimensions of various bone samples are best made with statistical methods as used by Kurtén, Simpson and others[2]. It has been argued that measurements of bones from archaeological sites cannot be used in calculations that require random samples because the animals were probably selected for killing. However some bias occurs in most palaeontological samples as the bones may get sorted (*a*) while the animals are still alive, (*b*) by burial or fossilization, (*c*) by exposure, and (*d*) by collection[3]. In the case of an archaeological sample of bones bias due to the first of these categories would have been caused by man (though perhaps less by hunting than by stock-rearing activities) but, on the other hand, bias due to the other possible causes is often minimized.

Correct identification of genus is obviously of the first importance. The bones most likely to be confused with those of *B. taurus* and *B. primigenius*

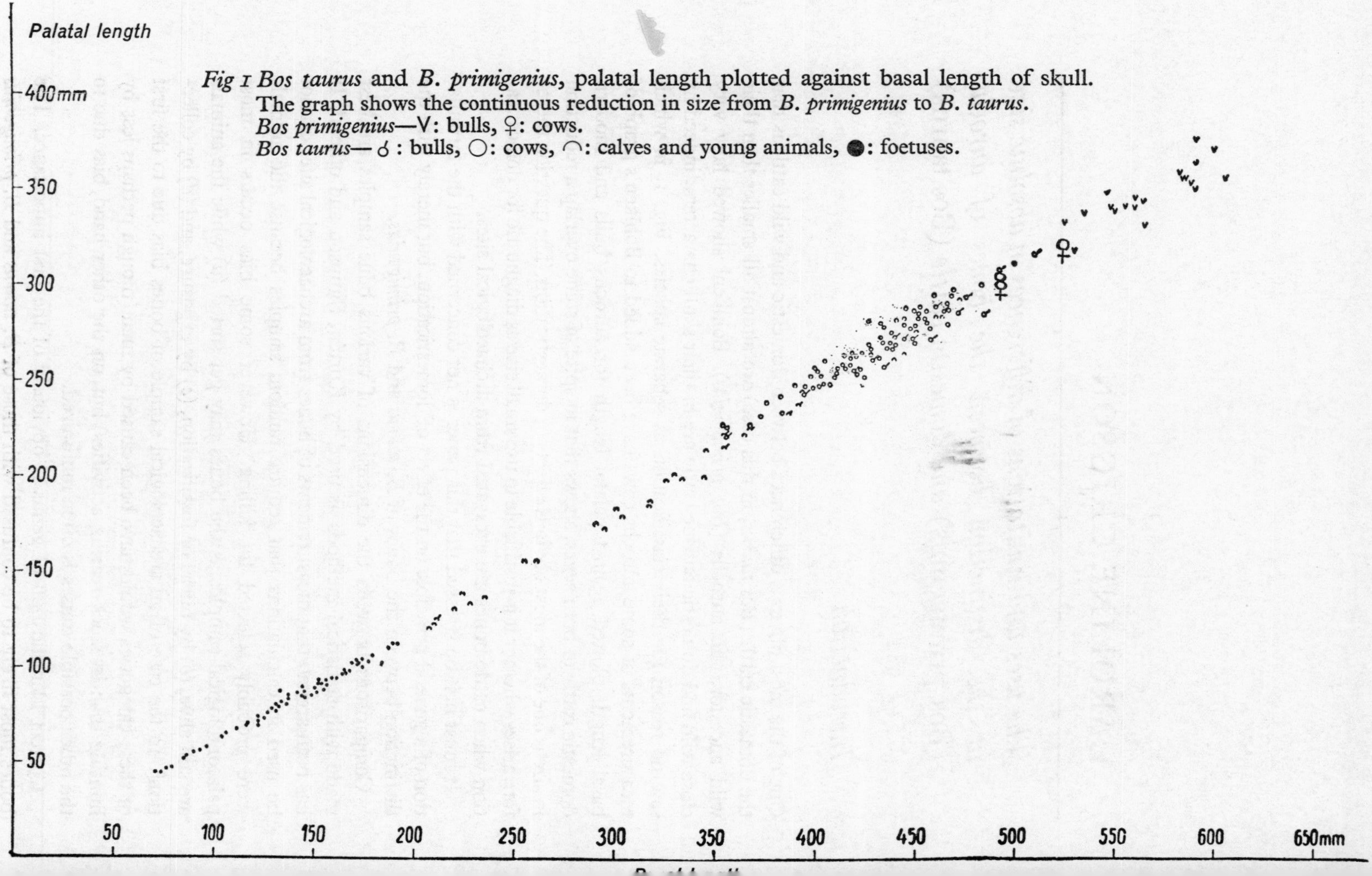

Fig 1 *Bos taurus* and *B. primigenius*, palatal length plotted against basal length of skull.
The graph shows the continuous reduction in size from *B. primigenius* to *B. taurus*.
Bos primigenius—∇: bulls, ♀: cows.
Bos taurus— ♂ : bulls, ○: cows, ◡: calves and young animals, ●: foetuses.

belong to the bison, but distinctive criteria for many parts of the skeleton have been worked out by Stampfli[4]. There are so few reports of post-glacial bison in Northern Europe, and those that do exist are from very early post-glacial times in Denmark and nearby[5], that the possible occasional presence of bison of a post-glacial date is very unlikely to interfere with the validity of the calculations. However bison were present in Switzerland (for example, some were identified by Stampfli at Burgäschisee-Süd[6]) and probably also in other parts of central and southern Europe.

Possible factors influencing the size of the aurochs

Sexual dimorphism and intrinsic variation

The remains have been found in Europe of two different forms of *B. primigenius* which differ from each other mainly in size. Rütimeyer[7] considered that domestic cattle of the "primigenius type" were descended from the aurochs and that "brachyceros" domestic cattle were descended from a smaller wild ancestor *yet to be discovered*. Hitscher[8] was the first to describe a small skull of *B. primigenius*, which he considered to be from a young animal. The same skull (and other similar ones) were variously described as adult dwarfs[9], as wild "*Bos brachyceros europaeus*"[10], as domestic *Bos taurus primigenius*[11], and as a small wild "*Bos urus minutus*"[12]. Hilzheimer[13] was the first to suggest that the small skulls might be from aurochs cows, a view which was confirmed by Leithner[14], who identified several aurochs cow skulls and one complete skeleton, and in spite of much controversy this view has come to be generally accepted on the Continent.

The position is not however the same in Britain: Jackson[15] writing on the aurochs skulls from Maiden Castle does not seem to have considered sexual dimorphism as a possible reason for their rather small size, and Bilton[16] re-identified the *B. primigenius* skull from Preston (Manchester Museum No. LL 144A) as domesticated and did not mention sex as a possible explanation for its relatively small size. The sexual dimorphism of the remains of aurochs from the mesolithic site of Star Carr is so doubtfully suggested in the report[17] that some authors[18] interpret the results as indicating that there were two different varieties of aurochs in Britain. Shawcross[19] compared a large, Bronze Age, aurochs skeleton with the remains of the smaller Star Carr aurochs without any suggestion that the difference between them might be sexual; on the other hand Jewell[20] considered that the two sizes of aurochs found in Britain are male and female, as on the continent.

The author[21] has drawn up provisional size ranges for many skull and some limb bone measurements for male and female aurochs in northern Europe in post-glacial times. A sexual dimorphism is obvious in almost all the measurements, the cows being the smaller. In most cases this is only a *partial* dimorphism[22], as the size ranges overlap, but nevertheless the ranges form a basis for the sexing of aurochs remains.

The aurochs was a rather variable animal, and this is particularly true of the skull where the variability is aggravated by wide sexual dimorphism. Some examples of the degree of variation are illustrated in Table 1.

Country	Measurement	Sex	Number	Mean mm.	V
N. Europe	length of front of skull	♂	24	685	4·9
N. Europe	length of front of skull	♀	7	600	5·1
N. Europe	length of front of skull	both	31	670	6·7
N. Europe	maximum occipital height	♂	46	219	5·0
N. Europe	maximum occipital height	♀	20	186	6·7
N. Europe	maximum occipital height	both	66	211	10·3
Britain	maximum length astragulus	both	12	87·08	4·28
Denmark	maximum length astragulus	both	31	87·52	4·96
Hungary	maximum length astragulus	both	96	84·12	4·81

Table 1 Coefficients of variation for various measurements of post-glacial *Bos primigenius*.
Measurements from Leithner, O. F. (1927). Der Ur, *Ber. int. Ges. Erhaltung des Wisents*, **2**, pp. 1–140, and Grigson, C. (In preparation).
The means and standard deviations were calculated from probability paper plots (Harding, J. P. (1949). The use of probability paper for graphical analysis of polymodal frequency distributions, *J. mar. biol. Ass. U.K.*, **28**, pp. 141–53.)

Various skull measurements of the two sexes taken separately, including those listed in Table 1, lie on straight lines when plotted on probability paper, showing that they were normally distributed—there is no suggestion that either the male or female group could be sub-divided on the basis of size, which strengthens the view that the existence of two size groups is merely the expression of a sexual dimorphism[23].

Geological age

There is some evidence, in Germany at least, that the aurochs was larger during the Pleistocene than in post-Pleistocene times[24]. British material has not been studied in detail and the situation is complicated by the assumption that the *B. primigenius* skulls in the British Museum (Natural History) are Pleistocene in date[25] although, in fact, the early dating of some of them is very doubtful: the Kirkcudbrightshire skull (36405) is labelled "turbary deposit", the Twickenham skull (M5970) was "dredged from the Thames" and the Atholl skull (M2245) is marked "Pleistocene?"; they are about the same size as those of definitely recent date in Denmark; but the undoubted Pleistocene specimens from Ilford are certainly enormous. The magnificent late-glacial skull from Faaborg (University Zoological Museum, Copenhagen) seems to belong to the Pleistocene rather than the Recent size group.

However it is the possible decrease in size *during* the post-Pleistocene period that is of more practical importance. Degerbøl[26] has produced a chart of various measurements of skulls and bones from complete skeletons of *B. primigenius* in Denmark which suggest that there was a slight decrease in size between the Pre-Boreal and Sub-Boreal periods. However when this chart is expanded (Figs. 2 and 2a) with measurements from archaeological sites and with recently dated skulls and skeletons (especially the Bronze Age skeleton from Lowes Farm[27]) from Denmark, N.W. Germany, and England no such diminution is apparent. Therefore it seems likely that the aurochs did not decrease in size in northern Europe between the Mesolithic and the Bronze Age.

Isolation

Interbreeding forms that are inter-fertile cannot diverge if they are able to breed freely, so that groups of animals of smaller stature than the members of the main population could only be set up if they were to be isolated from that population in one way or another. The main kinds of natural isolation are geographical, distance, ecological, and biological, but domestication by man might mimic the effects of natural isolation[28].

Geographical isolation

The past distribution of *B. primigenius* was extremely wide, ranging from N.W. Europe and N. Africa through Russia into eastern Asia, and into the Near East. Its eastern and southern extensions are still not clear partly because of the possibility of the spread of *B. namadicus* outside its Indian range; the distribution is particularly doubtful for the post-Pleistocene period. It is certainly possible that populations of aurochs could have become geographically isolated in particularly difficult or mountainous country within this huge area (as seems to have happened with another large ox—the kouprey (*Bibos sauveli*) in the mountains of the Laos–Cambodian border). A form of geographical isolation more likely to have occurred could have been on islands; for example, the aurochs remained on some of the Danish islands after they had become separated from the mainland. It has been said[29] that the reduction in gene flow caused by island isolation is likely to result in a decrease in stature in large mammals, including artiodactyls. However, if size changes occur as a result of geographical isolation the measurements of animals from such a population would still be normally distributed.

Distance isolation

Size differences might be expected to exist between potentially interbreeding animals which, although forming part of the same continuous geographical

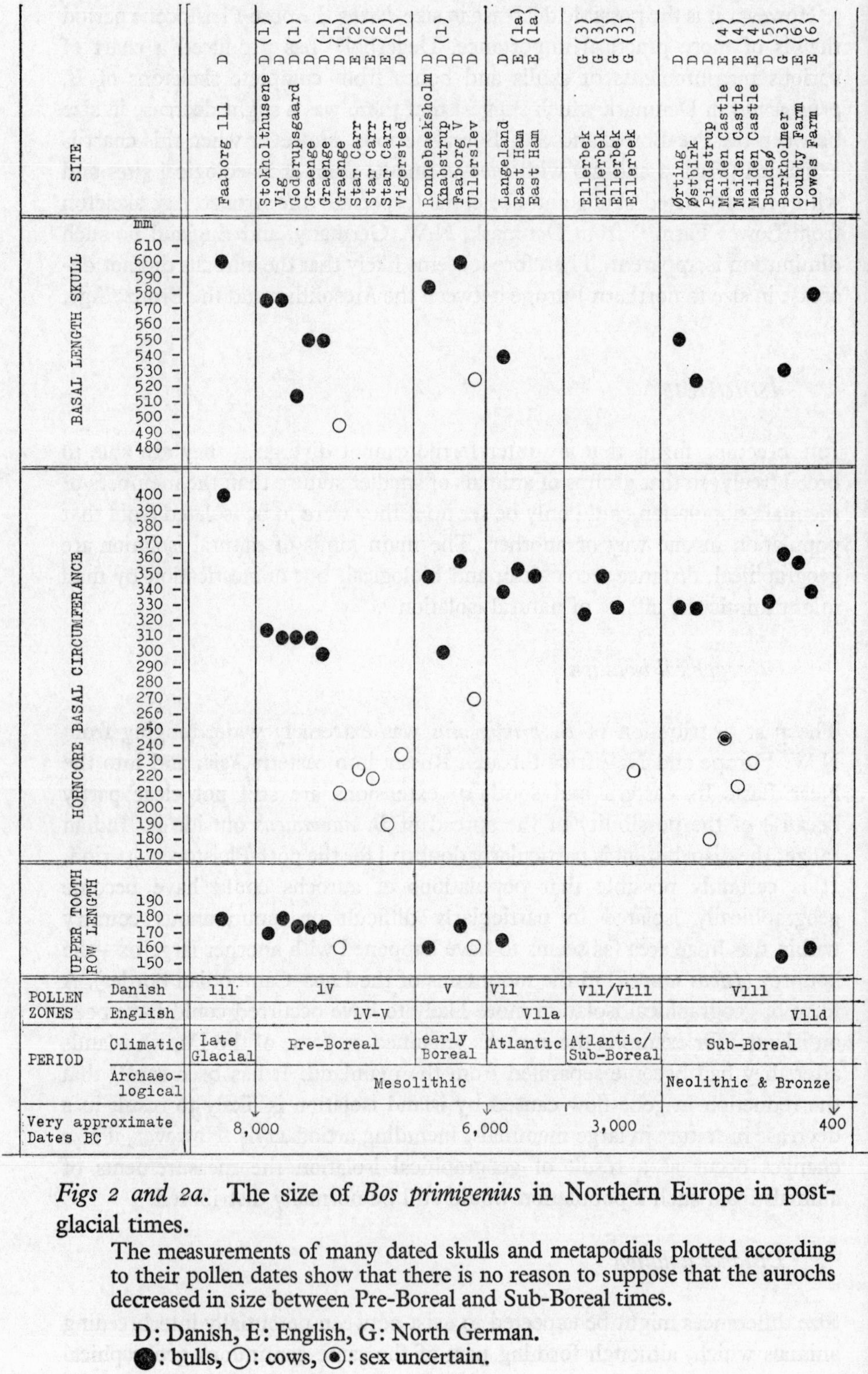
SITE
Faaborg 111 D
Stokholthusene D (1)
Vig D
Goderupsgaard D (1)
Graenge D (1)
Graenge D (1)
Graenge D (1)
Star Carr E (2)
Star Carr E (2)
Star Carr E (2)
Vigersted D (1)
Ronnebaeksholm D (1)
Knabstrup D
Faaborg V D
Ullerslev D
Langeland D
East Ham E (1a)
East Ham E (1a)
Ellerbek G (3)
Ellerbek G (3)
Ellerbek G (3)
Ellerbek G (3)
Ørting D
Østbirk D
Pindstrup D
Maiden Castle E (4)
Maiden Castle E (4)
Maiden Castle E (4)
Bundsø D (5)
Barkholmer G (3)
County Farm E (6)
Lowes Farm E (6)
BASAL LENGTH SKULL
mm
610
600
590
580
570
560
550
540
530
520
510
500
490
480
HORNCORE BASAL CIRCUMFERANCE
400
390
380
370
360
350
340
330
320
310
300
290
280
270
260
250
240
230
220
210
200
190
180
170
UPPER TOOTH ROW LENGTH
190
180
170
160
150
POLLEN ZONES
Danish
111
1V
V
V11
V11/V111
V111
English
1V-V
V11a
V11d
PERIOD
Climatic
Late Glacial
Pre-Boreal
early Boreal
Atlantic
Atlantic/ Sub-Boreal
Sub-Boreal
Archaeo- logical
Mesolithic
Neolithic & Bronze
Very approximate Dates BC
8,000
6,000
3,000
400

Figs 2 and 2a. The size of *Bos primigenius* in Northern Europe in post-glacial times.

The measurements of many dated skulls and metapodials plotted according to their pollen dates show that there is no reason to suppose that the aurochs decreased in size between Pre-Boreal and Sub-Boreal times.

D: Danish, E: English, G: North German.
●: bulls, ○: cows, ⊙: sex uncertain.

SITE		Stokholthusene (1) Vig Graenge Star Carr (1)	Ullerslev	Svaerdborg Svaerdborg Svaerdborg Holmegaard Holmegaard	East Ham (1a) Dyrholmen (5a) Dyrholmen (5a)	Pindstrup (4a) Woodhenge (6) Lowes Farm (7) Snail Down (7) Snail Down (7)
METACARPAL MAX. LENGTH	mm 270 – 260 – 250 – 240 – 230 –					
METATARSAL MAX. LENGTH	300 – 290 – 280 – 270 –					
POLLEN ZONES	Danish	1V	V	V1	V11	V111
	English	1V–V			V11a	V11d
PERIOD	Climatic	Pre-Boreal		Boreal	Atlantic	Sub-Boreal
	Archaeo-logical	Mesolithic				Neolithic & Bronze
Very approximate Dates BC		↳ 8,000		6,000	3,000	400

(Chart and all measurements based on Degerbøl, M. (1962). Ur und Hausrind, *Z. Tierzücht. ZüchtBiol.*, **76** (2–3), pp. 243–51, except where otherwise stated. 1: author. 1a: Banks, C. (1961). Report on the recently discovered remains of the wild ox (*Bos primigenius* Bojanus) from East Ham, *London Naturalist*, **41**, pp. 54–8, 2: Fraser, F. C. and King, J. E. (1954). Faunal remains, *in* Clark, J. G. D. *Excavations at Star Carr.* Cambridge. pp. 70–95. 3: Requate, H. (1957). Zur Naturgeschichte des Ures (*Bos primigenius* Bojanus 1827) nach Schädel- und Skelettfunden in Schleswig-Holstein. *Z. Tierzücht. ZüchtBiol.*, **70**, pp. 297–338. 4: Jackson, J. W. (1943). Animal bones—1 Neolithic, *in* Wheeler, R. E. M. *Maiden Castle, Dorset,* London, pp. 360–7. 5: Degerbøl, M. (1939). Dyreknogler, *in* Mathiassen T. Bundsø en yngre Stenalders Boplads paa Als, *Aarbøger for Nordisk Oldkundighed og Historie* **1939**. pp. 85–198. 5a: Mathiassen, T., Degerbøl, M. and Troels-Smith, J. (1942). Dyrholmen. En stenaldersboplads paa Djursland.*Kgl. Dansk. Vid. Selskab. Arkaeol.-kunsthist.* **1**. 6: Shawcross, F. W. and Higgs, E. S. (1961). The excavation of a *Bos primigenius* at Lowe's Farm, Littleport, *Proc. Camb. Ant. Soc.*, **54**, pp. 3–16. 7: Jewell, P. (forthcoming.))

distribution, were actually prevented from interbreeding by a great physical distance between them. The author, using various measurements, has prepared histograms of the size of the bones of post-glacial *B. primigenius* in various area (e.g. Figs. 3–5), although not all the measurements are available from each of the areas. The histograms suggest a close similarity in size between the aurochs found in different parts of N.W. Europe (Sweden, Denmark, Schleswig-Holstein, and Britain). Although the number of measurements available is rather small (except for the Danish material) it has been possible, in some cases, to apply tests of statistical difference. The results are given in Table 2 and show that there is no significant difference between

Country	Measurement	No.	Mean (mm.)	s (mm.)	t	Probability outside limits
Britain	least breadth	11	220·45	29·32	}0·0178	>90%
Denmark	frontal	23	220·65	31·50		
Britain	maximum	12	87·08	3·7281	}0·3091	70–80%
Denmark	length	31	87·52	4·3426		
Hungary	astragulus	96	84·12	4·0447	3·997	<0·1%

Table 2   A comparison of bone sizes of post-glacial *Bos primigenius* from different areas.
The table shows no significant difference between the aurochs of the N.W. European countries, but does reveal a significant difference between those from Denmark and Hungary.

the samples from Denmark and Britain and that the means of both samples are almost identical for frontal breadth and astragulus length.

The results are very different, however, when the size of the aurochs from Hungary is compared with that of the northern aurochs. A statistical test on astragulus length shows a very significant difference (measurements from Bökönyi[30]), the Hungarian animals being the smaller and such a difference is also apparent on the histogram (Fig. 5).

The apparently smaller size of the Hungarian aurochs might be an example of Bergman's rule that mammals decrease in size with increasing southerly latitude, although more research is needed before this can be definitely established. It suggests a north–south cline of decreasing stature, so great care must be taken when cattle remains from southern Europe, and more particularly from the Near East and Africa, are compared with those of north-western Europe.

Ecological isolation

B. primigenius is generally considered to be a woodland animal (although the wide spread of its horns would have prevented it from moving in dense forest), but the possibility (although there is no evidence for it) that there

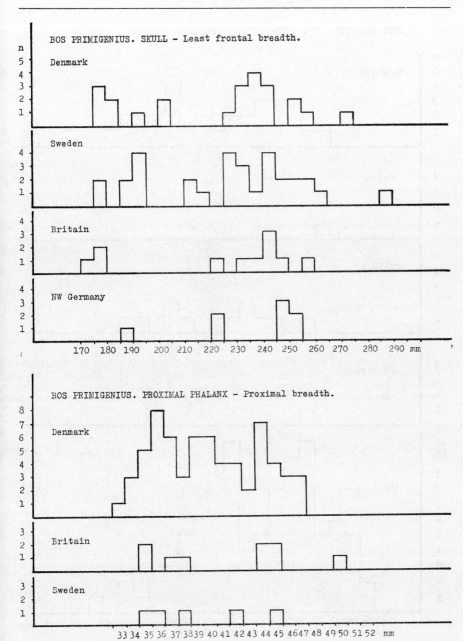

Figs 3 and 4 The size of post-glacial *Bos primigenius* in various parts of Northern Europe.

The histograms suggest, and this can be statistically confirmed, that the aurochs of Denmark, Sweden, N. Germany, and Britain were of the same size.

German measurements from Requate, H. (1957). Zur Naturgeschichte des Ures (*Bos primigenius* Bojanus 1827) nach Schädel- und Skelettfunden in Schleswig-Holstein. *Z. Tierzücht. ZüchtBiol.*, **70**, pp. 297–338.

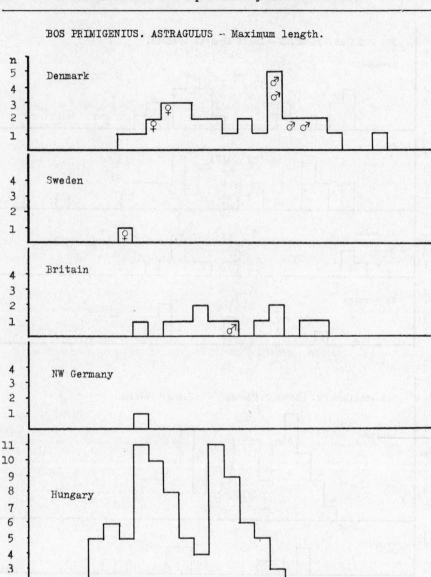

BOS PRIMIGENIUS. ASTRAGULUS - Maximum length.

Fig 5 The size of *Bos primigenius* in Hungary.

The histogram also shows that although the aurochs in different parts of Northern Europe were of the same size, it seems probable that the Hungarian aurochs was slightly smaller, at least in post-glacial times.

German measurements from Requate, H. (1957). ibid. Hungarian measurements from Bökönyi, S. (1962). Zur Naturgeschichte des Ures in Ungarn und das Problem der Domestikation des Hausrindes, *Acta Arch. Hung.*, 14, pp. 175–214.

were separate "woodland" and "plains" forms, as in the case of the American bison should not be overlooked.

Biological isolation

Since members of the various *Bos*, *Bibos*, *Bison* and *Bubalus* species can actually hybridize, it is often considered that they should be classified as varieties of the same species. It seems, however, very unlikely that such hybridization ever happened without the interference of man. Herds of two closely related *Bibos* species, the gaur and the banteng, came within one or two miles of each other[31] yet there are no recorded hybrids. It seems possible that such biological isolation could have occurred between groups within the same species; the aurochs must have been a herd animal and it is at least a theoretical possibility that preference for mating within the herd might have led to a reduction in gene flow and partial isolation.

Domestication by man

Interference by man in the lives of animals can be of many sorts and of varying degrees. Competition for land, forest clearance, agriculture and forest fires would have interfered with, and restricted the natural habitats of animals. Various forms of hunting, such as killing or maiming with missiles, trapping, driving into caves or pens or over cliffs must have had some effect on the natural animal populations.

It is only a small step from certain methods of hunting to following, or perhaps even controlling, the movements of cattle herds. Domestication is usually recognized when an animal breeds under artificial conditions, and it is at this point that real isolation from the wild form occurs[32]. However, one cannot say how early on in the process of man's interference with the herds normal gene flow would have been reduced nor how early on this would have had a recognizable morphological effect.

In addition to the reduction in size which would follow the isolation of animals, one would expect man to select for small size; to keep captive or handle a massive bull with horns several feet long would be anything but easy! If the wild and domestic forms were present in the same area, occasional crossings could be expected, whether intentional or accidental. Apart from the genetic effect of domestication there might be a phenotypic reduction in size caused by the possible deficiencies of primitive stock-keeping.

Conclusion

Only one of these various kinds of isolation is definitely known to have reduced the size of the aurochs: domestication by man, and where the presence of man can be assumed archaeologically this would be the most likely explanation for the presence of cattle that are smaller than local aurochs. Any such size change which was occurring naturally would have been a fairly slow process and would have resulted in a normal distribution of measurements within that population. The size range of animal bones from a single population, which had been preyed on by man and which are found in an archaeological site, will obviously not exceed the normal size range within the population as a whole. On sites where one finds a wide range of measurements from those of the aurochs downwards, one may suspect that domestication was in progress; although it does not seem possible on this type of data to distinguish between actual domestication and hybridization between imported domestic cattle and the local wild population. In either case, however, a wider than normal distribution of measurements occurs, and this may help to distinguish a "domestic" factor from other possible natural causes of small size in *B. primigenius*.

The recognition of domestic cattle bones

When cattle bones are found on archaeological sites how can one decide, on a metrical basis, whether they were those of wild or domestic animals? Ideally their measurements should be statistically compared to a large number of measurements of animals known to be "wild aurochs".

When working with any aurochs sample it is important to remember the wide sexual dimorphism of the aurochs so that the bones of cows are correctly identified. Any comparisons made must be between contemporary samples, for aurochs may differ in size in different periods (although such differences do not seem to have occurred in post-glacial N.W. Europe). Samples must also be from the same locality, for aurochs may have been of different sizes in different places. At the present time measurements of *B. primigenius* are usually too few to satisfy theses ample requisites and assumptions about the wild and domestic status of bones from archaeological sites must remain doubtful. However, it is to be hoped that with careful extrapolation of existing data, and the eventual collection of much more data, domestication in cattle will become easy to recognize metrically.

Some examples of the use of the size ranges of Bos primigenius

Burgäschisee-Süd

Histograms based on Stampfli's[33] *Bos* identifications at this Swiss Cortaillod site reveal (see Fig. 6) three main size groups. Stampfli interprets them

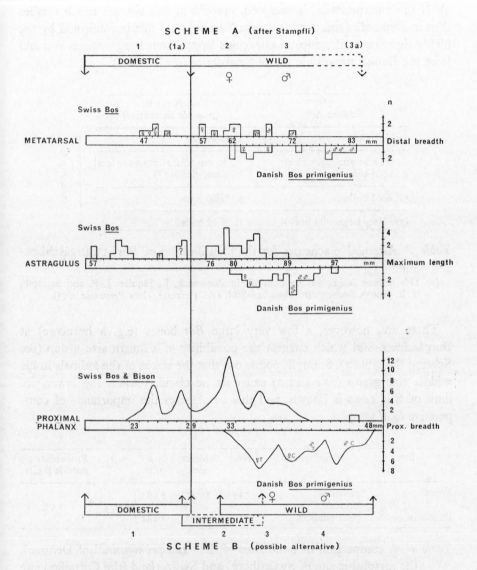

Fig 6 The distinction between *Bos primigenius* and *Bos taurus*—1.

The histograms show two alternative interpretations of the *Bos* measurements from the Swiss Cortaillod site of Burgäschisee-Süd: either the Swiss aurochs was much smaller than that of Northern Europe *or* animals intermediate in size between wild and domestic cattle were present. This demonstrates the difficulty of the use of absolute size in identification when the size of the local aurochs is not known.

Swiss measurements from Boessneck, J., Jéquier, J.-P., and Stampfli, H. R. (1963). Seeberg, Burgäschisee-Süd. Die Tierreste, *Acta Bernensia*, 2 (3).

as (1) domestic cattle, (2) wild cows, and (3) wild bulls (see Scheme A, Table 3). If this interpretation is accepted, aurochs at this site are much smaller than in Denmark (and north-western Europe), and this is confirmed by the highly significant difference in astragulus length from Burgäschisee-Süd and from the Danish mesolithic site of Sværdborg (see Table 4).

Scheme A[a]	Scheme B (possible alternative)	
1. Domestic	1. Domestic	↑ increasing size
(1a? Intermediate size) 2. Wild cows	} 2. Intermediate (crosses or local domestication?)	
3. Wild bulls	3. Wild cows	
(3a. Very large wild bulls)	4. Wild bulls	↓

Table 3 Alternative schemes for the identification of *Bos* at Burgäschisee-Süd.

(a) This scheme is implied by Stampfli in Boessneck, J., Jéquier, J.-P. and Stampfli, H. R. (1963). Seeberg, Burgäschisee-Süd. Die Tierreste, *Acta Bernensia*, **2** (3).

There are, however, a few very large *Bos* bones (e.g. a horncore) at Burgäschisee-Süd which suggest the possibility of a fourth size group (see Scheme B, Table 3). Stampfli points out that the status of the animals in his middle size group (1a? and 2) can only be clarified when the lower size limit of wild cows is known, and this emphasizes the importance of comparative *local* samples.

Site	Measurement	No.	Mean mm.	s mm.	t	Probability t outside limits
Sværdborg	proximal breadth	34	38·47	3·695	6·774	<0·1%
Burgäschisee-Süd	prox phalanx	51	33·37	3·181		

Table 4 A comparison of bone sizes of the "*Bos primigenius*" of Denmark (the mesolithic site of Svaerdborg) and Switzerland (the Cortaillod site of Burgäschisee-Süd).
(Swiss measurements from Boessneck, J., Jéquier, J.-P., and Stampfli, H. R. (1963). Seeberg, Burgäschisee-Süd. Die Tierreste, *Acta Bernensia*, **2** (3).)

Bos primigenius *in British Neolithic sites*

Measurements of cattle bones from British neolithic sites plotted against measurements of north-western European aurochs show that the Fussell's Lodge[34] *Bos* foot bones are of domestic size (Fig. 7), that wild cattle were hunted at Windmill Hill[35], and suggests that the special large British neolithic

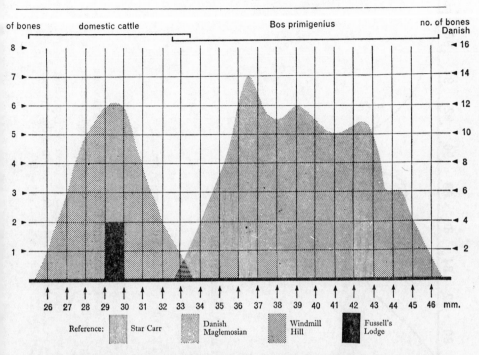

Fig 7 The distinction between *Bos primigenius* and *Bos taurus*—2.
The histograms show that the footbones from the possible hide burial at
Fussell's Lodge long barrow belong to the domestic size group and not with
the wild cattle (Grigson, C. (1966). The animal remains from Fussell's Lodge
long barrow, *in* Ashbee, P., The Fussell's Lodge Long Barrow Excavations
1957, *Archaeologia* **C**, 1966, pp. 62–73.)

domestic ox (proximal breadth of proximal phalanx 35 mm.) claimed for
Maiden Castle[36] was probably wild[37].

Neolithic cattle in Schleswig-Holstein

Nobis[38] was of the opinion that some of the cattle from the TRB site of
Fuchsberg-Südensee were intermediate in size between wild and domestic
cattle and therefore that local domestication was taking place. Histograms
using the north-west European size ranges of *B. primigenius* confirm that there
were animals of intermediate size in Fuchsberg-Südensee and also in the two
nearby TRB sites of Weissenfels[39] and Bundsø[40]. The wide range of variation
suggests that domestic animals are somehow involved. However, considerations of size alone are not enough to decide between the various possibilities;
(1) that there was crossing between small domestic cattle (which might have
been imported) and local wild aurochs, (2) that actual domestication was
taking place, or (3) that both processes were in operation together.

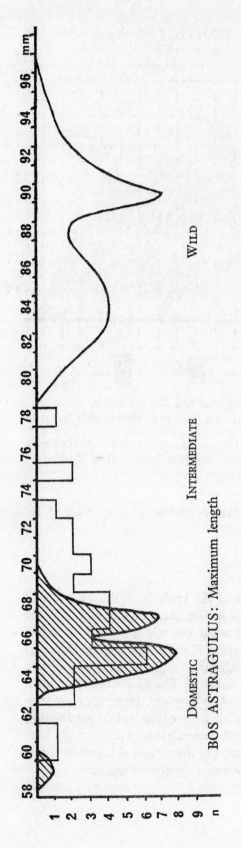

DOMESTIC

INTERMEDIATE

WILD

BOS ASTRAGULUS: Maximum length

▨ Domestic cattle bones from English neolithic sites (Windmill Hill and Maiden Castle).

︿ Postglacial Aurochs bones from northern Europe.

▭ Bones of domestic and intermediate size from northern European TRB sites (Bundsø, Fuchsberg-Südensee and Weissenfels).

Fig 8 The distinction between *Bos primigenius* and *Bos taurus*—3.
The histogram shows that some of the cattle from the TRB sites of North Germany and Denmark were intermediate in size between wild aurochs and neolithic domestic cattle. This probably indicates that either domestication or hybridization between local wild and imported domestic cattle was taking place.
German measurements from Nobis, G. (1962). Die Tierreste prähistorischer Siedlungen aus dem Satrupholmer Moor (Schleswig-Holstein), *Z. Tierzucht. ZüchtBiol.*, 77, pp. 16-30 and Nobis, G. (1954). Zur Kenntnis der ur- und frühgeschichtlichen Rinder Nord- und Mitteldeutschlands, *Z. Tierzücht. ZüchtBiol.*, 63, pp. 155-94.

Notes

1 Bohlken, H. (1962). Probleme der Merkmalsbewertung am Säugetier-schädel, dargestellt am Beispiel des *Bos primigenius* Bojanus 1827, *Morph. Jahrbuch*, **103** (4), pp. 509–661.

2 Kurtén, B. (1955). Sex dimorphism and size trends in the cave bear, *Acta Zool. Fennica*, **90**, p. 48; Simpson, G. G., Roe, A. and Lewontin, R. C. (1960). *Quantitative Zoology*. (2nd ed.). New York.

3 Simpson, G. G., Roe, A. and Lewontin, R. C. (1960). op. cit. p. 114.

4 Boessneck, J., Jéquier, J.-P. and Stampfli, H. R. (1963). Seeberg, Bur-gäschisee-Süd. Die Tierreste, *Acta Bernensia*, **2** (3).

5 Degerbøl, M. (1945). The bison in Denmark, *Danmarks Geol. Unders.*, **2** 73, pp. 1–62.

6 Boessneck, J., Jéquier, J.-P. and Stampfli, H. R. (1963). ibid.

7 Rütimeyer, I. (1867). Versuch einer natürlichen Geschichte des Rindes in seinen Beziehungen zu den Wiederkauern in allgemein, *N. Denk. Allgem. Schweiz. Ges. ges. Naturwiss.*, **22** (2), pp. 1–176.

8 Hitscher, K. (1888). Untersuchungen von Schädeln der Gattung Bos, unter besonderer Berücksichtigung einigerin ostpreussischen Torfmooren gefunderer Rinderschädel, *Diss.Königsberg*.

9 Nehring, A. (1889). Uber Riesen und Zwerge des *Bos primigenius*, *Sitzungsber. Ges. naturf. Freunde Berlin*, pp. 5–7.

10 Adametz, L. (1898). Bos (brachyceros) Europaeus n. sp. (Resumé), *Bull. int. Acad. Sci. Cracowie*, pp. 88–103.

11 La Baume, W. (1909). Beitrage zur Kenntnis der fossilen und sub-fossilen Boviden, *Schrift. naturf. Ges. Danzig*, **12**, pp. 45–80.

12 Malsburg, K. von. (1911). Uber neue Formen des kleinen diluvialen Urrindes *Bos (urus) minutus* n. spec., *Bull. int. Acad. Sci. Cracowie*, pp. 340–8.

13 Hilzheimer, M. (1909). Wisent und Ur im Naturalkabinett zu Stuttgart, *Jahresheft Vereins, vaterl. Naturk. Württemburg*, **65**, pp. 241–69.

14 Leithner, O. F. (1927). Der Ur, *Ber. int. Ges. Erhaltung des Wisents*, **2**, pp. 1–140.

15 Jackson, J. W. (1943). Animal bones—1 Neolithic, *in* Wheeler, R. E. M. *Maiden Castle, Dorset*. London. pp. 360–7.

16 Bilton, L. (1952). The History of the Chillingham Herd of Wild White Cattle. *M.Sc. Thesis, University of Manchester*.

17 Fraser, F. C. and King, J. E. (1954). Faunal remains, *in* Clark, J. G. D. *Excavations at Star Carr*. Cambridge. pp. 70–95.

18 e.g. Piggott, S. (1954). *The Neolithic Cultures of the British Isles*. Cambridge.

19 Shawcross, F. W. and Higgs, E. S. (1961). The excavation of a *Bos primigenius* at Lowe's Farm, Littleport, *Proc. Camb. Ant. Soc.*, **54**, pp. 3–16.

20 Jewell, P. A. (1962). Changes in size and type of cattle from prehistoric to medieval times in Britain, *Z. Tierzücht. ZüchtBiol.*, **77**, pp. 159–67.

21 Grigson, C. In preparation.

22 As defined by Kurtén, B. (1955). ibid.

23 Grigson, C. In preparation.

24 Leithner, O. F. (1927). ibid.; Requate, H. (1957). Zur Naturgeschichte des Ures (*Bos primigenius* Bojanus 1827), nach Schädel-und Skelettfunden in Schleswig-Holstein, *Z. Tierzücht. ZüchtBiol.*, **70**, pp. 297–338.

25 Fraser, F. C. and King, J. E. (1954). ibid.; Shawcross, F. W. and Higgs, E. S. (1961). ibid.

26 Degerbøl, M. (1962). Ur und Hausrind, *Z. Tierzücht. ZüchtBiol.*, **76** (2–3), pp. 243–51.

27 Shawcross, F. W. and Higgs, E. S. (1961). ibid.
28 Berry, R. J., this volume, pp. 207–17.
29 Berry, R. J. ibid.
30 Bökönyi, S. (1962). Zur Naturgeschichte des Ures in Ungarn und das Problem der Domestikation des Hausrindes, *Acta Arch. Hung.* **14**, pp. 175–214.
31 Lydekker, R. (1898). *Wild Oxen, Sheep, and Goats of all Lands*. London. p. 46.
32 See Berry, R. J. ibid. and Bökönyi, S., this volume, pp. 219–29.
33 Boessneck, J., Jéquier, J.-P. and Stampfli, H. R. (1963). ibid.
34 Grigson, C. (1966). The animal remains from Fussell's Lodge long barrow, *in* Ashbee, P. The Fussell's Lodge Long Barrow Excavations 1957, *Archaeologia C* **1966**, pp. 63–73.
35 Grigson, C. (1965). Faunal remains: measurements of bones, horncores, antlers and teeth, *in* Smith, I. F. *Windmill Hill and Avebury: Excavations by Alexander Keiller 1925–39*. Oxford. pp. 145–67.
36 Jackson, J. W. (1943). ibid.
37 Jewell, P. A. (1962). ibid.; Grigson, C. (In press). The domestic animals of the earliest neolithic in Britain, *in* Schwabedissen, H. *Die Anfänge des Neolithikums vom Orient bis Nordeuropa*.
38 Nobis, G. (1962). Die Tierreste prähistorischer Siedlungen aus dem Satrupholmer Moor (Schleswig-Holstein), *Z. Tierzücht. ZüchtBiol.*, **77**, pp. 16–30.
39 Nobis, G. (1954). Zur Kenntnis der ur- und frühgeschichtlichen Rinder Nord- und Mitteldeutschlands, *Z. Tierzücht. ZüchtBiol.*, **63**, pp. 155–94.
40 Degerbøl, M. (1939). Dyreknegler, *in* Mathiassen, T. Bundsø en yngre Stenalders Boplads paa Als, *Aarbøger for Nordisk Old kundighed og Historie* **1939**, pp. 85–198; Grigson, C. (In press). ibid.

SEBASTIAN PAYNE

A metrical distinction between sheep and goat metacarpals

The osteological separation between sheep and goats presents considerable difficulties: thus Reed[1] writes, "The greatest obstacle to an analysis of the origin and spread of prehistoric sheep and goats is my complete disbelief in the validity of most of the published identifications." In order to be fully useful, a method for the separation of sheep and goat bones should satisfy four conditions:

1 The relevant part of the skeleton should occur with reasonable frequency in archaeological contexts.
2 The relevant part of the skeleton should not, *per se*, be likely to present a biased figure for the relative proportions of the two animals: horn-cores, for example, are often used, but some of the sheep or goats, especially the females, may well be hornless, and the horn-cores of the animals differ so much (not only in shape, but also in structure and in size) that their resistance to destruction must surely also differ considerably: any figure thus obtained must therefore be treated with caution.
3 The separation obtained should be clear, demonstrable, and easily reproduced by different observers; ideally, therefore, the difference on which it is based should be capable of measurement.
4 The distinction should be able to be applied to immature as well as to adult bones.

It is not however necessary that such a method should separate all sheep from all goats. All that is needed is a way in which the sheep and goat bones at any one site can be separated into two discrete groups, with a low proportion of intermediate specimens.

In this paper a method is described which, it is hoped, goes some way towards filling this need, using the ratio between two measurements on each distal metacarpal condyle: this fragment occurs very frequently on most sites.

The method

Two measurements are taken on any distal metacarpal condyle (Fig. 1): the medio-lateral width of the condyle (*W. cond.*), and the antero-posterior width of its external trochlea (*W. troch.*). The first measurement cannot be taken accurately unless one arm of the callipers is narrow enough to fit between the two condyles, if both are present. Replicate measurements from

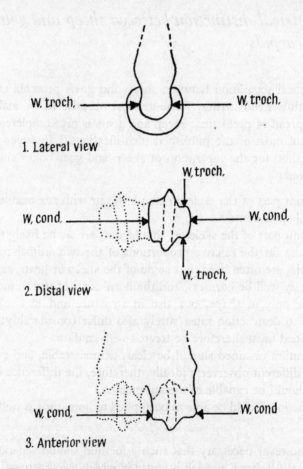

Fig 1 Distal metacarpal, showing the measurements.

the same series of metacarpals taken by the same observer, and by different observers, have given results consistent to within 0·3 mm. These two measurements are then plotted against each other for all the available distal metacarpal condyles. The medial condyle is normally larger than the lateral condyle, and the ratio *W. cond.* : *W. troch.* tends to be higher in the medial condyle: for this reason, different symbols are used for the medial condyles (triangles), and the lateral condyles (squares), whenever they can be distinguished. Similarly, fused and unfused condyles are differentiated in the plots.

Excavated samples

Results are presented for samples of metacarpals taken from five archaeological sites. In each case the same conventions are observed. In the first four plots (Figs. 2–5) two clusters can be seen. The samples are admittedly small, and the appearance of clustering may be exaggerated by the fact that a single animal may be represented by as many as four symbols. If, however, these clusters have any significance, and in at least one case (the sample from neolithic Nea Nikomedeia, Fig. 2), this seems a safe conclusion, a number of alternative explanations are available:

(*a*) That they represent different age-groups of a single population. This seems unlikely, especially as both groups contain immature (unfused) individuals.

(*b*) That they represent different sex-groups of a single population. This seems unlikely, first because the relative positions of the groups are not similar in the four examples, and secondly because a small sample of modern sheep and goats of known sex showed no similar sexual dimorphism.

(*c*) That they represent two separate populations, either of the same, or of different species.

The last seems to be the most reasonable explanation on the basis of the available data. As both sheep and goat seem to be present, using other accepted criteria, especially the shape of the horn-cores, and the skull sutures, the two clusters can probably be identified as sheep and goats. An obvious test is to examine a modern sample of sheep and goats, to see whether they show the same difference.

A modern sample

A sample of modern sheep and goats of known identity was collected by Mr. E. S. Higgs in 1963 in Verroia, a town in northern Greece near the site of Nea Nikomedeia, about fifty miles west of Thessaloniki. The plots for the metacarpals in this sample (Figs. 6–7) show a clear difference between sheep and goats: there is no clear separation into two discrete clusters, but there is no overlap between them either. This result confirms the earlier conclusion, that the two clusters in the excavated samples are to be identified as sheep and goats.

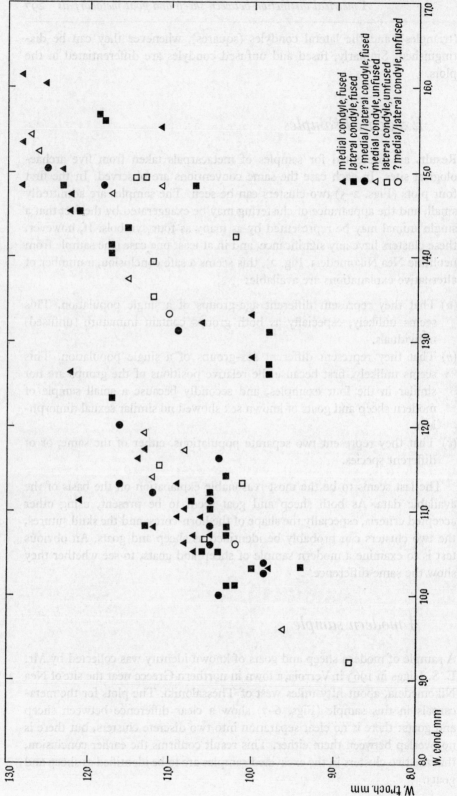

Fig 2 Metacarpal sample. Nea Nikomedeia, Greece. Neolithic.

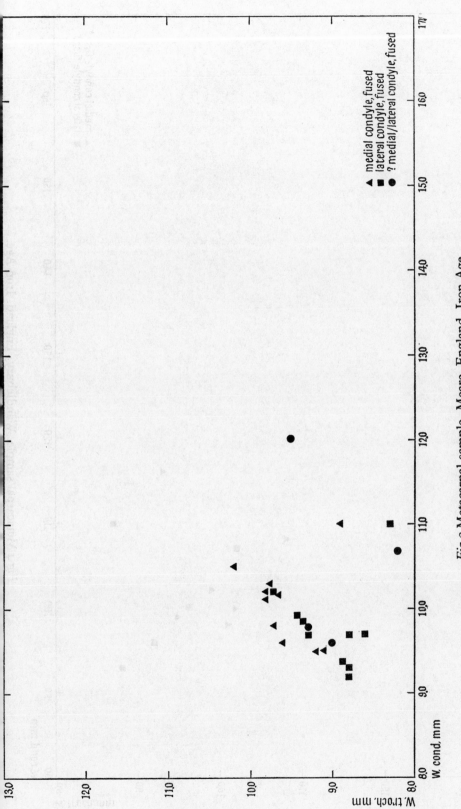

Fig 3 Metacarpal sample. Meare, England. Iron Age.

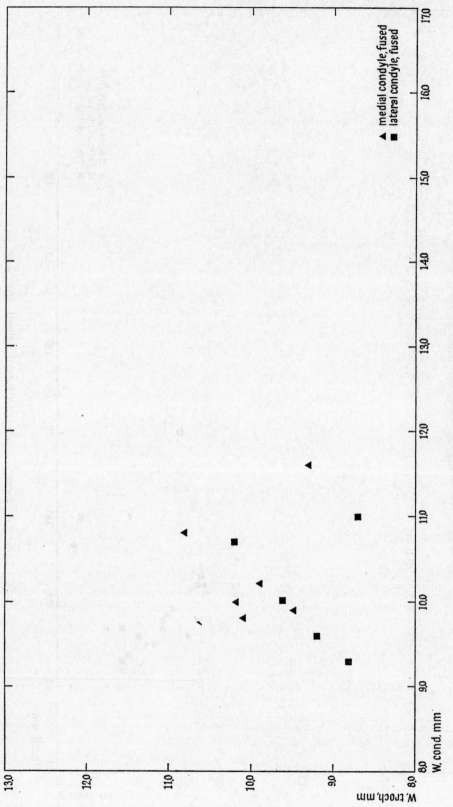

Fig 4 Metacarpal sample. Wandlebury, England. Iron Age.

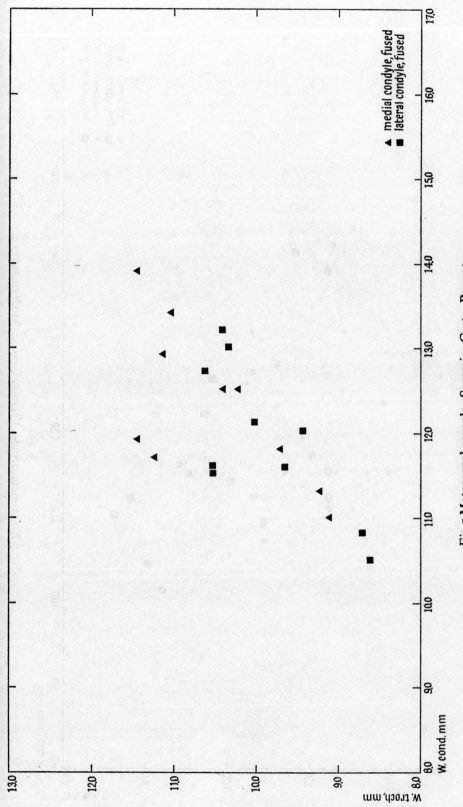

Fig 5 Metacarpal sample. Samaria, Crete. Recent.

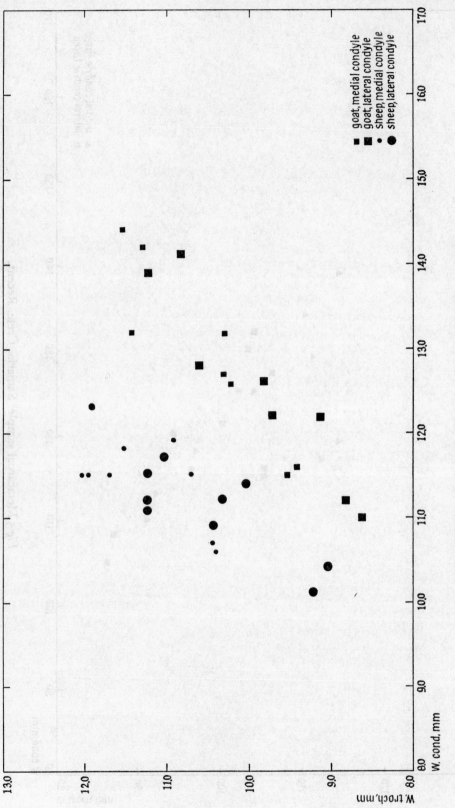

Fig 6 Right metacarpals. Verroia, Greece. Modern sample.

goat, medial condyle
goat, lateral condyle
sheep, medial condyle
sheep, lateral condyle

W. cond, mm

W.troch, mm

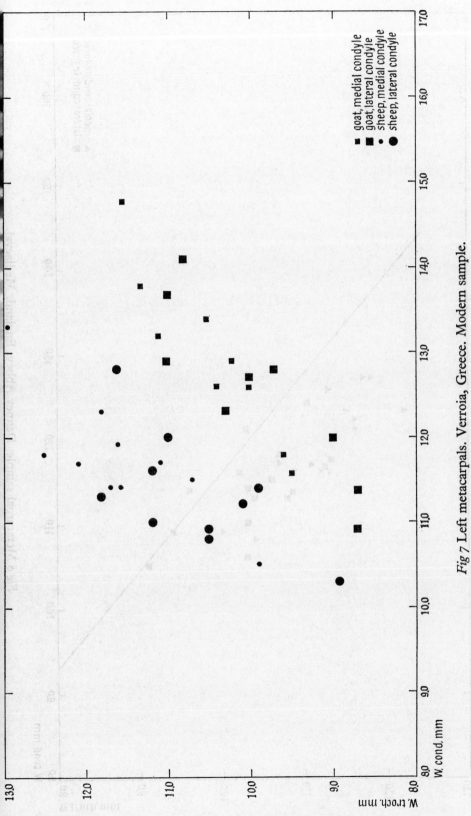

Fig 7 Left metacarpals. Verroia, Greece. Modern sample.

goat, medial condyle
goat, lateral condyle
sheep, medial condyle
sheep, lateral condyle

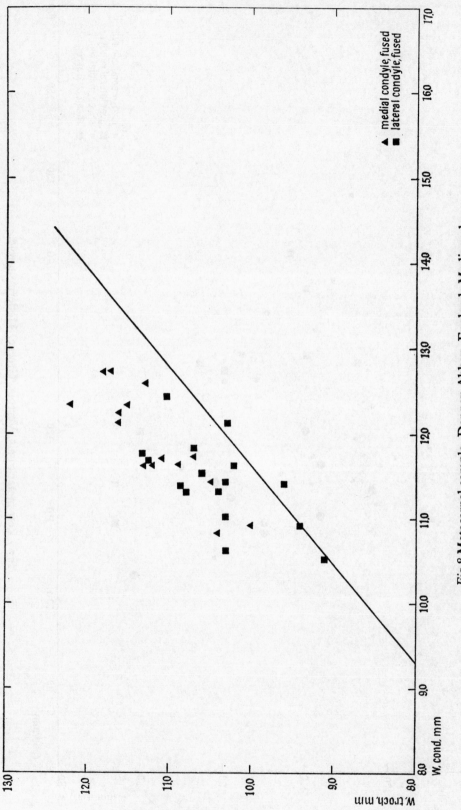

Fig 8 Metacarpal sample. Denney Abbey, England. Mediaeval.

Conclusions

It is important to stress that it is *not* suggested that a diagnostic ratio, based on these two measurements, can be used to identify every individual sheep/goat distal metacarpal condyle. All that is claimed is that if this method is applied to the sheep/goat metacarpals from a reasonably homogeneous archaeological context, the sheep and the goats, if both are present, are likely to form two distinct clusters, and can thus be identified. It is likely that, if a sample is large enough, there will be some intermediate specimens; what is important is that the bulk of material will fall into two distinct clusters. If only one species is present, only one cluster is expected: in a sample from an English mediaeval site (Fig. 8), a single cluster is observed: if a diagnostic ratio is used, on the basis of the modern sample, to separate the sheep from the goats, it might be concluded that a few of the bones are of goats (as is shown by the line drawn in the figure), but it seems more reasonable to interpret the cluster as a single population of sheep, and this is historically not improbable.

This method is presented here, in an unfinished state, in the hope that it can be put to the test on a wider range of material than has yet been available. The author would be grateful to see the results of any attempt to apply it[3].

Notes

1 *in* Braidwood, R. J. and Howe, B. (1960). Prehistoric investigations in Iraqi Kurdistan, *Studies in Ancient Oriental Civilisation*, Oriental Institute, Chicago, **31**, pp. 1–184.
2 The author wishes to thank Miss Fiona Gilmore for allowing him to examine material from Meare, and Mr. E. S. Higgs for providing material from Wandlebury, Denney Abbey and modern comparative material from Verroia. The work was done as part of the British Academy–Cambridge University Early History of Agriculture Project; the author especially wishes to thank its Director, Mr. E. S. Higgs, for help and encouragement.

H. S. SMITH

Animal domestication and animal cult in dynastic Egypt

The writer is not a prehistorian, and has no specialist knowledge of animals, even from the purely antiquarian point of view. He was asked merely as a general egyptologist to suggest the relevance of dynastic Egyptian evidence to the problems of animal domestication in the ancient world. It follows that this short paper is highly eclectic, and that it has no claim to independent worth, being based entirely on the work of others. It does not present more than a small part of the evidence from Egypt which is important to this subject.

Scientific study of the beginnings of animal domestication in the Nile valley has not advanced far, though as the result of the Nubian campaign some teams of prehistorians have begun to interest themselves specifically in the subject. In general, however, largely owing to the lack of well-excavated predynastic settlement sites in the alluvium, such anatomical material as we have from earlier work may well be marginal to the main problems, and as much of it was excavated forty years or more ago, identifications doubtless leave much to be desired. Moreover the culture contexts in which these specimens were found are not dated on an absolute time scale, and even their relative dating may be disputed in some cases. As there is at present no means of judging how far the desert edge sites from which these specimens come represent the level of achievement in the valley, it seems best at present not to propose on inadequate evidence an account of the early history of domestication there, which may only mislead.

Dynastic Egypt, however, throws a few side-lights on the state of domestication and various forms of animal-keeping in a particular sophisticated urban culture, that may be of some value for purposes of comparison. Scientific study of the magnificent Egyptian portrayals of animals in sculpture, relief and painting, is in the first place the work of two men, Schweinfurth and Keimer, and this work has been principally devoted to identification of species, often a delicate matter, rather than to the specific study of domestication. The field is too vast for any summary here, and the author is incompetent by training to make it. Animal domestication may have been as specialized in the ancient world as in the modern. In the third and second millennia B.C. in Egypt, the bull preferred for sacrifice and for the table was called *ỉwz*; exceedingly fat with pendulous belly, it stood relatively low on its haunches, and had wide everted horns, which however were often deliberately twisted asymmetrically or even removed during youth. Texts suggest that these bulls were normally imported from the south, perhaps mainly from the Dongola bend and adjacent territories. On arrival by river in Egypt, these animals were kept tethered in stables or fenced paddocks under constant surveillance; there they were fattened methodically for slaughter. The native wild bull of the Delta marshes and the hill country bordering the valley, the Egyptians called *ng*; it is depicted as lean and standing relatively high on its haunches, with wide everted horns like those of the *ỉwz*, which are, however, never deformed or removed. The *ng* was captured by lassooing, and once tamed, appears to have been allowed to graze freely, being caught for service by use of sticks and the lassoo. It was the draught animal par excellence used for pulling the plough, stone blocks, funeral sarcophagi, etc. The Egyptians bred from the females, and also naturally used them for milking, whereas in the case of the *ỉwz*, females do not seem to be often represented and breeding in Egypt was probably less common. The *ng* was in the natural course of events also used for sacrifices and killed for meat (usually, one suspects, animals that had done good service), but was never apparently deliberately fattened. The cult animal of the bull-god Apis was a *ng*; probably this is true also of other bull-gods, but is not demonstrable[1].

Perhaps the most remarkable case of over-specialization is that of a particular race of fat-tailed sheep in which, Herodotus (III, 113) tells us, the tail became so heavy that the sheep was unable to drag it about without serious difficulty and consequent ulceration; so the shepherds supported the tail on a wheeled trailer drawn by reins. This apparent fantasy has been shown to be literal truth by Keimer, who has traced a series of references in Arabic and European sources to these sheep from the mediaeval period to the last century, and discovered that the trailer was still used in the Menufiyah province of the Delta in recent times[2]. The fat-tailed woolly sheep, *Ovis platyra*, with horns curved down and forward, was introduced in the Middle Kingdom, and lived for a short time side by side with the ancient Egyptian fleeceless sheep, *O longipes*, which, however, became extinct by the early New Kingdom. *O. longipes* had laterally-twisted horns almost parallel to the ground, and it is with these horns that the ram-headed deities Khnum and Amun and Herishef are always shown. When in the later period incarnation animals were required, these had to be culled from *O. platyra*, but the mummies of these animals show that they were provided with a gilded wooden crown in the form of the horizontally-twisted horns of *O. longipes*, so as to maintain the original sacred appearance of the deity. In the particular case of the ram god of Mendes in the Delta there is evidence to show that for a time a species of goat with horns similar in shape to *O. longipes* was used for incarnation animals, but subsequently *O. platyra* was used here too[3].

That the third millennium was a time when the Egyptians were making experiments with the surrounding fauna is shown by the scenes of feeding tethered animals in fenced paddocks already referred to; for ibex, oryx, antelope, addax, gazelle, and hyaena are shown being fed in the same paddock with *iwz* bulls[4]. In the first three cases the motive is clearly fattening for sacrifice, but the case of the hyaenas, who had to be forcibly fed (Fig. 1), is

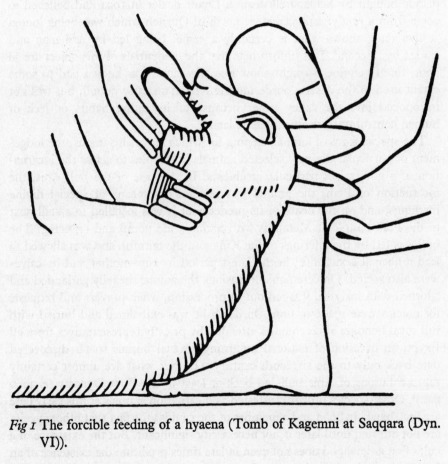

Fig 1 The forcible feeding of a hyaena (Tomb of Kagemni at Saqqara (Dyn. VI)).

strange, for they do not normally seem to appear in offering scenes or lists[5], and there is no evidence that scavengers formed part of the Egyptian diet except in time of famine, nor do they figure in cult. Another example is that of cranes, who are shown in the bird-pens of nobles' estates being forcibly fed (Plate II)[6]. Such scenes do not recur after the Old Kingdom. While the keeping and forcible feeding of animals cannot of course be equated with domestication for use, some of the same processes are involved. We should perhaps then examine prehistoric material for signs of incipient or experimental utilization of species which never became fully domesticated. In this connection reference should be made to the camel, which as is well-known does not appear among the dynastic fauna of Egypt until the Roman period. There are, however, indubitable representations of the camel from the predynastic period, and one most remarkable theriomorphic vase in the form of a camel from an allegedly intact tomb at Abusir el-Meleq, which contains a (to me) disconcertingly wide range of material, but may date from the First Dynasty[7]. None of this proves early use of the camel, but a terracotta plaque bought by Schiaparelli from a Luxor dealer in 1904 and believed to come from a predynastic cemetery north of Qurneh which was being looted at that date, shows what is certainly a camel being led by one man and ridden by a second. It is unfortunate that the credentials of this object are so poor, for if genuine it might show that the camel was known and to some extent used in the deserts bordering the Nile at an early period, but was not introduced into the valley either because of its eating habits or lack of human control until three millennia later[8].

The special form of animal keeping for which Egypt is famous, the lodgement of particular divinely selected animals in temples to act as the incarnation of a god, raises particular problems. In the case of the bull Apis, the incarnation of Ptah, the animal was selected by means of special divine markings, and on the death of its predecessor it was installed in a stall next to the Ptah temple at Memphis with nation-wide pomp and rejoicing. The bull was fed by the offerings of the King and the faithful, and was allowed to lead a normal sexual life; in the latest period its cow-mother and its calves were also sacred. On ceremonial occasions the animal, heavily garlanded and adorned with insignia, was led out in procession, when prayers and requests for oracles were made to him. On death he was embalmed and buried with full royal honours at ceremonies attended by priestly representatives from all Egypt, an occasion of national mourning. Actual burials so far discovered date back only to the sixteenth century B.C., but what are almost certainly representations of Apis bulls go back at least to the First Dynasty (*c.* 3000 B.C.)[9]. Other species probably attested as incarnation animals at this early date are ibis, hawk, baboon and a member of the canids; the fact that other species are not attested until later is not necessarily significant. But the existence of a cult of an animal god does not even in late times predicate the existence of an incarnation animal; in the case of savage species statues were always used for cult purposes. Evidently the practical measures necessary to keep an animal in good health in captivity for cult purposes are similar to those required for domestication for use.

In Table I are listed some important Egyptian genera, selected on an arbitrary basis, with details of their utilization by the Egyptians for sport, offering and sacrifice, domestication, as pets and as cult animals. This table, of course, drastically over-simplifies the complexity of the phenomena, ignoring species, date, tabu and other important considerations. It does serve to show, however, that the group of animals worshipped in Egypt has (i) no direct relation with the group of domesticated animals; (ii) no direct relation with the group of animals favoured for offerings and sacrifices in tomb or temple cult. Most genera hunted by the king and the nobility in the Old Kingdom for sport recur among those worshipped; it is notable that some forms of such hunting and harpooning continued to be represented long after they had passed out of practice, because they signified ritually the victory of the king over his enemies, or in mythical terms of Horus over Seth (Typhon)[10]. Many genera not in this group were of course worshipped. Most of them were, however, wild, while those common domesticated fauna of Egypt, the goat, the pig, the donkey and the duck were never associated with cults.

In view of this, it might seem that any connection between the keeping of animals for cult purposes and domestication for use might be ruled out. Yet I doubt whether the possibility can be dismissed so lightly. As seen above, many of the fauna worshipped belong to the uplands or were the object of hunting. The German school of historians of religion led by H. Kees has made it probable, by careful study of individual cults and their mythology, that behind even some of the cults which seem most closely connected with domesticated animals and the agricultural life of the valley, there stand precursors belonging to an earlier stage of the economy. For instance, in dynastic times the cult of Min of Coptos, who appears both as a white bull and as an ithyphallic anthropomorphic deity, is concerned almost entirely with the fertility of the crops and herds; yet certain titles and strands of myth appear to show that originally Min in the form of a rampaging wild bull was lord of the eastern desert. Likewise, there are indications that the anthropomorphic female deities of the first cataract, Anukis and Satis, were originally a dorcas gazelle and an oryx respectively. Certain bull and cow cults appear also to have originally been addressed to wild species, and the object of one cult, the baboon, *Papio hamadryas*, appears to have been extinct in Egypt by the third millennium B.C. One important deity, Seth, the god of storm and desert, is represented by a strange mythical animal, unknown among live and fossil fauna, which yet may represent some of the traits of okapi or aardvark. It seems possible that this representation may be a stylization of some creature or a cross between creatures once known to predynastic Egyptians or a strain of them, at a time when they lived in the deserts of North Africa, or indeed elsewhere. Kees in fact sees the history of animal-cult in predynastic Egypt as a gradual adaptation of cults which had originated among people hunting, gathering, fowling, fishing and grazing over a wide area, to the changed circumstances of intensive agricultural life in the valley dependent on the Nile flood. This system of interpretation is far from proven, but there is a considerable body of textual and iconographical evidence to support it, and it is of course welcomed by the considerable body of religious historians who

Genus	Hunted by Royalty and Nobility	Kept for fattening	Offered or Sacrificed	Kept as pets or in gardens	Domesti- cated	Object of cults	Notes
Lion	x	–	–	–	–	x	
Baboon	–	–	–	–	–	x	a
Monkey	–	–	–	x	–	–	b
Oryx (antelope)	x	x	x	–	–	?	c
Addax (antelope)	x	x	x	–	–	–	c
Buffalo	x	x	x	–	–	–	c
Gazelle	x	x	x	–	–	?	c, d
Ibex	x	–	–	–	–	–	
Fallow Deer	x	–	–	–	–	–	
Hyaena	–	x	?	–	–	–	
Wild Dogs (Wolf, Jackal)	–	–	–	–	–	x	e
Fox	–	–	–	–	–	–	f
Domestic Dog	–	–	–	x	x	–	
Cattle: *iwz*	–	x	x	–	x	x	
Cattle: *ng*	x	–	x	–	x	x	
Sheep	–	–	–	–	x	x	
Goat	–	–	–	–	x	–	g
Pig	–	–	–	–	x	–	h
Horse	–	–	–	–	x	–	
Donkey	–	–	–	–	x	–	h
Cat	–	–	–	x	x	x	i
Hare	x	–	x	–	–	–	
Mongoose	–	–	–	–	–	x	
Hippopotamus	x	–	–	–	–	x	j
Crocodile	–	–	–	–	–	x	j
Fish (Lepidotus)	–	–	–	–	–	x	k
Fish (Oxyrhynchus)	–	–	–	–	–	x	k
Frog	–	–	–	–	–	x	
Vulture	–	–	–	–	–	x	
Falcon	–	–	–	–	?	x	l
Kite	–	–	–	–	–	–	m
Crane	–	x	–	–	–	–	
Stork	–	–	–	x	–	–	n
Heron	–	–	–	–	–	x	
Ibis	–	–	–	–	–	x	o
Goose	–	–	x	–	x	x	p
Duck	–	–	x	–	x	–	
Ostrich	x	–	–	–	–	–	

GENERAL. Phenomena are very much more complex than shown in this chart. In particular the related factor of tabu is omitted, species are not distinguished, and date of introduction and of first attestation of cult are left out of consideration.

(a) No longer native in Egypt during dynastic period.

(b) The baboon is shown adoring the sun at dawn, but had no cult of its own.

(c) These animals were considered (at least from the New Kingdom) as "Typhonian", and were in the context of royal rituals sacrificed as enemies.

(d) No cult in dynastic times: some inferential evidence for predynastic cults.

(e) Wepwawet of Siut, appears on early monuments erect and armed. Elsewhere the wolf/dog occurs prone on a shrine, typically as necropolis god and embalmer of Osiris (Anubis).

(f) A human figure disguised as a fox appears playing the flute on a predynastic hunting palette: it is suggested that it may be a decoy.

(g) No original goat cults: through similarity of the horns to *Ovis longipes* the goat was for a time after the extinction of this species substituted for it in the cult of the ram of Mendes.

believe that animal and plant cults belong to an earlier stage of religious development than anthropomorphic cults[11].

If Kees is right, animal cults of some sort must have existed among the inhabitants of north-east Africa before the main "neolithic revolution" and before the intensive agricultural settlement of the Nile valley. It follows that they were in being during the times in which animals were being domesticated for use. Of course there is nothing to show that at that early time special incarnation animals were kept and fed; however, as the main point of animal cult of this sort appears to be that the powerful *numen* to be propitiated or appeased was felt to be manifest in the animal, the possibility that man attempted from the first to approach the spirit through the living exemplar cannot be ruled out. And if so the means he used would be very much those used in the process of domestication.

The most that can be said for the above tendentious argument is that it points one more of the factors that *could* have played a part in the keeping or domestication of particular species in a particular culture-context. For while it is certainly right and necessary to regard the whole process of the domestication of animals as an evolutionary event, that "event" is surely the sum of many particular historical occurrences, which may well have been due to individual combinations of cultural and environmental causes.

Notes

1 Montet, P. (1954). Les boeufs Egyptiens, *Kemi*, **13**, pp. 42–58.
2 Keimer, L. (1953–4). Notes diverses, *Bull. de l'Institut d'Egypte*, **36** pp. 466–76.
3 Keimer, L. (1938). Remarques sur quelques representations de béliers, *Annales du Service des Antiquités d'Egypte*, **38**, pp. 297–332; Zeuner, F. E. (1963). *A History of Domesticated Animals.* London. p. 184 and Fig.

(h) These animals were considered "Typhonian", but were normally avoided even for sacrifices: eating them was tabued.
(i) The early African cat may have been used for retrieving, but the evidence is difficult to interpret. This species died out after the Middle Kingdom: the domestic cat of the New Kingdom replaces some lionesses in cult, e.g. Bastet.
(j) Considered "Typhonian". Crocodile hunting not shown after the Old Kingdom. Hippopotamus-hunting scenes occur in the context of royal ritual to the latest period but can hardly have taken place after the Middle Kingdom.
(k) Considered "Typhonian". Generally fished for and eaten, but tabu in the context of certain festivals and certain local cults.
(l) There is some evidence for falconry in ancient Egypt, see Keimer, L. (1950). Falconry in ancient Egypt, *Isis*, **41**, p. 52.
(m) The sisters Isis and Nepthys as mourners for Osiris appear as kites, but there is no cult of the bird.
(n) Kept in royal gardens as exotic specimens.
(o) Is cult-incarnation of the same god, Thoth (the moon), as baboon.
(p) The goose plays a role in the myths of creation, and is identified with Amun, but the existence of a cult is dubious.

Table 1 Utilization of selected genera in dynastic period.

7.17, corrects an error in his chapter (1954). Domestication of animals, *in* Singer, C. *et al.* (eds.) *A History of Technology*. Oxford. pp. 345–6 and Fig. 222.

4 Zeuner, F. E. (1954). op. cit. p. 341 and Fig. 220; see also von Bissing, K. (1905). *Die Mastaba des Gem-ni-kai*, 1, Berlin. pl. XI; see also Keimer, L. (1956). Notes de lecture, *Bull. de l'Institut Francais d'Archéologie Orientale*, 55, pp. 13–20.

5 The hyaena is found once in an Old Kingdom mortuary offering scene. A hyaena is seen in the hunting scenes of the Pyramid temple of Sahuré being tackled by a dog, and they are occasionally seen led to and from the hunting field. A suggestion that they were used as decoys has no direct support.

6 Duell, P. (1938). *The Mastaba of Mereruka*, 1. Chicago. pl. 52.

7 Möller, G. and Scharff, A. (1926). *Die Archaeologischen Ergebnisse des Vorgeschichtliches Gräberfeldes von Abusir el-Meleq*, 209. Berlin. pp. 40–1 and pl. 24.

8 Keimer, L. (1929). Bermerkungen und Lesefrüchte zur altägyptischen Naturgeschichte, *Kemi*, 2, pp. 85–90.

9 Otto, E. (1964). *Beiträge zur Geschichte der Stierkulte in Aegypten*. Hildesheim. An ivory from the Hierakonpolis deposit in the Petrie Collection, University College London, has recently been cleaned, and has proved to show a bull with a disk between the horns, probably Apis or Mnevis.

10 Säve-Södebergh, T. (1953). *Egyptian Representations of Hippopotamus Hunting as a Religious Motive*. Uppsala.

11 Kees, H. (1956). *Der Götterglaube im alten Ägypten*. Berlin. Especially the first chapter.

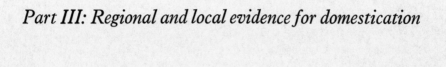

Part III: Regional and local evidence for domestication

F. R. ALLCHIN

Early domestic animals in India and Pakistan

Considering that the Archaeological Survey of India recently celebrated its centenary, and that in the past two decades there has been such a spate of excavations, the available archaeological evidence bearing on the domestication of animals in the subcontinent is regrettably sparse (see map, p. 324). Before 1947 scarcely any excavation reports thought fit to mention animal remains. The work of Sewell and Guha for Mohenjo-daro (1931)[1], and Prasad for Harappa (1936)[2] were happy exceptions. Since 1950 a growing number of reports has appeared in which at least some reference to animal remains is made. The principal published data relates to the excavations at Hastinapur (1950–2)[3], Piklihal (1952)[4], Maheshwar (1952–3)[5], Rangpur (1953–6)[6], Maski (1954)[7], Mundigak (1951–8)[8], Nevasa (1954–6)[9], Utnur (1957)[10], and Langhnaj (1944–63)[11]. There is further a considerable volume of hitherto unpublished material relating to other excavations. In some instances the scale of the excavations, or the quantity of animal remains discovered, were such that their potential usefulness is limited. Further, some of the reports provide little more than bare identifications of species, and the number giving attention to other matters, such as the changes brought about by domestication, is still very small. One of the upshots of this note is to point to the need for national centres where animal remains can be preserved and made available for study. One fears that in the past the field archaeologist often did not trouble to collect animal remains; but cases have certainly occurred in which he did so, only to find that they were later disposed of by the custodian in whose care they were placed. Finally it may well be that small collections have been retained, but their whereabouts have ceased to be generally known. My aim in this note is to draw attention to the potential interest of this subject, and to suggest some of the problems which are ripe for consideration.

The first problem must be to discover what animals were utilized at different periods and what was the history of each species. A second problem would seem to involve the origin of each domestic species, and whether it was introduced from outside in an already domesticated condition, or was locally domesticated from indigenous wild species. A third problem would be to find out what changes, if any, were consequent upon domestication. And a fourth general problem would concern the utilization of different species, for food, traction, etc., at various periods.

For the general history of domestic species in India the data available are still so slight that there is a serious danger of misinterpreting them. It is known that the final stage of the stone age, now generally referred to as the late stone age, persisted in certain refuge areas until very recent times. Proof has however been lacking that its origin was in absolute time anterior to the arrival of the first food-producing communities even if this has been generally accepted as a working hypothesis. Recently a number of excavations of late stone age caves or rock shelters have been made, and one, at Adamgarh in Hoshangabad district, has produced a radiocarbon date suggestively earlier than those of any neolithic sites so far known in India and Pakistan[12]. Peculiar interest now centres upon this and other such sites, because among the animal remains are several species, some of which were potentially domestic. At Langhnaj these include a canid, a pig (*Sus cristatus*), buffalo and perhaps another species of bovine[13]; and at Adamgarh dog, *Bos indicus*, buffalo, sheep, goat, and pig are reported[14]. It is clearly a matter of great interest to examine such sites carefully with a view to discovering the sequence in which these species appear in the sections, and to obtain absolute dates. The publication of the report on Adamgarh is eagerly awaited. The first appearance of domestic species in more orthodox "neolithic" contexts is only slightly better known. It appears that in Baluchistan and adjacent areas bones of cattle, sheep and goat occur during the first stage of settlement, the stage of semi-permanent camping sites represented by the lowest levels of Rana Ghundai, Kili Ghul Mohammad, Mundigak, etc. A single radiocarbon date from Kili Ghul Mohammad suggests that this period comes to an end around the middle of the fourth millennium. It is inferred that the cattle were mainly of the humped zebu variety, as terracotta figurines both during this and subsequent periods in this area almost always show cattle with a prominent hump. So far there is very little if any anatomical information about remains from any of these sites. Chronologically the next earliest information comes from far to the south at Utnur where a largely pastoral people kept cattle, sheep and goats during the last quarter of the third millennium B.C. With the civilization of the Indus plains much more information is available on a whole series of domestic species. The history of domestication in India and Pakistan is therefore likely to involve the relationships of two rather separate groups of peoples, the late stone age hunting and collecting groups, widely scattered over the whole subcontinent, and *perhaps* independently taking to domestication of certain species; and the groups of largely nomadic pastoralists who spread from the west, probably as the result of population expansion in the relatively earlier centres of West Asia. These people, if they brought with them herds of animals, would have been obvious targets for the "hunting" activities of the earlier inhabitants whom they encountered[15].

My second question relates to the origins of the domestic species attested in early contexts; briefly these include the zebu, buffalo, sheep, goat, pig, horse, elephant, camel, dog, cat and fowl. The problem of the origin of *Bos indicus* is bound up with that of its relationship to *Bos primigenius* and is really quite beyond the scope of this paper[16]. In India and Pakistan (with the single exception of the Indus civilization) representations in terracotta and painting, on either rock or pottery, suggest that the former was the universal type of cattle. Only in Harappan and pre-Harappan contexts in the Indus valley do we encounter, alongside the zebu, "unicorn" seals and terracotta figurines of humpless beasts which resemble the primigenius type, and the formula used to depict them appears to be of Mesopotamian origin[17]. Further the study of the animal remains from Harappa, no less than from Utnur, seems to indicate, whenever diagnostic characters are available, that they belong to humped cattle[18]. It is evident that by the end of the third millennium there were several breeds of *Bos indicus* widely dispersed. The breed depicted on the Harappan seals corresponds remarkably with the modern breed in Sindh and Gujarat, with its heavy build, pronounced dewlap, and shortish simple curved horns: that depicted in the oldest stratum of rock paintings and in neolithic terracottas in the southern Deccan was evidently of much lighter build, with inconspicuous dewlap and long double curved horns, and with a pronounced hump, and appears to be closer to the modern cattle of Central India. There is thus a suggestion that such regional varieties are sufficiently ancient. These things, together with Alur's observations on medullosis (to be referred to below) seem to indicate that *Bos indicus* was already clearly differentiated from *Bos primigenius*, and that its domestication must have been from an indigenous species.

The relationship of the Indian buffalo (*Bos bubalus*) to its wild counterpart leaves little doubt that it was domesticated locally. To this day the buffalo is regarded as only semi-domestic, and as Watt so well remarked "Few domestic animals have in fact changed less than the buffalo". Cross mating with wild beasts is still common[19]. This means that there is little likelihood of clear differentiation of wild or domestic animals, and that the identification in archaeological assemblages will have to rely on other criteria. There has not as yet been sufficient study of sheep and goat bones in our contexts to indicate the nature of the early specimens, but Prasad concluded that the Harappan sheep could have been locally domesticated from the feral *Ovis vignei*[20]. The position is no clearer with regard to the goat. Prasad also concluded that the Harappan pig was a domestic version of the Indian wild pig, *Sus cristatus*[21]. Hence here too it may be difficult to determine whether at any given site the bones of pig are domestic or feral. I am not aware of any study of the relationship of the two in modern examples. The bones of horse are clearly those of an imported animal. It can be agreed with Zeuner that the teeth obtained by Ross from the surface of the section of Rana Ghundai I should be regarded with suspicion, and that in any case they are more likely to be those of the onager, *Equus hemionus*[22]. The earliest clear evidence comes from a late level at Mohenjo-daro, and terracotta figurines from Harappan contexts are at best equivocal. A recent find of horse bones from a site in Mysore, dated by radiocarbon to *c.* 1300 B.C. and of equine teeth at a neighbouring site dated by radiocarbon to *c.* 1600 B.C.[23] is very suggestive; and need in no way go against the earlier view associating the appearance of the horse in the subcontinent with the arrival of Indo-Iranian speaking peoples. There is still no proof that the bones of elephant found in Harappan and later sites are those of domesticated beasts, and the nature of breeding and taming makes it unlikely that they would be easily recognizable if they were. But it can at least be reasonably affirmed that the domestication at whatever date took place locally. Indeed the elephant seems to call for special glossing of the definition of the word "domestication". The remains of camel at Harappan sites are surely certain proof that the single humped camel was domestic[24]. New and more abundant material is understood to be available in the recent excavations at Kalibangan[25]. It may be expected that *Camelus dromedarius* formerly existed in a feral state in Sindh and Rajasthan, and that it was locally domesticated. That the jungle fowl was locally domesticated seems certain, but more study will be required if its history is to be made clear. So too is there need for more information about the reported remains of cat and dog, and their relations to wild species, such as the jackal or wolf.

My third major problem has to do with changes which may have arisen as a result of domestication. As yet insufficient material is available, or insufficient study has been made, to enable such changes to be described. Some work has been done for *Bos indicus*. Thus Sewell proposed that the complexity or simplicity of the enamelling patterns of molars from Mohenjo-daro might show by reference to modern domestic (or recently feral) herds evidence of progressive change[26]. He also mentioned progressive reduction of size of teeth. Later writers have not adduced further evidence in support of his views. More recently Alur (in an as yet unpublished study of material from Utnur) has noticed a significant variation in the medullosis of certain bones, suggesting that by comparison with those of modern cattle they show a relatively earlier evolutionary stage[27]. Another aspect which deserves closer study than it has hitherto had is of progressive reduction of size in succeeding periods. Alur's study of the bones from Utnur revealed the presence, alongside a majority of bones of normal size, of smaller percentages of very large, large and even small (though mature) bones, and my own preliminary survey of the bones from the excavation revealed a progressive increase in the percentages of small animals in succeeding periods[28].

My fourth problem concerns the study of man's utilization of his domestic animals. How neglected this aspect has been can be seen from the fact that so far there has been no study of the animal remains from any of the great cities of the Ganges valley (except Hastinapur). Thus we are unable to use the evidence of archaeology to throw objective light upon the developing food habits of North India during protohistoric or early historic times. The significance of such a research project is obvious: even though it goes far beyond the range of domestication as hunted animals, fish and fowl must also be recorded. Alur has recently confirmed my comment that the many split bones from Utnur indicated that cattle formed an item of diet at that time. There is growing evidence of the use of cattle bones for tools. He has also drawn attention to a somewhat unexpected evidence of utilization of the Utnur cattle. He points out that the anchylosis of the bones of the hock joint is typical of that occurring in modern draft animals, and must here too indicate that the cattle were used for heavy draft or weight bearing purposes[29]. What these may have been demands attention.

In conclusion it seems worth repeating that the stage is now set, in this as in palaeobotanical and other environmental studies, for substantial advances in our knowledge in both India and Pakistan, provided that suitable centres for collecting data can be established, and that a few specialists are able to give their attention to these questions.

Notes

1 Sewell, R. B. S. and Guha, B. S. (1931). Being Chapter XXXI of Marshall, J. (1931). *Mohenjo-daro and the Indus Civilization*. London. pp. 649–73.
2 Prasad, B. (1936). Animal remains from Harappa *Memoirs of the Archaeological Survey of India*, 51.
3 Lal, B. B. (1955). Excavations at Hastinapura, *Ancient India*, 10 and 11.
4 Allchin, F. R. (1961). *Piklihal Excavations*. Hyderabad.
5 Sankalia, H. D., Subbarao, B. and Deo, S. B. (1958). *Excavation at Maheshwar and Navdatoli*. Baroda.
6 Rao, S. R. (1963). Excavation at Rangpur, *Ancient India* 18 and 19.
7 Thapar, B. K. (1957). Maski 1954. *Ancient India* 13.
8 Casal, J.-M. (1961). *Fouilles de Mundigak*; and Poulain, J. B. (1966). Etude de la faune, *Bull. de l'Ecole française de l'Extrême Orient*. 53, pp. 119–35.
9 Sankalia, H. D. et. al., (1960). *From History to Prehistory at Nevasa*. Poona.
10 Allchin, F. R. (1963). *Excavations at Utnur*, Hyderabad.
11 Clutton Brock, J. (1965). *Excavations at Langhnaj: 1944–63. Pt. II. The Fauna*. Poona.
12 Joshi, R. V. (1961). *Indian Archaeology a review 1960–61*, pp. 12–16 and ibid. (in press) "Late Mesolithic culture in Central India". I am indebted to Dr. Joshi for his kind permission to refer to the unpublished paper. I understand that the study of the animal remains has been made by Sri Bholanath, but that it is also unpublished.
13 Clutton-Brock, J. (1965). ibid.
14 Joshi, R. V. (In press). ibid.
15 My wife and I have discussed the hypothetical relations between the earliest "Neolithic" cultural groups and the late stone age inhabitants of peninsular India in a paper which is still in press.
16 Zeuner, F. E. (1963). *A History of Domesticated Animals*. London. pp. 236–40.
17 Zeuner, F. E. (1963). op. cit. p. 236. We have discussed the art historical

aspect in greater detail in *Birth of Indian civilization*. London (1968). pp. 306–7.

18 Prasad, B. (1936). op. cit. p. 37, and Alur, K. R. in his unpublished study of the animal remains from Utnur. Alur expressly mentions the occurrence of the supraspinous process on a number of thoracic vertebrae.

19 Watt, G. (1908). *The Commercial Products of India*. London. pp. 732–3.

20 Prasad, B. (1936). op. cit. pp. 51–2.

21 Prasad, B. (1936). op. cit. p. 56.

22 Zeuner, F. E. (1936). op. cit. p. 332.

23 The sites are Hallur and Sangankal respectively. I am indebted to Dr. Nagaraja Rao for the information.

24 Prasad, B. (1936). op. cit. pp. 58–9.

25 Information from Shri B. K. Thapar.

26 Sewell, R. B. S. and Guha, B. S. (1931). op. cit. pp. 655–8.

27 Alur, K. R. (Unpublished) 1967. Note on the animal remains from Utnur. Professor Alur has recently made a study of remains from a number of other excavations of Neolithic-Chalcolithic sites in southern India, and reports that similar variations in the medullary cavities of cattle bones occur at more than one site.

28 Allchin, F. R. (1963). op. cit. pp. 62–3.

29 Alur, K. R. (Unpublished) 1967. ibid.

F. R. ALLCHIN

Early cultivated plants in India and Pakistan

Until recently the history of early cultivation in the Indian subcontinent depended entirely upon textual references. During the 1930s reports were published of plant remains at Mohenjo-daro and Harappa; and in the past two decades more than twenty excavations of later prehistoric or proto-historic sites have produced plant materials, now in various stages of publication. The aim of this short paper is to present an outline of the picture supplied by this evidence, to draw attention to the wealth of material in India and Pakistan (Fig. 1), and to suggest the need for further research, both in the field and the laboratory. For the purposes of this discussion the Indian sub-continent may be divided into three major provinces: a western or Indus province, roughly corresponding to modern West Pakistan; a southern or Peninsular province; and a north-eastern or Gangetic province. All the finds so far reported belong to one or other of these three.

Western or Indus province

This province includes the great alluvial tracts of the Indus system, and the upland valleys of Baluchistan. It is throughout an area of low rainfall and considerable variation of temperature between winter and summer. It is also that part of the subcontinent in which the earliest evidence of settlements of cultivators or pastoralists is to be found. The reported plant remains are as follows:

1 *Cereals.* The principal grains so far recorded are wheat and barley, but as comparatively little excavation has been done the picture is probably far from complete. At Mundigak (in period II? late fourth millennium B.C.) grains of club wheat (*Triticum compactum*) are reported[1]. No evidence is yet available from pre-Harappan levels in the Indus valley, but from the excavated Harappan sites (*c.* 2200–1750 B.C.) there is more evidence. Two varieties of wheat, the club wheat and an Indian dwarf wheat (*T. sphaerococcum*) are

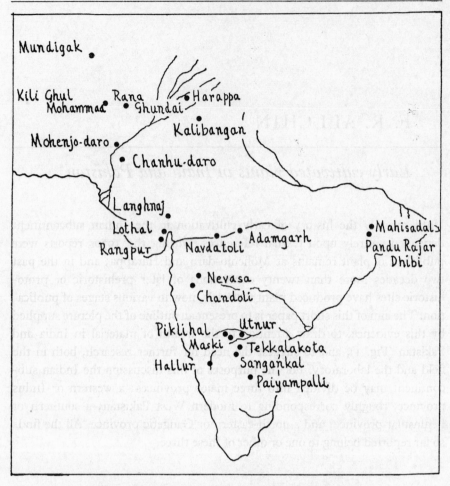

Fig 1 Map of India and Pakistan showing sites mentioned.

reported, as well as two varieties of barley, a small seeded six rowed variety (*Hordeum vulgare*) and a sub-species (*H. vulgare* var. *nudum*)[2].

2 *Leguminous plants.* From the Indus civilization the field pea (*Pisum arvense*) is reported[3].

3 *Oilseeds.* Also from the Harappan civilization two oilseeds are recorded. From Harappa came a lump of *sesamum,* a plant whose antiquity in India may be judged from the fact that it gave its name *tila* to all kinds of oil (*tel,* etc.)[4]. From Chanhu-daro seeds of mustard, identified as most probably *Brassica juncea* were obtained[5].

4 *Fruits.* Several varieties are reported from Harappan times, and one from an earlier context. From Mundigak II comes evidence of *Zizyphus*

vulgaris, then probably as now wild or only semi-domestic[6]. From Harappan contexts come dates and seeds of melon[7].

5 *Other crops.*   There is evidence that a variety of cotton (*Gossypium* sp.) was cultivated in the Indus civilization. Apart from actual fibres surviving in contact with copper tools and a silver vessel, at Mohenjo-daro and Harappa, numerous woven textile impressions are reported on faience vessels, etc.[8] It is also reported that the fibres from Mohenjo-daro had been dyed with some substance, probably a madder. The European madder (*Rubia tinctorum*) is still cultivated in Sindh[9].

Southern or peninsular province

This province is comparatively more varied in climate, rainfall in particular varying between tropical rain and semi-desert precipitation. The evidence is from recent excavations and much is as yet incompletely published.

1 *Cereals.*   Early evidence of wheat cultivation is restricted to the north-west of the province. Both *Triticum vulgare* and *T. compactum* have been identified by Dr. Vishnu Mittre throughout the chalcolithic occupation at Navdatoli (*c.* 1800–1200 B.C.)[10]; and its cultivation seems to have spread towards the south to occur at Sonegaon towards the end of this period[11]. The province produces the earliest evidence so far for rice cultivation. Rice husks and spikelet impressions on pottery and clay are reported at both Lothal and Rangpur IIA (that is, probably towards the end of the Harappan period)[12]. Rice (*Oryza sativa*) is again reported in phases II–IV at Navdatoli (*c.* 1600–1200 B.C.)[13]; and spread to the south to appear at Hallur in an early Iron Age context (*c.* 900–800 B.C.)[14], and yet later in Iron Age graves from the Tamil coastal plains. Rice husk impressions are not infrequently encountered in sites of the Gujarat coast during the second millennium B.C. (personal observation), but these have not yet been studied. Rice is further reported at Kaundinyapur in Maharashtra (*c.* 500 B.C.)[15]. From the peninsula comes the first evidence in India of another important group of cereal crops. At both Hallur and at Paiyampalli grains of finger millet (*Eleusine coracana, rāgī*) are reported, in the former case dating to about 1800 B.C.[16] Another grain from Rangpur III (*c.* 1200 B.C.) has been identified as possibly the bulrush millet (*Pennisetum typhoideum, bājrā*)[17], and the same millet has been tentatively identified at Hallur, although in both cases there is a possibility that it may rather be *Paspalum scrobiculatum, kodon*[18]. Firm evidence of both the bulrush and finger millets, as well as of *kodon*, comes from Nevasa at the opening of the Christian era, from where too comes the earliest archaeological occurrence in India of the great millet (*Andropogon sorghum*), evidently a late arrival upon the scene[19]. Kaundinyapur also yields the first evidence of maize

(*Zea mays*) in the subcontinent, in the form of grain impressions on pottery.
It is not clear from the published sources what is the date of its occurrence,
one source referring it to a house of the Bahmani period (*c.* fifteenth century
A.D.), another assigning the type of pottery to the eighth to ninth century A.D.[20]

2 *Leguminous plants.*   The peninsula also provides the first evidence of the
cultivation of several species of leguminous plants. From Tekkalakota I (*c.*
1800–1600 B.C.) and Paiyampalli come examples of horse gram (*Dolichos
biflorus*)[21], and from the latter site and from Navdatoli comes green gram
(*Phaseolus radiatus*)[22]. Navdatoli yielded a very rich series of plants from its
chalcolithic levels, including black gram (*Ph. mungo*), lentil (*Lens culinaris*),
the grass pea (*Lathyrus sativus*), the field pea (*Pisum arvense*), and several
other leguminous weeds[23]. Evidently another late arrival in India was the
chick-pea or *canā* gram (*Cicer arietinum*), which first appears in period IV
at Nevasa (third to first century B.C.)[24].

3 *Oilseeds.*   The only early oilseed so far reported in the peninsula is linseed
(*Linum usitatissimum*) which occurred throughout the occupation at Navdatoli[25]. That one of its uses may have been to prepare flax may be inferred
from the discovery of spun fibres in a string of beads from a burial at Chandoli
(*c.* 1400–1200 B.C.)[26].

4 *Fruits.*   The Indian jujube (*Zizyphus jujuba, ber*) is reported at Navdatoli;
and the myrobalan (*Phyllanthus emblica, āmalaka*) at the same site[27]. Whether
either of these were strictly cultivated is open to doubt. Wood of the date
palm is probably reported at Utnur, and date palm matting impressions also
at Tekkalakota, but no date stones have been reported[28]. In modern times
the date is cultivated, in the Deccan, rather for its juice which is fermented
to make *tādī* than for its fruit.

5 *Other crops.*   The cultivation of cotton in the peninsula is first attested
by the second half of the second millennium at Nevasa, where a thread of
silk and cotton was discovered in a string of beads from a burial[29]. I have also
recently noticed textile impressions, apparently of cotton, on a number of
early Iron Age sherds from southern Mysore.

Northern or Gangetic province

This province coincides with the alluvial plains of the Ganges system. It
witnesses a marked increase in rainfall and corresponding moderation of
winter cold as one moves eastwards to the delta. Although much excavation
has taken place comparatively little plant evidence has so far been reported.

1 *Cereals.* Only one grain has so far been discovered, rice. At Hastinapur and at Noh rice is found during the period of the Painted Grey ware (*c.* 1000–500 B.C.)[30]. My own observation suggests that rice husks were frequently added to pottery of this and the following period in the central Ganges valley. Rice is again reported at Sonpur (*c.* 800–600 B.C.)[31] and from the western margins of the delta at Mahisadal and Pandu Rajar Dhibi already before the arrival of iron (i.e. prior to 700 B.C.)[32]. The importance or rice for the economy of North India is evident from the frequent references in later Vedic literature, from the time of the Yajur Veda Saṃhita onwards, and by the opening of the Christian era Suśruta distinguishes no less than thirty-nine varieties[33].

2 *Other crops.* There is as yet no other evidence for other cultivated plants in this province.

The evidence so far assembled prompts one to form a number of tentative conclusions both on the plants themselves and on the related subject of their discovery, study and preservation. As far as I am aware there is no single centre, or group of centres to which this material may be sent and where it may be studied and preserved. Dr. Vishnu Mittre of the Birbal Sahni Institute at Lucknow has been responsible for many of the published identifications, and it would seem that this centre might well form a national home for archaeological plant remains of this kind. It is evident that not all field archaeologists are equally interested in collecting this sort of material, and it is to be hoped that its considerable importance may become generally appreciated. A number of the principal grains and plants found in the Indus province, and even in adjacent parts of the peninsula, appear to have been first domesticated in West Asia and to have entered South Asia probably along with the spread of cultivation in subsequent centuries. On the other hand, Professor Sir Joseph Hutchinson has pointed out to me the probability that certain of the millets, notably *Eleusine* and *Pennisetum*, were first domesticated in Africa[34]. It will be interesting to enquire whether they reached the Indian peninsula by land (in which case it may be expected that traces will be found in intermediate areas) or by some other route, perhaps by sea. Several of the plants are almost certainly indigenous. Among those we notice rice, cotton, sesamum, and Indian mustard. There is regrettably no archaeological evidence as yet for the antiquity of a number of other important Indian plants, and it is still necessary to rely upon the evidence afforded by literature. Among these plants we may cite sugar cane, first mentioned in the Atharva Veda (before 800 B.C.), and the black pepper (*Piper nigrum*), for which the earliest references are in the *Āpastambha Dharmasūtra*, probably before 500 B.C. Archaeological evidence is still awaited for a number of other cultivated plants, for example yams (*sūrana*) for which the earliest literary evidence is in Caraka (first to second century A.D.). There are, however, as we have seen, several instances in which evidence so far available appears to support the literary record. For example, respecting the relative lateness of the introduction of *Cicer arietinum*, for which the earliest references are in *Rāmāyaṅa Uttara-kāṇḍa Baudhyāyana Gṛhya Śeṣasūtra*, and *Susruta saṃhita* (suggesting collectively dates between the first and fourth centuries A.D.); or of Sorghum millet, whose earliest references are in *Caraka*, *Bhela* and Kaśyapa *Saṃhitas* (suggesting collectively a similar range of dates). The new perspectives provided by archaeology hold out great hopes for a reappraisal of other types of evidence. It is evident that much useful work could still be done in plotting the modern dialect names for different species and considering them in a historical light. Such "linguistic palaeontology" is likely to yield useful information, now that the chronological dimensions are beginning to appear.

Notes

1 Casal, J.-M. (1961). *Fouilles de Mundigak*. Appendix XIII by R. Porteres, Paris. pp. 259–60.
2 Marshall, J. (1931). *Mohenjo-daro and the Indus civilization*. London. vol. 2. pp. 587–9; Mackay, E. J. H. (1943). *Chanhu-daro excavations*. New Haven. p. 250; Vats, M. S. (1940). *Excavations at Harappa*. Delhi. pp. 466–7.
3 Mackay, E. J. H. (1943). ibid.; Vats, M. S. (1940). op. cit. p. 467.
4 Vats, M. S. (1940). ibid.
5 Mackay, E. J. H. (1943). ibid.
6 Casal, J.-M. (1961). op. cit. p. 260.
7 Vats, M. S. (1940). ibid.
8 Marshall, J. (1931). op. cit. pp. 585–6; Mackay, E. J. H. (1938). *Further Excavations at Mohenjo-daro*. Delhi. pp. 583, 591–4; Vats, M.S. (1940). op. cit. p. 466.
9 Watt, G. (1908). *The Commercial Products of India*. London. pp. 926–7.
10 Vishnu Mittre (1961). Plant economy in ancient Navdatoli and Maheshwar, *Technical reports on archaeological remains*. pp. 15–17.
11 *Indian archaeology—a Review*, 1964–5.
12 Rao, S. R. (1963). Excavations at Rangpur, *Ancient India*, 18 and 19. The note on the plant remains is by S. S. Ghosh and Krishna Lal, p. 168.
13 Vishnu Mittre (1961). op. cit. pp. 18–19.
14 Information by courtesy of Dr. Nagaraja Rao.
15 Vishnu Mittre (1966). Kaundinyapur plant economy in proto-historic and historic times, *Palaeobotanist*, 15, pp. 152–3.
16 For Hallur, information by courtesy of Dr. Nagaraja Rao, and for Paiyampalli information by courtesy of Shri S. R. Rao.
17 Rao, S. R. (1963). op. cit. p. 169.
18 For Hallur, information by courtesy of Dr. Nagaraja Rao.
19 Sankalia, H. D. *et al.* (1960). *From History to Pre-History at Nevasa*. Poona. pp. 529–30.
20 Vishnu Mittre (1966). op. cit. pp. 152–6; Vishnu Mittre and Gupta, H. P. (1966). Pollen morphological studies of some primitive varieties of maize (Zea mays L.) with some remarks on the history of maize in India, *Palaeobotanist*, 15, pp. 176–84.
21 Information by courtesy of Dr. Nagaraja Rao and Shri S. R. Rao.
22 Vishnu Mittre (1961). op. cit. pp. 21–2.
23 Vishnu Mittre (1961). op. cit. pp. 20–3.

24 Sankalia, H. D. *et al.* (1960). ibid.
25 Vishnu Mittre (1961). op. cit. pp. 23-4.
26 Deo, S. B. and Ansari, Z. D. (1965). *Chalcolithic Chandoli*. Appendix iv, by Gulati, A. N. A note on the early history of flax. Poona. pp. 195-201.
27 Vishnu Mittre (1961). op. cit. pp. 24-5.
28 For Hallur, information from Dr. Nagaraja Rao. The observation for Utnur was our own, and has not so far been substantiated by further examination of specimens.
29 Gulati, A. N. (1961). A note on the early history of silk in India, *Technical reports on archaeological remains.* pp. 53-9.
30 Lal, B. B. (1955). Excavation at Hastinapura, *Ancient India*, **10** and **11**. Appendix J, on plant remains by Chowdhury, K. A., and Ghosh, S. S. pp. 120-35; For Noh see *Indian Archaeology—a Review*, 1963-4, and ibid. 1964-5.
31 *Indian Archaeology a review*, 1960-1, p. 5.
32 For Pandu Rajar Dhibi see Das Gupta, P. C. (1964). *Excavations at Pandu Rajar Dhibi*. Calcutta. p. 14; for Mahisadal see *Indian Archaeology—a Review*, 1963-4.
33 Om Prakash (1961). *Food and Drinks in Ancient India*. Delhi. pp. 262-3.
34 On the origin of *Eleusine coracana* see Mehra, K. L. (1963). Considerations on the African origin of *Eleusine coracana* (L), *Current Science*, **32**, p. 300.

J. BURTON-PAGE

The problem of the introduction of
Adansonia digitata *into India*

The subject-matter of this paper relates to a period considerably later than that of most of the others presented here. But, as an archaeologist working in a comparatively late historical period, I welcome the opportunity to demonstrate that identity of interest, and *a fortiori* of approach, may occur when purely historical documents fail. The period primarily concerned, the late fourteenth and early fifteenth centuries, is well documented for political history and for the development of religion, and the main features of the cultural and social institutions of both the autochthones and the foreign ruling classes are clear. But this documentary evidence can do little more than provide a general background to my problem, which seems to have some connexion with a foreign menial class about whom all information (save their occasional involvement in political history) is scanty in the extreme.

The baobab, *Adansonia digitata*, is commonly "not supposed to be a native", says Nairne[1], although the family Bombaceae is well represented in India by other genera. Hooker[2] is more specific: the baobab, says he, is "a native of Africa, not truly wild in India", and in giving its distribution as "tropical Africa" he mentions that it is "cultivated in various parts of India and Ceylon". But here "cultivated" must be interpreted with caution: the tree has certainly been planted, as a specimen, in the botanical gardens of Calcutta, Madras and Bombay, presumably under British direction; and there seem to have been older plantings around Delhi and Allāhābād which may be attributed to the Mughal taste for curiosa around the end of the sixteenth century. I can find no other evidence of its deliberate planting in modern times. We can, however, be a little more precise concerning its Indian distribution: Birdwood[3] notes it as "generally found most abundant about the old ports frequented by the early Mahommedan traders", and it has indeed been reported as growing in and around Janjīrā, Chaul and Sūrat, all towns which would fall into this category. It does however also occur inland: where it is found in any numbers (apart from the specimen trees already mentioned) its greatest concentrations appear to be in Bīdar and Bījāpur in the Deccan; in Burhānpur in the former principality of Khandēsh; and above all in

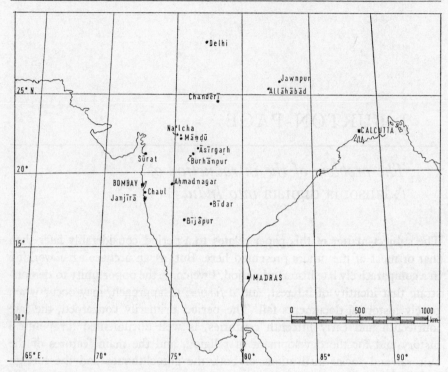

Fig 1 Location of places mentioned in the text.

Mālwā, in the towns of Chandērī and Māṇḍū and its suburb Na'lcha. All of these places (see Fig. 1) were towns of some importance under the mediaeval Muslim sultanates.

The baobab's onomastic status is suggestive. In Mālwā it is known as *Khurāsānī imli*, in Bījāpur as *Gōrakh imlī*, in both cases taking part of its name from the Tamarind, the true *imlī*. The confusion is already found in *c.* 1595 in Abu'l-Faẓl's description of Mālwā[4]: "here the tamarind grows as large as a coconut, and its fruit is extremely white". I can imagine no two trees less likely to be confused from the appearance of stem, leaf or fruit; perhaps the common feature of a fruit with an acid pulp is responsible for the baobab's sobriquet. The epithet *Khurāsānī* is fanciful, for the tree is unknown in Khurāsān; it seems to be no more than an elegant word meaning "foreign", as in *American cloth, Russian salad*; and I can find no reason for the Deccan association with Gōrakh (= Gorakṣanātha, the patron saint of an order of yogīs) unless there may be some association with death, for here the baobab was traditionally the tree under which executions took place (why? from its being merely an easy landmark for a rendezvous, or because its leaflessness all the year, except for the rains, suggested also lifelessness?). The tree cannot be identified in any old Indian flora, and appears to have no Sanskrit name. Such negative linguistic evidence is of course inconclusive by itself, but it does seem to support the suggestion of an introduction in Islamic times.

If, then, we assume that the baobab is an introduced species, the questions which arise are three: (*a*) when was it brought in? (*b*) for what purpose? (*c*) by what means? The date I shall refer to later; but we may observe here that local tradition in Māṇḍū[5] supposes it to have been brought in to the area under Maḥmūd Khaljī (1436–69). As to the means, Birdwood suggests that it was either introduced by traders or carried across the Indian Ocean by currents and winds, as certainly happened with *Kigelia pinnata*; but perhaps militating against this latter suggestion is the apparent reluctance of the baobab to regenerate naturally, even though the fruit germinates readily when planted. And even if the fruit had arrived on the Indian shore by such an accident, its transfer some 400 km. inland to the Mālwā plateau can only have been effected by man.

The last question, for what purpose it was introduced, is more puzzling. The tree now appears to have little value to man in India (even its natural role as an inherently comic vegetable seems to be little appreciated), although it appears somewhat surprisingly[6] as one of the possible crude materials of paper manufacture. I suspect that this happened merely because the tree happened to be there; in any case if the early fifteenth-century introduction can be supported, paper-making could not have been the prime purpose on chronological grounds. I have found no evidence of its hollow trunks being used as receptacles for water storage, as happens in certain African areas; and in any case this would seem pointless in such a region as Mālwā, where surface water is not hard to find. Nor is there any evidence, as far as I am aware, for the use of the hollow trunks for burial purposes, also reported from parts of Africa. I have seen deer feeding on its fallen petals, but I know of no instance of the petals being collected as cattle fodder (as with *Bombax*, for example), nor yet for use in dyeing, as with a variety of Indian trees. The only reference to other uses are of its fruits being "made into a refreshing sherbet by Muslim women" in the Deccan[7].

A clue to its date and an adumbration of its connexion with a particular class may be forthcoming from the fact that its distribution coincides strikingly with those areas under Muslim control (Mālwā, Khāndēsh, the Deccan, the western ports) where Ḥabshīs were settled in considerable numbers. The term Ḥabshī, literally "Abyssinian", refers in early Islam to slaves of Abyssinian origin, but in India is applied to African slaves of other races, Bantu and Somali, imported from the Horn of Africa[8]. The evidence for a total terrestial correspondence is incomplete, as information is lacking on the baobab in other Ḥabshī-colonized areas: Bengal, Jawnpur, Aḥmadnagar, Āsīrgaṛh. Even so, the coincidence is suggestive, and if we may thus associate the baobab with the Ḥabshīs we are given a *terminus a quo*: while there is some evidence for Ḥabshī slaves in north India as early as the beginning of the thirteenth century, the great period of their expansion all over India was the fourteenth; for example, the traveller Ibn Baṭṭūṭa[9] comments on their presence from north India to Ceylon on his journeys made between 1333 and 1342, as guards and men-at-arms on land and sea. There is evidence that they were in Gujarāt in large numbers in the mid-fourteenth century, and well established in the Deccan at the time of Fērōz Shāh Bahmanī (1397–1422). The island of Janjira was a Ḥabshī possession from the early sixteenth century, although Ḥabshīs had long before that been prominent in the Muslim navies on the west coast of India. For Mālwā there is no definite evidence of their presence before the time of Mahmud Khaljī, although they are known to have been employed at the court in his and his son's reigns to the tune of thousands. This adds weight to the Māṇḍū tradition reported above.

If, as seems possible, there is a connection between the baobab and the Ḥabshīs, the African tree and the African people, a powerful reason for the tree's introduction is still wanting. A slave people would hardly introduce it as a specimen to remind them of home; the craving for a "refreshing sherbet" is hardly convincing, as India is well provided with other natural resources for such purposes (the modern instance of a powerful Western nation who have been unable to sustain their existence overseas without a revolting sherbet made from the stimulant *coca* and *cola* plants is scarcely an exact parallel; fourteenth-century transport problems, especially for a slave people, are not comparable with our own). It does seem possible, however, that its importation for a cult purpose might have been permitted. What such a cult purpose might have been does not seem possible to say; colleagues at the School of Oriental and African studies concerned with African anthropology have not yet been able to throw any light on possible baobab cults in east Africa or along the coast[10].

It is obvious that more work needs to be done on the baobab and its attendant problems. There has been no investigation of the age of the Indian baobabs; although I understand that the Indian specimens, imposing though many of them be, do not approach the African ones in size. More work needs to be done on defining the distribution of the Indian baobabs. As I have shown, I fear only too clearly, there is need for more investigation, if the data are still ascertainable, on the anthropological side.

Notes

1 Nairne, A. K. (n.d.). *Flowering Plants of Western India*. London. s.v.
2 Hooker, J. D. (1872–5). *Flora of British India*, 1. London. p. 348.
3 Birdwood, C. (1886). Communication to Yule, H. (ed.) *Hobson-Jobson*. London. s.v. *Monkey-bread tree* (this name, however, is not used in India).
4 Abu'l-Faẓl (*c.* 1596). *Ā'īn-i Akbarī*, 2. (ed. Bibl. Ind.). p. 197.
5 Yazdani, Gh. (1929). *Mandu: the City of Joy*. Oxford. p. 2.
6 Watt, G. (1908). *Commercial Products of India*. London. p. 868.
7 Cousens, H. (1916). *Bijāpur and its Architectural Remains*. Bombay. p. 57.

8 For their history in India, see Burton-Page, J. (1965). "Ḥabshí", art, *in Encyclopaedia of Islam.* 2nd edition, 3. pp. 14–16.

9 Defrémery, C. and Sanguinetti, B. R. (1853–8). (eds.) *Voyages d'Ibn Batouta,* 4 (Arabic text and French trans.). Paris. pp. 31, 59–60, 93 and 185.

10 My thanks are due to Professor P. H. Gulliver and Dr. D. J. Parkin for allowing me to pester them with questions of Adansoniology.

JULIET CLUTTON-BROCK

Carnivore remains from the excavations of the Jericho Tell

The extensive period covered by Dr. K. Kenyon's[1] excavations of the Jericho Tell from the Mesolithic to the Byzantine provides an exceptionally favourable opportunity for the study of animal remains. It is possible to assess the composition of the wild faunal assemblage and to trace man's exploitation of this fauna and his introduction of exotic domesticated species. Carnivore remains were found in every main habitation level except the mesolithic and although specific identification has, in some cases, proved to be difficult, an analysis of the number of carnivore bones and teeth has enabled assertions to be made about the relative importance of the several genera that were present throughout periods of habitation of the site. The absolute numbers[2] of remains of each species are shown in Fig. 1.

The carnivore remains can be divided into three main groups, a wolf/jackal/dog complex, foxes, and cats. These are described in systematic order. A metrical comparison has been made of the canid remains from Jericho with those from prehistoric cave sites in Palestine studied by Kurtén[3].

Canidae

Canis spp. Thirty-six bones and teeth of *Canis* spp. were found dispersed throughout all levels of the excavations representing thirty-two individual animals. Three of these specimens were burnt. The remains of *Canis* consist mainly of isolated jaws or limb bones but there are four groups of articulated bones that may be remnants of whole carcases, either purposefully buried or thrown out on a rubbish pit. One nearly complete skeleton with jaws was retrieved from the Pre-Pottery Neolithic A, and a nearly complete forelimb from the same period. Another complete limb was found in the Pre-Pottery B, and a fragmentary skull and articulated long bones from a disturbed area between the Early and Middle Bronze Age.

Zeuner[4] has said about his preliminary investigation of the canid remains from the Pre-Pottery and Pottery Neolithic of Jericho that "... it is certain

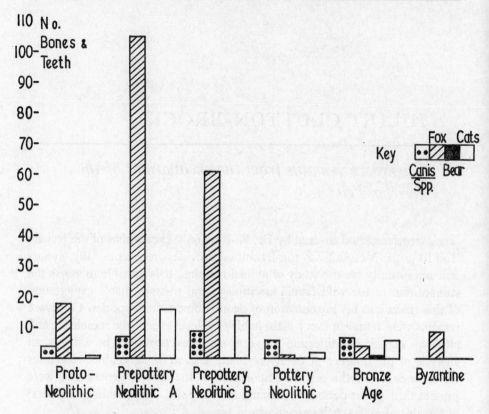

Fig 1 Absolute numbers (see text note (2)) of carnivore bones and teeth from the main phases of habitation of the Jericho Tell. Polecat and marten included with the cats.

already that there was considerable variation in size which suggests the presence of several breeds (of domestic dog). One was of fox terrier size, another that of the pariah dog." This report was based on the examination of mandible fragments and isolated teeth of which Plate VI(ii) is one. Contrary to Zeuner's statement, careful measurement of all the Jericho specimens does not show any great diversity in size of bones and teeth. Many are indeed the size of pariah dogs as represented by skulls in the British Museum (Natural History) but a disconcerting fact is discovered when a survey is made of skulls of the jackals, wolves, and dogs that are found at the present day in the Near East. This is that each species overlaps the others in size, and morphological differentiation on skeletal or dental structure is in many cases impossible. Fossil evidence suggests that two sub species of jackal occurred in the Palestine area in post Pleistocene times. These were *Canis aureus lupaster*, a large jackal, now confined to North Africa, and the common jackal, *Canis aureus aureus*.[5] *Canis aureus lupaster*, the Egyptian jackal, is considerably larger than the common jackal, and overlaps in size of bones and teeth the pariah dog and the local Arabian wolf, *Canis lupus arabs*. No canid remains were found at Jericho that can be identified as *Canis aureus aureus*.

In recent years much discussion has been given to the problem of specific identification of canid remains from early prehistoric sites in the Near East, and the general pattern that is emerging shows that these specimens often cannot be distinguished as dog, wolf, or jackal. In 1937 Bate[6] described the discovery of a Natufian "dog" from Mount Carmel and for many years this was thought to be one of the earliest records of domestication. Reinvestigation of this "dog" skull has shown however that it cannot be distinguished from *Canis lupus arabs*[7]. Further discussion of the problems of identification of Near Eastern canids has been provided by many authors[8].

Measurement of the *Canis* bones and teeth from Jericho shows that their size overlaps that of present day pariah dogs, *C. lupus arabs*, and *C. aureus lupaster*. The most commonly found tooth was the lower carnassial (M1) of which there were nine, representing seven individuals (four comprise two pairs). The labial length of these teeth are given below (in the case of the pairs the mean of the two is given) and compared with measurements of the teeth of post-glacial canids given by Kurtén. Kurtén measured all the carnivore skull and tooth specimens from excavations of the Palestine caves of Mount Carmel, Kebarah, Shukbah, Zuttiyeh, and Ksâr 'Akil, that are in the British Museum (Natural History) and made a statistical comparison with present day specimens. In the case of the wolf, measurements show that there has been a very marked post-glacial dwarfing. The fossil wolf of the late Pleistocene in Palestine was the same size as the present day European wolf but at the end of the Pleistocene a drastic reduction in size occurred that was probably stabilized by Mesolithic times. In the past confusion arose over the identification of canid remains from archaeological sites in Palestine because this post-Pleistocene dwarfing was not recognized. The Natufian canid remains from Mount Carmel are the same size as those from prehistoric Jericho, and the same size as the living wolves to be found in the Palestine area.

It can be seen from the table that on size the lower carnassial teeth from Jericho fall most closely within Kurtén's observed range for fossil specimens of *C. aureus lupaster* from Palestine.

Measurement of the bones and teeth of *Canis* spp. from Jericho gives no clear indication of which species are present nor of sure evidence for domestication. There are, however, two mandibles in which the premolar teeth have been so crowded and displaced that they may have belonged to tamed wolves if not to domesticated dogs. For it is now generally recognized on anatomical and behavioural grounds that the progenitor of the dog was the small Asiatic wolf.

In early societies such as the Pre-Pottery Neolithic of Jericho there must have been a sequence of wild to tamed wolf to dog, that is to a definite breed that can be said to be fully domesticated after generations of breeding in captivity. Osteological characters cannot provide evidence for distinguishing tamed wolf from early domestic dog and it is in fact still doubtful how clear are the distinctions between wild and tamed wolves. But it is of course possible to distinguish wild wolf from fully domestic dog. There is no evidence for such a dog from any of the Jericho levels.

One of the two mandibular rami, No. M.15.10A, that shows crowding of the teeth (Plate VI (iii)) comes from the earliest level to contain animal bones, the Protoneolithic, dated at earlier than 9000 B.P. It is a smaller jaw than any of the other specimens and the alveoli of the 1st and 2nd premolars are considerably displaced. It is however only a fragment of charred bone without teeth and specific identification cannot be made from such a small piece of jaw. In fact the possibility that it belonged to a member of the genus *Cuon* rather than *Canis* cannot be discounted.

Species	N.*	O.R. mm.	M. mm.	S.D. mm.	V. mm.
Canis aureus aureus					
Recent only	11	16·1 –18·9	17·77 ± 0·28	0·93	5·2
Canis aureus lupaster					
Fossil	6	20·4 –23·7	21·75 ± 0·61	1·37	6·3
Recent	7	19·5 –22·5	20·86 ± 0·37	0·99	4·7
Canis lupus arabs					
From Würm	6	25·1 –31·6	28·20 ± 1·00	2·50	8·9
Post-glacial	2	23·8 –24·3	24·05	—	—
Palestine Recent	5	21·7 –24·2	23·10 ± 0·50	1·10	4·6
Canis spp. Jericho					
Pre-Pottery A—EB/MB	7	20·65–23·75	22·03 ± 0·41	1·09	4·95

* *Abbreviations:* N—number of specimens measured; O.R.—observed range; M—mean ± tandard error of the mean; S.D.—standard deviation; V—coefficient of variation.

Table 1 Labial lengths of the lower first molar of *canis* spp. from Jericho compared with those of *Canis aureus aureus*, *Canis aureus lupaster*, and *Canis lupus arabs*, quoted from Kurtén.[a]

(a) Kurtén, B. (1965). The carnivora of the Palestine caves, *Acta Zool. Fenn.*

The second mandibular ramus, No. O.6.21J (Plate VI(i)), that shows crowding of the teeth was found in the Pottery Neolithic. The cheek teeth are very large in relation to the length of the ramus (Length of M1, 23·25 mm.), and they had come to be compacted in order to be accommodated in the jaw. It is generally recognized that this compaction and displacement of large teeth is a diagnostic character of early domestic dogs, but there are as yet no statistics to show how often it may occur in wild populations of canids.

All the remaining *Canis* jaws have large well spaced teeth and there is no justification for claiming that they belonged to domesticated dogs. There is so little evidence for the specific identification of the *Canis* remains from Jericho that it has been decided that for the present they should only be described as *Canis* spp.

Vulpes vulpes

A total number of 203 bones and teeth of fox have been collected from all levels, representing 134 individual animals. Remains of foxes greatly outnumber those of any other carnivore. The great majority of these fox bones comes from the earliest levels. There are no mammalian bones and teeth from the Mesolithic but in the Proto-Neolithic there are eighteen fox bones and teeth representing thirteen individual animals, whereas all other mammalian remains from this period only number nine specimens. In the Pre-Pottery A levels, the 105 fox specimens still outnumber those of any other species. From the Pre-Pottery B levels onwards the number of foxes represented steadily decreases.

It can only be assumed that foxes were eaten and hunted for furs by the Proto-Neolithic and Pre-Pottery people along with any other wild animals that could be caught. Fox bones and teeth are found as individual specimens

Period	N.*	O.R. mm.	M. mm.	S.D. mm.	V. mm.
Post-glacial	55	13·6 –17·1	15·24 ± 0·11	0·81	5·3
Shukbah A	6	14·0 –15·0	14·37 ± 0·15	0·37	2·6
Recent	9	12·2 –14·8	13·76 ± 0·30	0·91	6·6
Jericho Pre-Pottery Neolithic	3	13·19;13·35; 16·0	14·15	—	—
Jericho Pre-Pottery A	17	12·55–15·80	13·85 ± 0·22	0·92	5·4
Jericho Pre-Pottery B	2	12·00–14·90	13·45	—	—
Jericho Pre-Pottery A/B	1	15·65	—	—	—
Jericho Byzantine	1	14·10	—	—	—
Jericho all levels	24	12·00–16·00	13·94 ± 0·22	1·09	7·82

* *Abbreviations:* N—number of specimens measured; O.R.—observed range; M—mean ± standard error of the mean; S.D.—standard deviation; V—coefficient of variation.

Table 2 Labial length of the lower first molar of *Vulpes vulpes*[a] from Jericho compared with those measured by Kurtén both fossil and recent.

(a) Kurtén, B. (1965). The carnivora of the Palestine caves, *Acta Zool. Fenn.*

widely dispersed through the early levels of the excavations and 7% of the bones are burnt. This is approximately the same percentage as is found for the remains of other food animals. The nine bones and mandible fragments from the Byzantine may however represent a single animal that was killed as a pest and not eaten but thrown out, for the bones were found together in a rubbish pit.

Kurtén[9] also found that foxes outnumbered in their remains all other species from the cave excavations, Kurtén's statistical analysis of the measurements of fox teeth from these caves has shown that there has been a marked change in size of the fox since the last glaciation. In post-mesolithic times there has been a reduction in size of the fox similar to that found by

Kurtén for the wolf and the wild cat. The population represented by fossils from level A at Shukbah is intermediate in size between the large mesolithic form and the present day fox. Shukbah A is of uncertain date but it is later than the underlying mesolithic strata and could be similar to the Proto-neolithic of Jericho, that is it is later than 7800 ± 210 B.C.

A comparison may be made with Kurtén's measurements of fossil foxes from the Palestine caves and with those of the Jericho specimens. As with *Canis* spp. the most commonly found tooth was the lower carnassial. A table is therefore given below of Kurtén's measurements for this tooth compared with those from Jericho.

Unfortunately the sample of teeth from the Proto-Neolithic is too small to reflect any size change from fox teeth of later periods but it is noteworthy that in agreement with Kurtén's measurements the largest fox carnassial (L.—16·00 mm.) does come from the earliest levels and it is possible that these Proto-Neolithic foxes were rather larger animals than the Palestinian fox of the present day.

Zeuner[10] notes that the remains of foxes that have been killed for food are not uncommon finds from early archaeological sites. In the neolithic lake-dwellings of Switzerland fox bones were common and bore cutting and tooth marks that showed they had been eaten by humans. Fox remains have also been recorded in large numbers by Degerbøl from the Maglemose of Denmark. Flannery[11] also comments on the remains of foxes amongst food debris from prehistoric sites in Iran.

Ursidae

Ursus arctos. Only a single bone of bear has been retrieved from the Jericho excavations. With the absence of lion remains and the scarcity of leopard this is surprising and suggests that throughout the long period of habitation over which the excavation extended, there was very little hunting of large carnivores.

Incertae sedis

Vormela peregusna. The complete facial and maxillary region of the skull of a small carnivore was found in the Middle Bronze Age. The cranium is missing and most of the teeth except for two canines and two premolars. This skull has been provisionally identified as belonging to the marbled polecat, *Vormela peregusna.*

Martes martes. A single metapodial bone, provisionally identified as marten was found in the Pre-Pottery A.

Felidae

There are at least four types of wild felid represented by fragmentary bones and teeth. The lack of complete bones however makes it difficult to differentiate the species with the exception of the leopard. Three bones of leopard have been identified; a second phalanx from the Pre-Pottery B, a charred calcaneum from the Pottery Neolithic, and a first phalanx from the Middle Bronze Period. This bone was severely damaged during life, only the anterior surface of the shaft remains and there is no marrow cavity.

The leopard (*Panthera pardus*) is the largest felid present; it is surprising that there are no lion remains, for lions must have been abundant in the mountains of Palestine throughout prehistoric times as they were in historic times until at least the Roman Period[12].

Apart from the leopard bones there are thirty-six other felid bones and teeth representing twenty-nine individual cats. The majority of these come from the Pre-Pottery levels and the bones were found with other food remains.

It is extremely difficult to determine the species of these cat bones, which are mostly in a very fragmentary condition. It was decided that the most practicable way of dealing with the specimens was to grade them according to size and suggest the species present on this basis. The largest of the bones and teeth may belong to the caracal lynx, *Felis caracal*, although the teeth are not identical in cusp shape with those of caracal skulls in the British Museum (Natural History).

The next group of cat remains, smaller than those ascribed to the caracal lynx, falls most closely within the size of *F. chaus*. Twelve skeletal bones of this species were found in the Pre-Pottery periods, the Pottery Neolithic and the Middle Bronze Age.

The smallest cat bones and teeth have been identified as belonging to *F. lybica*. Fourteen specimens of this cat have been found from the Protoneolithic and Pre-Pottery Neolithic periods but none from later levels. The Libyan cat has been suggested as being the ancestor of the domestic cat[13] and it has similar body proportions to the domestic cat. Zeuner[14] has considered the possibility that the small cat remains from Jericho could have been those of domesticated animals but there is no osteological evidence for this.

Kurtén[15] measured the teeth of all the fossil cats from excavations in Palestine caves that are in the collection of the British Museum (Natural History). He made a statistical comparison of these fossil cat teeth with those of recent specimens and found that, as with the other carnivores, there was a drastic reduction in size of the wild cat of Palestine at the beginning of the Mesolithic.

It is not practical to compare Kurtén's measurements with those of the

Jericho cats because of the small number of specimens from Jericho and the uncertainty of their specific identification.

Discussion

It can be seen from the above descriptions that the numbers of carnivore remains from Jericho, with the exception of minor finds such as the few leopard and bear bones, comprise a total of thirty-six specimens of *Canis* spp., two hundred and three of foxes and thirty-six of cat. Were any of these animals domesticated ? The osteological evidence for the presence of domestic dogs is slender and rests on the few jaws that had compacted teeth. The very large number of fox bones in the Pre-Pottery Neolithic implies that this canid was the most heavily exploited carnivore during these early periods. It is however more likely that scavenging foxes were killed (perhaps by trapping) for meat and skins rather than that they were tamed or domesticated. The same must be true of the cats, and wolves and jackals would have been killed and eaten whenever they could be caught.

The lack of domestic dog bones in the Bronze Age periods remains a mystery. A comparison may be made here with the Bronze Age site of Emporio on the island of Chios, Greece[16] where remains of undoubted domestic dog were common. At Emporio there were forty bones and teeth of Bronze Age dogs, whereas, amongst the very much larger total number of bones at Jericho, there are only seven Bronze Age specimens of *Canis* spp. This does not necessarily mean, of course, that the Bronze Age people of Jericho did not keep dogs, only that they did not eat them. It is possible that dogs were considered to be "unclean" animals and that their carcases were thrown outside the city walls. In this case their remains would not be found with those of food animals in the habitation levels[17].

Notes

1 Kenyon, K. M. (1957). *Digging up Jericho*. London; Kenyon, K. M. (1960). *Archaeology in the Holy Land*. London.

2 Where two or more bones were found in articulation these were counted as one specimen. Because of the dispersion of the bones over the very wide range of levels it is reasonable to assume that these absolute numbers do in fact represent the minimum number of individuals present.

3 Kurtén, B. (1965). The carnivora of the Palestine caves, *Acta Zool. Fenn.*

4 Zeuner, F. E. (1963). *A History of Domesticated Animals*. London. p. 94.

5 Bodenheimer, F. S. (1935). *Animal life in Palestine*. Jerusalem; Harrison, D. L. (1968). *The Mammals of Arabia*, II. Carnivora, Hydracoidea, Artiodactyla. London.

6 Bate, D. M. A. (1937), *in* Garrod, D. A. E. and Bate, D. M. A. *The Stone Age of Mount Carmel, Excavations at the Wady El-Mughara*, I. Oxford. pp. 157–253.

7 Clutton-Brock, J. (1962). Near Eastern canids and the affinities of the Natufian dogs, *Z. Tierzücht. ZüchtBiol.*, **76**, pp. 326–33.

8 Degerbøl, M. (1961). On a find of a Preboreal domestic dog (*Canis familiaris* L.) from Star Carr, Yorkshire, with remarks on other domestic dogs, *Proc. Prehist. Soc.*, **27**, pp. 35–55; Kurtén, B. (1965). ibid.; Lawrence, B. (1956), *in* Field, H. An anthropological reconnaissance in the Near East, 1950, *Papers Peabody Mus. Harvard*, **48** (2), App. E., pp. 80–1; Lawrence, B. (1967). Early domestic dogs, *Sonderdruck aus Z. f. Saügetierkunde*, **32** (1), pp. 44–59; Reed, C. A. (1960). A review of archaeological evidence on animal domestication in the prehistoric Near East, *in* Braidwood, R. J. and Howe, B. Prehistoric investigations in Iraqi Kurdistan, *Studies in Ancient Oriental Civilisation*, Oriental Inst., Chicago, **31**, pp. 119–45; Reed, C. A. (1961). Osteological evidence for prehistoric domestication in South-western Asia, *Z. Tierzücht. ZüchtBiol.*, **76**, p. 38.

9 Kurtén, B. (1965). ibid.

10 Zeuner, F. E. (1963). op. cit.

11 Flannery, K. V., this volume, pp. 73–100; Flannery, K. V. (1967), *in* Hole, F. and Flannery, K. V. The prehistory of Western Iran: a preliminary report, *Proc. Prehist. Soc.*, **33**, pp. 147–207.

12 Bodenheimer, F. S. (1960). *Animal and Man in Bible Lands*. Leiden.

13 Bodenheimer, F. S. (1935). ibid.; Zeuner, F. E. (1963). op. cit.

14 Zeuner, F. E. (1958). Dog and cat in the Neolithic of Jericho, *Palestine Exploration Quarterly*, pp. 52–5.

15 Kurtén, B. (1965). ibid.

16 Clutton-Brock, J. (In press). Animal remains from the Bronze Age Excavations of Emporio, Chios, *in* Hood, M. S. F. *Excavations at the Bronze Age Site of Emporio, Chios, Greece.*

17 The work for this report was aided by a grant from the National Environmental Research Council to Dr. Kathleen Kenyon, to whom I am additionally indebted for the time she spent answering my many queries on the complicated phases of the excavation. My thanks are due to Professor Dimbleby of the Department of Human Environment, Institute of Archaeology, London, for the use of one of his research rooms and to Dr. F. C. Fraser and Miss J. E. King of the Osteology Room at the British Museum (Natural History) for the facilities that they offered me during the course of the work.

G. W. I. HODGSON

Some difficulties of interpreting the metrical data derived from the remains of cattle at the Roman settlement of Corstopitum

Metrical data have been obtained on the bones of domestic *Bos brachyceros* and *Ovis aries* excavated from the Roman settlement of Corstopitum in the years 1966[1] and 1967[2]. These data, when treated with those published by Meek and Gray[3] for the excavations from 1906–10, provide a major source of metrical data referring to the long bones of sheep and cattle from the Romano-British period. The indications are that the site will continue to yield more skeletal material for several years to come[4].

Cattle long bones

The validity of treating the 1911 published data together with those data obtained by the author may seem open to question. However, "Student" *t* tests, to establish the significance between the means of samples of measurements published for the distal widths of cattle metapodials[3] and those excavated in 1966 and measured by the author, suggest that the differences between the means are *not* significant at probabilities of 0·05 and 0·01. The test employed applies to a normal distribution, so an investigation was made to see if the distribution of measurements about their mean values was similar to a normal curve. Cornu's criterion[5] was applied to the distal width measurements of cattle metapodials. This test compares the standard deviation (s.d.) with arithmetic mean deviation from the average values (*e*); for Cornu's Value:

$$\frac{\text{s.d.}}{e} = 1·25$$

$$e = \frac{\Sigma |x - \bar{x}|}{n}$$

$$\text{s.d.} = \sqrt{\frac{\Sigma x^2}{n} - \left(\frac{\Sigma x}{n}\right)^2}$$

The values obtained were:

(a) metacarpals $\dfrac{\text{s.d.}}{e} = 1\cdot29$ for 155 specimens

(b) metatarsals $\dfrac{\text{s.d.}}{e} = 1\cdot45$ for 173 specimens

These values express the positive skewing which is seen in Figs. 1 and 2, where the same data are expressed in histogram form. The positive skewing may be due to one or more of the following causes:

1 there could have been a mixed population of cows, steers and bulls in which the more massive bull bones may skew the curve. Application of Howard's[6] so-called metapodial indices, $\dfrac{\text{distal-breadth}}{\text{length}} \times \dfrac{100}{1}$ and $\dfrac{\text{mid-breadth}}{\text{length}} \times \dfrac{100}{1}$ indicates that some bulls were present but that the bulk of the material is from steers and/or cows. The sample size is necessarily smaller for the MB/L index as most of the metapodials cannot be included because they have been smashed as if for marrow extraction. We cannot be certain to what extent castration was practised.
2 the introduction of *larger* forms in order to improve stock or to provide draught animals.
3 because of slaughtering of a preferred class of animal as regards size, age or maturity. At a given age class we would expect a normal distribution for any single dimension, but preference for killing at a particular age would give a skewed distribution rising to a peak at bone dimension appropriate to that preferred class, e.g. veal. We cannot consider bones of specific age groups but can only assume that the sum total of bones covers the sum total of age groups at which the animals were killed. There were no obvious signs of any very young or very aged cattle having been slaughtered and these curves may reflect the preferred class for slaughter.
4 the sample of 155 metacarpals and 173 metatarsals may be atypical.

Jewell's[7] work of comparing the length or width ranges of certain bones from various sites has been extended. The Corstopitum metacarpal length ranges from 15·7 cm. to 20·3 cm., the distal width of the metacarpals from 4·5 to 7·3 cm. and distal width of the humerus from 4·7 to 8·1 cm. These include specimens which are *shorter* and *narrower* than any reported from all those sites, extending from the mesolithic to the mediaeval period, which are listed in Appendix II, except for a single metacarpal from the Iron Age village of Catcote[1] which is 0·2 cm. shorter than the smallest from Corstopitum.

When the upper limits of the ranges of the same three dimensions are considered the Corstopitum ranges include specimens which are *longer* or *wider* than those described from any of the Iron Age and Romano-British

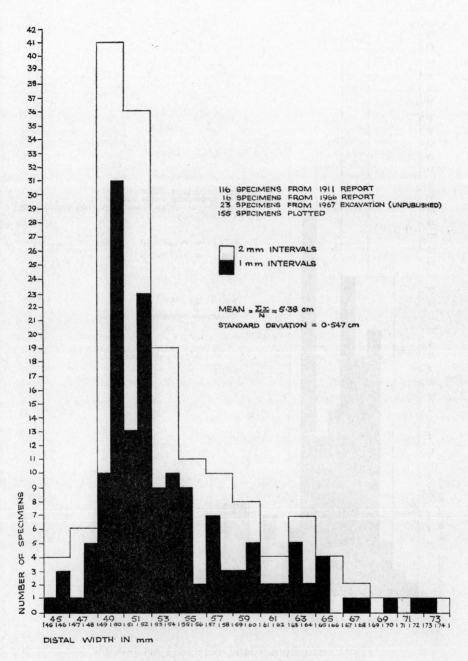

Fig 1 Corstopitum. Cattle metacarpal distal widths.

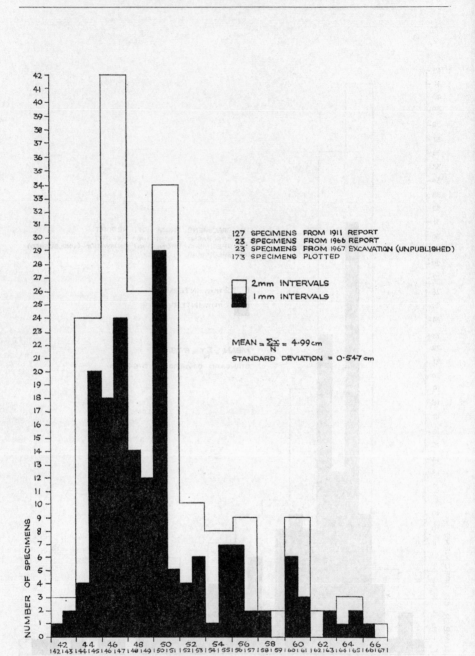

Fig 2 Corstopitum. Cattle metatarsal distal widths.

sites cited, except for a single metacarpal from Rotherley[32] which exceeds the longest Corstopitum specimen by 0·2 cm.

Jewell[7] has commented on the gradual diminution in size of cattle from British ancient sites from the neolithic ox, of earlier sites, to the Celtic Shorthorn of Iron Age and Romano-British times and of the diversity of types of cattle from Roman sites with the emergence of beasts larger than those which commonly existed in the preceding centuries. Whether the small forms at Corstopitum represent an unimproved stock or a diminution in size due to domestication and the larger forms represent an improvement of the stock by selective breeding or the importation of large draught animals, or whether the larger size is merely residual from an ancient stock, cannot be ascertained. It may be that the *larger* and *smaller* specimens merely represent the upper and lower limits of a single population and that because the Corstopitum sample is large, more of the extreme forms are found here. At the time of writing the bones have been treated as being all Romano-British but an attempt is being made to distinguish the different occupational levels from which the bones are found with a view to finding how size varied during an occupational time of several centuries[1].

Appendix I

Statistical data referring to bones of cattle excavated at Corstopitum in 1966[1] and 1967[2] and for those published in 1911[3]

Cattle. Bos taurus longifrons

	Number	Mean	Standard deviation
Metacarpals (distal width)	155	5·38 cm.	0·539 cm.
Metatarsals (distal width)	173	4·99 cm.	0·546 cm.
Tibia (distal width)	93	5·34 cm.	0·535 cm.
Radius (distal width)	68	5·9 cm.	0·65 cm.
Scapula			
(a) minimum width of neck	332	4·75 cm.	0·49 cm.
(b) maximum "diameter" glenoid cavity	203	5·08 cm.	0·37 cm.

Appendix II

	Reference		Reference
Mesolithic		Matignons	10
Star Carr	8	Puddle Hill	11
Neolithic		Skara Brae	12
Maiden Castle I	9	Stonehenge	13

	Reference		Reference
Neolithic		Catcote	1
Whitehawk Bay	14	Glastonbury	27
Windmill Hill	15	Little Woodbury	28
Woodhenge	16	*Romano-British*	
Bronze Age		Caerleon	29
Boscombe Down	17	Eastwood-Fawkham	30
Castle Hill	18	Highdole Hill	31
Jarlshof Sumburgh,		Rotherley	32
Shetland	19	The Rumps	33
Lowes Farm	20	Woodcuts	32
Maiden Castle II	9	Woodyates	32
Minnis Bay	21	*Mediaeval*	
Ogbourne West Enclosure	22	Kirkstall	34
Ratfyn	23	Northolt	34
Skendleby	24	Petergate	34
Snail Down	25	Pontefract	34
Iron Age		Well Street	35
All Cannings Cross	26		

Notes

1 I am indebted to Professor Birley of Durham University and to John Gillam, M.A., F.S.A., of Newcastle University for allowing me to work on the material excavated at Corstopitum during 1966 and 1967.

Notes to Appendixes

1 Hodgson, G. W. I. (1967). A comparative account of faunal remains from some ancient sites in the North of England. *M.Sc. Thesis, Durham University.*

2 Hodgson, G. W. I. Unpublished data on faunal remains from 1967 excavation at Corstopitum.

3 Meek, A. and Gray, R. A. H. (1911), *in* Forster, R. H. and Knowles, W. H. Corstopitum, *Archaeologia Aeliana*, 3 ser., 7, pp. 78–125.

4 The material, identified, measured and catalogued is now stored in the Hancock Museum, Newcastle-upon-Tyne.

5 Brooks, C. E. P. and Carruthers, N. (1953). *Handbook of Statistical Methods in Meteorology.* H.M.S.O. p. 42.

6 Howard, M. M. (1963). The metrical determination of the metapodials and skulls of cattle, *Roy. Anthropol. Inst., Occasional Paper*, **18,** pp. 91–100.

7 Jewell, P. A. (1962). Changes in size and type of cattle from Prehistoric to Medieval Times in Britain, *Z. Tierzücht. Zücht Biol.*, 77. pp. 159–67.

8 Fraser, F. C. and King, J. E. (1954), *in* Clark, J. G. D. *Star Carr.* Cambridge. pp. 70–95.

9 Jackson, J. W. (1943), *in* Wheeler, R. E. M. *Maiden Castle, Dorset.* London. pp. 360–71.

10 Poulain-Josien, T. (1966), *in* Burney, C. and Case, H. Les Camps Néolithiques des Matignons, *Gallia Prehist.*, **9.** Fig. 1, pp. 210–38.

11 Field, N. R., Mathews, C. L. and Smith, I. F. (1964). New neolithic sites in Dorset and Bedfordshire (Puddlehill), *Proc. Prehist. Soc.*, **15**, pp. 364–6.

12 Watson, D. M. S. (1931), *in* Childe, V. G. *Skara Brae. A Pictish Village in Orkney*. London. pp. 198–204.

13 Jackson, J. W. (1935). The animal remains from the Stonehenge excavations of 1920–26, *Antiq. J.*, **15**. pp. 434–40.

14 Jackson, J. W. (1934), *in* Curwen, E. C. Excavations in Whitehawk Neolithic Camp. Brighton 1932–3. *Antiq. Journ.*, **14**. pp. 127–9.

15 Jope, M. and Grigson, C. (1965), *in* Keiller, A. *Windmill Hill and Avebury*. Oxford. pp. 141–67.

16 Jackson, J. W. (1929), *in* Cunnington, M. E. *Woodhenge*. Devizes. pp. 61–9.

17 Jackson, J. W. (1936), *in* Stone, J. F. S. An enclosure on Boscombe Down East, *Wilts. Arch. Mag.*, **47**. pp. 484–7.

18 Jackson, J. W. (1939). Report on the animal remains from the late Bronze Age site of Castle Hill, *Sussex Arch. Coll.*, **80**. pp. 267–8.

19 Platt, I. P. (1933), *in* Curle, A. O. Excavations at Jarlshof, Shetland, *Proc. Soc. Antiq., Scot., 1932–3*, **67** 6th series, 7, pp. 127–35, and also 1933–4, **68** 6th series, 8, pp. 313–18.

20 Higgs, E. S. and Shawcross, F. W. (1961). The excavation of a *Bos primigenius* at Lowes Farm, Littleport, *Proc. Camb. Ant. Soc.*, **54**. pp. 3–16.

21 Jackson, J. W. (1943), *in* Worsford, F. H. Late Bronze Age Site at Minnis Bay, Birchington, Kent, *Proc. Prehist. Soc.*, **9**. pp. 41–4.

22 Jackson, J. W. (1942), *in* Piggott, C. M. Five late Bronze Age Enclosures in North Wilts, *Proc. Prehist. Soc.*, **8**. pp. 54–9.

23 Jackson, J. W. (1935), *in* Stone, J. F. S. Some discoveries at Ratfyn, Amesbury, *Wilts. Arch. Mag.*, **47**. pp. 66–7.

24 Jackson, J. W. (1935), *in* Phillips, C. W. The Excavations of the Giant Hills, Long Barrow, Skendleby, Lincs, *Archaeologia*, **85**. pp. 95–9.

25 Snail Down. Reported as being in preparation by Jewell, P. A. (1963). Cattle from British Archaeological Sites, *Roy. Anthrop. Inst.*, *Occasional Paper*, **18**. pp. 80–1.

26 Jackson, J. W. (1923), *in* Cunnington, M. E. *The Early Iron Age Site at All Cannings Cross Farm, Wilts*. Devizes. pp. 43–50.

27 Dawkins, W. Boyd, and Jackson, J. W. (1917), *in* Bulleid, A. and Gray, A. St. G. The Glastonbury Lake Village, *Glastonbury Antiquarian Soc.* pp. 643–72.

28 Fraser, F. C. (1948), *in* Brailsford, J. Excavations at Little Woodbury, *Proc. Prehist. Soc.*, **14**. pp. 19–23.

29 Watson, D. M. S. (1928), *in* Wheeler, R. E. M. and Wheeler, T. V. Report on the animal bones from Caerleon, *Arch.*, **78**. pp. 214–15.

30 Chaplin, R. E. and Coy, J. P. (1963), *in* Phillip, B. J. The Romano-British Farmstead at Eastwood Fawkham, *Archaeologia Cantiana*, **78**. pp. 70–2.

31 Jackson, J. W. (1936), *in* Holleyman, G. A. An early British agricultural village site on Highdole Hill, Tescombe, *Sussex Arch. Coll.*, **77**. pp. 202–21.

32 Pitt-Rivers, A. (1888). *Excavations at Cranbourne Chase*, **1. 2, 3**. London. (*I*, pp. 171–88; *II*, pp. 209–28; *III*, pp. 233–9.)

33 Chaplin, R. E. and Coy, J. P. (1964), *in* Brooks, R. T. Report of the 1963 excavations at the Rumps, St. Minver, *Cornish Arch.*, **3**. pp. 26–34.

34 Ryder, M. L. (1961). Livestock remains from four mediaeval sites in Yorkshire, *Agricultural Hist. Rev.*, **9**. pp. 105–10.

35 Chaplin, R. E. (1966). The animal remains from the Well Street Site, Coventry, *Birmingham Arch. Soc.*, **81**. pp. 130–8.

MARIA HOPF

Plant remains and early farming in Jericho[1]

Excavations in the Middle East and Asia Minor since 1950 have brought to light cereals from the Pre-Pottery settlement layers which go back to the beginning of farming. Both barley and hulled wheats were found. Without exception the barley belonged to the hulled two-rowed form, *Hordeum distichum*, in so far as it is distinguishable—with its fragile rachis—from *H. spontaneum*. Naked and multi-rowed hulled barley first occurred in the later layers. Helbaek[2] concluded that the two-rowed barley must have been the original form, from which the multi-rowed forms arose through the mutation of a single gene causing the lateral flowers to become fertile.

Similar observations have been made with wheat. In Jarmo (6500 B.C.) Helbaek[3] found a hulled wheat closely related to *Triticum dicoccoides* as well as *T. dicoccum*, and in Ali Kosh (6900 B.C.), Beidha (6500 B.C.) and Hacilar (6500 B.C.) there was also emmer. *T. monococcum* occurred together with emmer in places of equal age, though always only in small numbers, so that it seems to have been of secondary importance. It is only absent from Beidha, the most southerly site, which lies outside the area of distribution of wild einkorn, *T. boeoticum*. There may be two reasons for these findings: either the wild cereals were brought into cultivation in more than one place at more or less the same time, and the crop was related to the local wild plants; or the culture spread from a centre in the Middle East in which all three above-named primitive forms occurred. Where the local conditions of the secondary territory did not suit one or other of the species, as for instance at Beidha, perhaps it died out.

In the light of the complex questions outlined here, the observations on the plant remains from early Jericho (Pre-Pottery to Bronze Age) are of particular interest, for it lies in the range of distribution of *H. spontaneum* and *T. dicoccoides*, though *T. boeoticum* is absent here—at least at the present day[4]. The Pre-Pottery layers here began—according to carbon-14 dating—*c.* 7000 B.C.

In addition to the impressions in mud-brick—which there is not space to discuss here—there are altogether 110 samples of carbonized cereal grains, legumes and fruits, which can be divided up according to the observed period of settlement as follows:

Species	Pre-Pot. A	Pre-Pot. B	Pot. Neol.	Chalco-lithic	Early Bronze	Early Middle	Middle Bronze
% of total nos. of samples	4%	9%	6%	2%	60%	7%	12%
H. distichum	x	x	x	x	x	x	x
H. nudum						x	x
T. monococcum		x	x		x	x	x
T. dicoccum	x	x	x		x	x	x
T. aestivum s.l.					x	x	x
Vitis { pips					x		x
Vitis { fruits					x		x
Ficus	x			x	x		x
Pisum		x				x	x
Lens		x			x	x	x
Vicia cf. faba		x					x
Cicer		x?			x	x	
Avena		x?			x		x
Bromus			x		x	x	x
Linum					x		
Punica							x
Phoenix					x		
Allium					x		x
Cruciferae			x		x		x

Leaving aside the few very small Bronze Age grains of naked barley (3·7 × 1·8 × 1·4 mm.) all the finds of barley belong to the two-rowed hulled form *H. distichum*. The grains are long and relatively flat (6·2 × 3·2 × 2·3 mm.) and rachis segments with weak marginal hairs were repeatedly observed, carrying the strong median florets but with the lateral florets only represented by small weak stalks. In the Pre-Pottery A two simple rachis segments and a total of six small grains (5·2 × 2·5 × 1·8 mm.) were found, while by the following period B the grain size had increased considerably (6·0 × 3·0 × 2·3 mm.) and with *c.* 1200 grains there were also found rachis segments with 2 or 3 connected internodes, evidence for the cultivated form with a tough rachis which probably did not occur in the previous phase.

Of the hulled wheats the oldest period yielded only two single grains of emmer, *Triticum dicoccum*. This species is also represented in all the later periods by grains, rachis segments, spikelets and a number of obliquely inserted terminal spikelets. Considerable difficulties arise in distinguishing it from einkorn, *T. monococcum*, which occurs regularly and abundantly from the Pre-Pottery B level of Jericho onwards. Einkorn occurs largely in the two-grained form; the length of the fruit does not exceed that of emmer, its ventral side is not arched outwards, and the width of the grain usually corresponds with that of emmer. Therefore the characteristically curved embryo-end of einkorn must serve as the distinguishing character. Furthermore, emmer alters on carbonizing, in contrast to einkorn, so that the upper half swells up and it becomes drop-shaped, as was found in all the settlement phases at Jericho. No significant difference could be detected in the width of the rachis segments of einkorn and emmer. Typical grains of naked wheat,

T. aestivum s.l., with short straight rounded scutellum, occur from the Early Bronze Age, while a piece of a strong twisted awn in the Pre-Pottery A, and subsequently also a fruit in the Early Bronze Age, indicate the presence of (? wild) oats, *Avena* sp.

The roundish horse-bean, *Vicia* cf. *faba*, resembles those shown by Feinbrunn[5] (see below); with a mean diameter of 5·3 mm. it is only a little larger than the largest peas, *Pisum* cf. *sativum* (min. 3·0, max. 5·5 mm.). The size of the palisade cells and stalk cells in their testa makes it possible to refer material to *Vicia* with safety. The lentils, *Lens culinaris*, have a diameter of 3·0 mm., smaller than the Bronze Age examples described by Feinbrunn[6] from Beth-Shean and by Helbaek[7] from Lachish.

Chickpea, *Cicer arietinum*, occurred in great quantities in the Early Bronze Age; fragments without shells, from the Pre-Pottery B, could also belong here.

Carbonized fig-pips, *Ficus* cf. *carica*, could be detected in many samples after the first settlement; only once was any of the flesh of the fruit found. In addition to the innumerable pips of the vine, *Vitis vinifera*, with their short, clearly thickened stalk, many carbonized berries also occurred, mostly containing 2–4 pips. It is a moot point whether the shape of the pips or the number in each berry are indicative of the primitive state. On the other hand, a cultivated form certainly appeared at the same time in flax, *Linum usitatissimum*; in addition to seeds (4·2 × 1·9 mm.), separate carpels and a complete capsule (6·2 × 5·5 mm.) were found. It is only dehiscent at the very tip, along the suture of a carpel; the wild form usually bursts open in the middle of the carpel as well. Kenyon[8] reported the occurrence of fragments of wall of pomegranate, *Punica granatum*, and in support of this were found pips (3·8 × 2·0 mm.) which are considerably smaller than those of modern varieties on the market today. The only date-stone, *Phoenix dactylifera*, from the Early Bronze Age measured 12·75 × 6·75 mm. The "onions" are long and slender, and could originate from *Allium* cf. *ampeloprasum*. The occurrence of weeds is very slight, from which it is evident that only threshed and winnowed harvest products are present at the actual centres of settlement; the waste material will have been left behind at the threshing place.

From Phase A only 6 barley grains, 2 grains of emmer, 46 fig pips, and 3 broken pieces (at least 3·5 mm. long) of a legume were found, so it is doubtful whether this represents the complete stock of the earliest fruit, nuts and cultivated plants from Jericho, and one does not know whether einkorn and several species of legumes in the Pre-Pottery B are to be looked upon as additional new species or whether they are old forms which have only not been recovered previously. The full Neolithic, in spite of technical progress (pottery), surprisingly shows a remarkable paucity of species, which in turn is even more conspicuous in the Chalcolithic. There is a complete change in the Early Bronze Age, in which, in addition to the species already known from the Pre-Pottery B, no less than six new records were produced: *Triticum aestivum, Vitis, Linum, Phoenix, Allium* and *Cicer* (if *Cicer* were not already present in Pre-Pottery B). Neither of the following periods show any further new introductions (apart from *Punica*). The reappearance in the Middle Bronze Age of beans with a somewhat larger seed (5·6 mm.) than in the Pre-Pottery B (5·2 mm.) could indicate equally either a reintroduction or a continuation of its use.

If one considers the wild plants occurring in the nearby or more remote surroundings of the settlement[9], the finds in general indicate they did not originate from the native flora. For instance, *Triticum boeoticum* is absent in Palestine. If einkorn should actually first occur in the Pre-Pottery B (c. 6250 B.C.) in Jericho, the destroyers of the tower and the builders of the third and fourth walls must at least have invaded through the area of distribution of wild einkorn which lies to the north, whilst the tower builders of Phase A (c. 6800 B.C.) had at their disposal in the countryside wild barley and wild emmer for domestication and the fig for gathering.

The newly arrived potters of the first half of the fifth millennium do not seem to have practised intensive farming; the plant remains therefore give no clue to the origin of these inhabitants. Among the plants of the Early Bronze Age (from 3200 B.C.) on the other hand, vine (in 28 samples!) and a single grain of naked wheat indicate connections with the north or north-east, whilst *Linum, Cicer, Phoenix* and *Allium* do not need to be of foreign origin. However, the flax capsule must be considered to have a shape modified by cultivation, so these other plants or at least their products, though they have not previously appeared in the tell, could also have been a valued commodity of the newcomers.

On the basis of the finds described, cultivation in Jericho during the Pre-Pottery A phase could possibly be traced to the taking into cultivation of native wild plants. In phase B an alien northern element shows itself in *Triticum monococcum*, but whether it actually occurred earlier could not be determined with certainty because of the small amount of material found. For this reason the hypothesis of a local development of farming is weak, although the fragility of the *Hordeum* rachis is also evidence of an early stage of domestication; this characteristic could nevertheless be related to the invasion of a local wild barley into an already highly developed system of field crops.

Notes

1 cf. Kenyon, K. M. (1960). *Excavations at Jericho*, 1. Palestine Exploration Society, London; Kenyon, K. M. (1965). *Excavations at Jericho*, 2. Palestine Exploration Society, London.
2 Helbaek, H. (1966). Commentary on the phylogenesis of *Triticum* and *Hordeum*, *Econ. Bot.*, 20. pp. 350–60.
3 Helbaek, H. (1966). Pre-Pottery neolithic farming at Beidha, *Palestine Exploration Quarterly*, 98, pp. 61–6.

4 Zohary, D. (1966). Distribution of wild wheat and barley, *Science*, 153, pp. 1074–9.
5 Feinbrunn, N. (1938). New data on some cultivated plants and weeds of the early bronze age in Palestine, *Palestine J. Bot., J. Ser.*, I, pp. 238–40.
6 Feinbrunn, N. (1938). ibid.
7 Helbaek, H. (1958). Plant economy in ancient Lachish, *in* Tufnell, O. (1958). *Lachish IV*. London. pp. 309–17.
8 Kenyon, K. M. (1960). op. cit. pl. XVII.
9 Zohary, M. (1962). *Plant Life of Palestine*. New York.

CHARLES A. REED

The pattern of animal domestication in the prehistoric Near East

Agriculture, which includes animal domestication, is a part of the long history of human cultural adaptation whereby man, probably more by trial and error than purposeful forethought, achieved increasing control of his environment. Viewed in this light, the cultivated plants and domestic animals are as much artifacts of human culture as was an Olduwan pebble tool or is any modern tool; each of these was wrought from nature by man and allows him to divert more of the energy in his ecosystem to his own purposes. Through the increase of foodstuffs after the beginning of the Agricultural (Neolithic or Food-Producing) Revolution, the human species has incredibly multiplied its own population at the expense of the rest of the world's biota.

Archaeological and natural-historical evidences combine to place this earliest agriculture in the lower hills and adjacent plains of the area east of the Mediterranean into south-western Iran. Here grew the wild emmer and einkorn wheats and the wild two-rowed barley[1] first cultivated and here occurred also the wild mammals—wolf, goat, sheep, pig and cattle—which were the earliest domesticants. Here too—in the Levant, in southern Turkey, and along the western edges of the Zagros ranges—the earliest evidences of agriculture, including the bones of the first domesticants, are being recovered by archaeologists. We must not, of course, overlook the possibilities that other men in many places may have been doing similar things. There is for instance the report of independent domestication of sheep in Dobrogea, Rumania[2], at about the same time this process was happening in the foothills of the Zagros Mts.

For more than 99% of their co-existence, man and other animals came together as hunter and prey, man more often being the hunter. The change to man the domesticator was thus a major behavioural shift in human adaptation for the utilization of animal resources. In analysing this basic change in the man–animal situation, the relations between four possible variables must be considered: 1 the evolving morphology, intelligence, and innate behaviour of the animals; 2 the evolving morphology, intelligence, and innate behaviour of the particular men involved; 3 pertinent changes in the environment; 4 changes in human culture.

The first two of these potential variables can be discounted. The plants and animals did not together evolve to a stage of potential domesticability; indeed, they undoubtedly could have been cultivated and/or domesticated for several millions of years before they were. Man had been modern in form and behaviour, in so far as can be determined, for some 25,000 years before domestication occurred. However, in the area involved and at the time (some 11,000 years ago) of the earliest evidences of the intensive use of cereal grains, a use which presumably preceded the beginnings of agriculture, both the physical environment and human culture were changing rapidly, the cultural innovations probably occurring in correlation with a marked climatic shift from colder to warmer.

The Würm–Weichselian–Wisconsin period of world-wide temperature depression, producing massive continental glaciers in the nearer polar regions of both northern and southern hemispheres, had run its course. The Taurus–Zagros Mts. of the Near East had been heavily glaciated[3], but by 12,000 years ago these glaciers were melting back toward their highland sources. While the climate on the plateaux inland from the mountains remained somewhat cool and dry for another 6000 years[4], indicating the relative slowness of the change from the ice-age to a climate typical of the present, man in the Near East began moving out of caves and living more in open sites after some 12,000 years ago.

Human culture, as we know it from the recovered remnants of the tools (mostly stone but occasionally of bone), was changing rapidly; the blades, burins and scrapers which had dominated the Near Eastern tool kit for the major portion of the Upper Palaeolithic were being supplanted in part by microlithic tools, often of such preciseness of shape as to be termed "geometrics". These microliths are usually so small that they must have been hafted to have been used, and their variety and popularity presumably indicate an increased use of available perishable materials—wood, skins, hair, horn, and perhaps vegetable foodstuffs.

We do not know the full story, but we do know that within a period generally falling between eleven and ten thousand years ago, after approximately a thousand years of the intensive use of microliths, men were settling into semi-permanent villages. We find these present as part of the Natufian culture[5] of the Levant (best exemplified at the site of Mallaha[6] on the edge of Lake Hulah in Palestine's Jordan Valley), at Zawi Chemi Shanidar[7] beside the Greater Zab (a branch of the Tigris) in northern Iraq, and even on the cold-steppe of the Iranian Plateau at the site of Ganj-Dareh Tepe[8].

All of these near-contemporaneous sites indicate permanent occupation, and all have some degree of house-building, although the type of structure is difficult to detect at Zawi Chemi. The Natufian sites and Zawi Chemi have mortars and pestles and/or querns and hand-held milling stones; at Ganj-

Dereh some broken stone was found which may be pieces of querns. The Natufian sites and Zawi Chemi had sickles (or at least sickle blades) and microliths; these were not found at Ganj-Dareh. Nowhere had pottery been made or metal yet utilized.

In so far as the evidence has been recovered, the Natufian people of the Levant had the more complex culture, but had no domestic animals[9], whereas the simpler people of Zawi Chemi did. These latter had domestic sheep[10].

The time has come to pause, take stock, and ask ourselves some questions.

1 South-western Asia, although still colder than it is at present, was in a period of more rapid warming than had been that of the prior few thousand years. Indeed, so rapid was the world-wide climatic warming that the continental glaciers were melting back at such an increased rate that modern scientists designate 11,000 B.P.[11] (Before Present) as being approximately the end of the "ice-age" (Pleistocene) and the beginning of the post-Pleistocene (Recent). Studies of pollen, particularly, and of other remains from bottom-cores at Lake Zeribar in the Iranian Zagros[12] show that south-western Asia shared in this world-wide change of climate during and following the end of the Pleistocene. Warming is noticeable by about 14,000 B.P.; particularly for the Zagros at approximately 11,000 B.P., trees (primarily oak and pistachio) were beginning to re-invade the foothills, an area from which they had been eradicated during the cold of the terminal glacial period.

Questions:

(a) Did this period of climatic change influence and/or accelerate human cultural evolution toward the microlithic type of tool production, or did the pattern of cultural change have such inherent tendencies as to be relatively independent of environmental shifts, so that the microlithic phase would have occurred in south-western Asia when it did even if the climatic change had not been accelerated?[13]

(b) Was the introduction of microlithic tools merely accompanied by, or perhaps directly associated with, a more intensive utilization of the available food resources, particularly the seeds of certain grasses (wild barley and wheats)? We have no evidence to answer directly, but the introduction of sickles and milling stones in south-western Asia within the subsequent few hundred years would suggest some period of use of these nutritious grains prior to the invention of specialized tools for reaping and milling them.

2 From the Kom Ombo plain of Upper Egypt we have milling stones (handstones) and oval or irregular-shaped, slightly concave querns which were in use there by or before 13,000 B.P.[14] Indeed, the preparation of vegetable foods by the use of pounding and grinding stones seems to have had a long history in Africa[15], and such practices may have already begun

some two million years ago, on the evidence of hammer-stones found at Makapansgat in Transvaal[16]. While there is generally little evidence for cultural contact between Egypt and the Asiatic Levant in the Late Palaeolithic, this priority of typical querns and hand-stones in Egypt by at least two thousand years is intriguing.

Questions:

(*a*) If milling stones were introduced from Africa, do we need to think of that introduction as being correlated with a period of rapid climatic change? Or, possibly, did both the culture and the environment in south-western Asia favour utilization by the end of the Pleistocene of milling stones, whether introduced or home invented?

(*b*) Is the preparation of vegetable food on grinding stones in any way associated with the first domestication of the hoofed mammals? If it is, other factors are also present, as such domestication did not occur amongst the Natufians or, until millennia later, among the Egyptians or Nubians.

The symbiotic association of a primate species, man, with other mammalian species, his domesticants, is a part of evolutionary history, and contemplation of the biological factors which allowed or influenced that history is as necessary as is consideration of the environmental and cultural factors.

The earliest domesticants were mammals of the Orders Carnivora (dogs) or Artiodactyla (pigs, sheep, goats, cattle). The last three of these five are ruminants from one family, the Bovidae. Each of the five and each wild ancestor had in common a well-developed intra-specific social life[17], which has undoubtedly been of aid in their adjustments to living with members of another species. Two of them, dog and pig, have the ability to eat a wide variety of plant and animal materials, including offal and carrion: the bovids, in company with all ruminants, consume materials such as leaves or grass not directly available as food to man.

Of the wild ancestors, the cattle (*Bos primigenius*) are extinct and so not available for experimentation. The other four, however, are readily tamed if caught when young and treated with consideration; wolves and dogs interbreed readily and produce fertile offspring, as do wild and domestic pigs. I have no data on the breeding of domestic and wild goats, but would expect them to do so, in as much as their physical similarities are such that we include them in the same species, *Capra hircus*. Similarly I would expect that any Old World sheep, all of which are now often put in the single species *Ovis ammon*, would mate successfully with any domestic sheep.

Judging from evidence of the bones exhumed from early prehistoric village-farming sites in the Near East, the dog was seemingly never an important factor in the economy, and the domestic pig was presumably only slightly more important; at least the bones of these two domesticants are rare in comparison with those of sheep and goat. Indeed, in many sites, bones of gazelles outnumber those of pigs. The possibility remains of course that the gazelles were tamed and kept in herds, to be killed as needed, but we have no evidence of this.

The failure of any vertebrate to have evolved an enzyme or enzymes to digest cellulose remains an enigma in the study of biochemical evolution. This failure, however, has meant that cellulose, one of the most common organic materials in the terrestrial world, has been denied to all vertebrate herbivores as a direct source of energy. Only by evolving internal fermentation vats, often quite complex in structure and function, can a mammal utilize cellulose; in such vats, anaerobic bacteria (aided in some instances by certain Protozoa) process the ingested food and break down the cellulose to simpler molecules which are then available to the mammal's digestive system.

The most efficient of such fermentation-vats are those which have evolved anterior to the intestine, by modification of the stomach or of the stomach plus adjacent parts of the oesophagus; of these the ruminants (camels, deer, giraffes, bovids) are the best known, but others (hippopotamus, kangaroos, and possibly some rodents and primates) have independently evolved similar anatomical and physiological specializations[18], but without rumination.

Cud-chewing, thus, is not the important factor in cellulose utilization, but seemingly is an auxiliary device, evolved in the ruminants, which increases the efficiency of the fermentation-vat. Some other mammals (the horse and other perissodactyls, pigs, rabbits, and many rodents) have evolved a fermentation-vat in the caecum, posterior to the small intestine. This relatively inefficient arrangement may well be a factor in the gradual near-replacement since the Oligocene of Perissodactyla and Suina by ruminants.

A secondary advantage to having a fermentation-vat anterior to the true stomach, known to be true at least for ruminants, is that urea can be secreted from the blood into the stomach, thus recycling the body's nitrogen, with the result that the animal can survive on low-nitrogen fodder. Another advantage is that the bacteria produce all the necessary vitamins, except A and D, a situation which again allows the animals to survive on what would generally be regarded as a sub-minimal diet.

Two concepts, one merely of interest but the other of value to our thinking, emerge from the above considerations of ruminant physiology. The first is that, while the ruminants eat roughage (grass, leaves, etc.) they do not live directly from this ingested material; for the most part the micro-organisms in the internal fermentation-vat consume that food, but the ruminant lives then on the by-products of bacterial metabolism and on the surplus population of the micro-organisms. A thought more valuable to the solution of problems concerning the beginnings of domestication is that ruminants were, by the very nature of their anatomical and physiological organization, pre-adapted to survive on food high in cellulose, which is not directly available to man or dog, and can be utilized only inefficiently by pigs.

Dog, man, and pig are, however, direct competitors for food; even wolves, ancestors of dogs are (in common with many of the Canidae), much more omnivorous than many people realize. It is true that pigs and dogs in pre-historic times, as well as today, might seek out food (earthworms, acorns, bulbs for pigs; carrion, camp scraps for dogs) not ordinarily eaten by man, but none of these food items was impossible for man to eat, and many of them were sometimes eaten by him. Particularly under conditions of scarcity was man in direct competition with two of his early domesticants and might even rob the dog of its wild prey. Furthermore, man would derive more energy from direct consumption of such food than he would by diverting it to pig or dog and then eating them. Only in a community where there is an excess of human food can pigs and dogs be tolerated as a part of the biosocial community. Thus to cycle grain through a pig before consumption by man is to lose more than three-fourths of the potential energy originally present in the grain[19], although man may gain to a lesser degree by the concentration of the protein and by the aesthetic pleasure derived from eating meat.

With early man's bovid domesticants there was typically no necessity, and in practice little possibility, of competition for food. Zeuner[20] has termed these animals the "crop-robbers", and that they undoubtedly were when wild, but once under human control they could be kept away from the fields until after the harvest. The basic point is that ruminants in general and sheep, goats and cattle in particular (to limit our discussion to the prehistoric Near East) eat materials such as dry grass, leaves, straw, twigs, etc., with green fodder when available, which would be a starvation diet for man, dog, or pig. The domestic bovid (as well as domestic camels and reindeer, later in time) is thus a converter of cellulose-rich materials, otherwise unavailable to man, into carbohydrates, fats, and proteins by way of milk and flesh, and is also a converter of those same materials, generally useless otherwise, into such valuable commodities as hides, hair, and wool. In time, the dung, particularly of cattle, also came to be utilized, both as fuel for humans and as a fertilizer for the fields.

In summary, the ability to survive on a diet high in cellulose and low in proteins is a pre-adaptive factor in the successful domestication of bovids by early villagers and later of camels and reindeer by nomads. (The same primary adaptations, too, are of course present in those camelids, llama and alpaca, which were later and independently domesticated in South America.) These factors, 1 a multi-chambered "stomach" with a fermentation-vat anterior to the functional digestive tract; 2 rumination; and 3 recycling of nitrogen from urea, in correlation with the various anatomical similarities and the evidence of the fossil record, indicate to me a common ancestry for the Ruminantia (including the camels) by the middle of the Eocene or earlier. Thus the beginnings of the physiological adaptations which allowed sheep, goats, and cattle to survive under conditions of probably minimum diet and poor care in early Recent villages had had their evolutionary origins, in however preliminary form, some fifty million years earlier.

Undoubtedly the ruminants' neural and endocrine adaptations for sociability, and their anatomical and physiological adaptations for high cellulose and low protein diet, had been perfected for millions of years prior to the evolution of any anthropoid biped identifiable as *Homo*; why then were no ruminants—or the omnivorous pigs or the semi-omnivorous wolves for that matter—not domesticated earlier in human prehistory?

The animals were obviously ready, but man was not. Since by the time we are considering, *c.* 12,000 to 11,000 years ago, modern man had been the only type present for some 25,000 years, the changes in men necessary to bring them to a state of readiness to domesticate animals must have been primarily cultural. Some factor had to tip the balance of behaviour to change them from hunters of wild animals to keepers and defenders of tame ones.

We cannot *prove* that relatively rapid climatic change was a direct or indirect factor in the origin of cultivation and domestication, but the environmental change *may* indeed have been an important even if indirect influence. Climatic warming certainly meant a slow but continuous shift of vegetational zones upward on hill and mountain, and a correlated slow movement of animal populations to maintain themselves in the environments in which they could exist. These biological changes, depending upon end-of-Pleistocene warming, may well have stimulated cultural innovations in south-western Asia, quite as did floral and faunal changes in Europe at this same time. We know that in the Near East, within a period of little more than a thousand years, microliths were invented or introduced, people began to move out of caves and build villages of various types, people began reaping and milling wild cereals, people began cultivating cereals, and animals became domesticated. (Not all of these events necessarily occurred in the order designated, as the sequence was different in some places and some events occurred simultaneously.)

I believe that, on the basis of present evidence, a primary requirement for the earliest domestication of the ruminants, and for pigs, is that man settled down to village life. A necessity for village life is an established food source for man, which, by the invariable association of early villages with milling stones, would mean dependence upon cereal grain, acorns, or some such highly nutritious plant food which could be gathered in quantity, fragmented or powdered, dried if need be, and stored.[12]

I believe that the archaeological record, although incomplete as yet, is in preliminary agreement with the above proposition, but many sites in different environmental areas, from the Jordan's mouth to the plateaux of Iran and Anatolia, will have to be dug meticulously and have their discoveries analysed carefully to test the hypothesis.

Villages with housing and milling stones do not necessarily have to have had cultivated grains and/or domesticated animals. Mallaha and other Natufian settlements seemingly did not, nor did the sites of Mureybat and

Bouqras, on the Euphrates in northern and eastern Syria, respectively[22]. At Mureybat, seventeen occupation levels, dated between 10,200 B.P. and 9500 B.P., succeeded each other; at Bouqras the early level is thought to be coincident with the PPNA settlement at Jericho and the village persisted late enough to have coarse, unpainted pottery. The C-14 determinations are 8240 ± 100 to 7840 ± 60. The villages seemingly maintained themselves completely by hunting and gathering, with some evidence for animal husbandry at Bouqras at the very end of its existence.

Palestine remains an enigma in this early history of animal domestication. The problem has been discussed particularly by Perrot[23] and by Ducos[24]. The basic fact remains, after considerable investigation, that cereal cultivation and animal domestication cannot be demonstrated for much of Palestine (particularly the upper Jordan Valley) and southern Syria prior to the late fifth millennium B.C. Between *c.* 8000 B.P. and perhaps *c.* 6500 B.P., an occupational hiatus of fifteen hundred years seemingly exists, as if Palestine had been deserted. Perrot suggests a period of desiccation, to correlate in part with the Boreal Period of Europe (*c.* 9500–7600 B.P.). However, the chronological synchrony is not close, and one suspects that the extremes of environmental change necessary to have caused such human desertion cannot have occurred; even if the population abandoned their villages for the most part, and abandoned Jericho also (as seems to have happened), Palestine must have been occupied, and I suggest occupied by people who had some domestic mammals even if only goats or goats and sheep. We must remember that, prior to this supposed cultural hiatus, and in the millennium between 9000 and 8000 B.P., Beidha (at the southern end of the Dead Sea drainage) had cultivated barley[25] and probably also had domestic goats[26] at the same time. The people of Jericho, later in the same millennium, seem definitely to have had cultivated barley[27] and perhaps reared domestic goats[28]; the evidence on this latter point is being re-evaluated by Clutton-Brock and we must delay any decision until her results are known. However, in that same millennium, domestic goats have been reported from El Khiam[29], a site in the Wadi Khareitoun between Bethlehem and the Dead Sea. With goats and barley known from the lower part of the drainage of the Dead Sea after 9000 B.P., and cultivated wheat at Jericho *c.* 8000 B.P.[30], I cannot believe that cultivation and domestication were absent from Palestine until 6500 B.P. The evidence must exist, yet to be found in spite of the lack of success of careful search already made for it.

Summaries of individual species

In my previous reviews on prehistoric domestication in the ancient Near East[31] I tried to weigh the evidence as then existing, and decided that many prior statements on the subject could not be accepted. The result was that the earliest known representatives of each of the domesticants in many areas were necessarily put at a time obviously some thousands of years later than that domestication had occurred. I believe that the resulting practice, of demanding proof of domestication before accepting claim for it as valid, was a healthy one, and the intervening decade has seen numerous workers who have helped to fill the chronological voids I had left.

The dog (*Canis familiaris*): An increasing number of behavioural studies confirm the relationship between dog and wolf, as based on morphological similarities, while at the same time excluding the jackal or any other canid from the dog's ancestry. Many of these studies of behaviour are included in a recent issue of the *American Zoologist* (May 1967) devoted to the subject. A few points are worth discussing.

Several authors[32] separately considered various aspects of the evolution of canid behaviour in general or that of wolf and dog in particular. Although their work was independent, a general consensus emerges that the behaviour of wolf and dog differs from that of other members of the family primarily in the possession of adaptations to increase sociability and decrease friction, competition, and fighting in the group. My own further conclusion is that such behaviour can only have evolved in the free-living pack-life of the wolf, to be then inherited and largely retained by the domestic dog throughout that animal's relatively short span of existence since first domesticated.

The rearing of tame wolves is not new, but Woolpy and Ginsberg[33] have analysed the problem by experiments. Before six weeks of age, wolf pups show no fear of man, and indeed are usually all friendliness, with much tail-wagging, nosing, licking, and exploratory play-biting[34]. After six or seven weeks of age, taming becomes increasingly difficult, although seemingly a wolf of any age can be "socialized" to accept man as a comrade if one has the time and patience. The important aspect which emerges from these experiments, and from the description of the rearing of a wolf-pup to socialized adulthood[35], is that pups acquired prior to six weeks of age and hand-reared would behave toward man much as a large dog does.

There are some few behavioural patterns of adult tamed wolves not found in dogs, but the latter of course have been subjected to artificial selection, and at least one action selected against may well have been the affectionate muzzle-bite greeting of the tamed wolf[36]. Additionally, Scott[37] made the important suggestion that selection in the dog has been "for a highly protected neonatal existence", which I translate to mean the retention of the trustful and friendly behaviour of the wolf pup. (Different breeds of dogs vary of course, due to special selection in each, and individual training and experience is another variable.) Certainly the experiment with Elsa the lioness shows how much of the wildness of a large social carnivore can be lost in one generation when the individual is hand-reared by humans[38].

Prehistoric experiments of raising wolf pups may have been tried dozens or hundreds of times before a breeding population was established which remained in the human environment, but there would seem now no difficulty in believing in the feasibility of this process of domestication of dog from wolf.

Fentress[39] made the concluding statement that dogs were not derived from wolves that exist today, but that primitive man domesticated his first dogs from a common ancestor. This statement will appeal to, and be repeated by, dog-lovers and people in dog-clubs, who have an emotional bias against accepting the living wolf as typical of the ancestor of their pets, but in actuality the population (or populations) of Old World wolves from which dogs were derived some 11,000 or more years ago were probably little different, except possibly by slightly larger size, than are the wolves of those same regions today.

Scott suggested that dogs may have been domesticated only once, since the up-curved tail or the curly tail held over the back is characteristic of all dogs but not of wolves. He proposed that the mutation occurred early in the history of dogs and was retained by artificial selection. A common ancestry of all dogs would necessarily be an ancient one in the history of domestication, to have dogs at Star Carr in England by approximately 9500 years ago[40], in Anatolia[41] 9000 years ago, and in Idaho by 10,400 B.P.[42] There remains work to be done, but the major outlines of the domestication of the dog do seem to be more discernable through the mists of antiquity than was true a few years ago.

For south-western Asia, I had previously[43] indicated doubt concerning proof of the presence of domestic dogs until a relatively late date. The problem now is happily being clarified by the discovery of dogs at Çayönü[44] in south-western Anatolia, a site dated at *c.* 9000 B.P.[45] Further examination, by Miss Lawrence and myself, of the remains of the large canids from Jarmo, about which I was puzzled previously[46] reveals that they too undoubtedly represent dogs and not wolves.

Zeuner[47] had published on the presence of dogs at Jericho from the lower levels of the Pre-Pottery Neolithic B period (*c.* 8300? B.P. as I extrapolate the radiocarbon determinations there). With the evidence of earlier dogs already in south-western Asia, their presence in the PPNB levels, and even in the earlier PPNA, would seem reasonable. However, Clutton-Brock[48] has re-examined the canid material from Jericho and has not been able to certify that any of the bones or teeth are definitely from dogs and not from the local wolf. Obviously, we need more material, which need demands more excavation.

The fact remains that bones of dogs from prehistoric villages in south-western Asia are generally rare, but we now must realize that such rarity does not necessarily preclude the presence of dogs in those same villages. Probably dogs were not eaten, and possibly dead dogs were not allowed to lie in the village, so few of their bones are preserved for us.

Possibly the earliest drawing of a dog is that represented in a hunting scene from level III (*c.* 7500 B.P.) at Çatal Hüyük[49] in south-central Anatolia. The "dog" however would probably not have been recognized as such if out of the context of the scene of a man hunting deer, as the actual figure of the small carnivore could as easily be that of a mustelid or viverrid.

The pig (*Sus scrofa*): No emotional problems arise in accepting the wild pig as the ancestor of the domestic pig, nor do we find international symposia convened to discourse on the comparative behaviour of wild and domestic pigs, and on the problems in taming the former. I can, however, report that the striped young of the wild pig, two of which I kept for several weeks at Jarmo in 1955, behave exactly as do the unstriped young of domestic pigs, and they smell the same, too.

Stampfli[50] has given a good resumé of the prehistoric domestication of the pig in south-western Asia, which need not be repeated here since his studies will be published. He found that pigs, prior to the period of Sumerian cities, were found at numerous sites but rarely represented more than 5% of the bones of food animals; they were however more numerous (25%) at Matarrah.

Stampfli verified the unpublished work of Flannery[51] that remains of only wild pigs were recovered from the lower, pre-ceramic levels at Jarmo, and that there had been a transition to smaller domestic pigs (with some large presumably hunted pigs still remaining) in those upper layers with pottery. The implication, thus, is that domestication of the pig was a process happening at Jarmo *c.* 8500 B.P., but not a process necessarily limited to that site. Actually, domestic pigs were already present, although a minor part of the village fauna, at Çayönü, several hundreds of years earlier in south-western Anatolia[52]. These latter are the earliest domestic pigs known, but we should not thereby imagine that they necessarily will retain that distinction. However, if settled villages were a prerequisite for domestication of artiodactyls, pigs at Çayönü may be close in time to that period of origin.

The sheep (*Ovis aries*) and the goat (*Capra hircus*): The sheep identified by Perkins[53] remain the earliest-known domestic animals, perhaps in correlation with the fact that the site, Zawi Chemi, is one of the earliest definite villages (*c.* 10,800 B.P.). Domestic sheep are now known also from Çayönü, *c.* 9000 B.P.[54] However, to illustrate the continuing problems of identification of broken pieces of bones of Caprinae as recovered from prehistoric sites, Stampfli[55] could not be certain that any of the sheep bones found at Jarmo were from domestic sheep, although he thinks they probably were. In any case, goats seemingly were much more important than sheep at Jarmo, outnumbering them by a wide margin.

The time of introduction of domestic animals into Africa has long been a gnawing problem, but recently Higgs[56] has presented some definite evidence from the upper (neolithic) levels of the cave of Haua Ftea in Cyrenaica, Libya. Again, in illustration of the difficulties inherent in zoo-archaeology, the butchering practices of the neolithic people seem to have resulted in their discarding outside the cave the taxonomically diagnostic bones, so that

Higgs was unable to distinguish sheep from goats[57]. (His problem was further complicated by the presence in the same deposits of the closely-related wild audad or "Barbary Sheep", *Ammotragus*.) However, he definitely stated that domestic sheep or goats or both were living in Cyrenaica before *c.* 6800 B.P., and possibly as early as 8400 B.P. Since both domestic sheep and goats were well known in south-western Asia by this earlier time, and goats presumably this early or earlier were at Beidha[58] in the southern end of the Dead Sea drainage, there would seem to be little difficulty in accepting the probability that domestic goats and/or sheep could have been herded by easy stages across Sinai (not such a desert then, certainly, as it is now, and not such a desert now as many believe[59]) and the northern coast of Egypt into the mountains of Cyrenaica. They could also have been moved up the Nile valley and into the oasis of Fayûm, but we have no evidence of their presence in these areas until later.

The earliest history of domestic goats in south-western Asia is not much more clear than when I wrote on the subject ten years ago. They are the dominant food animal at Jarmo[60], and are listed as being abundant in the earliest or Bus Mordeh phase at Tepe Ali Kosh, Deh Luran, Iranian Khuzistan, where their identification as domesticants is based on the high proportion of yearlings there[61]. Since the lower levels of this site may date well before 9000 B.P., these domestic goats, already outside the area of their natural range in the mountains, may represent the earliest record yet known. Tepe Ali Kosh is one site where domestic goats would definitely seem to precede sheep, as the latter are reported only as possibly present in the second phase at the site, but then become more numerous later, as indeed also do the goats.

Lawrence cannot be certain that domestic goats were present at Çayönü, *c.* 9000 B.P., but their wide-spread distribution within a relatively short time after, from Beidha[62] (where there are no native true goats) to Khuzistan[63] would imply the beginnings of their domestication at least by 9000 B.P., if not earlier.

Domestic goats, but not sheep, were reported from the levels of Pre-Pottery Neolithic B at Jericho[64], but on limited evidence. While I had previously accepted this as a valid record, I am happy that Clutton-Brock is now making a thorough study of all the bones from Jericho, and hopefully we shall soon have available the results of her investigations. The bones from numerous other sites in south-western Asia also await study, or have been studied but the results not yet published. Some of these studies may change the pattern as here presented for the prehistoric chronology of domestic sheep and goats, and for other species also.

Cattle (*Bos taurus*): Accumulating evidence indicates that cattle were the last of the four major food-animals of the prehistoric Near East to have been domesticated. Indeed, the earliest known cattle for which we have clear evidence of domestication, *c.* 8500 B.P., were not in south-western Asia; they were from the site of Argissa-Maghula, in Greek Thessaly[65]. The next oldest site for what seem to be domestic cattle is also in Greece, only a relatively short distance from the first, at Nea Nikomedeia, in Macedonia[66]. The date here is *c*. 8100 B.P. We do not know whether cattle were first domesticated in south-eastern Europe and then moved as domesticants to Asia, or whether the pattern was in the reverse direction and we have not found the early sites in Asia as yet, or whether independent centres of domestication of cattle occurred, sparked perhaps by people who travelled in trade and saw what others were doing.

Possibly there was more of an act of purposeful domestication in bringing cattle into the villages than there had been with the earlier domesticants. After some 2000 years of increasingly intense domestication of sheep and goats particularly, the thought may have occurred that the big wild cattle, hunted only occasionally I would say, from the record of the sparsity of their bones in most village sites of the period, might be worth taming and keeping. I know of no way of proving or disproving such a supposition.

Isaac[67], following the pioneer ideas of Eduard Hahn in the late nineteenth century, has argued that domestication of cattle emerged from religious practices based on awe, fear, and admiration of the great bulls, which sometimes stood two metres at the withers. He has proposed that cattle might have been driven into large enclosures, from which certain males were isolated for sacrifice as occasion demanded, but leaving others free to breed. Gradually those which did not meet the standards of the sacrificial animals would be diverted to other purposes.

While admiring Isaac's broad scholarship and skilful presentation, I had previously tended to discount this religious approach to the origins of cattle domestication on the basis that his supporting data were drawn almost entirely from late prehistoric representations or from representations and writings of historical periods. All of this evidence, while definitely portraying cattle in religious contexts, was too long after the fact, I thought, to have bearing on the actual time of domestication. Additionally, there seemed little hope of finding archaeological evidence which would shed light on such a theory.

I am less certain than I used to be that no archaeological evidence can be found, and the reason for tending to change my mind is the obvious importance of the cattle, and what certainly seems to be a cattle-cult, at Çatal Hüyük[68]. Here perhaps is the place to test, with actual stratified archaeological material, the possibility of religious practices involving wild cattle leading to the use of cattle as the servant of man[69].

The introduction of cattle into village-farming and town-farming economy may have caused some important cultural changes, although not necessarily immediately. Cattle were the first domestic animals capable of pulling a plough. The earliest representations of ploughs are from Warka IV (I am quoting Isaac), *c*. 5200 ? B.P.[70] The question is, how much earlier were ploughs

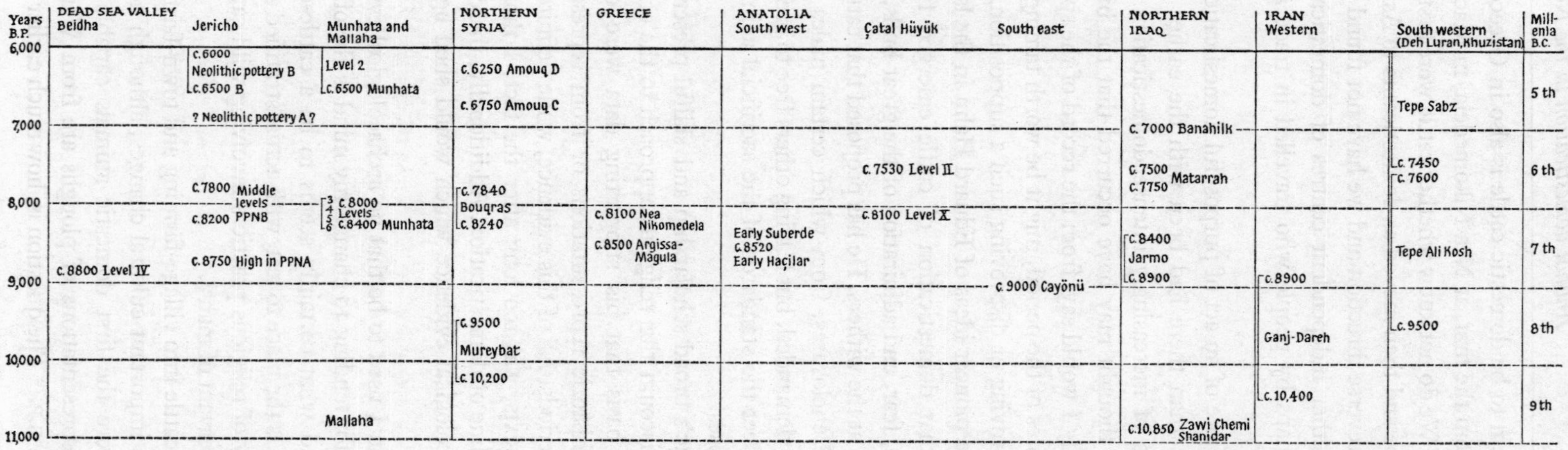

Years B.P.	DEAD SEA VALLEY Beidha / Jericho	Munhata and Mallaha	NORTHERN SYRIA	GREECE	ANATOLIA South west	Çatal Hüyük	South east	NORTHERN IRAQ	IRAN Western	SOUTH WESTERN (Deh Luran, Khuzistan)	Millennia B.C.
6,000	c.6000 Neolithic pottery B c.6500 B	Level 2 c.6500 Munhata	c.6250 Amouq D c.6750 Amouq C							Tepe Sabz	5th
7,000	? Neolithic pottery A?					c.7530 Level II		c.7000 Banahilk c.7500 Matarrah c.7750			6th
8,000	c.7800 Middle levels c.8200 PPNB	c.8000 3-4 Levels c.8400 Munhata 5-6	c.7840 Bouqras c.8240	c.8100 Nea Nikomedeia c.8500 Argissa-Maghula	Early Suberde c.8520 Early Haçilar	c.8100 Level X		c.8400 Jarmo c.8900	c.8900	c.7450 c.7600 Tepe Ali Kosh	7th
9,000	c.8750 High in PPNA c.8800 Level IV		c.9500 Mureybat				c.9000 Çayönü		c.9500 Ganj-Dareh	c.9500	8th
10,000		Mallaha	c.10,200						c.10,400		9th
11,000								c.10,850 Zawi Chemi Shanidar c.10,900			

Fig 1 Chronological chart for sites mentioned in the text. All C-14 determinations have been calculated on the basis of a half-life of 5570 years.

intensively used? Lacking remains of ploughs, which were wooden, archaeologists might well look for changes in settlement-patterns and for possible population increases after the domestication of cattle. These changes could have been initiated by more intensive cultivation following the introduction of the plough. Possibly too some evidence of stables, not so necessary for the smaller artiodactyls, will be found coincident with the appearance of cattle. Today amongst some of the mountain nomads of south-western Asia, cattle are used as pack animals. Is there any archaeological evidence of increased volume of trade after the appearance of cattle?

As mentioned, domestic cattle are found later in south-western Asia than are sheep and goats. The first known Asiatic domestic cattle, those reported from Tepe Sabz at Deh Luran in Iranian Khuzistan[71], may have been as early as 7450 B.P. Another early date is for the site of Banahilk, a Halafian site in the mountains of northern Iraq, as I stated in 1961[72]. The date of Banahilk is *c.* 7000 B.P.[73] Stampfli[74] could not find any evidence of domestic cattle at Jarmo or Matarrah, and in the 'Amuq sequence near Antioch he cannot discern domestic cattle prior to Phase C, and then only tentatively. Only with Phase D (*c.* 6200 B.P.) does he find definite evidence of domestic cattle.

Thus the problem of the origin and spread of domestic cattle, as with other problems in the prehistory of south-western Asia, presents us with a mystery. The cattle are found first in Greece, and then in far-distant Khuzistan, and then in northern Iraq, but not until later on the eastern Mediterranean coast. However, numerous Anatolian sites (Hacilar, Çatal Hüyük, Suberde) have sequences in the time range of that of the early cattle in Greece. From Suberde, at least, some 25,000 bones were salvaged[75], and the study of these and of the bones from other Anatolian sites should do much to unravel the mysteries of early domestication of cattle in south-western Asia[76].

Notes

1 Harlan, J. R. and Zohary, D. (1966). Distribution of wild wheats and barley, *Science*, **153**, pp. 1074–80; Zohary, D., this volume, pp. 47–66.

2 Radulesco, C. and Samson, P. (1962). Sur un centre de domestication du mouton dans le Mesolithique de la grotte "La Adam" en Dobrogea, *Z. Tierzücht ZüchtBiol*, **76**, pp. 282–320.

3 Wright, H. E., Jr. (1961). Pleistocene glaciation in Kurdistan, *Eiszeitalter und Gegenwart*, **12**, pp. 131–64.

4 Wright, H. E., Jr. (1968). Natural environment of early food production north of Mesopotamia, *Science*, **161**, pp. 334–9.

5 Garrod, D. A. E. (1957). The Natufian culture: The life and economy of Mesolithic people in the Near East, *Proc. Brit. Acad.*, **43**, pp. 211–27.

6 Perrot, J. (1966). Le gisement Natoufien de Mallaha (Eynan), Israël, *L'Anthropologie*, **70**, pp. 437–83.

7 Solecki, R. L. (1964). Zawi Chemi Shanidar, a post-Pleistocene village

site in northern Iraq, *Rep. VIth Inter. Congr. Quaternary, Warsaw, 1961,* **IV,** pp. 405–12.

8 Young, T. C., Jr. and Smith, P. E. L. (1966). Research in the pre-history of central western Iran, *Science,* **153,** pp. 386–91; The site of Ganj-Dareh Tepe, on the "inner" (north-eastern) side of the Zagros range, would seem to have been too early, some ten thousand five hundred years ago, and at too high an altitude, which implies harsh winter cold at that period, to have been a permanent village with definite house-walls. The earliest carbon 14 determination may be found to be erroneous, or— we will have to change our minds as to what is right and proper for pre-historic peoples to have done. We have had to change before.

9 The Natufian "dog", which had become firmly entrenched in some books and monographs, was shown, independently, by Clutton-Brock, J. (1962). Near Eastern canids and the affinities of the Natufian dog, *Z. Tierzücht ZüchtBiol.,* **76,** pp. 326–33; and Reed, C. A. (1961). Osteological evidences for prehistoric domestication in south-western Asia, *Z. Tierzücht ZüchtBiol.,* **76,** pp. 31–8, to be within the range of variation of the local Palestinian wolf.

10 Perkins, D., Jr. (1964). Prehistoric fauna from Shanidar, Iraq, *Science,* **144,** pp. 1565–6.

11 I use dates in B.P. (Before Present), in preference to the common practice of stating them as B.C. (Before Christ), because the latter usage indicates to most people an accuracy and validity which we cannot yet know in pre-historic studies. The "radiocarbon year" is not necessarily the same length as the calendric year, being sometimes longer and sometimes shorter. There is considerable literature on this subject which I have summarized (1966). Organic remains from the Yale University Nubian Expedition's archaeological sites DI-21B and WO-2A, with a discussion of the radio-carbon determinations, *Postilla, Yale Peabody Museum,* **102,** pp. 35–46, for myself and others who do not understand everything published in journals of geophysics.

12 van Zeist, W. and Wright, H. E., Jr. (1963). Preliminary pollen studies at Lake Zeribar, Zagros Mountains, south-western Iran, *Science,* **140,** pp. 65–7; Wright, H. E., Jr. (1966). Stratigraphy of lake sediments and the precision of the palaeoclimatic record, in *Royal Meteorological Society Proceedings of the International Symposium on World Climate from 8000 to 0 B.C.* London. pp. 157–73; Wright, H. E., Jr., McAndrews, J. H. and van Zeist, W. (1967). Modern pollen rain in western Iran, and its relation to plant geography and Quaternary vegetational history, *J. Ecology,* **55,** pp. 415–43; Megard, R. O. (1967). Late-Quaternary Cladocera of Lake Zeribar, western Iran, *Ecology,* **48,** pp. 179–89; van Zeist, W. (1967). Late Quaternary vegetation history of western Iran, *Rev. Palaeobot. and Palynol.,* **2,** pp. 301–11.

13 The proposal that a period of rapid climatic change coincided with, and may have had some stimulating effect on, the change from hunting and gathering cultures to early agricultural and/or herding ones runs counter to the thought of the past fifteen years that relatively little climatic change had occurred in most of south-western Asia at the close of the Pleistocene. As one of the proponents (Reed, C. A. and Braidwood, R. J. (1960). Toward the reconstruction of the environmental sequence in north-eastern Iraq, *Studies in Ancient Oriental Civilization,* **31,** pp. 163–73) of that theory, I do wish to call attention to the fact that Braidwood and I stated that the mammalian fossils upon which we were then basing our conclusions would not be as accurate palaeoclimatic indicators as would pollen, when and if a pollen record could be found. It has now, with much supporting evidence. I, for one, bow to Lake Zeribar, although I have no intention of reviving any suggestion of the desiccation theory of

animal domestication. For a list of references to the recent theory of climatic continuity in south-western Asia, see Hole, F. (1966). Investigating the origins of Mesopotamian civilization, *Science*, 153, pp. 605–11, footnote 8. I agree with Hole that true urbanization probably was little influenced by any climatic changes, although obviously such an early site as Jericho may now be more explicable than some of us have found it priorly, on the basis that the climate during the Pre-Pottery periods (A and B) was probably cooler, even if not wetter than it is today.

14 Vignard, E. (1923). Une nouvelle industrie lithique, le "Sebilien", *Bull. Inst. fran. Arch. orient.*, 22, pp. 1–76, pl. XIV bis; Reed, C. A., Baumhoff, M. A., Butzer, K. W. Walter, H. and Boloyan, D. S. (1967). Preliminary report on the archaeological aspects of the research of the Yale University Prehistoric Expedition to Nubia, 1962–3, *Antiq. Dept. Egypt, Fouille en Nubie, (1961–1963)*, pp. 145–56; Butzer, K. W. and Hansen, C. L. (1968). *Desert and River in Nubia*. Madison, particularly pp. 135–6 and 170–2.

15 Clark, J. D. (1965). The later Pleistocene cultures of Africa, *Science*, 150, pp. 833–47.

16 Maguire, B. (1965). Foreign pebble pounding artifacts in the breccias and the overlying vegetation soil at Makapansgat Limeworks, *S. Afr. Arch. Bull.*, 20, pp. 117–30; Dart, R. A. (1965). Pounding as a process and the producer of other artifacts, *S. Afr. Arch. Bull.*, 20, pp. 141–7.

17 Zeuner, F. E. (1963). *A History of Domesticated Animals*. London. pp. 1–560.

18 Moir, R. J. (1965). The comparative physiology of ruminant-like animals, *in* Dougherty, R. W. *et al* (eds.) *Physiology of Digestion in the Ruminant*. Washington.

19 Cottrell, F. (1955). *Energy and Society*. New York. p. 20.

20 Zeuner, F. E. (1963). ibid.

21 The field experiments of Harlan, J. R. (1967). A wild wheat harvest in Turkey, *Archaeology*, 20, pp. 197–201. indicate the necessity of having a somewhat permanent place of living once harvesting of cereals had become common. Working in south-western Turkey where wild einkorn wheat grew densely, Harlan used a prehistoric flint sickle and harvested the equivalent of two pounds or more of clean grain per hour. In the three-week period typically available for such harvesting of wild wheats a family could have gathered enough seed to last them for a year. With some 330–50 pounds of grain per person (equal to a ton or more for a family of six), the harvesters were obviously going to have to store their newly-gained food and to stay around to protect and eat it. The first simple villages may have grown up around such storage places.

22 van Loon, M. N. (1966). Mureybat: An early village in inland Syria, *Archaeology*, 19, pp. 215–16; van Loon, M. N. (1966). The Euphrates Valley Expedition, *Report for 1965–66*, The Oriental Institute, Univ. of Chicago, pp. 17–22; de Contenson, H. (1966). Découvertes récentes dans le domaine du Néolithique en Syrie, *L'Anthropologie*, 70, pp. 388–91.

23 Perrot, J. (1967). Munhata, *Bible et Terre Saint*, 93, pp. 4–16; also Personal communication.

24 Ducos, P. (1965). Contribution à l'étude de l'histoire de la domestication: etude des faunes post-paléolithiques de Palestine, du Mésolithique à l'Age du Bronze. *Thèse de Doctorat de Sciences de l'Université de Bordeaux*. pp. 1–324. (I have not seen the original of this thesis, but Dr. Ducos very kindly sent me an extended summary of his results; Ducos, P., this volume, pp. 265–75.

25 Helbaek, H. (1966). Pre-Pottery Neolithic farming at Beidha, *Palestine Exploration Quarterly*, Jan.–June 1966, pp. 61–6; Helbaek, H. (1966).

Commentary on the phylogenesis of *Triticum* and *Hordeum*, *Econ. Bot.*, **20**, pp. 350–60.

26 Perkins, D., Jr. (1966). The fauna from Madamagh and Beidha, *Palestine Exploration Quarterly*, Jan.–June 1966, pp. 66–7.

27 Hopf, M., this volume, pp. 355–9.

28 Zeuner, F. E. (1955). The goats of early Jericho, *Palestine Exploration Quarterly*, 1955, pp. 70–86.

29 Ducos, P. (1966). Los huesos de animales, *in* Gonzales-Etchegarroy, J. *Excavacions en le Terrazee le El Khiem* (*Jordania*), **2**.

30 Hopf, M., this volume, ibid.

31 Reed, C. A. (1959). Animal domestication in the prehistoric Near East, *Science*, **130**, pp. 1629–39; Reed, C. A. (1960). A review of the archaeological evidence on animal domestication in the prehistoric Near East, *in* Braidwood, R. J. and Howe, B. Prehistoric Investigations in Iraqi Kurdestan, *Studies in Ancient Oriental Civilization*, Oriental Institute, Chicago, **31**, pp. 119–45, Fig. 7.

32 Schenkel, R. (1967). Submission: Its features and function in the wolf and dog, *Amer. Zool.*, **7**, pp. 319–29; Kleiman, D. G. (1967). Some aspects of social behaviour in the Canidae, *Amer. Zool.*, **7**, pp. 365–72; Scott, J. P. (1967). The evolution of social behaviour in dogs and wolves, *Amer. Zool.*, **7**, pp. 373–81.

33 Woolpy, J. H. and Ginsberg, B. E. (1967). Wolf socialization: A study of temperament in a wild social species, *Amer. Zool.*, **7**, pp. 357–63.

34 I can testify to the truth of this innate friendliness of young wolves, as I once handled four of them in northern Iraq; their parents had been killed by a Kurdish hunter, who was taking the young to Kirkuk to be sold. (Such practices, even though uncommon, must inject a certain minimum of genes from wolves into the population of Iraqi dogs.) The pups—appealing balls of fur some four or five weeks old—were all friendliness with no sign of distrust in spite of having been separated from home and parents, carried for some hours in a bag, and then dumped out helter-skelter on the ground. One had lost a forepaw when captured, but not even such an injury evoked hostility.

35 Fentress, J. C. (1967). Observations on the behavioral development of a hand-reared male timber wolf, *Amer. Zool.*, **7**, pp. 339–51.

36 Woolpy, J. H. and Ginsberg, B. E. (1967). ibid.

37 Scott, J. P. (1967). ibid.

38 Adamson, J. (1960). *Born Free, a Lioness of Two Worlds*. New York. pp. 1–220.

39 Fentress, J. C. (1967). ibid.

40 Degerbøl, M. (1961). On a find of a pre-boreal domestic dog (*Canis familiaris* L.) from Star Carr, Yorkshire, with remarks on other Mesolithic dogs, *Proc. Prehist. Soc.*, **27**, pp. 35–55.

41 Lawrence B. (In press). Evidences of animal domestication at Çayönü, *Bull. Turkish Hist. Soc.*

42 Lawrence, B. (1967). Early domestic dogs, *Z. Sauget.*, **32**, pp. 44–59.

43 Reed, C. A. (1961). ibid.

44 Lawrence, B. (In press). ibid.; Lawrence, B. (1967). ibid.

45 Braidwood, R. J. (1966). The Prehistoric Project, *Report for 1956/66*, The Oriental Institute, Univ. of Chicago, pp. 24–6.

46 Reed, C. A. (1961). ibid.

47 Zeuner, F. E. (1958). Dog and cat in the Neolithic of Jericho, *Palestine Exploration Quarterly*, 1958, pp. 52–5.

48 Clutton-Brock, J., this volume, pp. 337–45.

49 Mellaart, J. (1967). *Çatal Hüyük: A Neolithic town in Anatolia*. New York. pl. 57.

50 Stampfli, H. R. (1966). The fauna of the prehistoric archaeological sites of

Jarmo, Matarrah, Karim Shahir, and the Amouq in south-western Asia. (Manuscript to be published by the Oriental Institute, Univ. of Chicago.)
51 Flannery, K. V. (1961). Skeletal and radiocarbon evidence for the start and spread of pig domestication. *Thesis for the degree of Master of Arts, Dept. of Anthropology, Univ. of Chicago.*
52 Lawrence, B. (In press). ibid.
53 Perkins, D., Jr. (1964). ibid.
54 Lawrence, B. (In press). ibid.
55 Stampfli, H. R. (1966). ibid.
56 Higgs, E. S. (1967). Early domesticated animals in Libya, *in* Bishop, W. W. and Clark, J. D. (eds.) *Background to Evolution in Africa.* Chicago. pp. 165–73.
57 Prehistoric people often did diabolic things which thwart modern prehistorians.
58 Perkins, D., Jr. (1966). ibid.
59 Darwish M. Al-Far, a Bedouin from Sinai who is now an Egyptian geologist, has told me that modern Bedouins often drive sheep from the interior of Sinai to towns along the Suez Canal to sell them. Additionally he stated that, following winters and springs with more than average precipitation, the crossing of the whole of Sinai on foot with flocks of sheep and goats would present no trouble.
60 Stampfli, H. R. (1966). ibid.
61 Hole, F., Flannery, K. V. and Neely, J. (1965). Early agriculture and animal husbandry in Deh Luran, Iran, *Current Anthropology*, **6**, pp. 105–6; Flannery, K. V., this volume, pp. 73–100.
62 Perkins, D., Jr. (1966). ibid.
63 Hole, F., Flannery, K. V. and Neely, J. (1965). ibid.; Flannery, K. V. this volume, ibid.
64 Zeuner, F. E. (1955). ibid.
65 Boessneck, J. (1962). Die Tierreste aus der Argissa-Magula vom präkeramischen Neolithikum bis zur mittleren Bronzezeit. In Milojcic, V., Boessneck, J. and Hopf, M., *Die Deutschen Ausgrabungen auf der Argissa-Magula in Thessalien*, **I**. Beiträge zur ur- und frühgeschichtlichen Archaeologie des Mittelmeer-Kulturraumes, **2**, pp. 37–99. (Not seen; quoted from Stampfli.)
66 Higgs, E. S. (1962). Excavations at the early Neolithic site at Nea Nikomedeia, Greek Macedonia (1961 season). Part II. The biological data: Fauna, *Proc. Prehist. Soc.*, **28**, pp. 271–4, Fig. 3.
67 Isaac, E. (1962). On the domestication of cattle, *Science*, **137**, pp. 195–204.
68 Mellaart, J. (1967). ibid.
69 Additionally, Ducos (1966). ibid., has suggested that the goats which he thinks to have been domestic at El Khiam, in southern Palestine, had been killed as part of a sacrificial rite. The majority of the goat bones were from animals only a month old, and the long bones, delicate at that young age, often remained unbroken, as if the animals had not been eaten.
70 Ehrich, R. W. (ed.) (1965). *Chronologies in Old World Archaeology.* Chicago. pp. 1–557.
71 Hole, F., Flannery, K. V. and Neely, J. (1965). ibid.
72 Reed, C. A. (1961). ibid.
73 Ehrich, R. W. (1965). ibid.
74 Stampfli, H. R. (1966). ibid.
75 Bordaz, J. (1966). Anatolian Research Project, Suberde excavations: Preliminary report, *New York Univ., Dept. of Classics, Bull.*, **66–2**, pp. 1–3.
76 My field work in south-western Asia was initiated and thereafter encouraged by Professor Robert Braidwood of the Oriental Institute, University of Chicago. To him, and his financial sponsors, I am most grateful. My own ideas develop slowly, and indeed may often be borrowed

from others without memory of the original source. Both in the field in the Nearer Orient and at many conferences and random meetings in the United States I have discussed the problems of Near Eastern prehistory with Robert and Linda Braidwood, Bruce Howe, Herbert Wright, Patty Jo Watson, Barbara Lawrence, Hans Helbaek, Jack Harlan, Frank Hole, Kent Flannery, Dexter Perkins and many others.

RUTH TRINGHAM

Animal domestication in the Neolithic cultures of the south-west part of European U.S.S.R.

My aim in this paper is to present analyses of the animal bone material from a number of early prehistoric sites in the south-western part of the U.S.S.R., since these are only rarely available to research workers in this country (Figs. 4 and 5); I have also tried to indicate their archaeological context (Figs. 1 and 2). I have not attempted, however, to put forward or support any claims for early independent domestication of any animals.

It may be said for certain that the forest/steppe and steppe north of the Black Sea in the Ukraine and Moldavian republics is, so far, the region where domesticated animals first occur on prehistoric sites in the U.S.S.R., apart from the settlements of the Džeitun culture in Turkmenia in central Asia. This was probably a result predominantly of the early prehistoric settlements of this region being closest to the early agricultural settlements of south-east Europe, although it seems from the early post-glacial period to have been an area rich in wild pigs in particular, and also wild cattle.

In this region a number of claims have been put forward by Soviet archaeologists for the possible evidence especially in the Crimea and Moldavia for an early independent development of domestication of animals before the introduction of pottery manufacture, for what may be termed an "aceramic neolithic" culture. However, before the north Pontic aceramic neolithic sites are accepted as indubitable proof of an early centre of animal domestication, it should be questioned firstly whether the sites are as early as they have been claimed; that is, earlier than the introduction of a productive agricultural economy from western Asia to south-east Europe, as represented in the Karanovo I/Starčevo/Körös/Criş group of cultures; and secondly whether the animal bones show definite traces of domestication.

This applies particularly to the claims for very early domesticated pigs in the cave sites of the south Crimean mountains: Taš Ayir and Zamil Koba[1]. Both caves have late palaeolithic material at the base, overlain by two mesolithic strata, the earlier referred to as the "Crimean Azilian" industry, and the later as the "Crimean Tardenoisian" industry. Above these are two neolithic layers, the lower with a few shreds of coarse undercoated pottery

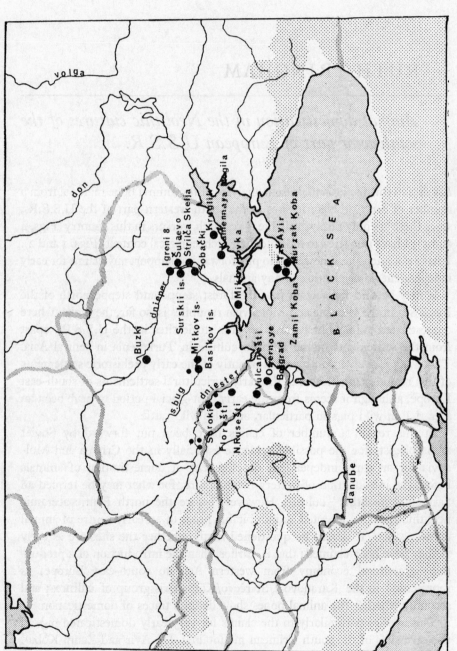

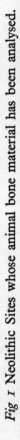

Fig 1 Neolithic Sites whose animal bone material has been analysed.

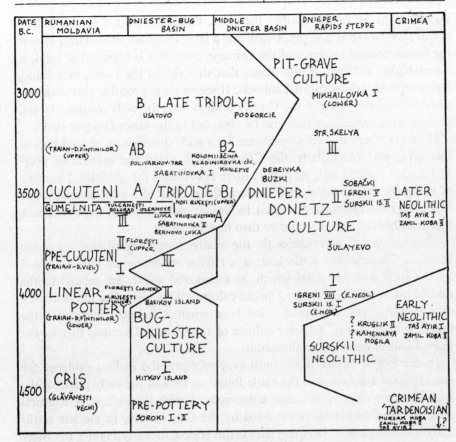

Fig 2 Cultural contexts of the sites referred to in the text.

similar to the Kukreks ware of north Crimea, and the upper representing a culture very similar to the middle phase of the Dnieper–Donetz culture of the lower and middle Dnieper basins, and may be compared to such sites as Buzki and Vovnigi. The flint blade industry of both neolithic layers continues the traditions of the preceding mesolithic layers. Above the neolithic strata, are layers representing cultures from the Bronze Age to the mediaeval period. A large number of pig bones have been found in all but the two uppermost layers. Even in the earliest layers domesticated, as well as wild and undistinguishable immature, animals have been identified.

It is worth noting, however, the difficulty in distinguishing between wild and domesticated pigs, since they are easily domesticated and as easily revert to the wild state[2]. In the Soviet Union, the distinction is made especially on a basis of size, the larger animals being identified as wild, and the smaller animals as domesticated[3]. Moreover, it has been noted that the wild pigs excavated in the upper palaeolithic cave settlements were small animals compared with the large wild pigs of the later, neolithic layers[4]. As mentioned above, in these latter layers, the smaller animals have been identified as domesticated. It seems possible, therefore, that there existed in the Crimea at this time two strains of pig, a small and a large one, both wild. Thus, even if the stratigraphical evidence of the Crimean cave-sites is regarded as valid, it seems highly unlikely, at this stage, that the pigs in the lower, mesolithic, layers represent domesticated animals. It seems more probable that domesticated pigs do not occur in the Crimea until at least the early neolithic layers, or even later, when they may also be observed in the lower Dnieper basin.

However, there is definite evidence for a wide distribution of wild pigs in this area, and particularly the Crimea itself, since the immediate post-Pleistocene period; and, moreover, there is evidence for specialized hunting of wild pigs during this period. In fact, the process of a local domestication of pigs in the Crimea, as described by Stoljar, may very well have occurred, but probably at a rather later date than he envisaged[5].

There is, as yet, no evidence for the relative chronological position of the Crimean Tardenoisian settlements apart from an *ante quem* date provided by the later neolithic dates which, as mentioned above, are related to the middle phase of the Dnieper–Donetz culture[6]. This phase, by the discovery of a Tripolye pot at Nikolskii, has been equated chronologically with the middle phase of the Tripolye culture of the western Ukraine; that is, the second half of the fourth millennium.

In the Bug–Dniester basin, until very recently, the earliest evidence for domesticated animals were the cattle found on sites of the early phase of the Bug–Dniester culture, at a time contemporary with the earliest agricultural settlements of Rumania, represented by the Criş culture, in the late sixth/early fifth millennium. On many sites in this region, the early phase of the Bug–Dniester culture was preceded by what was termed an "aceramic neolithic" culture, quite unjustifiably since there was no evidence for the domestication of any plants or animals; however, its geometric microlithic blade industry, which seems typologically related to the Crimean Tardenoisian flint industry, quite clearly provided the antecedents for the flint blade industry of the early phase of the Bug–Dniester culture. Recently, however, in the lower levels of two stratified sites in Moldavia, Soroki (Trifautski les land 2), the bones of domesticated, as well as wild, pig, have been found in association with this mesolithic or "aceramic neolithic" industry and dated by carbon-14 to the late sixth millennium B.C., earlier than any dates yet obtained from the earliest agricultural settlements of south-east Europe, even of Bulgaria[7].

However, it should be noted that in the later phases of the locally-developed Bug–Dniester culture, bones from domesticated pigs have not been identified[8]. It is conceivable, therefore, that the same situation as that observed in the Crimea may also exist in the Bug–Dniester basin.

An independent development of cattle-breeding in the Ukraine was claimed for the north Pontic steppe, but this is even more dubious. In the lowest layers of the stratified site of Kamennaya Mogila, north-west of the Sea of Azov, in two aceramic layers, levels I–III and IV–V, again in association with

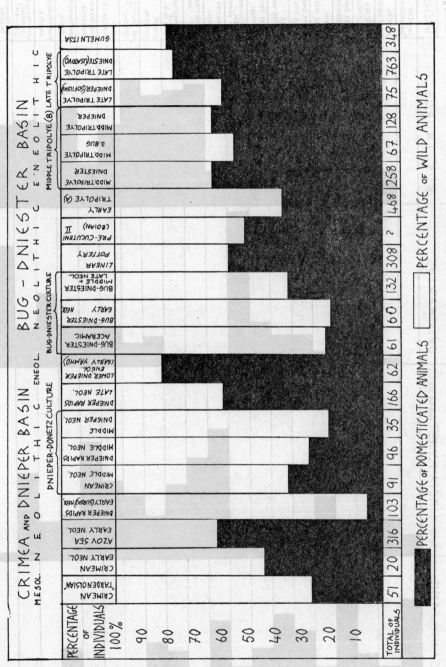

Fig 3 Percentages of individuals in the animal bone material of the early prehistoric sites of S.W. European U.S.S.R.

(See *Fig 4* for sites included.)
Sus scrofa L. is included in the percentages of domesticated animals of the Crimean sites.

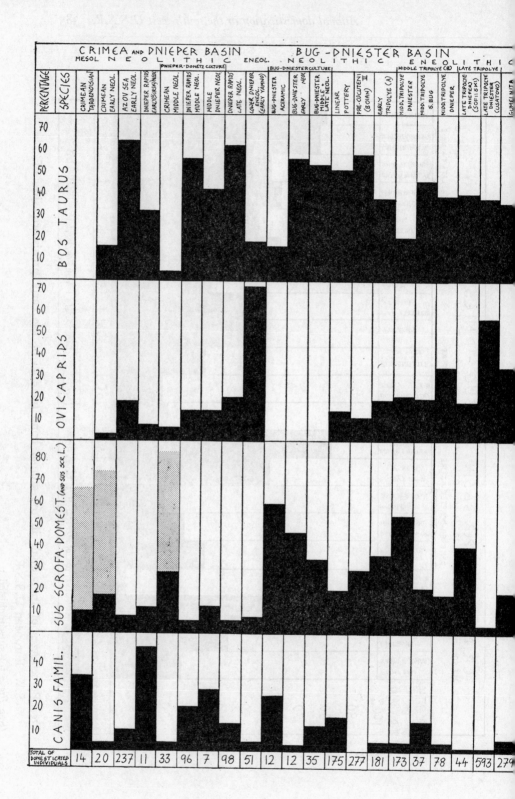

the local geometric microlithic blade industry, a large number of cattle bones have been excavated and claimed by Pidopličko as belonging to domesticated animals[9]. Ovicaprid bones, likewise claimed as domesticated, are also present in relatively large numbers. Danilenko has suggested that the aceramic layers at Kamennaya Mogila are at least as early as the Crimean Tardenoisian sites and that their evidence indicates a centre for the initial development of cattle breeding in the lower Don basin, immediately west of the Sea of Azov, although no sites of this kind, apart from Kamennaya Mogila, have yet been discovered[10]. He moreover suggests that it was the westwards spread of cattle breeding from this region which caused the increase in cattle breeding in the later neolithic cultures of south-east Europe and its introduction to central temperate Europe in the Linear Pottery cultures. Most other Soviet archaeologists, however, deny this possibility and prefer one of two alternatives: either the so-called domesticated cattle bones do not belong to the aceramic layers but to later levels, since originally the different levels were not distinguished by Pidopličko in his analysis; or the aceramic levels are not as early as they have been claimed, but are contemporary with the Dnieper–Donetz culture, where domesticated cattle often occur[11].

The earliest more conclusive evidence for cattle domestication in Moldavia and the Ukraine is that associated with the early phase of the Bug–Dniester culture, as seen in the animal bone material from Mitkov island on the Dniester[12]. This culture bordered directly on the distributional area of the Criş culture which spread to Rumanian Moldavia from the Danube basin in the early fifth millennium. The animal bone material from the Criş site of Glăvăneşti Vechi shows a predominance of domestic cattle, with rather less domesticated ovicaprids and very few pigs[13].

Sites of the Criş culture have not yet been discovered east of the Prut river, but a certain amount of contact with the Criş settlements is observable in the early phase of the Bug–Dniester culture[14]. No other domesticated animals

---

Fig 4 Percentages of individuals among the domesticated animals of the early prehistoric sites of S.W. European U.S.S.R.

The sites included are: 1. Crimean Tardenoisian: Murzak Koba, Zamil Koba II, Taš Ayir I; 2. Crimean early neolithic: Zamil Koba II, Taš Ayir I; 3. Azov Sea early neol.: Kruglik, Kamennaya Mogila I–III; 4. Dnieper Rapids early neol.: Surski is. I, Igreni VIII, Sulayevo; 5. Crimean middle neol.: Zamil Koba II, Taš Ayir I; 6. Dnieper Rapids middle neol.: Sobački is. II, Igreni V; 7. Middle Dnieper middle neol.: Buzki; 8. Dnieper Rapids late neol.: Strelča Skelya; 9. Lower Dnieper eneolithic (early pit grave culture): Mikhailovka I (lower layer); 10. Bug-Dniester culture, aceramic phase: Soroki 1:2, Soroki 2:2 and 3; 11. Bug-Dniester culture, early phase: Soroki 1:1b, Soroki 2:1, Soroki 3, Mitkov is.; 12. Bug-Dniester culture, middle and late phases: Soroki 1:1a, Basikov is., Soroki 5, Tsikinovka I; 13. Linear Pottery culture: Novia Ruseşti I, Floreşti (lower layer), (Tsira); 14. Pre-Cucuteni II: Floreşti (upper layer); 15. Tripolye A (early Tripolye): Luka Vrublevetskaya, Bernovo Luka; 16. Middle Tripolye (Dniester): Polivanov Yar; 17. Middle Tripolye (southern Bug): Sabatinovka I; 18. Middle Tripolye (Dnieper): Kolemiiščina II, Khalepye; 19. Late Tripolye (middle Dnieper): Podgorcie; 20. Late Tripolye (lower Dniester): Usatovo; 21. Gulmeniţa culture: Bolgrad, Ozernoye, Vulcaneşti.
Sus scrofa L. is included in the percentages of domesticated animals of the Crimean sites and is shown by lighter shading in the appropriate column.

apart from cattle and dogs have yet been found in the settlements of this phase. Nor have they been found in the sites of the middle phase of the Bug–Dniester culture as seen in the animal bone material from Basikov island on the Dniester river[15].

The middle phase of the Bug–Dniester culture has been shown to be contemporary with the Linear Pottery culture of the Ukraine and Moldavia whose settlements are distributed in the forest/steppe of the upper Dniester basin, generally rather north and west of those of the Bug–Dniester culture[16]. The material of the Dniester basin Linear Pottery settlements is very closely related to that of the central European Linear Pottery sites, as seen at Bylany[17], especially to the late phase of this culture which has been dated by the carbon-14 method to 4100–3900 B.C. The bone analyses from the lower layers at Floresti[18] and Novi Ruseşti[19] in Soviet Moldavia, and Traian (Dealul Fintinilor) in Rumanian Moldavia[20], show a definite increase in the proportion of wild animals as compared with that of the central European Linear Pottery settlements, although this proportion is nevertheless considerably smaller than that of the wild animals in the Bug–Dniester settlements (Fig. 3). Among the domestic animal bones, cattle predominate (at Floreşti, 93% of these belong to the long-horned variety), pig are of rather less importance, whereas ovicaprids are almost negligible (Fig. 4).

The later neolithic cultures which spread to Moldavia and the western part of the Ukraine from the Balkans, which were partly evolved from the Linear Pottery cultures but which also had very strong elements from the Danube basin, and which are referred to as the Pre-Cucuteni/Cucuteni–Tripolye complex, show a similar predominance of domesticated animals over wild ones (Fig. 3); the proportion of domesticated animals increases in the later phases, especially in the Dniester basin[21]. A similar increase may be observed in the extension of the more southern copper-using Gumelniţa culture, as at Bolgrad, Vulcaneşti and Ozernoye in the lower Dniester basin[22]. Domesticated cattle, ovicaprids, and pigs are present on all the sites of the Cucuteni/ Tripolye and Gumelniţa cultures, generally with cattle predominating although in the later Tripolye sites and Gumelniţa sites of the lower Dniester basin there is a marked increase in the importance of sheep (Fig. 4).

Further east in the middle and lower Dnieper basin, the sites of the Dnieper/Donetz culture, which in its middle phase is contemporary with the middle phase of the Tripolye culture, do not show such a high proportion of domesticated animals until the latest neolithic, as at Strelča Skelya[23] and especially the beginning of the pit-grave culture in the lower Dnieper steppes, as at Mikhailovka I[29]. On these latter sites a large increase and predominance of ovicaprids may be observed among the domesticated animals, similar to the eneolithic sites of the lower Dniester steppe at Usatovo and Sandraki[25].

Domesticated horses are attested among the animal bone material of the eneolithic sites of the lower Dnieper and Dniester steppes, and would seem

LATE MESOLITHIC AND EARLY NEOLITHIC SITES OF THE CRIMEA AND LOWER DNIEPER BASIN

The four numbers in each cell (where present) are, in order: (1) total number of bones; (2) percentage of bones; (3) number of individuals; (4) percentage of individuals.

Species	TAŞ AYIR I (Tardenoisian)	ZAMIL KOBA II (Tardenoisian)	MURZAK KOBA	TAŞ AYIR I (early neol.)	ZAMIL KOBA II (early neol.)	KAMENNAYA MOGILA I–III	KAMENNAYA MOGILA IV–V	SURSKII IS. I	IGREN VIII	KRUGLIK II	SULAYEVO
BOS TAURUS					1 / 0.2 / 1 / 3.1			4 / 0.8 / 2 / 1.94		38 / 61.3 / 3 / 25	7 / 1.1 / 1 / 1.62
CAPRA/OVIS					2 / 0.4 / 1 / 3.1					3 / 4.8 / 1 / 8.3	4 / 0.6 / 1 / 1.62
SUS SCROFA DOM.	35 / 24 / 2 / 16.4			24 / 13 / 4 / 18	7 / 1 / 2 / 6.2	136 / 16.8 / 48 / 15.8	8 / 4.3	2 / 0.4 / 1 / 0.97		3 / 4.8 / 1 / 8.3	
CANIS FAMILIARIS			4 / 4 / 2 / 9.5	3 / 0.24 / 3	3 / 1 / 1 / 3.1			2 / 0.4 / 1 / 0.97		2 / 3.2 / 1 / 8.3	8
EQUUS SP.						140 / 11.2 / 50 / 16.4	5 / 2.7				
CERVUS ELAPHUS	25 / 17 / 2 / 15.4	8 / 11 / 1 / 12.5	22 / 22 / 3 / 14.3	29 / 17 / 2 / 9	27 / 5 / 2 / 6.2	10 / 1.2		84 / 16.6 / 19 / 16.5	7 / 12 / 2 / 11.1	1 / 1.6 / 1 / 8.3	101 / 16.4 / 3 / 4.84
CAPREOLUS CAPR.	5 / 3 / 1 / 7.7	4 / 5 / 1 / 12.5	10 / 10 / 2 / 9.5	13 / 7 / 2 / 9	80 / 16 / 6 / 18.6	10 / 1.2			3 / 2.7 / 1 / 5.6	1 / 1.6 / 1 / 8.3	6 / 0.8 / 2 / 3.24
SUS SCROFA FERUS	17 / 12 / 1 / 7.7	9 / 12 / 3 / 33.5	10 / 10 / 3 / 14.3	26 / 15 / 4 / 18	60 / 12 / 4 / 12.4	19 / 1.5 / 10 / 3.3	1 / 0.54	15 / 2.96 / 4 / 3.9	1 / 1.78 / 1 / 5.6	1 / 1.6 / 1 / 8.3	1 / 0.2 / 1 / 1.62
URSUS (?ARCTOS)			1 / 1 / 1 / 4.8								
BOS PRIMIGENIUS	59 / 40 / 4 / 30.8			7.10 / 6 / 1 / 4.5		915 / 73.4 / 180 / 58.4	160 / 86.5	79 / 15.6 / 11 / 10.6	65 / 58 / 4 / 22.2	8 / 12.9 / 1 / 8.3	
SUS SCROFA L.		51 / 69 / 2 / 25		48 / 28 / 6	287 / 57 / 9 / 22.9		4 / 2.2				
CANIS LUPUS	1 / 1 / 1 / 12.5	1 / 1 / 1 / 12.5				1 / 0.1 / 1 / 0.33		20 / 4 / 8 / 7.7	2 / 1.78 / 2 / 11.1	1 / 1.6 / 1 / 8.3	18 / 2.9 / 2 / 3.24
VULPES VULPES	1 / 1 / 1 / 7.7		4 / 4 / 2 / 9.5			1 / 0.1 / 1 / 0.33		2 / 0.4 / 1 / 0.9	1 / 0.9 / 1 / 5.6		18 / 2.9 / 3 / 4.84
MELES MELES	2 / 1 / 1 / 4.8		2 / 2 / 1 / 4.8			3 / 0.2 / 2 / 0.66					3 / 0.5 / 2 / 3.24
FELIX SILVESTRIS	2 / 1 / 1 / 7.7		4 / 4 / 2 / 9.5								4 / 0.6 / 1 / 1.62
LEPUS EUROPAEUS	2 / 1 / 1 / 7.7				1 / 4.5 / 4 / 1	2 / 0.2 / 2 / 0.66	3 / 1.6	20 / 4 / 10 / 9.7	9 / 8 / 3 / 16.6	4 / 6.5 / 1 / 8.3	13 / 2 / 2 / 3.24
MARMOTA BOBAK											
MARTES FOINA						1 / 0.1 / 1 / 0.33	3 / 1.6				
CASTOR FIBER						7 / 0.7 / 2 / 0.66		1 / 0.2 / 1 / 0.9	3 / 2.7 / 3 / 16.6		1 / 0.2 / 1 / 1.62
SPALAX PODOLICUS						1 / 0.54					
LUTRA LUTRA											7 / 1.1 / 2 / 3.24
SILURIS GLANIS					17 / 3 / 4 / 12.4	5 / 0.4 / 2 / 0.66		142 / 28.2 / 28 / 27	16 / 1 / 5.6		120 / 19.4 / 14 / 22.6
EMYS ORBICULARIS								134 / 26.5 / 19 / 18.4			235 / 37.8 / 18 / 29
LYNX LYNX											
CRICETUS CRICETUS			30 / 30 / 4 / 19			3 / 0.2 / 1 / 0.33					
?OVIS SP.			12 / 12 / 1 / 4.8								
AVES								13 / 9	20 / 4		14 / 4
PISCES								2 / 1			52 / 3
TOTAL	146 / 13	73 / 8	99 / 21	173 / 22	488 / 32	1247 / 304	185	505 / 103	112 / 18	62 / 12	621 / 62
DOMESTIC ANIMALS	35 / 24 / 2 / 15.4	– / –	4 / 4 / 2 / 9.5	46 / 26 / 6 / 27	13 / 2.6 / 4 / 12.4	193 / 15.8 / 73 / 23.8	171 / 92.4	8 / 1.58 / 4 / 3.9	– / –	46 / 74 / 6 / 50	91 / 18 / 7 / 11.2
WILD ANIMALS	111 / 75 / 11 / 84.6	73 / 11 / 8 / 100	95 / 96 / 19 / 90.5	127 / 74 / 16 / 73	475 / 98.4 / 28 / 87.6	1054 / 84 / 231 / 76.2	14 / 7.6	493 / 98.2 / 99 / 96.1	100 / 18 / 100	16 / 26 / 6 / 50	510 / 82 / 55 / 88.8

Fig 5 Analyses of animal bones from late mesolithic and early neolithic sites of the Crimea and Lower Dnieper Basin.

The four columns of each site (from left to right) represent: (1) total number of bones of the species; (2) percentage of the total; (3) number of individuals represented by the total; (4) percentage of individuals. Grand totals apply only to mammals. *Sus scrofa* L. refers to immature animals aged from 5 weeks to 1 year which cannot be determined as definitely wild or domesticated and which have been classed together with the wild animals.

	MIDDLE AND LATER NEOLITHIC of the MIDDLE and LOWER DNIEPER BASIN																											BUG-DNIESTER NEOLITHIC								LINEAR POTTERY CULTURE							
	SURSKI IS. II				IGRENI V				TAŠ AYIR I (LATER NEOLITHIC)				SOBAČKI				BUZKI				STR. SKELYA				MIKHAILOVKA I (LOWER LAYER)				MITKOV IS. (EARLY NEOL.)				BASIKOV IS. (MIDDLE NEOL.)				NOVI RUSEŠTI I (LOWER LAYER)				FLOREŞTI (LOWER LAYER)			
BOS TAURUS	274	30	59	27.3	29	3.7	11	5.9	37	5	1	3.3	56	26	5	13.2	42	14.2	3	8.6	1058	60	357	21.7	18.6	9	14.5	?40	4.9	2	5.2	1090	38.2	58	23.5	231	44.2	26	37
CAPRA/OVIS	3	0.33	3	1.36						0.1			54	25	8	21	3	1.01	1	2.9	106	21	12	7.6	6.5	3	6.8					473	16.7	36	15.1				
SUS SCROFA DOM.	5	0.55	3	1.36					143	22	5	16.5	10	4.6	5	7.9	4	1.3	1	2.9	13	6	3.5	20	1.4	4	6.4					325	11.5	36	15.1	44	8.7	12	17
CANIS FAMILIARIS	19	2	10	4.5			1	5.9	5				9	4	3	7.9	8	2.7	2	5.7	35	11	6	3.5	0.4	2	3.2	4			0.4	18	0.6	5	2.1	23	4.5	4	5.7
EQUUS SP.	37	4	12	5.4					3		0.3	2	48	22	3	6.6					85			10	6	104			2	0.2	1	2.6	128	4.5	17	7.1				
CERVUS ELAPHUS	313	34	54		75	30.7	2	11.7	68	8	3	9.9	167	76	3	7.9	16	5.4	3	8.6	281	28	17.6		8.9	4	6.4	474	50.8	51	4	63.2	167	5.9	12	5.0	75	15	10	14.2
CAPREOLUS CAPR.	5	0.55	5		5	2.05			47	6	2	6.6					28	9.5	4	11.4	4	4	2.52					142	15.2	56	6.9	7	190	3.2	14	5.9				
SUS SCROFA FERUS	1	0.11	1	0.45	78	31.9	3	5.9	399	47	12	34.6	3	1.3	1	2.63	23	9.15	4	11.4	3	1.7	50		4.2	3	4.8	221	23.8	180	22.1	8	208	7.3	10	4.2	52	10	10	14.2
URSUS (? ARCTOS)	7	0.77	3	1.36	1	0.41	1	5.9			0.1																		6			0.6					27	0.9	5	2.1
BOS PRIMIGENIUS					11	4.5	1	5.9	2	10	6	1	3.3	2	0.09	1	2.63	1	0.34	1	2.9	5			2	1.16	4	0.3	1	1.6	17	1.92	235	8.3	18	7.6	92	17.6	8	11.4
ALCES ALCES																																		10	0.3	3	1.3				
CANIS LUPUS	9	0.99	5	2.25	1	0.41	1	5.9									1	0.34	1	2.9	2			2	1.16			3	0.3			3	3	27	0.9	6	2.5
VULPES VULPES	12	1.32	4	1.8									3		1.3													1			0.1			25	0.9	8	3.4
MELES MELES	2	0.22	1	0.45						0.1						3.3																1			0.1	2.6	32	1.1	6	2.5
FELIX SILVESTRIS	3	0.33	1	0.45	1	0.40	16.4	4	23.5	1		0.1				1		1.3	2	0.4	1	2.63											3	0.1	1	0.4
LEPUS EUROPAEUS	22	2.3	13	5.9	2	0.82	1	5.9	23	3	2	6.6	4	1.86	2.5	5.2	5	1.7	2	5.7	5	3	1.7									66	2.3	11	4.6
MARMOTA BOBAK																																								
MARTES FOINA																																		9	0.3	1	0.4
CASTOR FIBER	5	0.55	4	1.8									3	1.3	2	5.2	34	11.5	5	14.2	2	2	1.16					5	0.6	2	5.2	6	0.2	2	0.8
SPALAX PODOLICUS	1	0.11	1	0.45																																	
LUTRA LUTRA																					2				0.2												
SILURIS GLANIS	57	6.2	15	6.75									7	3.35	2	5.2					8	6	3.5									3	0.4	1	2.6
ENYS ORBICULARIS	45	4.9	24	10.8	22	9.05	2	11.7	2		0.9	2	5.2	126	42.6	8	22.2	15	4	4.52				2	0.2	2	5.2				
LYNX LYNX																																10	0.3	3	1.3
CRICETUS CRICETUS																																2	0.09	1	0.4
SAIGA TATARICA																						3	0.3			1	1.6								
BISON BONASUS																																13	0.5	4	1.7
AVES	30				2				67				2				6				17	9														
PISCES	58				11								5				1																			
TOTAL	911				244				784				275				295				1649	1166						815				2825				517	70		
DOMESTIC ANIMALS	301	36	75	34	14	5.75	2	11.8	232	27.1	6	20	129	60	19	50	57	19.5	7	20	1212	74.6	98	60	100	85.8	51	40	5	2	5.2	1896	67.1	133	55.8	298	57.7	42	59.7
WILD ANIMALS	522	64	145	66	230	94.2	15	88.2	552	72.9	24	80	86	40	19	50	239	80.5	28	80	420	254	68	40	164	14.2	11	775	95	36	948	929	32.9	105	432	219	42.3	28	40.3

Fig 6 Analyses of animal bones from the middle and late neolithic sites of S.W. European U.S.S.R. The four columns of each site (from left to right) represent: (1) total number of bones of the species; (2) percentage of the total; (3) number of individuals represented by the total; (4) percentage of individuals. Grand totals apply only to mammals.

to be earlier further east in the Dnieper basin if the evidence for domesticated horses from Dereivka[26] is valid; this site on the middle Dnieper, belonging to the middle phase of the Dnieper-Donetz culture, is contemporary with Tripolye BI on the Dniester where, so far, no domesticated horse bones have been excavated from this period. In Figs. 3–6, horses have been included with wild animals although, as has been mentioned above, those from Mikhailovka and the late Tripolye sites may be identified as domesticated animals.

Notes

1 Krainov, D. A. (1960). Peščernaya Stoyank Taš Ayir, kak osnova periodizatsii poslepaleolitičeskikh kultur Krima, *Materiali i Issledovaniya po Arkheologii*, **91**. Moscow.
2 Krainov, D. A. (1960). op. cit. pp. 131–3.
3 Dimitrieva, E. L. (1960). Fauna Krimskikh stoyanok Zamil Koba II i Taš Ayir I, *Mat. Issled Arch.*, **91**, pp. 166–87.
4 Dimitrieva, E. L. (1960). op. cit. p. 173.
5 Stoljar, A. D. (1959). Ob odnom ceentre odomašnivaniya svini, *Sov. Arkh.*, **3–4**, pp. 3–18.
6 Telegin, D. J. (1961). K voprosu o Dnepro-Donetskoi neolitičeskeikulture, *Sov. Arkh.*, **4**, p. 26; Telegin, D. J. (1967). Istoriya plemen Dnepre-Donetkulture (5th–3rd mill.), *Avtoreferat dissertat. na soisk. ucen. Doctora Ist. Nauk. Kiev.*
7 Markeyevič, V. I. (1965). Issledovania neolita na Srednem Dnestre, *Kratkiye Soobiščeniya Inst. Arkh.*, **105**, pp. 85–90. Moscow; Markeyevič, V. I. (1968). Neolit Moldavii, *Avtoreferat dissertat. na Kand. Ist. Nanka, Moscow.*
8 Bibikova, V. I. (1963). Iz istorii goletsenovoi fauni pozvonočnikh v Vostečnoi Evrope, *Prirodnaya obstanovka i fauni prošlovo I*, **132**, Kiev, pp. 119–47.
9 Pidopličko, I. G. (1956). *Materiale do Vivčeniya minulikh faun URSR.* Kiev. pp. 54–5; Danilenko, V. M. (1952). Priazovskaya ekspeditsiya 1947 g., *Arkh. Pam. URSR*, **4**, Kiev, pp. 67–9.
10 Danilenko, V. M. In discussion at Institute of Archaeology, Kiev, June 1967.
11 Telegin, D. J. (1967). ibid.
12 Bibikova, V. I. (1963). op. cit. p. 132.
13 Comša, E. (1959). La civilisation Criş sur le territoire de la R. P. Roumanie, *Acta Arch. Carpathica*, **1** (2), Kracow, pp. 173–84.
14 Passek, R. S. (1962). Relations entre l'Europe Occidentale et l'Europe Orientale à l'epoque néolithique, *Atti del Congrese ISPP*, Rome, pp. 126–44.
15 Bibikova, V. I. (1963). op. cit. p. 132.
16 Passek, T. S. (1962). ibid.; Passek, T. S. and Černyš, E. K. (1963). Pamyatniki kulturi linieno-lentočnoi keramiki na territorii SSSR, *Arkheologiya SSSR*, **B 1–2**, Moscow.
17 Soudsky, B. (1966). *Bylany.* Prague.
18 Passek, T. S. and Černyš, E. K. (1963). op. cit. pp. 31–2.
19 David, A. I. and Markeyevič, V. I. (1967). Fauna mlekopitayuščikh poselenia Noviye Rusešti I, *Izvestia Akademii Nauk Mold. SSSR*, **4**, Kišinev, pp. 3–26.
20 Necrasov, C. and Haimovici, S. (1962). Studiul restorilor de fauna

descoperite în 1959 la Traian (D. Vieii şi D. Fîntinilor), *Materiale*, **8**, Bucureşti, p. 262.
21 Passek, T. S. (1962). ibid.
22 Bibikova, V. I. (1963). ibid.
23 Pidopličko, I. G. (1956). op. cit. p. 14.
24 Passek, T. S. (1962). ibid.
25 Pidopličko, I. G. (1956). op. cit. pp. 33–5.
26 Bibikova, V. I. (1963). op. cit. pp. 14, 132.

WILLIAM WATSON

Early animal domestication in China

The bones of domestic animals (or of the animals susceptible of domestication) have been excavated on many neolithic sites, but not yet in sufficient quantities to allow inference as to regional differences or indicate conclusively a pattern of development in the various neolithic traditions. A detailed analysis of the animal remains is available for only one place, the Yang Shao culture site of Pan-p'o in south Shensi, other reports merely naming species by common terms and giving no statistical information.

By far the commonest of domestic animals are dogs and pigs, which are found at Yang Shao, Proto-Lung Shan and Lung Shan sites. Cattle and sheep/goats have also been identified at sites of each of these types, but are so rare as to leave the question of complete domestication in doubt[1]. There is no reliable report of horse associated with the Yang Shao, but a site in the Fen Ho valley of south Shensi, with pottery of Lung Shan type, contained bones of horse[2]. This site adjoins the upland area where the beginnings of horse-raising would naturally be looked for. In Manchuria horse has been identified in association with pottery of derived Yang Shao type, but of presumed later date than the Yang Shao culture of the Yellow River valley[3]. There are general indications from excavation that the proportions of sheep/goats and cattle is greater at sites of Lung Shan culture, where the scapulae of both are frequently found used in a method of divination. This would indicate the expected trend, the local domestication of these animals falling later than that of the dog and pig and contributing to the broad differentiation of the Yang Shao and the Lung Shan traditions.

The Kansu branch of the Yang Shao culture is now shown to be retarded by comparison with the development along the Wei River valley and the middle course of the Yellow River, and certainly continues in local variant forms as late as the beginning of the Bronze Age in the first half of the second millennium B.C. The appearance of a majority of sheep/goat bones at sites in Kansu therefore does not necessarily indicate priority over their appearance in Lung Shan context farther east, although the nature of the uplands of Kansu and adjacent regions to west and south-west being well suited to sheep raising (particularly in the conditions of greater warmth and rainfall indicated for the high neolithic period in north China), would incline one to look there for the earliest domestication[4]. At Huang-niang-t'ai in Kansu cattle bones were found as well as those of pig and sheep, but so far this association has been exceptional for the western branch of the Yang Shao culture[5].

At Pan-p'o in south Shensi, a large village site fully excavated and fully representative of the developed Yang Shao culture, all the domesticable species were present[6]. The domesticated pig was ubiquitous, its bones being found in nearly every one of the 200+ numbered features of the site. Nearly all the animals had been killed young, very few bones belonging to individuals estimated at more than one year of age. The skeletal characteristics fall within the range of wild *Sus scrofa*, but they do not come close to wild species surviving in China, so that there is no presumption in favour of local domestication. The dogs (six individuals identified) are small boned with raised forehead, so markedly different from *Canis lupus* that there can hardly be question of recent local domestication. Only three sheep were identified, with dental features suggesting close alliance to the *Ovis shangi* found at the Bronze Age capital of Anyang (*c.* 1650–1027 B.C.) and known as the Yin sheep. Indeterminate bovid and horse were represented by only one tooth apiece. The very small proportion of the last three specimens in the total of bones found at the site supports no more than the inference of a beginning of domestication, if that, and they can have played only a small part in the Yang Shao economy. The horse tooth resembles closely that of Przewalski's horse, to which are also related all the horses known in the pre-Han period and before the introduction of superior breeds from the far west.

Among the wild animals which were hunted by the Yan Shao farmers the spotted deer (*Pseudaxis hortularum*) was second only to the pig in frequency; it is identical with the deer still found wild in north, south and east China. The roebuck (hornless river deer, *Hydropotes inermis*), also sufficiently frequent to imply regular hunting for food, is identical with the surviving animal, which is now found only in the well-watered terrain on the lower Yangtze. Its presence at Pan-p'o implies a nearby terrain of pond and marsh, such as exists no longer, with surrounds of high grass, and a somewhat warmer climate than that at present experienced in the Yellow River valley. The bamboo rat (*Rhizomys sinensis*) is no longer to be found in the vicinity of Pan-p'o, and its ancient presence is a further indication of warmer weather, greater abundance of surface water and thickets of bamboo.

At Pan-p'o was found also evidence of a fowl (*Gallus* sp.) which may hint at a beginning of domestic poultry, but that inference needs confirmation. At a Lung Shan site in Hupei some pottery models of ducks and geese, accompanying others of sheep, dogs, turtles and fish, put domesticated fowl almost, but not quite, beyond question. It is perhaps to be expected that this step in animal husbandry should accompany the adoption or at least notable expansion in cattle and sheep raising which has been attributed to the Lung Shan culture and period.

Notes

1 Andersson, J. G. (1943). Prehistory of the Chinese, *Bull. Mus. Far Eastern Antiquities*, 15, p. 43; Bylin-Althin, M. (1946). Ch'i Chia P'ing and Lo Hant'ang, *Bull. Mus. Far Eastern Antiquities*, 18, p. 458; T'ung Chu-ch'ên (1957). The distribution and chronology of neolithic culture in the lower courses of the Yangtze and Yellow River, *K'ao ku hsüeh pao*, 2, pp. 7–21.

2 At the site of Kuang-shê; see Shou Tien (1957). Discovery of the neolithic site at Kuang-shê, *Wen wu ts'an k'ao tzŭ liao*, 1, pp. 57–9.

3 Hamada Kosaku and Mizuno Seiichi (1938). *Ch'ih-fêng, Hung-shan-hou*. Tokyo; Lü Tsun-ê (1958). Report of an archaeological reconnaissance at Hung-shan (Chih-fêng), Inner Mongolia, *K'ao ku hsüeh pao*, 3, pp. 25–40.

4 Kuo Tê-yung (1958). An archaeological reconnaissance in Wei-yüan hsien, Lung-hsia-hsien and Wu-shan hsien on the upper Wei river in Kansu province, *K'ao ku t'ung hsün*, 7, pp. 6–160; Kuo Tê-yung (1960). Report on excavations of the site of Huang-mang-mang-t'ai, in Wu-wei-hsien, Kansu province, *K'ao ku hsüeh pao*, 2, pp. 59–60; Chêng Nai-wu and Hsieh Tuan-chu (1960). A brief report of excavations at two sites of the Chi-Chia culture at Ho-chuang and Chin-wei in Lin-hsia, *K'ao ku*, 3, pp. 9–12.

5 Chang Yun-p'êng (1956). A short report of archaeological excavations at Ching-shan and T'ien-men in Hupei, *K'ao ku t'ung hsün*, 3, pp. 11–21.

6 Institute of Archaeology of the Academy of Sciences of China (1963). *Hsi-an Pan-p'o*. Peking. pp. 255–69.

WILLIAM WATSON

Early cereal cultivation in China

As there is no absolute or even developed relative chronology for the neo-lithic period in China it is only possible to make broad distinctions in the early history of cereal cultivation. The exiguous evidence this far available comes in all cases from excavated levels assigned to comparatively advanced forms of neolithic culture. The initial phases of neolithic culture in its local varieties are still poorly defined and there is no argument for associating the introduction of agriculture closely with the adoption of other characteristic neolithic practices; nor, among the reported specimens, have any primitive strains been identified such as to imply an initial stage in local domestication. The example of Japan, where the pottery-using Jomon culture subsisted for some six millennia (on radiocarbon evidence) before the arrival of rice as the first cereal in the second century B.C., suggests that a comparable dislocation of neolithic techniques may have occurred in China. Apart from the survival of grain and seeds in archaeological contexts, the wide distribution in China of characteristic flat stone knives, pierced or notched for hafting and often abraded, is taken as evidence of grain harvesting, and where they occur in a full neolithic context, or on sites where grain has been recovered, the inference appears sound. These knives are distributed mainly along the middle course of the Yellow River, to the north-east as far as Liaotung, through the eastern coastal provinces as far south as northern Fukien, and along the Yangtze valley into Szechwan. The differences in distribution of the main varieties of the knife, oblong and crescentic, do not coincide with the limits of the main divisions of neolithic culture as defined in ceramic terms, and so cannot be related closely to the differences of cultivated grains that are noted below[1].

The terms of the problem are set by the climatic and pedological distinction between north and south. The primary loess reaches from the north-west to a limit just south of the Yellow River and as far east as Honan, and beyond to the coast the soil is formed of the fluviatile extension of the loess. Loessic soil is on the whole alkaline, poor for holding water, but when water is supplied to it it brings active constituents towards the surface by capillary action, and is thus to some extent self-fertilizing. This property must have encouraged the large size and settled character of neolithic sites in the Yellow

River valley. The extent of the primary loess coincides closely with the distribution of the Yang Shao neolithic tradition. East of Honan and down the
coast from Liaotung to Chekiang is the preserve of the Lung Shan culture,
which in part occupies the redeposited loess but in part also is found on the
terrain characteristic of the lower lying regions extending from the Yangtze
basin southwards. This region is well-watered, with much permanent water,
and has soils of acid type. Towards the south it enjoys increasingly heavy
rainfall. Precipitation is less in the north and less seasonally confined, and
there is a long cold winter.

The cereals identified in neolithic contexts are millet, rice and wheat. The
first two are preserved in the grain, placed in pots with burials, and rice
survives as husk included in baked clay[2]. Cultivation on the deep primary
loess requires a cereal able to stand long rainless periods, and the millet
which was the staple of the Yang Shao farmers meets this requirement
admirably. Foxtail millet (*Setaria italica* var. *germanica*) and broom corn millet
(*Panicum miliaceum*) have been identified at Yang Shao sites in Shensi and
southern Shansi[3]. The dominant position of the millet varieties along the
middle and upper courses of the Yellow River in the neolithic period is fully
established, and they remain an important crop today. The question of
the cultivation of rice in the Yang Shao region and on the primary loess
remains problematic. The difficulty of providing sufficient water on this
terrain might be thought prohibitive, but *Oryza sativa* was identified at the
eponymous site of Yang Shao Ts'un in Honan[4] and it is reported from Liu
Tzŭ Chen in Shensi[5]. The context is however doubtful at the first site, and
at the latter, where *Setaria italica* was recognized with certainty, the identification of rice was tentative ("husks resembling rice"). Only at this site has
there been the suggestion of the presence of both cereals. Thus the case for
the cultivation of rice in the context of the Yang Shao neolithic and on the
primary loess is not yet proven.

Apart from these sites, neolithic rice is reported only from places in the
eastern part of the Yangtze basin (Anhui, Kiangsi, Chekiang, Hupei) in the
well-watered region of southern soil and climate, in each case in a context
of local Lung Shan type[6]. These sites are believed to be later than the main
Yang Shao Lung Shan development of the Yellow River zone, possibly
little before the beginning of the Shang Bronze Age (*c.* 1650 B.C.). The rice
husks recovered from baked clay at sites on the Chiang Han Plain, Hupei,
belonging to the same late neolithic period, resemble the Keng sub-species
(*Oryza sativa* ssp. *spontanea* Roschev), cultivated at the present day in east
China, differing sharply from the other modern variety, subsp. Hsien Ting,
cultivated in the same region. The neolithic rice is distinguished by the width
of the grain (length to width ratio 2·01) and the prominent fine hairs on the
husk surface and the ridges[7].

Wheat has only once been identified with certainty in neolithic context,
at Tiao Yu T'ai in northern Anhui, accompanied by Lung Shan pottery[8].

In the Shang Bronze Age, to judge from the divinatory texts excavated at Anyang, wheat was still of minor importance compared with millet. Where these texts specify the grain, the ideographs used to do so are interpreted in most cases as varieties of millet (yellow and black). The ideograph for wheat is securely identified, but appears rarely. There seems to be no instance of the ideograph interpretable as rice[9].

Regarding kaoliang (*Andropogon sorghum*) the position is obscure and tantalizing. In recent syntheses of Chinese archaeology we read that it was cultivated both in neolithic times and in the Shang and Chou periods[10]. For the neolithic K. C. Chang can only cite Bishop's statement of 1928, in an article dealing generally with the neolithic period in north China: "from one site (Ching Ts'un) grains of *Sorghum vulgare* have been identified. If these date in reality from neolithic times, as appears certain, this discovery is of decided interest; for hitherto it has generally been believed that this valuable food plant, the kaoliang or 'grand millet' of the modern Chinese, was introduced from India about the sixth century A.D."[11] Other authorities cited base their conclusion on the interpretation of grain characters in Shang oracle texts, a process beset with doubt[12]. Unfortunately the systematic excavations undertaken on early sites since 1950 have yielded only one identification of sorghum: the excavators of San Li Tun report that "some stalks of kaoliang sorghum were also preserved"[13], and even here we lack detailed publication of criteria of determinations, cultural context and the manner of association.

In his recent paper Dogett does not entertain the possibility of an introduction of domesticated sorghum into China so early as the neolithic period. He doubts also the suggestion made by Burkill in 1953 that it reached China direct from its African home across the Sabaean lane and not before the thirteenth century A.D.[14] He prefers Ball's opinion of 1913 that kaoliang, having some affinities with Indian sorghums, developed from a variety which reached China from India "some ten or fifteen centuries ago". This theory assumes a coastwise spread. In a subsequent verbal communication Dogett has however allowed that sorghum may have arrived in China earlier, particularly as it has been recovered in India earlier than the beginning of the Christian era. The distinct characteristics of the Chinese kaoliangs may, he believes, have been acquired through hybridization with the native wild *Sorghum propinquum*. Sorghums are to be found all through Central Asia. Thus one must reckon with the possibility that they spread thence into China at a time early enough to allow for the development of the kaoliangs as a distinct race[15]. Meanwhile it is well to suspend judgement on the question until better excavated evidence is available in China. Dogett accepts a date for the arrival of sorghum in India between 1500 and 1000 B.C. Even in Central China neolithic culture may extend in places below the first of these dates, and Bishop's report, if substantiated by other finds, would not clash with the chronology inferred for India.

There appears to be no difficulty in accounting for the other sorghum race found in China: the Amber Canes, *Sorghum dochna*. These are related to Amber Canes found spread along the coasts from East Africa around India, and south-east Asia to China, and their uniformity along the whole of this route points to a rapid and recent spread[16].

It is not uncommon for seeds of other food plants and fruit trees to be recovered in excavations. At the site of Ch'ien Shan Yang in Chekiang, in addition to rice, the following were identified: *Prunus persica*, *Cucumis melo* (gourd), *Trapa natans* (water chestnut), *Arachis hypogea*, *Sesamum indicum*, *Vicia faba*[17]. At the large village site of Pan-p'o in Shensi a pot was found filled with seeds described as edible vegetable. The pollen recovered at this site has been interpreted as indicating a wide grassy plain around the village with a scatter of elm, persimmon, and other deciduous trees possibly providing animal fodder but not human food. Seeds of hazel, pine and chestnut, found at depth on the site, were probably brought from a distance, for no pollen of the nut trees was found, and the far-carrying pine pollen, though present, does not necessarily indicate that the trees were near[18].

In sum, the archaeological evidence for the character and distribution of cereals in China in the neolithic period prefigures not unexpectedly the modern distribution, with this main difference, that wheat, now become the main crop in the loessic region from Kansu to Shantung and extending beyond the loess north-east to Manchuria and at places reaching south towards the Yangtze, was of minor importance in the neolithic period, when the staple on the loessic soil was varieties of millet. Today only a comparatively small area grows both wheat and rice, and in early time also it seems that millet and rice were largely mutually exclusive, this arising no doubt then as now from difference of terrain and soil rather than climate, and from the local incompatibility of the field system of each. What is known of the neolithic cereals reinforces the cultural division recognized on other grounds between the Yang Shao and the Lung Shan traditions. All that has been said above must be qualified by the following considerations, apart from the still unsatisfactorily limited number of determinations on which the broader inferences are based:

1 The lack of a reliable chronology for the neolithic period. This applies even to the relation of the Yang Shao and Lung Shan cultures: these have been seen hitherto as broadly contemporary in origins at least in west and east respectively, but are now arguable as broadly successive, the Lung Shan being the later facies of the Yang Shao, in fully developed form coming to occupy exclusively the fluviatile loess as it formed and became habitable on the lower Yellow River.

2 There is no archaeological evidence for early cereals in Manchuria, Szechwan (both specially favoured for agriculture) and the region of south-east and south China where the ceramic tradition of the so-called "south-

eastern neolithic" persisted very late, and where agriculture also made a tardy appearance.

3 The study of the historical pedology and climatology of east Asia is still little advanced, and results are hardly available for archaeological interpretation.

4 In China archaeologists are denied the evidence provided elsewhere by the survival of fossil field systems. As regards rice cultivation progress in this matter should prove possible, as the antiquity of existing field systems is realized and excavation is undertaken specifically to determine it. There has been a presumption in the past that the focus of domestication for rice, if it should prove definable, will lie in south-east Asia. The investigation of ancient fields in that area may throw light on the problem. No theory has been expressed as to the geographical origin of domesticated millets.

Notes

1 An Chih-min (1955). The stone knives of ancient China, *K'ao ku hsüeh pao*, 10, pp. 27–51.
2 The possibility of identifying grain impressions in pottery has not yet been exploited. While it can hardly be doubted that evidence of this kind must exist, the careful levigation to which the clay is subjected in most of the advanced neolithic areas must tend to minimize it.
3 Yellow River Catchment Archaeological Commission (1959). Brief report of archaeological excavations at Liu Tzu Chên, Hua Hsien, Shensi, *K'ao ku*, 2, pp. 71–5; also Anon. (1955). Discoveries at a neolithic village —Pan-p'o near Hsi-an, *K'ao ku t'ung hsün*, 3, pp. 15–16; Bishop, C. W. (1933). The neolithic age in northern China, *Antiquity*, 28, pp. 389–404; Institute of Archaeology of the Academy of Sciences of China (1963). *Hsi-an Pan-p'o*, Peking. p. 124, pl. LV–LVIII.
4 Andersson, J. G. (1947). Prehistoric sites in Honan, *Bull. Mus. Far Eastern Antiquities*, 19, pp. 21–2.
5 Yellow River Catchment Archaeological Commission (1959). ibid.
6 Hu Yüeh ch'ien (1957). Reconnaissance of neolithic sites in Anhui, *K'ao ku hsüeh pao*, 1, pp. 21–30; Hsieh Ch'un-chu and Chu Chiang (1955). Examination of the neolithic site at Hsien li tun in Wu hsi, Kiangsu, *Wen wu*, 8, pp. 48–59; Chekiang Cultural Properties Control Commission (1960). Excavations of Ch'ien Shan Yang in Wu Hsing, *K'ao ku hsüeh pao*, 2, pp. 73–91; Andersson, J. G. (1946). ibid.; Yellow River Catchment Archaeological Commission (1959). op. cit. pp. 71–5.
7 Ting Ying (1959). Examination of rice husk found in red baked earth of the neolithic period in the Chiang Han plain, *K'ao ku hsüeh pao*, 4, pp. 31–4.
8 Hu Yüeh-ch'ien (1957). ibid.
9 Ch'ên Mêng chia (1956). *Yin hsü pu tz'ŭ shu*, Peking. pp. 525–32.
10 Cheng, T. K. (1960). *Archaeology in China*, II, Shang China, Cambridge. p. 197; Chêng, T. K. (1963). *Archaeology in China*, III, Chou China, Cambridge. p. 22; Chang, K. C. (1963). *The Archaeology of Ancient China*. New Haven and London, p. 59.
11 Bishop, C. W. (1933). op. cit. pp. 395–6.
12 For evidence of crop cultivation in the Shang period Chêng, T. K. (1960). ibid., cites Yu Shêng-wu (1957). Agricultural products of the Shang

Dynasty, *J. Humanistic Studies: Peoples' University of the North East*, 1, pp. 81–107 (not available to the writer); and Wu Ch'i-ch'ang (1937). Yin agricultural practices as seen in the oracle records and bronze inscriptions, *in Studies presented to Chang Chu-shêng*, Shanghai. pp. 323–368 (but in this there is no mention of kaoliang); Ch'ên Mêng-chia (1956). ibid., does not identify any oracle text character with kaoliang.

13 Yin Jan-chang and Li Chung-i (1960). Preliminary report on the second season of excavations on the site of San Li Tun, Hsin I Hsien, Kiangsu, *K'ao ku*, 7, pp. 20–2; the reference reads: "Being carbonized through burning the external appearance of the stalks was well-preserved. They were examined by Li Yang-han, Director of the Department of Agriculture at the Nanking Institute of Agriculture, and determined as stalks of kaoliang from near the roots. Traces of leaves of kaoliang were also discovered stratified in the cultural level." The pottery (*ting*) and bronze knives found on the site indicate a date between the tenth and eighth centuries B.C.

14 Dogett, H. (1965). The development of the cultivated sorghums, *in* Hutchinson, Sir J. (ed.) *Essays on Crop Plant Evolution*. Cambridge. p. 62.

15 According to Dogett, H., Personal communication from Sir Joseph Hutchinson.

16 Dogett, H. (1965). ibid.

17 Chekiang Province Cultural Properties Control (1960). Report on the first and second seasons of excavations at the site of Ch'ien-shan-Yang in Wu-hsing hsien, Chekiang, *K'ao ku hsüeh pao*, 2, pp. 84–7.

18 Institute of Archaeology of the Academy of Sciences of China (1963). op. cit., pp. 270–2.

Part IV: Studies of particular taxonomic groups

Section 1: Plants

J. ALEXANDER & D. G. COURSEY

The origins of yam cultivation

Introduction

After the cereal grains, the staple food crops of most of the peoples of the world are the so-called "root" crops, which include stems, rhizomes, corms, bulbs, tubers and other types of organ as well as true roots. The origins and the beginnings of the cultivation of these crops are generally obscure, although in most cases, clear botanical evidence exists as to the continent of origin (e.g. cassava or manioc is unquestionably of tropical American origin). The yams present one of the most difficult and interesting cases for study.

Yams are still important food crops, the annual world production being estimated at twenty to twenty-five million tons[1], and before the introduction of American crop plants to the Old World, must have played a relatively more important role than they do today. Ethnographic evidence from Africa and Asia supports this, for the past importance of yams to many communities is shown by the part they play in socio-religious events. A very wide range of societies still have yam-based economies; some are comparatively primitive, being until recently stone tool-using and organized in small isolated settlements; others have developed high civilizations (amongst the highest in Africa) based upon population densities of more than five hundred to the square mile.

To the study of yam domestication three kinds of evidence, botanical, ethnographic and archaeological, are relevant, but each kind is complicated by special problems. The botanical by the presence of wild and cultivated varieties through almost the whole of the humid and sub-humid tropics; the ethnographic by the failure of observers to distinguish between yam species; and the archaeological by the inability, at present, of field-workers to recover direct evidence of yam cultivation[2].

Botany

The yams, in the true sense of the word, are plants of the natural family Dioscoreaceae, in the monocotyledonous order Liliales. By far the largest genus of this family is *Dioscorea* itself, containing some six hundred species in all, among which are numbered all the important species of edible yams. Two other small genera, however, deserve passing mention: the tropical American *Rajania* and the European *Tamus*, which contain the Carib Yam, *R. cordata* and the Black Bryony, *T. communis* respectively. There are also a few other minor genera (*Avetra*, *Trichopus* and *Stenomeris*), of no economic importance, in the Dioscoreaceae[3].

Before proceeding, it may be useful to clear up a misconception that exists over the use of the word "yam". Strictly, the word is applied only to members of the genus *Dioscorea* and it is in that sense that it is used here. It is often misapplied, however, especially by American writers, to include numerous other tropical and sub-tropical root and tuber crops, principally the sweet potato (*Ipomoea batatas*) but also to aroids such as cocoyams or taros (*Xanthosoma* and *Colocasia* spp.) and arrowroots (*Maranta* spp.). The "Elephant Yam" of India (*Amorphophallus campanulatus*) is also an aroid and not a true yam. The so-called "yam belt" of the southern U.S.A. is actually a region where sweet potatoes are extensively grown. In West Africa, a tuberous-rooted legume (*Sphenostylis stenocarpa*) is commonly referred to as the "yam bean", on account of the form of its root, as are also species of *Pachyrhizus* in Asia and Central America. The word "yam" is derived from the West African Mande "niam" or Temne "enyame", which was adopted as "ynhame" in fifteenth-century Portuguese, or "ñame" in Spanish and spread thence into other European languages[4].

Most species of *Dioscorea* and all those of importance as food crops develop as underground tuber or group of tubers, from which an herbaceous "vine" is produced annually, to die away at the end of the growing season. The yam tubers are, organographically, derived from the stem. They are natural storage organs, which enable the plant to survive during periods of inclement conditions—e.g. from one rainy season to the next—and it is these tubers that form the edible part of the plant.

In all *Dioscorea* which are normally used as food plants, the tuberous system is renewed annually, the old tuber, in the natural state, withering away as the vine develops during the growing season, to be replaced by a new one formed towards the end of the phase of active growth. In some wild species the underground system is perennial, and survives for the whole life of the plant, becoming more or less lignified. Some of the *Dioscorea*, such as those of the section Stenophora, are rhizomatous.

The stem of the yam plant consists of a twining vine, adapted for climbing among bushes, savannah trees or even forest trees. In the smaller species, it may reach only two or three metres, but in the stronger-growing species, ten metres is not unusual, and even more may be achieved. The male and female flowers are borne separately, usually on different plants, and are inconspicuous: they are, none the less, insect pollinated and not wind pollinated, as has been suggested. The fruit, when formed, is a dry capsule, containing seeds winged for dispersal by the wind. In many of the cultivated forms, centuries of vegetative propagation has so reduced the sexual fertility of the plant, that flowering is rare, and fertile seed is hardly ever, if at all, set.

When grown as a crop plant, propagation is invariably by means of vegetative "setts", which consist of small tubers—in the case of those species which produce many tubers; from bulbils, when these are formed; or, most usually, from small pieces of large tubers.

Stakes or ropes tied to trees are normally provided for the vines to twine upon, to replace the support provided by the "bush" in the wild state. Such staking is necessary in order to maximize yields.

Representatives of the genus *Dioscorea* are to be found in most parts of the tropics. A number of species also penetrate into the temperate parts of the world, while a few are alpine in habitat. It is only among the tropical and sub-tropical species, however, that yams of any value as food crops are found. The natural distribution of the Dioscoreaceae in the world is shown in Fig. 1.

Within the tropics, species of *Dioscorea* are to be found almost wherever the rainfall is sufficient for their growth—about 120 cm. annually—in both Old and New Worlds, and in Australia. Various members of the genus are adapted to rain forest and to savannah. A considerable proportion of the members of the genus provide edible tubers, and some of these occur in most parts of the non-arid tropics. Others provide poisons which are widely used for hunting and fishing.

The evolutionary history of the genus has been discussed fully by Burkill[5]. It is sufficient for the purpose of this paper to note that the ancestors of the *Dioscorea*, having evolved originally in what is now South-east Asia, appear to have achieved world-wide distribution as early as the end of the Cretaceous era. An alternative theory, based on cytological considerations, suggests an evolutionary origin in Central Africa: this, however, is difficult to reconcile with morphological taxonomy. Subsequently, evolution followed somewhat varying paths in the Old and the New Worlds with the result that botanical differences are marked between the species of the two hemispheres. Separation of the Asiatic from the African ancestral forms appears to have taken place later, during a period of desiccation in the Miocene era. There are therefore closer relationships between the species of Asia and those of Africa, and a single species occurs wild in both continents. This is *D. bulbifera*, of the section Opsophyton, and there are appreciable differences between the two continental forms: the African form has been separated by some botanists as a different species.

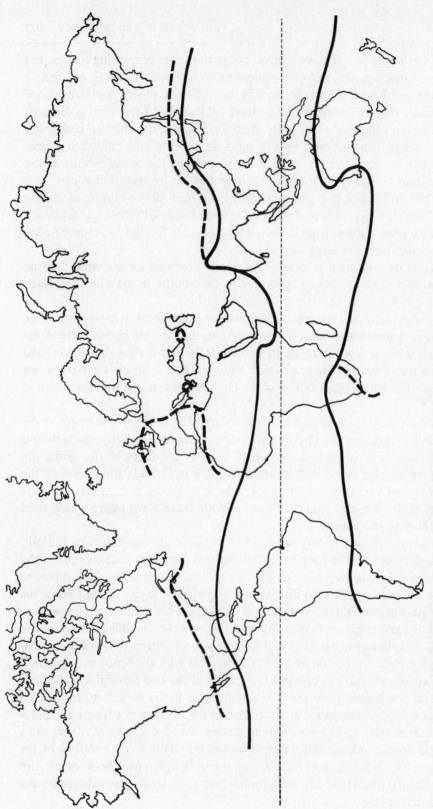

Fig 1 The natural distribution of the Dioscoreaceae in the world. The full line encloses the tropical area in which the edible yams occur. Within the extensions enclosed by dashed lines, only atypical species, of no value as food crops, occur (e.g. *Tamus*, and sections such as *Stenophora* and *Testudinaria*)

Nearly all the *Dioscorea* of the Old World, except for a few aberrant species which, not being food crops, do not enter the present discussions, have chromosome numbers based on multiples of 10, and in a large number of species, $2n = 40$. The New World species which have been examined to date, have all been found to have chromosome numbers based on 9. Some of the cultivated species are high polyploids, with chromosome numbers ranging up to $2n = 140$. These high chromosome counts have been recorded principally in those species which are most highly developed in cultivation, *D. alata* and *D. cayenensis* (the latter species including *D. rotundata*, according to the taxonomy followed by the author in question). A few cultivated forms appear to have abnormal counts, based on multiples of 9, e.g. $2n = 36$ or 45. It has been suggested that such high polyploidy in cultivated forms is associated with long periods of continuous vegetative propagation[6].

Of the many species of yam known, only comparatively few are of importance as crop plants. These fall naturally into three groups, according to their geographical origins.

Asiatic Yams

The Greater Yam (also known as Water Yam or Winged Yam)	*D. alata*
The Lesser Yam (also known, incorrectly, as the Chinese Yam)	*D. esculenta*
The Chinese Yams	*D. opposita* and *D. japonica* (both often known by the invalid taxon *D. batatas*)
The Aerial or Potato Yam	*D. bulbifera*
Other Asiatic species utilized to some extent are:	*D. hispida*
	D. pentaphylla
	D. nummularia

African Yams

The White, or White Guinea, Yam	*D. rotundata*
The Yellow, or Yellow Guinea, Yam	*D. cayenensis*
The Cluster or Bitter Yam	*D. dumetorum*
The Aerial or Potato Yam	*D. bulbifera* (the African form of this species has been separated by some as *D. latifolia*)
African species of minor use are:	*D. preussii*
	D. praehensilis
	D. sansibarensis
	D. colocasiifolia

American Yams

The Cush-cush, Yampi or Mapuey	*D. trifida*
Other American species, cultivated to some extent, and more in times before the introduction of Asiatic and African species, include:	*D. convolvulacea* *Rajania cordata*

The most widely grown species are the Asiatic *D. alata* and the African *D. rotundata*: these, together with *D. cayenensis*, *D. nummularia*, *D. opposita* and *D. japonica* all belong to the section Enantiophyllum of the genus *Dioscorea*. One of the characteristics of the yams of this section is the formation of a single tuber—rarely two or three, and extremely seldom more—in each season. The tubers often weigh as much as five to ten kilograms each, and in exceptional cases may weigh more than fifty kilograms, and be two to three metres in length. These are the most typical yams: together, the six species mentioned probably account for more than 90% of all the yams that are actually grown for food, in the world. The minor African species, *D. praehensilis*, *D. preussii* and *D. colocasiifolia* also belong to this section: all its members have vines which twine to the right, whereas the other species of yam mentioned twine to the left.

The Asiatic *D. hispida* and the African *D. dumetorum* belong to the section Lasiophyton, and form a cluster of medium-sized tubers, more or less fused together. Their vines twine to the left, and bear compound leaves, usually with three leaflets (most *Dioscorea* leaves are simple). These two species are so similar that they have been classified as sub-species, but are now regarded as distinct. Wild forms of both species are extremely toxic, owing to the presence of alkaloids, but can be detoxicated by prolonged soaking in water. Many less toxic or non-toxic cultivars exist. To this section also belongs *D. pentaphylla*, which is generally similar.

D. bulbifera (including *D. latifolia*). This yam, which belongs to the section Opsophyton, differs from most others in that it is the aerial bulbils, which are freely borne in the leaf axils, which provide the edible product: the underground tuber is either small or absent. Many wild forms are toxic, though others produce bulbils so succulent that they can be eaten raw. Although widespread in cultivation throughout the tropics, it is nowhere a major food crop, to the same extent as some other species.

The Lesser Yam, *D. esculenta*, is the only member of the section Combilium. Unlike the species discussed so far, it forms a large number of individually small tubers, each usually weighing only a few hundred grams: the underground system of a newly-lifted plant superficially resembles that of the potato. The whole plant, although of climbing habit, is of smaller stature than the Enantiophyllum yams. It is seldom cultivated to such a large extent, although known and appreciated in most tropical countries.

D. sansibarensis, of the section Macroura, hardly ranks as a cultivated plant, although somewhat improved forms are known: it freely produces small bulbils, as well as tubers which, in wild forms contain an alkaloid and are highly toxic. It is a very large-growing species, believed, in many parts of Africa, to possess magical properties.

The indigenous American yams are today of minor economic importance, having been largely displaced in cultivation by Asiatic and African species. The most widely grown, *D. trifida* (section Macrogynodium) produces a group of smaller tubers, rather after the manner of *D. esculenta*. The related genus *Rajania*, which is restricted to tropical America, forms long, single tubers, not dissimilar to those of the Enantiophylla.

Ethnography

The ethnographic evidence for the use of yams may now be considered.

Wild yams are harvested by hunter/gatherers and domesticated yams are cultivated today in Africa, Asia and South America. No comparative study of their social/religious customs and methods of cultivation seems to have been published but the following generalizations can be made:

In *South-east Asia* wild yams are known and prized by hunter/gatherers, in Ceylon, the Andaman Islands, Malaya, the Pacific Islands and Australia. In some areas slices of the tuber are even reburied for propagation. The toxins are removed by pounding, shredding and soaking[7] and are sometimes used in fishing and hunting.

Cultivated yams are grown from India to Fiji and from China to New Guinea. They are major food crops in parts of Indonesia, New Guinea and the islands of Oceania. The general technique after clearing and burning is to fence a plot and then to plant tuber-fragments in mulched mounds. The work is hard, continuous (both men and women taking part) and extremely skilful, many species and cultivars being used to suit varying soils and climatic conditions. Digging sticks and hoes are the commonest tools used, but communities are small and some were purely stone-using at the coming of Europeans[8]. Cooking is usually by pounding or roasting. Religious ritual and belief are often linked with the yam agricultural cycle and yams are much used in ceremonies.

Literary evidence shows yams to have been known in India in the sixth century A.D. and in China in the second century A.D.

In *South America* wild yams are eaten by hunter/gatherers in Eastern Brazil and Venezuela. Shredding and soaking are employed to remove the toxins[9].

Cultivated yams are widely grown as a secondary crop in Brazil and Venezuela but nowhere are they a major crop[10]. After clearing and burning the tuber-fragments are planted in low mulched mounds and regularly tended.

They are interplanted with other crops and yields are low and communities are small (0·6 per square mile). Only stone axes and hoes were in use prior to European contact. Cooking processes include grating and soaking[11]. Yams have no special religious connections, as far as is known, in America.

In *Africa* wild yams are known and searched for by hunter/gatherers in the rain-forests[12]. They are also used in time of famine by cultivators at the fringes of the forest[13] and in the savannah. The toxins are removed by soaking and are sometimes used in hunting.

Cultivated yams are grown from Guinea to Kenya and from Angola to Uganda, but their importance varies greatly. Only in West Africa from the Ivory Coast to the Cameroons are they at present a major food crop. There have been suggestions that in Uganda and the Congo they were once much more widely grown[14].

After clearing and burning, tuber-cuttings are planted in mounds or ridges. These are mulched and the growing vines carried by living trees or by poles. Population densities of up to 500 per square mile are supported[15]. Hoes and rakes are the commonest tools used. Yams are usually interplanted with other crops, great skill being shown in the choice of soils and species. The apportioning of work between men and women varies greatly from region to region[16]. Iron tools were commonly in use at the coming of Europeans but some groups were still stone-using in the nineteenth century A.D., and memories of a stone-using period were preserved by others[17]. Cooking is usually by pounding and mashing. Yams are used extensively in religious ceremonies and some varieties are credited with magical properties. Events in the yam agricultural cycle are widely celebrated[18].

Archaeology

It is apparent from this evidence that both wild and cultivated yams were being utilized for food in most parts of the tropical world before historic times and that only archaeology can solve the problems of their domestication. The archaeological evidence is best considered separately in the three great regions into which the botanical evidence divides (Fig. 2).

Area I: South-east Asia

This region is the home of many species of cultivated yams. The principal ones are *D. alata, D. esculenta, D. nummularia, D. bulbifera, D. hispida* and *D. pentaphylla,* the first two named being the most widely grown. Many other species are also cultivated but to a limited extent and in restricted areas. The relative importance of the species vary greatly from one district to another, although *D. alata* usually predominates, and throughout the area the relative importance of yams to other crops also varies. Most peoples in the

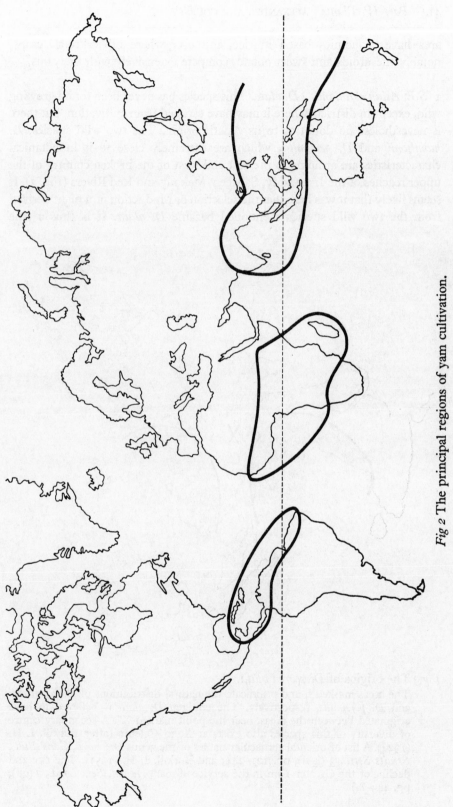

Fig 2 The principal regions of yam cultivation.

area have economies based in rice, and everywhere other "root" crops, notably the aroids and sweet potato, compete extensively with the yams.

1 *S.E. Asian mainland.   D. alata.* This species has never been found growing wild, except in districts where it may have escaped from cultivation, but there is nevertheless no doubt as to its Asiatic origin. The two wild species, *D. hamiltonii* and *D. persimilis*, which are extremely close to it in botanical characteristics are at home to the east and west of the broken country of the upper reaches of the Irrawaddy, Salween, Mekong and Red Rivers (Fig. 3). It seems likely that it was here that the selection or production of a plant derived from the two wild species mentioned became *D. alata*. It is thus a true

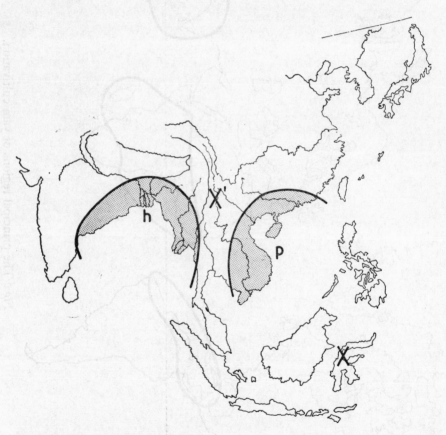

Fig 3 The origins of *Dioscorea alata.*
   The areas marked h and p indicate the natural distributions of *D. hamiltonii* and *D. persimilis*, respectively. The cultigen *D. alata* is believed to have originated between the areas, near the point marked X'. A secondary centre of diversity of this species also exists at X, in Celebes (after Burkill, I. H. (1924). A list of oriental vernacular names of the genus *Dioscorea*, *Gdns' Bull., Straits Settl.*, 3 (4–6), pp. 121–244; and Burkill, I. H. (1951). The rise and decline of the Greater Yam in the service of man, *Advmt. Sci., Lond.*, 7 (28), pp. 443–8.)

cultigen, or product of cultivation. A more southerly origin, in the Malay peninsula itself, is unlikely as it is an area with rainfall spread almost evenly throughout the year and the wild yams of that area, having no severe dry season to survive, do not possess large, esculent tubers like those of *D. hamiltonii* and *D. persimilis*.

D. esculenta has no closely related wild species, so its exact origin is somewhat obscure. Botanically it is certainly Asiatic, although not Chinese in origin, and it would appear likely that it was first taken into cultivation in the same area as *D. alata*, while its subsequent spread also followed similar paths.

Much closer to the wild forms are *D. pentaphylla* and *D. hispida*. *D. pentaphylla* is a highly variable species as far as the quality of its tubers is concerned: some are pleasant and harmless to eat, others nauseous and highly toxic. It has been suggested that this wide variation may well have provided a stimulus to selection by the more primitive cultivators, and this species is currently at the early stages of ennoblement[19].

Most forms of *D. hispida* are highly toxic, owing to the presence of the alkaloid, dioscorine, in the tubers, and are used as food only in times of famine, after a lengthy processing to remove the alkaloid, involving alternate soaking and drying of the shredded tubers. For this purpose, tubers are collected mainly from wild plants, although it is possible that some ennoblement of the less toxic forms has taken place.

The archaeological evidence from this area is still very scanty but a number of relevant generalizations may be made.

In Southern and Eastern Asia in the third and second millennia B.C., only two distinctive complexes of cultural equipment have been recognized. Both are first recognizable in the warm-temperate climatic zones; one in Central/North China, the other in West Pakistan/North-west India; and both are based on the cultivation of cereals. In the second millennium B.C. cultivated wheat, millets and rice are present in both zones[20]. The ground stone tools and pottery which are the commonest durable evidence in both complexes are quite distinctive. In the region between them, that in which the domestication of *D. alata* and *D. esculenta* probably took place, artifacts of both traditions have been found and recent absolute dates indicate that some of them belong to the late third and second millennium B.C.[21] Excavation in Eastern India has recently reinforced existing evidence of a movement of stone tool-types, and probably pottery-types, westwards from the Chinese/Indo-Chinese province at this time[22]. Whilst there is no indication of what, if anything, these tool- and pot-makers were growing, the general nature of the equipment is that associated with agriculture elsewhere in India and China and provides a context in which the domestication of local tubers might have taken place. There is so far no earlier evidence from this entire region which suggests agriculturalists of any kind.

Further south in Malaya the present evidence from the second millennium B.C. suggests connections with cultures further north in Indo-China[23]. There are no distinctive local cultures which might be associated with agriculture nor is there any evidence suggesting any early or indigenous domestication of yams. In this the archaeological evidence supports the botanical evidence[24].

2 *The Philippine, Malaysian and Indonesian islands.*   Here *D. alata* and *D. esculenta* exist in an enormous variety of cultivars and have longer and more deeply buried tubers than the local varieties. The latter are sufficiently numerous for a secondary centre of domestication in Celebes and the neighbouring islands to have been suggested[25]. The following deserve special comment.

D. nummularia is used as a food plant mainly in Indonesia and some of the Pacific islands where it is of secondary importance. Nowhere does it seem to be greatly ennobled, nor does it exist in any great variety of cultivars; although it has considerable ritual significance in some areas[26].

D. pentaphylla is occasionally met with as a cultivated plant in many parts of India, the Malay peninsula, the Philippines, Indonesia and Fiji. It is nowhere an important crop plant and would appear to have been brought rather fortuitously into cultivation at a number of widely separated places.

D. bulbifera. The practices adopted for the cultivation of this species are radically different from those used for other yams. The edible portion of the plant is the aerial bulbil, which may be "harvested" from the vines of the growing plant, after the manner of a fruit. Such an easily available food must have attracted the attention of man at a very early date, and as might be expected, the use of this plant as food occurs in many districts. As there are no very great numbers of cultivars concentrated in any one part of Asia or Africa, it is not unreasonable to assume that this species was brought into cultivation in many places, independently.

The archaeological evidence from this region shows stone and pottery artefacts of the two mainland cultural traditions; the Chinese/Indo-Chinese type being widespread through the coastal islands and the Indian/Pakistani type through Indonesia[27]. There is at present no evidence to suggest an independent development of agriculture earlier than the mainland[28]. This appears to support the botanical evidence that the original domestication of the main yam cultivars should not be looked for here.

3 *Central and North China, most of Japan, the Ryukyu Islands and parts of Korea.* This is not today a very important yam-growing region, but deserves mention as substantial quantities of the two very closely related species *D. opposita* and *D. japonica* are grown here. Only a small number of cultivars are known and they are not cultivated to a significant extent anywhere else in the world. They are to be regarded as warm-temperate, rather than as tropical, crops, in spite of their close botanical relationship to many of the major tropical food yams. They are members of the section Enantiophyllum, and so normally produce only a single, large tuber, which in most forms drives deeply

into the soil, making harvesting a laborious process. They are well adapted to the area in which they grow, and where, without doubt they originated. They have not, within the historical period at least, been crops of major importance. In modern times they have been taken in cultivation to the Hawaiian Islands, America and even, during the time of the mid-nineteenth century potato famines, to Europe: in none of these areas, however, have these yams ever become much more than horticultural curiosities.

There is at present no archaeological evidence to suggest when they were brought into cultivation. Literary evidence attributes their cultivation in China to the mythical period before *c.* 1500 B.C.

4 *The Pacific Islands east of Indonesia and Australasia.* In this region yams of S.E. Asian types (notably *D. alata, D. pentaphylla, D. bulbifera* and *D. nummularia*) were widespread at the time of the first European contacts. They are not indigenous to the islands and botanical, ethnographic and archaeological evidence all support a movement of people and cultivated plants eastwards in the first and second millennia A.D.[29] There is therefore no reason to consider this region further, in connection with agricultural origins.

5 *The westward spread of S.E. Asian yam cultivars.* Some cultivars (notably *D. alata* and *D. esculenta*) are found in India, Ceylon, Madagascar, the coast of East Africa, Central and West Africa, the Caribbean islands and in Central and South America. Since Madagascar, Africa and South America have indigenous wild and cultivated yams of their own, the problems of the origins of cultivation are different from those of the eastern spread and primarily relevant to the problems of local cultivars there. They may be considered in three regions:

(a) *The coastlands of the Indian Ocean.* Here the only certain evidence is literary, and it is established that cultivated yams were known in India by 600 A.D. (probably earlier) and in Madagascar well before 1450 A.D.[30] There seems no doubt that the references are primarily to *D. alata.*

The archaeological evidence for this spread is twofold: firstly from the third millennium B.C. onwards there is considerable evidence for long distance trade between the highly sophisticated societies of W. Pakistan, N.W. India, the Persian Gulf and Arabia, but it is only in the first millennium B.C. that Ceylon, Indonesia and the S.E. Asian mainland can be shown to take part in it. An earlier participation by Malays and Indonesians seems unlikely on present evidence for no highly developed societies of the kind likely to be interested in trans-Indian Ocean trade have been recognized at this period. Secondly from 300 B.C. onwards historical evidence makes such contacts more likely and from *c.* 150 B.C. onwards direct sailing across the ocean is well attested.

There is considerable archaeological evidence that the manufactures of the Chinese and Roman Empires were being exchanged by this route in the first two centuries A.D.[31] Since yams were used from at least this time onwards by Malay sailors, this trade provides a context for the arrival of yams, and perhaps bananas (another S.E. Asian food favoured by sailors), on the east coast of Africa. These voyages would have been contemporary with the great Pacific voyages to the east[32].

On quite different evidence, linguistic and racial, a date between 300 B.C. and 400 A.D. is generally accepted for the settlement of Madagascar by Malaysian people. These might well have brought *D. alata* to the island.

(*b*) *The spread into Central and West Africa.* When records began to distinguish the yam species growing here (in the last century) *D. alata*, alone of the S.E. Asian cultivars, was to be found in a few areas of the Congo Basin and in the "yam zone" of West Africa, and in many areas was distinguished linguistically from "proper yams" i.e. the local species[33]. Two other S.E. Asian cultivated plants, bananas and *Colocasia* were found in the same regions[34].

There seem to be two possible explanations for this: *D. alata* may have spread by land from the Kenya-Tanzanian coast at some time after 400 B.C.; or it may have been carried by sea round the Cape of Good Hope. If the latter, then it is likely to have arrived after 1498, when Portuguese are known to have been using it for sea-stores, rather than have been carried by Malay/Madagascans for whom there is no evidence of sailing in the Atlantic. If the former, then the African archaeological evidence for the early first millennium A.D. is important. Whilst there is general evidence of long distance trade eastwards from Katanga and Rhodesia in this millennium[35], and of folk movements out of the Congo Basin to the east and south, there is no evidence of any trade or movements into West Africa, especially across the Cameroon Mountains, which to this day form a major ethnic boundary. Indeed such evidence as there is suggests rather a southward movement from that region[36]. If *D. alata* reached West Africa at this time there is no archaeological context at present in which to place it; it must also have been adopted very readily and local wild forms quickly brought into cultivation.

(*c*) *South America and the Caribbean islands.* Cultivars of Southeast Asian species (*D. alata* and *D. esculenta*) reached this region, together with some African ones, in and after the sixteenth century A.D. There is literary evidence that they were deliberately imported by Spaniards and Portuguese.

Area II: West and Central Africa

This area is the home of a large group of cultivars of which *D. rotundata* and *D. cayenensis* are principal[37], and *D. dumetorum, D. praehensilis, D. colocasiifolia* and *D. preussii* lesser, varieties.

The limits of the main zone, growing 90% of all the yams in Africa, are remarkably sharp (Fig. 4). The northern and southern are climatic, represen-

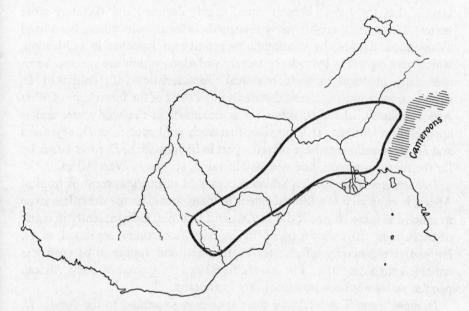

Fig 4 The West African yam zone.
The full line encloses the area where yams are, traditionally, the staple food crop (after Miège, J. (1954). Les cultures vivrières en Afrique occidentale, *Cah. d'Outre-Mer*, 7 (25), pp. 25–50; Coursey, D. G. (1965). The role of yams in West African food economies, *Wld Crops*, 17 (2), pp. 74–82; and Coursey, D. G. (1967). *Yams*. London. pp. 28–67.)

ting the boundary of minimum rainfall in the north, and the coastal swamps and lagoons in the south. The western boundary coincides closely with the Bandama River of the central Cote d'Ivoire, and the eastern to the Cameroon Mountain chain[38].

In the remainder of Central and West Africa, yams are only cultivated to a very limited degree, and they are only major crops in very restricted localities. The same species are grown as in the main zone, but *D. rotundata* is less important and the minor African yams more so.

D. rotundata and *D. cayenensis* are best considered together, as they are extremely close botanically, and the techniques of cultivation are virtually identical. Most of the French botanists who have worked with the genus

Dioscorea regard the former as being merely a subspecies of the latter[39]: the term *D. cayenensis* in most French writing therefore includes yams that British authors would refer to as *D. rotundata*. A detailed discussion of the taxonomy would be out of place here, but it may be noted that *D. cayenensis sensu strictu* is a forest species, adapted to a short dry season, and a correspondingly brief period of dormancy: the forms that may be referred to as *D. rotundata* have a longer dormant period, adapted to the longer, fiercer dry season of the savannah: they therefore tend to build up larger reserves in their tubers, and are thus better suited for use as crop plants (an incidental advantage is that the tubers become more deeply dormant and therefore store better). However, there are many intermediate forms, which have been fixed as apomictic clones, by continuous vegetative propagation in cultivation, which may represent hybrids, or merely variations within the species. Yams essentially identical in their botanical characteristics with cultivated *D. cayenensis* are known in the wild state through most of the forest zone of West Africa. Like *D. alata*, *D. rotundata* is unknown in the wild state, and is apparently a cultigen. It is possible that such wild species as *D. abyssinica* and *D. praehensilis* may have played a part in its formation. *D. rotundata* is by far the most important, and widely cultivated, species in West Africa.

D. bulbifera. This species, which occurs wild throughout most of tropical Africa, is cultivated to a limited extent in many areas. Its use doubtless arose in much the same way as it did in Asia and Oceania, independently in many districts. The African forms of the species (sometimes separated as *D. latifolia*) are generally inferior to Asiatic ones, and appear to be even less ennobled than the latter. The Asiatic forms are recognized by some African peoples as having been introduced by Europeans.

D. dumetorum. The wild and toxic species is so similar to the Asiatic *D. hispida* that it was formerly regarded as a sub-species: it is now known to be distinct. In parts of West Africa it has been ennobled in cultivation to a considerable degree, and virtually non-toxic forms are quite extensively grown, especially in the former Eastern Provinces of Nigeria. The process of acculturalization of this species is still continuing: in 1901 Chevalier observed plants of this species being collected from the wild state in Ubangui-Shari, and those which were not immediately required for food being planted around village compounds.

Like *D. esculenta* the properties of the starch of this yam render it unsuitable for the making of the traditional West African dish, "fufu": it is, nevertheless much appreciated for other culinary uses.

It is only in recent years that botanical research has shown this complex of cultivars to be certainly African and in so doing has made much of the previous theorizing invalid[40].

The ethnographic and archaeological evidence complement each other particularly well in this region, for the ethnography shows that at the coming of the Europeans there was no evidence of staple food crops other than yams in the "yam zone" of West Africa. It is likely therefore that agriculture began here only after local yams had been ennobled or foreign ones introduced. The archaeological evidence is interpreted below as suggesting the former:

In the savannahs immediately south of the Sahara, cereal-based agriculture is attested in the third millennium B.C. and in the eastern and southern savannahs early in the first millennium A.D. (but might have been there well before this)[41]. This may mean that "domestication" as a concept was available to forest dwellers in West Africa as early as the third millennium B.C. This is supported by finds of savannah-type artifacts far south into the forest margins at that period[42].

In the third and second millennia B.C. therefore, the contemporary situations in West Africa and in the interior of S.E. Asia have more parallels than was previously suspected. In both there was the possibility of contact with well established cereal growing communities and there were hunter/gatherers who in all probability then as now, knew and prized wild tubers, including yams, which were suitable for cultivation[43].

A similar parallelism may be noted in the archaeological evidence, for on the forest margins in Ghana and Nigeria as in S.E. Asia, complexes of ground stone tools and pottery related to cereal agriculturalists' types, are found in the second and first millennia B.C.[44] Whilst these cannot yet be associated directly with agriculture, similar artifacts in the African savannahs certainly were in the previous millennium. It may be, as Davies suggests[45], that yams were already being cultivated in Africa.

If this were so then the later events in the area fall into place. At the coming of the Europeans in the fifteenth century A.D. dense populations organized into urbanized societies existed in southern Nigeria and around the mouth of the Congo. The traditions of these societies stretch back to twelfth century A.D. apparently based upon the yam cultivation[46] which is still, as it was in the seventeenth century, so interwoven with their religious and social life. The complexity of the cultivation and the variety of cultivars of the indigenous species might well mean that three millennia of development, rather than the single one since the earliest possible introduction of *D. alata*, are represented. That other urbanized societies developed in West Africa during and possibly before the first millennium A.D. is well documented in ancient Ghana.

It would seem that a good case exists for regarding the domestication of yams in West Africa as being contemporary with and quite separate from that in South-east Asia.

Area III: South America and the Caribbean islands

The yams most cultivated in America today are Asiatic and African introductions of the sixteenth and seventeenth centuries; *D. alata*, *D. cayenensis*, *D. rotundata*, *D. esculenta* and *D. bulbifera* are all grown, especially in the West Indies. The first named is generally the most popular, but in Jamaica and elsewhere in the Western Caribbean the African species are more favoured.

Although there are more species of *Dioscorea* indigenous to the New World than to the Old, man in the Western Hemisphere has paid little attention to them as potential crop plants, probably because of the availability of more easily cultivated "root" crops such as manioc or cassava (*Manihot esculenta*), tanias (*Xanthosoma* spp.), sweet potato (*Ipomoea batatas*) and in the cooler areas, *Solanum* spp. The one species that was fairly widely cultivated and to some extent ennobled was *D. trifida*. This species appears to have a centre o origin on the borders of Guyana and Brazil, where many forms are known, and to have spread in cultivation through Trinidad northward along the island chain, becoming progressively more highly selected, until in Jamaica only one or two forms are known[47]. This pattern of distribution suggests an original domestication and dispersal by the Arawak, but no very definite information appears to be available.

In one of the two surviving Carib communities, in Dominica, species of *Rajania* (a small genus of the Dioscoreaceae, whose members are of similar anatomy to the yams) are still grown to a limited extent. It is not highly ennobled, and although common in the wild state, is not now cultivated elsewhere in the Caribbean[48].

A form of "protoculture" of *D. convolvulacea*, which is encouraged in orchards and cocoa plantations, using the trees as supports, has been mentioned in Costa Rica[49].

American yams have not been taken in cultivation to the Old World to any significant extent, in marked contrast to the westward movement of both Asiatic and African cultivars. There is at present no indication of how long these have been in cultivation or whether the "Aje" referred to by Columbus was *D. trifida*, another indigenous *Dioscorea*, or possibly some other crop[50].

It is certain, however, that root crops, in particular *Manihot esculenta* were widely cultivated in pre-Hispanic times and that yams, which today play a subsidiary role within that agricultural system, may well have played it then. This is made more likely by the knowledge and use made of wild tubers, including yams, by local hunter/gatherers. Since suggestions that roo. cultivation might have been practised in the third millennium B.C. in this region[51] yams, as a minor crop, may well have a respectable antiquity here and domestication may have been generally contemporary with that in the other two areas. The parallelism between this and the African and Asian regions also includes contiguity with an area which, by the third millennium B.C., already had established an agricultural pattern (in this case Meso-American), and the presence of hunter/gatherers appreciative of wild tubers including yams.

It may be therefore that there was an independent centre of yam domestication in the New World not far removed in time from those of the Old World.

Conclusions

On the basis of the evidence presently available, there is no reason to suppose that the introduction of yams into cultivation occurred initially only in a single area. Instead, the prerequisites of domestication are clearly seen to have existed in three widely separated regions—South-east Asia; West Africa and tropical America—and different species of yam were actually brought into cultivation, and subsequently ennobled, in the three areas. Subsequent movement of the cultivated forms has taken place, in historic times, the Asian species being taken in cultivation to both Africa and America, and the African species to America: this has tended to obscure the original pattern.

The conditions which favoured the domestication appear to have been, in all three regions, cultural interaction between people possessed of primitive grain-based agricultural systems with others, still in the hunter/gatherer stage, who were utilizing wild yams. These contacts seem to have occurred approximately simultaneously, in all three regions, during the third millennium B.C.[52]

Notes

1 Coursey, D. G. (1965). The role of yams in West African food economies, *Wld. Crops*, **17** (2), pp. 74–82.
2 Alexander, J. (In press). The domestication of yams, *in* Brothwell, D. R. and Higgs, E. S. (eds.) *Science and Archaeology*. 2nd ed. London.
3 Coursey, D. G. (1967). *Yams*. London. pp. 28–67.
4 Burkill, I. H. (1938). The contact of the Portuguese with African food plants which gave words such as "Yam" to European languages, *Proc. Linn. Soc.*, **150** (2), pp. 84–95; Corominas, J. (1954–7). *Diccionario Critico Etimologico de la Langua Castellana*. Madrid; Coursey, D. G. (1967). op. cit. pp. 5–27.
5 Burkill, I. H. (1960). The Organography and the Evolution of the Dioscoreaceae, *J. Linn. Soc. (Bot.)*, **56** (367), pp. 319–412.
6 Sharma, A. K. and De, D. N. (1956). Polyploidy in *Dioscorea, Genetica*, **28** (1–2), pp. 112–20; Martin, F. W. and Ortiz, S. (1963). Chromosome Numbers and Behaviour in some Species of *Dioscorea, Cytologia*, **28** (1), pp. 96–101; Martin, F. W. and Ortiz, S. (1966). New Chromosome Numbers in some *Dioscorea* Species, *Cytologia*, **31** (1), pp. 105–7.
7 Forde, C. D. (1964). *Habitat, Economy and Society*. London.
8 Barrau, J. (1956). Les ignames alimentaires des îles du Pacifique sud, *J. Agric. trop. Bot. appl.*, **3** (7–8), pp. 385–401; Forde, C. D. (1964). ibid.
9 Sauer, C. O. (1952). Agricultural origins and dispersals, *Amer. Geog. Soc., Bowman Memorial Lectures, Series 2*.
10 Stewart, L. and Farron, M. (1959). *The Native Peoples of South America*. New York.
11 Metraux, A. (1948). *in* Steward, J. H. (ed.) *Handbook of South American Indians*, III. *Bureau of American Ethnology*, **143**; Forde, C. D. (1964). ibid.
12 Burkill, I. H. (1939). Notes on the genus *Dioscorea* in the Belgian Congo, *Bull. Jard. bot. Etat., Brux.*, **15** (4), pp. 345–92.
13 Okiy, G. E. O. (1960). Indigenous Nigerian food plants, *J. W. Afr. Sci. Sci.Assoc.*, **6** (2), pp. 117–21; Corkill, N. L. (1948). The poisonous wild

cluster yam, *Dioscorea dumetorum Pax.*, as a famine food in the Anglo-Egyptian Sudan, *Ann. trop. Med. Parasit.*, 42 (3–4), pp. 278–87.

14 McMaster, D. (1960). A subsistence crop geography of Uganda, *Ph.D. Thesis, Univ. of London*; Burkhill, I. H. (1939). ibid.

15 Gourou, P. (1966). *The Tropical World.* 4th ed. London.

16 Irvine, F. R. (1963). *A Textbook of West African Agriculture.* London: Torto, J. O. (1956). The cultivation of yams in the Gold Coast, *New Gold Cst. Fmr.*, 1 (1), pp. 6–8.

17 Clark, J. D. (1963). Africa south of the Sahara, *in* Braidwood, R. J. and Willey, G. R. (eds.) *Courses toward Urban Life.* Edinburgh.

18 Coursey, D. G. (1967). op. cit. pp. 197–203. A more detailed study of this subject is currently under preparation.

19 Burkill, I. H. (1924). A list of oriental vernacular names of the genus *Dioscorea*, *Gdns' Bull., Straits Settl.*, 3 (4–6). pp. 121–244; Burkill, I. H. (1951). The rise and decline of the Greater Yam in the service of man, *Advmt. sci., Lond.*, 7 (28), pp. 443–8.

20 Watson, W., this volume, pp. 397–402; Allchin, F. R., this volume, pp. 323–9.

21 Sharma, T. (1966). Neolithic cultures of Assam, *Ph.D. Thesis, Univ. of London*; Sieveking, G. (1954–5). Excavations at Gua Cha Kalantan, *Fed. Mus. J. (Malaya).* 1–2, p. 75; Clark, J. D. (1964). *World Prehistory.* Cambridge; Solheim, W. G. (1968). Early Bronze in North-eastern Thailand, *Current Anthropology*, 9 (1), pp. 59–62.

22 Sharma, T. (1966). ibid. See especially under Daojali Hading.

23 Tweedle, M. (1953). The stone age in Malaya, *J. R. Asiat. Soc.*, 26 (2).

24 Sauer's theory should, therefore, be abandoned.

25 Burkill, I. H. (1924). ibid.; Burkill, I. H. (1951). ibid.

26 Barrau, J. (1965). Histoire et préhistoire horticole de l'Oceanie tropicale, *J. Soc. Océanistes*, 21 (21), pp. 55–78.

27 van Heekeren, J. (1957). *The Stone Age in Indonesia.* The Hague.

28 With the possible exception of Taiwan (see Solheim, W. G. (1968). ibid.). The evidence is, however, too uncertain to be acceptable at present.

29 Barrau, J. (1965). ibid.

30 Burkill, I. H. (1924). ibid.; Burkill, I. H. (1951). ibid.; Wrigley, C. (1960). Speculations on the economic prehistory of Africa, *J. Afr. Hist.*, 1 (2), pp. 189–203; Jumelle, H. and Perrier de la Bathie, H. (1910). Fragments biologiques de la flore de Madagascar, *Ann. Mus. colon., Marseilles* (2° Ser.), 8, pp. 1–96; Jumelle, H. (1922). Ignames sauvages et ignames cultivées à Madagascar, *Rev. Bot. appl. Agric. trop.*, 2 (9), pp. 193–7.

31 Wheeler, R. E. M. (1958). *Rome beyond the Imperial frontiers.* London.

32 Barrau, J. (1963). *Plants and migrations of Pacific peoples. 10th Pacific Science Congress.* Hawaii.

33 The other important Asiatic species, *D. esculenta*, was introduced only within the Colonial period in Africa. The Asiatic form of *D. bulbifera* is recognized by some African people, e.g. the Floup of Portuguese Guinea, as having been "brought by white men"; see Coursey, D. G. and Alexander, J. (1968). African agricultural patterns and the sickle cell, *Science*, 160 (3835), pp. 1474–5.

34 Simmonds, N. W. (1962). *The Evolution of the Banana.* London; The other crop, *Colocasia*, may, as suggested by Burkill, I. H. (1938). ibid., have come down the Nile valley, but there is no archaeological evidence which makes such a move likely. There is also no reliable evidence that Malay navigators ever penetrated into the Atlantic.

35 Fagan, B. (1966). *Southern Africa.* London. (See especially Ingombe Ilede); Poznanski, M. (1961). Pottery types from archaeological sites in East Africa, *J. Afr. Hist.*, 2 (2), pp. 177–98; Fagan, B. (1966). The Iron Age of Zambia, *Current Anthropology*, 7 (4), pp. 453–62.

36 Stevenson, W. Unpublished information.
37 Torto, J. O. (1956). This author suggests that about 80% of the yams grown in Ghana at that time were derived from two cultivars of *D. rotundata;* Coursey, D. G. (1967). op. cit. pp. 134–44. The figure given by Torto for Ghana is probably at least approximately correct for the West African yam zone as a whole; Chevalier, A. (1936). Contribution a l'étude de quelques espèces africaines du genre *Dioscorea, Bull. Mus. Nat. Hist. Nat., Paris* (2ᵉ ser.), 8 (6), pp. 520–51.
38 Miège, J. (1954). Les cultures vivrières en Afrique occidentale, *Cah. d'Outre-Mer,* 7 (25), pp. 25–50; Coursey, D. G. (1965). ibid.; Coursey, D. G. (1967). op. cit. pp. 22–5.
39 Chevalier, A. (1936). ibid.; Burkill, I. H. (1939). ibid.; Coursey, D. G. (1967). op. cit. pp. 59–60.
40 Murdock, G. P. (1959). *Africa: its peoples and their culture history.* New York. There is no point in discussing a wholly Asiatic origin for African yam cultivation, as this concept has now been discredited (see Coursey, D. G. and Alexander, J. (1968). ibid.)
41 Fagan, B. (1966). ibid.; Clark, J. D. (1963). ibid.
42 Davies, O. (1960). The neolithic revolution in tropical Africa, *Trans. Hist. Soc. Ghana,* 4 (2), pp. 14–20. Unpublished evidence from W. Stevenson suggests that derivation of these artifacts from local palaeolithic sources, as proposed by Davies, is unlikely.
43 Isolated hunter/gatherer communities in both these areas still make extensive use of such wild yams and other "roots".
44 Davies, O. (In press). *Ntereso.* Paper presented at the 8th Congress on Pre- and Proto-history, Prague (1966); Shaw, T. (1968). *Radiocarbon dating in Nigeria.* Ibadan. p. 10.
45 Davies, O. (1967). *West Africa before the Europeans.* London.
46 Coursey, D. G. (1967). op. cit. pp. 197–203, and further work under preparation. Festivals associated with yam cultivation were the major events in the annual socio-religious cycle in much of this area.
47 Henry, V. C. R. (1967). Studies on botanical and agronomic characteristics of cush-cush (*Dioscofea trifida L.f.*), *Ph.D. Thesis, McGill Univ.,* and Private communication.
48 Chevalier, A. (1946). Nouvelles recherches sur les ignames cultivées, *Rev. int. Bot. appl. Agric. Trop.;* 26 (279–80). pp. 26–31.
49 Leon, J. Private communication, from Instituto Interamericano de Ciencias Agricolas.
50 According to Leon, basing his opinion on Oviedo's *Historia General y Natural de las Indias,* "aje" refers definitely to a white-fleshed form of sweet potato, not to any of the *Dioscorea.*
51 Rouse, I. (1962). The intermediate area; Amazonia and the Caribbean area, *in* Braidwood, R. J. and Willey, G. R. ibid.; Rouse, I. (1964). The Caribbean Area, *in* Jennings, J. D. *Prehistoric Man in the New World.* Chicago.
52 One of us (D.G.C.) is required to state that the opinions expressed here are his own and not necessarily those of the Tropical Products Institute.

A. KRAPOVICKAS[1]

The origin, variability and spread of the groundnut (Arachis hypogaea)

The origin and spread of the groundnut are of equal interest to ethnologists, botanists and crop-scientists. Knowledge of this subject is certainly basic to soundly based programmes for improving this important economic crop. Several years have been occupied in the study of a large collection of South American varieties maintained at the Experimental Station of Manfredi (I.N.T.A. Cordoba, Argentina) and the time is opportune for a presentation of conclusions drawn from this study. The material used consists of land races (unimproved strains) collected from relatively unsophisticated cultivators in some of the less readily accessible areas of Mexico, Peru and Bolivia. There are, in addition, 1000 accessions collected in two expeditions to Paraguay, Bolivia and Central Brazil with W. C. Gregory and J. Pietrarelli. The prime object of these journeys was to collect material to clarify the taxonomy of the genus *Arachis* and visiting the type localities of wild species. One area not visited was the N.E. of Brazil, the original location of *A. pusilla* Benth.

The author's studies of variability within the cultivated species began with descriptions of local varieties cultivated in central Cordoba Province, the most important area of groundnut cultivation in Argentina[2] and an analysis of introgression in N.E. Argentina[3].

Material collected in Paraguay, Brazil and Bolivia has also been analysed and this paper presents some of the results of this work and further observations on Mexican and Peruvian material.

Origin of Arachis hypagaea

The genus *Arachis* is confined to South America. It includes thirty species and occurs in an area between the River Amazon and the Rio de la Plata and from the Atlantic to the foothills of the Andes. The centre of origin of the genus is probably in the Mato Grosso (Brazil) close to the Gran Pantanal. Representatives are found there of all the sections into which we divide the genus[4].

The outstanding morphological feature of this genus is the geocarpic fruit produced by all species. In *A. hypogaea* the fruit has a single cavity which contains 1–5 seeds. The characteristics of the fruits of wild species were first described by Burkart[5], the development of these fruits was interpreted by Krapovickas and Rigoni[6]. In all wild species the fruit is articulated with two single-seeded compartments, separated from each other by a filamentous isthmus, the length of which varies according to species from a few millimetres to about 20 cm. This must be due to the presence of two meristems in the ovary one at the base, the other between the two ovules. In *A. hypogaea* only the basal meristem functions which grows after fertilization to produce a peg which buries the tip of the ovary. The ovules, once buried below ground, grow and mature. The intercalary meristem normally fails in *A. hypogaea* and for this reason the biarticulate pod may be considered as a wild character.

The growth of the peg and isthmus is horizontal in the majority of species from Central Brazil and may reach a length of one metre, flowers may be aerial or subterranean. In *A. hypogaea* flowers are normally aerial and the peg grows vertically both in the aerial and subterranean portions. This I believe is important; from an area at approximately 57°W and westwards there is an increase in the number of species with vertical peg development, such types are commoner in the more peripheral areas.

In attempts at interspecific hybridization attempted so far between *A. hypogaea* and wild species more success is obtained when the wild species pollen parent also has vertical peg growth than when this is horizontal[7].

The great majority of wild *Arachis* species are perennial but annual forms are found in two district areas 2500 km. apart in the N.E. of Brazil and N.W. Argentina and areas near the Bolivian frontier. In the latter area four species have been found of which three are diploid and one *A. monticola* Krap. et Rig. is tetraploid with $2n = 40$ chromosomes. This species (from altitudes 1400–2800 m. above sea level in Argentina) is the only wild species to give fully fertile hybrids with *A. hypogaea*. The only perennial species which can cross with *A. hypogaea* to give viable hybrids are those with a taproot similar to *A. villosa* Benth, $2n = 20$ chromosomes and more or less vertical pegs. Such hybrids have three genomes and are more or less sterile. The range of *A. villosa* and its relatives is somewhat peripheral to that of the genus as a whole, they occur to the west of the 57° meridian, that is west of a line marked by the Rivers Paraguay and Uruguay. This evidence indicates that *A. hypogaea* has originated farther to the west than had been thought previously and that it arose in the periphery of the area occupied by this genus.

It seems likely that *A. hypogaea* originated in Bolivia, at the base or in the foothills of the Andes. There exists in this area a very important centre of variability of *A. hypogaea* subsp. *hypogaea*. This subspecies we believe has the greatest affinity with the wild annual species and the perennials of the *A. villosa* group shown by the occurrence of the runner habit, similar branching pattern and absence of compound spikes.

It is curious that Bolivia is scarcely mentioned in older literature on the groundnut yet it is not only an important centre of variation of the cultivated forms but the area in which this crop plant arose. The diversity of use to which groundnuts are put in the area indicates also that it has been present there for a long time. In addition to the more customary uses it is employed in the preparation of chicha de mani[8] a refreshing non-alcoholic drink. In Santa Cruz de la Sierra a soap is produced from it. In the woodland zone of Northern Bolivia the natives eat the entire soft fruit with relish at the stage when the pericarp is thick and juicy[9].

Intraspecific taxa of A. hypogaea

Earlier systems of classification have taken into account characters of the fruit only[10] or characters of the fruit together with habit, erect or prostrate[11]. Since the importance of branching systems was recognized more rational classifications have been produced[12] and comparable results have been obtained from cultivated peanuts of North America, Africa, Venezuela and Argentina.

The study of branching habit and other vegetative characters is best carried out on living plants which have been grown at low plant population densities. Branching pattern has been correlated with the form and size of the fruit, growth habit, the duration of the vegetative period, with seed dormancy and with other characters. In this way it is possible to interpret the taxonomic contributions of previous authors and understand their illustrations.

In a previous work[13] we proposed a taxonomic system dividing *A. hypogaea* into two subspecies according to branching habit, alternate (subsp. *hypogaea*) or sequential (subsp. *fastigiata*). A new varietal entity (var. *hirsuta*) which has recently come to light should be added to this scheme.

Arachis hypogaea L.
  subspecies *hypogaea*
    var. *hypogaea* (= *A. africana* Lour.), the Brazilian type of Dubard[14], the Virginia type of Gregory *et al.*[15]
    var. *hirsuta* Kohler (= *A. asiatica* Lour.) the Peruvian type of Dubard[16] in part.
  subspecies *fastigiata* Waldron
    var. *fastigiata* the Peruvian type of Dubard[17] in part, the Valencia type of Gregory *et al.*[18]
    var. *vulgaris* Harz, the Spanish type of Gregory *et al.*[19]

The two subspecies are distinct entities, in addition to their morphological differences they show divergence in physiological and genetical characters. Groundnuts of subspecies *hypogaea* are generally prostrate, their seeds have considerable dormancy, their vegetative period is long with a duration of from 5–10 months. In subspecies *fastigiata* plants are erect, the seed has no dormancy and the vegetative period is short, 3–5 months, which permits two crops per annum in some tropical areas. In crosses between the two subspecies we have observed progeny with lethal characters (albinos) or with malformations. This confirms the observation of Hull[20]. Forms intermediate between the subspecies are encountered much less frequently than those intermediate between botanical varieties.

The genocentres of groundnuts in South America

It has been possible by using Anderson's method[21] to analyse the patterns of variability found in the indigenous strains of South America. It has been shown for example that the great variability found in the Guarani region is most probably due to introgressive hybridization. This has produced a typical hybrid swarm from which we were able to determine the probable prototypes which crossed freely among themselves and have as a result given this region a special character. By extending this method to other areas of South America we have identified different prototypes and we can delimit distinct genocentres from a study of the patterns of variability produced.

Although we are dealing with forms in cultivation at the present time, it is possible to explain why the genocentres are static. In the localities visited groundnuts were grown almost exclusively for subsistence, there was no appreciable export trade nor had any cosmopolitan varieties been introduced to these areas.

At the present time we can recognize the following genocentres

1 The Guarani region, the basins of the Paraguay and Parana rivers
2 Goias and Minas Geraes (Brazil)
3 Rondonia and N.W. Mato Grosso
4 The Eastern foothills of the Andes in Bolivia
5 Peru.

1 *The Guarani region*

This includes a large part of the basins of the rivers Paraguay and upper Parana bordering N.E. Argentina (Corrientes and Misiones), the East of Paraguay, southern Mato Grosso and western Sao Paulo in Brazil. The extent of this region eastwards is uncertain but it probably extends to the Brazilian States of Parana, Santa Catarina and Rio Grande do Sul.

The groundnuts of this region are almost entirely erect (subspecies *fastigiata*); Valencia is the commonest form. The subspecies *hypogaea* is very rare and is represented by two indigenous races, Guaycuru or Guanaco and Rasteiro. These are very similar but are differentiated by testa colour, salmon or reddish in Guaycuru and white with red streaks in Rasteiro; the latter is characteristic also of the Overo variety of Argentina (Manduvi Cabara or Mani cabra of Paraguay). These groundnuts occur along the length of the upper Parana River and also in Ceres (Goias, Brazil). Rasteiro was described as a species by Chevalier[22] from fruits originating in Santa Catarina (Brazil).

In the Guarani region there is very little evidence of introgression between the two subspecies of *A. hypogaea*, but there does exist a swarm of forms intermediate between the races belonging to subspecies *fastigiata*. In the course of analysing this introgression we were able to identify the following prototypes, all belonging to subsp. *fastigiata*

var. *fastigiata* Valencia and Porto Alegre
var. *vulgaris* Negrito and Spanish.

Of these Porto Alegre and Negrito with dark violet testa colour are only found in the Guarani region and their distribution can be regarded as coinciding with the extent of this region. Valencia also occurs in the region of Goias and Minas Geraes but specimens from this area show no evidence of introgression. We have not found Valencia groundnuts in any of the other three regions. It is possible that it has spread throughout the world from an original location in Paraguay or Central Brazil and has given rise to numerous cultivars, e.g. "Colorado de Cordoba" in Argentina and "Tatu" in Brazil.

The "Spanish" groundnut characteristically has fruits with two seeds, the testa is pale pink or light chestnut and abundant foliage is produced. We have found it only in the Guarani region where it is most frequently found in N.E. Argentina. It is not absolutely certain whether this race is truly indigenous in this region or is a recent introduction. However, the Guarani region is a centre of variation of the variety *vulgaris* and it is a reasonable assumption that the Spanish groundnut has been disseminated from this region. There are numerous cultivars of Spanish conformation, e.g. Macspan, Blanco Manfredi, Dixie Spanish and Natal Common.

2 *The region of Goias and Minas Geraes*

Our travels only covered the south of Goias and N.E. Minas Geraes but here we met with a varietal pattern quite distinct from that of the Guarani region. This region coincides with the basin of the River Tocantins and the river San Francisco marks its eastward extent, here erect groundnuts (subsp. *fastigiata*) predominate. We came upon only one example of subsp. *hypogaea* in the vicinity of Ceres (Goias) which was like Rasteiro in having a red and white testa.

Cultivated races in this region belong in the main to subsp. *fastigiata*, both varieties *fastigiata* and *vulgaris* are represented with little indication of introgression between them. An important feature of this region is the remarkable increase in frequency of the variety *vulgaris*, fruit size is larger than in region 1 and is similar to that of the North American cultivars Tennessee Red and Tennessee White. In our collection we have similar material from Venezuela and Mexico. No material of Spanish type has been collected in the area.

3 *The region of Rondonia and N.E. Mato Grosso (Brazil)*

This region is not as yet well defined and requires further study, nevertheless the data we have collected so far show that it has some very peculiar features. The type specimen of *A. nambyquarae* Hoehne was collected in Pimenta Bueno (Rondonia); this has a bi-coloured testa and we consider it belongs to *A. hypogaea* subsp. *hypogaea* var. *hypogaea*. *A. villosulicarpa* also occurs in the Mato Grosso[23] cultivated by natives of Juruena and Diamantino. This species is not closely related to *A. hypogaea*; it is diploid and perennial.

In central Mato Grosso we have collected a number of erect groundnuts with yellow testas, a colour not previously observed.

This region is part of the Amazon basin and further exploration of this river system will greatly increase our knowledge and enable us to elucidate further its importance.

4 *The eastern foothills of the Andes in Bolivia*

The outstanding feature of this region is the abundance of forms belonging to subspecies *hypogaea* var. *hypogaea*. There is a great range of variability to be found in habit and size of plant, in fruit characters and testa colour.

The four representatives of var. *fastigiata* that we have collected from this area are distinctly different from those of the other regions. We have not collected any representative of var. *vulgaris*.

In this region the groundnut is grown over a range of ecological conditions and at altitudes up to 2000 metres above sea level.

In Bolivia we have observed several instances of introgression between the two subspecies. The groundnut "Overo" or "Pintado" with red and white testa occurs throughout the whole of Bolivia, this is frequently encountered in the markets of La Paz, Cochabamba and Santa Cruz de la Sierra. It is a different groundnut from Rasteiro or from Nambyquarae, because of its semi-erect habit and its segregation for branching habit and seed coat colour. It is possible that this form has arisen from crosses between var. *hypogaea* and var. *fastigiata*. In Santa Cruz de la Sierra, we collected a form we have called "Cruceño" with plant habit and fruits similar to those of var. *fastigiata* but with some features of "Pintado". This could well be a product of introgression.

5 *The region of Peru*

In Peru we have collected two distinct types of groundnut, one very similar to Virginia Runner, a common North American cultivar and the other with fruits very similar to those found in the pre-Columbian tombs on the coast of Peru. We presume that Virginia Runner is of recent introduction to the area, the numerous collections made show little or no variability.

The situation with regard the second type is very different. These are characterized by very large fruits with marked constrictions between seeds, very prominent veins and at the distal extremity a marked, parrot-like beak. This type of fruit has been illustrated repeatedly in reports on pre-Columbian remains from coastal Peru[24] and is represented on pottery of the Mochica culture. This groundnut may well be that which Monardes[25] described from the shores of the River Maranon thus "it is of the size of the middle finger, round, twisted throughout, with a very neat design, its colour brownish, it has inside a seed which rattles when dry somewhat like an almond with a light-tan husk, it is white and breaks into two parts like an almond".

The fruits of the pre-Columbian type which we obtained in the Lima market proved to belong to distinct types of plant, this suggests that we are in a centre of variability for this groundnut. The fruits most like those of pre-columbian tombs belong to the subspecies *hypogaea* that is to say they are prostrate, with alternate branching and late maturity and otherwise conform to the description of the variety *hirsuta* Kohler (= *A. asiatica* Lour.). This variety may show some peculiarities in its growth, for example the main axis may grow to a length of a metre or more, far exceeding that of the runner groundnuts of var. *hypogaea*. These groundnuts are still grown on the Pacific coast.

We have also found similar fruits, frequently coarser and with heavier veins, belonging to subspecies *fastigiata* var. *fastigiata*. These have been described and illustrated by Mazzani and Cobo[26] under the name of "Tingo Maria". "Tingo Maria" does not appear to be the typical pre-Columbian groundnut and probably originates in the woodland zone in Eastern Peru.

Radiocarbon datings of groundnuts from Huaca Prieta in the valley of the River Chacama at 850 B.C. have been obtained.

There is general agreement on the nature of prehistoric Peruvian groundnuts; however Towle[27] points out that a smaller variety had also been found with a slightly reticulated pericarp and without a dorsal ridge. This seems to be rather similar to several cultivated varieties actually grown |in the U.S.A. at the present time. This material was obtained in Lupe and is of the early Ancon period.

Dubard[28] termed all these groundnuts "Peruvian type" but because he used the number of seeds per pod as his principal diagnostic character, he included Valencias in his Peruvian group. Valencias also have 3–4 seeds but the fruit has no beak, no prominent ridges on the dorsal surface nor prominent veins. Dubard's "Peruvian type" includes both sequentially branched and alternately branched forms. The alternately branched forms with 3–4 seeds, rough pod with a parrot-like beak, the runner habit, fairly hairy and very late maturing can be distinguished by the sum of these characters from Virginia, Spanish or Valencia groundnuts.

The relation between groundnut genocentres and indigenous tribes

A comparison of the genocentres described and the distribution of indigenous ethnic groups in South America enables us to draw some very timely conclusions. The existence of genocentres can be explained by geographical isolation due to the great distances and the lack of contact between primitive settlements. There is at the present time a dearth of information on the groundnuts of the Amazon basin and the eastern foothills of the Andes from Bolivia to Venezuela. Study of these regions would undoubtedly extend our knowledge of the processes of domestication and spread of the groundnut.

If we superimpose on the ethnic and linguistic map of South America[29] the present scheme of variation patterns of the groundnut we can see that genocentre no. 1 coincides broadly with the distribution of the Guarani Indians and no. 2 with that of the Gé people. The other three genocentres each cover a mosaic of tribes. However it can be shown that there is some affinity between genocentres no. 1 and no. 2 and none between these and the remainder. In addition there is very little apparent affinity between groups 3–5.

The establishment of relationships between these genocentres and the indigenous cultures, although outside the scope of the present treatment, is worth further detailed ethnological study. We suggest that for such a study these possible correlations might serve as a useful working hypothesis.

Spread of the groundnut

The groundnut is one of a number of American cultivated plants which almost immediately after Columbus were disseminated and became established in the Old World. The rapidity of this spread has led some to postulate an African origin, an opinion still to be seen repeated in some technical works, but which has been discarded for the past century. The description of precolumbian groundnuts from coastal Peru[30] established the South American origin of this plant[31]. Several theories have been elaborated to explain its mode of spread.

Right from the start comparative studies were made of the archaeological groundnuts of Peru and those found in lands bordering the Pacific and Indian Oceans (the Philippines, China, India, Madagascar, etc.) This aroused interest in pre- and post-Columbian trans-oceanic relationships.

Dubard[32] was among the first to attempt an explanation of the spread of groundnuts. He differentiated two types, the Peruvian with 3–4 seeds and the Brazilian with 2 seeds per fruit. According to Dubard, the Peruvian type similar to the pre-Columbian form of the tombs, must have been spread by the Spanish in the Pacific basin and to Mexico and from there introduced to Spain. The Brazilian type must have been distributed along the West African coast by early Portuguese slave traders who bought it there.

Bois[33] split *A. hypogaea* into subspecies *africana* (Lour.) with prostrate branches and *asiatica* (Lour.) with erect branches. According to Bois these two subspecies correspond to the Brazilian and Peruvian types respectively, of Dubard.

Fruits similar to Peruvian archaeological groundnuts were mentioned and illustrated by Skyortzow[34] and by Ames[35] from China. Anderson[36] said "—the most primitive type of peanut, the same narrow little shoestrings which are found in the Peruvian tombs, are commonly grown today, not in Peru but in South China. How did they get there?" The resemblances between Asiatic and Peruvian groundnuts have been used to support theories of trans-Pacific land connections. Merrill[37] however denies the possibility of such connections and supports the hypothesis that the spread of groundnuts occurred along the old Portuguese trade route from Brazil to Goa and thence to Canton and later Macau. This opinion of Merrill's has been generally accepted and illustrated in maps[38].

Spread in South America

Much light can be shed on this problem by studying the vernacular names of *A. hypogaea*. The following list is based principally on information gathered by I Gilii and Xuarez[39], II Valdizán and Maldonado[40] and III Rivet in Chevalier.[41]

Betaca Pole	Mocobí[42]
Cacahuali	Piro, Chontaquiro (II)
Cacahuete	Mexican Spanish (I)
Cacuali	Piro (II)
Curiquieré	Mojos (I)
Chemnakjai	Lenguas[43]
Choccopa	Aymará (II and III)
Chocopan	Araucanos[44]
Inchic	Keshua (II)
Inchig	Kichua quiteno (III)

Inchik	Peruvians and natives of Quito (I)
Inchis	Kichua (III)
Inci	Campa (II)
Inqui	Antis (II)
Kadyahati	Hianakoto (Caribe) (III)
Kupekana	Arawak (Tariana) (III)
Maguá	Guaná[45]
Mandobi	Brazilian Portuguese (I) Tupi (III)
Mandovi	Pilagá[46]
Manduví	Chiriguano[47]
Maní	Spanish American (I); Haiti (III); Aparai (Caribe) (III)
Manobi	Brazilian Portuguese (I) Tupi (III)
Manubi	Guarani (I)
Maytapa	Pacaguara (II); Pano (Pakaguara) (III)
Mondowi	Tupi (III)
Mundubi	Tupi (III)
Munui	Tupi (III)
Naaquis	Chiquitos (I)
Nioskita	Choroti[48]
Sil'ari	Itonama (III)
Tágalatic	Toba[49]
Tama	Pano, Shipibo, Conibo (II)
Tlalcaca-huatl	Mexican
Torali	Colorado (III)
Yapiopeka	Tukano (Kobena) (III)
Yatubu	Tukano (III)
Yaxtutu	Tukano (Tuyuka) (III)
Yolique	Mbayá (I)
Zebé	Yurakaré (II and III)

The commonest names in use are "cacahuate" in Mexico, a name which in Spain was transformed into "cacahuete", in Brazil "amendoin" and in Paraguay "manduví" and "maní". The latter is in fairly general use in the rest of Spanish America, it is also the name mentioned by Oviedo[50] from Hispaniola. Reference to the above list shows that in the Tupi–Guarani region there are numerous variants differing little from the actual name "manduví". In the remainder of South America the names show little affinity one with another. A large number of variants of "manduví" occurs in the languages from the eastern foothills of the Andes and between these linguistic groups there are others having affinities with the Arawak tongues. The Arawaks inhabit the area which extends from the Caribbean to the heart of South America as far as the border of Bolivia with the Chaco.

The presumed area of origin of *A. hypogaea* is in a region in which Arawak linguistic influences predominate and it is rather remote from those of the Guarani. In spite of this coincidence and also their wide dispersion in America, I do not necessarily conclude that the Arawaks are responsible for the spread of the groundnut from its centre of origin as far as the Caribbean islands. Such a hypothesis is however consistent with the evidence available at the present time.

Spread outside South America

The progenitors of the whole range of cultivars now widely dispersed throughout the world originally came from South America. It is possible to place all of them in the botanical varieties described previously, groups lower in the taxonomic hierarchy require further study.

The runners of coastal Peru (var. *hirsuta*) appear to have had their origin in this area. Similar forms however are still cultivated in Mexico where they are called "chino". This name has no geographical significance but signifies in the vernacular "wrinkled", referring to the prominent veins and ridges of the pod. "Chino" varieties of Mexico conform to the Peruvian type in having alternate branching, runner habit, similar fruit and seed with violet testas. These are long established cultigens in Mexico and are illustrated in Clavigero[51]. Only fruits are shown but this author mentioned a vegetative period of seven months which confirms that this groundnut belonged to the subspecies *hypogaea*.

Heiser[52] commented on the lack of historical information on pre-columbian cultivation of the groundnut in Mexico but mentioned the discovery by MacNeish of a groundnut found at Tehuacan of the period 200 B.C.–700 A.D. According to Hernandez[53] the groundnut was probably taken from Haiti to Mexico by the Spanish; if this was so the introduction was probably of the Virginia type, evidently the form grown in the Antilles.

The groundnut was soon taken across the Pacific by the Spaniards. The first introduction to the Malayan archipelago was between 1521–9 or perhaps some time after 1579[54]. According to Bolhuis the first crops were of the variety Katjang tjina, a runner plant with small two-seeded pod, without strong markings and a vegetative period of 8–10 months.

The groundnut probably reached China (Fukien province) in the early seventeenth century, possibly even before 1608[55].

The observations and more particularly later descriptions and illustrations of material from the Western Pacific and Indian Oceans indicate that it was the Peruvian groundnut which spread throughout these regions. It has been variously named *Chamaebalanus japonicus*[56], *Arachis asiatica*[57], l'Arachide de l'Inde[58], and *Arachis hypogaea*[59].

Virginia groundnuts of runner habit (var. *hypogaea*) were apparently introduced to the South-eastern United States with the slave trade[60]. A range of improved forms have been produced in this area (e.g. Virginia Bunch) which have become widespread. In general morphology the Virginia ground- nut agrees with the descriptions and illustrations of groundnuts from the Antilles of seventeenth-century authors du Tertre, Labat and Plumier[61]. As yet no mainland locality has been found in South America in which the Virginia type has been of ancient cultivation nor in which it shows any appreciable variation, it should be pointed out that studies of variability are lacking in the N.E. of Brazil and in the Caribbean. (The Virginia type does however show a very considerable range of variation in the African continent[62].)

There is more information about the Spanish type (var. *vulgaris*). Gilii and Xuarez[63] record its introduction to Europe. The plant is illustrated under the name *Glycine subterranea* and came from seed sent in 1784 from Brazil to Don Jose Campos in Lisbon part of which was sent on to Rome. The greater part of the variability of var. *vulgaris* has been recorded in Paraguay and the Brazilian States of Goyaz, Minas Geraes and Sao Paulo, and therefore Brazil is a very likely source of the original Spanish type. There is no evidence against the view that the Spanish type was that which was spread by Tabares de Ulloa[64] (1799) in Valencia and from there it was taken to the South of France at the beginning of the nineteenth century. According to Higgins[65] this groundnut was introduced to the U.S.A. from Spain in 1871 and to Africa early in the present century.

Information on the Valencia type (var. *fastigiata*) in the literature is of more recent date. Dubard[66] described the fruit but the first use of the name "Valencia" was by Beattie[67] referring to a new introduction to the U.S.A. from Spain. Tonnelier[68] referred to a groundnut with 3–4 seeds/pod from Cordoba Argentina which is probably the present cultivar "Colorado de Cordoba" a Valencia type groundnut. The centre of variation of the Valencia group is in Paraguay and Central Brazil and it is possible that spread took place from South America in the present century, via Spain as the name suggests. The Valencia type has actually been cultivated on the Mediter- ranean coast and from this area it has been sent not only to the U.S.A. but to other parts of Europe in addition to Asia and Africa.

Notes

1 This paper was originally given in Spanish to the XXXVIIIth *Congreso Internacional de Americanistas* in September 1966 at Mar del Plata, Argentina. The translation is by J. Smartt.
2 Rigoni, V. A., Krapovickas, A., and Pietrarelli, J. (1960). Las variedades cultivadas de maní en la provincia de Cordoba, *Rev. Invest. Agríc.*, 14 (2), pp. 177–96.
3 Krapovickas, A. (1960). Hibridación introgressiva en manies de la región guarantica argentina, *Rev. Invest. Agríc.*, 14 (2), pp. 161–75.
4 Krapovickas, A. and Gregory, W. C. (In press).

5 Burkart, A. (1939). Estudios sistemtáicos sobre les Leguminosas-Hedisareas de la Rep. Argentina y regiones adyacentes, *Darwiniana*, 3 (2), pp. 117-302.

6 Krapovickas, A. and Rigoni, V. A. (1957). Nuevas especies de *Arachis* vinculadas al problema del origin del maní, *Darwiniana*, 11 (3), pp. 431-55.

7 Smartt, J. and Gregory, W. C. (1967). Interspecific cross-compatibility between the cultivated peanut *Arachis hypogaea* L. and other members of the genus *Arachis*, *Oléagineux*, 22, pp. 455-9.

8 Weddell, H. A. (1853). *Voyage dans le Nord de la Bolivie*. Paris.

9 Scolnik and Luti, Personal communication.

10 Burkart, A. (1939). ibid.; Chevalier, A. (1933). Monographie de l'Arachide, *Rev. Bot. Appliq.*, 13, pp. 689-789; Dubard, M. (1906). De l'origine de l'arachide, *Mus. Nat. Hist. Nat. Paris, Bull.*, 5, pp. 340-4; Hermann, F. J. (1951). A synopsis of the genus *Arachis*, *U.S. Dept. Agric. Agriculture Monograph*, 19; Hoehne, F. C. (1940). Arachis, *Flora Brasilica*, 25 (122).

11 Bois, D. (1927). *Les Plantes Alimentaires chez tous les Peuples et a travers les Ages*, I. Paris; Chevalier, A. (1929), L'origine botanique et l'amélioration des Arachides cultivées, *Rev. Bot. Appliq.*, 9, pp. 97-197; John, C. M. Venkatanarayana, G. and Sheshadri, C. R. (1954). Varieties and forms of groundnuts, *Indian J. Agric. Sci.*, 24 (4), pp. 159-93.

12 Bunting, A. H. (1955). A classification of cultivated groundnuts, *Emp. J. Exptal. Agric.*, 23, pp. 158-70; Gregory, W. C., Smith, B. W. and Yarbrough, J. A. (1951). Morphology, Genetics and Breeding, *in The Peanut, the Unpredictable Legume*. Washington; Krapovickas, A. and Rigoni, V. A. (1960). La nomenclatura de las subespecies y variedades de *Arachis hypogaea* L., *Rev. Invest. Agric.*, 14 (2), pp. 197-228; Mazzani, B. and Cobo, M. (1957). Características varietales del maní, *Agronomía Tropical*, 7 (3), pp. 109-49.

13 Krapovickas, A. and Rigoni, V. A. (1957). ibid.

14 Dubard, M. (1906). ibid.

15 Gregory, W. C., Smith, B. W. and Yarbrough, J. A. (1951). ibid.

16 Dubard, M. (1906). ibid.

17 Dubard, M. (1906). ibid.

18 Gregory, W. C., Smith, B. W. and Yarbrough, J. A. (1951). ibid.

19 Gregory, W. C., Smith, B. W. and Yarbrough, J. A. (1951). ibid.

20 Hull, F. H. (1936). Inheritance of rest period of seeds and certain other characters in the peanut, *Florida Agric. Exper. Station Bull.*, 314.

21 Anderson, E. (1949). *Introgressive Hybridisation*. New York.

22 Chevalier, A. (1929). L'Arachide Rasteiro du Brésil, *Rev. Bot. Appliq.*, 9, p. 487.

23 Hoehne, F. C. (1944). Duas novas espécies de Leguminosas do Brasil, *Arq. Bot. Est. Sao Paulo*, 2, pp. 15-18.

24 Costantin, J. and Bois, D. (1910). Sur les graines et tubercules des Tombeaux péruviens de la Période Incasique, *Rev. Gen. Bot.*, 22 (258), pp. 242-65; Dubard, M. (1906). ibid.; Towle, M. A. (1961). *The Ethnobotany of Pre-Columbian Peru*. Chicago; Wittmack, L. (1887), *in* Reiss, W. and Stuebel, A. *The Necropolis of Ancon in Peru*, 3. Berlin.

25 Monardes, N. (1574). *Historia Medicinal de las Cosas que se traen de Neustras Indias Occidentales que sirven en medicina*. Sevilla.

26 Mazzini, N. and Cobo, M. (1957). op. cit. Fig. 4B.

27 Towle, M. A. (1961). ibid.

28 Dubard, M. (1906). ibid.

29 Steward, J. H. (ed.) (1950). *Handbook of South American Indians*, 6. map 18.

30 Squier, E. G. (1877). *Peru Illustrated*. New York.

31 de Candolle, A. L. P. P. (1884). *Origin of Cultivated Plants*. London.

32 Dubard, M. (1906). ibid.

33 Bois, D. (1927). ibid.
34 Skvortzow, B. V. (1920). On some varieties of peanuts grown in China, *J. N. China Branch Roy. Asiat. Soc.*, **51**, pp. 142–5.
35 Ames, O. (1939). *Economic Annuals and Human Cultures*. Cambridge, Mass.
36 Anderson, E. (1952). *Plants, Man and Life*. Boston.
37 Merrill, E. D. (1954). *The Botany of Cook's Voyages*. Waltham, Mass.
38 Olivier, M. (1954). Le marché mondial des arachides, *Oléagineux*, **9** (2), pp. 125–8; Johnson, F. R. (1964). *The Peanut Story*. Murfreesboro, N.C.
39 Gilii, F. L. and Xuarez, G. (1789). *Osservazione Fitologiche sopra alcune Pliante Esotiche Introdotte in Roma fatte nell'anno 1788*. Rome. Translated in Furlong, G. (1954). *Gaspar Juares, S. J. y sus Noticias Fitologicas*. Buenos Aires.
40 Valdizan, H. and Maldonado, A. (1922). *La Medicina Popular Peruana*. Lima.
41 Chevalier, A. (1933). ibid.
42 Zapata Gollán, A., (1945). Nomenclature mocobí de animales y plantas, *Bol. Dep. Estud. Etnogr. y Coloniales*, **1** (1), pp. 51–62. Santa Fé.
43 Cerviño, P. A. (1910). *Vocabulario Español y Lenguas, en Catal. Razonado de las Secc. Lenguas americanas por B. Mitre*, **2**. Buenos Aires. (MSS. of 1839.) pp. 145–60.
44 Abregú, V. C. (1942). *Idiomas Aborígenes*. Buenos Aires.
45 Cominges, J. de (1892). *Vocabulario de Algunas Palabras en Idioma Guaná*. Obras escogidas de Juan de Cominges. Buenos Aires. pp. 247–9.
46 Da Rocha, A. C. (1938). Vocabulario comentado Pilagá-Castellano, *Comisión Honoraria de Reducciones de Indios*, **7**. Beunos Aires.
47 Metraux, A. (1930). Etudes sur la civilisation des indiens Chiriguano, *Rev. Inst. Etnol. Univ. Nac. Tucuman*, **1** (3), pp. 295–494.
48 Hunt, R. (1915). El choroti o yofuaha, *Rev. Mus. La. Plata*, **10** (2nd series), pl. 23.
49 Tebboth, T. (1943). Diccionario Castellano-Toba, *Rev. Inst. Antropol. Univ. Nac. Tucumán*, **3** (2), pp. 35–221.
50 Oviedo y Valdés, G. F. de (1535). *Primera Parte deai Historia Natural y General de las Indias*. Madrid.
51 Clavigero, F. S. (1787). *The History of Mexico*, **1**. London.
52 Heiser, C. B., Jr. (1965). Cultivated plants and cultural diffusion in Nuclear America, *Amer. Anthrop.*, **67** (4), pp. 930–49.
53 Hernandez, F. (1790). *Opera*, **2**. Madrid.
54 Bolhuis, G. G. (1955). La culture de l'arachide en Indonésie, *Oléagineux*, **10**, (3), pp. 157–60.
55 Currington Goodrich, L. (1936–7). Early notices of the peanut in China, *J. Orient. Stud. Cath. Univ. Peking*, **2**, pp. 405–9.
56 Rumphius, G. E. (1747). *Herbarium Amboinense*, **5**. Amsterdam.
57 Loureiro, J. (1790). *Flora Conchinchinensis*. Lisboa.
58 Cordemoy, C. J. de. (1866). Note sur L'Arachide (Île de la Réunion), *Adansonia*, **6**, pp. 249–53.
59 Blanco, M. (1878). *Flora de Filipinas*. (3rd ed.), **2**. Manila.
60 Higgins, B. B. (1951). Origin and early history of the peanut, *in* Gregory, W. C., Smith, B. W. and Yarbrough, J. A. (1951). ibid.
61 Chevalier, A. (1933). ibid.; Higgins, B. B. (1951). ibid.
62 Gibbons, R. W. and Harkness, C. In preparation; Bunting, A. H. (1955). ibid.; Bunting, A. H. (1958). A further note on the classification of culti-vated peanuts, *Emp. J. Exptal. Agric.*, **26**, pp. 254–8; Meikle, J. O. (1965). A survey of African-grown groundnut varieties in Rhodesia, *Rhodesia Agric. J.*, **62**, pp. 109–13; Smartt, J. (1961). Groundnut varieties of Northern Rhodesia and their classification, *Emp. J. Exptal. Agric.*, **29**, pp. 153–8.

63 Gilii, F. L. and Xuarez. G. (1789). ibid.
64 Tabares de Ulloa, F. (1799). *Relación Sucinta en que se explica sencillamente el nuevo descubrimiento de sacar el aceyte del cacahuate o Maní de America.* Valencia.
65 Higgins, B. B. (1951). ibid.
66 Dubard, M. (1906). ibid.
67 Beattie, W. (1911). The peanut, *Farmers Bull.*, **431**. Washington.
68 Tonnelier, A. C. (1912). Informe sobre el mani, *Bol. Min. Agric.*, **14** (5), pp. 460–8.

BARBARA PICKERSGILL

The domestication of chili peppers

Introduction

Chili peppers share with *Phaseolus* beans and the Cucurbits the distinction of being among the first plants cultivated in the New World. Unlike the latter crops, peppers never formed a staple part of the diet, but have always been much-prized condiments. Both fresh and dried fruits contain a phenolic compound, capsaicin, in the placentas, which gives them their characteristic pungency.

Several of the cultivated species of *Capsicum* are extremely variable. Bell peppers, paprika, cayenne and the Mexican chilis are all forms of a single species, *C. annuum*. This is the only species known to most Europeans, although at least three others, *C. baccatum*, *C. chinense* and *C. pubescens*, are still widely cultivated in South America, which is the centre of origin of this genus.

These species could be of recent origin; the products of a single domestication followed by evolution and divergence under cultivation. Alternatively, there may have been several distinct species before the development of agriculture, each of which was subsequently domesticated from wild plants of that species. These multiple domestications may have occurred independently or the idea may have spread from one area to another, leading to experimentation with the rather different wild material available in different regions.

Distribution of the domesticated chili peppers

Table 1 shows the probable pre-Conquest distribution of the principal cultivated species of chili pepper. The most likely ancestor of cultivated *C. annuum* is the wild bird pepper (*C. annuum* var. *minimum*). This has a fairly wide distribution, whereas cultivated *C. annuum* was limited to Middle America in pre-Conquest times[1]. *C. baccatum*, on the other hand, has always been restricted to South America. Wild plants (var. *baccatum*) occur only in southern Peru and Bolivia. Cultivated types (var. *pendulum*) presumably developed from these wild plants and are most frequent in Peru and Bolivia but extend north up the west coast to southern Colombia. *C. chinense* has a distribution which is complementary to that of *C. baccatum*, since *C. chinense* attains its greatest diversity east of the Andes, in the Amazon Basin. It extends also to the West Indies, and its range overlaps that of *C. baccatum* in Ecuador, Peru and Bolivia. *C. chinense* is closely related to, and possibly originated from, a fourth species, *C. frutescens*. The latter includes the cultivated Tabasco peppers and is widespread both as a weed and in cultivation throughout Middle America and lowland South America. In highland South America these species give place to a more hardy pepper, *C. pubescens*, of which no wild forms are known.

Species		Probable pre-Conquest distribution
C. annuum		
var. *minimum*	wild	Southern U.S., West Indies, Mexico, Central America, Colombia.
var. *annuum*	cultivated	Southern U.S., Mexico, Central America.
C. baccatum		
var. *baccatum*	wild	Southern Peru, Bolivia.
var. *pendulum*	cultivated	Southern Colombia, Ecuador, Peru, Bolivia, southern Brazil, northern Chile, and Argentina.
C. chinense	cultivated	West Indies, lowland South America south to Bolivia and southern Brazil.
C. frutescens	wild and cultivated	Mexico, Central America, lowland South America south to Bolivia and Brazil.
C. pubescens	cultivated	Highland South America.

Table 1 Pre-Conquest distribution of the cultivated species of *Capsicum*.

Since there are wild plants related to most of the cultivated varieties, and since the different species are separated by well-marked barriers to gene exchange[2], it is probable that these species existed before the development of agriculture and that each was domesticated independently. Moreover, since the species have somewhat distinct ranges even today, they were probably domesticated in different areas by different groups. It is, of course, possible that the wild varieties found today represent weedy plants descended from cultivated varieties, but studies on their cytology and ability to intercross[3] suggest that the wild varieties are more closely related to one another, and hence closer to any common ancestor of this group, than are the cultivated varieties.

Little is known about a number of other species of limited distribution. In Bolivia, fruits of *C. cardenasii* and *C. eximium* are collected and sold in the markets, and the same is true of *C. praetermissum* in south-eastern Brazil. Toleration rather than cultivation of useful but weedy peppers is characteristic also of primitive agricultural systems in Amazonia, where peppers seldom seem to be sown deliberately but spontaneously germinating plants are preserved even if they come up in the middle of the manioc patch or banana grove. Peppers probably occupied a similar privileged status as tolerated weeds in the initial stages of their domestication.

Changes occurring under domestication

Chili peppers are particularly favourable for studying evolution under domestication since so many of the species contain both wild and cultivated varieties. These can be crossed and the genetic bases of the differences between them studied. The archaeological record, although incomplete, may date some of the stages in their domestication.

Wild peppers all have in common small, red, pungent fruits, which may be spherical, oval, conical or elongate, borne erect on the plant, and deciduous, i.e. readily separating from the persistent calyx. The seeds are probably dispersed by birds, attracted by the bright colour of the exposed fruits and seen feeding avidly on the flesh of even the most pungent varieties. Under cultivation, one of the first changes to occur was loss of this dispersal mechanism. Since man was growing the plants for their fruits, he selected, consciously or unconsciously, for non-deciduous fruits which would remain on the plants until harvested. This character is controlled by a single major gene, and the dominant allele produces deciduous fruits[4], so once a mutation to the recessive, non-deciduous allele had occurred it would be relatively easy to eliminate deciduous fruits by selection. The position of the fruits also changed from erect to pendant. This was perhaps in part a consequence of the increased size and weight of the fruit in cultivated forms, but a mutation to pendant would again protect the crop from bird damage, since pendant fruits are hidden amongst the foliage and not conspicuous.

Size, shape and colour of the fruits also varied enormously under human selection. Observations of this type have repeatedly been made on cultivated plants, leading to the generalization that variability is greatest in that part of the plant that is of economic importance. Red, orange, yellow and brown fruits developed independently in all four cultivated *Capsicum* species and there is also much parallel variation in fruit shape.

Another effect of domestication seems to have been a shift to increased self-pollination. Comparison of wild and cultivated varieties shows that wild plants have relatively long styles exserted beyond the anthers, while in cultivated plants the stigma is at or near the level of the anthers, so that self-pollination is more likely. Self-incompatibility, reported for some wild species of *Capsicum*, is unknown in cultivated varieties. Increased inbreeding could have been caused by selection by man for high fruit set, or for plants which bred true from seed, or by movement of the crop into an area in which natural pollinating agents were uncommon. Once self-pollination is established, several distinct types can be grown in a small area without losing their identities by intercrossing. Standley[5] reported a practice among the Indians of

Guatemala which, if widespread, would also increase the amount of inbreeding. He stated that varieties of maize and beans "are often very local and carefully guarded, but not because they are believed superior to varieties grown by neighbours. The Indians cherish a firm belief that it is best to plant seeds grown on the premises. Otherwise the plants would never be happy; they would become homesick, as it were, pine away, and the crop would fail."

The archaeological record

Chili peppers have been identified from sites in both Middle and South America. In Mexico, peppers have been recorded from MacNeish's excavations in Tamaulipas[6] and Tehuacán[7]. In both areas peppers are present in the earliest levels, dating back to about 7000 B.C. This antedates the development of agriculture and implies that wild plants were being exploited. These Mexican specimens have sometimes been assigned to *C. frutescens*, but I have seen photographs of broken fruits from Palo Blanco levels at Tehuacán (700 B.C.–A.D. 200) and these relatively large fragments with the calyx still attached look to me more like cultivated *C. annuum*.

In South America, chili peppers have been found in sites on the coast of Peru. Peppers are thus far unknown from pre-agricultural sites in this region, which suggests that they did not occur wild here but were introduced from elsewhere. The first plants cultivated were apparently gourds and squashes[8], but by 2000 B.C. peppers were grown in the Ancón area on the central coast[9] and at Huaca Prieta on the north coast[10]. I have studied material from both areas and consider that these specimens came from cultivated, not wild, plants. Fruits from the lowest levels in both areas had the calyx attached, which suggests that the non-deciduous character, typical of cultivated plants, was already established. At Huaca Prieta, both red and orange fruits were present in the lowest levels, which again suggests selection under cultivation, since orange fruits are unknown among wild forms. Seed width also falls within the range of cultivated rather than wild plants.

If the material is in good condition it is possible to identify more precisely the cultivated species represented in sites in South America. *C. pubescens* can be distinguished from *C. baccatum* and *C. chinense* by its black seeds, but it has not yet been recorded archaeologically. *C. baccatum* and *C. chinense* both have straw-coloured seeds, but *C. baccatum* has a toothed calyx with prominent veins, while in *C. chinense* the calyx is entire and the veins less conspicuous. The fruits from Ancón and the lower levels of Huaca Prieta represent *C. baccatum*. This species was domesticated in southern Peru or Bolivia[11]. The material from both Huaca Prieta and Ancón belongs to the late Preceramic Stage and during this stage cotton, *Canna* and *Canavalia* beans also reached the coast, probably spreading from the same centre as *C.*

baccatum. This suggests that southern contacts played an important part in the development of coastal cultures at this time.

The Huaca Prieta specimens show that *C. baccatum* was gradually improved under human selection. Seeds and fruits increased in size and deciduous fruits were eliminated. However, in H.P.3 D2 and succeeding levels, mean seed width decreased, deciduous fruits reappeared, and the shape and calyx characters of some of the fruits suggest that a second species, *C. chinense*, at a less advanced stage of domestication, was introduced. The centre of diversity of *C. chinense* today is east of the Andes and its domestication was probably connected with the development of agriculture in the tropical forests. It may well have spread in association with manioc, which apparently reached the coast of Peru at about the same time as this pepper.

As more archaeological material becomes available, it should be possible to assess more accurately the interplay between different areas of the New World on the basis of changes in the cultivated plants. Present evidence indicates that agriculture developed along surprisingly independent lines in Mexico and Peru[12]. Even when the same crop was cultivated in the two areas, it was often represented by different species, as for example the amaranths, chenopods, *Canavalia* beans and chili peppers. In Peru, on the other hand, although one might expect the desert coast and the Amazon jungles to have been effectively isolated by the barrier of the high Andes, contact between the different regions seems to have been effective and prolonged, as shown by the presence of manioc, peanuts and *C. chinense*, domesticated in the tropical forests, in prehistoric sites on the coast.

The historical record

Chili peppers were a new and valuable spice to Europeans at a time when the desire to obtain spices was providing a considerable impetus to exploration. They were the most important spice encountered by Columbus in his unsuccessful attempt to find a route to the East Indies. Several of the Spanish chroniclers thus devoted considerable space to these peppers.

Perhaps Cobo[13], who travelled throughout much of Spanish South America early in the seventeenth century, has given the best description of the variability then present in chili peppers. He reported that "one is as large as limes or large plums; another, as small as pine nuts or even grains of wheat, and between these two extremes are many different sizes. No less variety is found in colour. . . . The same difference is found in form and shape; for one is round; another, elongated, and others, of many other forms. . . . Finally, the different kinds of peppers found in these Indies are so many that they exceed forty." Garcilaso de la Vega[14] mentioned both yellow and brown fruited forms and both Acosta[15] and Oviedo[16] reported sweet varieties. It is thus clear that the great variability in these peppers was established by the time of the Spanish Conquest and was not a product of the trade and opportunities for hybridization created by European colonization.

It is difficult to identify the species recognized today in the chroniclers' descriptions. The rocoto, described by Cobo[17] as having a leaf "very different from the other kinds of pepper, for it is much larger, not as smooth, of a dark green" is probably *C. pubescens*, since this species has hairier leaves than most cultivated varieties and is still called rocoto today. Oviedo[18] described a pepper which "has (small green fruits) mottled with black, . . . not the whole fruit, but some part of it". This is almost certainly *C.annuum* var. *minimum*, which in Colombia is gathered while the fruits are still green. It has not proved possible to distinguish between *C. chinense* and *C. baccatum* in the chroniclers' accounts.

All the chroniclers agree on the importance of peppers to the Indians. According to Cobo[19], "pepper holds first place, after maize, as the plant most common and of greatest esteem amongst the Indians". The fruits were used in stews or soups, with meat or fish, and the leaves could be used to make a sauce similar to parsley[20]. Salt and tomatoes were sometimes used to temper the pungency of the fruits[21]. Besides being used fresh, the fruits were preserved by pickling, which was the form preferred for sea voyages[22], or by drying.

The value of pepper fruits to the Indians, and the fact that they could be preserved and stored for some time, may have led to their becoming a form of money in Peru, in the same way that cacao beans did among the Aztecs. According to Valcárcel[23], "under the Inca money was not known and certain preferred products like peppers were perhaps the rudiments of a monetary system. Until a few years ago one could shop in the plaza of Cuzco with the so-called 'Rantii', which was a handful of peppers."

Not surprisingly, in view of their secular importance, chili peppers also figured in religious belief and custom. One form of the Inca creation myth names the four brothers who emerged at the beginning of the world as Manco Capac, who became the first Inca, Ayar Cachi (Cachi = salt), Ayar Uchu (Uchu = chili pepper) and Ayar Sauca (Sauca = pleasure). The allegorical interpretation given by Garcilaso[24] is that "by the salt they say that the instruction which the Ynca gave in the rational life is to be understood. The pepper represents the delight they received from this teaching, and the word for pleasure is to show the joy and satisfaction in which they afterwards lived."

Summary

The evolutionary history of chili peppers is being traced by a combination of morphological, cytogenetical and archaeological studies. At least four species were grown in the New World at the time of the Spanish Conquest and these species seem to have undergone parallel but independent domestication and selection in different areas. Chili peppers are among the most ancient cultivated plants and may prove as valuable as some inorganic artifacts in tracing cultural contacts in the Americas[25].

Notes

1 Smith, P. G. and Heiser, C. B., Jr. (1957). Taxonomy of *Capsicum sinense* Jacq. and the geographic distribution of the cultivated *Capsicum* species, *Bull. Torrey Bot. Club*, **84**, pp. 413–20.
2 Smith, P. G. and Heiser, C. B., Jr. (1957). Breeding behaviour of cultivated peppers, *Proc. Amer. Soc. Hort. Sci.*, **70**, pp. 286–90; Eshbaugh, W. H., III. (1964). A numerical taxonomid and cytogenetic study of certain species of the genus *Capsicum*, *Ph.D. thesis, Indiana University*; Pickersgill, B. (1966). The variability and relationships of *Capsicum chinense* Jacq., *Ph.D. thesis, Indiana University*.
3 Pickersgill, B. 1966). ibid. and unpublished data.
4 Lippert, L. F., Smith, P. G., and Bergh, B. O. (1966). Cytogenetics of the vegetable crops. Garden pepper, *Capsicum* sp., *Bot. Rev.*, **32**, pp. 24–55.
5 Standley, P. C. (1946). Food plants of the Indians of the Guatemalan highlands, *J. Arnold Arbor.*, **27**, pp. 395–400.
6 Kaplan, L. and MacNeish, R. S. (1960). Prehistoric bean remains from caves in the Ocampo region of Tamaulipas, Mexico, *Botanical Museum Leaflets, Harvard University*, **19**, pp. 33–56.
7 MacNeish, R. S. (1964). Ancient Mesoamerican civilisation, *Science*, **143**, pp. 531–7.
8 Lanning, E. P. (1965). Early man in Peru, *Scientific American*, **213**, pp. 68–76.
9 Moseley, M. E., Personal communication.
10 Bird, J. (1948). America's oldest farmers, *Nat. Hist.*, **57**, pp. 296–303 and 334–5.
11 Pickersgill, B. Unpublished data.
12 Heiser, C. B., Jr. (1965). Cultivated plants and cultural diffusion in Nuclear America, *Amer. Anthrop.*, **67**, pp. 930–49.
13 Cobo, B. (1653). *Historia del Nuevo Mundo*. Reprinted in 1956 in *Biblioteca de Autores Españoles*, **91**. Madrid. The quoted passages have been translated from this reprint.
14 Garcilaso de la Vega, I. (1609). *Comentarios Reales*. Primera parte. Translated and edited by C. R. Markham for the *Hakluyt Society Works*, **2** (45), London. 1871.
15 Acosta, J. de. (1590). *Historia Natural y Moral de las Indias*. Translated in 1604 by E. Grimston and edited by C. R. Markham for the *Hakluyt Society Works*, **60** and **61**, London. 1880.
16 Oviedo y Valdés, G. F. de. (1547). *Historia General y Natural de las Indias*. Reprinted in 1959 in *Biblioteca de Autores Españoles*, **117**, Madrid. The quoted passage has been translated from this reprint.
17 Cobo, B. (1653). ibid.
18 Oviedo y Valdés, G. F. de. (1547). ibid.
19 Cobo, B. (1653). ibid.
20 Cobo, B. (1653). ibid.; Oviedo y Valdés, G. F. de (1547). ibid.
21 Acosta, J. de. (1590). ibid.
22 Cobo, B. (1653). ibid.
23 Valcárcel, L. E. (1925). *Del ayllu al imperio*. Lima. The quotation has been translated from the Spanish.

24 Garcilaso de la Vega, I. (1609). ibid.
25 The work reported here was supported in part by a grant from the National Science Foundation of the United States to Dr. C. B. Heiser, Jr., who supervised the thesis from which this paper has developed. I should like to thank the Instituto Nacional de Antropologia e Historia, Mexico City, for photographs of pepper fruits from Tehuacán; Dr. M. Towle for loan of the specimens from Huaca Prieta in the Harvard Botanical Museum; and Mr. M. E. Moseley for making available specimens and unpublished data from his excavations at Ancón.

J. SMARTT

Evolution of American Phaseolus *beans under domestication*

Introduction

Studies of crop plant evolution are of interest to both the plant breeder and the archaeologist. The plant breeder cannot hope to understand the present state of his crop plants without some knowledge of their evolutionary history while the archaeologist needs to know the role which specific crops played in the life of human communities in the past and for how long they have been significant in them.

Many botanists, geneticists and agriculturists have been interested in studies of crop plant evolution. Typical of the kind of work which has been done is that of Simmonds[1] on bananas, Hutchinson *et al.*[2] on cotton and several others[3]. Most evolutionary studies of crop plants have been a by-product of straightforward plant breeding projects. In the effort to broaden the genetic base of a given crop plant land races or relatively "unimproved" varieties were first exploited followed by ancestral wild forms and related species. As a result of such work a more or less clear picture of probable phylogenetic relationships has frequently emerged over a period. In the present study this approach could not be used. The great mass of taxonomic and genetical data necessary simply was not available.

In the present world food situation the actual and potential importance of the protein rich grain legumes is such that much more detailed study is required before much improvement can be made in them. To form some idea of the evolutionary history of a group of plants such as the New World species of *Phaseolus* it has been necessary to consider the published evidence available and where necessary to try to fill gaps as far as possible by further experiment and observations. This work began in early 1965 at the School of Agriculture, Cambridge under the direction of Professor Sir Joseph Hutchinson. A considerable range of *Phaseolus* material had already been assembled and this was added to quite considerably during the course of the work.

Taxonomy

The genus *Phaseolus* belongs to the tribe Phaseoleae of the Leguminosae and is related to other genera with cultigens such as *Vigna* and *Dolichos*. The more conservative authorities consider that the genus *Phaseolus* contains about 150 species[4]. This number is probably inflated by synonyms, Mackie[5] listed 18 for one species (*Phaseolus lunatus* L.) alone and this is probably not exceptional.

Four distinct groups can be recognized easily within the genus namely

1 *Phaseolus* proper or *Euphaseolus*[6]: the large seeded American beans
2 *Macroptilium*[7]: very small seeded American forms
3 *Azukia*[8]: rather small seeded Asiatic forms
4 *Caracallae*[9]: forms with characteristic "snail flowers".

These groupings consist of forms which have similar flower and pod morphology which have been grown at Cambridge and are by no means a complete breakdown of the genus. The taxonomic treatments of the genus available at the present time are not only unhelpful but positively misleading; de Candolle, Taubert and Piper[10] all place some closely related species in different sections of the genus. The quality of much of the herbarium material available is very poor, without flowers very often and inadequate for reliable determination in many cases. A modern taxonomic revision of this important genus is long overdue.

The New World cultivated species *Phaseolus vulgaris* L., *Ph. coccineus* L., *Ph. lunatus* L. and *Ph. acutifolius* A.Gr. were selected for study because they are most widely disseminated members of the genus and adequate material was available. Although accurate figures of the world production are not available, it is probable that *Ph. vulgaris* is the most widely cultivated, followed by *Ph. lunatus* and *Ph. coccineus* in that order with *Ph. acutifolius* in the lowest rank. These beans have all come to the Old World in post-Columbian times.

Archaeological record

The archaeological record for *Phaseolus* in the New World is most impressive. Kaplan[11] has reported radiocarbon datings of 7000 B.P. for *Ph. vulgaris* from Tehuacán, Mexico, 5300 B.P. for *Ph. lunatus* from Chilca, Peru, 5000 B.P. for *Ph. acutifolius* from Tehuacán, Mexico and 2200 B.P. for *Ph. coccineus* also from Tehuacán with a possible earlier dating of 7500–9000 B.P. from Ocampo in Mexico. These dates take us up to early agricultural times in America, yet Kaplan has reported that seed and pod material of *Ph. vulgaris* was basically similar to modern beans. This suggests that the development of beans similar to modern types occurred quite rapidly in early agricultural times.

Kaplan has also concluded that *Ph. lunatus* was domesticated independently in Peru and Mexico, these different domesticates can be distinguished easily on seed size, the large, Peruvian *macrospermus* and the smaller Mexican *microspermus* type. It seems quite probable that domestication of *Ph. vulgaris* has been equally if not more complex; the present complex pattern of morphological variation in *Ph. vulgaris* could be perhaps a result of a complex pattern of domestication.

Because beans have such a long history under domestication it is possible that the divergence between the cultivated and wild forms has been so great as to make it difficult to relate cultigens to their wild progenitors. There is the additional possibility that the four species now in cultivation had a single wild progenitor. Both questions can be resolved easily; wild forms of all four species, obviously related to the forms in cultivation can be found. We can conclude that the origin of specific rank differences between the four species, all of which incidentally are diploid with $2n = 22$ chromosomes, preceded domestication.

Kaplan has also pointed out the dietary importance of beans. Bean seeds are rich in lysine and tryptophane, two essential amino-acids deficient in maize. The two crops complement each other and together produce a reasonably balanced diet. In the absence of domesticated animals this combination of crops is highly advantageous and even at the present time, notwithstanding the introduction of cattle and other domestic animals, *Phaseolus* beans still make an important contribution of protein to the Mexican diet.

Comparative morphology of wild forms

1 Growth habit

The wild forms of the four *Phaseolus* species we are considering have basically the same growth habit. This they share with other wild species such as *Ph. polystachyus* (L.) B.S.P., which have produced no cultigens. *Ph. polystachyus* is called the thicket bean and its habit of growth enables it to become established and survive in such a plant community. The main axis is slender and ascending and may reach a length of several feet, six or even more. Lateral branches are produced profusely which initially are not ascending but grow out more or less horizontally and straight for considerable distances (two or three feet, perhaps more) before assuming the twining and ascending pattern of growth. In this way thicket vegetation can become thoroughly infiltrated by the growth of these plants in a relatively short time.

Some differences in response have been observed in experimental cultivation. The primitive form of *Phaseolus coccineus* (*Ph. formosus* H.B.K.) when grown in open ground does not climb or scramble but first covers the soil with a mat of vegetation, only when this is done will it climb. On the other hand primitive *Ph. vulgaris* (ssp. *aborigineus* Burk.) is climbing in open ground; in greenhouse cultivation however both forms are climbing from the outset.

2 *Flower, fruit and seed characters*

Lilac flowers are found in all four species in the wild. In addition red and pink flowers are found in wild *Ph. coccineus* (the pink flowered individuals are hybrid) and white flowers are found in some northern collections of *Ph. vulgaris* ssp. *aborigineus*.

Basic flower structure is very similar indeed in all four species. Size of flowers is greatest in *Ph. coccineus*, least in *Ph. lunatus*. The stigmatic surface is outwardly directed or nearly terminal in *Ph. coccineus* (*Ph. formosus*) and inwardly directly in the others. This is associated with a greater tendency to cross-pollination in *Ph. coccineus*. Self-pollination is perfectly feasible, the stigmatic surface however requires scarification before pollen will grow in *Ph. coccineus*; this is not required in the other three species. The young pod is rather fleshy in *Ph. vulgaris* and *Ph. coccineus* but fibrous in *Ph. acutifolius* and *Ph. lunatus*. The number of seed per pod is characteristically never more than four in *Ph. lunatus* but may range up to eight or nine in the other species.

Testa colour and pattern is basically similar throughout the four species (and also *Ph. polystachyus*). This is basically grey or brown with a dense pattern of darker spots and blotches. Self-coloured testas do occur, black-seeded *Ph. lunatus* and *Ph. vulgaris* and buff-seeded *Ph. coccineus* (*formosus*) have been collected from the wild.

Seed dormancy occurs as a rule due to "hard-seededness", in addition *Ph. acutifolius* requires a post-harvest maturation period before germination can occur.

Flowering and fruiting in *Phaseolus* may be affected by day length, a common enough occurrence in plants from low latitudes. In the Cambridge collection of *Phaseolus*, wild representatives of *Ph. vulgaris* have the most rigid photoperiodic requirement; one accession from N.W. Argentina does not flower before October under normal day lengths in England. Other lines will flower earlier than this but not usually until the summer solstice is past. It is possible to induce such forms to flower in Spring by early sowing in the greenhouse. Two distinct types of photoperiodic response have been observed, the first for a specific day length and the second for a declining day length. This subject merits detailed study under carefully controlled conditions.

In addition to photoperiod-sensitive lines, day-neutral strains can be found which will flower at almost any time of the year under long or short days.

3 *Variability in wild populations*

The sampling of wild populations we have been able to make is much smaller than we would have liked but it does indicate that the variability within each species in the wild may be quite considerable. Some of the conclusions we might draw from the changes we believe to have followed domestication must be subject to the proviso that such differences might already have existed in wild populations, though perhaps not extensively. There can be little doubt however that in the early days of domestication, progress in the improvement of beans was assisted by the variability which existed in the populations of the wild form of a given species.

Ecological considerations

In nature all four species do not occur together in the same habitat. A range of habitats is exploited from the cool, moist montane conditions in which *Ph. coccineus* flourishes to the arid, semi-desert conditions in which *Ph. acutifolius* is found. Warm temperate conditions are optimal for *Ph. vulgaris* whereas *Ph. lunatus* grows best in the tropics and sub-tropics.

The environments which the members of this genus can exploit cover an enormous geographic range from Scandinavia to New Zealand; it is regrettable that these valuable plants are not exploited more fully, especially in the tropics where they could provide additional protein for human nutrition.

Response to domestication

The New World cultigens in the genus *Phaseolus* provide an opportunity to test Vavilov's principle of homologous variation. One would expect responses to be qualitatively similar and to a considerable extent they are. Of course the selection pressures to which the different species have been exposed are different and the differences in response under domestication will in all probability reflect this. This does not of course exclude the possibility that the species have inherently different capacities to respond. The actual response must therefore depend on both the capacity for response and the intensity of selection imposed.

1 *Morphological responses*

(*a*) *Growth habit*. The most obvious effect of domestication on most *Phaseolus* is the modification of growth habit. To take *Phaseolus vulgaris* as an example, the physical difference in growth form between the wild ssp. *aborigineus* and a cultivated dwarf French bean variety is enormous. The differences between climbing or "pole" varieties and the wild forms are less but they are none the less real.

The major difference between wild and climbing beans on the one hand and the dwarf varieties on the other is principally in branching pattern. In the wild and climbing forms growth is indeterminate, the axes continue to grow indefinitely whereas in most dwarf varieties after the production of seven or eight nodes or less, growth of the main axis is terminated by an inflorescence. Lateral branches are terminated in a similar fashion. This difference is under very simple genetic control, by a single locus. Typical 3 : 1 ratios are given in F_2 for crosses indeterminate × determinate in *Ph. vulgaris*, *Ph. coccineus* and *Ph. lunatus*[12].

The differences between primitives and climbers are rather more subtle. In both the main axis is ascending and behaves similarly. The behaviour of the lateral branches is quite different. In the primitives these are numerous and can grow to enormous lengths. In cultivated climbers these are very considerably reduced in number and if they grow to any considerable length are ascending from the outset, there is no diageotropic tendency. In the most advanced climbers the growth form is pyramidal, the first laterals are the longest, successive branches are progressively shorter. Laterals are often produced only at the first seven or eight nodes.

The selection of growth habits has been related to development of agricultural practice. It is generally believed that maize and beans were grown together. The maize stalks provided support for climbing beans. However if beans with the wild growth habit were grown, unless the maize plants were well separated the whole plot would become an enormous tangle by the time either the beans or maize were mature. A reduction in the production of lateral branches is clearly advantageous in these circumstances. This seems to have come about by selection at the polygenic level. Among domesticated climbing beans there is a considerable range of variation in the extent to which lateral branching is suppressed.

After a period of mixed cropping of maize and beans, single crop cultivation was probably attempted and in these circumstances the dwarf-determinate growth habit was advantageous. In nature or in mixed cultivation the dwarf determinate mutation would have been effectively lethal. It is of course on the dwarf-determinate form that the present commercial production of beans for canning and processing is based. Man has here preserved and propagated a key mutant in *Phaseolus* on which its future as a crop plant has depended. Kaplan[13] has mentioned vegetative remains of a dwarf bean 800 years old which was found in Tamaulipas. Since differences in seed characters are not correlated in any way with growth habit nothing can be inferred in regard to the growth form of more ancient material.

Ojehomon[14] at Cambridge studied comparatively the development of indeterminate and determinate forms of *Ph. vulgaris* and has suggested that the terminal inflorescence of a determinate is equivalent to the axillary inflorescence of an indeterminate at the seventh or eight node on the main axis. That is the lowest node which bears an inflorescence. Froussios (unpublished) has classified three distinct growth forms on the basis of both growth habit and branching pattern these are:

1 Indeterminate climber
2 Indeterminate bush or dwarf
3 Determinate bush or dwarf.

To this list the class indeterminate-scramblers represented by the primitive forms can be added.

The full range of growth forms can be found in *Ph. vulgaris*. No dwarf-indeterminates have been reported in *Ph. coccineus* and *Ph. lunatus*; however, all cultivars of *Ph. acutifolius* are of this type.

(*b*) *Size of vegetative plant parts.* We have considered how under domestication the production of lateral branches has been reduced in the climbers and the length of the main axis and lateral branches has been curtailed in dwarf forms. Without compensating increases in the size of plant parts, stems and leaves principally, it is doubtful whether the plant could have responded successfully to selection. A determinate mutation in the genetic background of *Ph. vulgaris* ssp. *aborigineus* would have produced a spindly plant perhaps six inches high with very low productive capacity. It seems probable that what has happened is that selection for increase in leaf and stem size proceeded hand in hand with that for reduction in production of lateral branches. The genetic control of these could well be independent. Certainly experimentally produced F_2 progeny from the cross *Ph. coccineus* cr. Hammond's Dwarf Scarlet × *Ph. coccineus* (*Ph. formosus*) show segregants combining the determinate dwarf habit of the cultivar with the small leaf of the primitive parent.

The consequences of domestication have been reductions in the number of branches and leaves with a compensating increase in leaf size together with correlated increases in stem diameter. When the new balance was struck in the climbers, the determinate mutant became viable in cultivation because the individual plant had sufficient leaf area to produce an adequate yield of crop.

The response pattern outlined has been recorded in all species but *Ph. acutifolius*. In this species leaf and stem size have not increased, the plant habit is bushy rather than climbing and no determinate forms have become established.

(*c*) *Changes in reproductive plant parts.* Flower size is appreciably larger in cultigens of *Ph. coccineus* and *Ph. vulgaris* than in primitive forms but little or no change has apparently occurred in *Ph. acutifolius* and *Ph. lunatus*. Changes in flower colour have occurred: white flowers are found in cultivated *Ph.*

coccineus, *Ph. lunatus* and *Ph. acutifolius* but not in the wild, and lilac flowers are found among the cultigens of all species except *Ph. coccineus*. Every species therefore has two common flower colour variants, red and white in *Ph. coccineus* and lilac and white in the other species.

The most important change which has taken place in the reproductive parts is pod and seed size. Seed number per pod has not changed significantly except in *Ph. acutifolius* in which up to nine seeds may be found in wild forms but rarely more than six in cultivars. Pod and seed size has increased most in *Ph. coccineus*; primitive pods rarely if ever exceed three inches in length. Pods of cultivars with the same number of seeds may be well over a foot in length. The weights of individual seeds of any wild species do not usually exceed 0·1 gm. by very much; the seed of cultivars of *Ph. coccineus* may be as much as 1·0 gm. in weight. Seed weight has increased by a factor of about eight. In the other species increases in pod and seed size have not perhaps been as great but in *Ph. vulgaris* and *Ph. lunatus* they are none the less striking and a five- or six-fold increase at least has been achieved in some cultivated varieties. In *Ph. vulgaris* there is a continuous range of seed size from the primitive to the largest seeded cultivated form. In both *Ph. coccineus* and *Ph. lunatus* there is at the present time a very sharp discontinuity between primitive and cultivated races in seed size. A much less striking increase in seed size has occurred in *Ph. acutifolius*, probably only by a factor of three.

Preliminary studies have begun on the inheritance of seed size in *Ph. coccineus*. The indications are that it is determined polyfactorially but no estimate of the number of effective factors can be made at the present time.

One of the most remarkable features of cultivated beans is the enormous range of testa colours and patterns which can be found. Four main colour groups have been identified in *Ph. vulgaris*; similar groups doubtless occur but have not been studied as extensively in other species. They are white, black, red and brown. Superimposed on these ground colours may be various patterns of spots, flecks, stripes and eyes. The genetics of basic testa colours is fairly simple with probably at least two loci involved; that of the patterns is more complex.

An important property of the testa is its permeability to water. Wild species are characteristically hard-seeded and unless the seed surface is abraded do not absorb water readily. Kaplan[15] considered that the loss of this property was an important factor in the domestication of beans. Cultivated beans as a rule absorb water readily through the testa without abrasion. Rathjen[16] at Cambridge has found that hard seed may be produced by F_1 intervarietal hybrids in *Ph. vulgaris*. These hybrids were between lines of poor genetical combining ability and much of the seed was rather poorly developed. It has been suggested that the relative growth of embryo to testa is greater in cultigens than in wild forms and that stretching increases permeability. In the reported instances where embryo growth is poor the testa is unstretched and may be impermeable as a result.

Pod structure is basically similar in wild forms and the more primitive cultigens. In cultigens generally there is a tendency for dehiscence to be reduced without necessarily any gross change in anatomical structure. Apart from this consideration no other change has occurred in the pods of *Ph. lunatus* and *Ph. acutifolius*, under domestication both are very fibrous. Pods of *Ph. vulgaris* and *Ph. coccineus* are even in the wild state less fibrous than those of *Ph. lunatus* and *Ph. acutifolius*. Under domestication the fibre content of the pods has been further reduced, more so in *Ph. vulgaris* than in *Ph. coccineus*. Three distinct pod textures are found in *Ph. vulgaris* namely:

1 parchmented—very fibrous—dehisces strongly at maturity
2 leathery—less dehiscent—splits readily along the sutures
3 stringless—indehiscent—does not split readily along the sutures.

Varieties with parchmented pods are used entirely for dry seed production, leathery podded varieties can be used either for green pod production when young or haricot production when fully mature. Stringless beans are used entirely for the production of green pods.

2 *Change in life form*

Ph. coccineus and *Ph. lunatus* are perennial species fundamentally although in cultivation frequently treated as annuals. The determinate forms of both species show a tendency towards the annual life form. *Ph. vulgaris* ssp. *aborigineus* includes both annual and perennial forms, the accessions in the Cambridge collection from Argentina are annuals, a single accession from Mexico is perennial and produces a similar type of root-tuber to *Ph. coccineus* and *Ph. lunatus*. *Ph. acutifolius* is a strict annual.

There is a tendency under domestication for selection towards the annual life form, this is reinforced by the ever increasing use of determinate dwarf forms.

3 *Physiological responses*

(a) *Photoperiod sensitivity*. The genus *Phaseolus* in America has its centre of distribution in tropical and sub-tropical latitudes. Collections of cultivars from this area almost invariably include forms which are photoperiod sensitive. Photoperiodic response shows a range from day-neutral to a requirement for a twelve hour day for flower induction. In *Ph. vulgaris* photoperiod sensitivity is not confined to any particular morphological type and is found in them all, likewise day-neutrality. The occurrence of varying degrees of photoperiod sensitivity in wild forms suggests that the alleles for day length sensitivity have never been fixed. The migration of *Ph. vulgaris* into North America in pre-Columbian times ensured that day-neutral alleles were fixed in these populations but not in those near the centre of origin.

Segregations in F_2 of hybrids between a photoperiod-sensitive primitive and a day-neutral cultivated type gave typical monofactorial ratios of 3 sensitive : 1 day-neutral. The range in photoperiod sensitivity suggests that other genetic loci may influence the expression of this character.

(*b*) *Seed dormancy.* In addition to dormancy imposed by hard seed, there is dormancy in primitive *Ph. acutifolius* which is apparently imposed by a post-harvest maturation period. There is some evidence that this may also occur in *Ph. vulgaris* ssp. *aborigineus*. In general, however, no difficulty has been found in germinating fairly fresh seed (i.e. within two months of harvest) of other species.

Experimental hybridization

Crosses have been made experimentally between primitive and cultivated forms of all four species. Fertility of the F_1 hybrids has been perfectly normal with very few exceptions and F_2 progenies have been raised and examined. Simple monofactorial segregations have been observed for branching pattern, photoperiod sensitivity and flower colour. Seed size and seed coat colour segregations are more complex and require much more detailed study. Certainly there are no grounds to suppose that there is any kind of fertility barrier between primitive and cultivated forms. Flower and seed morphology differs most widely between *Ph. coccineus* cultivars and the presumed primitive ancestral form *Ph. formosus*. The stigma of *Ph. coccineus* is lateral, elongate and outwardly directed; in *Ph. formosus* it is capitate and terminal. The seeds are nearly circular in outline, the hilum a broad oval in *Ph. formosus*, whereas *Ph. coccineus* seeds are more kidney-shaped and the hilum is elongate. In the three other species there is very close correspondence in flower and pod morphology between primitive and cultivated forms. Although de Candolle more than a century and a quarter ago suggested that *Ph. formosus* was ancestral to *Ph. coccineus*, it is possible that an undescribed form may yet exist which is actually closer to the ancestral type.

Conclusion

In conclusion it can be said that the response of New World *Phaseolus* species does provide a good illustration of Vavilov's principle of homologous variation. In three of the four species, dwarf determinate forms occur and in two of them it is possible to demonstrate that an homologous locus is probably involved. In F_2 progeny from an interspecific hybrid *Ph. vulgaris* (dwarf determinate) × *Ph. coccineus* (dwarf determinate) no segregation for branching habit was observed. It is not possible to cross either of these species with *Ph. lunatus* and establish genetic homology directly, but morphologically the result is the same and a homologous locus in all probability does control branching habit in the three species.

The suppression of lateral branching in domesticated climbers accompanied by an increase in size of leaf and stem has followed a similar pattern in *Ph. vulgaris*, *Ph. coccineus* and *Ph. lunatus* although the most perfect pyramidal form is developed in *Ph. vulgaris*. In physiological terms the cultivated types show more pronounced apical dominance. The dwarf indeterminate growth form is subject to environmental modification. *Ph. vulgaris* varieties and cultivated *Ph. acutifolius* which develop this habit of growth out of doors may under greenhouse conditions behave as indeterminate climbers. It is possible that this change in form is controlled by the production of a growth substance, most probably a gibberellin, which is suppressed under conditions of high incident ultraviolet light.

Some question might also be raised on the question of determinate *vs.* indeterminate growth habits. The typical determinate dwarf cultivated bean bears its terminal inflorescence after not more than seven or eight nodes have been produced on the main axis. In both *Ph. vulgaris* and *Ph. coccineus* climbing forms occur in which growth in length of the main axis is terminated by an inflorescence after twenty or even more nodes have been produced. This suggests that growth habit may be controlled by genes affecting in the first place internode length and secondly node number.

A general response in all beans to domestication has been increased seed size. Segregation data of F_2 progeny studied so far indicate that this is probably polyfactorial. Detailed biometrical study of this important character is most certainly needed.

There is little doubt that in domestication *Ph. vulgaris* has proven to be the most versatile. It has produced the greatest range of variants, in growth habit, seed shape, seed-coat colour and pod texture. The environmental range is however restricted to warm and cool temperate climates and herein lies the greatest potential for future improvement. A versatile legume such as *Ph. vulgaris* could be exploited very intensively in the tropics if it could be grown there satisfactorily. There is the possibility that the production of amphidiploids between *Ph. vulgaris* and *Ph. acutifolius* might be a step in this direction, if they possessed the heat tolerance of *Ph. acutifolius* without serious loss of the pod and seed quality of *Ph. vulgaris*.

Kaplan[17] has pointed out that in recent historic times the cultivation of *Ph. acutifolius* has contracted to a marked degree in Mexico and it seems quite likely that this species will disappear from cultivation in a relatively short while. The possibility of making use of it in hybridization should however be borne in mind. There seems to be no immediate danger of the remaining two species going out of cultivation, largely because these species extend beyond the effective range of *Ph. vulgaris* cultivation, *Ph. coccineus* into cooler climatic zones and *Ph. lunatus* into tropical regions.

We are still unable to pinpoint any single decisive factor which has established *Ph. vulgaris* in its pre-eminent position among *Phaseolus* beans but the following factors are probably the most important.

1 an inherent capacity to respond to selection
2 the heavy selection pressures applied
3 an early wide dispersion and selection over a range of temperature environments in pre-Columbian times favouring a very rapid spread in post-Columbian times.

The factor which has limited the spread of *Ph. vulgaris* has of course preserved the range of four species now in cultivation. There is no doubt that Gause's law can be applied to crop plant species as well as those in the wild. Just as two very similar species cannot coexist indefinitely in the same natural habitat and exploit it in exactly the same way so two very similar crop plants will not persist indefinitely in cultivation under any given set of environmental conditions; one or other will fall by the wayside.

Notes

1 Simmonds, N. W. (1962). *The Evolution of the Bananas*. London.
2 Hutchinson, J. B., Silow, R. A. and Stephens, S. G. (1947). *The Evolution of Gossypium*. Oxford.
3 Darlington, C. D. (1956). *Chromosome Botany and the Origins of Cultivated Plants*. London; Hutchinson, Sir J. (ed.) (1965). *Essays on Crop Plant Evolution*. Cambridge; Schwanitz, F. (1966). *The Origin of Cultivated Plants*. Harvard.
4 Rendle, A. B. (1925). *The Classification of Flowering Plants*, 2. Cambridge.
5 Mackie, W. W. (1943). Origin, dispersal and variability of *Phaseolus lunatus*, *Hilgardia*, 15, pp. 1–29.
6 Bentham, G. (1862). *Genera Plantarum*, 1. Hookerian Herbarium, Kew.
7 Hutchinson, J. (1964). *The Genera of Flowering Plants*, 1. Oxford.
8 Ohwi, J. (1953). *Flora of Japan*. (Japanese.) (Eng. trans. 1965.) Smithsonian Inst., Washington.
9 de Candolle, A. P. (1825). *Prodromus*, 2. Paris.
10 de Candolle, A. P. (1825). ibid.; Taubert, P. (1891), *in* Engler, A. and Prantl, K. *Die Natürlichen Pflanzen familien*, 3. Leipzig; Piper, C. V. (1926). American genera of *Phaseolineae*, *Contributions*, *U.S. National Herbarium*, 22, p. 9.
11 Kaplan, L. (1965). Archaeology and domestication in American *Phaseolus* beans, *Econ. Bot.*, 19. pp. 356–68.
12 See also Allard, R. W. (1953). Inheritance of morphological characters in lima beans, *Hilgardia*, 22, pp. 283–9.
13 Kaplan, L. (1965). ibid.
14 Ojehomon, O. O. (1966). The development of flower primordia of *Phaseolus vulgaris* (L.) Savi, *Ann. Bot.*, 30, pp. 487–92.
15 Kaplan, L. (1965). ibid.
16 Rathjen, A. (1965). *Ph.D. thesis, Cambridge.*
17 Kaplan, L. (1965). ibid.

W. R. STANTON

Some domesticated lower plants in South-east Asian food technology

The philosophy underlying the subject of the domestication of lower plants has come under close scrutiny as part of the rapid expansion of research in recent years into various novel methods of satisfying man's requirement for food, that is, in the face of a rapidly increasing world population.

I have used, in the title to this paper the broad taxon "lower plants" to distinguish this process of plant evolution under the influence of man from that of the previous speakers who have all been dealing with higher plants, that is Angiosperms. The so-called lower plants comprise a very wide variety of life forms most conveniently distinguished from the higher plants by their reproductive system, but they may be considered from the point of view of the present discussion as *plant forms which do not normally occupy the environments provided by agriculture*, except to interfere with the normal course of agriculture by causing diseases of higher plants, deterioration and spoilage, and superficially interfering with man's agricultural efforts.

However, on closer inspection of agricultural evolution in its broadest sense, including fertility improvement, food harvesting, storage, and processing (and in this context I include both the harvest of animals as well as the gathering of plant parts), it is realized that a great diversity of autotrophic, heterotrophic and parasitic plant forms associated with the main economic species have undergone concomitant changes. As with higher plant breeding, it is only within very recent times that a positive breeding approach has been directed towards the secondary organisms involved in natural-product production and utilization.

The term "plant" is of great antiquity as applied to the micro-organisms of Western food technologies. One has only to think of such terms as "vinegar plant" and "ginger-beer plant"; mushrooms and seaweeds used for food have also been described in this way. Otherwise, the lay classification made the distinction between "moulds", "slimes", and "ferments", the recognition of the role of lower-plants in the last category being of relatively recent origin.

The constructive role of micro-organisms under domestication is almost as diverse as that of the higher plants of agriculture. This has not been solely a consequence of higher plant and animal domestication. Lower plants have opened up new possibilities in terms of food production and recovery, flavour improvement, toxic component removal, utilization of waste for food, supply of essential secondary food constituents, and such activities as binding by their thread-like structures, or disintegration from the activity of their extra-cellular enzymes as the need arose. Extra cellular enzyme processes are familiar in the technology of retting and the saccharification of starches.

A major part of the work of the microbiology department at the Tropical Products Institute is concerned with the diversity of constructive roles of micro-organisms as will be seen from Fig. 1.

I have confined my discussion to particular aspects of South-east Asian food technology for reasons which I will explain in a moment.

Even if one excludes the technologies of the manufacture of cheese, bread, beers, wine, vinegar and so on, lower plant domestication is not exclusively a tropical phenomenon. For instance, seaweeds are of very ancient usage in Welsh (lava-bread)[1] and Norwegian food technology; lactic acid fermentations are important in the fermentation of temperate zone vegetables, although they assume a greater importance in the tropics[2].

However, in a tropical and sub-tropical environment the food preservation methods of chilling, salting, and drying are impossible or less freely available. Even after treatment of the harvest by the second two methods, infection of the products with micro-organisms is likely to occur.

It is this interaction, that is "the presence of high salt concentration plus partial dehydration", which is employed in the characteristic fermented fish sauces and pastes of South-east Asia. These products are daily items of diet and contribute as much as one third of the daily protein requirement, other than rice, to the diet. For this reason I have chosen a tropical region with a long history of food technology, and that is, an area with "millennia of history of fungi, food and fermentation" to quote the title of Hesseltine's classical review of the subject[3].

In Indonesia, at the heart of the region, fermented cakes of soya beans and groundnut provide about one-third of the total crude protein requirement of the population and these fermentation processes have been particularly studied in our laboratory because they can be applied to fermenting low-protein agricultural products to synthesize microbial protein *in situ* with added mineral nitrogen and other salts[4].

Mushrooms, although a very common constituent of the South-east Asian diets, contribute a small proportion of the protein, and recent studies of the Basidiomycetes have shown that it would not be possible to meet the whole of the human protein requirement from the culture of this type of organism even by modern industrial methods. Nevertheless, the Dutch have recently considered it worthwhile to investigate the growing of the classical mushroom of South-east Asia, the paddy-straw mushroom (*Volvaria* species)[5] as part of the diversification of their industrialized food economy. The Basidio-

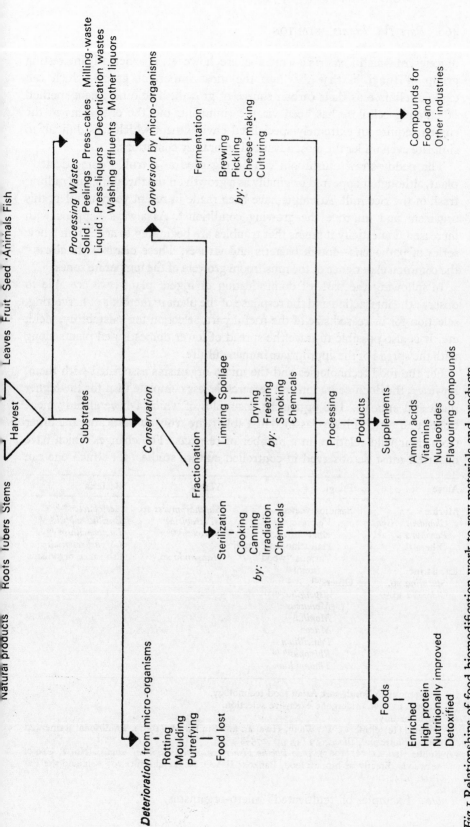

Natural products   Roots Tubers Stems   Leaves Fruit Seed Animals Fish

Harvest

Substrates

Processing Wastes
Solid : Peelings Press-cakes Milling-waste
Liquid : Press-liquors Decortication wastes
Washing effluents Mother liquors

Conversion by micro-organisms

by:
Fermentation
Brewing
Pickling
Cheese-making
Culturing

Compounds for
Food and
Other industries

Conservation

Fractionation

Limiting Spoilage

by:
Drying
Freezing
Smoking
Chemicals

Sterilization

by:
Cooking
Canning
Irradiation
Chemicals

Processing

Products

Supplements

Amino acids
Vitamins
Nucleotides
Flavouring compounds

Deterioration from micro-organisms

Rotting
Moulding
Putrefying

Food lost

Foods

Enriched
High protein
Nutritionally improved
Detoxified

Fig 1 Relationships of food biomodification work to raw materials and products.
The harnessing of micro-organisms to *improve* tropical foods, *produce* foods from tropical wastes, to *convert* natural raw materials to useful products.

mycetes, of which *Volvaria* is a member are, however, a particularly interesting group of fungi in that they are the most important group which can exploit cellulose as their carbon source of growth. The other main method of utilizing cellulose has been via the ruminant, but the organisms in the rumen require an extremely specialized environment which it is difficult to simulate even under the most advanced laboratory conditions.

The paddy-straw mushroom can be regarded as a truly "domesticated" plant, although it appeared originally as a growth on the threshing and milling trash of the rice mill. Attempts have been made in recent years to select this organism and improve the growing conditions[6]. As always happens with increased domesticity it seems that troubles are beginning to arise from a new series of pathogens—fungi, bacteria and viruses. These diseases are already the common experience of the mushroom growers of the temperate zones.

In following the path of domestication of higher plants, we are able to observe the interaction and the response of the plant to methods of harvesting, selection for increased size of the useful part, selection for palatability, yield, etc. It is also possible to trace the spread of lower domesticated plants along with the spread of the appropriate human culture.

For the food technologies and the micro-organisms associated with them, however, the documentation and research is less complete than for the higher plant and animals. The organisms, examples of which I have already mentioned and which I have classified in Table 1, are truly domesticated and differ from their wild relatives in a number of respects. The changes which have occurred must be observed in controlled culture studies, for which one can

Algae	Fungi	Yeasts	Bacteria
Marine	Basidiomycetes	*Saccharomyces* sp.	*Acetobacter*[a,b]
Chondrus crispus	e.g. *Volvaria*[a,b]	*S. cerevisiae*[a,b]	*Bacillus subtilis*[a,b]
Porphyra sp. [a]	*Amanita* sp.	*S. rouxii*[a,b]	*Lactobacillus*[a,b]
Others[e]	Hallucinogenic fungi		*Corynebacterium*
	Various "wood"	*Hansenula* sp.[a]	fish sauce organisms
Lacustrine	fungi[a]		
Spirulina sp.	Others[d]		
Chlorella sp.[c]	*Aspergillus*[a,b]		
	Monascus[a]		
	Monilia[a]		
	Mucor		
	Penicillium		
	Rhizopus[a,b]		
	Thamnidium		

(a) Indigenous to South-east Asian food technology.
(b) Known to have undergone extensive selection.
(c) Japan mainly.
(d) See also Hesseltine, C. W., Wang, Hwa, L. and Smith, M. (1967). Traditional fermented foods, *Biotechnol. Bioeng.*, **9** (3), pp. 275–88.
(e) Subba Rao, G. N. (1965). *Indo-Pacific Fisheries Council Regional Studies*. No. 2. Use of seaweeds directly as human food, Bankok; F.A.O. Regional Office for Asia and the Far East, p. 32.

Table 1 Examples of "cultivated" micro-organisms.

use the equivalent of the Clausen transplant-experiment technique[7], studies of growth rate, interaction with substrate, biochemical pathways, and the biochemistry and organoleptic character of the end products. Taste is still an important aid to the selection of the organisms involved in the fermentation in spite of all the refinements of analytical chemistry.

The end-product of the micro-organic culture consists of the micro-organism mass itself such as the sporophores of Basidiomycetous fungi, and the algae[8], including seaweed. Even bacteria such as the *Acetobacter* sp. are stimulated to form a jelly-like mass on fruit juice and coconut water in a Philippine fermentation process to produce Nata. Alternatively, a mixture of the original material with mycelium threads of fungi such as *Rhizopus*, *Mucor* and other species may be produced[9], or a more complex fermentation may occur such as is used in the manufacture of *miso*, a fermented soya bean paste of Japan[10], in which a number of organisms have taken part at different stages. This particular paste is of interest in that three-quarters of the households in Japan use this fermented product as a main soup component daily, according to a recent survey report. The Japanese products represent a northward and eastward migration of the "sho" processes (a general term in Japan for the high salt fermentations). Today these fermentations are carried out under highly industrialized conditions, the organisms being given the benefit of highly specialized environments, and the domestication in consequence has proceeded here further than it has elsewhere in the region. Further, due to the extensive Japanese investigations of these industrialized organisms and their associated production methods, more is known about the variation in character between different strains in Japan than in other parts of the region. Japanese, American, Indonesian and our own study of the organisms used in the village-factory and domestic economies in the south and east of the region show that these food micro-organisms, which are conserved from one process batch to the next, differ considerably in many characters from their wild counterparts.

The types of variation which we found in different isolates in response to different substrates and controlled conditions are shown in Table 2.

I feel that we are on the verge of a large development in domestication of these organisms, in order to make a better use of the limited food resources of the Tropical World, and we shall require all the modern techniques of agronomy such as the statistical methods of response surfaces to achieve optimum growing conditions, and plant breeding which has great possibilities with micro-organisms, in order to achieve optimum results. We have however the advantage with the cultivation of these lower plants that we can control with relative ease the environment in which they are grown, and we can employ specialized environments which will protect them in part from harmful elements of the rest of the biota, that is, from the effects of unwanted micro-organisms such as those which produce mycotoxins and which are the analogues of weeds in higher plant agriculture.

General genetic and cytological stability: probably increases (true of brewing yeasts).

Growing rate: increased in the selected substrate, but decreased in comparison with "wild types" on the general range of substrates. Probable loss of capacity to overcome naturally occurring growth inhibitors.

Environmental adaptability: growth of cultivated strain inferior to wild type outside the range of conditions normally provided for the fermentation, e.g. temperature, humidity, salinity, oxygen, tension, nutrient concentration.

Reproductive capacity: selection for early and heavy sporulation under the processing conditions employed.

Food acceptability: improved palatability and acceptability of end-product (selection against unacceptable metabolites).

Increased tolerance: to growth inhibiting factors occurring in the cultivation process, e.g. metal ions (Cu^{++}, Zn^{++}), specific glycosides, NO_3, urea, organic acids, phenolic compounds.

Contrived growth: in presence of its own metabolites; the loss of enzyme feed-back inhibitions.

Advanced industrial processes: strains with highly selected segments of biosynthetic pathways with removal of feed-back inhibitions.

Table 2   Examples of known and postulated changes in fungi due to selection under cultivation.

Micro-organism cultures may be regarded as components of a two stage phytosynthetic process and, apart from the disadvantage of an obligatory requirement of non-solar energy, they have many advantages over higher plant cultures in features such as short cultivation time, low demand on land and fresh water (sea-water and saline water can be used) and simplicity of mutual adjustment of organism to environment with consequent precise control over the character of the synthetic product. Analysis of the classical process impresses one with the degree of understanding which early technologies achieved in harnessing the ferments.

As with higher plants, it is pertinent to advance domestication initially with the recognized food species of micro-organisms, though because we can now create chemically and physically controlled environments not available to earlier food technologists, we may be able to cultivate previously untamable species.

Notes

1 Duddington, C. L. (1967). *Seaweeds and Other Algae.* London. p. 207; Glabe, E. F., Goldman, P. F. and Anderson, P. W. (1957). How Irish moss extractive improves protein-content foods, *Fd. Engng.,* 29 (1), pp. 65–7; Larsen, B. A. and Hawkins, W. W. (1961). Nutritional value as protein of some of the nitrogenous constituents of *Chondrus crispus* and *Laminaris digitata, J. Sci. Fd. Agric.,* 12, pp. 523–9; De Guerin, B. C. (1946). Carrageen in the Channel Isles, *Fd. Mf.,* 21, pp. 95–8; Sieburth, J. McN. and Jensen, A. (1967). Effect of processing on the microflora of Norwegian seaweed meal with observations on *Sporondonema minutum* (Høye), Frank and Hess, *Appl. Microbiol.,* 15 (4), pp. 830–8.

2 Etchells, J. L., Jones, I. D. and Lewis, W. M. (1947). Bacteriological changes during the fermentation of certain brind and salted vegetables, *U.S.D.A. Technical Bull.,* 947, Oct. 1947.

3 Hesseltine, C. W. (1965). A Millennium of fungi, food and fermentation, *Mycologia*, **57**, pp. 149–97; Hesseltine, C. W., Wang, H. L. and Smith, M. (1967). Traditional Fermented Foods, *Biotechnol. Bioeng.*, **9** (3), pp. 275–88.
4 *Annual Rep. Tropical Products Inst.* (1967). H.M.S.O., London. p. 49.
5 Chang, S. T. (1965). Cultivation of the straw mushroom in S.E. China, *World Crops*, **17** (3), pp. 47–9.
6 Madic, V. R. and Roldan, E. F. (1965). A preliminary test on the effect on mushroom production of straws rendered sterile with fumigant dowfume MC–Z, *Araneta J. Agric.*, **12**, pp. 233–8.
7 Clausen, J., Keck, D. D., Hiesey, W. M. (1939). The concept of species based on experiments, *Amer. J. Bot.*, **26** (2), pp. 103–6.
8 Subba Rao, G. N. (1965). Use of seaweed directly as human food, *Indo-Pacific Fisheries Council Regional Studies*, **2**, F.A.O. Regional Office for Asia and the Far East, Bangkok. p. 32.
9 Hesseltine, C. W. *et al.* (1964). Tempeh: Nutritive value in relation to processing, *Cereal Chem.*, **41** (3), pp. 173–81.
10 Standal, B. R. (1963). Nutritional value of proteins of oriental soyabeans' products, *J. Nutr.*, **81** (3), p. 279 and p. 285.

Section 2: Animals

M. S. DROWER

The domestication of the horse

The four main species of the genus *Equus* appear to have been distributed over the forests and plains of the Old World during the Pleistocene period in separate geographical zones: the onagers or half-asses (hemiones) in Hither Asia (Arabia, Persia and India), the asses in northern and north-east Africa, the zebras in the south and east of Africa and the caballine horses in Europe and in Central Asia north of the great mountain ranges. All these species are capable of producing hybrids, and all but the zebras have been domesticated by man[1].

Of the species of *Equus caballus*, three wild races, all rather small, have survived until fairly recently. These are Przewalski's horse, a native of Mongolia, of which a few specimens only are preserved in zoological gardens; the tarpan, which became extinct in the middle of the nineteenth century A.D.; and the forest wild horse, which survived in Poland until the eighteenth century. Whether the wild horses depicted in cave-paintings as the quarry of hunters were all of one sub-species, or of several different strains, is in dispute; the existence of a much larger horse in palaeolithic times has been postulated[2]. It appears at any rate certain that neither palaeolithic nor mesolithic man domesticated the horse.

First domestication

There is little evidence, written or archaeological, for the presence of the domesticated horse in the Middle East until a little before 2000 B.C. Domestication, necessarily a gradual process, must have been achieved earlier and elsewhere. The distribution of the wild species suggests that horses were first tamed on the grass steppe-lands to the north, in the Ukraine or somewhere further east, between Turkestan and China. The tamers are likely to have been nomadic herdsmen to whom rapid mobility would have given many advantages. It is however difficult to establish evidence for the early domestication of the horse, since precise indications of morphological change, such as are present in the skeletons of cattle and sheep[3], are absent from the bones of Equidae[4]. Bones of horses occur at all levels of the Tripolye culture of the Ukraine, but become numerous only in the later phases; the sharp increase in numbers in other sites contemporaneous with Tripolye B has been thought to be evidence for domestication about 2700 or 2800 B.C.[5] In the so-called Timber Grave culture of the Volga region, ceremonial horse burials occur, together with sacrifices of cattle, in a context of the middle of the second millennium[6].

One or two isolated examples of bones formerly identified as *E. caballus*, found in Persia in an early context at Sialk and Anau, are now generally considered to be onagers[7], and this is probably also true of the remains found in Beersheba and dated to the fourth millennium B.C.[8], though the possibility cannot be ruled out that this was an early breed of wild horse which later died out. Horses are not however depicted in prehistoric rock-drawings in Palestine or Egypt[9]. The bone tablet from Susa which appears to be a tally of domesticated equids with short bristle-manes must depict onagers[10].

The first literary mention of the horse (in Sumerian ANŠE KUR.RA) occurs in a text of the Third Dynasty of Ur, *c.* 2100 B.C., in which the animal is described as "of the (caravan) route" (i.e. not wild), and "with flowing tail"; the latter epithet distinguishes it from the onager and ass[11]. The word ANŠE.KUR means "foreign ass" or "ass of the mountains"; it is found in its literal meaning in the Sumerian story of "Enmerkar and the Lord of Aratta", in which asses of the mountain are used as beasts of burden (a purpose for which the horse was not employed)[12]. Though horses are not mentioned in the Code of Hammurabi and cannot therefore have been a domestic animal frequently owned and used by Babylonians of the early eighteenth century B.C., they make their appearance at about that time as costly and much-desired objects of trade between the Amorite princes, Hammurabi's near contemporaries, whose correspondence is preserved in the Mari letters. Carchemish on the Euphrates was one of the centres of distribution and Kharsamma in Cappadocia was a source of supply[13]. Horses are several times mentioned in the texts from Kanesh (modern Kültepe, near Kayseri) where the form used is the Akkadian *sisu*, a word of undoubtedly Indo-European origin ($>$aś^{w}as, ek^{w}os)[14], and although they do not receive mention in the tablets from Alalakh of the eighteenth century B.C., they were known at the same time in Brak and Chagar Bazar, on the river Khabut, where there are models of equids, evidently horses, with painted or modelled bridles, and the tablets mention "yokes" of horses: the quantities of fodder allowed for a yoke show that two, or three (two and a spare), horses are meant[15]. For their role was not to replace the ass as a pack animal, but to draw, yoked in pairs, the light *biga* with spoked wheels which was now revolutionizing warfare.

The horse and chariot of the Bronze Age

This mobile vehicle[16], in build quite unlike the cumbersome solid-wheeled Sumerian chariot drawn by onagers which it superseded[17], is everywhere in the Near East associated with the newcomers—Kassites, Hittites, Hurrians— who during the early years of the second millennium B.C. were establishing their rule over the kingdoms of Western Asia. Its use must have given tactical superiority to the newcomers. In particular it is associated with the Indo-Aryan aristocracies among the Hurrian and Kassites. Texts pertaining to the art of horse-breeding use technical terms akin to Sanskrit, and the chivalry of Mitanni and the Hurrian-dominated city-states of Syria and Palestine were known by the Indo-Iranian name *maryannu*[18]. It may therefore be suggested that mounted Aryans brought the horse south of the Caucasus, and that in some well-wooded[19] but not too rugged terrain, a new and more mobile form of chariot was devised, perhaps by the Hurrians of the region who already knew and used the heavier onager or ass-drawn vehicle[20].

The new technique spread rapidly: by the sixteenth century horses and chariots were known and used in Greece and Egypt. The first European horse is that depicted in the fifth shaft-grave at Mycenae, and the earliest representations of horses in Egypt appear at the beginning of the eighteenth dynasty, about 1570; they are mentioned in texts referring to the war of liberation from the Hyksos a decade or so before, and the single horse whose skeleton was found in the debris of the destroyed Middle Kingdom fortress at Buhen[21] may have been buried as early as the seventeenth century B.C. Remains of horses have been found in India in contexts of the sixteenth century and the horse and chariot reached China at least by 1300 B.C.[22]

Technical treatises which have survived among the cuneiform tablets of the Late Bronze Age show that in Anatolia[23], North Syria[24] and Mesopotamia[25] the breeding, training and veterinary care of horses was well understood: there are directions for exercising and grooming horses, stressing the importance of careful diet, and remedies for sick animals. At Ugarit what appeared to be an indoor riding school[26] was found. When sent from one country to another, the animals needed to be acclimatized. In a letter to the King of Babylonia[27], a Hittite king asks for fresh supplies of horses, since those which the former Kassite king had sent have gone lame: "In Hatti-land the cold is severe, and an old horse does not last long. So send me, my brother, young stallions!" Horses are listed at Alalakh and Nuzi according to sex, age and colour; in Nuzi[28], Hurrian words are used for the various colours, and in the Kassite texts[29] stallions are given names such as "Foxy", "Starry",

"White", "Piebald". The name of the sire is often added (X., son of Y.), showing that pedigrees were remembered and perhaps stud-books kept. White horses were especially prized, in the Ancient Near East as among the Persians, Romans and Germans of a later age[30]; they were destined to draw the chariots of kings and of gods and in Assyria were accorded divine honours[31].

Ownership of horses and a chariot was a matter of rank and privilege. Only kings and nobility are shown in the lightest type of vehicle, the mono-place chariot in which extraordinary skill and balance were needed. Looping the reins round their waist, they let fly their arrows at a gallop after fleeing targets, whether enemy soldiers or wild game. Ramesses III in the later New Kingdom is shown in an open-fronted chariot with one foot on the chariot pole, but this was unprecedented virtuosity (Pl. III). The breed was small, in general not exceeding the dimensions of a pony: skeletal remains, and the dimensions of the stables at Ugarit[32], confirm the reliability of the artists in this respect. It has often been remarked that horses are seldom shown being ridden, and that in such representations (Fig 1), the riders appear to be

Fig 1 Riding groom, from the tomb of Horemheb at Memphis, *c.* 1345 B.C.
(after Aldred, C. (1951). *New Kingdom Art in Ancient Egypt during the 18th dynasty B.C.* London. Fig. 141.)

grooms or stable lads[33]. The explanation that they were too small to bear full-grown men cannot be correct, for donkeys were ridden; the reason may lie rather in the difficulty an inexperienced bareback rider without stirrups would have in keeping his balance, and his dignity, on a short-striding animal at the trot[34]. Nevertheless Astarte, the Syrian goddess who protected charioteers, is herself shown riding bareback[35], and it may be suspected that there were larger breeds which were more suitable for riding. The Buhen horse was larger than a pony, and a horse found buried at Osmankayasi near Boghazköi[36] was about fourteen and a half hands (150 cm.), the size of a modern Arab, and able no doubt to pull the heavier, three-manned chariot of the Hittites. For horses must have been bred for size as the weight of the chariot increased. The armour-plating of chariots and horses and of their riders, was no doubt made necessary by the spread of penetrating weapons such as the composite bow; the *sariam* frequently mentioned in the Nuzi texts (the word is probably Indo-Iranian) appears to have been a leather jerkin or cover sewn with metal scales[37].

The Iron Age

By 1000 B.C. new and larger breeds of horse were making their appearance and superior harness had evolved. A second wave of Indo-European immigration brought horse riders to the Iranian highlands. To Azerbaijan and to Gilan and Mazanderan on the well-watered southern shore of the Caspian Sea came the Mannaeans and the Medes, and Iran soon became the land of "fine horses and fine men". Horses figure largely in the animal style of Luristan and bronze cheek-pieces, horse-bits and other harness elements are the most common objects found[38]. Pottery models show saddles. The horses the newcomers rode were relatively big: horse-bones from Hasanlu in Azerbaijan (Early Iron Age) examined by Bökönyi were those of animals about 140 cm. in height[39] and those found in early Scythian graves at Szentes-Vekerzug in Hungary studied by him were of a similar size[40]. Zamua and the Mannai territories south of Lake Urmia were sources whence the Assyrians obtained fresh supplies of horses, and from the ninth century onwards mounted cavalry formed an essential part of the Assyrian fighting force. At the same time, according to the palace reliefs, the chariot was getting heavier and larger; so, too, were the horses that drew it (Fig. 2).

Fig 2a War chariot: relief from the palace of Ashur-nasir-pal, ninth century B.C.
(after Layard, A. H. (1849). *Nineveh and its Remains*, 2. London. p. 350).

According to Hilzheimer[41] several breeds of horse are represented in these reliefs, but he probably puts too much reliance on the accuracy of the draughtsman; similarly, Ghirshman's attempt to deduce from the painted pottery horses from Susa and Makou the existence of two distinct breeds[42] is unwarranted. There is however good evidence for the coexistence of two

Fig 2b Ashur-bani-pal's state chariot, seventh century B.C.
(after Layard, A. H. (1849). *Nineveh and its Remains*, 2. London. p. 137).

races of horse in the remarkably-preserved burials of the fifth century B.C. at Pazyryk[43]: in each *kurgan* a number of short-headed ponies were found, which Professor Vitt considered to have been descended from a wild Mongolian stock of Przewalski descent, and also at least one thoroughbred horse of greater stature (over 140 cm.); these were all geldings and had been fed on corn and carefully tended, and they wore fine trappings. It is suggested that the larger animals, which were similar in size and build to those from Szentes, mentioned above[44], may be descended from tarpan stock. Antonius also classes Scythian horses as descendants of tarpans, basing his theory largely on the horses depicted on the Chertomlyk vase[45].

Archaeology and the testimony of Herodotus (Bk. VII) have told us much about the Scythians, and it is in this remarkable people that the fullest development of a pastoral economy in which the horse played a leading part may be pictured. They rode and shot with skill; they ate salted horse flesh and drank fermented mare's milk. In the barrows of South Russia the wholesale sacrifice of horses described by Herodotus can be vividly reconstructed[46]. It may be that the way of life of these nomads reflects the original symbiosis of man and horse, developed on the steppe-lands perhaps two thousand years earlier.

The Western horse

It is not possible to discuss here the vexed question of the horses depicted in the rock-engravings of North Africa, nor is the present writer competent to do so. The date of the drawings, of which some thousands survive, has been much discussed and there have been various attempts to classify them. Henri Lhote in his studies of the Tassili group[47] distinguishes a "chevaline period" in which horses are shown in pairs drawing a light-wheeled chariot, in the attitude of the "flying gallop"; in these he sees similarities with

Mycenaean art and he suggests that the Sea Peoples, after the failure of their attacks on Egypt, moved westwards with their Libyan allies and penetrated the Fezzan, bringing with them the horse and chariot. Another theory would associate the Tassili charioteers with the Garamantes and other tribes known to the Romans. Neither takes account of the theory, discussed by Zeuner[48], that there may have been a separate western centre of domestication in Spain or North Africa which gave rise to the North African "barb" or Barbary horse. Here too there seems to be much scope for further enquiry. Whatever the truth may be, it seems certain that the idea of the domestication of the horse, and of harnessing it to a wheeled vehicle, must have reached the Western Mediterranean from the Levant.

Notes

1 Zeuner, F. E. (1963). *A History of Domesticated Animals*. London.
2 Zeuner, F. E. (1963). op. cit. p. 306.
3 See Bökönyi, S. and Grigson, C., this volume, pp. 219–46 and 277–306.
4 Zeuner, F. E. (1963). op. cit. p. 316.
5 Dr. S. Bökönyi's dating (in discussion).
6 Clark, G. and Piggott, S. (1967). *Prehistoric Societies*. London. p. 275.
7 See Noble, D. S., this volume, pp. 485–8.
8 Anati, E. (1963). *Palestine before the Hebrews*. London. p. 241.
9 Anati, E. (1963). op. cit. p. 208; Winkler, H. (1938–9). *Rock Drawings of Southern Upper Egypt*. E.E.S. Archaeological Survey.
10 Amiet, P. (1966). *Elam*. Anvers-sur-Oise. p. 97.
11 Falkenstein, A. (1952). Sumerische religiose Texte 2: Ein Šulgi-Lied, *Z. Assyriologie*, **16**, pp. 64 ff.
12 Salonen, A. (1956). Hippologica Accadica, *Annales Academiae Scientiarum Fennicae*. Sarja. Ser. B. Nide. **100**. Helsinki. p. 19.
13 Salonen, A. (1956). op. cit. p. 23; Dossin, R. (1938). Aplahanda, Roi de Carkémiš, *Rev. d'Assyriol.*, **35**, p. 120.
14 Salonen, A. (1956). op. cit. p. 21.
15 Gadd, C. J. (1940). Tablets from Chagar Bazar and Tell Brak, *Iraq*, **7**, pp. 22 ff.
16 Yadin, Y. (1963). *The Art of Warfare in Biblical Lands*. London. pp. 86 ff.
17 See Noble, D. S., this volume, ibid.
18 O'Callaghan, R. T. (1948). Aram Naharaim, *Analecta Orientalia*, **26**, pp. 64 ff.
19 The chariot preserved in Florence is built of oak and elm and has tyres of birch-bark . . . all northern woods.
20 Crossland, R. A. (1967). Immigrants from the North, *C.A.H.II²*, Cambridge, ch. 27.
21 Emery, W. B. (1960). A preliminary report on the excavations of the Egypt Exploration Society at Buhen, 1958–9, *Kush*, **8**, pp. 7 ff.
22 Dewall, M. von. (1964). Pferd und Wagen im frühen China, *Saarbrücker Beiträge zur Altertumskunde*, **I**, pp. 109 ff.
23 Kammenhuber, A. (1961). *Hippologia Hethitica*. Wiesbaden.
24 Virolleaud, Ch. (1934). Fragments d'un traité phénicien de thérapeutique hippologique, *Syria*, **15**, pp. 75 ff.
25 Ebeling, E. (1951). Bruchstücke einer mittelassyrischen Vorschriftensamlung fur die Akklimatisation und Trainierung von Wagenpferden, *Deutsche Akad. d. Wiss., Inst. f. Orientforschung*, **7**.

26 Schaeffer, C. F. A. (1938). Les fouilles de Ras Shamra-Ugarit: neuvième campagne (printemps 1937), *Syria*, 19, p. 314.
27 See Salonen, A. (1956). op. cit. p. 28 for references.
28 Pfeiffer, R. and Speiser, E. A. (1936). One hundred new selected Nuzi texts, *Ann. Am. Sch. Or. Research*, 16.
29 Balkan, K. (1954). Kassitenstudien I, Die Sprache der Kassiten, *Amer. Or. Series*, 37, pp. 11–40 and pp. 127 f.
30 Herodotus, 7, 40 and 7, 113; Livy, 5, 28, 5; Tacitus, *Germania*, 10, etc.
31 Weidner, E. A. (1952). Weisse Pferde im alten Orient, *Bibliotheca Orientalis*, 9 (5–6), pp. 157 ff.
32 Schaeffer, C. F. A. (1949). *Ugaritica*, 2 (Mission de Ras Shamra, 5). Paris. p. 13.
33 Schulman, A. R. (1957). Egyptian Representations of Horsemen and Riding in the New Kingdom, *J. of Near Eastern Studies*, 16, pp. 263 ff.
34 I have to thank Mr. H. J. Case for this explanation; he says further "to keep his balance he instinctively tries to close his calves and heels round the belly. This excites the animal and makes him trot faster; and places the rider (with his pelvis tilted forward) in a highly uncomfortable position and one in which he has little control, should the pony suddenly break into a fast canter or gallop. Chariot-horses were equally spectacular and less liable to lapses of dignity."
35 Leclant, A. (1960). Astarte à cheval d'après les représentations égyptiennes, *Syria*, 37, pp. 1 ff.
36 Bittel, K., Heere, W. and Otten, H. (1958). *Die hethitischen Grabfunde von Osmankayasi. Bogazköy-Hattusa*, 2. pp. 60–4.
37 Oppenheim, A. L. (1950). Review of Figulla, H. H. (1949). *Business Documents of the New Babylonian Period*. London, *J. Cuneiform Soc.*, 4, pp. 191 ff.
38 Porada, E. (1965). *Ancient Iran*. London. pp. 75 ff. and pp. 234 ff.
39 In discussion.
40 Bökönyi, S. (1954). Les chevaux scythiques de Szentes-Vekerzug 2. Les fouilles de 1952–3, *Acta Arch. Hung.*, 4.
41 Hilzheimer, M. (1955). The evolution of the domestic horse, *Antiquity*, 9, pp. 133 ff.
42 Ghirshman, R. (1954). La village perse-achémenide, *Mém. de la Mission archéologique en Iran*, 36, pp. 38 ff.
43 Golomshtok, E. A. and Griaznov, M. P. (1933). The Pazirik burial of Altai, *Amer J. Archaeology*, 37, pp. 30 ff; Talbot Rice, T. (1965). *The Scythians*. London. pp. 70 ff.
44 Bökönyi, S. (1954). op. cit. pp. 100 ff.
45 Antonius, O. (1922). *Grundzüge einer Stammesgeschichte der Haustiere*. Jena. p. 287.
46 Recently Talbot Rice, T. (1965). ibid.
47 Lhote, H. (1953). Le Cheval et le Chameau dans les peintures et gravures rupestres du Sahara, *Bull. de l'Inst. français de l'Afrique noir*, pp. 1138 ff.
48 Zeuner, F. E. (1963). op. cit. pp. 330 ff.

J. G. EVANS

The exploitation of molluscs

Molluscs have been exploited by man from the earliest times and for a wide variety of purposes. For instance, the extraction of the crimson dye, Tyrian Purple, from the dog winkles *Murex* spp. and *Nucella* spp., was known to both the Phoenicians and the Minoans[1]. A vast quantity of shells was needed for this process (about 8000 per gram of dye). Each shell was struck at a particular point to remove the small gland which yields the dye, and such a technique leaves clear evidence of the use to which the animals were put[2]. Another pigment used in antiquity was Roman Sepia, obtained from the cuttlefish. Where stone was scarce, strong shells were often used for raw materials as in the manufacture of adze-blades from *Tridacna* on the coral islands of Polynesia. The shell of *Cardium*, the cockle, was used by neolithic people of the Mediterranean for stamping their impressed-ware pottery (cardial decoration)[3] though it should be pointed out that not all cardial decoration was necessarily produced in this way, other sharp implements being used to produce a similar effect. Mother-of-pearl, the nacreous lining of bivalve shells, has always been a popular material, for inlay as in the Standard of Ur and some of the grave furniture from Tutankhamen's tomb, and more recently for buttons and knife handles. Shells are often found far from the sea in contexts which, at least on the basis of some modern ethnographic parallels, suggest some sort of magico-religious association with the place of origin of the culture[4]. A classic example is that of the mussel, *Spondylus gaederopus*, found on Danubian sites as far north as the Rhineland from its source in the Eastern Mediterranean[5]. From this may have evolved the idea of shell trade or currency, although it is very possible that the latter developed in some instances independently where there was a lack of metals. There are innumerable examples too in prehistory of the adornment of the living and the dead with shells, those of *Dentalium*, the tusk shell, being particularly favoured. It is important in this connection to recognize however that the perforation of shells may be done not by man but by certain predatory molluscs[6]; this does not, of course, exclude the collection and use of such perforated shells for necklaces and bangles. Among the earliest objects used by man for personal adornment were pearls.

It is for their exploitation as a supply of food, however, that molluscs are particularly noted and with which this paper is mainly concerned. The more important food molluscs are the bivalves such as oysters, cockles and mussels; the marine snails such as whelks, periwinkles and abalones; the cephalopods—cuttlefish, octopus and squid; and the land snails[7]. The bivalves and marine snails comprise part of the group popularly known as shellfish; the rest of this group includes animals such as the crab and lobster which are not molluscs but crustaceans and will not be discussed here.

In the palaeolithic period shellfish were eaten by coastal-dwelling people when and where available—for example by Mousterians at Devil's Tower, Gibraltar[8]—but there seems never to have been any special emphasis on shellfish as a basic part of the economy. It was in the mesolithic period that shellfish were exploited to their fullest, in some cases to the virtual exclusion of all other types of animal food, and people who subsisted by this means have been given the name "strandloopers". Among the more important of these are the Canaliño culture of California[9], the Hoabhinians and Toalians of the Far East[10], the Capsians of North Africa and the Tagus Valley in Spain[11], the Asturians of Cantalabria[12], the Tardenoisians of Brittany[13], the Ertebølle people of Denmark[14], and the Larnians and Obanians of North-west Britain[15].

The origin of this mode of life may be argued to have been a quite normal one for coastal-dwelling people. However, in Western Europe the adoption of a strandlooping existence is associated with the spread of the forests after the end of the last glaciation, and a restriction of open areas available to mesolithic man for hunting who is thus driven to the coasts to seek a livelihood. In California it is associated with a decrease in the area of forest and a consequent reduction in the amount of game. In some cases there is an association with an island or coastal economy, where a ready supply of food of larger animals was not available. Thus the rise in sea-level during the post-glacial period increased the length of coastline per surface area of land; and a close association is found for instance between sites of the Ertebølle culture with the ancient shore-line of the Littorina sea[16]. Perhaps too, strandloopers were peoples driven to the coasts by others living inland better able to cope with the conditions there. In some cases a shellfish economy is a seasonal occupation.

The point at any rate seems clear: some kind of environmental change causes the mode of life of a people to be changed, from a primarily hunting or mixed economy to one based largely on food-gathering. Shellfish are as nourishing as a meat diet, if eked out by vegetable food; they contain large quantities of glycogen and need not be added to by animal flesh; moreover, their abundance per unit area is greater than that of any other food animal. But they do involve a lot of wasted labour in collecting since they produce the greatest bulk of refuse for a given quantity of edible substance[17]. The situation is neatly summarized as follows: "One suspects . . . that shellfish, as a main article of food, were eaten for lack of something better rather than from choice—perhaps in bad seasons, in winter or when in unfamiliar surroundings, so that the better potentialities of the place had still to be learned"[18]. Indeed in certain cases, for example the Hoabhinians, strandloopers became better able to cope with a variety of environments, with time evolving from an economy based solely on shellfish to a mixed one of food-gathering and hunting.

An economy based to a large extent on shellfish occurred in many places during the neolithic and later periods, but not to the universal extent of the mesolithic period. Most characteristic are the impressed-ware sites where poverty-striken peasants subsisted on a diet of shellfish but eked out also by domestic cattle, as for example with the Sipontiano culture of Coppa Nevigata in Italy[19].

The effect of man and other environmental factors on shellfish populations can be studied on archaeological sites, and this is particularly so with sand middens where a technique known as *column sampling* can be applied[20]. This involves taking bulk samples at intervals through a vertical column of deposits and analysing them for shellfish remains. The results can then be plotted in the form of a histogram as has been done in Fig. 1 for a prehistoric site in the Isle of Harris, Inverness. The basic diet on this site was of marine shellfish with domestic animals, and certain foods (possibly delicacies) such as the oyster, *Ostrea edulis*, and the freshwater mussel, *Margaritifera margaritifera*.

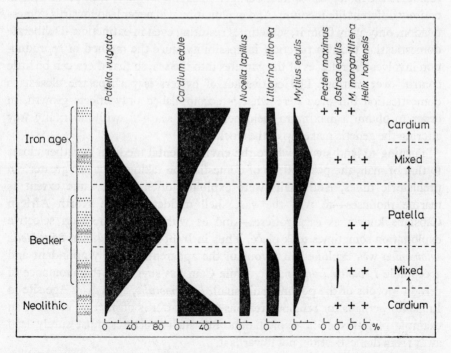

Fig 1 Diagram showing changes in relative abundance of various food molluscs in a prehistoric midden at Northton, Isle of Harris, Scotland.

Similarly on a Californian site of the Canaliño culture a change from an economy based largely on abalone to one on mussels took place. Changes such as these reflect differences in availability of the various species. In the Californian case this was caused by man for the abalone was eaten out of existence. But availability may also depend on environmental factors; *Cardium*, for example, is most abundant in estuaries on a muddy substratum, while *Patella* and *Mytilus* are more common on rocky shores. Changes in the availability of such substrata may relate to changes of sea-level and thus be reflected in man's economy. Man may also exploit a small number of shellfish species to a much greater extent than the majority for reasons perhaps of seasonal availability, ease of collection or edibility, and severe depletion of the stock may eventually lead to extinction and enable other species to build up their numbers which are then taken over as a food supply[21]. Changes caused thus by man may be accentuated by the natural enemies of shellfish, while climatic changes, notably of temperature, may also result in population changes[22].

But while exploitation may lead to changes in the composition of shellfish populations there is no evidence to suggest that shellfish have ever been "domesticated"; i.e. selectively bred to produce a stock which differs genetically from the wild ancestor. Domestication as a natural process under conditions of association with man is highly unlikely when one considers how remote is the biological contact between man and mollusc, each occupying an entirely different life medium. And exploitation will never lead towards domestication, only away from it, sometimes resulting even in extinction. Deliberate domestication too is a practical impossibility since the method of reproduction involves the releases of the gametes into the sea, so that there can be little control over mating. The cultivation of oysters is perhaps the closest to domestication but even here what is accomplished only affects growth, in order to obtain a maximum yield per area of sea bed, without in any way altering the genetic make-up of the stock.

Turning to land snails, where the environmental medium is rather closer to that of man, the possibilities of domestication taking place are greater. In prehistoric times, land snails were exploited often to the same extent as marine molluscs—to wit, the vast shell middens of the North African Capsians known as escargotières—and as with marine molluscs selective exploitation sometimes took place. Thus in Iran, Reed has shown how *Helix salomonica* was exploited in favour of the apparently equally abundant and acceptable *Levantina diulfensis*[23], while Cain has suggested the avoidance of certain morphs of the polymorphic snail, *H. nemoralis*, at an Iron Age site in England, perhaps for religious reasons[24]; this latter is of interest in being an example of intraspecific exploitation. But such processes must surely lead away from domestication, not towards it.

Deliberate domestication of a species of large snail (probably *H. pomatia*) seems to have been accomplished by the Romans, variations being kept separate in vivaria and bred for such characters as size, colour, and fecundity[25]. This practice, however, has not been maintained and one suspects that it was from the first more of an academic experiment rather than a policy engendered by economic hardship.

Under more natural conditions, the association of snails and man has not led to domestication but it is interesting to see how this association has become closer since the neolithic period and along lines which might well have resulted in domestication. The greatest initial impact of man on the environment was during the neolithic period and such changes as were produced affected the snail population more then than at any subsequent time. At first, changes in the populations of mollusca were a direct reflection of environmental changes. Shade- and moisture-loving species were either greatly suppressed, becoming restricted to area undisturbed by man, or were eliminated totally. Xerophiles and heliophiles, however, flourished and colonized large tracts of previously wooded country. With time, certain species of both the shade-loving and the xerophile/heliophile groups altered their ecology to the extent that they came to live in such close association with human habitations as to become almost entirely dependent on man for their existence[26]. Such molluscs are distinguished as synanthropic and it is these, if any, which might have become domesticated. But this is as far as the process has gone. Thus the synanthropic species, *H. aspersa* and *H. pomatia*, are both edible and eaten to the present day in Britain and the Continent; but there is no question of domestication, only of collection during certain seasons.

Thus while the example of the Romans shows that the potential is there, land snails have not become domesticated either through deliberate selective breeding or through a more natural association with man. The reasons for this are various but connected perhaps with the fact that molluscs are of little hindrance to man in the wild state, and yet are sufficiently abundant to be profitably collected on a mesolithic food-gathering basis.

Notes

1 Jackson, J. W. (1916). The geographical distribution of the shell-purple industry, *Memoirs and Proc. Manchester Lit. and Phil. Soc.*, **60** (7).
2 Information from W. T. Stearn (in discussion).
3 Childe, V. G. (1957). *The Dawn of European Civilization*. London. p. 58.
4 Jackson, J. W. (1917). *Shells as evidence of the migrations of Early Culture*. London.
5 Clark, J. G. D. (1952). *Prehistoric Europe: The Economic Basis*. London. pp. 241–3. It appears to be uncertain whether *Spondylus gaederopus* does in fact occur in the Black Sea as quoted by Clark. (N. Shackleton, Personal communication).
6 Ansell, A. D. (1960). Observations on predation of *Venus striatula* (da Costa) by *Natica alderi* (Forbes), *Proc. Malacol. Soc.*, **34**, pp. 157–64.

7 Symposium on Edible Molluscs (1960). *Proc. Malacol. Soc.*, **34**, pp. 113–56.

8 Garrod, D. A. E. *et al.* (1928). Excavation of a Mousterian rock-shelter at Devil's Tower, Gibraltar, *J. Roy. Anthrop. Inst.*, **58**, pp. 34–113.

9 Meighan, C. W. *et al.* (1958). Ecological interpretation in archaeology: part I, *Amer. Antiq.*, **24**, pp. 1–23.

10 Cornwall, I. W. (1964). *The World of Ancient Man*. London.

11 Balout, L. (1955). *Prèhistoire de l'Afrique du Nord*. Paris; Obermaier, H. (1925). *Fossil Man in Spain*. Yale.

12 Obermaier, H. (1925). ibid.

13 Just Pequart, M. and St. (1954). *Hoëdic*. Anvers.

14 Clark, J. G. D. (1936). *The Mesolithic Settlement of Northern Europe*. Cambridge.

15 Lacaille, A. D. (1954). *The Stone Age in Scotland*. Oxford; Movius, N. J., Jr. (1942). *The Irish Stone Age*. Cambridge.

16 Clark, J. G. D. (1936). ibid.

17 Townsend, M. (1967). The common limpet (*Patella vulgata*) as a source of protein, *Folia Biologica*, **15**, pp. 343–51.

18 Cornwall, I. W. (1964). op. cit. p. 223.

19 Puglisi, S. M. (1955). Industria microlitica nei livelli a ceramica impressa di Coppa Nevigata, *Riv. Sci. Prehist.*, **10**, pp. 19–37.

20 Meighan, C. W. *et al.* (1958). ibid.

21 For instance, in France today, the oyster which is mainly cultivated is *Ostrea angulata*; before 1914 only the more northerly *O. edulis* was present: while in the mesolithic period, both species were present. See Just Pequart, M. and St. (1954). ibid.

22 Thus in the shell mounds of the Asturians, *Monodonta* (*Trochus*) *lineata* replaces *Littorina littorea*, the latter being the characteristic form of the Upper Palaeolithic and Azilian middens; this change is said to be climatically caused.

23 Reed, C. A. (1962). Snails on a Persian hillside: Ecology, Prehistory-gastronomy, *Postilla:Yale Peabody Mus.*, **66**.

24 Cain, A. J. (1967). The large snails, in Avery, M. *et al.* Rainsborough, Northants, England: Excavations 1961–5, *Proc. Prehist. Soc.*, **33**, pp. 305–6.

25 Pliny's *Natural History*. **9**, p. 173.

26 Kerney, M. P. (1965). Snails and man in Britain, *J. Conchol.*, **26**, pp. 3–14.

DUNCAN NOBLE

The Mesopotamian onager as a draught animal

The Mesopotamian onager is an extinct member of the family of half-asses now represented by the common or Persian onager and the Indian onager. It became extinct in the early twentieth century when it succumbed to the effects of continued hunting and the depredations of troops in the First World War. The last reported sighting of Mesopotamian onagers was by the traveller Carl Raswan[1] in the late twenties of this century near the Jebel Sinjar. In 1928 one was in the Schönbrunn Zoo, Vienna[2], and a photograph survives.

The Mesopotamian onager was a light, swift, animal standing one metre (nine hands three inches) at the withers according to Antonius[3] and was as fast as the horse, if without its staying powers. Its ears were longer than the horse's but shorter than those of the ass and the Indian onager. It had the erect mane of the wild horse but was distinguishable by the tail which was tufted from half way along its length. It appears from its muzzled representations to have been a difficult animal to use and not ideal for draught purposes. The Director of Whipsnade Park of the Zoological Society of London states[4] of the Persian onagers in his keeping that they are unhandleable and indeed unapproachable with inherently intractable dispositions and, while reasonably fleet of foot, are narrow-chested—not the sign of a good draught animal.

From evidence of onagers' bones at Anau, level I[5], c. 4800 B.C., and Sialk II[6] c. 3500 B.C. there is no doubt that onagers[7] were hunted for food in prehistoric times, as they were later by the Assyrians and the Arabs. But it is from Sumerian levels (c. 2500 B.C.) and the Uruk period preceding that the Mesopotamian onager appears as a draught animal.

It may be that clay discs from Tepe Gawra XVIII c. 4000 B.C. represent wheels and a Halaf sherd from level XVI c. 3900 B.C. shows two onagers. Thereafter the first clear indication of the use of wheeled vehicles is in pictograms from tablets from Uruk level IV c. 3100 B.C. Terracotta model wagons and chariots appear in Tepe Gawra VIII in the Jemdet Nasr level c. 3000 B.C. and in Sumerian Early Dynastic times (2370–2900 B.C.) vehicles occur in considerable numbers as models, paintings on pottery, and chariot burials at Ur, Kish, and Susa. That a considerable number of these wagons and chariots were pulled by onagers is clear from the shell inlay called the Standard of Ur[8] (Plate IA) and the mother-of-pearl fragments of the Standard of Mari[9], and from a scarlet ware vase from Khafaje from an E.D.I. level and a bronze model from Tell Agrab (E.D.III.) (Plate IB).

That the onager was ridden is less certain and we depend for our information on terracotta models of riders from Susa from which the animal is not easily identified. It appears likely that if the onager was ridden, it was not so used as a regular means of transport.

The war panel on the Standard from the Royal Tombs of Ur shows in its lowest register four successive stages of the charge of a chariot against a barbarian enemy. It is a heavy vehicle with four solid wheels, each made of three planks. The body has a wooden framework and a high front to which is lashed a quiver of javelins. The framework is panelled in leather or basketwork and models from Susa[10] have markings indicating that basketry was used. The vehicle is drawn by four onagers harnessed abreast to a yoke lashed to the curved pole which is attached to the base of the chariot. On the pole is a double ring through which the reins pass and the onagers are yoked by their collars from which hang pointed streamers which would increase their frightening aspect. Also from Ur comes a rein ring surmounted by a statuette of an onager. As the yoke is not visible in the inlay, it is most likely that it extends over the withers of the inner beasts only and the collars of the outer animals are lashed to its extremities. This interpretation is borne out by the chariot from Tell Agrab described below. The animals have headstalls whose nosebands extend forward, partially to muzzle them. This conclusion is reinforced by the heads of onagers shown on the fragments of the stylistically similar inlays found in the temples of Ishtar and Ninni-Zaza at Mari. The fragment from the early dynastic temple of Ishtar shows a headstall essentially identical to the Ur one, and those from the slightly later temple of Ninni-Zaza illustrate headstalls with muzzles of plaited material covering the lower jaw and also the whole muzzle—a subsequent modification.

The question of how the animals were controlled has been discussed. A ring is shown in front of the Ur onagers' noses and Woolley[11] considered that it represented the rings of a bit, while noting that the oxen which pulled the king's essentially similar car found in grave PG/789 were guided by a ring through the nostrils. Hilzheimer[12] thought that the reins were attached to the headstall. But Schaeffer[13] has come to what appears to be the correct conclusion in finding from a comparison of the Ur and Mari inlays that the ring was in fact passed through the flesh of the upper lip.

The crew consisted of the driver who wielded a long forked goad to urge on his animals and standing behind him a soldier shown carrying at one time a javelin and at another an axe.

To gain an idea of the size of the vehicles we note that the ox wagons of grave PG/789 had wheels of diameter between 60 and 100 cm. From the Y cemetery at Kish in grave Y237 (E.D.III) comes a burial with a four-wheeled wagon pulled by equids of which the excavator was able to distinguish the wheels and the chassis and curved hoops on the sides which suggest that it was a freight vehicle. It had wheels of 50 cm. diameter with axles 90 cm. long and the chassis was 45 cm. wide. This suggests that the chariots were long narrow vehicles and with hardwood being used in their construction the Ur Standard ones would have had a tare weight of 275 kg. (605 lb.) or up to 410 kg. (900 lb.) with crew. The Kish chariot had bronze nails studded round the rim of the wheels although these are not shown in the Ur and Mari chariots. But round the wheels of the Ur ox waggons Woolley was able to distinguish a grey powder which he took to be the remains of leather tyres.

Terracotta models from Tepe Gawra[14] and Kish A cemetery[15] (E.D.III) and Susa[16] show two-wheeled versions of the type of conveyance described above with a high front often with two holes for the reins to pass through. But a different type is evidenced by a bronze model found in an E.D.II context at Tell Agrab[17] and by a terracotta model from the A cemetery at Kish[18]. The Tell Agrab model portrays four onagers yoked as were the Ur Standard beasts to a two-wheeled chariot with a straight pole which forms also the body of the car astride which sits the driver who has before him a high wooden protection of two upright timbers with a semi-circular top. The wheels are again solid, made of planks, and protected by pointed bronze nails round the rim.

The Kish model has a body which is rounded like a saddle with the marks of a fleece thrown over it while the front is square with crossed struts like the Ur chariots. A limestone plaque from the Third Dynasty of Ur[19] shows a chariot pulled by felines and it is also like a saddle with a leopard skin thrown over it.

We notice that there are no nails in the wheels of the four-wheeled Ur and Mari chariots which are definitely used for war, while they are found on two-wheeled chariots and also on the four-wheeled chariot on the Khafaje vase which appears to be a processional vehicle. As there is no evidence of a swinging front axle, it may be that while in a light two-wheeled chariot or peaceful wagon the nails contributed greatly to lateral stability, in a fighting chariot smooth leather tyres gave adequate protection to the wheels and yet allowed them to slide sideways when cornering at speed. But turning must have been difficult as from the Tell Agrab model we know that the lip ring on the outer animal on the left was attached by a single rein to the ring through its companion's lip from which led a rein which the driver held in his left hand while he guided the other pair in similar fashion with a rein in his right hand. To turn to the left the driver pulled in on his left-hand rein, thereby checking his left pair and at the same time pulling it to the right and away from the direction of the turn. The collar, pressing on the animals' wind pipes and jugular veins would at the same time reduce the control and their tractive effort.

The chariots which the driver sat astride can hardly have been used against an enemy as the driver would have been fully occupied with his team and unable to defend himself. Rather must they have been used for scouting or as a commander's personal transport. With the four-wheeled chariots little manoeuvre can have been possible. We may consider that the onagers were pointed in the desired direction and held by grooms until the opportune moment when they were launched against the foe. The soldier's axe and spear can only have been for personal defence as four animals would cut a swathe two and a half metres wide through the enemy ranks and any persons within reach would already have been trampled over. As the enemy line was approached the spearman can have had time to throw only two spears before the chariot passed through the opposing forces or was brought to a stand-still. The real weapon was the onagers' hooves and the effect was psychological rather than material.

And then in Akkadian times, *c.* 2300 B.C., with the introduction of the more dependable horse, the onager for ever passed out of use as a draught animal.

Notes

1 Raswan, C. R. (1935). *Black Tents of Arabia.* Boston.
2 Antonius, O. (1928–9). Der syrische Halbesel, *Der zoologische Garten,* 1, pp. 19–25.
3 Antonius, O. (1928–9). ibid.
4 Personal communication.
5 Pumpelly, R. (1908). (1908). *Explorations in Turkestan, Expedition of 1904.* 2. Washington.
6 Ghirshman, R. (1938–9). *Fouilles de Sialk.* Paris.
7 The excavators identify the Anau and Sialk equids as horses but Zeuner, F. E. (1963). *A History of Domesticated Animals.* London. p. 316, identifies them as onagers.
8 Woolley, C. L. (1934). *Ur Excavations II, The Royal Cemetery.* London. pp. 269–73 and pl. 92.
9 Parrot, A. (1956). *Mission archéologique de Mari, I: Le Temple d'Ishtar.* Paris. pp. 136–46 and pl. LVI.
10 Mecquenem, R. de. (1943). *Mémoires de la Mission Archéologique en Iran,* 29. Archéologie Susienne, Paris. Fig. 91b.
11 Woolley, C. L. (1934). op. cit. p. 270.
12 Hilzheimer, M. (1931). Die Anschurrung bei den alten Sumerien, *Praehistorische Z.*
13 Schaeffer, C. L. (1938). Contribution à l'étude de l'attelage Sumerien et Syrien aux IIIe et IIe millénaires, *Préhistoire,* 6.
14 Speiser, E. A. (1935). *Excavations at Tepe Gawra,* I. Philadelphia. pls. XXXIVc and LXXVIII.
15 MacKay, E. (1929). *A Sumerian Palace and the A cemetery at Kish, Mesopotamia,* Chicago. pl. XLVI.
16 Mecquenem, R. de. (1943). op. cit. pl. XLVI. 3.
17 Frankfort, H. (1937). Revelations of early Mesopotamian culture, *Illustrated London News,* 6 (Nov.); Frankfort, H. (1943). *More Sculpture from the Diyala Region.* Chicago. p. 12.
18 MacKay, E. (1929). op. cit. pl. XLVI. 7.
19 Woolley, C. L. (1934). op. cit. pl. 181b.

CLIFFORD OWEN

The domestication of the ferret

The three lines of investigation used in studying domestication are archaeological, zoological, and historical.

In studying the ferret only the second two have been pursued. This communication suggests ways in which attention to the problem by archaeologists might be of real value.

A very brief outline of what is known will be given and suggestions made for work needing to be done.

Historical material starts with a mention by Aristophanes[1], *c.* 450 B.C., in a comedy, of an animal which might have been the ferret, followed by Aristotle[2], *c.* 350 B.C., but the correct translation of the Greek word used has been the subject of much argument. Although Aristotle states that this animal could become very mild and tame, there is reason to suppose that other members of the weasel tribe may have been kept in a semi-domesticated state for the control of small rodents. These references gave rise to considerable philological discussion in the sixteenth century but the issue remains undecided.

The first reference which can be said with any probability to relate to the ferret is that of Strabo[3] (fl. about 63 B.C. to A.D. 24). He states that a Libyan animal, bred purposely, was muzzled and put into rabbit holes when it either pulls out the rabbit with its claws or causes it to bolt to the men and dogs standing ready. The fact that this method is still used by the Ruafa of Morocco suggests that it is an accurate and authentic description, and that the animal used was the ferret.

The use of the ferret for rabbit catching would appear to have been the reason for the domestication of this somewhat troublesome animal and its use is associated with the spread of the rabbit as a semi-domesticated food animal and, later, a feral species. The rabbit appears originally to have been indigenous to Spain and possibly North Africa; the occasion for Strabo's remarks was a plague of rabbits in the Balearic Islands, to which they had been introduced. The use of the ferret for killing rats is not mentioned until later. It appears to have been less important than its use in rabbiting, and this contribution will be confined to a discussion of the latter use. However, ratting should be borne in mind in the appropriate contexts.

Pliny[4] (A.D. 23–79) also mentions the rabbit and the ferret. The next reference is in A.D. 600, by Isidore of Seville[5], to the ferret and rabbit-hunting. After this, as is to be expected, references are scarce until mediaeval manuscripts. Many of these contain variations of what Aristotle said; little of real value can be found until the habit of observation and reporting of contemporary life became established.

Then, some idea of the extent of the spread of both rabbit and ferret can be gathered. Illustrations in manuscripts provide evidence for the breeding of domesticated rabbits of different colours (black and white) by 1516, and for the existence of rabbit warrens and the use of ferrets. The most important of these is a splendid copy of the Livre de Chasse of Gaston, Comte de Foix[6], who reigned over two principalities in Southern France and Northern Spain. This copy shows ferreting in full swing with purse nets, and a ferret wearing a muzzle. Gaston de Foix wrote this book between 1st May 1387 and his death about four years later.

In the thirteenth century references to ferrets show that they had spread northwards to Germany before 1245. It is frequently stated that Genghis Khan used ferrets at Termed in 1221. Termed is probably Termez, on the Oxus river, about 160 miles south of Samarkand. The statement comes from an English book of 1826[7], derived from a French work of 1722[8], quoting from a compilation attributed to the Imam Mehemet bin Ahmed Azzahabi, born in Cairo and died in Samarkand in 1345. It is important that the work by Azzahabi be traced if possible. Dr. M. Lings of the British Museum has kindly offered to look into the problem. Until the result of his investigation is known it would perhaps be advisable to treat this evidence of the use of the ferret in Afghanistan with reserve.

Queen Mary's Psalter of about 1340 shows ferrets being used by well-dressed women but the translation of Gaston de Foix, made by Edward 2nd Duke of York during his captivity in Pevensey Castle between 1406 and 1413, has an interpolation to the effect that no one hunts rabbits except fur-hunters—indicating that this form of the chase may not have enjoyed the same esteem as it did on the continent of Europe by that period.

Earlier references to the ferret can be found in laws and court rolls. The first known in England is for 1223 and there are references to a ferreter attached to the Court in 1281. References to the ownership of ferrets by a Bishop and a Prior indicate the importance of rabbits to church establishments; a law limiting the ownership of ferrets to those with an annual income of forty shillings, passed in 1390, indicates that by that time poaching was a problem. Warrens were carefully designed; sometimes walled or paled; and where necessary had raised banks to provide dry quarters for the rabbits. It can be taken that wherever warrens were established ferrets were used, and were therefore important items in the domestic economy.

The circulation of printed books marks another increment in the information on the ferret. It was accurately described in Conrad Gesner's[9] work on quadrupeds, published at Zurich in 1551. Gesner describes it as the colour of wool stained with urine—which gives a very good impression of the colour of the white ferret, here mentioned for the first time. The original ferret was undoubtedly the colour of a wild polecat and we do not know at what period the break to white occurred. The only earlier reference to colour is by implication in the poem "The Siege of Thebes" by John of Lydgate[10] (probably written in 1421) where the red eyes of the ferret are mentioned. As only white ferrets have red eyes it is probable that a white ferret is meant.

Consideration of the colour of the animal brings us to an appraisal of the zoological evidence on the possible origin of the domestic form. The ferret's ancestor is the wild polecat. There are two forms—eastern and western. The present distribution of these forms is not accurately known; nor is their taxonomic position, their previous distribution, nor the precise region where the animal was domesticated. It has been claimed that the ferret was domesticated in Morocco from a wild species; the writer does not think this is proven and his evidence for this view is in preparation[11]. Attempts to equate the ferret with one or other of these wild forms have mostly depended on comparison of skull measurements, and opinions have varied. The most sophisticated of these attempts has used multivariate analysis. In the view of Udo Rempe the ferret is derived from the western form of polecat. The present writer has endeavoured to compare the behaviour and ease of taming and breeding of the two forms but has unfortunately been unable to obtain live specimens of the eastern polecat. If (as discussed by Rohrs[12]) the idea of domestication travelled rather than the animal itself it is possible that both the eastern and western forms were domesticated.

The material used has been skulls of modern polecats and ferrets from museum collections and this leads naturally to the question of the skull characteristics of ferrets used in the earlier period of its use.

The archaeological material bearing on this problem is remarkable for its complete absence. Out of all the activity, year in year out, of providing considerable quantities of food by the use of the ferret—nothing remains. The whole purpose of this communication is to bring to light material unknown to the writer and to make it more likely that relevant material is not overlooked. The bones of ferrets, like those of the rabbits they pursue, are difficult: first, many archaeologists do not save small bones or may not record them adequately—this practice, though diminishing, regrettably persists; secondly, rabbits are the most intrusive creatures and ferrets have to follow them. Only in exceptional cases is one able to exclude the possibility of contamination by later burrowing. It is therefore vital to treat with extreme care any rabbit or ferret bones underneath sealed layers, and to save carefully every piece of skeletal material and any possible associated objects.

Objects which could be associated with ferreting are not many and their identification is difficult. Those most frequently mentioned are muzzles and nets—both unlikely to survive. However, there are some more robust items.

Bells were frequently used to alarm the rabbits and to cause them to run before they could be caught.

Although ferret bells are not recorded this is not as surprising as it might seem. They would be difficult to distinguish from bells used as ornaments of dress or for falconry and hawking—they might be readily linked with the merlin, sparrowhawk or kestrel.

However, the illustration of a ferret in Gesner (Pl. IV B) perhaps shows it wearing what may be the type of bell used—which is not like bells used for falconry today. In 1378 eight white iron chains for ferrets are included in an inventory of a haberdasher's shop. It would be impossible to determine their use if recovered from the site today.

Muzzles may have been made of metal, though the practice of tying the lips of a ferret together through a hole in the upper and nether lip on each side would make these superfluous. There is an interesting mention of silver rings being used for this purpose in Lower Germany and a report that gipsies in England knew of this practice in the present century is of interest. A number of patterns of metal muzzle are in use today but the date of their introduction is unknown—several of them appear to be of nineteenth-century origin. Ancillary tools, for digging out ferrets which "lay up", often of a special shape, were commonly used—but these are difficult to separate from agricultural implements or tools used for digging out foxes or badgers. Boxes and bags were used for carrying ferrets and these might be identifiable.

In order to assist in the classification of these objects it would help if sites of mediaeval establishments of importance could be searched for the place in which ferrets were kept. Objects found in such places would possibly be for use with ferrets and themselves might establish the use of the building. The household books of the Lord William Howard of Naworth Castle[13] (1618–33) give some idea of what might be found. The Warrener had a house with a slate roof which may have had a brick floor. He had a wallet for his ferrets, seven yards of coarse cloth for his bed, eight yards of cloth for a pair of blankets, a hank of yarn for mending his net, a paddle staff with iron on it, traps made by the man who mended the wains, probably of wood, but possibly of iron, a ferret line and, in 1622, a room was made for the ferrets at Cumrach. This, and the wages paid to him, indicate that he was a servant of some importance and that a warrener might occupy a house sturdy enough to present substantial remains. Among these, or in the room for the ferrets, might be found objects related to his work. The accommodation for the ferrets in this case seems to have been distinguishable but in many cases they may have been kept in wooden hutches, or in barrels—a common practice for hundreds of years.

Careful watch for evidence of ferreting can then be expected to yield results in remains of houses of servants, in outhouses, and in the raised banks of made warrens which, it is suggested in "The Countrie Farme"[14], should be sited between the hilly and the fertile ground of a Park, and near to the Lodge, and possibly represented in Britain by the "pillow-mounds" of Crawford[15].

In earlier or simpler communities the ferret may have been tethered, as in Morocco today, in a section of cork-oak bark hung from the roof of the dwelling house. The use of nets or metal accessories would be unknown. Under these circumstances ferret skeletons within the house area would be of significance.

The writer would be most grateful for notice of any known material evidence of the use of the ferret, up to and including the mid-nineteenth century.

Notes

1 Aristophanes. *The Acharnians.*
2 Aristotle. *Historia Animalium.*
3 Strabo. *Geographica*, Book III 2. 6.
4 Pliny's *Natural History*. 8, 55.
5 Isidore. *Patrologie.* 1850. Paris.
6 Gaston Phébus, Comte de Foix. MS Francais 616, Bibliotheque Nationale, Paris.
7 Ranking, J. (1826). *Historical Researches on the Wars and Sports of the Mongols*. London.
8 Croix, Petis de la (1722). *The History of Genghizcan the Great*. London.
9 Gesner, C. (1551). *Historiae Animalium*. Zurich.
10 Lydgate, John. (*c*. 1421). *Siege of Thebes*. Early English Text. Soc. Extra Series, 1911.
11 Owen, C. E. In preparation.
12 Rohrs, M. (1961). Biologische Anschauungen über Begriff v. Wesen der Domestikation, *Z. Tierzücht. Zücht Biol.*, 76 (i), pp. 7–23.
13 Selections from the Household books of the Lord William Howard of Naworth Castle. 1878. *Surtees Soc.* 68.
14 Estienne, C. (1586). *Maison Rustique.*
15 Crawford, O. G. S. and Keiller, A. (1928). *Wessex from the Air*. Oxford.

M. L. RYDER

Changes in the fleece of sheep following domestication (with a note on the coat of cattle)

Although it seems clear that the coat of cattle has changed far less than that of sheep since domestication, it is fortunate that the wild form of sheep is still in existence to demonstrate the extent of the change in sheep, which has been brought about mainly through the selective breeding by man towards different kinds of fleeces suitable for textiles.

The main changes that have occurred in the coat of the sheep are as follows:

1 *Pigment has been lost*; wild sheep, and some primitive domestic breeds are coloured, whereas most modern breeds are white, at any rate in the main fleece area. Apart from being unwanted in white garments, pigment interferes with dyeing, and so the desire to eliminate naturally-coloured wool fibres from fleeces could have begun with the development of dyeing. The mode of inheritance of colour in different breeds is likely to throw light on their affinities and evolution.

2 *Domestic sheep no longer moult*; wild sheep moult their coat completely each spring, and many primitive breeds show considerable fleece shedding, but the more highly evolved breeds have almost lost the tendency to shed wool. Fleece shedding can mean considerable loss of wool to the farmer, and so man would wish to select against it, but a satisfactory means of obtaining the wool would first have to be available in the form of iron sheep shears.

3 *Hairiness has decreased*; hairiness is undesirable because of the coarse fibre diameter, the harsh "handle", and the difficulty of dyeing hairy fibres.

Early changes

The coat of the wild sheep consists of a relatively short hairy outer coat, and an even shorter woolly undercoat, which is obscured by the outer coat[1]. The hairy fibres are about 6 cm. long, and are bristly in character, being known as kemps (Fig. 1). The main change in fleece structure since domestication can therefore be regarded as a development of the wool at the expense of the kemp (Fig. 2). The wool of sheep provides a paradox which leads to considerations like that of Flannery[2] on why it should have appeared. Wool was not a product of domestication, yet it was insufficiently developed in the wild animal to provide a reason for domestication.

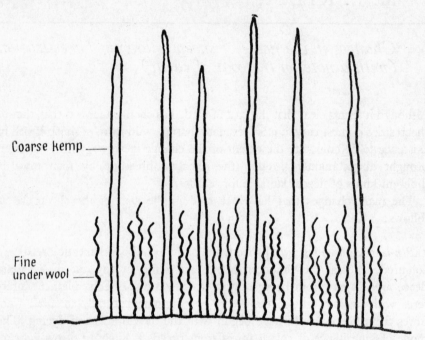

Coarse kemp

Fine under wool

Fig 1 Structure of the double coat in wild sheep.

So far as I am aware, no sheepskin or wool from the neolithic period is available for examination. Neolithic textiles usually turn out to be flax. One assumes therefore that the coat of the first domestic sheep would have been little different from that of the wild sheep before domestication. And, in fact, some of the most primitive sheep in existence today, the so-called "hair" sheep of tropical Africa and the hot plains of India, have a short kempy coat with an undercoat of fine wool[3]. Although some of these breeds are brown, the wild colour pattern has apparently been lost, and some are black and others white. This type of coat has been interpreted as an adaptation to a hot environment[4], but the more likely explanation is that it has undergone little change from that of the wild sheep although there is evidence of a reduction in the undercoat in some. It may be that man lacked the stimulus to select for wool to provide clothing in a hot environment.

It is unlikely as suggested by Flannery[5] that a woolly coat developed as a result of natural selection towards a coat providing insulation in a hot environ-

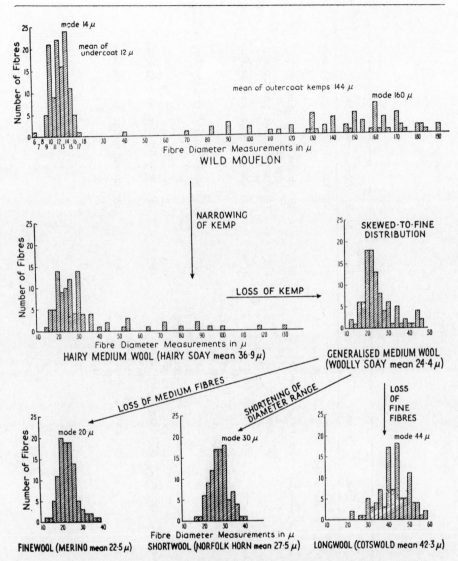

Fig 2 Changes in fibre diameter distribution during fleece evolution. Measurements from fleece of sheep remaining today have been given, but the last five distributions have been found in textiles of the Roman period.

ment. Wool is more likely to have been developed by man in a relatively cold environment, the insulation of the sheep against heat being a purely secondary and incidental feature of a fine-woolled fleece.

White as well as black and piebald sheep are depicted in Ancient Egypt before 2000 B.C., and the animals appear to have a short, kempy coat, although the rams have a throat fringe like that found in wild rams[6]. The only wool examined from this period was from a tomb of the "Old Kingdom". This was unspun, white, and had a length of 2 cm. which may not have been the full

Source	Site	Date		Pigment	Diameter Range	Mean Diameter	Mode	Distribution	Fleece Type
K. Schlabow (Neumünster Textilmuseum)	Unterteutschenthal (Germany)	Early Bronze Age		xx	12–32 36, 42, 46, 48	22·3	18	skewed-to-fine	gen. medium
K. Schlabow (Neumünster Textilmuseum)	Harrislee (Germany)	1600 B.C.	(a)	xx	8–26 2 of 32	16·6	16	almost symmetrical	fine
(Neumünster Textilmuseum)			(b)	xxx	10–28 2 of 40	18·7	14	skewed-to-fine	gen. medium
British Museum	Rylstone, Yorkshire — (England)		(a)	xxx	10–30 44, 48, 62, 74 (fine, medium and hairy fibres)	21·00	18	skewed-to-fine	hairy medium
			(b)	xxx	10–34 42, 44 (fine and medium fibres)	19·6	18	skewed-to-fine	gen. medium
			(c)	xxx	12–30 (fine only)	19·4	18	symmetrical	fine†
Danish National Museum (B5067, Draegter T.244)	Guldhoj, Vester Varndrup (Denmark) (a)	1200 B.C.	(a)	xxx	10–32 (96%) 40–44 (3%) 74 (1%)	18·7	18	skewed-to-fine	hairy medium
			(b)	xxx	8–28 (97%) 50 (1%) 62, 88 (2%)	16·3	14	skewed-to-fine	hairy medium

			wool	kemp	
Danish National Museum (B5067, Draegter T.244)	Skrydstrup (Denmark)[b]	head band xx 13–26 + kemp	20·5	102	— apparently intermediate between wild type and hairy Soay
		skirt xx	24·1	222	—
		large cloth xx +42–54 + kemp	24·3 + kemp	174	—
Universitets Oldsaksamling, Oslo	Bloheia (Norway)[c] 1200 B.C.	no info.	14·7	15	skewed-to-fine gen. medium
			8–27 35, 43		

Table 1 Fibre diameter measurements of Bronze Age wool textiles (microns)*.

In this and subsequent tables: the letters (a), (b), (c) and so on indicate different yarns; pigmentation is indicated as follows:

x slight
xx moderate
xxx heavy

* one micron = 0·001 mm.
† the three Rylstone yarns could be from the same fleece type, and the differences be due to the exclusion of coarser fibres from the sample. See discussion in text.

(a) Broholm, H. C. and Hald, M. (1940). *Costumes of the Bronze Age in Denmark*. Oxford.
(b) Figures from Steensberg, C. M. (1939). Undersogelser over Harr fra Skrydstrupgraven, *in* Broholm, H. C. and Hald, M. *Skrydstrupfundet*. Copenhagen. pp. 31–41.
(c) Figures from Rosenqvist, A. M. (1964). Investigations of woollen fibres in the Oseberg find, *Proc. Int. Conf. on Conservation*. Delft. pp. 133–6.

length of the fleece[7]. The mean fibre diameter was 34·6μ and there was a skewed-to-fine distribution, but there was a continuous range in fibre diameter from 12 to 110μ making it comparable with a hairy sheep (see below) rather than a kempy sheep, which has a discontinuous diameter distribution (see Mouflon in Fig. 2).

Most of the major variations in sheep, i.e. in the horns, tail length, and the appearance of a white, woolly type of fleece seem to have taken place by the time that illustrations and records first appeared in Mesopotamia about 3000 B.C., i.e. during the first half of the period since domestication. This seems to be an example of the principle that evolution along a new line at first proceeds rapidly, and then slows down[8]. In addition, the fact that evolution progresses more rapidly in smaller populations may have been a contributory factor.

It is likely that those characters such as colour, and the absence of horns, which seem to be controlled by relatively few genes, were introduced as a result of mutations. But most characters of economic importance such as fleece structure, and fleece weight are controlled by many genes, and show continuous variation. Thus subsequent changes wrought by man can be explained as due to a gradual selection of animals with the desired characters, such as a woollier fleece. Once some divergence had taken place, human migrations allowed wide out-breeding, and cross-breeding of this sort has been an important factor in the development of modern breeds.

Evidence from textile remains

The earliest wool, from textiles, that it has been possible to examine was from the Bronze Age of northern Europe. The first workers who examined such wool described it as mixed with deer hair. It is now realized that, at any rate in most instances, the "deer hairs" are really the kemp fibres found in the fleeces of primitive sheep. Details of the Bronze Age wool examined are given in Table 1. The Danish Bronze Age wool from Guldhøj dated 1200 B.C., was densely pigmented and had an unusual distribution of fibre diameters, which was unlike any known fleece type[9]. This had a very high proportion of fine fibres, and only a few medium and hairy fibres. That this was not a fortuitous result is shown by the finding of the same unusual diameter distribution in some Norwegian Bronze Age wool by Rosenqvist[10].

In primitive hand-spinning, the wool is taken direct from the staple, so one expects the distribution of fibre diameter in the yarn to be the same as that in the fleece. This unexpected distribution was therefore puzzling until moulting was investigated in the Soay sheep remaining on St. Kilda off north-west Scotland. Although the fine wool, and some of the hairy fibres, shed in the spring, many of the hairy fibres remain in the skin to shed later. Sheep that moult are plucked to obtain their wool, and this retention of the hairy fibres suggests that the plucking of primitive breeds might yield wool with a greater proportion of fine fibres than would be obtained if the fleece was shorn, and the hairy fibres included.

The similarity of sheep bones from excavations with those of the Soay[11], and the similarity of wool in textile remains with the fleece of the Soay[12] suggest that the Soay type is a survivor of the prehistoric sheep of Europe.

Soay fleeces range from a hairy type in which the hairy (outer coat) fibres are fine kemps, to a woolly type in which the outer coat fibres are of only medium diameter (Fig. 2). These probably correspond to the two types that have been described in textile specimens as hairy medium, and generalized medium, wool[13]. Irrespective of the extent of hairiness there are also dark and light brown types of Soay[14]. Dark, hairy animals more closely resemble the wild Mouflon, and are possibly the most primitive, while light, woolly animals may be the least primitive. The coat length is comparable to that in the Mouflon, being about 5 cm., and longer in hairy than woolly animals.

This range of fleece type in a single population indicates that a similar variation could have existed within flocks in the past. Thus the finding of different fleece types in textiles from a particular site could indicate a range of variation rather than the existence of distinct breeds.

Evidence from skin

By the Iron Age in the West, and probably before in the Near East, much wool was white, and a specimen from central Asia dated about 400 B.C. comprised a complete sheepskin with the wool intact[15]. This came from a Scythian burial at Pazirik in the Altai Mountains, and is of interest in having an outer coat of hairs instead of the kemps or medium fibres found in the Soay (Pl. VI A and Table 2). So far only two types of fibre, kemp and wool, have been mentioned, but some modern breeds have a third fibre type, long hairs. These are also known as heterotype hairs because they are intermediate in character between kemp and wool. They are coarse and kemp-like in summer, but in winter hairs grow thinner, and appear like true wool fibres: when kemps cease growing preparatory to shedding, hairs merely thin down and continue to grow.

The hairs of the Pazirik sample were longer and finer than kemps, but were unusual in showing evidence of shedding in the skin. They may represent a stage of evolution towards the much longer and usually continuously growing heterotype hairs found in the fleeces of modern hairy hill sheep such as the Scottish Blackface. Such fleeces have been thought of as being primitive, but having this specialized type of hair fibre, they are apparently highly evolved.

The origin of hairs would seem to be associated in some way with the change from a moulting fleece to one of continuous growth. Whether man began to select against moulting before or after starting to clip the wool is not

Source	Site	Date	Pigment	Length	Diameter Range	Mean Diameter	Mode	Distribution	Fleece Type
Inst. of Archaeology, Moscow	Pazirik (Central Asia)	4th–5th cent. B.C.	none	12 cm.	12–42 62–82	28·2	22 & 70	skewed-to-fine	hairy
Nat. History Museum, Vienna	Hallstatt (Austria)	800–500 B.C.	none	3 cm.*	20–80 96–100	35·5	22	skewed-to-fine	hairy

* see text

Table 2 Fibre measurements of Early Iron Age wools (**microns**).

known, but it is thought that shears were invented in the Near East about 1000 B.C.

In order to investigate the possibility that heterotypes had originated by crossing a woolly with a kempy sheep, some Merino sheep were crossed with a Mouflon, but the offspring had kemp and wool like the Mouflon parent[16].

The Pazirik specimen introduces the skin as a new source of evidence, and fibre length as a new dimension. Textile specimens, although readily studied, provide only fibre diameter values; it would be virtually impossible to obtain measurements of fibre length from them. The wool fibres on the Pazirik skin were 8 cm. long, and the hairs extended to 12 cm. That this was the maximum length was shown by observing in sections of the skin that the fibres had "brush ends" i.e. they had ceased to grow. This length of coat is longer than that of the wild sheep, or the Soay, but is comparable with only the shortest hairy fleeces of today. A sheepskin from the Iron Age Hallstatt salt workings in Austria had brush ends in the skin, but the length of 3 cm. seems too short to be the maximum coat length, and so this had probably become shortened through fibre breakage. The coarse fibres of this specimen appeared to be kemps rather than hairs (Table 2). The way in which fibre length can alter the appearance and nature of the coat was shown with some goats by Ryder[17]. Most goats have a short woolly undercoat obscured by a kempy outercoat, and when such animals were crossed with an Angora goat (the source of mohair) the progeny grew long wool, like that of the Angora parent, which completely obscured the kemp.

But if remains of woolled sheepskins are rare, remains of skin in the form of leather and parchment are not, and these frequently contain fibre remains that can not only provide measurements of fibre diameter, but give different evidence from the way in which they are arranged in the skin[18].

The outer coat hairs are formed first in the foetus, and are known as primary fibres. The fibres of the underwool are formed later and are known as secondaries. In most mammals the fibres are not distributed at random in the skin, but are arranged in characteristic groups. Primary fibres lie in rows of three, and the smaller but more numerous secondaries are grouped on one side of them so that each fibre group, which is the smallest unit of the coat, consists of a trio of outer coat primaries with their associated finer secondaries.

In the wild sheep (Fig. 3a) there is a tendency for the secondary fibres to lie between the primaries. The kempy sheep of the tropics, and the goat, have a similar grouping, but the secondaries have begun to move from between the primaries. The remaining three groups in Fig. 3 were found in parchment from the Dead Sea Scrolls[19]. The group shown in Fig. 3b is from a hairy sheep comparable with the Pazirik animal, but only a few were of this type. Most had a grouping like that in 3c which corresponds to the generalized medium wool type found in the Soay, but the Dead Sea samples had no pigment.

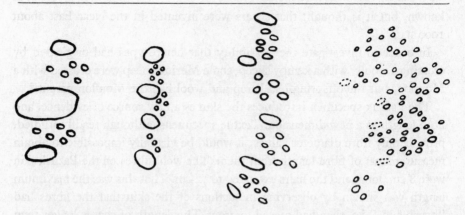

Fig 3 Wool fibre groupings in the skin (*a*) in wild sheep, (*b*), (*c*), (*d*) in parchment from the Dead Sea Scrolls; (*b*) hairy sheep; (*c*) generalized
medium wool; (*d*) fine-woolled sheep.
(from Ryder, M. L. (1962). The histological examination of skin in the study
of the domestication of sheep, *Z. Tierzücht. ZüchtBiol.*, **77**, pp. 168–71.)

There were two specimens of true fine-woolled type (3*d*) which is interesting
because it showed that a possible ancestor of the modern fine-woolled Merino
breed was in existence in the Near East about 2000 years ago.

The evolutionary trend in the wool fibre groups of domestic sheep therefore
seems to have been a movement of the secondaries from between the
primaries, accompanied by a tendency for the primary fibres to become less
hairy, and then finer. As more secondaries have developed in finer-woolled
types, these have spread away from the primaries. Thus fleece type can be
inferred from the type of fibre grouping in the skin from the relative sizes of
the primary and secondary fibres, and from the relative number of secondary
fibres in the group, i.e. the S/P ratio[20]. There is too little evidence as yet to
enable one to associate these changes with distinct areas of the Near East and
particular dates as attempted by Flannery[21].

The generalized medium wool (ancient fine wool) as an evolutionary link

Some samples of leather from water skins found in the Cave of the Letters
near the Dead Sea by Yadin[22] and dated second century A.D. gave results
similar to those from the Dead Sea Scrolls, viz. they were predominantly from
a generalized medium wool sheep[23]. But some pieces of dyed cloth with the
leather were of immense interest because to the naked eye they were apparently made of fine wool. This wool would therefore seem to be the ancient
fine wool to which classical writers refer. A microscopic examination gave a
different result, however, which made all the earlier findings fall into place

medium wool, but one medium sample had a symmetrical distribution and so could represent the evolution towards the true medium type proposed above. Four yarns were of true fine type, and ten, although having a skewed-to-fine distribution like the generalized medium wool, were finer and perhaps intermediate between the generalized medium and fine types. It is possible, however, that these were generalized medium wools that had become finer owing to poor nutrition.

No.	Range	Mean	Mode	Distribution	Fleece Type
No. 4	10–24	16	16	symmetrical	true fine
A. (b)	10–26	17	16	symmetrical	true fine
C. (a)	10–36	19	16	symmetrical	true fine
I 8 (d)	12–32	19	16	symmetrical	true fine
No. 6	12–32	21	20	symmetrical	true fine
D. (b)	12–34	22	22	symmetrical	true fine
No. 2	12–36	24	22	symmetrical	true fine
A. (a)	10–32 1 of 40	22	20	symmetrical	true fine
B. (b)	14–34 3 of 40	21	20	skew fine	fine/gen. medium
II (2) (b)	12–46	23	20	skew fine	gen. medium
D. (a)	14–48	25	20	skew fine	gen. medium
B. (a)	14–46 3 of 50	27	24	skew fine	gen. medium
II (1) (a)	10–42 2 of 52	23	20	skew fine	gen. medium
II (2) (a)	12–42 1 of 54	21	16	skew fine	gen. medium
I 8	12–40 56 & 58	24	22	skew fine	gen. medium
II (1) (b)	12–48 54 & 80	21	16	skew fine	hairy medium
C. (b)	12–46 1 of 50	27	22 & 28	symmetrical	gen. med./medium
Z weft	14–50	33	30	symmetrical	shortwool
tent (b)	12–140	36	20	continuous	hairy

Table 4 Wool fibre diameter measurements in yarns from Daliyeh (microns).

In contrast, eight of the yarns from Daliyeh were of true fine type, and only one was a fine generalized medium wool. If, as is suggested, some of the fine yarns (Nos. 2, 4 and 6) in fact date back to the fourth century B.C., then the origin of the true fine wool can be pushed back several centuries. Five of the Daliyeh yarns were generalized medium wool, and one was of the hairy medium type, which is more common on sites in northern Europe. There was again one possible true medium type, and also one shortwool. These types are somewhat unexpected in this region because they became predominant later in Britain, but there is no reason why they should not have evolved independently in other areas. Finally, one yarn from a tent was of hairy type (the other tent yarns being camel hair). This suggested that three samples of

Source	Site	Date	Pigment	Diameter Range	Mean	Mode	Distribution	Fleece Type
National Museum Scot. FA14	Balmaclellan twill		(a) –	16–30	20·6	18	skewed-to-fine	fine
			(b) –	10–34 2 hairs 70μ	21·2	16	skewed-to-fine	hairy medium
National Museum Scot. FRA1180	Newstead		(a) ×	12–36 1 hair 80μ	23·3	20	skewed-to-fine	hairy medium
National Museum Scot. FRA483	Falkirk (Scotland)		(b) ×	12–50	28·3	30	symmetrical	true medium
Ryder(a)			(a) –	10–30	16·7	16	symmetrical	fine
			(b) ××	10–36 1 hair 80μ	18·2	14	skew fine	hairy medium
			(c) ××	12–34	17·8	14	skew fine	fine/gen. medium
Dr. J. P. Wild	Huntcliffe twill (Yorkshire)	c. A.D. 370	(a) ×	8–32 1 of 40μ	17·8	18	symmetrical	fine
			(b) ×	8–56	20·3	20	skew fine	gen. medium
	St. Albans (England) (8 yarns probably same cloth)			6–32 1 at 36 & 42	14	12	skew fine	fine
Ryder(b)	Xanten (Germany)	1st half (1)	(a) ××	10–40	22·7	18	skew fine	fine/gen. medium
		1st cent.	(b) ××	10–40 hairs 52 and 60	20·7	20	skew fine	hairy medium
		(2)	(a) ××	10–44	25·6	22	skew fine	gen. medium
			(b) ××	14–44	22·7	20	skew fine	gen. medium
Dr. J. P. Wild	Schillerplatz Mainz	No. 22	(a) –	10–32	19·3	20	symmetrical	fine
			(b) –	10–32	20·97	20	symmetrical	fine
		No. 26	(a) – ×	14–40	22·3	20	skew fine	fine/gen. medium
			(b) – ×	14–44	22·9	20	skew fine	fine–gen. medium
		No. 31	(a) – ×	12–38	20·4	20	skew fine/ symmetrical	fine/gen. medium
		No. 35	(b) – ×	10–36	19·4	18	skew fine	fine/gen. medium
			(a) –	10–38	18·5	16	skew fine	fine/gen. medium
		no No.	(b) –	12–38	19·3	20	skew fine	fine/gen. medium
			(a) –	12–40	23·7	26	skew fine/ symmetrical	fine/gen. medium

Source	Sample					Range (microns)	Mean (microns)	Quality
Mainz (Germany)		(b)	warp	–	20	skew fine	12–30 plus 1 of 44	20·7	fine/gen. medium
			warp	–	20	skew fine/symmetrical	14–34	20·4	fine
Saalburg (Germany)			weft	–	18	skew fine/symmetrical	14–36	21·2	fine
British Museum	Mainz 1910-7-7-145	(a)		–	18	skew fine	12–32	19	fine
		(b)		–	20	skew fine	12–40	24	fine
		(a)		x	20	skew fine	12–36 plus 1 of 40	21·5	fine/gen. medium
		(b)		x	24	symmetrical	10–50	25·9	short wool ("Down"?)
		(c)		xx	28	symmetrical	10–52 hair 60μ	27·6	true medium
	Mainz 1910-7-7-146	(a)		x	20	skew fine	10–46	26·1	gen. medium
	London 1956-12-1A	(a)		xx	18	skew fine	10–52 hair 60μ	24·3	hairy medium
	London 1956-12-1B	(a)		xx	20	skew fine	12–46 2 hairs 58μ	24·3	hairy medium
		(b)		xx	22	skew fine	14–52 1 hair 60μ	27·7	hairy medium
Hull covering of Nemi boats (c)	1st cent. 1st boat	III	?white			—	60's quality	say 24μ	—
	2nd boat	IV	(a)				16–60 microns	24 microns	
			(b)				range not so great	16 microns	
		I & II					?	16 microns	
							20–24 microns	? 22 microns	

(a) Ryder, M. L. (1964). Fleece evolution in domestic sheep. *Nature, Lond.* **204**, pp. 555–9.
(b) Ryder, M. L. (1965). Report on the wool, *in* Wild, J. P. Zwei Textilproben aus Xanten, *Bonner Jahrb.*, **165**, pp. 275–6.
(c) Ucelli, G. (1950). *Le Navi di Nemi.* (2nd ed.) Rome.

Table 5 Summary of wools examined from Roman period in Europe (microns).

leather which were from hairy animals were in fact from hairy sheep and not from goats.

The generalized medium wool is probably the same as the fine-woolled sheep referred to in Roman records, which apparently originated in the Near East, and spread around the Mediterranean[27]. It may have been brought to northern Europe by the Romans.

Table 5 summarizes the findings from European textiles of the Roman period, and these in general accord with the results from the Near East (above). Of thirty yarns examined five were of true fine type, and eleven were fine generalized medium wools. There were only four typical generalized medium wools, but seven of hairy medium type. Again evolution towards the true medium (two yarns) and the shortwool (one yarn) had occurred.

The remainder of the first millennium A.D. is represented in the Mediterranean region by Coptic and other textiles from North Africa. Although these were of the same general type as the earlier wools from the Near East, they were appreciably hairier, and some yarns from Tripoli dated about A.D. 1000 had natural pigmentation like wools of similar date from northern Europe. The measurements are summarized in Table 6 from which it can be seen that there was only one relatively fine type, and seven generalized medium wools, but there were seven of hairy medium type and two hairy ones.

Wools of similar date from northern Europe similarly had more hairy representatives, and even more pigment than during the Roman period (Table 7). There were fifteen hairy medium wools, ten generalized medium wools and one of true medium type. There were only three intermediate fine wools, but as many as nine of true fine type, which came mainly from English Saxon sites.

The mediaeval period in North Africa is represented by twenty-four yarns from Nubia supplied by Miss E. Crowfoot. These came from burials at Qasr Ibrim dated tenth to fourteenth century, excavated by Prof. J. Plumley.

The generalized medium type predominated with nine examples and there were six of hairy medium type. Two more hairy specimens had a mean diameter and distribution more in keeping with the true hairy type. There were two yarns comparable with the shortwool of northern Europe, and two of fine to generalized medium type, but only three true fine wools. Only three specimens, three hairy medium wools and one fine to generalized medium wool, had natural pigmentation (Table 6a).

British breeds of sheep

The main type of sheep in Britain before the Roman occupation was probably brown and of Soay type. Historical evidence suggests that the Romans introduced a white sheep with a finer fleece. Textile evidence summarized above supports this conclusion, and suggests that the sheep was basically of generalized medium type.

It is possible that crosses between the white, Roman sheep, and the brown, native Soay produced types that later emerged as breeds such as the Cheviot of the Scottish Border, and the Welsh Mountain breed. These are (or were) horned in the males only, any pigment is usually brown, and they remain today in the northern and western parts of Britain which received least Roman influence (Fig. 5).

The Roman generalized medium type could itself have evolved into a primitive longwool, by the coarsening of the fine fibres, already discussed.

Source	Range	Mean	Mode	Distribution	Fleece Type
Coptic wools in the British Museum					
T13 (b)	8–44	20	20	symmetrical/ skew fine	fine/gen. medium
T10 (a)	8–46	21	14	skew fine	gen. medium
T9 (b)	10–46	21	16 & 20	skew fine	gen. medium
T8 (b)	8–40 2 of 50, 56	22	20	skew fine	gen. medium
T8	10–30 2 of 44, 56	19	16	skew fine	gen. medium
T10 (b)	8–42 50, 60	22	20	skew fine	hairy medium
T9 (a)	10–44 50, 60	22	14	skew fine	hairy medium
T8 (a)	10–44 3 of 50, 2 of 60	27	20	skew fine	hairy medium
T12 (b)	16–52 2 of 60 & 68, 72	31	20	skew fine	hairy medium
T13 (a)	10–52 58	26	20	skew fine	hairy medium
T12 (a)	10–60 64 & 76	32	30	continuous	hairy
Coptic wools in Halifax Museum					
E9–331	12–54 58	25	20	skew fine	gen. medium
E9–329	14–16 50	25	22	skew fine	gen. medium
Ghirza, Tripoli, A.D. 1000 GH41 natural brown					
warp	14–50 56, 60	26	22	skew fine	hairy medium
yellow weft GH45 natural brown	12–54	26	24	skew fine	gen. medium
warp GH55	20–64	37	26	skew fine	hairy medium
pigmented xxx 8–50	2 of 58, 60, 76	26	22	skew fine	hairy

Table 6 Diameter measurements of North African wools of the first millennium A.D. (microns).

The appropriate diameter range has been found in at least one textile from Britain, and the white-faced, polled, Romney breed, whose original home was Kent, is an example of a primitive longwool.

A shortening of the diameter range probably produced the shortwool of English mediaeval fame, and most mediaeval illustrations show white-faced polled sheep like that surviving today as the Ryeland breed. Surprisingly, Romano-British textiles include the true fine type rather than this shortwool, i.e. the type that would be derived by a shortening of the diameter range[28]. The true fine wool, which could have been derived by a narrowing of the medium fibres emerged in Spain as the modern Merino breed (Fig. 5).

The third main British sheep is the black-faced horned type. This has a long hairy fleece, and first appeared in northern and eastern England[29]. When it arrived is not known, but it appears to have had an ultimately Asiatic origin,

No.	Pigment	Range	Mean	Mode	Distribution	Fleece Type
36/1 (a)	–	8–24	16	14	symmetrical	fine
(b)	–	8–24 2 at 30	16	14 & 18	symmetrical	fine
21b	–	14–34	22	16	skew fine	fine
15c	–	14–38	23	16	skew fine	fine/gen. medium
15a	xxx	14–36 42	22	16	skew fine	fine/gen. medium
2	–	14–40	23	26	skew fine	gen. medium
21a	–	16–38 50	26	27	skew fine	gen. medium
44	–	16–42 46	28	24	skew fine	gen. medium
21c	–	16–42 48	28	24	skew fine	gen. medium
29c	–	14–48	27	24	skew fine	gen. medium
4a	–	16–48	29	24	skew fine	gen. medium
4b	–	14–52	26	20	skew fine	gen. medium
28b	–	14–52	27	18	skew fine	gen. medium
29a	–	14–54	58	20	skew fine	gen. medium
9a	–	14–44	25	24	symmetrical	shortwool
46	–	18–44	27	26	symmetrical	shortwool
18b	xxx	14–66	27	20	skew fine	hairy medium
9b	–	16–48 60 & 86	26	24	skew fine	hairy medium
28a	–	16–48 60, 62, 66, 68	32	28	skew fine	hairy medium
15b	xxx	16–54 76	29	20	skew fine	hairy medium
29d	x	16–52 74	31	24	skew fine	hairy medium
18a	–	16–58 94	30	22	skew fine	hairy medium
28a	–	18–48 54, 56, 82	32	30	symmetrical	hairy medium/ hairy
29b	–	10–64	36	30	symmetrical	hairy medium/ hairy

Table 6a Diameter measurements of mediaeval wools from Qasr Ibrim Nubia (microns).

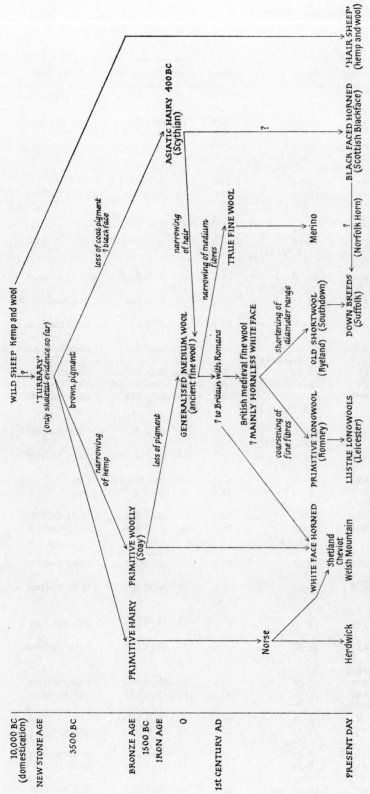

Fig 5 Suggested lines of evolution of fleece types. The dates given are approximate ones based on the earliest date for the beginning of each period at the centre of domestication in South-west Asia, although for instance the Bronze Age fleece evidence comes entirely from Northern Europe at a later date.

Source	Pigment	Range	Mean	Mode	Distribution	Fleece Type
Germany						
Steinfeld						
T43 (a)	xx	12–30	16·6	16	skew fine	gen. medium
		1 of 50				
(b)	xx	10–34	17·1	16	skew fine	gen. medium
		40 & 48				
Schleswig						
T33 (a)	xx	14–54	29·0	30	symmetrical	medium
(b)	xx	12–30	22·9	22	skew fine	hairy medium
		2 of 58, 66				
Schleswig						
T34 (a)	xxx	14–78	29·7	22	skew fine	hairy medium
(b)	xxx	16–48	28·6	30	symmetrical	hairy medium
		68, 70, 78				
Schleswig						
T35 (a)	xxx	14–36	25·0	20	skew fine	hairy medium
		46, 64 & 76				
(b)	xxx	16–48	28·5	22	skew fine	gen. medium
Schleswig						
T36 (a)	x	14–38	22·5	20	skew fine	hairy medium
		1 at 60				
(b)	x	14–34	22·4	20	skew fine	hairy medium
		some hairs				
(c)	xx	16–44	26·2	20	skew fine	gen. medium
(d)	xx	14–46	26·2	26	symmetrical	shortwool
(e)	xxx	18–42	28·5	20	skew fine	hairy medium
		54, 58, 64				
Netherland varves						
T37 (a)	xx	14–58	29·0	24	skew fine	hairy medium
Groningen		62, 76, 80				
(b)	xxx	14–52	25·7	26	symmetrical	hairy medium
Ezinge		66 & 80				
T38 (a)	xx	10–26	18·1	20	symmetrical	fine
(b)	xx	8–34	18·6	18	symmetrical	fine
Leens						
T39 (a)	xxx	14–62	33·4	22	skew fine	hairy medium
(b)	xxx	12–46	24·6	20	skew fine	hairy medium
		52, 54, 76				
Leens						
T40 (a)	xxx	12–58	27·7	22	skew fine	hairy medium
		1 of 64				
(b)	xxx	12–52	26·6	20	skew fine	hairy medium
		1 of 70				
Leens						
T41 (a)	xxx	14–44	21·7	18	skew fine	gen. medium
		50 & 56				
(b)	xxx	14–58	24·1	18	skew fine	hairy medium
		64, 66, 78				
Norway (Saetrang)						
P20 skin	xxx	10–42	21·4	20	skew fine	gen. medium
hair	xxx	12–50	27·1	20	skew fine	gen. medium
England (Saxon sites)						
Combe, Kent						
1 (a)	–	12–44	21	16	skew fine	gen. medium
		50–56				
(b)	–	8–44	21	18	skew fine	gen. medium
2 (a)	xx	8–44	22	16	skew fine	hairy medium
		64				
(b)	xx	10–46	22	16	skew fine	gen. medium

Table 7 (cont.)

Source	Pigment	Range	Mean	Mode	Distribution	Fleece Type
Broomfield Barrow						
B1 (a)	xx	10–34	20	18	symmetrical	fine
(b)	xx	12–34	22	22	symmetrical	fine
		44				
B3 (a)	xx	8–38	18	14	skew fine	fine/gen. medium
		44				
(b)	–	10–28	18	18	symmetrical	fine
B4 pile	–	10–32	17	16	symmetrical	fine
Sutton Hoo						
SH1 (a)	–	8–38	15	10	skew fine	fine
(b)	–	8–32	16	13	skew fine	fine
SH2 (a)	–	8–36	17	16	skew fine	fine/gen. medium
		40, 42				
(b)	–	10–38	18	18	skew fine	fine
SH10 pile	–	10–40	20	20	skew fine	fine/gen. medium

Table 7 Diameter measurements of northern European wools dating from
A.D. 300 to 900 (microns).

possibly going back to the Pazirik sheep already discussed, and there are similar breeds on the continent, notably the Heidsnucke of Germany[30].

The relative fineness of Saxon wools has already been mentioned. Although mediaeval wools examined from Scotland were fine, earlier (Viking) and later wools from Scotland tended to be hairy[31]. It has been possible to examine surprisingly few mediaeval wools, and with progressively later date one is less certain of local manufacture. Nahlik[32] studied many textiles from Novgorod in Russia dating from the tenth to the fifteenth centuries, and one can see from his figures that all types from true fine to very coarse fleeces are represented, but he acknowledges the difficulty of deciding which were local cloths, and which were imported.

Evidence from various sources allows the following tentative suggestions to be made regarding the fleece types of European sheep. The first wave of sheep to spread through Europe were probably of Soay type, and in addition to the Soay itself remaining on the very edge of the continent its influence apparently remains in the Scandinavian "northern short-tailed" breeds (including the Orkney and Shetland sheep in Britain) which have a range of colours (black, grey and white) with relatively few brown animals[33]. The Roman fine-woolled sheep was apparently a big influence in western Europe, and the black-faced, hairy, Asiatic type is another main type, but with which Asiatic invasion it entered Europe is as yet unknown. Investigation of more material, particularly from south-eastern Europe, may help to fill-in the details of this sketchy framework.

The three main biological problems in fleece evolution that remain to be solved are, first, what changes took place during the several thousand years between domestication and the earliest (Bronze Age) wool samples examined ? Neolithic samples are needed to investigate this question.

Second, how did the long, continuously-growing heterotype hair originate ? The occurrence of a hairy fleece (the N-type) in the New Zealand Romney provides a similar problem, but this has usually been thought of as a "throw-back" rather than a new mutation[34]. Further Asiatic samples of similar date to the Pazirik skin may provide a range of types that might help to elucidate this change.

Thirdly, what was the origin of the long, lustrous, coarse but non-medul-lated fibres of the longwool ? The diameter changes that seem to lead towards the lustrous longwool fleece, which apparently emerged in its present form in England in the seventeenth century, have been discussed in the present account, but the type of specimen available precludes length measurements. A mutation may well have been important in this change, a similar mutation having been described in the Merino breed[35].

The coat of cattle

The coat of cattle presents a more difficult problem than that of sheep because wild cattle are now extinct, and far less is known about variation in the coat of modern cattle than in the fleeces of sheep. In addition, the relative wealth of material from wool textiles is lacking, the main source of material being leather, and this has fewer hair remains even than parchment. It is clear, however, that the variation is less in cattle, presumably because the coat has undergone little or no selection.

All the hairs of cattle are in fact comparable with the primary fibres of sheep, and they are distributed at random in the skin, and not in groups as in sheep. Roman and mediaeval leather examined indicated a coat similar to that of modern cattle. Where hairs remained, the density of pigment granules could be discerned, but not the actual colour. Those examined had little pigmentation (at least in the area from which the skin had come) being either grey or dun.

The first difference from what was obviously cattle skin was found in a fragment of skin from a neolithic bow from Meare, Somerset, dated 2600 B.C. This had hairs, which, although apparently bovine, were much finer than those of modern cattle[36]. Bronze Age burials have yielded other bovine hair samples because human bodies were often buried in a skin[37], and where this has decayed excavators have sometimes been able to retrieve the hairs. Some of these examined have been similar to those of the modern ox, whereas another group found in Scotland were finer like the Meare sample (Table 8).

The identity of this bovine animal is puzzling. It has a skewed-to-fine distribution of fibre diameter, and an asymmetric distribution of pigment within the hair, which are characteristics found in the bison. But the bison is thought to have died out in Britain before the land bridge with the continent was broken. The wild ox (*Bos primigenius*), a cousin of the bison, on the other hand is known from skeletal remains to have persisted until the Bronze Age[38], and so it is possible that this unidentified bovine with finer hair was in fact the wild ox.

It may be therefore that, in contrast to sheep, which have clearly been selected for fine wool, the change following domestication in cattle has been towards hairiness. The mean diameter of cattle hair from ancient and modern samples including that from the supposedly primitive Highland cattle, falls within the range 35 to 50μ (Table 8). This range is supported by unpublished measurements made on a number of British breeds by Dr. D. McEwan Jenkinson, who did find, however, that the few Galloway cattle investigated had a mean hair diameter of about 30μ, which could possibly indicate a primitive status for this breed. The Walcheren, King Fergus Isle and Chillingham samples, are, on the other hand much coarser than the normal cattle range (Table 8).

But until more evidence becomes available, the possibility that these unidentified ancient specimens are wild cattle must remain a tentative suggestion, and their true identity must remain a mystery.

Appendix

Methods and criteria on which fleece type is decided

The method of examining skin is a modification of the normal histological technique[39]. Wool fibres are examined in whole mount, and the diameter of 100 fibres from each sample is measured using a projection microscope at a magnification of 500×.

The criteria on which fleece type is decided have evolved as more and more samples have been examined, and are based on the measurements found in modern breeds. Although the mean diameter, and the diameter distribution are taken into account, the upper limit of the diameter range is the deciding factor (see Fig. 2). Thus a fleece with a symmetrical (statistically normal) distribution, and a maximum fibre diameter between 30 and 40μ (one μ (micron) = 0·001 mm.) would be regarded as a true fine type. The shortwool, too, has a symmetrical diameter distribution, but has a mean diameter of about 25μ compared with a mean of about 20μ in the fine wool. A skewed-to-fine diameter distribution appears to be a primitive feature and if this occurred in a fleece with an upper limit above 35μ, it would be regarded as a fine variety of the generalized medium wool (i.e. fine/generalized medium wool).

The generalized medium wool is characterized by a skewed-to-fine distribution, and a maximum diameter about 55μ. The true medium wool has a symmetrical diameter distribution with an upper limit of about 60μ, whereas

Source	Site	Date	Pigment	Medullation	Diameter Range	Mean	Distribution
DEFINITELY OX							
Ancient							
Danish National Museum (S.369)	Mogelmore (Denmark)	? Stone Age	xx	much	8–104	37	continuous [a]
Danish National Museum	Skrydstrup, Denmark	Bronze Age	xx	much	—	c. 60	— [b]
Neumünster Textilmuseum	Harrislee (Schleswig, Germany)	Bonze age (1600 B.C.)	x	moderate	12–90	39	continuous/skew fine [c]
National Museum, Scotland (EQ55)	Collessie (Fife)	Bronze Age	xxx	little	10–108	49	continuous/normal [d]
National Museum, Scotland	Corrydown (Aberdeen-shire)	Bronze Age	xx	much	10–112	38	symmetrical [e]
	Sebay (Orkney)	Bronze Age	xxx	little	10–124	35	symmetrical [f]
Neumünster Textilmuseum	Windeby (Schleswig, Germany)	A.D. 100	xxx	little	10–150	40	continuous/skew fine [g]
Dr. P. J. van der Feen, Zoologisch Museum, Amsterdam	Walcheren (Netherlands)	A.D. 1000	xx	much	28–118	75	continuous/normal [h]
National Museum, Scotland	King Fergus Isle, (Inverness)	not known	xxx	much	14–186	79	continuous [i]

	Period		Amount	Range	No.	Distribution
Modern						
Chillingham herd of "wild" white cattle, Northumberland		—	much	22–160	56	continuous (j)
Highland breed Edinburgh Zoo		xx (brown)	much	14–72	41	continuous (k)
Shorthorn *		xx (red)	much	14–100	44	continuous (l)
Hereford *		xx (red)	not recorded	—	42	— (m)
"BOVINE"						
Prehistoric						
Meare, Somerset	Neolithic	x (asymmetric)	none	20–46	33	to few hairs (n)
Masterton, Fife	Bronze Age	xx (asymmetric)	moderate	8–42	19	skew-fine (o)
Methil, Fife	Bronze Age	x	little	8–46	18	skew-fine (p)
Ashgrove, Fife	Bronze Age	x	little	8–46	18	skew-fine (q)
Pyotdykes, Angus	Bronze Age	—	little	6–38	14	skew/fine (r)
Modern						
Munich Zoo "bred-back" Aurochs		—	moderate	10–60	30	symmetrical (s)
European Bison (*Bison bonasus*)		xx (asymmetric)	moderate	12–66	30	skew-fine (t)

(There is no reason to believe that these are other than superficially like wild oxen)

Table 8 Summary of cattle hair measurements (microns).

(a) Ryder, M. L. (1964). Report on the skin, *in* Coles, J. M, Coutts, H. and Ryder, M. L. A Late Bronze Age find from Pyotdykes, Angus, Scotland, *Proc. Prehist. Soc.*, 30, pp. 193–7.
(b) Steensberg, C. M. (1939). Undersøgelser over Haar fra Skrydstrupgraven, *in* Broholm, H. C. and Hald, M. *Skrydstrupfundet*. Copenhagen. pp. 31–41.
(c) Ryder, M. L. (1966). Report on hair and skin remains from Ashgrove Farm, Methil, Fife, and other Bronze Age sites, *Proc. Soc. Antiq. Scot.*, 97, pp. 175–6.
(d) Ryder, M. L. (1966). ibid.
(e) Ryder, M. L. (1964). ibid.
(f) Ryder, M. L. (1964). ibid.
(g) Ryder, M. L. (1966). ibid.
(h) Ryder, M. L. (1966). ibid.
(i) Ryder, M. L. (1964). ibid.
(j) Ryder, M. L. (1964). ibid.
(k) Ryder, M. L. (1964). ibid.
(l) Ryder, M. L. (1964). ibid.
(m) A.B.R.O. Unpublished data.
(n) Ryder, M. L. (1963). Report on the Meare skin, *Proc. Prehist. Soc.*, 29, p. 98.
(o) Ryder, M. L. (1964). ibid.
(p) Ryder, M. L. (1964). ibid.
(q) Ryder, M. L. (1966). ibid.
(r) Ryder, M. L. (1964). ibid.
(s) Ryder, M. L. (1964). ibid.
(t) Ryder, M. L. (1964). ibid.

the hairy medium wool has a skewed-to-fine distribution with a few hairs greater than 60μ in diameter. The hairy type has a continuous (although often skewed-to-fine) distribution with a relatively high proportion of hairy (i.e. medullated) fibres that are often over 100μ in diameter.

Notes

1 Ryder, M. L. (1960). A study of the coat of the Mouflon *Ovis musimon* with special reference to seasonal change, *Proc. Zool. Soc. Lond.*, 135, pp. 387–408.
2 Flannery, K. V., this volume, pp. 73–100.
3 Ryder, M. L. and Stephenson, S. K. (1968). *Wool Growth*. London.
4 Wright, N. C. (1954). The ecology of domestic animals, *in* Hammond, J. (ed.) *Progress in the Physiology of Farm Animals*, 1. London. pp. 191–251.
5 Flannery, K. V. ibid.
6 Ryder, M. L. (1959). Sheep of the ancient civilizations, *Wool Knowledge*, 4 (12), pp. 10–14.
7 Ryder, M. L. Unpublished data.
8 Mayr, E. (1942). *Systematics and the Origin of Species*. New York.
9 Ryder, M. L. (1964a). Fleece evolution in domestic sheep, *Nature, Lond.*, 204, pp. 555–9.
10 Rosenqvist, A. M. (1964). Investigations of woollen fibres in the Oseberg find, *Proc. Int. Conf. on Conservation*, pp. 133–6. Delft.
11 Ryder, M. L. (1964b). The history of sheep breeds in Britain, *Agric. Hist. Rev.*, 12 (1), pp. 1–12 and (2), pp. 68–82; Ryder, M. L. (1968a). The evolution of Scottish breeds of sheep, *Scot. Stud.*, 12.
12 Ryder, M. L. (1964a). ibid.
13 Ryder, M. L. (1964a). ibid.; Ryder, M. L. (1968a). ibid.
14 Ryder, M. L. (1966a). Coat structure in Soay sheep, *Nature, Lond.*, 211, pp. 1092–3; Ryder, M. L. (1968b). Fleece structure in some native and unimproved breeds of sheep, *Z. Tierzücht. ZüchtBiol.*, 85, pp. 143–170.
15 Ryder, M. L. (1961). A specimen of Asiatic sheepskin from the fourth or fifth century B.C., *Aust. J. Sci.*, 24, pp. 246–8.
16 Ryder, M. L. (1966a). ibid.
17 Ryder, M. L. (1966b). Coat structure and seasonal shedding in goats, *Anim. Prod.*, 8, pp. 289–302.
18 Ryder, M. L. (1963a). Remains derived from skin, *in* Brothwell, D. R. and Higgs, E. S. (eds.) *Science in Archaeology*. London.
19 Ryder, M. L. (1962). The histological examination of skin in the study of the domestication of sheep, *Z. Tierzücht. ZüchtBiol.*, 77, pp. 168–71.
20 Ryder, M. L. (1962). ibid.; Ryder, M. L. and Stephenson, S. K. (1968). ibid.
21 Flannery, K. V. (1965). The ecology of early food production in Meso-potamia, *Science*, 147, pp. 1247–56.
22 Yadin, Y. (1963). *The Finds from the Bar-Kokhba Period in the Cave of the Letters*. Jerusalem.
23 Ryder, M. L. (1964a). ibid.
24 Fraser, A. S. and Hamada, M. K. O. (1952). Observations on the birth-coats and skins of several breeds and crosses of British sheep, *Proc. Roy. Soc. Edin.*, B, 64, pp. 462–77.
25 Bowden, P. J. (1962). *The Wool Trade in Tudor and Stuart England*. London.
26 Ryder, M. L. Unpublished data.

27 Ryder, M. L. (1959). ibid.
28 Ryder, M. L. (1964a). ibid.
29 Ryder, M. L. (1964b). ibid.
30 Ryder, M. L. (1968b). ibid.; Ryder, M. L. (1968c). The wools of Britain. (Paper presented at Brit. Ass. 1967) to be published in *The Wool Textile Industry in Great Britain*. London.
31 Ryder, M. L. (1968a). ibid.
32 Nahlik, A. (1963). The textiles of Novgorod, *Akedemi Nauk*, **123** (IV), p. 228.
33 Ryder, M. L. (1968b). ibid.
34 Ryder, M. L. and Stephenson, S. K. (1968). ibid.
35 Short, B. F. (1958). Dominant felting lustre mutant fleece-type in Australian Merino sheep, *Nature, Lond.*, **181**, pp. 1414-15.
36 Ryder, M. L. (1963b). Report on the Meare skin, *Proc. Prehist. Soc.*, **29**, p. 98.
37 Piggott, S. (1962). Heads and hoofs, *Antiquity*, **36**, pp. 110-18.
38 Shawcross, F. W. and Higgs, E. S. (1961). The excavation of a *Bos primigenius* at Lowe's farm, Littleport, *Proc. Cam. Ant. Soc.*, **54**, pp. 3-16.
39 Ryder, M. L. (1963a). ibid.; Ryder, M. L. and Stephenson, S. K. (1968). ibid.

Part V: Human nutrition

N. A. BARNICOT

Human nutrition: evolutionary perspectives

The domestication of plants and animals initiated major changes in human ecology. These changes, leading to larger settled communities and ultimately to the amenities of urban life, may be regarded as beneficial, but they also had dangers. Settled cultivators must face the threat of famine due to the vagaries of weather and the onslaughts of pests, whereas hunter-gatherers, exploiting a wider range of foodstuffs and with fewer mouths to feed, are likely to be more secure in this respect. It is true that incidents of starvation have been recorded among Eskimos and among aborigines of the Central Australian Desert but these habitats are rather extreme and probably atypical of the long hunting-gathering phase of human history. Plant domestication can also lead to over-emphasis of a single staple such as rice, maize, cassava or plantain; if this staple is poor in certain nutrients deficiency disease may result.

Apart from the direct effects on nutrition, the change from food collecting to food production obviously involved a host of secondary changes in human ecology and these may have greatly altered the nature and magnitudes of evolutionary selective pressures to which human populations were exposed. The creation of novel micro-environments by human interference led in some cases to closer contact with disease vectors, such as mosquitoes carrying malaria or rats carrying plague-infected fleas. The larger communities made possible by efficient agriculture provided a more stable reservoir for various pathogens and crowded, sedentary conditions favoured transmission of microbial diseases.

If domestication was a revolution in the human food quest it was not the first, at least if we take man's more remote ancestors into account. At some stage there must have been a transition from a largely vegetarian diet to a hunting economy providing significant amounts of meat. On an even longer evolutionary time scale the change was more complex. Many primitive mammals, including some lemurs, eat a variety of small animal food. Presumably the monkeys and apes, which are predominantly vegetarian, evolved from such creatures and it is a reasonable inference that the earlier members of the hominid lineage were also vegetarians, though the evidence is scanty

In the last twenty years or so much new evidence relating to these problems has come to hand and it may be useful to mention some of it briefly. First, there have been important discoveries of fossils showing features transitional to man and second, there has been a resurgence of studies on wild primates.

According to Petter[1], some Madagascar lemurs such as *Phaner furcifer* and *Microcebus murinus* eat considerable amounts of small animal food. *Daubentonia*, a highly specialized nocturnal form, lives mainly on insect larvae. On the other hand *Lemur* was never seen to eat animal prey, while *Lepilemur* and the Indridae are vegetarians restricted to a rather narrow range of plant foods.

Baboons, which differ from most other non-human primates in living on the ground and usually, though not exclusively, in open savannah, are predominantly vegetarians, eating a great range of plant species. At the Cape[2] they live on certain flowers, bulbs, and cones, varying their diet according to seasonal availability. In the Kenya grasslands they subsist mainly on the seeds, shoots and rhizomes of grasses throughout the year. Insects are usually a minor dietary component and young mammals are only occasionally killed and eaten. Troops living near the shore at the Cape often ate mussels and limpets. Evidently baboons show a good deal of dietary adaptability. Observation on the Japanese macaque[3] showed that troops living in essentially the same habitat might differ considerably in the plant foods habitually exploited and also in their propensity to adopt new foods introduced by humans. Some species of monkey are more specialized in their dietary habits. The Colobidae are leaf eaters, sometimes gaining their water supply from this source as well as solid nutrients and showing anatomical modifications of the stomach.

Monkeys are of course only distantly related to man but these studies may provide some basis for informed speculation about the food habits of the Oligocene or early Miocene forms from which the Hominidae evolved.

The anthropoid apes of today, notably the chimpanzee and gorilla, show many resemblances to man at the gross anatomical, chromosomal and molecular levels and, according to some workers, may have diverged from the hominid lineage as late as the Pliocene. Chimpanzees in the rain forest of Uganda[4] ate many species of vegetable food and very seldom insects. In more open deciduous woodland, however, Goodall[5] saw them eat gall-fly larvae, ants and termites and they occasionally killed small mammals. Here again we have evidence of local variation in dietary habits. Mountain gorillas according to Schaller[6] live in country ranging from lowland rain forest to mountain forest and bamboo, exploiting a different range of plants in each habitat.

Turning to the fossils the most interesting in relation to human evolution are the Australopithecinae recovered from early Pleistocene deposits in South and East Africa. The evidence of the pelvis and lower limb shows that these small-brained and large-jawed creatures were capable of bipedalism. It has long been recognized that bipedalism, by freeing the hands for manipulation, may have been a critical factor in the emergence of tool using and making. At Makapan in South Africa Dart found many ungulate bones associated with australopithecine remains and he suggested that some were used as tools and may have inflicted the fractures found on baboon skulls from these deposits. Pebble tools have been found at Sterkfontein, another australopithecine site and at Olduvai, Leakey[7] found them on a living floor along with an australopithecine skull and the broken bones of small mammals, birds and reptiles which he regarded as the food debris of this creature. Two species of *Australopithecus* are commonly recognized. One (*A. robustus* or *Paranthropus*) has massive jaws and molar teeth, while in the other (*A. africanus*) these features are less pronounced. Robinson[8] has suggested that the former retained the ancestral vegetarian habit while in the latter hunting for meat was more developed. However the Olduvai form mentioned above (*Zinjanthropus boisei* or *A. boisei*) is of the *robustus* type despite its apparent association with tools and animal food. Later more remains were found at this horizon and also above and below it. These are claimed to be significantly more advanced (i.e. man-like) than *A. boisei* and it is suggested that this form, named *Homo habilis*, was the tool maker. Similarly it has been suggested that a more gracile jaw found at Sterkfontein (*Telanthropus*) represents the tool making population at this site. It is apparent that the interpretation of these very interesting fossils is not unequivocal and it is still a subject for much controversy.

Remains of still earlier hominids are much less abundant. Simons[9] has recently re-examined fossil primate material from the Upper Miocene and Lower Pliocene of Northern India which includes jaw fragments assignable to *Ramapithecus*. The small canine teeth, molar cusp pattern and short face lead him to classify this form as a hominid and to conjecture that some of the features in which the australopithecines approach man were already foreshadowed in this fourteen million year old fossil.

There is of course much archaeological material testifying to the hunting activities of man from the Middle Pleistocene onwards. The remains of hearths at Choukoutien indicate that cooking, at least in the form of roasting, may have been practised half a million years ago. This practice certainly distinguishes man from other primates. While making accessible certain foods which would otherwise be rather indigestible it may, like other types of food processing, lead to loss of nutrients. Archaeological sites sometimes yield good evidence of the kinds of large mammals most hunted but it is difficult to form a quantitative picture of the diets of prehistoric man, especially the significance of vegetable foods. As Brothwell[10] suggests a search for human faecal remains might yield valuable evidence but it is not likely to be successful unless conditions were unusually dry.

When we turn to the literature on modern hunter-gatherers we find lists of the plant and animal species exploited but very little about the amounts of each consumed and their nutritional value. The reasons for this are obvious. Quantitative surveys are not easy to conduct on settled communities and even more difficult on nomadic hunters who may seek food individually or in small groups over an extensive area and may consume significant amounts in the bush rather than in camp. The nutritional values of most of their foods will not be found in standard food tables and must be determined by laborious analyses. The availability of major foods is likely to vary with season so that a satisfactory study must extend over at least a year. There are some studies of Eskimos, for example that of Høygaard[11] at Angmassalik in East Greenland, but Eskimos, although nutritionally very interesting, exemplify a rather special type of hunting economy. There is also McArthur's[12] fine attempt to study Arnhem Land aborigines. These people, although living for much of their time in settlements, still retained the skills necessary for periodic episodes of bush life. The survey lasted only twenty-two days and therefore gives only a glimpse of the nutritional economy of this type of existence. Data on African hunter-gatherers such as Kalahari Bushmen and the Hadza of Lake Eyasi are to be expected in the next few years.

Yudkin[13] has raised the interesting question of the factors determining food choice and the possibility that man retains an innate predilection for certain kinds of food. Obviously human diets are immensely varied and the things which are regarded as fit to eat differ greatly from one culture to another. Whether or not certain innate appetites exist it is clear that custom and belief play a great part in determining food habits. Not infrequently they lead to neglect of nutritionally valuable foods such as eggs and fish. Animals, such as pigs in New Guinea and cattle in many African pastoral peoples are often desired more for prestige than as sources of meat[14]. The human psyche is apt to surround matters concerning food with values foreign to textbooks of nutrition.

I have spoken of the evolutionary background of human food habits. The mechanisms of evolutionary change are now better understood than they were in Darwin's time, thanks largely to great advances in genetics, both experimental and theoretical. The discovery of many simply inherited variations of proteins and blood group substances in man, has given us a vivid picture of the great amount of genetical variability both between individuals and between one population and another. For the most part we do not know how this intrapopulation variability is maintained or what has caused regional variation in gene frequencies but we suppose that natural selection must have played an important role and we are always on the look out for functional differences that may give particular genes selective value. It is virtually certain that diet, as a major component of the human environment, must have exerted such effects but we still have very little good evidence. One case in point is the condition known as favism[15] in which a mutant gene causing deficiency of an enzyme, renders males, and some females, liable to serious haemolytic attacks if they eat fava beans. We may also mention galactosemia, a rare inherited condition in which the metabolism of the sugar of milk is defective. The problem of diabetes, a disease with both genetical and nutritional components, is too complex to be more than mentioned here. There must be many other inherited variations in enzymes and other physiologically important proteins which influence individual efficiency in digesting, absorbing and metabolizing various nutrients. Many of these effects may be slight and difficult to detect but a search for them may open up new pathways connecting nutrition with genetics and evolutionary studies.

Notes

1 Petter. J. J. (1965). The lemurs of Madagascar, *in* De Vore, I. (ed.) *Primate Behaviour: field studies of monkeys and apes,* New York. pp. 292–319.
2 De Vore I. and Hall, K. R. (1965). Baboon ecology, *in* De Vore, I. (ed.) op. cit. pp. 20–52.
3 Kawamura, S. (1963). The process of sub-culture propagation among Japanese macaques, *in* Southwick, C. H. (ed.) *Primate Social Behaviour.* London and New York. pp. 82–90.
4 Reynolds, V. and Reynolds, F. (1965). Chimpanzees of the Budongo forest, *in* De Vore, I. (ed.) op. cit. pp. 368–424.
5 Goodall, J. (1965). Chimpanzees of the Gombe Stream Reserve, *in* De Vore, I. (ed.) op. cit. pp. 425–73.
6 Schaller, G. B. (1965). The behaviour of the Mountain Gorilla, *in* De Vore, I. (ed.) op. cit. pp. 324–67.
7 Leakey, L. S. B. (1959). A new fossil skull from Olduvai, *Nature, Lond.,* 184, pp. 491–3.
8 Robinson, J. T. (1964). Some critical phases in the evolution of man, *S. African archaeol. Bull.* 19, pp. 3–12.
9 Simons, E. L. (1964). On the mandible of Ramapithecus, *Proc. Nat. Acad. (Wash.),* 51, pp. 528–35.
10 Brothwell, D. R., this volume, pp. 531–45.
11 Hoygaard, A. (1941). *Studies on the Nutrition and Physiopathology of Eskimos.* Oslo.
12 McArthur, M. (1960). Food consumption and dietary levels of groups of aborigines living on naturally occurring foods, *in Records of the American-Australian Scientific Expedition to Arnhem Land,* II, pp. 90-135.
13 Yudkin, J., this volume, pp. 547–52.
14 Cranstone, B. A. L., this volume, pp. 247–63.
15 For further details see Brothwell, D. R., this volume, ibid.

D. R. BROTHWELL

Dietary variation and the biology of earlier human populations

Studies on the biology of earlier human populations are relevant to a full consideration of the impact of domestication in two ways:

1 The detailed examination of actual human remains may help to reconstruct the nutritional status of an early population, including dietary insufficiency. Early textual evidence of population health can at times help to substantiate or even extend our knowledge in this respect.
2 From an archaeological point of view, the most significant factor of all in the study of domestication, is that it greatly modified the living and livelihood of earlier groups, so that the demography of these populations underwent marked changes, and in some respects there probably emerged greater heterogeneity in terms of population composition than had been possible in earlier cultures. This may be tentatively deduced from the theoretical extrapolation back in time from historical facts about populations, and from modern demographic and palaeodemographic findings (which includes certain archaeological distribution data).

An examination of human remains usually amounts to the study of skeletal material, although in a few regions of the world soft tissues may remain (Egypt, Peru, American South-west, Aleutian and Canary Islands). In recent years, coprolites have been recognized as another valuable source of information on man, and one especially relevant to a consideration of earlier diets[1]. Regrettably, earlier archaeologists, in their hypnotic pursuit of habitations and pottery, have ignored these "coarser" aspects of human life, and thus only now are dried faeces being actively searched for at New and Old World sites. What little information I shall have time to present will, I hope, help to persuade more excavators to become enthusiastic about the lavatories as well as the villas and palaces of earlier populations.

But first, what sort of information can be derived from skeletal remains? Again, some comment of omission is necessary, for until recently, more time was given to craniometry than to exploring possible ways in which the environment might have influenced skeletal growth and variation. Thus, we know practically nothing about the variations in bone density or thickness of cortical tissue, and to what extent the differences which do occur are determined by nutritional as well as genetic and age factors. That bone density differences occur in modern human populations seems reasonably established[2], and recently attempts have been made to get comparable results on excavated skeletal material (on the now extinct Sadlermiut Eskimo group). Mazess[3] concludes that their high bone densities may be influenced in part, but not wholly, by their specialized animal food diet.

Similarly, there is growing information on the thickness variation in compact bone of some modern groups, where again age, sex and race, as well as diet, are clearly important factors[4]. It may well be that this type of investigation will be more applicable to the study of early skeletal series[5] than density analyses, owing to the added problem of post-mortem changes in prehistoric and protohistoric skeletons (Pl. VII, *b, c*). In any case, it is obvious that such lines of enquiry must in future be considered when investigating earlier populations, especially where racial similarity but marked dietary divergence are suspected. From the point of view of results meaningful to the archaeologist, discussion of this subject is alas five or ten years too soon!

Perhaps the link between studies on ancient diets and skeletons can be most convincingly demonstrated by reference to certain well defined abnormalities detectable in bones or teeth, and to certain historic references to early population health. Again, I want to emphasize problems and possibilities, as well as present facts.

Vitamin D deficiency

This results in rickets in children and osteomalacia in adults, and can certainly produce the most pronounced skeletal deformities of any dietary deficiency condition. In particular, marked bowing of the femur, tibia and fibula may result. On theoretical grounds, one might reasonably expect that the early cereal cultivators may at times have relied too heavily on high carbohydrate diets, and if too few fish and dairy foods (or sunlight) were available then rickets would appear. Surprisingly, however, although vast numbers of prehistoric and protohistoric skeletons have been examined in Europe and North Africa alone, evidence of this deficiency disease is very scanty. In sum, there are only one or two possible cases of bowing, and post-mortem deformation may account for some. Possibly the only convincing prehistoric case in Northern Europe is seen in a pair of tibiae from the Danish neolithic site of Raevehøj. This rarity of the condition during much earlier times contrasts noticeably with city samples dated to the industrial revolution, and for instance the St. Bride's Church skeletal series (London, *c.* 1750–1850) shows some degree of rickets deformity in 6·9% of 233 individuals[6]. However, I would not wish to argue that periodic and localized rickets did not occur earlier, and it may perhaps be significant that Soranus of Ephesus (A.D. 98–138) refers to rachitic-like deformities of the legs in children in Italy, while Chinese literature of the third century B.C. refers to crooked legs and hunchback[7].

Scurvy

As well as a marked deterioration in oral health, vitamin C deficiency (scurvy) can sometimes result in post-cranial changes, including vertebral collapse (though none are pathognomonic). The broad omnivorous diet of early hunting and collecting peoples and the probable availability, at least seasonably, of fruit and vegetables to the early cultivators would certainly not encourage this condition. However, it would be worth making a search for possible evidence of this disease, and indeed I have been recently debating whether some of the relatively numerous cases of vertebral collapse in Amerindian skeletons might have resulted from scurvy. Certainly they are not all the result of senile osteoporosis. In Europe, both Hippocrates and Pliny were acquainted with the disease, but whether it occurred in villages and towns ordinarily, or only in times of war and unrest, is debatable.

Vitamin A and B-complex deficiencies

Deficiencies in vitamin A and B do not result in marked bone changes, but there is some information about them nevertheless. Inadequate vitamin A commonly results in nyctalopia. Possibly the earliest reference to this "night blindness" is in the *Ebers Papyrus* (*c.* 1600 B.C.), followed by Hippocrates, and later in Chinese literature (A.D. 610). Early communities specializing in intensive cereal cultivation with minimal hunting or stockbreeding, would be especially likely to this health hazard. Beriberi (B_1 deficiency) may have been a serious problem in eastern Asia for some millennia; at least it is mentioned in the *Su Wen*, a Chinese text of *c.* 2690 B.C. A good example of mass involvement in such a disease is recorded in the long siege of T'ai Ch'eng (A.D. 529), when nine-tenths of the population of 120,000 developed swelling of the body, shortness of breath and died[8]. Similarly, Strabo mentions the condition in Roman troops.

Pellagra (B_2 deficiency) is not known for sure from earlier New World cultures, but might be inferred from its occurrence in some parts of Central America today, and the great reliance placed upon maize by Maya and Aztec economies.

Iodine insufficiency

This is a localized phenomenon, related to iodine deficient soils in various parts of the world. One might question, however, whether the more sedentary nature of many populations during post-mesolithic times might have further encouraged thyroid malfunction. Certainly skeletal evidence of cretinism would be worth searching for in areas recently affected. Pliny was certainly aware of endemic goitre in some Alpine areas.

General famine

Whereas in palaeolithic hunting and collecting economies there must have been a continual "trimming away" of the older and less healthy members of the group, relative to the abundance of food in a particular area, the neolithic revolution encouraged vast changes. Extended food resources, and perhaps better storage methods, permitted survival to the point where severer climatic fluctuations or plant and animal disease precipitated a general food crisis on a scale rather unlikely in earlier cultures.

There is of course textual and even art evidence (Fig. 1) for famines, extending back patchily over four thousand years. China, a country famous for its food shortages, has over 1800 famines recorded just for the more recent period 100 B.C. to A.D. 1910. Indeed, the populace, according to a first century B.C. publication[9] attempted to adapt to the food crises after the agricultural revolution by intentionally growing the water darnel, a weed tolerant to drought and flood, and thus a valuable provision in times of shortage.

At times, famines must have been sufficiently long term to have markedly influenced child growth in the communities affected. However, although such crises may have impeded growth, and even resulted in mean adult statures less than potentially realizable (given a better nutritional standard), it is still not easy to demonstrate nutritionally induced differences by reference to skeletal studies. Prior to any such enquiry, one must be fairly confident that the populations to be considered are derived from the same "stock" (whether the samples are spatially or temporarily separated). To my knowledge, Steffensen[10] is the only one so far who has been brave enough to try to relate probable changes in nutritional level with estimated mean stature, in this case in early Icelanders (Fig. 2). In view of the fact that neolithic and later prehistoric stature estimates show variation in Europe and South-west Asia, this type of investigation deserves following up, although much caution needs to be exercised.

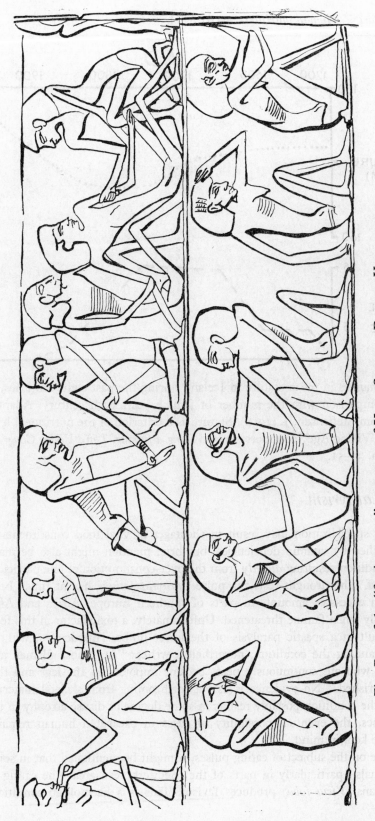

Fig 1 Part of the "famine scene", causeway of Unas, Saqqara. Dynasty V, c. 2350 B.C.
Drawing by Rosemary Powers

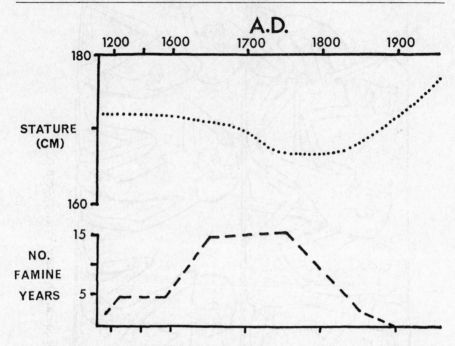

Fig 2 Changes in mean stature in Iceland during the past eight centuries, in comparison with the number of famine years each century. Adapted from Steffensen, J. (1958). Stature as a criterion of the nutritional level of Viking Age Icelanders, *Prieji Viking a fundur*, Third Viking Congress, pp. 39–51.

Lathyrism

Dietary specialization may result in shortages of vital food constituents as exemplified by vitamin deficiencies, but brief mention might also be made of a condition resulting *directly* from the over-consumption of one particular foodstuff. The drought-resistant pulse *Lathyrus sativus* has at times been eaten in excessive amounts in parts of southern Europe, Africa and Asia, especially when famine threatened. Unfortunately, a toxic factor in this food can result in a spastic paralysis of the lower limbs. Hippocrates, without understanding the condition, nevertheless writes: "At Ainos, all men and women who ate continuously peas, became impotent in the legs and that state perished." No evidence is as yet forthcoming from skeletal material, but as the condition possibly results in some degree of disuse atrophy in the leg bones, the eventual possibility of cases in excavated human remains must be kept in mind.

While on the subject of eating pulses, it might be mentioned that in some individuals—particularly in parts of the Mediterranean area—the eating of fava beans (*Vicia faba*) produces favism. This is a haemolytic condition, which can be quite serious, and which seems to be connected with the sex-linked gene producing the glucose-6-phosphate dehydrogenase deficiency disease. However, although there is clearly a "diet-based" selection pressure operating against these bean eaters, the favism/G6PD deficiency situation also seems to confer some advantage in resisting malaria. There is thus a balance of the negative and positive factors, at least in the relevant malarial areas. The example nevertheless demonstrates that diet can have close genetic-microevolutionary associations.

Oral health

I need not establish the fact here that diet can be detrimental to oral health, and in particular is a major contributing factor in caries development. The disease certainly occurred even in fossil man (Pl. vIIa). Differences in caries frequency in earlier populations and the possible influence of diet has also been discussed in various journals[11]. By far the most dramatic increases in dental decay have in fact taken place during the past two or three centuries, without doubt as a result of the increased and widespread use of refined flours and sugar. What happened as a result of the advent of agriculture does not make such an exciting picture, indeed, although I think it had its effect, there would seem to have been rather a delayed reaction. Of the various neolithic dental samples so far studied, there is no significant increase in caries rate above those for palaeolithic and mesolithic groups and a total sample (*c.* 3000–1000 B.C.) of nearly 30,000 teeth show a caries percentage of only 3·1[12].

By Iron Age times there are noticeable increases in some samples, although these late prehistoric groups did not simply show a trend in ever higher figures. The British Bronze Age caries figure is in fact noticeably smaller than the neolithic one, and I have already questioned whether this might give support to Childe's[13] suggestion that the former people were more pastoral and less dependent upon cereals in their diet than the latter group[14]. To what extent related geographical/agricultural zones might show caries rate differences has recently been questioned by Isobel Smith[15], from the point of view of British neolithic "highland" and "lowland" zones. So far, the regional British neolithic figures I have assembled, for the most part on inadequate samples, do not seem to suggest any significant variation in this respect. Again, however, it is the type of enquiry which might eventually prove revealing in some areas, and by Saxon times in England, there is certainly evidence of regional variation (Fig. 3).

Perhaps I should briefly mention certain other aspects of oral health Enamel hypoplasia has been noted in hominid teeth from early pleistocene to recent times. It can result from nutritional disturbances, but also from infective disease, and until this basic problem is explored further—with a view to possible ways of differentiating infective and more chronic malnutritional types of hypoplasia pattern, then useful conclusions are impossible.

Diet may influence periodontal diseases in two ways: (*a*) by direct but local effects, such as in the increased calculus deposition and irritation resulting from a high carbohydrate diet; (*b*) by systemic effects, as in protein deficiency periodontitis[16]. Information on periodontal disease in earlier populations rests on the careful assessment of alveolar bone loss, and of course any frequency will greatly underestimate a true frequency of all degrees of periodontal disease in the living. However, useful comparisons can still be

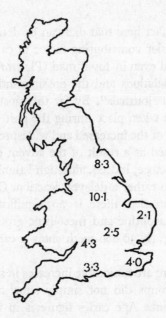

Fig 3 Regional variation in caries frequencies during Saxon times, as seen in the total caries percentage for seven cemetery groups.

made between skeletal series, but as yet there is little standardization of rating methods, or for that matter results. In a study I have been undertaking with colleagues[17] on early Egyptian groups we are able to demonstrate a marked increase in alveolar bone loss from predynastic to late dynastic times, and it would seem reasonable to blame diet in part for this.

As Alexandersen[18] has reviewed the published data in detail, I need not expand further here, except perhaps to say that alveolar bone loss in early skeletons may, in certain circumstances, specifically suggest one form of dietary inadequacy. Thus, Mellquist and Sandberg[19] tentatively concluded that the poor periodontal health in many Norsemen might well have resulted from scurvy.

Coprolite studies

I have considered at some length the question of dietary variation, and possible ways in which skeletal and dental studies may assist in "reconstructing" the food resources of a population. Far less coprolite material is available than skeletons, and very little information on diet as yet forthcoming from such remains; but analysis of such material promises much for the future. As I say, this depends upon the extent of archaeological interest and cooperation. The laboratory of physical anthropology at the B.M. (N.H.) is only just beginning investigations of this sort, and I am finding it very difficult to get a series of coprolite samples for comparative purposes. Incidentally, there might be other possibilities of food residue collection from the alimentary tract of long decomposed bodies. Hazzledine Warren[20] as long ago as 1911 reported on a prehistoric British skeleton buried in sand in which seed remains were identified and removed from the abdominal area. Although the burials were not ideal, I have recently tried removal of grave earth from the lower abdominal region of Dark Age skeletons, and by differential flotation, the removal of organic remains. However, where the grave fill contains a variety of organic debris, as in this case, the task of food residue identification is doubly difficult.

Coprolite studies have quite blossomed out in the past ten years. The excellent work of Callen and Cameron[21] and Callen[22] has been followed by such detailed work as Watson and Yarnell[23] and the various papers given in No. 70 of the *University of California Archaeological Survey* (1967) on Nevada cave coprolites. Parasitological studies on ancient faeces have been made[24] and even faecal deposits from northern European soils can be rewarding (Pl. VIId).

Coprolites have begun to give precise information on the wide range of foodstuffs consumed by individuals of differing cultures, and of course have assisted in establishing the spread and antiquity of certain domesticated plants. The breadth of potential information is enormous, and even such data as the number and size of fish bones consumed have clear relevance to a consideration of calcium intake or the degree to which foods were chewed or bolted. Work in progress on coprolites from Asiab, Iran by J. R. Harlan, R. B. Stewart and colleagues, seems to show evidence of geophagia[25].

Diet, demography and microevolution

"Population" wrote Huxley[26], "is the problem of our age." Though on a more modest scale, one just wonders whether the same might be said of the period following the agricultural revolution? World population estimates for palaeolithic and mesolithic times vary from five to under twenty millions[27].

By 3000/4000 B.C. it has been estimated, mainly by extrapolating from the demographic information on different economic groups today and historic records, that world population numbers had possibly increased to over twenty million and as much as ninety million. We now tolerate, three thousand million! The trouble with using population data on modern "primitive" populations, as Cook[28] emphasizes, is that such people may no longer have a truly pre-contact diet and have probably been influenced by the diseases of civilized communities. Thus, however neat the graphs of early population increase appear, the estimates are really very crude, and we really have no idea of fertility or what proportion of neolithic people survived into the reproductive period. The inadequate nature of neolithic skeletons prevents direct assessment of this latter problem, although this material does enable us to establish that survival into middle and late adult age groups was not common. Mean life expectancy for neolithic adults was only about 31–34 years for males and 28–31 years for females (considering data by Angel, Kobayashi, and Brothwell[29], but in fact there was no significant increase of life expectancy anywhere until about a century ago (when the world population had quietly increased to one thousand million).

I do not wish to argue that, given the right environment, the temporal and spacial mosaic of plant and animal domestication did not encourage varying degrees of population expansion. But I must confess to a gnawing doubt as to whether, in the case of population growth in post-glacial times we really put the egg before the chicken. I don't wish to labour the point, but simply state the question, in view of its relevance to future palaeodemo-graphic interpretation. At present we visualize the early cultivators bursting forth in their new found fertility, but what of the hunters and collectors in more favourable environments? Why shouldn't a fully exploited and adequate "natural harvest", permit a many fold expansion of group size, especially if a few basic methods of food storage were known? Given increased density, more effective social organization could arise, and with it pooled ideas for economic improvements, such as experimental planting of seeds or group round-up of larger mammals. Jaffe[30] gives the population of China in A.D. 2 as *c.* 59,000,000, and one wonders to what extent the population was already tottering by the time rice was introduced perhaps as early as 3000 B.C.

Clearly, China has tolerated a high density/sub-starvation level at least back into protohistoric times, so that one might well ask whether in this case domestication did more than provide temporary relief, and simply permitted greater population/environment disequilibrium. One tends to forget that minimal subsistence calorie requirements (preventing serious malnutrition) can be as low as 1900 for males, ranging down to 1000 in women and children[31]

My contribution to this book seems to be a remarkably gloomy one. The more direct relationships between diet and disease have already been mentioned, but cultivation and stock rearing resulted in other human health problems. Polunin[32], for instance, argues that the high frequency of malaria in some Malayan aborigines (who practise a shifting agriculture), results from the fact that the vector, *Anopheles maculatus*, is able to breed well in the sunlit streams following forest clearance for cultivation. Similarly, Audy and Harrison[33] show that shifting cultivation encourages the spread of mite-borne scrub typhus.

Any tendency for numbers of individuals to cluster together raises health problems, so that the early farmers possibly encouraged as never before the build up of certain strains of bacilli and streptococci, as well as parasites of the roundworm-hookworm type. Food storage and village or longhouse development must have initiated rodent infestation, and with it plague and other killers. Perhaps, even, the association was sufficient for mutant forms of murine leprosy to become adapted to man? The development of African pastoralism must in parts have been bedevilled by trypanosomiasis[34], while South-west Asia and the Mediterranean world may have been the earliest centres for the transfer of bovine tuberculosis and brucellosis to man. Animal disease recorded by Middle Kingdom Egyptians is thought to have included anthrax[35], and this may well be referred to by Homer, Pliny, and others[36]. In historic times, anthrax has reached epidemic proportions in man, and clearly may also have threatened late prehistoric peoples.

Little of this can be confirmed by reference to early skeletons, although it is significant that tuberculosis seems to have been early established in Egypt[37], and I have very tentatively suggested the presence of brucellosis in Bronze Age Jericho[38].

The relationship between dietary change, following the neolithic revolution, and human microevolution is both a new and dangerous field. Kelso and Armelagos[39] have been brave enough to suggest a relationship between blood group frequency and dietary habit; high A being linked with fat intake, and carbohydrate consumption with B. The hypothesis is interesting but at present difficult to substantiate[40]. Shatin[41] has also considered the possible genetic consequences of dietary changes and population increase. Neolithic cultural development and contacts, he suggests, might have influenced outbreeding. Like Livingstone[42] he believes that the sickle-cell polymorphism has probably undergone its most intensive selection among African food-producing groups during the past 5000 years. He further debates the repercussions of neolithic and later dietary change on the progress diseases as divergent as treponematoses, peptic ulceration and coronary disease. This, as I say, is a difficult field, but in view of the profound dietary changes which have taken place, clearly merits serious attention.

Finally, a few words about human populations and possible adaptive variation resulting from the neolithic economy changes. Coon[43] has argued that the earliest Old World farmers, which he says were "presumably light-skinned, bearded Caucasoids similar to those still inhibiting the Near East", migrated in bands into northern Europe, North Africa, India and China.

The reason why they are not now to be seen in countries such as China he states is because these people hybridized with the indigenous population—who were adaptively more successful and thus emerged as the conspicuous type again. Somehow, this view doesn't seem satisfactory, and surely the picture must have been far more complex? Certainly, there must have been varied movements of people in search of new productive lands, but at the same time a cultural "chain reaction" must have ensured the handing on of domestication ideas and products far more rapidly than human movements. I am reminded, for instance, of the spread of the banana in the Amazonian area of South America, where it has reached isolated tribes deep in the interior.

It would seem reasonable to say that the agricultural revolution encouraged a differential increase and expansion of some groups. Population size in the Mexican and Andean civilizations grew to far more than the total for the rest of the New World prior to European contact[44]; African Negro groups also flourished, and in movements southwards compressed the Khoisan peoples into far more restricted territories. In South-east Asia, mongoloid expansion must have been encouraged if not dictated by population pressures, and perhaps the non-mongoloid Ainu of Japan represent one of the other Asiatic stocks brought near to extinction by mongoloid economic competition.

In populations which expanded too much and too fast, and where environmental factors caused periodic crop failure, there is the possibility that some groups may have started to become "famine adapted" for smaller body size and smaller calorie needs. I state this only in a very tentative way, having found no convincing data so far to support it. Unfortunately, microevolutionary factors pull in various ways and directions at once, so that what may result in body form may be rather a biological "compromise". Perhaps a recent speculation by Brues[45] is also relevant here, for she debates the possibility of physical variation having differential survival value in markedly contrasting earlier cultures and economies. Alas, these are still only ideas, but perhaps eventually laboratory or field studies may show that here also, the history of domestication and human biology have significant links[46].

Notes

1 Callen, E. O. (1963). Diet as revealed by coprolites, *in* Brothwell, D. and Higgs, E. S. (eds.) *Science in Archaeology*. London. pp. 186–94; Heizer, R. F. (1967). Analysis of human coprolites from a dry Nevada cave, *Reps. Univ. Cal. Archaeol. Survey*, Berkeley. 70, pp. 1–20.
2 Baker, P. T. and Angel, J. L. (1965). Old age changes in bone density: sex and race factors in the United States, *Hum. Biol.* 37, pp. 104–21; Baker, P. T. and Little, M. A. (1965). Bone density changes with age, altitude, sex and race factors in Peruvians, *Hum. Biol.*, 37, pp. 122–36.
3 Mazess, R. B. (1966). Bone density in Sadlermiut Eskimo, *Hum. Biol.*, 38, pp. 42–9.

4 Garn, S. M., Pao, E. M. and Rihl, M. E. (1964). Compact bone in Chinese and Japanese, *Science*, 143, pp. 1439–40; Garn, S. M., Rohmann, C. G. and Nolan, P. (1964). The developmental nature of bone changes during aging, *in* J. E. Birren (ed.) *Relations of Development and Aging*. Illinois. pp. 41–61; Garn, S. M. (1966). Malnutrition and skeletal development in the pre-school child, *in Pre-school child Malnutrition*. Nat. Acad. Sci.-Nat. Res. Coun. Washington. pp. 43–62.

5 Brothwell, D. R., Molleson, T. I. and Metreweli, C. (1968). Radiological aspects of normal variation in earlier skeletons: an exploratory study, *in* D. R. Brothwell (ed.) *The Skeletal Biology of Earlier Human Populations*, pp. 149–72. Oxford.

6 Powers, R. Personal communication.

7 Lee, T'ao (1940). Historical notes on some vitamin deficiency diseases in China, *Chinese Med. J.*, 58, pp. 314–23.

8 Hou, H. C. and Yu, C. M. (1940). Beriberi in ancient medical literature, *Chinese Med. J.*, 58, pp. 302–13.

9 Shêng-Han, S. (1965). Translated. On *"Fan Shêng-Chih Shu"*. An *Agriculturistic Book of China Written by Fan Shêng-Chih in the First Century B.C.* Peking.

10 Steffensen, J. (1958). Stature as a criterion of the nutritional level of Viking Age Icelanders, *Prioji Vikingafundur, Third Viking Congress*, pp. 39–51.

11 See Brothwell, D. R. (1959). Teeth in earlier human populations, *Proc. Nutr. Soc.*, 18, pp. 59–65; and Brothwell, D. R. (1963). The macroscropic dental pathology of some earlier human populations, *in* Brothwell, D. R. (ed.) *Dental Anthropology*, pp. 271–88. Oxford, for earlier literature.

12 Brothwell, D. R. (1963). ibid.

13 Childe, V. G. (1949). *Prehistoric Communities of the British Isles*. London.

14 Brothwell, D. R. (1960). The Bronze Age people of Yorkshire; a general survey, *Adv. Sci.*, 16, pp. 311–32.

15 Smith, I. F. (1964) *in* Field, N. H., Matthews, C. L. and Smith, I. F. New Neolithic sites in Dorset and Bedfordshire, with a note on the distribution of Neolithic storage-pits in Britain, *Proc. Prehist. Soc.*, 30, pp. 355–60.

16 Bradford, E. W. (1959). Food and the periodontal diseases, *Proc. Nutr. Soc.*, 18, pp. 59–65.

17 C. Wood Robinson and H. G. Carr. Unpublished data.

18 Alexandersen, V. (1967). The pathology of the jaws and the temporomandibular joint *in* Brothwell, D. R. and Sandison, A. T. (eds.) *Diseases in Antiquity*. Illinois. pp. 551–95.

19 Mellquist, C. and Sandberg. T. (1939). Odontological studies of about 1400 Mediaeval skulls from Halland and Scania in Sweden and from the Norse Colony in Greenland and a contribution to the knowledge of their anthropology, *Odont. T. Supp.*, 3B.

20 Warren, S. H. (1911). On a prehistoric interment near Walton-on-Naze, *Essex Naturalist.*, 16, pp. 198–208.

21 Callen, E. O. and Cameron, T. W. M. (1960). A prehistoric diet revealed in coprolites, *New Scientist*, 8, pp. 35–40.

22 Callen, E. O. (1963). Diet as revealed by Coprolites, *in* Brothwell D. R. and Higgs, E. S. op. cit., pp. 186–94; Callen, E. O. (1965). Food habits of Some Pre-Columbian Mexican Indians, *Econ. Bot.*, 19, pp. 335–43.

23 Watson, P. J. and Yarnell, R. A. (1966). Archaeological and Paleoethnological investigations in Salts Cave, Mammoth Cave National Park, Kentucky, *Amer. Antiquity*, 31, pp. 842–9.

24 Samuels, R. (1965). Parasitological study of long-dried fecal samples, *Mem. Soc. Am. Archaeol.*, 19, pp. 175–9; Tubbs, D. Y. and Berger, R.

(1967). The variability of pathogens in ancient human coprolites, *Reps Univ. Cal. Archaeol. Survey, Berkeley*, **70**, pp. 89–92; Pike, A. W. (1967). The recovery of parasite eggs from ancient cesspit and latrine deposits: an approach to the study of early parasite infections, *in* Brothwell D. R. and Sandison, A. T. op. cit., pp. 184–8.

25 Braidwood, R. V., Personal communication.

26 Huxley, J. (1957). *New Bottles for New Wine*. London.

27 Huxley, J. (1957). ibid; Deevey, E. S. (1960). The human population, *Scientific American*, **203**, pp. 194–204.

28 Cook, S. F. (1947). Survivorship in aboriginal populations, *Hum. Biol.*, **19**, pp. 83–9.

29 Angel, J. L. (1947). The length of life in Ancient Greece, *J. Gerontol.*, **2**, pp. 18–24; Kobayashi, K. (1967). Trend in the length of life based on human skeletons from prehistoric to modern times in Japan, *J. Fac. Sci. Univ. Tokyo.*, Sect. V, **3**, pp. 109–60; Brothwell, D. R. (1968). The human biology of the Neolithic population in Britain (in press).

30 Jaffe, A. J. (1947). Notes on the rate of growth of the Chinese population, *Hum. Biol.*, **19**, pp. 1–11.

31 Davidson, S. and Passmore, R. (1967). *Human Nutrition and Dietetics*. Edinburgh.

32 Polunin, I. (1960). The effects of shifting agriculture on human health and disease, *Symposium on the impact of man on humid tropics vegetation*. UNESCO Science Co-operation Office for S.E. Asia, Goroka, Territory of Papua and New Guinea. pp. 388–93.

33 Audy, J. R. and Harrison, J. L. (1951). A review of investigations on mite typhus in Burma and Malaya, 1945–50, *Trans. R. Soc. Trop. Med. Hyg.*, **44**, pp. 371–404.

34 Lambrecht, F. L. (1964). Aspects of evolution and ecology of tsetse flies and trypanosomiasis in prehistoric African environment, *J. Afr. Hist.*, **5**. 24 pp.

35 Steele, J. H. (1962). *Animal Disease and Human Health*. Food and Agriculture Organization of the United Nations, Roma. Freedom from Hunger Campaign.

36 Vaughan, V. (1923). *Epidemiology and Public Health*. London. **2**, pp. 851–61.

37 Morse, D., Brothwell, D. R. and Ucko, P. J. (1964). Tuberculosis in Ancient Egypt, *Am. Rev. Resp. Dis.*, **90**, pp. 524–41.

38 Brothwell, D. R. (1965). The palaeopathology of the E.B.-M.B. and Middle Bronze Age remains from Jericho (1957–8 excavations), *in* Kenyon, K. M. *Excavations at Jericho*. II. London. pp. 685–93.

39 Kelso, A. J. and Armelagos, G. (1963). Nutritional factors as selective agencies in the determination of ABO blood group frequencies, *Southwestern Lore*, **29**, pp. 44–8.

40 Otten, C. M. (1967). On pestilence, diet, natural selection, and the distribution of microbial and human blood group antigens and antibodies, *Current Anthropology*, **8**, pp. 209–26.

41 Shatin, R. (1967). The transition from food-gathering to food-production in evolution and disease, *Vitalstoffe Zivilisationskrankheiten*, **12**, pp. 104–7.

42 Livingstone, F. B. (1962). Anthropological implications of the Sickle-cell gene distribution in West Africa, *in* Ashley Montague, M. F. (ed.) *Culture and the Evolution of Man*. New York.

43 Coon, C. S. (1959). Race and ecology in Man, *Cold Spring Harbour Symposia on Quantitative Biology*, **24**, pp. 153–9.

44 Dobyns, H. F. (1966). Estimating aboriginal American population, *Current Anthropology*, **7**, pp. 395–449.

45 Brues, A. (1959). The spearman and the archer—an essay on selection in body build, *Amer. Anthrop.*, 61, pp. 457–61.

46 I am most grateful to Professor N. A. Barnicot, for comments pertinent to the final preparation of this paper. Miss Theya Molleson kindly hunted out certain references, and Mrs. Irene Copeland continued her secretarial support.

JOHN YUDKIN

Archaeology and the nutritionist

The domestication of plants and animals is concerned with man going into the business of producing his food instead of hunting and gathering his food. The nutritionist is interested in this for three practical reasons:

1 The "ideal" diet. The first is that to know what man ate before he invented agriculture is to know his diet during the millions of years during which he adapted to a particular choice of foods. We may thus assume that this choice represents something like his "ideal" diet, and might well form the basis of the advice that the nutritionist is asked to give in formulating diets for health.

2 Diets and diseases of civilization. The second reason for the nutritionist's interest is that he needs to know what the pre-agricultural diet was in order to ascertain the dietary changes produced by the introduction of agriculture. A study of these changes may possibly then afford a clue as to the causes of diseases that appear to be associated with civilization.

3 Factors determining food choice. The third reason for wishing to know what dietary changes followed man's domestication of plants and animals is that these may give clues as to the factors that determine man's choice of food. We are still not very knowledgeable as to why people eat some foods and reject other foods, and a study of dietary changes with time can provide useful pointers.

We have a long way to go before we can answer all the questions I have just raised. In the meantime, let me summarize my own views that relate to the three general problems I have outlined[1]. Many of these views are no doubt based on slender or non-existent evidence, or even on quite incorrect assumptions.

1 The "ideal" diet

As I understand it, man and his immediate ancestors, emerging as a distinctive species two million years ago and perhaps much longer, were hunters as well as gatherers of food. Their diets contained an unknown but not insignificant proportion of animal foods. Being omnivorous, he was not so likely to suffer from food shortages as those species that had very restricted diets. But it does look as if, when conditions allowed, his diet contained quite a lot of meat and in some circumstances also quite a lot of fish. It seems that he was not nearly so fussy as we are today in the sorts of meat that he ate; he did not insist on fillet steak, but polished off the liver, kidneys and the entrails with relish. Nor was he averse from chewing the cartilage and soft bones, and breaking open the bones for marrow.

In terms of its major constituents, then, his diet when the hunting was good was relatively rich in protein, reasonably rich in fat, and not very rich in carbohydrate. It would be poorer in protein and fat, and richer in carbohydrate especially starch, at those times when he was not very successful in hunting or scavaging for food.

It seems a reasonable assumption that the particular ecological niche in which man found himself some 9000 years ago was one to which he had become pretty well adapted, and that this adaptation included the foods that he chose to eat. On this basis, the nutritionist would suggest that a diet that contained a fairly high proportion of meat would be basically the diet most suitable for human animals. This is supported by a consideration of recent changes in diet. We know[2] that once man began to produce his food rather than hunt or gather it, his total food supplies increased and these were mostly the high-yielding vegetable foods rich in starch. As a result, his numbers grew and it soon became impossible for him to revert to the low-yielding method of hunting and gathering. Thus, from some 9000 years ago until the recent industrial revolution, agricultural man has in general been unable to eat anything more than small quantities of meat. However, when there is no limitation imposed by economic factors, or cultural factors such as vegetarianism, people tend to have a diet that contains quite a high proportion of meat.

I have been talking about man's food preferences. The fact is of course that, if his preferred foods are not available, man can eat from a wide range of animal and vegetable foods. One feature of man's inherently omnivorous habit, incidentally, is that it enabled him to live in a wide range of environments, in which he found and later produced a very wide range of foods. It is this factor more than any other that made it possible for man to inhabit ultimately almost every corner of the world.

A second point of interest is that the adoption of the largely vegetable diet that followed the development of agriculture 8000 or so years ago was only possible because man had much earlier learnt how to make and control fire. Unless they are cooked, most of the cereal and root crops would have been indigestible except in very small quantities; some like cassava would even have been poisonous.

2 *Diet and diseases of civilization*

If these considerations relating to man's "ideal" diet are correct, we must conclude that the present-day diets of the majority of mankind differ considerably from the ideal diet. The changes began only 9000 years ago[3], at most only one half of 1% of man's existence as a distinct species—and it is unlikely that he has become completely adapted to these changes.

One dietary consequence of the introduction of agriculture was, as we saw, a change in the proportion of the major constituents—a fall in the proportion of protein and fat, and a rise in the proportion of carbohydrate. In addition, cereals and especially root crops, as well as being relatively short in protein, may in varying degrees also be short in some of the B vitamins. Thus, maize is short of nicotinic acid which is needed to prevent pellagra; man learnt to mill and polish rice thus reducing the content of thiamine which is needed to prevent beri beri. Moreover, all cereals contain phytate, the consumption of which conduces to rickets as it interferes with the absorption of calcium. To this we may add the suggestion that the agricultural diet no doubt contains less calcium than the pre-agricultural diet, in which man ate the soft bones of animals and fish.

If, as I suggested earlier, it is reasonable to assume that nutritional disease was rare during the two million years or more when man was consuming the diet to which he had become adapted, we are entitled to say that widespread nutritional diseases such as protein deficiency (the commonest nutritional deficiency), beri-beri, pellagra, riboflavin deficiency and rickets stem largely from the dietary change brought about by the neolithic revolution.

As well as producing nutritional deficiency, the neolithic diet high in carbohydrate is more likely to produce dental caries. It is widely believed that dental caries began to be prevalent after man took to his carbohydrate-rich agricultural diet[4]. As Brothwell[5] says, however, there is still a great deal to be done in order to determine, for example, the relationship between dental caries and the adoption of diets based largely on animal breeding on the one hand, or on cereal production on the other hand.

A second direct consequence of the introduction of agriculture is, I believe, due to the new foods themselves, rather than to the nutrients they contain. What I am suggesting is that there is evidence that man is still not completely adapted to the consumption of cereals or cows' milk, two foods that were consumed in very much smaller quantities if at all in preneolithic times. For it is a fact that the commonest allergies found in the countries where there have been most studies are allergies to wheat and to milk.

3 Factors determining food choice

There has been a great deal of research, and even more armchair discussion, as to why people eat what they do. I believe that most of the theories are inadequate in the light of what we know about nutritional requirements. My own views are best set out in a series of propositions:

(*a*) The cells of all species of animals require the same chemical substances for their continuing life and function.

(*b*) Many of these substances can be made from other substances, but there remain some forty or fifty that the animal needs to have provided for it in the forms in which it uses them. Different species require these in roughly the same proportion.

(*c*) In most species, all of these essential substances must be supplied by the diet, though there are some species in which a few of the essential substances may be supplied by microbial synthesis in the gut.

(*d*) Species vary very much in the foods that they consume. Some animals are almost entirely carnivorous, some herbivorous, some omnivorous. And within these groups, some species choose quite different diets from others, and some are much more restricted than others.

(*e*) But since all species require the same, or nearly the same, substances in their diets, and in roughly the same proportion, it follows that it cannot be the nutrient composition of the foods that determine that they shall or shall not be consumed by different species.

These considerations lead to the suggestion that there are properties of shape, colour, smell, taste and texture that cause a particular species to choose particular foods. For these properties, I use the word palatability, in a perhaps excessively wide sense. It is axiomatic that, during the course of evolution, a developing species must have continued to choose foods that gave it the required nutrients, but it chose foods within its own ecological niche that had particular attributes of palatability for that species.

As far as man is concerned, it appears that the foods that are most palatable are of two sorts. The first are those with the texture, savoury taste and other qualities of meat; the second are those with the smell and colour, and sweet, acid and aromatic taste of fruits. It is possible too that he likes to intersperse these with rather neutral foods such as seeds, shoots, leaves and roots, which prevent the palate becoming excessively jaded with the strong tastes of the other foods. If this is so, it would suggest that the diet that to developing man was most attractive was a diet of meat, fruit and some roots, seeds and leaves. These would have given him—as it were incidentally—all the protein, vitamins, mineral elements and calories that he required. When he ate what he liked, he ate what he needed.

As I suggested earlier, this hypothesis that palatability is a major deter-

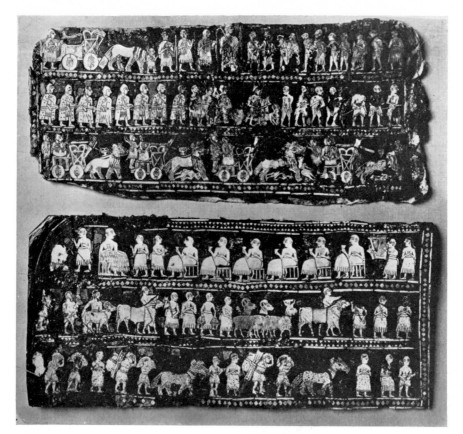

a

b

NOBLE: A "Peace" and "War" panels of the Standard of Ur (see p. 486).
B Copper chariot from Tell Agrab drawn by four onagers (see p. 486).

(Both these illustrations are reproduced by courtesy of the Trustees of the British Museum)

PLATE I

SMITH: The forcible feeding of cranes (Tomb of Mereruka at Saqqara (Dyn. VI) (see p. 309).

PLATE II

DROWER: Pharaoh Ramesses III hunting wild cattle in his chariot, Twentieth Dynasty, *c.* 1190 B.C. (from Medinet Habu II: Later Historical Records of Ramesses III. Epigraphic Survey of the Oriental Institute of Chicago, 1932) (see p. 474).

PLATE III

STURTEVANT: A Plantation slaves preparing cassava bread in the Lesser Antilles about 1660. 5: Peeling manioc roots; 6: Pulping the roots with a rotary grater; 7: Pulping the roots with the old-style grater; 8: Grated pulp in bags in press; 9: Sifting flour; 10: Cooking cassava on griddle; 13: Cassava cakes drying. (From J. B. du Tertre (1667). *Histoire générale des Antilles . . .*, **2**, facing p. 419) (see p. 182.)

OWEN: B Domestic ferret (from Gesner, C. (1551). *Historiae Animalium*) (see p. 492.)

PLATE IV

a

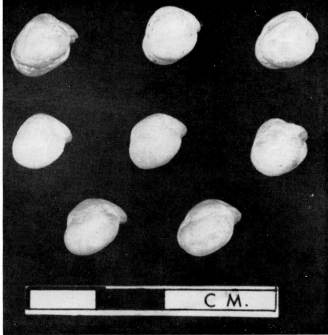

b

DIXON: a Gold hawk's head from Hierakonpolis, Upper Egypt (from
Schaefer, H. and Andrae, W. (1925). *Die Kunst des Alten
Orients*. Berlin. pl. 234 top) (see p. 137.)
b Chick peas (see p. 137).   PLATE V

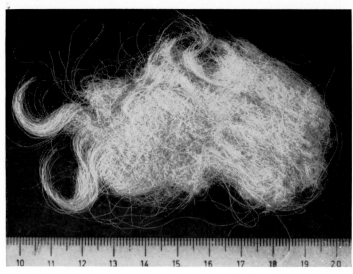

RYDER: A Sample of Scythian sheepskin from Pazirik in central Asia dated
about 400 B.C.
(from Ryder, M. L. (1964). Fleece evolution in domestic sheep, *Nature*,
Lond. **204**, pp. 555–9) (see p. 501)

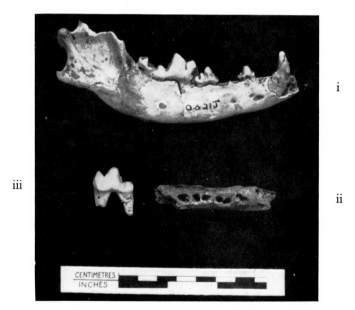

CLUTTON-BROCK: B *Canis* spp. from the Jericho Tell.
(*i*) No. O.6.21J. Pottery Neolithic. Right mandibular
ramus with large compacted teeth: young animal. (*ii*)
No. D.5.3c. Pottery Neolithic. Lower left carnassial
tooth. Described by Zeuner[1] (*iii*) No. M.15.10A. Proto-
neolithic. Anterior portion of left horizontal ramus of a
canid mandible: the bone is charred: the alveoli of the
premolar teeth are much displaced (see pp. 338, 340)
[1] Zeuner, F. E. (1963). *A History of Domesticated Animals.* London.

PLATE VI

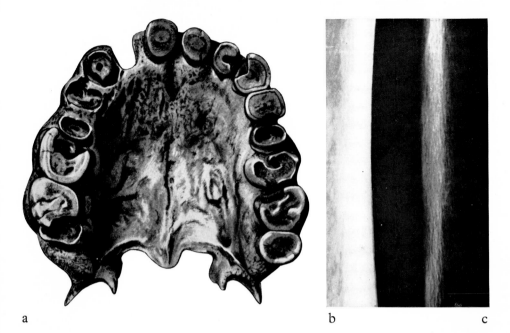

a   b   c

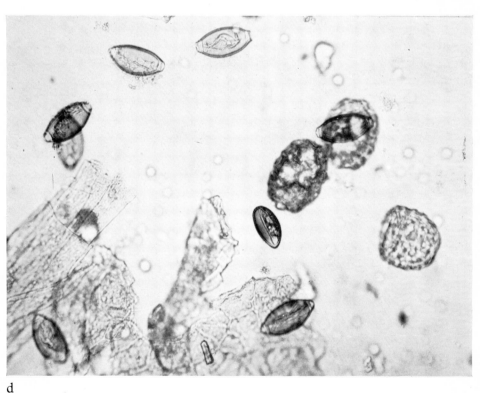

d

BROTHWELL: a Palate of Rhodesian Man, showing severe caries; b and c X-rays of part of the cortical tissue of early femora from Jericho, showing marked differences in density; d faecal residue from a medieval English site, showing plant tissue and eggs of *Trichuris* sp., Ascaris sp. and *Dicrocoelium dendriticum* (×200, preparation by courtesy of Dr. A. Pike) (see pp. 532, 537, 539.)

PLATE VII

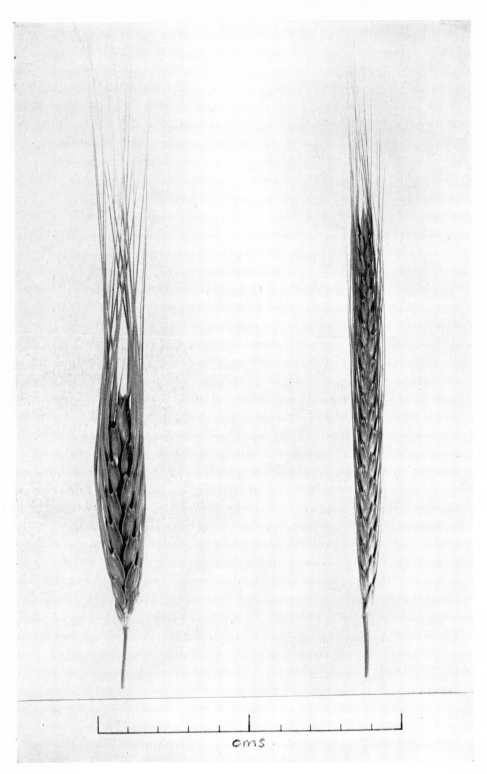

ZOHARY: Cultivated and wild emmer and wild einkorn (see p. 49).

PLATE VIII

minant in an animal's food choice, and that in man the most palatable foods are meat and fruit, is supported by the dietary trends that occur when there are no economic or other restrictions on man's food choice. It is a basic nutritional concept that increasing affluence in man is associated with an increased consumption of the highly palatable meat and fruit, and a decreased consumption of the less palatable cereals and roots.

Finally, I would like to bring this story up to date, although we now have to deal with recent history rather than prehistory. I have said that a major revolution in man's diet occurred when he invented agriculture, and this has been the thesis of my paper so far. But a second revolution in man's diet occurred with the introduction of industrialization, and the development of science and technology, some 200 years ago. This had two tremendous effects on man's food, with results that were I believe to some extent of opposite effects on man's nutritional health.

The first effect was the development of methods of food production, storage, preservation and distribution. This made much more food available to the industrialized countries with their increasing wealth, and made it available too entirely independently of geography and of season. As a result, for the first time in the story of man or indeed of any species of animal, there is now a small but significant proportion of the world's human population that can look forward to living their whole lives without ever really being hungry. In this way, because of the availability of more food, and especially more of the more nutritious foods like meat and fruit, the industrial revolution could be expected to have produced nothing but an improvement in man's nutritional health.

But in addition to this, science and technology have made it possible to separate the two associated but distinct factors of palatability and nutrition. It is no longer true that when you eat what you like, you eat what you need. It will no doubt soon be possible to produce something that has the appearance, smell, taste and texture of a grilled steak, but with neither protein nor vitamins. More important, it is already possible to produce a drink that has the appearance, smell and taste of fruit juice, but with no vitamin C nor any other nutritional quality except the dubious qualities of sugar. Chiefly for technological reasons, it happens that we can produce sugar very cheaply, and with it make a very wide range of highly palatable foods and drinks. The effect of this is to increase our sugar consumption from 4 lb. a year in the middle of the eighteenth century to 120 lb. or more nowadays.

I have elsewhere produced evidence that this very large consumption of sugar plays a part in causing not only dental caries, but also obesity, diabetes, peptic ulceration, some skin diseases, and above all coronary thrombosis[6]. I might add here, as a final comment, that it was chiefly a consideration of pre-historic man's diet with its content of animal fat that more than any other single factor led me to dispute the widely held view that coronary thrombosis might be caused by this dietary constituent.

The industrial revolution then has made available to a substantial number of people, on the one hand a better range of nutritionally desirable foods than has ever before been possible, and on the other hand nutritionally undesirable foods that previously were consumed in much smaller quantities. For these people, the result has been simultaneously the almost complete elimination of nutritional deficiency disease, and the production in virtually epidemic form of a range of diseases that were previously quite rare. "The malnutrition of affluence" is more than a striking catch-phrase.

Notes

1 Yudkin, J. (1962). Nutrition in the affluent society, *Mem.s and Procs. Manchester Lit. and Philos. Soc.*, **104**; Yudkin, J. (1963). Nutrition and palatability with special reference to obesity, myocardial infarction, and other diseases of civilization, *Lancet*, **I**, p. 1335; Yudkin, J. (1964). Patterns and trends in carbohydrate consumption and their relation to disease, *Proc. Nutr. Soc.*, **23**, p. 149; Yudkin, J. (1967). Evolutionary and historical changes in dietary carbohydrates, *Am. J. clin. Nutr.*, **20**, p. 108.
2 e.g. Flannery, K. V., this volume, pp. 73–100.
3 As pointed out by Hawkes, J. G., this volume, pp. 17–29.
4 Bibby, B. G. (1961). Cariogenicity of foods, *J. Amer. med. Ass.*, **177**, p. 316.
5 Brothwell, D. R., this volume, pp. 531–45.
6 Yudkin, J. (1963). ibid.; Yudkin, J. (1964). Dietary fat and dietary sugar in relation to Ischaemic Heart Disease and Diabetes, *Lancet*, **II**, p. 4; Yudkin, J. (1964). Levels of dietary sucrose in patients with Occlusive Atherosclerotic Disease, *Lancet*, **II**, p. 6; Yudkin, J. (1967). Sugar and Coronary Thrombosis, *New Scientist*, 16th March; Yudkin, J. (1967). Why blame sugar ?, *Chemistry and Industry*, 2nd Sept.

Conclusion

STUART PIGGOTT

Conclusion

After a seminar of such complexity and concentration, an elaborate summing-up would be virtually impossible to prepare. I shall therefore limit my remarks to some aspects of early animal and plant domestication in a region where I know the material at first hand, namely Europe. *Ne supra crepidam sutor judicaret*: I will take Pliny's advice and not look beyond my Danubian shoe-last celt.

Conventionally, within the ecological modification of the Three Ages model of prehistory, the appearance of agricultural economies (in the widest sense) is equated with the beginning of a phase (of something) known as "neolithic". I have put this in rather laboured terms to make what I think is as valid point: "neolithic" is the verbalization of a mental construct designed, as we are currently using it, to accommodate certain archaeological data in a way in which they will appear to have significance when viewed in terms of a more general model in which the determinants are changes in technology and subsistence-economics in combination. It is not Lubbock's original "neolithic" of 1865, and hardly Childe's of the 1930s; it will surely not be that of the next generation of prehistorians, who may well have modified it beyond recognition if indeed they find an intellectual necessity to retain it at all. Much of our discussion has, in a sense, been either writing Notes Towards the Definition of the Neolithic, or expressing doubts about its existence.

It would seem to me that a significant difference is perceptible in the socio-economic changes inferred from archaeological evidence in this context in the Near East, and those in Europe. The cardinal problems in Western Asia are those of transition among indigenous societies; in Europe, those of the intro-duction and adoption of an already formed cultural complex in which the domestication of animals and plants, if the decisive economic factor, was not the total content of the new pattern. The European prehistorian has there-fore to consider the circumstances in which not only the techniques of domestication were acquired or disseminated, but in which an alien culture was accepted and adopted. The new social artifacts are expressed not only in the modification of inert substances as tools (in the widest sense, in which a stone or pottery bowl is a tool), nor in that of living organisms—domesticated plants and animals—but also in the more subtle and more profound modifications of belief and behaviour which would alter the very structure of society.

Of the intrusive nature of the first agriculturally based economies in Europe there seems on the present evidence little doubt. The absence of the necessary potential cultigens and domesticates such as cereals or ovicaprids in Europe as opposed to Western Asia is a commonplace, even if it has minor exceptions; the archaeological evidence demonstrates the introduction of a whole range of novelties in material culture in the earliest neolithic settlements. The fact that a secondary domestication of locally indigenous cattle or pigs could, or did take place, does not alter the intrusive character of the initial impact of the new group of closely knit cultural traditions reflected in the archaeological evidence for village settlements on an economic basis of mixed farming. It was not simply a process whereby hunting and gathering peoples adopted the sporadic cultivation of plants in the manner of much of the garden agriculture of the New World, nor the intermittent and partial domestication such as takes place with reindeer-herding communities, nor the idea of permanent settlements such as Lepenski Vir. The evidence from East Europe brought forward by Dr. Tringham in her paper to this seminar, and more directly in a study of the relationship of the latest Mesolithic to the earliest Neolithic in South-east and Central Europe[1], makes it clear that no initial acculturation of indigenous hunting and gathering communities by contact with those with agricultural economies can be detected. In other words, we are dealing not with animal and plant domestication as a technical increment adopted by cultures already established in East and Central Europe, but with the introduction, maintenance and comparatively rapid development and dissemination of a new and alien tradition, in a form sufficiently cohesive and viable as not only to establish itself, but to make the necessary adjustments which would allow of its pushing the initial domesticates beyond their natural climatic and geographical habitat, far to the West and North of Europe.

A few years ago I tentatively and briefly put forward a thesis that in antiquity it might be thought possible to perceive two types of society characterized respectively by their acceptance or rejection of circumstances leading to technological change. With such change, which alone can be documented by archaeological evidence, would go the accompanying social phenomenon, susceptible to perception by history alone, of changes in ideas, a flexibility rather than a rigidity of tradition, and a willingness to think empirically and if need be unconventionally. For such societies, developing such a character for themselves or welcoming the adoption of new ideas from outside, I suggested the term *innovating*; for those opposed to such disruptive processes within, or influences upon, their long established economies, that of *conserving*[2]. I was subsequently encouraged in my belief that such a distinction might have a certain validity by the discovery that the same concept had in fact been demonstrated at length in a quite different context, that of historical England before the Industrial Revolution, by an American anthropologist, Professor Margaret Hodgen, a dozen years earlier[3].

She examined the sociological assumptions which, "isolating technology from its matrix in the economic or social system, endow it with irresistible advance", and characterizing these philosophies of history as the "darling vice" of the nineteenth century, with roots in a long antecedent past of simplistic evolutionary thinking, criticizes them for separating "the innovator from his innovation . . . the agent of change from the fact of change". She contrasts those communities which have been receptive of innovation with those who have opposed it, and, summing up her detailed and precisely dated sequence of technological change and development in an historic context, notes how "the technologically new in England has emerged at particular epochs in the historical past under definite geographical conditions and in historical correlation with a fundamental break in custom, the intrusion of strangers".

It seems to me that the concept of innovators and conservers may be as usefully employed in thinking about the beginning of animal and plant domestication, or the transmission of the new cultural complex once achieved, as in historically documented situations. And perhaps it will not be out of place here to suggest that another thesis demonstrated by Professor Hodgen may be of value to us as prehistorians. She comments on the creation in pre-industrial England of centres or regions of technological adaptability and a ready acceptance of change. She notes "not only the efficacy of new blood in bringing about industrial changes, but the fertility of the old cultural ground that had long before received enrichment from foreign craftsmen", areas in which "after long years of experience in accepting changes in tools, an ancient rigidity of agricultural custom had been replaced by relative cultural elasticity", where "the obscure zeal of nameless pioneers linked with the presence of alien craftsmen . . . had 'broken the cake' of custom".

May one of the secondary effects of the adoption of agricultural techniques or their implantation *in partibus* by newcomers, have been not only the dramatic circumstances of the emergence of literacy and civilization in Western Asia, but the creation of areas far afield favourable to subsequent technological innovations of a quite different kind, such as the precocious initiation and development of non-ferrous metallurgy in Eastern Europe? And, although impossible to document by archaeological means, should not the necessity of accepting new and changing mental concepts be reflected in a corresponding enlargement and sophistication of language among these innovating societies?

I have strayed from the primary matter of the seminar and must return., The papers submitted fall into two groups, those dealing with methodology and those with inferences from the data that sound methodology can alone provide. More than one speaker dealt with the objective criteria our inter-disciplinary studies demand, and some very real problems were brought to our notice. It is perhaps worth while enlarging on one aspect whereby an element of uncertainty is introduced into our interpretations: it was touched on more than once but will bear re-statement. Our basic evidence for early agriculture is provided by animal and plant remains in archaeological con-texts, as organic artifacts side-by-side with the products of material culture in inert substances. Now in settlements or in burials we are dealing with socially determined situations—Childe's "fossilized behaviour"—and as archaeologists we should recognize that in these contexts we are not dealing with random assemblages representative of the whole nutritional spectrum of omnivorous man, but with part of the material evidence for human behaviour.

This is of course patently obvious in the case of evidence from burials: what goes into a grave is subject to selection not only in terms of the range of objects available within a given culture, but in terms of religious and there-fore social approval. Ignorant of the religion, and informed only inferentially of the social structure of a prehistoric community, the choice may seem to us meaningless or even capricious. I would remind you in passing that the archaeological phrase "grave-goods" itself conceals an unverifiable assump-tion as to motive and purpose, rather than demonstrates an inference. But whatever the irrecoverable reasons for the placing of objects in a grave, their presence is far from being the product of chance. They have been selected according to conventions of which we are ignorant, and this limitation of choice will operate on food remains as much as for pots or weapons, clothing or ornaments. We cannot take them as representing the whole nutritional potential of the culture of which they are a part.

It is perhaps less often realized that this may apply to settlement debris as well. But food refuse is the product of meals, and cooking, eating and drinking are essentially social activities with complex rules, conventions, tabus and prohibitions unrelated to nutrition as such. Religious dictates take no account of a nice balance of proteins and carbohydrates; Custom, not Calory is King. The Jewish and Muslim prohibition of pork is an obvious example, but what for that matter are we to make of the statement in Pausanias that, in the gross pork-eating Celtic world, it was tabu in Galatian Pesinus ? There were Celtic tabus against fish: these and their modern counterparts may be related to allergies, but throughout prehistory there must have been innumerable irrational restrictions on diet comparable with those so abundantly docu-mented in recent ethnography. Certain parts of animals may be accepted as food, others rejected: we need look no further than our own society to be reminded for instance of ambivalent attitudes towards what we uncompro-misingly call Offal, and American cook-books more delicately designate Variety Meats.

The more advanced modes of cooking which became at first necessary and

later desirable in the preparation of the diet available to the first agriculturalists inevitably affected material culture, and the development of pottery-
making techniques must have a primary relationship to the preparation,
storage and service of forms of food and drink not hitherto exploited.
Archaeologists on occasion get hooked on pots and take ceramic trips, forget-
ting that one should not rate the container above the contents, the stew-pot
over the stew. Food and drink may be perishable imponderables beyond
reach of even inferential recovery, but non-nutritional problems may be
illuminated in terms of cooking processes, as Rausing has recently suggested
in the instance of the composite archer's bow which needs animal glue and
prepared sinew which cannot be made except by prolonged boiling in a vessel
of pottery or metal. From this essentially culinary fact he argues that the
invention and development of this type of bow can only have taken place
among peoples employing such means of food production, rather than in the
aceramic contexts of most hunters and gatherers[4].

The last point I wish to make is that enshrined in a cliché so many of us
have turned to when setting examination papers on neolithic Europe. *Ex
oriente lux*, or *le mirage orientale*? An antithesis on paper, has it any solution
in practice? It is in miniature (and perhaps on a larger scale than that) a
crucial test of the diffusionist model of the relationship between the earliest
agriculture in Asia and Europe, and our seminar has suggested that the light
from the east is not an illusion, but may even be a fairly coherent beam. The
desire to believe it was a *mirage* led Salomon Reinach to support the fantastic
cause of the Glozel forgeries in the 1920s, and so to find pre-literate literacy
in neolithic France. If we are spared such excesses today, do not let us con-
gratulate ourselves too rapidly before remembering the emotive attempts of
more than European people of late to discover an indigenous origin for
agriculture within their own territories, and the keen competition for a
national aceramic neolithic; the Tartaria tablets and their interpretation form
a problem quite as interesting to students of human psychology as to prehistorians. But despite the nonsense, one thing does seem to stand up to the
assaults of reasoned scholarship. With perhaps minor exceptions, Europe
appears still to maintain its indebtedness for the initiation of agriculture to
peoples, crops and herds from the lands across the Hellespont and beyond
the Aegean. It is an old debt, standing now for some seven or eight thousand
years.

Notes

1 Tringham, R. (1968). A preliminary study of the early neolithic and latest
mesolithic blade industries in southeast and central Europe, *in* Coles,
J. M. and Simpson, D. D. A. (eds.) *Studies in Ancient Europe.* Leicester.
pp. 45–70.

2 Piggott, S. (1965). *Ancient Europe: from the Beginnings of Agriculture to Classical Antiquity*. Edinburgh and Chicago.

3 Hodgen, M. T. (1952). *Change and History: a Study of Dated Distribution of Technological Innovations in England*. Viking Fund Pubs. in Anthropology, **18**, New York.

4 Rausing, G. (1967). *The Bow: Some Notes on its Origin and Development*. Lund & Bonn. pp. 145 ff.

INDEX

General

Aardvark 311
Abalone (see also Mollusc) 480, 482
Abies cilicica (see also Fir) 38
Acacia 103
Acetobacter 466
Ackee 179
Acorn (see also Oak, *Quercus*) 78–9, 205, 366–7
Adansonia digitata (see also Baobab) 331–5
Addax (see also Antelope) 309, 312
Aegilops (see also Wheat) 56, 61, 64, 82, 88–90, 145, 152, 155–7, 162–3
   cylindrica 64
   longissima 64
   speltoides 64, 162
   squarrosa 60–3, 65, 163, 174, 176
   triuncialis 64
   variabilis 64
Ahaggar Tuareg (see Tuareg)
Akkadian 488
Alcelaphus 105
Alces alces (see also Deer) 102, 390
Alder (see also *Alnus*) 113
Allium (see also Onion) 356–8
Allouia (see also *Calathea*, Llerén) 10
Almond (see also *Prunus*) 38, 84, 86, 90
Alnus (see also Alder) 112–13
Alpaca 254, 366
Amalaka (see also Myrobalan, *Phyllanthus*) 326
Amanita 466
Amaranth 447
Amber canes (see also *Sorghum*) 400
Ammotragus (see also Sheep) 372
Amorphophallus campanulatus 406
'Amuq' 150–1, 154, 157, 166, 168, 374–5
Ananas comosus (see also Pineapple) 179
Andropogon sorghum (see also Kaoliang, Millet) 325, 399
Animal keeping 125–6, 219–21, 307, 310
Anopheles maculatus 541
Antelope (see also Addax, Oryx) 103, 312
Añu (see also *Tropaeolum*) 10, 23
Ape 525
   Chimpanzee 526
   Gorilla 526

Apocynaceae 17
Apodemus sylvaticus (see also Mouse) 211
Apple (see also *Malus*) 201, 205
   Crab 201–6
Arab 250, 485
Arachis (see also Groundnut, Peanut) 427–41
   africana 429
   asiatica 429, 433, 437
   fastigiata 431
   hypogaea 179, 400, 427–41
   monticola 428
   nambyquarae 432
   pusilla 427
   villosa 428
   villosulicarpa 432
   vulgaris 431
Arawak 178, 185, 422, 436–7
Arracacha (see also *Arracacia*) 10, 23
Arracacia (see also Arracacha) 23
   xanthorrhiza 10
Arrowroot (see also *Canna*, *Maranta*) 10, 178, 184–9, 406
   Fiji (see also *Tacca*) 10
Artemisia (see also Sagebrush) xix, 77, 112
   herba-alba 38, 40
Aryan 473
Asclepiadaceae 17
Aspergillus 466
Ass 102, 471–2, 485
Assyrian 485
Astragalus (see also Vetch) 82, 88, 155
Asturian 480
Aurochs (see also *Bos*, Cattle) 83–4, 86, 95, 222, 224–5, 227, 277–94
Australian Aborigine xviii
Australopithecus (see also *Homo*, *Paranthropus*, *Telanthropus*, *Zinjanthropus*) 527
   africanus 527
   boisei 527
   robustus 527
Avena (see also Oat) 56, 82, 88, 157, 160, 166, 356–7
   barbata 158
   byzantina 154

Avena—continued
　fatua 158
　ludoviciana 154, 157, 166
　sativa 154, 158, 166
　sterilis 52, 56
　strigosa 166
Avetra 406
Aztec 448, 533
Azukia 452

Baboon (see also *Papio*) 310–13, 526–7
Babylonian 472
Bacillus subtilis 466
Badener 227
Badger 492
Bajra (see also Millet, *Pennisetum*) 325
Banana 70, 179, 188, 191, 418, 444, 451
Banteng (see also *Bibos*) 287
Bantu 252, 333
Baobab (see also *Adansonia*) 331–5
Baradostian 144, 222
Barley (see also *Hordeum*) 19–20, 25–6,
　　44–5, 47–67, 71, 74, 80–1, 84, 87–8,
　　91, 125, 131–5, 137–40, 150–3,
　　156–7, 160–1, 164–5, 168, 324, 355–7,
　　368
　cultivated 53, 55, 64, 152, 165, 368
　four-row 134
　it 137–9
　multi-rowed 355
　six-row 55, 74, 90, 134, 150–1, 153,
　　155–7, 159, 165, 168, 324
　two-row 47, 55, 74, 82, 85, 90, 134,
　　150–3, 155–9, 163–5, 168, 355–6
　wild 45, 52–9, 61, 63–4, 82, 152–3, 158,
　　163–4, 168, 358, 361, 363
Basuto 256
Bavenda 258
Bean (see also *Phaseolus*) 13, 17, 22, 25,
　　139, 179, 358, 446, 451–62, 536–7
　fava 528
　soya 25, 464, 467
Bear (see also *Ursus*) 219, 338, 342, 344
Bedouin 260
Bedstraw (see also *Galium*) 88
Beer 71, 139–40, 464
Ber (see also Jujube, *Zizyphus*) 326
Berberidaceae 17
Beriberi 533, 549
Betula (see also Birch) 112–13, 116
Bibos (see also Banteng, Gaur, Ox) 287
　sauveli 281
Birch (see also *Betula*) 111
Bison 7–8, 279, 287, 516–17
　bonasus 390
Blesbok (see also *Damaliscus*) 105
Bombaceae 331
Bombax 333
Bos (see also Aurochs, Cattle, Ox) 287
　289–90
　brachyceros 347
　brachyceros europaeus 279
　bubalis 319

Bos—continued
　gaurus 105
　indicus 318–20
　namadicus 281
　primigenius 105, 270, 277–94, 319, 364,
　　389–90, 517
　taurus 74, 271, 277–94, 372, 386, 389–90
　taurus longifrons 351
　taurus primigenius 279
　urus minutus 279
Brassica juncea (see also Mustard) 324
Breadfruit 179
Bromus 356
Broomcorn (see also Millet, *Panicum*) 135,
　　153, 165, 398
bš3 139–40
Bubalus (see also Buffalo) 287, 309
　bubalus 106
Buck, African 106
Buckwheat 68
Budares (see also *Nanihot*, Manioc) 12
Buffalo (see also *Bos*, *Bubalus*, *Synceros*)
　　103–5, 312, 318–9
　African 105, 107
　Asiatic 106
　Indian 319
Bug-Dniester 382–8
Bushman xviii, 75, 528

Cactaceae 17
Calathea (see also Allouia, Llerén) 10
　allouia 178, 184
　Calluna 112–13
Camel (see also *Camelus*) 101, 208, 250,
　　252–3, 255–60, 262, 310, 319–20,
　　365–6, 506
　bactrian 250
Camelus dromedarius (see also Camel) 320
Canavalia 446–7
Canis (see also Dog) 337–40, 342, 344
　aureus aureus 338–40
　aureus lupaster 338–40
　familiaris 74, 214, 369, 386, 389–90
　latrans 214
　lupus 389–90, 394
　lupus arabs 339–40
Canna (see also Arrowroot, Tous-les-mois)
　　23, 178, 185, 192, 446
　indica 186
Cannabis sativa (see also Hemp) 19
Caper (see also *Capparis*) 86, 90
Capparis (see also Caper) 86
Capra (see also Caprinae, Goat) 267, 386,
　　389–90
　hircus 74, 267–8, 364, 371
Capreolus capreolus (see also Roe Deer)
　　236, 389–90
Caprinae (see also *Capra*, Goat) 267, 269,
　　272–4
Capsian 480
Chukchi 253
Capsicum (see also Pepper) 179, 443–50
　annuum 443–4, 446, 448

INDEX

Sites (in italics) and Localities

INDEX

Authors

Abad, J. R. 196-7, 199
Abbad y Lasierra, I. 199
Åberg, E. 132, 140, 142
Aberg, F. A. xxvi
Abregú, V. C. 440
Abu'l-Fazl 334
Acosta, J. de 447, 449
Adametz, L. 293
Adams, L. 128
Adams, R. M. 88-90, 92, 96, 98-9
Adamson, J. 378
Aldred, C. 474
Alexander, J. 423-5
Alexandersen, V. 538, 543
Allard, R. W. 462
Allchin, B. 128
Allchin, F. R. 321-2, 424
Allee, W. C. 97
Alur, K. R. 319-22
Ames, O. 435, 440
Amiet, P. 477
Amoroso, E. C. 256, 263
An Chih-min 401
Anati, E. 477
Anderson, E. 430, 435, 439-40
Anderson, J. 235, 244
Anderson, P. W. 468
Andersson, J. G. 395, 401
Angel, J. L. 540, 542, 544
Anghiera, P. M. d' 185, 190, 196, 199
Ansanus, T. 199
Ansari, Z. D. 329
Ansell, A. D. 483
Antonius, O. 476, 478, 485, 488
Arcikhowski, A. W. 221-2, 229
Aristophanes 489, 493
Aristotle 489-90, 493
Armelagos, G. 541, 544
Ashbee, P. 291
Ashton, H. 263
Audy, J. R. 544

Bachiller y Morales, A. 194
Bader, R. S. 217
Bailey, L. H. 196-7
Baker, H. G. 216
Baker, J. R. 128, 249, 262
Baker, P. T. 542
Balkan, K. 478
Balout, L. 484
Banks, C. 283
Barham, H. 186-7, 195, 198
Barker, H. 46, 197, 199
Barrau, J. 423-4
Barrett, O. W. 196
Bartlett, H. H. 185, 198
Bate, D. M. A. 97, 267, 274, 339, 344
Batten, C. A. 215
Baumhoff, M. A. 377
Beasley, A. B. 216
Beattie, W. 438, 441
Beckwith, M. W. 195, 198
Beer, G. R. De 215
Bell, G. D. H. 169, 172
Bendig, A. W. 210, 215
Bennett, W. C. 194
Bentham, G. 462
Benzon, P. E. 197-8
Berger, R. 544
Bergh, B. O. 449
Bernegg, A. S. von 196-8
Berry, R. J. 213, 215-16, 244, 294
Bertsch, F. and K. 166, 170, 172, 201, 203, 205-6
Beug, H. J. 46, 147
Bibby, B. G. 552
Bibikova, V. I. 391-2
Biddle, M. 128
Bigalke, R. C. 108
Billings, W. D. 14
Bilton, L. 279, 293
Binford, L. R. and S. R. 75-8, 81, 96-7
Bird, J. 449
Birdsell, J. B. 76, 96
Birdwood, C. 331, 333-4

Birkett-Smith, K. 262
Bishop, C. W. 399, 401
Bissing, K. von 314
Bittel, K. 478
Blanco, M. 440
Bligh, J. 108
Blumberg, B. S. 216
Bobek, H. 37-8, 41, 45-6
Bodenheimer, F. S. 344-5
Boessneck, J. 224, 226, 229, 289-90, 293-4, 379
Bohlken, H. 274, 277, 293
Bois, D. 196, 198, 435, 439-40
Bökönyi, S. 99, 215, 224, 229, 284, 286, 294, 475, 477-8
Boldingh, I. 197
Bolhuis, G. G. 437, 440
Boloyan, D. S. 377
Bond, G. 118
Bordaz, J. 379
Bose, S. 96
Botteina, S. 158, 171
Bottema, S. 42, 46
Bowden, P. J. 506, 520
Bowen, H. C. xxvi
Boyrie Moya, E. de 199
Bradford, E. W. 543
Braidwood, L. xxi
Braidwood, R. J. xx, xxi, 66, 68, 71-2, 97, 169, 305, 376, 378, 544
Braun, H. W. 210, 215
Brautlecht, C. A. 195, 197
Britton, N. L. 196-7, 199
Broadhurst, P. L. 210, 215
Broholm, H. C. 499
Brooks, C. E. P. 352
Brothwell, D. R. 216, 527, 529, 540, 543-4, 549, 552
Brown, W. H. 197-8
Browne, P. 195, 198
Brues, A. 545
Bryan, K. 32, 34
Buechner, H. K. 109